THE FORTUNES OF MONTAIGNE

MICHEL DE MONTAIGNE
From the painting in the Château de Montaigne

THE FORTUNES OF MONTAIGNE

A HISTORY OF THE ESSAYS IN FRANCE, 1580–1669

by

ALAN M. BOASE

Habent sua fata libelli

1970

OCTAGON BOOKS

New York

First published in 1935

New material © 1970 by Allan M. Boase

Reprinted 1970

by special arrangement with Methuen & Co. Ltd.

OCTAGON BOOKS

A DIVISION OF FARRAR, STRAUS & GIROUX, INC.

19 Union Square West

New York, N. Y. 10003

LIBRARY OF CONGRESS CATALOG CARD NUMBER: 70-119645

Printed in U.S.A. by

NOBLE OFFSET PRINTERS, INC.

NEW YORK 3, N. Y.

AUTHOR'S NOTE TO THE OCTAGON EDITION

It will soon be thirty-five years since this book was first published; it has been out of print for more than twenty. It is alas! in the nature of things that none of those whose help and inspiration I had then to acknowledge should still be alive. Because of the war, a projected translation into French foundered, and for a long spell I thought of the *Fortunes of Montaigne* as having perhaps been robbed of some of its interest by a whole series of works in which Montaigne's religious views have been more closely studied and his curious position more widely recognised. I surmised too (wrongly as it would seem), that Professor Pintard's definitive study of *Le Libertinage Erudit du 17-ième Siècle*, in which Gassendi, Naudé, the Du Puy brothers and many others figure even more largely than they do in my book, would be completed by a second volume, so that the story of the impact of the *Essais* on several generations of French readers would be retold in a wider context and with far more learning than I could ever command. Besides this, Molière and La Fontaine, Pascal, La Rochefoucauld and all the *moralistes* have been the subject of illuminating studies—I think of Benichon, Dagens, Moore and friends, colleagues or pupils, such as Moore, Krailsheimer, Odette de Mourgues and Lionel Gossman.

Nevertheless, when the occasion arose, after so long an interval of time, to reread oneself from cover to cover, I must confess that—despite some blushes, notably for my almost Shavian animosity to the use of the hyphen—I have still found the book surprisingly valid. To say the least, it completes the work for which (in its original thesis form) it provided also the source material, Pierre Villey's *Montaigne devant la Porstérité* (see p. vii, note 1, for an observation on Plattard's lack of acknowledgement), and it thus links up with the Abbe Dreano and Professor Donald Frame's continuation of the story of the *Essais*. Even after the elaborate studies of Montaigne's religion which we owe to Janssen, Sclafert, Citoleux Müller and Lebègue, and which have served to gain a general recognition of his fideism, my emphasis of the *vanitas* motif as an integral part of this fideism appears to me a feature insufficiently stressed. Nor it seems has anyone been willing to recognise that aesthetic slant in Montaigne's moral thinking which made him

AUTHOR'S NOTE TO THE OCTAGON EDITION

the *vade mecum* of *les Gens Honnêtes*, master of *l'art de vivre* and *l'art de plaire*.

No, I have no conclusions to change, only a regret that my far-reaching enquiry could not have been extended to include a proper consideration of echoes of the *Essais* in the theatre, or—more systematically—in the poetry of the period. If only because, instead of the rather timid allusion on pp. 74-5 to my *Criterion* article heralding Sponde and putting forward the tentative notion of a French metaphysical poetry, it could have led (as it now seems to me) to a recognition of the extent to which Montaigne's cult of the paradox—creating not only the relaxation of tolerance, but humour, wonder, insight—was a determining influence in what we now recognise as the age of the Baroque. It was also the age which for a minority at least, self-schooled by their study of Montaigne or Charron, saw the birth of what we may call liberal values and thus provided more surely than the Renaissance itself the real prolegomena to the Enlightenment. Indeed, the weakest pages of Paul Hazard's masterly *Crise de la Conscience Européenne* are those on Natural Law, an ubiquitous preoccupation of the 17th Century, as my book shows. But when it was written the civilised world had not yet realised how precarious a belief in those liberal values was to prove in our own times. That too may lend a new if melancholy interest to the reactions of individual Frenchmen to the organizational drive which culminated in the Fourteenth Louis' absolutism.

ALAN BOASE

November, 1969

PREFACE

THE mere mention of 'literary influence' is disquieting to many intelligent people. The academic world has seen too much of an unprofitable mixture of dissection and conjecture in this field. In the case of a book of such importance as Montaigne's Essays, so widely read, so praised and damned, so diverse in interest, such an inquiry hardly needs a defence. Apart from his unique qualities, Montaigne provides in many ways an epitome of Renaissance thought. With the exception of Rabelais, Montaigne was for the French Seventeenth Century the one great prose writer, the one prose-classic of an earlier age who had written an original work in their tongue. The Essays were republished in France every two or three years from 1580 to 1669. For eighty-nine years, then, the printers found Montaigne good business, and it is my purpose to show what those who bought the Essays during that period sought or found there.

In 1676 the Essays were placed upon the Index. For the next half-century, for fifty-five years, to be exact, no French printer thought it worth his while to place a new edition of Montaigne before the public. Even then the initiative came from England, from Lacoste, the friend of St. Evremond and the translator of Locke, who published in London a handsome quarto, backed by the subscriptions of the English nobility and members of the diplomatic corps. These facts, this reverse of fortune, I shall also attempt to interpret more briefly.

The main theme of this study is the development of Humanism as opposed to orthodox Christianity, and the part played by the Essays in that development. It reveals in some small measure a side of the seventeenth century in France, which, though more difficult to appraise, less visible on the surface, less homogeneous, less dramatic than Port-Royal—in the wide sense in which Sainte Beuve used that name—is certainly no less important in the history of ideas. Without a knowledge of this side of the *Grand Siècle* there is much in the succeeding Age of Reason that can hardly be seen in its true light.

If my design seems to me easily justified, I would crave the indulgence of the reader with regard to its execution. The questions I have attempted to answer are these. What are the general ideas of those who are particularly drawn to Montaigne—or who write against him ? What did these writers think of the Essays, and what specially interested them in the book ? And, finally, what did they borrow from him, or, more profitably, what are their less conscious borrowings, their adaptations of his ideas ? It has thus been part of my task to give an account of criticism and appreciation of the Essays, as distinguished from their influence ; to keep these two aspects of this study completely separate has proved impossible. Furthermore, it has been found undesirable to attempt some sort of analytical arrangement whereby the reader might have found assembled together a collection of all that concerns Montaigne and the relativity of custom, Montaigne and witchcraft, &c. It has been possible indeed to make a partial exception with regard to education and *honnêteté*. I do not think, however, that this is entirely a disadvantage. My study is of the impact of a whole mind upon other minds—of a man upon other men. The method adopted enables us to obtain a more concrete and, therefore, a truer picture of the age itself and the rôle which Montaigne's book played in it.

It must be added that *The Fortunes of Montaigne* was originally written as a doctoral thesis, and completed in 1929. Its publication has been delayed for a variety of reasons. A book is better without some of the para-

phernalia of reference which is expected in an academic
dissertation, especially as I had been anxious to prove
up to the hilt, by quotation of obvious reminiscence and
allusion, that I had the right to speak of ' influence '.
Before embarking on this task of pruning, my MS. was
sent to the late Professor Villey, to whom all students
of Montaigne are peculiarly indebted. He was kind
enough to speak well of it, and, with my permission,
made a most extensive use of my apparatus of references
in order to compile the dictionary of parallel passages
and *rapprochements* which may be found in an Appendix
to the *édition de luxe* published in 1929–30 by the Librairie
Alcan.   Since this is available to the public, it has seemed
permissible to dispense with more of these references
than I should otherwise have done.[1]

Within the last year M. Henri Busson's *La Pensée
Religieuse Française de Charron à Pascal* has covered
some of the ground dealt with in this book, and has
shown that the fideist tendencies of the seventeenth
century were even more widespread than is here suggested.   M. Busson, however, ignores a side of fideism
which is more particularly connected with Montaigne,
and which is explained in the Introduction. I am
indebted to his book for independent confirmation of
many points of interest, as well as for certain important
indications.

Finally, I should like to express my thanks to Professor Strowski of the University of Paris who originally
suggested that I should write this book, and to Mr.
Arthur Tilley of Kings' College, Cambridge, Dr. H. F.

---

[1] It is perhaps also necessary to draw attention to a posthumous
work of Professor Villey, which has just appeared : the first—and alas !
the only—volume of a grandiose work under the title of *Montaigne devant
la Posterité*.   The period under review only extends from 1580 to (roughly)
1610, but the author has dealt more copiously than I have with at least
one figure : J.-P. Camus.   I was much touched to hear from Mme. Villey
that the question of acknowledging his debt to my thesis was the subject
of their conversation a few hours before the tragic railway accident in
which he met his death.   I cannot help feeling, however, that had he
lived he would have found means of acquitting himself of this duty of
acknowledgement somewhat more explicitly than his literary executors
have done.

Stewart of Trinity College, Cambridge, and Professor
Forster of the University of Sheffield, who have all given
me many valuable hints and useful advice.

SHEFFIELD

CONTENTS

NOTE

It has seemed unnecessary in a study of the history of ideas to adhere rigidly to the archaic spelling of most of the authors quoted. This has been done only where obviously necessary to the meaning or where the flavour of a text has demanded it. With regard to the spelling of Montaigne's name, I have adopted the only sensible rule which can be applied to surnames of the sixteenth and seventeenth century, that is the employment of the form habitually used by the possessor of that name : *Montaigne* and not *Montagne*. Both forms are found, though the latter is more common in the seventeenth century, and naturally both were pronounced : *Montagne*.

The edition of the Essays quoted is that of P. Villey (Alcan, 1922–3) unless otherwise stated. The letters A B and C refer, respectively, to the text of 1580, the additions of 1588 (including the whole of the Third Book) and to the additions of *copie de Bordeaux* from which the 1595 edition was published.

CORRIGENDA

p. 124, 2 lines from bottom, *for* ' misfortune ' *read* ' misfortunes '

p. 127, 13 lines from bottom, *for* ' régentés ' *read* ' régentées '

p. 137, line 13, *for* ' Vergil ' *read* ' Virgil '

p. 168, note 2, line 2, *for* ' etait ' *read* ' était '

p. 169, 2 lines from bottom, *for* ' Thélogique ' *read* ' Théologique '

p. 171, line 11, *for* ' des Periers ' *read* ' des Périers '

ADDENDA

p. 338, note 5. It remains to be pointed out that Montaigne himself appears to be the origin of the expression, though perhaps not with the exact refinement of meaning of Méré and Mme de Sablé : for he writes of his two favorite authors : ' *Sénèque est plein de pointes et saillies ; Plutarque, de choses* ' (*Essais*, II, 10, p. 113).

p. 373, line 19. And Montaigne's phrase *avoir une arrière boutique* gives rise to Pascal's formula *avoir des idées de derrière la tête* (310, 336).

INTRODUCTION

MONTAIGNE'S name has a fairly definite meaning for every educated European, even for those who may never have opened a copy of the Essays. They know him for the sceptic, the smiling sage, tolerant and humanitarian, the follower of ' nature ', the first author of our own era to confess himself frankly to us and give us a ' self-portrait ' : and it is because he is all this that Montaigne has been called the first ' modern man '. Yet his book is one of those classics which for three and a half centuries has possessed something of an enigmatic character for many of those who are familiar with its pages. The controversy centres round Montaigne's religion, centres, therefore, round that strange Essay on the uncertainty of knowledge which is a treatise in itself, the *Apologie pour Raymond Sebond*, a defence, that is, of the fifteenth-century theologian whose ' Natural Theology ' Montaigne translated at his father's behest. Did La Bouderie, the priest who wrote of the Christianity of Montaigne just over a hundred years ago, deserve the discreet smile of Sainte Beuve, the shrug of the shoulders, the murmur of ' *o sancta simplicitas* ' ? Is M. André Gide correct when he sees in that natural conservative, Montaigne, the prototype of his own contemporaries, Barrès and Maurras—' the first Catholic who was not a Christian ' ? It is my purpose, first of all, to show that there is no longer an enigma ; that if we cease to pay our unconscious tribute to the charm of an author who can make us feel he is a possible friend, a man of our own age, if we will replace him in his own historical setting, this enigma disappears. It not only disappears but also gives us the best starting-point from which to show the fundamental unity of Montaigne's thought and the precise nature of his originality.

When the scholarship of M. Villey made it possible to date the majority of the Essays with accuracy, and to see what books Montaigne was reading in any particular month or year, it became the habit to speak of the period, at which most of the

Apology appears to have been composed, as the Sceptical Crisis. It was then, in February 1576, that Montaigne struck the famous medal with the balances and his motto ' *Que sais je ?* ', an action which is as much the declaration of a political neutrality as of a philosophical suspension of judgement. It was intensely topical. Hardly a month had passed since young Henry of Navarre had made his escape from Court, accompanied only by Montaigne's friend, Grammont, and had come to Agen. It was the moment when Monluc wrote the last pages of his Commentaries. ' I have heard ', he says, ' of the arrival of the young prince in the country. Knowing his great qualities, I foresee the struggle will be long. I have a mind to retire to a monastery in the topmost Pyrenees, which I remember having seen in my younger days, from whence I shall look down at once on France and Spain.' Montaigne's medal was a similar gesture, and, at the same time, the declaration of a philosophic creed.

The interpretation which the historical analysis of Montaigne's spiritual development often receives is too hasty and schematic. His infinite variety is reduced to a series of successive phases : the Stoic ; the Sceptic ; the Epicurean ; the Practical Sage, and so on. These may be useful labels, but they are in danger of corresponding to no psychological reality. Unless they are understood as partly cumulative, and not merely successive, steps, the evolutionary treatment of Montaigne's book will have done more harm than good. This misunderstanding is particularly acute in the case of this so-called Sceptical Crisis. The impression is apt to be given that Montaigne was more of a sceptic then than he was subsequently, or that he later ceased to be the sceptic which he had once been. The first of these alternatives is possible, the second is certainly false.

It is often implied that at this moment of his life Montaigne was in process of ' losing his faith ', or in danger of losing it. That may be true ; but, if so, it involves the paradox of holding that he was losing his faith at the precise moment at which he was engaged in writing an apologetical work in which scepticism was used in defence of religion according to a system then prevalent and widely approved. Paradox is not impossibility, but this paradox can only be explained away by maintaining either deliberate hypocrisy on Montaigne's part, or else a gradual realization, while he was still writing, of the weakness of his case. Of these I see no signs.

The fact is that the Apology, like the greater number of the apologetical works of the Renaissance [1] is based on the view of faith and reason known to modern Catholic theologians as the heresy of fideism : that is, the affirmation that not even the most important dogmas of the Church, such as the existence of God and the immortality of the soul, can be proved. They must be believed by faith, and, furthermore, it is dangerous to try to prove them.

That is the fully developed and properly defined fideist doctrine, and it brings with it a number of interesting results which carry us far beyond the sphere of theology.   Where it was held by sincere Christians, it was a natural step to a further doubt whether reason could establish any truths at all.   So far from being in a position to intrude into the sphere of faith, reason was put upon the defensive and its incompetence in its own domain was demonstrated.   This is precisely what Montaigne does in the Apology and—still more important—it had been done before him, around him, by his friends and by the friends of his friends.

In the following century, during the Counter-Reformation, fideism, at least in its more pronounced forms, was to some extent discredited, though it was far from disappearing, as M. Busson's more recent study has shown. [2]   The Scholastic theology had a certain revival under the auspices of the Jesuits and a series of Popes who favoured them, but orthodoxy implicitly placed less reliance on rationalism.   Fideism, however, had, or came to have, associated with it a certain ideology or attitude to life which, perhaps, corresponds to some of the most permanent psychological needs of man, and which is certainly of quite extraordinary importance in the history of modern thought. This attitude, of which Montaigne provides a first-rate example, often survived in the seventeenth century the doctrine with which it had been associated.   Hence the amusing spectacle of people who borrow from Montaigne with one hand and strike him with the other, while what they borrow and what they blame coexists in the Essays.   One of the lessons of Montaigne's influence is the extent to which his fideism, and the attitude which goes with it, is central in his work.   This attitude may be conveniently called, for the moment, his pessimism ; while this fideism, typical of the whole age, requires some further historical analysis, if we are to understand its full significance.

[1] Henri Busson : *Les Sources et le Développement du Rationalisme dans la Littérature Française de la Renaissance* (1533–1600).   Paris, 1922.   More recently, the fideism of Montaigne has been studied in detail and still more conclusively established by H. Janssen (*Montaigne Fidéiste*.   Leiden, 1930).
[2] H. Busson : *La Pensée Religieuse Française de Charron à Pascal,* 1933.

Pomponazzi and the Paduan Averrhoists are the chief but
not the only source whence the fideism of the Renaissance derives.
The thirteenth-century Averrhoists, who were condemned by the
University of Paris in the time of St. Thomas, stated with as
much intransigeance as Pomponazzi the innumerable contradictions of faith and reason, but, in the meantime, the thought
of Duns Scot, of Occam and the Nominalist Scholastics of the
fourteenth century had tended, by a continuous process of
criticism, to separate the domain of pure philosophy and a
natural science, which as yet hardly existed, from the sphere of
theology. More and more of the propositions of the latter were
recognized as dependent on faith and impossible to demonstrate.
This is inevitable, since, if you reject universals, as the Nomina-
lists and some Averrhoists did, and treat abstractions as mere
names, while clinging to the body of Christian doctrine, the division of two spheres of human knowledge, of *two kinds* of ' truth ',
is necessarily imposed upon you—the ' truth ' of faith and the
' truth ' of reason. It is this tendency which helps to explain
the prodigious influence of the Paduan school in the sixteenth
century. One has only to turn to Busson's work, just named,
to realize this influence, and also to see how the piled-up contradictions and the final declarations of incompetence, made almost
certainly in bad faith by Pomponazzi, were reproduced in good
faith by many genuine apologists.

This problem of sincerity, unfortunately, always arises when
faith is considered as opposed to reason, until we reach an age
of comparative freedom of expression in the 18th century. Whenever found, it has to be dealt with on the merits of each particular
case. Mere inconsistency is far more often due to an attempt
to reconcile beliefs, to which a man is deeply attached, with
rational views, to which his very honesty of thought forces him,
rather than to the intention of escaping disagreeable consequences. The problem, however, is complicated by the fact
that the words ' faith ' and ' revelation ' cover a multitude of
interchanging senses. Faith is used not only without the quali-
fications of ' explicit ' or ' implicit ', but as meaning the articles
or the content of faith ; an act of the will ; a divine illumination
in which man's part is conceived as essentially passive ; as something received on what is really human authority ; or as a peculiar kind of virtue. Practically the only honest attempt at
definition during the period dealt with in this book is that of
Lord Herbert in his *De Veritate*. So far as the seventeenth
century is concerned, this lack of ingenuousness, is of two kinds.

Many Catholic writers make a voluntary or involuntary confusion (which suits their case) between revelation proper, which must be something which directly reaches the individual, as Herbert truly says, and a *mediate* revelation, which is the authority of the Church. On the other hand, the distinction between faith and reason often indirectly serves a different purpose. Many of those who make a point of taking faith as something *purely* passive, totally outside the individual's control and completely dependent on God's grace, do so, merely in order to find a good basis for a plea for toleration or liberty of thought. But besides the extreme opposition of faith and reason, there is the attitude of prudence, adopted by most thinkers of the sixteenth and seventeenth century, the affirmation of the complete separation of theology and philosophy.

The immense importance of fideist ideas can only be understood when it is recognized that this habitual distinction between the sphere of faith and the sphere of reason alone rendered possible the development of independent thought and, along with it, of modern science. For those, like Bacon and Descartes, whose main interest was the advance of science, it provided a means of keeping their work clear of religion, of obtaining the right to free speculation just because their freedom was understood to be limited. Yet it is not merely the relation of the thinker to the society in which he lived, it is also a personal question which is involved ; the right which the individual feels himself to have of examining impartially certain philosophical problems ; and the desire which he also feels of preserving intact his religious beliefs. There was an uncomfortable disparity between the world-picture offered by Christian doctrine—a whole conception of life in which the emotional nature of the individual was anchored—and, on the other hand, the rational inferences to be drawn from certain features of his experience, certain scientific results, such as the Copernican astronomy, certain discoveries as to the inhabitants of the New World.

In other words, as Mr. Basil Willey has recently put it,[1] it is a question of the distinction between ' doctrines felt as facts '—traditional ' facts '—and the most plausible *explanation* of new facts. The ' double truth ' conception is at bottom a distinction between what is felt as true, and what is satisfactory as ' explanation '. The doctrines themselves are, of course, also explanations, but have become such fundamental assumptions that their character as explanation is no longer apparent to any but the most penetrating and philosophical minds of the day. What

[1] *Seventeenth Century Background,* Chapter I.

Mr. Willey has perhaps not succeeded in showing so clearly is the important rôle of a certain development of fideism which is present in the Essays.

Speaking of apologetics in France towards 1550, M. Busson says that Postel was the last of his generation to attempt to give to faith a rational basis.   After him all the apologists accept the fundamental doctrine of Pomponazzi, the powerlessness of reasoning in matters concerning religion.   Postel's contemporaries, the two great humanists, Marc-Antoine Muret and Adrian Turnèbe, are shown by Busson to be excellent examples of this change. And, he adds, a most important subsequent development leads us straight to Montaigne himself : ' *Voici par une extension toute naturelle on étend le doute à l'autorité même de la raison et des sens en matière philosophique.   L'origine en est chez les Padouans qui en opposant la raison à la foi l'ont rendue suspecte aux croyants* '.[1]

This extension of fideism, then, is often almost a guarantee of sincerity.   M. Busson, who is here speaking of Guy de Bruès, one of the recognized precursors of the Apology,[2] goes on to mention some of the other works which lead up to Bruès and eventually to Montaigne.   Among them we may notice Arnaud Du Ferron's dissertation ' against Maximus Tyrius '.[3]   It should not be forgotten that Du Ferron was the friend of Gouvéa, Montaigne's master at Bordeaux ;   friend, too, of Etienne de La Boëtie, his *inviolable frère et intime ami*.   Muret also was Montaigne's master ;   it was to *mon Turnebus* that the author turned for information about Sebond's *Theologia Naturalis* ; and Du Ferron is already a sceptic something after the manner of Montaigne.

When Etienne Pasquier, another friend of Montaigne's, made his famous pleading against the Jesuits before the Parliament of Paris in 1564, he accused their theologian Maldonat of impiety for attempting to prove the existence of God.[4]   It is an accusation made in bad faith, it may be said.   Granted, but the point is that it should have been thought profitable to make it.

In its more popular form a reaction against the dogmatism of the Protestants helped the acceptance of fideism everywhere, and Montaigne's weapons were borrowed more than once for an attack on the Huguenots.

---

[1] op. cit., p. 480.
[2] P. Villey : *Sources et l'Evolution des Essais*, II, 169, et seq.
[3] Busson, op. cit., p. 109 et seq.
[4] Prat. *Maldonat et l'Université de Paris*, p. 134.

The Apology, then, is less original and less paradoxical than it seems. The paradox lies, rather, in the fact that it is intended as a defence of a book which belongs to a rationalist system of apologetics—*Magnificat à matines*, as Joseph Scaliger called it.[1] Sebond, whose book was given to Montaigne's father by Bunel, himself a rationalist in theology, sets out to prove by natural reasons alone almost all the dogmas of the Church—even that of the Trinity. The preface, where his claim is made, was censured by the Council of Trent. Montaigne, in his translation of the *Theologia Naturalis*, shows himself perfectly cognizant of this exaggerated claim—if not of its censure—and accordingly modifies it.[2]

In Montaigne's own time, or, at any rate, in the first half of the century, the book had a good deal of success, as also an abridgement, made in 1551 at the request of Eleanore of Austria, the widow of Francis I. Perhaps this was partly due to the fact that, provisionally, the author makes no use of the Scriptures. The avoidance of what was acutely controversial matter may have recommended it in certain quarters.

It is as well, too, that we should be reminded by this popularity, that fideism was never quite general, nor was it accepted as orthodox. But the writings of the ' theological rationalists ' of the Renaissance, such as Postel, Ramus and Du Plessis Mornay, to name three names, show how great was the influence of the Paduans even among those who opposed them.

The revival of Aquinas at the close of the sixteenth century was a reaction which brought with it a very unsatisfactory state of affairs. Averrhoism and Nominalism had left their mark, and it was widely felt by apologists that the Aristotelian *tabula rasa* doctrine of knowledge, as interpreted by St. Thomas, afforded a somewhat precarious basis for demonstrating the immortality of the soul. Those circles which did not make concessions towards some system of innate ideas were averse from *apologiae* of any kind. An attitude of compromise with the Platonic-Augustinian idealism is to be found even in Suarez and the theological lectures of Coimbra.[3] There had, of course, been

---

[1] ' Extat Theologia Sebundi, Gallica : per Montanum, qui etiam fecit Apologium pro eo, et nihil ibi de illo ; eo omnia faciunt, ut *magnificat à matines* ' (*Scaligerana*, 1667, Cologne, p. 215, art. Raymundus).

[2] J. Coppin : *Montaigne traducteur de Raymond Sebond*. Lille, 1925, Chapter V. See also the same writer's article (*Revue du 16ᵐᵉ Siècle*, 1930, fasc 3–4), where the suggestion of H. Janssen (*Montaigne Fidéiste*) that Montaigne was unaware of the real character of Sebond's work is convincingly refuted.

[3] E. Gilson : *Etudes de Philosophie Médiévale : L'Innéisme Cartésien et la Théologie*.

plenty of interest in Plato and Neoplatonism during the whole
of the Renaissance, from the time of Ficino onward, though it
often had more of a poetical than of a philosophical significance.
The arguments of the *Phaedo* and the *Timaeus* were, however,
constantly brought into play by sixteenth-century apologists,
while Francesco Patrizzi boldly recommended the theologians
to replace Aristotle by Plato.

At the end of the century comes, too, the Stoical movement
led by Lipsius, with its revival of the notion of reason as a spark
of the divine nature and thus possessing an innate knowledge
of first principles. The *notitiae communes* of Herbert's *De
Veritate* (1624), later attacked by Locke, have the same character,
and, almost at the same time, we find grouped round Cardinal
de Bérulle, founder of the Oratorians, a band of apologists of
whose Platonism, though eclectic, there can be no doubt.
Two of these, Mersenne and Silhon, we shall meet again in
these pages. The former writes specifically against ' the pyrrhonists and sceptics ', that is, the fideists and those unbelievers
who cover themselves with this name, while the latter's chosen
enemy, in all his theological works, is Montaigne, whose sincerity and many other qualities he is, however, prepared to
admit.

The importance of Bérulle and his group is due to their relations with Descartes, who took from them, more or less as it
stood, this Augustinian Platonism.[1] The rigid dualism to which
his physics led him provided a new and improved basis for the
doctrine of innate ideas. The direct knowledge of itself which
the mind, according to the Platonic view, possessed, the purely
spiritual nature of knowledge, provided him with the elements
of a new rational apologetic, which it was necessary to substitute
for the scholastic doctrine of mediate knowledge. It was only
by showing official theology that he could do their job for them
better than they could themselves that he could hope to get his
new mechanistic physics accepted. The ' Meditations ' were
written with the precise intention of getting all those who were
not unduly prejudiced to accept, as it were unconsciously, the
new principles of physical science as being perfectly compatible
with the doctrines of the Church.[2]

It goes without saying that this Platonic doctrine of ideas
fitted in more or less with the results which Descartes might
have arrived at independently. It remains true that his first
interest lay in physical science. He gave back to the Oratorians

[1] E. Gilson, loc. cit.
[2] id., *La Liberté chez Descartes et la Théologie*, 1913, p. 95.

their Platonic idealism strengthened and improved by a new and simplified theory of the relations of soul to the body and of both to the external world.

The Oratory, which we have just seen linked with Descartes, stands for one side of an Augustinian revival of which the other is represented by the Jansenists, with their insistence on the dogma of original sin as involving a positive defect in human nature. Just as the theology of the Jesuits was a revival of Thomism, so, for their Molinist views, they could claim a supporter in Aquinas, who held that the nature of man was precisely what was contained in the definition of his essence, and that, at the Fall, only a special grace had been lost.[1] The only part, however, of the Jansenist-Jesuit controversy which will enter our field is that which centres round the question whether the virtue of the pagans had any merit in the eyes of God.

Although the Church eventually decided to reject Descartes (1674), and the theological manuals henceforth simply applied to him Aquinas's refutation of Plato, the Cartesians had as great an influence on religion—particularly on the question of the agreement of faith and reason—as they had on physics.[2] The new theological rationalism, which he encouraged, goes far to explain the disfavour into which Montaigne fell at the end of the seventeenth century. Theologians such as Arnauld, Régis, and Fénelon, apart from the Oratorians, adopted the Cartesian idealism, and even if Bossuet uttered a famous warning against the dangers of the ' use of reason ', he approved many elements of Descartes' teaching.[3]

The discredit into which fideist tendencies had fallen within the Church is admirably illustrated by the way in which Bossuet's friend, Pierre-Daniel Huet, Bishop of Avranches, thought it wise to keep to himself his *Traité Philosophique de la Faiblesse de l'Esprit Humain*, in which he openly declared a fideism which attentive readers of some of his earlier works had not been slow to perceive.

---

[1] *Revue Philosophique*, Mai–Juin, 1924, article of Etienne Gilson.

The semi-Pelagians did not accept, however, that other severer side of St. Thomas's moral doctrine, his notion of Predestination. It was, it should be noticed, the consideration of the Thomist interpretation of this dogma which produced a crisis in the early life of St. Francis of Sales. He and those who came under his influence, the *humanistes dévots*, form an intermediate party between Jansenists and Jesuits, but their moral teaching inclines towards the latter.

[2] Gilson : op. cit., p. 166, note 2. M. Busson's *Pensée Religieuse* shows that this influence did not begin to make itself felt until after 1660.

[3] cf. *Correspondance* (ed. Urbain), IV, 17, et seq.

Il était si persuadé que la plupart des gens désapprouveraient ses
sentiments sur la Faiblesse de l'Esprit humain, qu'il n'a pu se résoudre
à les publier pendant sa vie . . . quoiqu'il le regardât comme le
meilleur de tous ses ouvrages.

So writes the publisher of the posthumous work in 1723. The
scandal appears to have been great, and it was necessary for the
Abbé d'Olivet to prove that the manuscript published was really
by Huet. It was as inconceivable, apparently, to the Catholic
theologians, who had all become rationalists, as it was to Voltaire,
that such an attitude could be anything but a pretext.[1]

Of course, there were those like Bayle and others who held
that since the Cartesian proofs of God's existence and the soul's
immortality were—to say the least—open to dispute, les savants
libertins rightly preferred to consider such matters as certain
only by revelation.[2] But fifty years earlier such views were far
more widely held than among the savants libertins. In the Traité
du Vide, Pascal, himself a fideist, complains of the blindness of
those who appeal to authority in matters concerning reason and
experience, and to reason in those concerning religion. The first
part of this dictum is indisputably true. The Aristotelian physics
were the most outworn part of the old system, and could only
be maintained by the persecution and systematic stifling of all
who sought to overthrow them. It is hardly necessary to refer
to the burning of Bruno, the imprisonment of Campanella, the
prohibition against Copernican theory (1616), and the retractation extorted from Galileo, or the decree of the Parlement of
Paris against ' novelties ' in physics (1624).

The second part of Pascal's complaint was perhaps less true
than it appears.[3] Apart from the Oratorians and Descartes,
there was an unavowed tendency in official Catholic circles to
frown on all apologetics in which any philosophic considerations
were involved. Thus the mysterious Ives de Paris records, in
the first volume of his Théologie Naturelle (1635), the opposition
to its publication. This has forced him to add a preliminary
discourse : Qu'il est permis d'éclaircir les vérités da la Religion par

---

[1] K. S. Barach : P. D. Huet als Philosoph. 1862, p. 20, 1. Ch.
Bartholemess : Huet ou le Scepticisme Théologique, p. 44.

[2] While, as Bayle says, every Cartesian of his time would admit that
the principles of the old philosophy are incapable of giving any valid
proofs at all (Bayle : Dictionnaire, art. Charron. E. and O.).

[3] Of course, Pascal's remarks, apart from their general import, are
specially aimed at two people : Descartes, who was disposed to disregard
the importance of Pascal's experiments on the Void, because they did
not suit his general theories about matter : and the unfortunate Forton
de St. Ange (see below, p. 366).

raisons naturelles. The same tendency is revealed by the wide-spread attempt to prevent theology being treated in any language but Latin. The underlying idea is sufficiently evident in the comment of Garasse on the disapproval with which Coëffeteau's attempt at translating Aquinas was received : *C'est violer les mystères que de les révéler.*[1] In 1634 the Assembly of Clergy not only refused to accept the dedication of Marandé's *Théologien Français*, but refused to approve the design of such a book,[2]

In 1650 further testimony is provided in a book entitled *De l'Elévation de la Foi et de l'Abaissement de la Raison.* The author, Moyse Amirault (1596–1664), Descartes' fellow-student at Poitiers, and later the tutor of William Penn, was a well-known Calvinist minister, a friend of Conrart, and a man of conciliatory tendencies. A rationalistic attitude was, of course, more common among Protestants, but it should be noted what scandal Benjamin Whichcote, one of the Cambridge Platonists (known to their contemporaries as the ' Latitude Men '), caused among his conservative colleagues in that very same year by speaking of ' reason ' in the pulpit.[3] Amirault says the thesis of the Catholics is, that the more one renounces understanding with regard to all articles of religion the better, since blind belief is more meritorious. This view has been summed up in the formula the author takes as his title :

> Et bien que ceux qui ont ces sentiments soient en plus petit nombre que les autres, si sont ils fort considérables, pourtant. Car outre qu'il y a des gens de condition relevés qui tiennent ouvertement ce langage, il y en a plusieurs autres qui pour ne les dire pas si haute-ment, ne laissent pas pourtant d'avoir les mêmes mouvements en la pensée. Et je sais qu'entre les Docteurs, et même entre les Jésuites, il s'en trouve plusieurs qui suivraient cette maxime aux disputes de la religion, si les autres ne la rejetaient point comme dangereuse et scandaleuse.

Amiraut fears that this alleged respect for the heights of divine wisdom is often a mere excuse for indifference and for avoiding the obligation of accepting what actually had been demonstrated. He does not hope to convince those who are resolved to ignore

---

[1] Garasse : *Nouvean Jugement de ce qui a été dit . . .* p. 42, 3. N. Coëffeteau : *Premier Essay de Questions théologiques traités en nostre langue selon le stile de Saint Thomas et autres Scolastiques . . .* 1607.

[2] E. Jovy : *Pascal et Saint Ange,* p. 52, 3.

[3] It was one of the ' Latitude Men ', John Smith, who first introduced Descartes' teaching at Cambridge (E. T. Campagnac : *The Cambridge Platonists,* 1901).

what they really know, but he writes ' for those good souls who have had this opinion so dinned into them that they do not try to understand '.[1]

These remarks suffice, for the moment, to show that the different attitudes of seventeenth-century readers of Montaigne will be to a great extent influenced by their fideist or rationalist approach to religion. The century is, in this respect, a period of transition, but before its end the ecclesiastical world at least will be seen to have come to ignore the fact—inconceivable to them—that Montaigne was at once a sceptic and a Christian.

It has always been obvious that our author, by his scepticism, by his tolerance, and by his humanitarianism, must be numbered among the great-grandfathers of the *philosophes*. If, however, the pre-history of this movement is to be properly understood, a few words must be said about the different tendencies of philosophical liberalism from the end of the sixteenth century onwards. Here, again, may be perceived, though often in close connexion, the two currents of fideism and rationalism.

A fact, which is rarely recognized except, perhaps, in England and with regard to England, is that there was, for nearly a century after the Reformation, a large body of moderate and too often timidly inarticulate opinion which, in all countries, among both Roman Catholics and Protestants, still believed in the possibility of a really Catholic Church. The more optimistic of them still hoped for a general Council where schisms would be healed and where Rome would finally reject some of the abuses and superstitions which were the accretions of centuries. A good deal of the secret diplomacy of the modern Solomon, King James the First and Sixth, was dictated by some such hope, and it is only necessary to read the Journal of Pierre de l'Estoile, to note not only the interest of a conservative bourgeois of some enlightenment in this question, but the number of those he mentions as working for the ' re-union of the Churches ' in the time of Henri IV. The strength of this body of moderate opinion is generally underestimated, not only owing to their prudence, but also because later Roman Catholic and anti-clerical writers are apt to forget that many of those whom they brand as ' deists ' or ' atheists ', were certainly far from considering themselves outside the Church.

Deism, apart from the question of innate ideas, was chiefly

[1] op. cit., *Introduction*. Copious evidence is also afforded by Busson (*Pensée Religieuse . . . passim*).

concerned with universal consent as a criterion of truth. It thus forms part of the great empirical movement associated with the names of Bacon and Locke. The deists not only held that true belief in all essential matters is rational and, therefore, can and must be controlled in this way, but that the results of their investigations would inevitably coincide with their faith.[1]

The fideists, on the other hand, applied themselves to demonstrating the contradictoriness of phenomena or opinions, since they were equally confident that faith and reason were irreconcilable, and that reason must be made to work to its own discomfiture if their faith was to remain safe. Yet it also requires to be made clear that with Montaigne, already, this ' scepticism ', which went so far as to declare that *nous n'avons aucune communication avec l'être*, did not involve a similar belief with regard to ethics. From Charron onwards, too, we shall have the strange spectacle of a complete fideism as far as metaphysical problems and the major dogmas of religion are concerned, combined with a firm belief in a universal moral law. This combination of views was very common. It will be seen shortly that something of the kind is found even in the Essays, but there it is purely psychological, whereas the interest in natural law (furthered by a confusion of the Roman *jus naturale* and *jus gentium*) took its motive force from a kind of deification of such concepts as Nature, Reason, and Virtue—often identified—which is totally foreign to Montaigne's mind, in spite of his use of such expressions as *notre mère Nature*.

The attitude of those who, like Montaigne, not only oppose reason to faith but enlarge upon the impotence of reason, generally prevents them from doing any constructive thinking. Yet their function is rather to represent, far more, perhaps, than the Deists, the claims of toleration. It is clear that Montaigne's lists of diverse customs and beliefs have in view mainly the object of discouraging dogmatism, from the mere fact that he does not appear to realize how deeply such customs are rooted in the mentality of those who hold them. And quite apart from the works of La Mothe le Vayer, the great exponent of this manner of argument, there is a large body of literature in the seventeenth century which sets out, with more seriousness than meets the superficial eye, to advocate the claims of people of

[1] Herbert, the ' Father of the Deists ', illustrates all these aspects : sphere of revelation reduced, essential principles of religion and morality purely rational, and empirically verified by universal consent (in the *De Religione Gentilium*).

different tastes and character to enjoy these different tastes and interests, even in relatively unimportant matters.

I have spoken of an ' ideology ', connected with fideism. I had in mind all that side of the Essays which is concerned with the misery of man and the vanity of human nature. It is made up of various elements, partly borrowed : the *Omnia Vanitas* of Ecclesiastes, whose sayings, interspersed with those of Pyrrho, were carved on those beams under which Montaigne sat writing in his library ; the *Nihil miserius aut superbius* of Pliny ; and the Heraclitean obsession of flux and change. These elements and many more, which are, some of them, the commonplaces of all ages, are merged in Montaigne's scepticism, and give that scepticism its particular emotional colouring. It is profitable, how-ever, to examine more clearly the character which this ' pessimism ' really has and the place it fills in his philosophy of life.

' I should say ', wrote T. E. Hulme, in a much-quoted essay, ' that the starting point for the religious attitude was always the kind of discussion you find in Pascal (Frag. 139, Brun-schwicg's edition), and that is what I mean by a " critique of satisfaction." . . . My point is, it is not a separate subject. It is not philosophy, *nor* is it psychology. Always the subject is the " vanity of desire ".' [1] The *Pensée* in question begins by saying that ' the unhappiness of men comes entirely from not knowing how to remain quietly in a room '. Read on, and you will see that it is full of reminiscences of the Essays. What Hulme says of the ' vanity of desire ' is doubtless an adequate analysis as far as Pascal is concerned. The systematic way in which he set out to prove to his readers that they were utterly wretched—a thoroughness which sometimes defeats its own object—was the first step in his design of bringing them to faith. Pascal, too, is a fideist—' *le coeur a ses raisons* '—and Pascal's design was recognized as such and blamed in certain quarters from the moment the *Pensées* appeared.

In the case of Montaigne we have something more general. Meditation on the nothingness of man is common to all ages. Even at the time of the Renaissance, whose originality of thought, according to a recent writer,[2] consists precisely in a belief in the possibility of a moral code apart from any religious elements, and whose most typical representative in France is the epically optimistic Rabelais, we can find this ' vanity ' motif. Take, for instance, the popular comparison of Heraclitus and

[1] T. E. Hulme : *Speculations*, 1924.
[2] cf. J. Roger Charbonnel : *Revue du XVIme siecle*, 1924.

Democritus,[1] utilized by Montaigne himself, and which appears
in all the collections of *leçons*, those anthologies from which the
form of the ' essay ' was evolved.   One weeps, the other laughs,
but they are not two optimists ; they simply show, each in his
own way, their realization of the vanity of life.   In the *Académie*
of La Primaudaye they are both quoted as examples of the
irresolution and doubt which much learning engenders.
Take the *Théâtre du Monde* of Bouaystuau, another of the
company of compilators.   This book (which went into twenty
editions in twenty-five years) sets forth, with the help of Lucretius
and of the seventh book of Pliny's *Natural History*, a lurid picture
of the misery of man.   It is meant, however, to be taken along
with the same author's *Bref Discours de l'Excellence de l'Homme*,
where he pursues the opposite design.   It would be a mistake
to take this contrast as a mere literary exercise.[2]   Its primary
function is a satisfaction of the emotions by a dramatic device,
whose conventionality and agreement with two aspects of Christianity made it all the more effective with the greater public
of the time.   It is precisely this type of emotional meditation
on the misery of man, indulged in by an age which feels that
humanity is *not* totally miserable and *is* capable of new discoveries, new powers, new ambitions, which explains how the
' double truth ' theory worked, how the thinking man of that
time was able to hold in some sort of fluid synthesis a mental
world, which was, for most of them, as I have shown, divided
into two distinct and contradictory domains.[3]
Montaigne's ' pessimism ' was something more profound and
less purely emotional than what we find in Bouaystuau, and it
is interesting to see him react against the exaggerations of Lucre-

[1] See *Essais* (Edition Municipale, IV, p. 155).   Tahureau's *Democritic*
in particular has often been compared with Montaigne.   The popularity
of the two figures lasts on into the seventeenth century and gives us
the *Héraclite* of P. Du Moulin (1608) and the *Démocrite Chrétien and
Héraclite Chrétien* of Pierre de Besse (1615).   The popularity of the
two figures even at the time of the Fronde is attested by a Mazarinade
entitled : ' *Démocrite and Héraclite, riant et pleurant sur le temps qui
court* ' (cf. Bremond : *Histoire du Sentiment Religieux*, Vol. I, p. 308).
[2] e.g. George Boas in *The Happy Beast in French Thought of the
Seventeenth Century*, 1933.
[3] At times we can see in those who exploit these themes something
which is not far from that double aspect of language and meaning,
which it has been the service of Mr. I. A. Richards and Mr. C. K. Ogden
to point out in our time : the ' truth ' of poetry and religion, on the one
hand, the ' truth ' of science and commonsense, on the other—the
emotional and the ' referential ' use of language (see *The Meaning of
Meaning*).

tius and Pliny, as reproduced by the *Théâtre du Monde*, even in the course of making his famous comparison of men and beasts in the Apology. Montaigne's belief in the goodness of man and his scepticism are united to each other in a way which will be mentioned. It is clear that this ' vanity of man ' is, in the Apology and even elsewhere in the Essays, an integral part of Montaigne's fideism ; it does, so to speak, clear a space for his religion. And yet, though it has often in Montaigne this vaguely religious character, I think that Hulme's analysis will not always fit. This ' vanity of desire ' is merely one of the great tragic themes ; call it, with Unamuno, a ' tragic sense of life ', if you will—a realization of the dramatic and tragic doubleness of the universe—whose value is emotional—a *catharsis* in fact, to use a much-abused word.

There are two Montaignes, then : one who sees himself as the *scrutateur sans connaissance, le magistrat sans jurisdiction et après tout le badin de la farce* ; and another who cries with fervour : *J'accepte de bon cœur et reconnaissant ce que nature a fait pour moi, and m'en agrée et m'en loue. On fait tort à ce grand et tout puissant donneur de refuser son don, l'annuller et défigurer. Tout bon, il a fait tout bon.*[1]

The precise relationship between these two sides of Montaigne is admirably set forth in a couple of pages of the Apology.[2] All certain knowledge is impossible on account of the passions, which are constantly influencing the reason, the imagination and the senses. Nevertheless, the passions are the necessary conditions of virtue, and therefore good in themselves. They provide the initial energy, and virtue itself is valuable simply in proportion to its difficulty. Thus man is incapacitated as an instrument for the acquisition of knowledge by the same factor which makes him capable of virtue. This might be called a moral optimism coupled with an intellectual pessimism.

Montaigne's ethical ideas considerably changed in his later years, although he continued to stick to his fideism and his scepticism. Yet, note that, even while he is writing the Apology, he is surprised at the conduct of Pyrrho who refused to get out of the way of carts and walked on the edge of precipices. Even then his scepticism could be entirely summed up by this later formula : *La connaissance des causes appartient seulement à celui qui a la conduite des choses, non à nous qui n'en avons que la souffrance, et qui en avons l'usage parfaitement plein, selon notre nature, sans en pénétrer l'origine et l'essence.*

[1] *Essais*, III, 9, p. 292 B : III, 13, p. 443 B.
[2] *Essais*, II, 12, p. 321, et seq.

What appears to go further than this in the Apology is chiefly special pleading for the uncertainty of knowledge, and even this notion of making the passions responsible at the same time for human virtue and human ignorance, though it corresponds to a deeply felt connexion in the author's mind, is a little factitious in its symmetry. It reappears, nevertheless, even more clearly stated, after 1588, in the same part of the Apology :

> N'y a il point de la hardiesse à la philosophie d'estimer des hommes qu'ils produisent leurs plus grands effets et plus approchants de la divinité, quand ils sont hors d'eux et furieux et insensés. . .   Ceci est plaisant à considerer ; par la dislocation que les passions apportent à notre raison, nous devenons vertueux ; par son extirpation que la fureur ou l'image de la mort apporte nous devenons prophètes ou divins.   Jamais plus volontiers je ne l'en crus.   C'est un pur enthousiasme que la sainte vérité a inspiré en l'esprit philosophique, qui lui arrache, contre sa proposition, que l'état tranquille de notre âme, l'état rassis, l'état plus sain que la philosophie lui puisse acquérir n'est pas son meilleur état.

Fideism, then, as before, but Montaigne may say what he likes about this rejection of ' tranquillity ' as a rule of life, and the rôle of the passions in the virtuous life.   On the very page preceding this, he contradicts the first view.   The passions are no longer *sollicitations acheminant l'âme aux actions vertueuses.* They are *tempêtes qui débauchent honteusement l'âme de sa tranquillité.*   Of course, our appetites are necessary parts of us, but they are now good simply as parts and not because they provide us with an unruly element in whose control virtue alone consists. Virtue is not a matter of difficulty.   This change is the most important thing in the evolution of Montaigne's ethical ideas, and alone justifies the statement that he passed from a Stoical to an Epicurean view.

When Montaigne retired from public life, he turned to the task of setting his house in order, both in a literal, nay, even financial, and in a metaphorical sense.   The two key words to his ethical preoccupations at this moment were ' intention ' and ' *constance* '.   What astonishingly different results our actions have !   How little credit we can claim for what actually happens ;   and a man who lives in retirement must put away the thought of getting satisfaction from the admiration of others. So intention is the one thing that matters in ethics.   How interesting it is to look between the lines of the history-books and try to penetrate the motives of Plutarch's heroes !   How their most intimate and insignificant actions reveal them !   These are the considerations with which Montaigne begins the train of thought which leads him to his self-analysis.

As for *constance*, this has a double sense in the Essays. It sometimes means endurance, but it more often means consistency. Montaigne is afraid of death, of pain and of disease. With help of Seneca, he tries to harden himself against such thoughts. He is first and last a utilitarian, but a utilitarian who has already learnt that results, even psychological ones, are very precarious. To possess his soul in peace and quiet, it is to this alone that man can aspire, but in order to accomplish this, it is necessary for him to teach himself to be brave and to be happy in spite of possible misfortunes. Misfortunes, after all, depend largely on how we take them. It is necessary to feel that one will be the same, whatever happens. One must learn by habit and by discipline to be brave, to be self-controlled, to be just. However, it is not a matter merely of specific virtues but of a general direction in life. It is impossible to aspire to this self-possession except by consistency. It is necessary to choose one's road by reason, on which alone this consistency can found itself. Yet there is nothing so astonishing in life as its variety. Customs differ from country to country and from century to century, and few indeed are there even among the great men of the past who have had any internal unity in their lives.

Some such statement might serve as a picture of Montaigne's opinions round about the year 1574. Then came the so-called sceptical crisis. One side of this is connected with Montaigne's fideism. It does not matter here whether, in making the attempt to defend religion by reason, he realized that the new style in apologetics was the only line which he could honestly take , or whether he set out in the Apology as a fideist from the beginning. But there was another side to this crisis. A realization of the inter-dependence of contraries, an antinomianism or relativism, was forced on him by his reading of Sextus Empiricus and his preoccupation with the scepticism he was using to defend religion : παντὶ λόγῳ λόγος ἴσος ἀντίκειται. This relativism encouraged at the same time his interest in introspection.

The Essay on Cruelty, (II, 11), probably written towards 1578, shows us Montaigne face to face with one of the problems which he was beginning to realize by the light of his new relativism—a problem already mentioned. The Stoics had suggested to him the necessary connexion between virtue and the passions, but his relativism and his own self-analysis lead him to doubts upon this point. For virtue, then, is something different from mere goodness of heart, from innocence and an equable temperament. It is essentially a matter of overcoming difficulty. That is why God is called good, but not virtuous.[1] It seems clear to him, however, that virtue is good because of the psychological effect on the virtuous person; the ' manly pleasure ' of Cato in killing himself, and the realization of the beauty of the act, are insisted on. The later formula for this will be *la congratulation de bien faire*.

Yet, says the author, Socrates presents a real difficulty to this view. In all his acts there is a perfect ease which seems incompatible with this view. Montaigne leaves the question here unsettled and turns aside to consider his own natural hatred of cruelty, a mere good inclination for which he can take no credit. If we turn to the Third Book, the direction in which Montaigne is tending will be seen. Virtue is for him a harmony, a harmonious and regulated system of impulses. The suggestion that difficulty is an element necessary to moral goodness only appears once in the Third Book. Montaigne will hardly believe the familiar story of Socrates' original bad character, and he practically denies the dependency of virtues and vices:

> Tout ainsi que les Stoiciens disaient que les vices sont utilement introduits pour donner prix et faire épaule à la vertu, nous pouvons dire avec meilleure raison et conjecture moins hardie, que nature nous a prêté la douleur pour l'honneur et service de la volupté et indolence.[2]

Thus Montaigne's principle of contradiction, the complementary quality of apparent contradictions, holds good of pain and pleasure. It seems to him doubtful whether it is true of virtue and vice, and indeed a few pages later we find an explicit definition of virtue which excludes the notion of conflict or tension.[3] Just as Montaigne developed one of the favourite poetical themes of the Renaissance—the notion of Pastoral wisdom, the comparison of the peasants and the philosophers—into part of his fideism by contrasting an *ignorance abécédaire* and an *ignorance doctorale*, so there is an original innocence and an informed innocence, which are the two kinds of virtue, just as these two classes of peasants and sages are the two kinds of ' true believers '. It is in between, in the middle class, that the dogmatists and all those who trouble the world are found; and—if one may

---

[1] Compare with the discussion on the Epicurean God in the passage of the Apology just quoted (II, 12, p. 322 c).

[2] *Essais*, III, p. 418 B. See also the end of the Essay on ' Anger ' (II, 31), written already towards 1578.

[3] III, p. 444 c. ' La douleur, la volupté, l'amour, la haine sout les premières choses que sent un enfant ; si, la raison survenant elles s'appliquent à elle, cela c'est vertu.' See also *Essais*, III, 10, p. 312, Montaigne's comment on ' lest we be led into temptation '.

gloze—it is only there that the notion of virtue as a conflict has any application. The virtue of Socrates has the same harmony about it as the instinctive conduct of the peasant, the same perfection of instinct which Montaigne admires in animals.

Let us try to see how this change came about and the nature of several notions which Montaigne develops above all in the later Essays. Montaigne's scepticism was a *result* of searching for things stable, things constant. He rejected one hypostasis—a 'common-sense view' of virtue or truth—which had become unacceptable to him, only to look for another, and he retains to the very end a passion for what is fixed and what is universal, mitigated indeed by a keen realization of flux and variety. A painful disease and a riding accident which brings him to the brink of death help him to fix his attention even more upon himself. He realizes that he finds the pleasure of life precisely in this curiosity about himself, in his own character, and sees that he could not wish sincerely to be other than he is. He has found something stable in his own character, a *maîtresse forme*. Any consistency achieved at the price of ignoring this fixed element—which is itself hard to distinguish clearly and involves a discipline of introspection—is likely to be merely superficial. Suppressed rage may only have a worse effect on the feelings than if it were given some rein, and Montaigne is always more concerned with states of mind than with actions in themselves. Even his interest in the lives of the heroes of antiquity is concentrated on seeing what they are when they are most ' themselves '—that is, when the rock bottom of their characters appears in their most instinctive actions.

On this basis, Montaigne develops a new idea of consistency, which is, in its turn, balanced by the consideration of the value of adaptability. ' Order, moderation and consistency ', he writes, ' are the only things that a man who is but a poor fellow in general cannot achieve.' A man must choose what is fitting to him, fitting not only to his circumstances in life, his *état civil*, but appropriate to his individual nature with its physical basis, the ' humours ', if he wishes to carry out that general maxim : ' follow nature '.[1] Cato's death would not have been a fitting

---

[1] It is often said that Montaigne called himself a ' naturalist '. On the one occasion when he uses this term, applying it to himself, he is certainly not doing so precisely in the accepted sense of the word in those days (physical scientist). But the passage is concerned with style, and the word was originally brought into the sentence in contrast with the term ' scholastic ', afterwards suppressed. Writers who borrow without adapting are ' scholastic ', those who quote as he does are naturalists (*Essais*, III, 12, p. 367).

end to any other life than his.[1] *Notre grand et glorieux chef d'oeuvre est de vivre à propos.* To do this, we must even be prepared to sacrifice to some extent the way we have chosen for ourselves and our knowledge of what is, strictly speaking, right or wrong ; for Montaigne, like most other practical moralists, never doubts that, theoretically, we know very well what we should or shouldn't do. Thus Alcibiades, who can adapt himself to the ways of Athens or Sparta, and to the company of Lais as to that of Socrates, becomes one of those who command his admiration almost as much as Socrates himself.

In his insistence on harmony, not conflict, and on the importance of *individual* nature Montaigne revived two of the most important ideas of Epicurus, but the twist he gives them is a wholly personal one. Why, in his view, *should* we do this or that ? He is, and always was, a utilitarian and a hedonist, but with a difference. The notion of merit is quite foreign to his mind. Duty, that legalist conception of *la preud'homie scolastique*, he rejects. Its more purely psychological form, conscience, has, of course, some meaning for him, since vice is chiefly the result of ignorance and something negative, but it is the self-satisfaction of doing the right thing which weighs with him. It is interesting that Montaigne did not more completely abandon the idea of conscience, and supplies, I repeat, an indication that to some extent his views on the relativity of customs and laws were merely a much-needed argument for tolerance. He did not see the dangerous smugness which this notion of *acquiescientia in seipso* may acquire ; and this for two reasons. First, a certain realization of the concurrence of good and bad motives to produce any action, an *ambivalence des sentiments*, as it has been called, which is one of the many astonishingly modern things in Montaigne.[2] It is a realization, not an obsession, for he remains certain that whatever he does he does it whole-heartedly. The other reason is his preoccupation with consciousness. It becomes for him almost the ultimate test of value. The consciousness of being in tune with oneself and the world is the end of all endeavour. To be thus in tune necessarily implies consciousness. What is unconscious is not properly us, and all pleasures,

---

[1] After 1588, Montaigne borrows no less than nine passages on this one idea from the same section of Cicero's *De Officiis*.

[2] ' I find it not only difficult to reconcile our actions with one another, but I find it difficult, taking each one singly, to designate it by some leading quality, so ambiguous and motley do they appear from different angles ' (*Essais*, III, 13, p. 396 B). ' Dieu sait, à qui veut les étendre quelle diversité d' images ne souffre notre interne volonté ' (ib., I, 37, p. 297 B). See these passages in their context.

whether they are in well-doing or in mere well-being, depend on this. Others, he says, let their life slip by them without knowing the taste and savour of it ; for them it is just such a pleasure as sleep—sleep which he himself had tried to enjoy more exquisitely in his youth by making his servant wake him during the night.

To sum up, Montaigne absorbs ethics into a kind of general aesthetic of life. His personal system, almost as much as that of Shakespeare, is free from ethical bias.[1] His virtue has the artistic implication of the Italian *virtu*, himself a *virtuoso*. His goods and bads are the beautiful and the ugly. Art is in its essence a heightening of consciousness and a harmonizing of contrary impulses. Order and consistency are means to this end. This fittingness, this being adapted to oneself and one's circumstances, in which the concept of duty loses itself, is τὸ πρέπον, Cicero's *decorum*, the ' taste ' round which the battles of literary critics used to rage.

Montaigne himself confesses to us the defects of his views : *j'ai cette pire coutume, que si j'ai un escarpin de travers, je laisse encore de travers et ma chemise et ma cape : je dédaigne m'amender à demi.*[2] There speaks the artist. Like the artist, too, his views are not always intended to have a general application. He knows them to be true for himself, but would be cautious to recommend them to others.

J'ai pris bien simplement et cruement pour mon regard ce précepte ancien : que nous ne saurions faillir à suivre nature . . . je ne combats rien, mes deux maîtresses pièces vivent de leur grâce en paix, et bon accord : *mais le lait de ma nourriture a été, Dieu merci, médiocrement sain et tempéré.*

It is this same upbringing which has saved him, suckled as he was in a peasant's cottage, from the confusion of social, intellectual and moral superiority, so common to his time. The attitude of Renaissance humanism was an aristocratic optimism for the Sage, a pessimism as far as the Vulgar were concerned. Montaigne does not let this aristocratic prejudice invade the

---

[1] The distinction made here is on the lines of Jules de Gaultier's *Sensibilité Métaphysique*. Ethical systems are characterisically concerned with what *should be*, apart from *what is possible*. Once this is admitted, abstract Ethics are condemned. Only Personal Ethics, with their attempt to decide what is right in concrete cases and given personalities, can remain. Their procedure may be compared with that of the artist and his medium. This difference remains whether the reader chooses to think of ' beauty ' and ' goodness ' as value-concepts unrelated, or identified.

[2] *Essais*, III, 9, p. 218. See also p. 228 : ' Une rène de travers à mon cheval ', &c.

moral and intellectual part of life. He substitutes a new division, the peasants and the philosophers grouped together—extremes that meet—and on the other side, the semi-learned and the pedants.

It should further be noticed how strongly Montaigne must have felt that virtue was a harmony and not a conflict.[1] For, at the same time as his opinions were moving in this direction, he was becoming more and more conscious of the implications of his antinomianism. Everything, every concept of his thought, is becoming double, a balance of principles. This perception of antinomies and his aestheticism, are two essential points in estimating the originality of the Essays. The latter has been emphasized by two contemporary French critics, M. Elie Faure and M. Ramon Fernandez.[2] The chief importance of the essay of M. Fernandez rests on a distinction between the *moi*, or the affectivity at any given moment, and ' personality ', an organization of the succession of our states of mind, in which we accept, so to speak, the responsibility for the results of these states translated in terms of conduct ; a correspondence of feelings and acts, in accordance with which we can promise to ourselves how we shall feel and act in the future in any given set of circumstances.

The moral aestheticism of the Essays is just this organization. One of the demands of personality is an objective recognition of itself. It is the torment of a Rousseau that he cannot achieve this recognition, and it is impossible for him to do so just because he sets out with a false preconception of what he is. It is the achievement of Montaigne, says M. Fernandez, that even his enemies, the neighbour who tried to surprise him in his castle, the robbers who took him prisoner on one of his journeys, recognized him at once for what he was, inferring his character from his bearing. The ' self-portrait ' had a similar function in his life, and we shall see how contemporaries acknowledged the resemblance.

But the Essays have yet another rôle, a mirror held to himself, a method of self-knowledge necessary to the organization of the personality : *Encore se faut il têtonner* [peigner]*, encore se faut il ranger pour sortir en place.* M. Fernandez rightly makes great play with the resemblances of aesthetics and the psychology of personality. He adds, however, that these comparisons would

---

[1] Both these views, be it said in passing, are capable of being developed in a moral aestheticism, and differing more or less in the same way as what is dramatic and what is lyrical in art—whose value consists respectively in intensity or in comprehensiveness.

[2] Elie Faure : *Montaigne et ses Trois Premiers Nés* (1926) ; Ramon Fernandez : *De la Personnalité* (1928).

be dangerous unless there were some means of distinguishing these two domains. ' For if the mental processes of the artist and those of the " person " are similar sometimes to the point of identity, their respective objects cannot be confused, so that the psychological relationship only accentuates the objective differences.' That is, the artistic whole has only an indirect connexion with the life and conduct of the author. This may often be true, but Montaigne's book really is ' consubstantial with his life ', and this means not only that it is self-expression in the sense of being a description—a demand for the objective recognition of a personality conscious of itself—but also that it has been part and parcel of the acquisition of that consciousness. Montaigne's self-knowledge is chiefly retrospective, and it is this record of his own past which has helped him to know his *maîtresse forme*. So that it is true not only that Montaigne organized his personality on what are, in fact, aesthetic principles, but that the Essays form an integral part of this organization.

The most frequent failing of seventeenth-century appreciations of the Essays is their tendency to make Montaigne too much of a didactic moralist. The organization of the personality has no essential connexion with ethics. Spiritual unity, as M. Fernandez says, may be achieved by a bandit or a crook financier. So far from being a teacher or preacher, Montaigne, on the whole, prefers to draw no conclusions as to the wisdom either of the general maxim of ' follow nature ' or as to the advisability of following him in his organization of his character. Though he has no wish himself to be other than he is, he can conceive richer lives, more noble and more profitable. This side of Montaigne's relativism, the refusal to generalize his own experience, has been called by M. Brunschwicg, ' a mark of profound discouragement at the moral chaos produced by the civil wars '.[1] But surely, although a man may organize his own personality, he can hardly have the pretension to tell other people how to organize theirs, except indirectly by his own example.

Montaigne's influence as a master of living in this sense, of the personal life, is obviously a very difficult thing to follow. Its reflection in many cases may never cast its shadow across the printed page. The undoubted seventeenth-century interest in character was, to some extent, absorbed and side-tracked,

---

[1] L. Brunschwicg : *Le Progrès de la Conscience, II.* There is at least one well-known phrase in the Essays (III, 2, p. 27) which seems to belie M. Brunschwicg's remarks : ' chaque homme porte en soi la forme entière de l'humaine condition '. This claim should, however, be read in its context. Contrast *Essais*, II, 32, p. 530 c.

especially in the first fifty years, which chiefly concern us here, by the premature attempts to arrive at a rigid classification of types of character, on the basis of the Aristotelian theory of humours as elaborated by Galen, and embellished by the Spanish doctor, Juan del Huarte. In dealing with Charron and the elements other than the Essays which went to make up that *pot pourri* of his, there will be more opportunity for insisting on the importance of this generally ignored side of seventeenth-century psychology. It is in some of the writers on *honnêteté* that the aesthetic tendencies of Montaigne's ethics find their clearest echo.

Less original features of his ethics may seem, at first sight, to have a greater historical importance, since they are more easily linked up with the history of ethical theory. Thus if in the earliest Essays it is, above all, a preoccupation with motives which shows itself, it is pretty clear that Montaigne was naturally a utilitarian and a hedonist. Motivation, if considered to the exclusion of results, is an ethical position which may be called ' rigorism '. From the end of the Middle Ages an important refinement was taking place in religious ethics, a refinement whose influence within the Church is testified to both by the elaboration of casuistry and by the doctrine of the ' pure love ' of God : that is, an interest in purity of intention and an effort to condemn every form of mercenary spirit.

Contemporary with this rigorist tendency were others which, though compatible themselves with such views, helped by their very disagreement with each other to show the dangers which an absolutely consistent rigorism involved. The great service of rigorism was the realization it brought that the fear of hell was not a necessary or a desirable consideration. Some of these points in connexion with rigorism will cross our path, and it is desirable here and now to bring out clearly both Montaigne's utilitarianism and some of the implications of rigorism.

Though he is a utilitarian, Montaigne has not considered at all deeply the two alternatives just mentioned, nor realized their crucial nature, but the attitude of compromise which he adopts in dealing with the particular case of political honesty is very instructive (see III, i, *De l'Utile et de l'Honnête*). Machiavelli's political philosophy was the form in which utilitarianism was most familiar to the Renaissance mind, as the doctrine of Hobbes was to the seventeenth century. Montaigne stands neither with Machiavelli nor with his adversaries. Political necessity may demand a crime, but political authority has no right to command an honest man to perform it, because a part, at least, of the immorality consists in the honest man being forced to an act incompatible with his character. This formula may seem tautological, but it is what is at the bottom of Montaigne's mind, and is only another proof of how far he conceives morality in the terms of character. More important is the other reason— closely connected—which weighs with Montaigne both here and elsewhere, that is the *psychological* result on the man directly or indirectly responsible for such an act of political necessity : that is, not only remorse but the destruction of all possibility of trust, with consequent loss, from this reason alone, of peace of mind.

Similarly, Montaigne's utilitarianism with regard to personal, as opposed to political, action is only disguised by the fact that the most important result for him is the psychological result on the subject himself. That this result may depend largely on the ' principles ' or the ' conscience ' of the individual in question is a problem which he does not face simply because he does not doubt that a man knows well enough in general what is morally good or bad, and it is just in this belief that his moral optimism lies.

The moral optimism of Montaigne's contemporaries, however, has certain other features, those spoken of just now as difficult to reconcile with the more conventional forms of rigorism. These are the stock ideas of Renaissance and post-Renaissance humanism, the goodness of the passions and the life according to reason. With these one naturally connects the famous maxim : ' follow nature '.

It has already been shown that Montaigne makes some reserves as to this approved dogma about the passions. What must be insisted on, however, is that, during the period dealt with in this book, the passions are everywhere, even in the most orthodox circles, thought of as not merely indifferent but as good in themselves. In this period, during which, it is true, as has been often asserted, that some of the ideas of the Stoics enjoy considerable popularity, their ' apathy ' is a standing joke. Is not the love of God a passion ? We are here on dangerous ground, and the acuter minds of the day knew it, but such a subterfuge as Descartes' distinction of the passions of the mind and the passions of the body—presaged by a somewhat similar distinction of St. Francis of Sales [1]—was too unsound psychologically to have much success.

This interest in the passions, this licensing of them within certain limits, was obviously at variance, too, with the extreme intellectualism of the recommendation to live according to reason alone. The will must be determined only by reason ; yet, on the other hand, where it was so, if it ever was so, it was hard

[1] See p. 133.

to see what useful function the passions performed. Now, though obviously some satisfactory compromise is here to be attained simply by attention to the facts of psychology, the rigorist attitude of Christian ethics, where maintained, considerably complicated matters. Can actions motivated by the passions be considered of moral value ? Can actions dictated by reason be considered of moral value ? [1] These two questions pose themselves. The natural answer is : Both. In which case it is obvious that a ethical criterion must be sought elsewhere. Hence, perhaps, the discussions on moral taste and on conscience ; hence, also, those on the ' passions ' of gratitude and beneficence which fill the eighteenth century. Moreover, it was hard to see, when psychological analysis was attempted, how truly disinterested motivation, especially through the passions, was possible at all, except by invoking a supernatural act of grace for every virtuous action, as is done, for example, by the Jansenist, Jacques Esprit, in his *Fausseté des Vertus Humaines.*

Most seventeenth-century statements about ethics in general are concerned with these concepts of Reason, Nature and Virtue, often confused with each other and treated as emanations of the Deity. The actual formula, ' follow nature ', does not appear so often, except when used in condemnation by the *antilibertin* writers as merely the equivalent of a recommendation to self-indulgence. It should be noticed, however, that, even by those who use it in a favourable sense like Gassendi (the reviver not only of Epicurean atomism but of Epicurean ethics), it is commonly applied to the study of one's own aptitudes and not so much used in the general sense of the Stoics of antiquity. It is naturally among Gassendi's friends and followers, however, that we shall find the moral influence of Montaigne. Utilitarianism and rigorism are, however, still elements often to be found in the thought of the same man rather than self-conscious and consistently applied principles. In the first part of the seventeenth century, ethics is still struggling for the recognition of its independence of theology. The crucial question, already mentioned, was whether morality was really independent of piety and true belief. This is what underlay the quarrels about the Virtue of the Pagans, where fundamentally the conception of natural law is involved—a universal morality, inherent in human nature and independent of all revelation.

The question of lay-morals is also what lends real importance to the idea of *honnêteté*. At a certain level, *honnêteté* is only the

---

[1] The question may seem absurd ; but what, according to Christian ideas, is an action worth without charity ?

art of getting on in the world, but the very success of the idea, which has its repercussions on literary taste as well as on men's attitude to life, makes it far more than this. It is at once *sous-morale* and *sur-morale*—*sous-morale* as the proposal of a purely human ideal, which looks to the cultivation of virtues less heroic than those preached from the pulpit, to achieve some imperfect art or science of happiness ; *sur-morale*, because it also presents itself as a work of supererogation, the disinterested realization, in spheres of life which current Christian ethics hardly touch, of not merely the Good but even the Beautiful. It is through *honnêteté* alone perhaps that we can appreciate the real meaning which certain words such as ' reason ', *bon sens*, *bienséance* had for the seventeenth century. The ideals of an age may reveal by contrast the secret of what it is still but would fain cease to be. It is surely thus that the men of that century extolled reasonableness, moderation, elegance. Such words inevitably commanded the imagination of those generations whose hot blood and violent passions betrayed them as the sons and grandsons of the swashbucklers, fanatics and adventurers of the Wars of Religion. Such psychological factors help to explain the success of the whole trend of thought which may be called *honnêteté*.

But to explain the precise form which it took, it is, above all, to Montaigne's Essays that we must turn. *Honnêteté* is, in essence, a lay-morality, but if it is not hostile (in general) to religion, this is due to the fideist idea—because religious belief has been separated off from the rest of life, as being dependant purely on God's grace, concerned not with the here but with the here-after. The fideist idea brings with it a scepticism of reason, which is harnessed, above all, to the service of urging tolerance and forbearance. And forbearance is the real basis of the humanitarian ideal, already as prominent in the Essays as a certain social conservatism, which, oddly enough, proceeds from the same desire not to *judge*. If we proceed to ask how the *honnête homme* regards the problems of conduct, the answer must be that he came to see it, mainly through Montaigne's influence, as an *art*— or, might one say, a subtle equation whose fundamental term is the personality, the *maîtresse forme* of the individual. It is because this complex of ideas reappears again and again in those whose cult of Montaigne is most marked that we can even speak of a Montaigne tradition. If he appears to suffer an eclipse at the end of the century, it is due not only to the discrediting of the fideist idea, but to the very success of this tradition and even to its merging with the thought of those who are, in their several ways, his disciples.

CHAPTER I

THE RECEPTION OF THE ESSAYS—
I: MONTAIGNE AND THE MISCELLANY

Ce que ses écrits ont gagné de réputation publique jusqu'à ce jour, ce n'est pas par la meilleure de leurs parties, qui reste plusqu'à demi couverte, c'est par la moindre : comme exemples, histoires, et riches allégations : ces choses seulement les font rechercher du commun.

MARIE DE GOURNAY (1601).

THE two little volumes which left the press of Simon Millanges at Bordeaux in 1580, probably published at their author's expense, enjoyed a ready sale. So we may judge from the promptness with which a second edition followed only two years later, not many months after Montaigne's return from Italy (November 1581). It may seem, at first sight, unusual that so original a writer should find his public so quickly. But, apart from the very varied appeal which the Essays make to different types of reader, the edition of 1580 only here and there revealed the real Montaigne. For the most part, he appeared a new though interesting recruit to the vast band of sixteenth-century compilators.

The importance of Renaissance anthologies or treasuries of moral philosophy—miscellanies, *centos, exempla*—as popularizers of ideas is now widely recognized. It is nearly twenty years since Pierre Villey showed the genesis of the ' essay ', as we have it in Montaigne, from this successful *genre*. We may trace its line of descent from Antiquity; its survival in the Middle Ages has recently been studied.[1] Brought into new favour by humanists of the Renaissance such as Crinitus and Rhodiginus, treasuries in the vulgar tongue soon followed. Two of the most famous, both originally written in Spanish, Guevara's ' Epistles ' and Mexia's ' Forest of Divers Lessons ', were quickly translated into French and found innumerable imitators. The usual form

---

[1] P. Villey, *Sources et Evolution des Essais* and *Sources d'Idées* (Bibliothèque Française, XVIeme Siècle, Plon). J. Th. Welter : *L'Exemplum dans la Littérature Religieuse & Didactique du Moyen Age*, 1927.

I

of quotation or free reproduction of ancient instances and modern examples, preceded or followed by commentary or discussion, was varied by collections of apophthegms or proverbs, such as those published by Erasmus.   The main purpose of the authors, whatever the form adopted, was to provide short cuts to knowledge, and the vogue of even the feeblest reminds one of a thirst for learning and a credulity only paralleled by that of modern America.   It was natural that the compilators should recognize the form which Montaigne had enriched and transformed, and that they, in their turn, should pay him the compliment of extracting examples and opinions from the Essays.   It is among their works that we shall find evidence of what seemed most immediately provocative in Montaigne's work.

If the *genre* was recognizable, was not the title new ?   *Essai* —what did that mean ?   So far as I am aware, there is, prior to Montaigne, only one instance of the use of the word as part of a title :   *Le Coup d'Essai* of François Sagon, the poem in which he attacked Clement Marot.   It is Marot himself who claims the term as his own and makes his valet, Fripelipes, accuse the rhyming priest of stealing the only good thing in his pamphlet :

> Tu le grippas au prologue
> De l'Adolescence à mon maistre :
> Et qu'on lise à dextre ou senestre,
> On trouvera, bien je le sais,
> Ce petit mot de Coup d'essai,
> Ou Coups d'essai que je ne mente.

The sense here is clear enough and, apart from Montaigne, it is to poetry that the term is always applied as a title in the sixteenth century, and most frequently at the beginning of the seventeenth century.   All these instances are, however, posterior to 1580.   We may say therefore that, in spite of Sagon and Marot, in spite of the frequent description of such and such a piece of writing as a *coup d'essai*, Montaigne's title was a novelty, whose sense, however, seems perfectly clear.

Yet though Montaigne himself has given a sufficient gloss in such remarks as :   *Ce sont ici purement l'essai de mes facultés naturelles et nullement des acquises*, the title evidently intrigued early readers of the book.   One of the first references to the Essays is to be found in a letter of the great Scholar, Justus Lipsius.   He translates *essai* by *gustus*.   Another contemporary, Antoine de Laval [1] says this is an error, for it implies a reference

---

[1] See below, pp. 34–38.

to ' trial ' in the sense in which an ' essay ' is made of a prince's food, whereas *conatus*, a ' 'prentice effort ', gives the correct connotation. *Conatus* is the translation used by the historian, J. A. de Thou, and by Gaucher de Sainte Marthe (see p. 18), while later writers also employ such words as ' *Specimina* ' and ' *Tentamina* '.

La Croix du Maine, whose *Bibliothèque Française* (1584) contains the first published appreciation of Montaigne, is illuminating in his attempt to read a more precise meaning into the title than the author ever intended. Not satisfied with pointing out the sense of *coup d'essai ou apprentissage*, he goes on to suggest that it might also mean *essais ou expériences, c'est à dire, Discours pour se façonner sur autrui. Il sera encore bien pris en cette façon* he adds, rather mysteriously, *car le livre ne contient autre chose qu'une ample Déclaration de la vie dudit Sieur de Montaigne*, and it bears witness to his *grande doctrine et jugement émerveillable et encore de sa diverse leçon ou variété d'auteurs qu'il a lus*. In other words, La Croix tries to fit the definition of the moral anthology or miscellany as closely as possible to Montaigne's work. In such a book an author *fashions* his opinions and his judgement on what he reads, and implies that others might *fashion* themselves on him. This second and directly didactic intention is quite foreign to Montaigne, while the first can only be accepted with a restriction brought out by Saint Sernin, an obscure Protestant refugee, who writes forty years later :

Il y a diverses sortes d'Essais, car la plupart de ceux qui en font, n'ont d'autre but que pour montrer la profondité de leur savoir et tâchent d'épuiser toute la science des anciens auteurs pour acquérir le nom de docte et savant, mais ne nous dépeignent point ni ne découvrent les qualités de leur esprit ni leurs moeurs et conditions ainsi que fait le Sieur de Montaigne.[1]

[1] Jonatan de St. Sernin : *Essais et Observations sur les Essais du Seigneur de Montaigne* (London, 1625). For the history of the title ' Essay ' subsequent to Montaigne, it must suffice to repeat the conclusions I have arrived at elsewhere. With two exceptions, Bacon's Essays, translated in 1619 under the title of *Essais Moraux*, is the next prose-work to appear in France under that title. It is Descartes as much as Montaigne who creates the success of the term as applied to prose. The three treatises which follow the *Discours de la Méthode* are *Les Essais de cette Méthode*. Yet the step which marks the final passage from the primitive sense of ' trial '—which really needs no further explanation— to that of a piece of prose-writing on any subject, is the substitution of *Essai sur* for *Essai de*. This change took place only at the end of the seventeenth century and was probably originally made in England and thence passed to France.

To return to La Croix du Maine, we may note further that he has alluded to the self-portrait of the Essays—the fundamental originality of the book—and he tells a doubtless apocryphal story which shows how the idea of the portrait appealed to the imagination of contemporaries, even if its full significance generally escaped them. Montaigne, having presented a copy of the Essays to Henry III, the king told him how much he admired them :

Sire, (répondit l'Auteur) il faut donc nécessairement que je plaise à votre Majesté, puisque mon livre lui est agréable, car il ne contient autre chose qu'un Discours de ma vie et de mes actions.

Finally La Croix du Maine hints at a certain disagreement about the Essays. Some people have been rather lukewarm in their praise. He is too discreet to tell us the objections raised, but it may be suspected that the book seemed at once too outspoken and too frivolous to these critics, for, in reply, La Croix insists on the usefulness of the Essays and their resemblance with Plutarch's *Moralia*.[1]

Even if the self-portrait and the Plutarchan element are rightly distinguished by La Croix, he confirms what we have said of the place of the Essays in the minds of contemporaries, its place among the miscellanies.[2] To some of these we may now turn.

Take *Les Sérées* (1584) of Guillaume Bouchet, Juge et Consul des Marchands de Poitiers. They belong to the same branch of miscellany as Tahureau's *Dialogues* or Noël du Fail's *Baliverneries* : the subject matter is similar but the ' décor ' is humorous, with its Rabelaisian *bons buveurs* and *fesses tendues*. The monstrous and the salacious are here in evidence, but the book has its more serious side. It is true, however, that Bouchet has mainly used ' le Seigneur de la Montaigne ' as a source of curious anecdote rather than for his ideas. There are, however, discussions in which Montaigne's views are the centre

---

[1] The notice of La Croix du Maine contains some biographical details not wholly derived from the Essays. He is responsible, however, for the legend that Montaigne gave up his position as *Conseiller* at the Parliament of Bordeaux on the death of an elder brother. The brother in question died in infancy, probably before Michel himself was born, but his ' ghost ' was not laid until the nineteenth century.

[2] Another *Bibliothèque Française*, that of Du Verdier, produced quite independently, appeared in 1585. Here Montaigne is again allotted an honourable place and, according to Du Verdier's practice with the more important authors of the century, an extract of his work, the essay ' On Books ' (II, 10) is reproduced, but no critical comment is added.

of a debate. The question of the influence of spells on sexual impotence—or, as the phrase went, ' *les liaisons d'aiguillettes* ', —was a favourite topic of the day. According not only to Bodin, but to Wier, such cases are the work of the devil. Montaigne, who offers a psychological explanation, is the authority who is here confronted with the demonologists.[1]

In the later volume of *Les Sérées* (1597, 1598) we find a chapter on judicial torture, in which Bouchet makes use of Montaigne's eloquent protest against this abuse, and also records his regret that the plea of ' non proven ' is not admitted in the French Courts. In another chapter, it is the passage on kindness to animals which is reproduced : *Nous devons, selon de Montaigne, un devoir général non aux bêtes seulement, mais aux arbres mêmes et aux plantes.* The humanitarian rationalism of Montaigne is thus passably represented even in *Les Sérées*, though Bouchet does not always agree with views he makes his characters quote. Most of the company do not agree with Montaigne's disbelief in spells, but there is little opposition to his views on torture, and his ideal of humanity to animals is admired. Bouchet quotes with approval Montaigne's story of the Indians who criticize European maldistribution of riches, but in one of those attacks on the cruelty of the Spaniards to the Indians, which were common at this time, no allusion to Montaigne can be found, no hint of the ' children of nature ' theme which is what is specifically new in the Essays.[2]

Jean des Caurres, the author of certain ' Œuvres Morales ', published in 1575 and again with some additions in 1584, is a more serious-minded person than Bouchet. He was Principal of a College at Amiens and Canon of the Church of St. Nicolas. Here the one considerable passage taken from the Essays is again the protest against extortion of confession by torture. Des Caurres has added the second half of *De la Conscience* (II, 5), quotations and all, to his *Du Remors de Conscience* which

---

[1] *Les Sérées* (ed. Roybet, 1873), I, 190 et seq.

[2] Bouchet presents finally one intriguing problem. In two cases he is not content with what he can find in the Essays but *invents* for Montaigne (1) a protest against the physical tests provided for in pleas of annulment and (2) an incident showing the compassionate attitude of the Turks to animals. ' Ce que confirme de Montaigne, disant n'y avoir pas longtemps qu'il se trouva un Turc à Venise . . . lequel racheta tous les oiseaux de leurs cajots . . . *les Turcs ayant des aumônes et hôpitaux pour les bêtes.*' The words underlined are all that can be found in the Essays, but they were added in 1582 after Montaigne's return from Italy. Did Bouchet know him personally ? When he quotes Montaigne amiss, is he thinking of conversations which they had together ?

originally contained no reference to this subject. Nevertheless he had, in his first edition, already attacked the abuse in another chapter. It is indeed appropriate that in Des Caurres, as in Bouchet, we should have to record the borrowing of Montaigne's best-known attacks on unnecessary cruelty and injustice. There were, however, many others at the Renaissance who had made the same criticism of the use of torture—the passage below, for instance, certainly reflects Vives—and Des Caurres has merely welcomed in Montaigne one who felt as deeply on this point as he did himself. Already in 1575 we find him writing:

Je m'émerveille que les Chrétiens retiennent à belles dents, comme bonnes choses et saintes, ces façons de faire, qui ne sont pas seulement contraires à la charité et douceur Chrétienne mais aussi à toute humanité. Saint Augustin dit qu'on baille les tourments par une nécessité de la compagnie humaine. Mais qui ne voit qu'il parle avec les Gentils suivant les opinions des Gentils. Car quelle est cette nécessité si intolérable . . . Ne voyons nous pas tous les jours qui aiment mieux endurer la mort que les tourments, et confessent le crime feint, étants assurés du supplice, de peur qu'on leur baille la torture.[1]

And he closes his chapter with the words: *Les choses qui se disent contre les tourments sont bien fortes: mais celles qu'ils disent pour les tortures sont frivoles et très faibles.*

Des Caurres, a schoolmaster by profession, appropriately rounds off his work with a ' Bref Sommaire des Louanges d'un Collège ', in praise not only of his own but of schools in general. M. Villey once suggested that we might have here a reply to Montaigne's attack on the ' furious schoolmaster '. This cannot be so, for the ' Bref Sommaire ' appears in 1575 and does not appear to have been altered in any way. A similar suggestion has been put forward with regard to La Noue, who writes with enthusiasm and his usual practical sense about the advantages of schools in the fifth chapter of the *Discours Politiques et Militaires* (1587). La Noue composed his work in prison in Limburg between 1581 and 1585. His wife supplied him with books, and he certainly knew Bodin's *Démonomanie* (1580), but I cannot see any trace of Montaigne either in this chapter of the *Discours* or elsewhere.

On the other hand, there is a connexion between La Noue and Des Caurres, and both help to reveal by contrast the originality of Montaigne's *De l'Institution des Enfants*. Both enumerate the advantages of good schools, differing from Montaigne by

[1] *Œuvres Morales*, Livre I, chap. 23.

their insistence on the social side of education. Both speak of the benefits to the commonwealth which good schools procure, and both lay stress especially on the material profit and the economic advantages accruing to the towns which possess them.

Montaigne's ideas on education are, however, referred to by Tabourot des Accords (1547–90) in the Fourth Book of his *Bigarrures*. This miscellany, published in 1586, differs from the *Sérées*, Cholières' *Matinées* or Du Fail's *Eutrapel* [1] by a division, instead of a mixture, of what is serious and what is comic. Tabourot criticizes the ' direct method ' by which Montaigne learnt his Latin. He says, very sensibly, that it is a *recette de Grands Seigneurs* and that it is almost impossible to ' latinize ' the whole entourage of a child. It is perhaps possible, if executed by an arrangement between several families living in the same town. All his recommendations have this detailed and practical bent.

Tabourot, however, is not *influenced* by the Essays. He is still under the spell of those fetishes against which Montaigne reacts. Although he shows the customary solicitude for the education of the judgment, this is hardly more than mere lip-service, for he wishes his pupils to make collections of ' moral commonplaces ' when they read history, and the purpose of such collections is not to help them to live their lives, but to ' compose speeches and even whole books '.

In another chapter, Tabourot discusses the new interest in witchcraft. He is really concerned only with impostors and does not question the existence of sorcery. [2] On the other hand, he insists on the credulity and fear encouraged by obsession with this subject, and he roundly declares that *nouer l'aiguillette ne signifie autre chose qu'un couard amant*. [3] It would be too bold to say that he took this explanation from the Essays. What he found there was, more likely, the encouragement to say so. For he was a keen admirer of the Essays, as may be seen from the epigram on Montaigne which appears in his *Touches* : [4]

> Quiconque voit la nette pureté
> De tes écrits, les lit de tel courage
> Que si c'était quelque gentil ouvrage
> Qu'il eût jadis lui-même médité :

---

[1] *Les Neuf Matinées* (1585) and *Les Neuf Après-dinées* (1587) of Nicolas de Cholières show no traces of the Essays. Nor do the *Contes d'Eutrapel*, if I may trust the categorical negative of M. E. Philipot (*N. du Fail*, 1914, p. 460).
[2] op. cit., p. 76 et seq.   [3] ib., p. 84.
[4] *Quatrième et Cinquième Livres des Touches*, 1588.

Puis, tout ravi de sa simplicité,
Reconnaissant ton style inimitable,
T'adore ainsi qu'une divinité
Te voyant seul à toi-même semblable.

We shall find other examples of this feeling that the Essays are what one might have said oneself, expressed by a superior mind. They help to explain the speedy success of a book which contained much that was in advance of its time, apart from such topical subjects as magic and sorcery, torture and education.

Two more miscellanies, written when the popularity of this kind of composition was beginning to wane, may be mentioned here.

Louis Guyon first published his *Diverses Leçons* in 1604. Montaigne appears in the list of authors from whom he has drawn, but the one occasion of note on which one can say that this writer has taken anything from the Essays is a chapter entitled : *La vie n'est que trop longue*,[1] where a good deal of the Stoical essay *Que philosopher est apprendre à mourir* (I, 20) is reproduced. A Christian nuance is substituted for the Senecan one, and Montaigne's fine writing appears to be the reason for borrowing from him.[2]   The other compilation is Simon Goulart's *Trésor d'Histoires Admirables* (1600 and 1604).   This is a mere collection of textual extracts whose nature is sufficiently indicated by the title. About twenty-five or thirty passages from the Essays, often of considerable length, find their way into its pages, but they are merely Montaigne's ' examples ' and need not detain us here.

Goulart, however, is of far more importance in another connexion.   He is stated by Joseph Scaliger (who knew him well) to have been responsible for an expurgated edition of the Essays.[3] The edition in question is almost certainly that published at

[1] loc. cit., p. 894.

[2] Most of the chapters of this book are devoted to physical questions, but attention is paid to ' courtesy ', and Castiglione is very frequently quoted. This is the new interest to which every amateur and every literary hack is about to turn his attention.

[3] *Scaligerana editio altera*, Cologne, 1667, p. 79. *Goulart. Il a fait châtrer les œuvres de Montaignes : quae audacia in scripta aliena ?* See also p. 158. . . . *Ceux de Génève ont été bien impudents d'en ôter plus d'un tiers.* Goulart was the editor of the so-called *Histoire du Règne de Charles IX* in which La Boëtie's *Contr'Un* was published as a Protestant pamphlet. If the thesis of Dr. Armaingaud (cf. *L'Enigme du Contr'un*) that Montaigne was responsible for delivering La Boëtie's manuscript to the Calvinists, is accepted, it is possible that Goulart and Montaigne were acquainted with each other.

Lyon in 1595. A number of chapters are suppressed—including *Des Vers de Virgie* which, however, is often missing from copies of other editions—but adequate reason for taking this to be the publication mentioned by Scaliger is found on looking for one or two of the passages where Montaigne attacks the Protestants, which have been *omitted*. Whether Goulart was responsible or not, there can be no doubt that these are the Essays produced for Calvinist consumption.[1]

The *Apologie*, for example, in this edition, instead of beginning with the circumstances under which Montaigne's father came into possession of Sebond's *Théologie*, and speaking of Luther's heresy as a forerunner of an inevitable irreligion, begins in this abrupt manner :

Mon feu père quelques jours avant sa mort, ayant rencontré le livre de Raymond Sébond sous un tas d'autres papiers abandonnés, me commanda de le lui mettre en Français. Il fait bon traduire des auteurs comme celui là où il n'y a guère que la matière à représenter, &c.

Similarly in the last essay of Book Three, this sentence is omitted : *J'ai vu en Allemagne que Luther a laissé autant de divisions et d'altercations sur le doute de ses opinions.*[2] At the end of *De la Vanité* the charter of Roman citizenship has been suppressed, and with it a good deal of the praise of Rome itself. Other changes made in this same essay—treated as a sample of expurgation—are less easy to understand. Montaigne writes : *Mon père aimait à bâtir Montaigne.* This edition substitutes : *le lieu où il était né.* Yet there is apparently no general wish to cut out what is purely personal. Again, a good many Latin quotations are omitted, as also the praise of Montaigne's two friends, the *politiques*, Paul de Foix and Guy de Pibrac, which is contained in this chapter. Such treatment revolts the modern reader, but the trouble which has been taken to expurgate this edition is an indication either of high esteem for the merits of the book or, failing that, of an even more striking tribute to its popularity.

A final point of interest is that Expilly's sonnet on Montaigne first appeared in this edition.[3] In these fine verses it is as a Stoic that the author of the Essays is admired.

---

[1] Lyon. Fr. le Febvre 1595 12°. The text is founded on Langelier 1588. The preface 'Au Lecteur' is dated the first of March 1590 (instead of 1580).

[2] *Essais*, III, 13, p. 386 (in this 1595 edition see p. 974).

[3] *Les Poèmes de Claude Expilly*, 1596 (ed. 1624, p. 290). This sonnet was reprinted in the *L'Angelier* quarto of 1620. I have not found it elsewhere.

Que tu es admirable dans ce mâle langage,
Mais plus en ces raisons qui ornent tes écrits :
Capables d'enhardir les plus lâches esprits
A défier du Temps l'inconstance et l'orage.

Montagne, qui nous peins ta vie et ton courage,
En quelle antique école as tu si bien appris
De l'effroyable mort le glorieux mépris,
Que tu soutiens sans peur l'horreur de son visage ?

Magnanime Stoïque, en ces braves essais,
Tes fidèles témoins, tu montres que tu sais
Fouler dessous les pieds le soin qui nous dévore.

Les siècles à venir chanteront à bon droit :
Montagne, par lui-même, enseigna comme on doit
Et bien dire, et bien vivre, et bien mourir encore.

This is more or less the view of the Essays taken by Lipsius, and by Pasquier, as will be seen in a moment : Montaigne in his own person inculcates a Stoical morality. Here too is yet another reminder of the character of the ' First Essays ' of 1580.[1]

We cannot yet, however, leave Claude Expilly.[2] He appears to have been one of the few people at this time to take the ' children of nature ' view to which I have referred.   M. Chinard says in his ' Exotisme Américain ' : [3] Les défenseurs des Indiens ont été peu nombreux, s'ils ont été éloquents, mais tous, avant Montaigne, avaient fait intervenir dans le débat des questions religieuses ou légales. Towards the end of the century condemnation of the Spaniards was, indeed, very general, especially in France, where feeling ran high about the Spanish backing of the League.

[1] Compare also below, p. 119.

[2] Claude Expilly, born at Voiron in Dauphiné, studied at the famous Collège de Tournon, at Padua and at Bourges under Cujas. Councillor at the Court of Grenoble, where the League was in power from 1585 till 1590, Expilly remained in the town, guarding his precious library, when the Parliament fled to Romans. He was entrusted by the Leaguers with various missions but went over to Navarre when Lesdiguière took possession of Dauphiné. Famous for his learning and his gallantry, he was on the commission charged with the execution of the Edict of Nantes in that province, and was a friend of its rédacteur, Forget de Fresne. From D'Aubigné's correspondence we gather that he was entrusted with the manuscript of the Histoire Universelle, for its author suspected the Genevans of a wish to seize and destroy his papers. Expilly suffered like Montaigne from the stone.

[3] G. Chinard : L'Exotisme Américain dans la littérature française au XVIe siècle, 1911, p. 216.

Nothing I have met, however, comes so near to the attitude of the Essays as the following lines of Expilly :

Que ces avides mots de Tien et Mien nous coûtent :
Voyez ces Indiens innocents qui ne goûtent
Que le lait de Nature, ils jouissent de tout,
Car leurs possessions n'ont ni limite ni bout.
  Que cher vous coûtera, pauvre gent abusée,
De nos moeurs et nos loix la pratique rusée :
L'éclair de nos miroirs, l'usage des habits
Vous sera, pauvres gens, d'inestimable prix.
Le bruit de nos tambours, le son de nos trompettes,
Et le vain passe-temps des luths et des sonnettes,
Qui nous va decevant, ne vous voudra jamais
Le sein de la Nature, où vous étiez en paix.[1]

It is tempting then to imagine that Montaigne stands for something in the development of this theme by Expilly, for he shows himself fond of contrasting the nobility of the savage with the vices of the Christians. I am not quite sure that Chinard, however, does not overestimate the originality of the Essays on this point. A poet who has read Las Casas, who insists on the innocence of the natives, might pass naturally enough to the thought of a golden age. Nor should the legal nuance of one of the above verses escape the reader (*possessions sans limite ni bout*). The great lawyer, Francis à Victoria, had discussed some aspects of the property question in the New World. It is also a lawyer by training, Marc Lescarbot, whom Mr. Geoffroy Atkinson, in his *Relations de Voyages au XVII siècle*, takes as the earliest and one of the best examples of the ' happy savage ' view of the inhabitants of the New World.[2]

Lescarbot's *Histoire de la Nouvelle France* appeared in 1609, and the passages here quoted from Expilly were published thirteen years before.[3] Lescarbot, who shows no direct connexion with Montaigne, insists on the happiness of the Indian's life (recalling the Golden Age) and on the community of property [4] among them, and notes their social loyalty to one another. The loyalty of the ' savages ' to their chiefs is also contrasted with the perfidy of the Christians in the opening section of Coignet's *Instruction aux Princes* (1585), but the Essays seem

---

[1] *Poèmes* (1624), p. 221 et seq.

[2] See also M. Chinard's second volume : *L'Amérique et le Rêve Exotique au XVIIᵐᵉ et au XVIIIᵐᵉ Siècles*, pp. 100–115.

[3] See also Expilly, op. cit., p. 275, a poem written before 1608 and published in 1624.   [4] cf. Lescarbot, p. 759.

to me to provide the only parallel to such a passage as the following :

> Les cannibales fiers qui n'ont point d'autre loi
> Que l'instinct naturel, savent bien quelle foi
> Il faut garder aux Princes, eux qui, pour leurs Caciques
> Souffrent des Espagnols les rigueurs tyranniques,
> Se laissant déchirer à ces hommes cruels
> Plutôt que de trahir leurs Princes naturels.
> Et vous, nouveaux Scythes, vous armez pour détruire
> Le Roi qui dessus vous le grand Dieu veut élire.[1]

All things considered, it may be taken as likely that Expilly had profited by the ironical question of the ' Magnanime Stoique ' whose teaching he celebrates—*Mais quoi ! ils ne portent point de haut de chausses !*

We have seen certain views of Montaigne on education, on justice, on cruelty, on the savages, on the supernatural, discussed, adopted or rejected.   It was naturally the rationalist and humanitarian side of the Essays, expressed on recognized problems of the day, which was most immediately reflected in contemporary literature, for Montaigne's ' rich examples ' and his views on specific social topics were what could most conveniently be reproduced in the miscellany.   Another book, still vaguely belonging to the same *genre, Le Passe-temps de Messire François Le Poulchre de la Motte Messémé*, leads us to suppose that they may have appreciated other things in the Essays.

La Motte Messémé (1546–1596–7) was an amiable country gentleman who had seen some soldiering in his youth.   His *Honnêtes Loisirs* (1587), written in incredible doggerel, are of no little historical interest.   It is from this aspect alone that he has been adequately treated by M. Leo Mouton,[2] who almost ignores the entertaining *Passetemps* (1595 and 1597).   Both works are largely autobiographical—*les fruits cueillis dans ma vigne* ;   the first contains his life, the second his opinions.

Although La Motte has retouched his *Honnêtes Loisirs*, first written about 1572, I do not think they show any trace of Montaigne's influence.   It is important, therefore, to notice a similarity of character and a parallel design in writing.   Both have some of the same freedom of judgement, the same political outlook,[3]

---

[1] Expilly : *Poèmes* : ' Discours à M. de Silléry '.
[2] *Revue de l'Histoire Littéraire de la France*, 1931.
[3] La Motte insists on the civil obedience due to the king and holds out for liberty of conscience though not of public worship.   Of coercion he says dramatically : ' Non : au moins pour cela je n'ai ceint mon épée Vétu le corselet ni pris la lance en main ' (p. 69a).

and the rôle his book plays in La Motte's life corresponds closely to the earlier conception of the Essays : *de décrire ma fortune et mes exercises pour servir d'histoire privée en ma maison.* *Le Passetemps* is a record, not only of the author's opinions, but of his *diverse leçon* to use La Croix' phrase. A solitary meditation in his litter, as he returned across France from the baths of Plombières to his home near Loudun, has sent him to his tablets and his books ; the theme of that meditation is the antinomy of man's misery and his perfectibility, so characteristic of the Renaissance. Here the personal note is far more marked in spite of numerous passages taken from Plutarch and the Essays. It often reads like a free variation on the latter, whose phrases creep into La Motte's prose even when he appears to be opposing his views. The author passes from one subject to another on the flimsiest pretext (and, unlike Montaigne, he does not come back to the point) ; but the method of enunciating general themes discussed with ' examples ' taken chiefly from his own experience, is exactly that of the Essays.

La Motte accepts Montaigne's compromise between Machiavelli and Machiavelli's opponents such as Gentillet. Political necessity is a valid excuse for double dealing, but only in the last resort. Elsewhere he insists on the political use of religion and miracles *pour mener une commune* and holds it eminently justifiable. This euhemerism, characteristic of the Paduan School in general, and particularly associated with Machiavelli, is not typical of Montaigne, but La Motte's general political outlook is significant in the 1590's, when the terms *politique* and ' irreligion ' are widely used as practically synonymous.[1] More important is the development of Montaigne's attack, not this time on *la question*, but on punishment by torture, which La Motte makes in strong language derived from the Essays. He disclaims a wish, however, to change the accepted usage— prudently enough when it is remembered that Montaigne himself was taken to task by the Censorship at Rome for holding such an opinion as the following :

Je voudrais qu'on fît mille outrages au cadaver selon l'énormité du méfait, mais tandis qu'il est animé lui ôter la vie que tout simplement, cela sent son Chrétien à gros grain, à pleine la bouche. . . . Tirez à quatre chevaux votre criminel, tiraillez le, coupez lui une main, rompez le sur la roue, tout cela ne lui sert plus de rien pour son amendement, et cependant, vous, qui vous dites Chrétien, vous perdez possible son âme par la rage et le désespoir du mal que vous

[1] H. Busson, op. cit. p. 6.

lui faites souffrir, là où vous devriez tendre à la lui envoyer nette devant celui qui le rejugera et vous avec.[1]

On friendship, La Motte differs from Montaigne, and differs violently. The famous friendships of antiquity, to which he adds that of Montaigne and La Boëtie, are imperfect compared with the love of man and woman, and he arrives at a conclusion diametrically opposed to that of Montaigne : *Je ne puis croire qu'une si ferme et stable et ardente amitié puisse être entre les hommes.* La Motte clearly writes on this subject with a conviction formed by his own experience of a brief but happy marriage. It is therefore without any personal grievance that he holds strong views about divorce.[2]   They are indeed the most original thing in this little book, and their boldness may be contrasted with the learned and inconclusive debate on the subject in Bodin's *République* (I, 3).

To *Messieurs les Canonistes* he remarks that they, as celibates, can hardly have an adequate notion of what is implied by a marriage of this kind : *étant mieux d'offenser une fois (si c'est offence) plutôt que d'y retourner tous les jours en péché du souhait de la mort l'un de l'autre.*   The position is a strong one, and the author replies vigorously to possible theological objections, and concludes in a passage (reminiscent of Montaigne) which suggests that, but for the difficulty of succession and inheritance, the very contract of marriage would be better done away with.

The Essays are doubtless only responsible for encouraging La Motte to speak his mind on the subject of divorce, just as they have probably encouraged him to indulge in many neologisms. It is, however, in his general ideas that, despite constant echoes of Montaigne, we see most clearly the limits of Montaigne's influence on his mind.   Thus we find much discussion of the passions, acknowledged as *de l'origine et manutention de notre substance*, but it is always the conception of heroic virtue, abandoned by Montaigne, that appeals to La Motte. He shows clearly *which* Montaigne he prefers by refusing to admire Alcibiades.   La Motte is evidently fairly familiar with the ideas of the Paduan philosophy (perhaps not entirely through the Essays), but he is not in any marked degree a fideist. His religion is above all a practical one : *Rendre obéissance à son supérieur et ne prendre rien d'autrui sont les articles de ma foi ;* ‘ do as you would be done by ’, the foundation of lay morality which so many of the followers of Montaigne and Charron in

---

[1] op. cit., II, p. 31*a* et seq.   [2] ib., pp. 53*b* et seq.

the next century wish to substitute for the precepts of *la preud'-
homie scolastique*.[1]

When these views are read in their context, it is hardly possible
to doubt the general influence of the Essays on a congenial mind,
an influence which was not confined to humanitarianism or
purely practical problems, but whose exact extent is not easy
to estimate. It evidently excludes both Montaigne's notion of
virtue as a harmony, the importance of adaptability and also
the fideism of Montaigne's attitude to religion.

Another writer, born in the same year as La Motte Messémé,
but who was of a different social standing and education, must
now be dealt with : Pierre de L'Estoile, the author of the famous
' Journal '. Like La Motte, L'Estoile writes mainly for his own
satisfaction and that of his friends. It is only in 1606 that the
least reminiscence or mention of *le seigneur de Montaigne mon
vade mecum* is to be found, but from this time till five years later
we reach the pathos of that last entry : *tout est noir comme
noirci d'encre*, references to the Essays are not uncommon in
his pages, and become more numerous as the end is reached.
*Ce matin comme je passais le temps à lire les dits Essais que
j'aime et ay ordinairement à la main . . . Ces gens qui se
perchent à chevauchons sur l'épicycle de Mercure . . . m'arrachent
les dents, aussi bien qu'au sieur de Montagne, duquel est ce trait
que je lisais encores hier.*

Not that L'Estoile did not read Montaigne earlier, for it is
always the well-digested substance of the Essays, the quotations from memory, which flow from his pen. Rather it was
from this time that his interests are less purely political and he
begins to speak of his books. He had given up his charge of
audiencier at the Exchequer Court and in those last years, overcast by financial cares and ill health, his chief preoccupation
was the reunion of the churches by a General Council. He is a
good representative of the enlightened and moderate Catholic
opinion of the Renaissance. As such it is interesting to see the
old man in discussion with his cousin, the future Cardinal de
Bérulle, one of the great men of the Counter-reform, respectful
of the young theologian's learning but unconvinced that the
' Church cannot err '.[2] His serious reading at this time, apart

---

[1] Compare Sir Thomas Browne : "To do no injury or to take none
was a principle which, in my former years and impatient affection, seemed
to contain enough of morality" (*Religio Medici*).

[2] L'Estoile was the pupil of the Mattieu Béroalde who went over to
Geneva. His father on his death-bed said to the tutor : ' Maître Matthieu,
mon ami, je vous recommande mon fils que voilà. Je vous prie surtout

from the Essays, seems to have been religious, chiefly the Fathers and his other *vade mecum* the Bible, but it is remarkable to notice the place which reminiscences of Montaigne play on the fairly rare occasions when he allows himself to make some general reflexions.

It is Montaigne who supplies L'Estoile with the title-pages of his two penultimate ' Cahiers ' (the last is built up from the Bible with reflexions on the death of Henri IV).

En ces Registres (que j'appelle le Magasin de mes Curiosités) on m'y verra (comme dit le Seigneur de Montagne en ses Essais parlant de soi) tout nu et tel que je suis, mon naturel au jour le jour, mon âme libre et toute mienne, accoutumée à se conduire à sa mode, non toutefois méchante ni maligne, mais trop porté à une vaine curiosité et liberté (dont je suis marri).   Et laquelle toutefois qui me voudrait retrancher ferait tort à ma santé et à ma vie, parce qu'où je suis contraint je ne vaux rien, étant extrêmement libre et par nature et par art.   Je prie seulement mes amis et ceux qui me connaissent, d'excuser et supporter en moi ces vaines et chétives occupations, ces plaisirs où ma maladie et mon âge me pousse.   Auquel (pour éviter un plus grand mal) je fournis de jouets et d'amusements, comme à l'enfance, en laquelle je me sens retomber petit à petit. . . .[1]

L'Estoile thus sums up a dozen different ideas of the Essays.

Or again, he recalls an opinion of Montaigne—on the necessity of frankness about money matters—which he personally does not approve, in the middle of the prayer which ends his *Journal* for the year 1609 : he remembers elsewhere his saying that it is *plus aisé de porter une cuirasse toute sa vie qu'un pucelage* ; but in general, it is when he approaches the theme of vanity or *la fadaise de s'émouvoir du monde* that the words of Montaigne rise to his lips :

Mais quoi ! notre monde d'aujourd'hui (comme dit Montaigne en ses Essais) n'est formé qu'à l'ostentation. . . .   Ce n'est pas assez en ce monde d'avoir une connaissance en gros qu'on n'est guères sage : il faut en détail et en particulier, que chacun reconnaisse (comme je fais) qu'il n'est qu'un sot.

I think it may be said that it is the religion of Montaigne in so far as it consists in a certain emotional attitude—the vanity of life—the *catharsis* of which we have spoken in the Introduction, which reappears especially in the *Journal* of L'Estoile.

de l'instruire en la piété et la crainte de Dieu, et pour le regard de la Religion je ne veux pas que vous me l'ôtiez de l'Eglise : je vous le défends. Mais ne veux je pas que vous me le nourrissiez aux abus et superstitions d'icelle.' *Journal* (ed. Brunet, XI, 15).

[1] *Journal* (ed. cit.), VIII, 226. cf. ib., IX, 223, 4.

CHAPTER II

THE RECEPTION OF THE ESSAYS—
II : THE FIRST CRITICS

Si vous avez lu Montaigne, vous avez lu Plutarque et Sénèque, mais si vous avez lu Plutarque et Sénèque, vous n'avez pas lu Montaigne.

ANON (17th cent.)

U P till now we have been concerned mainly with the use to which certain features of the Essays were immediately put by a variety of writers. We may ask for more testimony and more direct testimony as to the merits which contemporaries saw in them as a whole. La Croix's function in his *Bibliographie* is to praise, and yet we have seen he implies that the book has had a varied reception. What attitude was adopted by those whose authority might count with their fellows, by the men of learning who had no need of short cuts to knowledge ?

One such man of learning has been quoted in the Introduction : Joseph Scaliger, whose *Magnificat à Matines* is a caustic comment on Montaigne's *Apologie pour Raymond Sebond*. He has also supplied us with reason for thinking that the mutilated Essays of 1595 were prepared by Simon Goulart. On the whole, he is much more interested in Sebond, whom Montaigne had translated in 1569, than in our author. He refers to Sebond several times in his letters, although (perhaps naturally) he never mentions Montaigne's translation to his learned correspondents, Isaac Casaubon and Richard Thompson.[1] We read, however, in the *Scaligerana* :

> Monsieur de Montaigne. Son père était vendeur de hareng. La grande fadaise de Montaigne qui a écrit qu'il aimoit mieux le vin blanc. Monsieur Du Puy disoit que diable a-t-on à faire de savoir ce qu'il aime ?

Scaliger is also said to have called Montaigne *un hardi ignorant.*[2]

[1] *Scaligeri Epistolae,* I, 93 ; III, 241.

[2] *Scaligerana* (ed. 1667), p. 215. The *hardi ignorant* is questioned by Charles Sorel (*Bibliothèque Française,* 1644), but, although I cannot find an early reference to it, it was widely accepted. (Cf. Méré : *Lettres,* I, 22.)

Ignorance (or disregard) of the finer points of scholarship, in-dulgence in the trivial or personal—it is easy to see that such would seem the faults of Montaigne in the eyes of a master of textual criticism, as also to a grave lawyer like his friend, Claude Du Puy, the father of the two Royal librarians and historians of the following century. And indeed the reserves made by an admirer like Etienne Pasquier or Dominicus Baudius are much on the lines of Du Puy's remark.

We may say then that there is a certain disdain in Scaliger's attitude, and he would naturally remember Montaigne, first, for his translation of the *Theologia Naturalis*, and secondly, for his Essays.[1]   Other distinguished writers thought first of the man, the Mayor or the diplomatist.   Such is the attitude of the his-torian, J.-A. de Thou, who saw something of him in 1582, when a special Chamber of Justice was sent from Paris to Guienne. It is to the Mayor of Bordeaux that Antoine Loisel, another member of that court, dedicates one of the speeches of his *Oeil des Rois* ; it is the skilful negotiator whom D'Aubigné admires in his History.[2]   Or else Montaigne is celebrated, above all, as a friend, the friend of La Boëtie—which is only in part a tribute to the essay *De l'Amitié*.   Such is the case with the *Elogia* of Scévole de Sainte-Marthe, which is a mere literary exercise.   It praises Montaigne indeed, but, in claiming for the Essays an inter-national reputation, shows an imperfect knowledge of the work. Sainte-Marthe imagines that Montaigne received his diploma of Roman citizenship in 1581 for the celebrity his book already enjoyed ' among the learned and wise of other lands '.[3]

That is, of course, untrue.   Yet a letter, written from Leyden in May 1583 and published three years later, had not a little to do with Montaigne's fame even in France.[4]   Montaigne him-self wrote later, perhaps in reference to this fact :

---

[1] See J. Coppin: *Montaigne, traducteur de Raymond Sebond*, 1925.   It is worth noting that Montaigne's translation of this very solid work (1569) was republished in 1581, and also later in 1603, 1605, 1611 and 1641.

[2] J.-A. de Thou : *De Vita Sua*, II, p. 58 ; III, p. 136 (ed. française 1717) : *Historia temporis sui* (ed. Roveriana, 1630), V, 104, p. 266.   A. Loisel : *De l'Oeil des Rois* (1596), dedication from Agen, Nov. 1582. Montaigne returned the compliment by sending Loisel a copy of a new edition of the Essays (in 1588) which contains a MS. dedication (Bib. Nat. Coll. Payen 17) : D'Aubigné, *Histoire Universelle* (Ruble), VIII, 329.

[3] *Elogiarum Libri*, II, 5 (1598).   (On Paolo Sarpi's admiration of *De l'Amitié*, see p. 297.)

[4] The present writer intends to publish later a full account of Lipsius, Van Veen and Baudius, in relation to Montaigne.

D'autant que la connaissance qu'on prend de moi s'éloigne de mon gîte, j'en vaux d'autant mieux. J'achète les imprimeurs en Guienne ; ailleurs ils m'achètent.

The letter was that of Scaliger's great rival and friend, Justus Lipsius (1547–1607). Lipsius first read the Essays towards the end of 1582 or the beginning of 1583. He recognized in Montaigne a great writer, a man after his own heart, and evidently wrote and spoke of him to many of his friends. He urged Christopher Plantin, the printer, to instruct his Paris correspondents to obtain information about the author, and it is not impossible that Plantin may have thought of reprinting the book.[1] *Thales Gallicus* : such was the title with which Lipsius honoured Montaigne, and, from the publication of Lipsius' letters in 1586, the phrase had no little success. Despite Lipsius' well-known failing for adulation, there can be little doubt of the impression the letter made. We may realize this better by remembering that this professor's ' reconversion ' to Catholicism (in 1591) was a European event. It is not only the pupils of Lipsius like Pieter van Veen and Dominicus Baudius who repeat the phrase, or Besoldus, Campanella's friend,[2] but the praise of Lipsius saves Marie de Gournay, a girl of twenty, who first read the Essays about 1585, from being laughed to scorn by her family and friends for her wild enthusiasm about Montaigne.

We have seen, too, the somewhat scoffing attitude of Scaliger. It has been suggested that he was piqued by the way in which Montaigne, returning ' Thales of Gaul ' in kind, had called Lipsius in his 1588 edition *le plus savant homme qui nous reste . . . vraiment germain à mon Turnebus.* Be this as it may, Montaigne and Lipsius entered into a desultory correspondence about

---

[1] The Essays were not printed outside France under 1602 (Leyden).
[2] Van Veen's interesting annotated copy of the Essays (Brit. Mus. C2897) contains a long appreciation of Montaigne which begins thus : ' Estant en France en ma jeunesse en l'age de 27 ans . . . cest Autheur cy est tombé en mes mains ; [in 1589]. Duquel en ce temps là j'ai fait selon ma capacité grand estat principalement entendant que le Sieur Lipsius l'osa bien nommer *Thaletem Gallicum.* Et comme volontiers la jeunesse s'attache à des authorités (et que j'avais en ma jeunesse ouï à Leiden le dict Sieur Lipsius et le tenu (come de raison) pour un des plus grands personnages de nostre temps principalement qu'il m'avoit aussi pour son Client, escrivant certaines lettres à moi qui ne sont imprimés [sic]) je ne m'en pouvais depetrer de le lire et relire. Puis après en ma vieillesse ne le prenant plus par authorité je l'ai toutefois admiré et aimé . . .' : Baudius : *Epistolae Centuria,* I, iv. ; Besoldus : *Opera Politica,* p. 86. Besoldus, writing about 1620, adds that these Essays contain ' much tending to Atheism '.

the end of 1587—a correspondence probably begun by the latter.

These letters reveal in some measure his view of the book. He praises the *practical* judgement of the author (*ad usum vitae*) ; he feels that he agrees with all his opinions, especially his love of Seneca and his disdain of ambition, and sees in the book the true image of his mind. At bottom, however, what he valued was the Stoicism of the Essays. This is made clearer in a letter written in April 1595 to his friend, Rémacle Roberty of Brussels, who had borrowed a copy of the Essays and wished to borrow any letters Lipsius might have. He claims that Montaigne is *maxime factus ad robur animis ingignendum sine quo quid nisi fluctus haec vita* ? And since Lipsius made his first acquaintance with the Essays of 1580, his impression is far from unfounded, while it is natural that he, the great Renaissance reviver of Stoical doctrine, should take this view.

The importance of Stoical ideas during this period is well known. It was an age of personal insecurity like that in which the ancient Stoicism itself arose, productive of the desire for preparation against misfortune in a limitation of desire to those blessings, such as peace of mind and consciousness of moral worth, of which no external event can rob us. Although such ideas are in no wise peculiar to Montaigne, they are represented in his earlier work, and we are bound to ask whether the Essays had anything to do with the Stoicism of the younger man. It is in Lipsius' dialogue *De Constantia* (1583), if anywhere, that we should expect to find traces of such influence, for it was written at the very moment when he first read the Essays. It was, however, the struggle in the Netherlands, the deception of the Antwerp massacre following D'Alençon's intervention, on which such hopes had been built by Lipsius among others, which prompted the book, and it centres round the personal problem of what part a *clerc* (as M. Benda would say) should play in a national calamity. Is it compatible with his duty to fly the country ? For it is doubtful whether he can do any good by remaining. Hence the main theme of the *De Constantia* is a discussion on Free Will and Providence. The subject is one which Montaigne has practically never touched, and there is little common to the two books. It is none the less just possible that the Senecan essays of the First and Second Books may have helped Lipsius to clarify his own views. For any *rational* attempt, such as his, to reconcile Christianity and Stoicism must attack the problem of Providence—the theological form of the problem of Free-will. Lipsius' later treatises on Stoicism, published in 1604,[1] with the special attention devoted to Stoical pantheism or materialism, show his keen realization of the character of his self-imposed task. It is precisely for this reason that he is the most important representative of the Stoical revival. No doubt the first Essays show the debt of Montaigne to Seneca in the working-out of an ideal of lay-morality, of virtue as its own reward, an ideal whose principle is not only a heroical *sustine*, a conflict whose merit may be measured by its difficulty, but that of living ' according to reason '. Yet this aspect of Montaigne is just what is least peculiar to him, and most typical of his century in general ; and in his later work what remains Senecan is only the exploitation of certain *emotional* themes. But even the *emotional* Stoicism of D'Urfé's *Epîtres Morales* (1598) or of Du Vair's *De la Constance* (1594) is astonishingly different, above all in its pious tone, from the spirit of the Essays.

On the other hand, Montaigne later built the second part of his essay *Des Coches* (III, 6), with its description of Roman spectacles, round a passage from Lipsius' *De Amphitheatro*, and Villey has suggested that *De la Vanité* (III, 9), with its praise of travel—and travel in order to escape from the troubles of one's own country—may be a reply to Langius, the Stoical protagonist of the *De Constantia*, who eventually induces his friend to stay at home—the rejoinder of the later ' Epicurean ' Montaigne to his Stoical admirer.

If Lipsius understood Montaigne in his own way, the importance of their relationship is seen even in the attitude of the latter's closest friends to the Dutch scholar. Marie de Gournay (whom Montaigne met in 1588), Pierre de Brach who, with her, prepared the 1595 edition for the press, Florimond de Raemond, all in their turn, enter into correspondence with him. By a strange chance, it is from him that Marie learnt of Montaigne's death. He it is whose offices she uses to convey the best text of the Essays, that of 1595, to certain foreign printers. And when she visited Brussels in 1597 she received a public welcome from a group of citizens headed by the same Councillor of Brabant and Quartermaster-General, Rémacle Roberty, who borrowed Montaigne's Essays and wished to borrow his letters from Lipsius. Furthermore, apart from Van Veen, who defends Montaigne's self-portrait in his MS. memoir (written about 1620), a more illustrious pupil of Lipsius, Dominique Baude or Baudius, has left a remarkable appreciation of the Essays.

Baudius, born at Lille in 1561, was by language and by long

[1] *Manducationis ad stoicam philosophiam lib. III : Physiologiae stoicorum lib. III* (1604).

residence more than half a Frenchman. He first mentions ' the Gallic Thales ' in a letter to one of his college friends (1588) [1] and in his poems we find, appended to some Latin verses addressed to Mademoiselle de Gournay, a long criticism of Montaigne in prose.[2] He too draws attention to the curious difference of opinion about the Essays. Both Montaigne's admirers and his enemies can count great names among them. Some praise him to the skies. Others take him for a mere cumberer of the literary world, an amateur, who is deservedly considered by the learned (e.g. Scaliger ?) as a waster of time and type. Baudius admits that Montaigne has faults ; but he has also genius, and may claim the freedom of genius. Indeed this very difference of opinion is in itself a tribute.

The important contribution, however, of Baudius is his admiration of Montaigne's unrivalled gift for expressing subtle psychological truths.[3] It is just this quality which ought to have struck intelligent contemporaries in reading the Essays— the most evident originality which a mere desultory perusal could make them realize—and Baudius certainly deserves to be remembered for pointing out this quality as Montaigne's greatest gift ; though indeed, when he wrote, Mademoiselle de Gournay had already commented on this feature of the Essays. Montaigne has the gift of reconciling everyday words and phrases with dignity and beauty of expression. He is above all a master of metaphor, and errs where only the greatest err—in too much daring. As for his titles (this perpetual pedantic objection is to dog our steps) the deception is generally so pleasant that we forgive him and the digression is often the best part of an essay.

Montaigne's one affectation, says Baudius acutely, is to pretend to have none. In spite of his professed negligence, his care for style is quite apparent. As for the opinion that learning is unworthy of a gentleman, and his pretended ignorance, we cannot take these for anything more than a device to claim the credit of achieving so much with so little study. Montaigne's constant refrain that he has no memory is puerile in the presence

1 *Epistolarum Centuria*, I, iv. Baudius (as professor at Leyden) found his Dutch inadequate. He came to England on a diplomatic mission in 1585, where he knew Sir Philip Sidney. After this he was resident in France for many years, became barrister at the Paris Bar, where he had many distinguished friends. In 1601 he returned to Leyden as Professor of Poetry and Law, where he died in 1606.

2 *Poemata*, 1607, Leyden, p. 359 et seq.

3 " Si punctum omne fert scribendi dicendique recte, qui facillime felicissimeque cogitata nostra mentis enunciare novit, vix quisquam hac facultate cum nostro Montano conferri potest."

of his many apt quotations, and his remark that he cannot remember the names of his servants except by the names of their posts is worthy of the parvenu, Eumolpus, of the *Satyricon*.[1] Some critics have naïvely imagined that the intimate and trivial details of his daily life are unfitting to his dignity. ' I gather,' says Baudius, ' that he never thought more highly of himself and less so of posterity, if he imagined it was his duty to inform them at what hour, for example, he took his siesta.'

Finally, as to Montaigne's religious opinions, the following significant ending should be noticed. It was this which incensed Mademoiselle de Gournay to the scornful reflexion that their author was only a Protestant after all.

Of his religion it is not for me to speak. Such examination belongs to those who make *inquisition* into the crime of heresy. If they should spare from their own concerns the leisure to peruse the volume, they will find without a doubt matter to scratch out with their cruel pens.

This and a parting gibe at the meddling Jesuits is all. It was a clever touch to avoid praise or censure of the ' doctrine ' of the Essays, and to put the responsibility for criticism of these upon the ' Loyolan dogs ', yet one cannot but wish that Baudius was a little less reticent.

There was no need, either, to draw the attention of the Inquisition to the Essays. One Jesuit had already attacked Montaigne in a book on sorcery and witchcraft. This was Marc Anthony Delrio, who, there is some reason to suppose, may have been a relation of Montaigne himself,[2] and who certainly was a close friend of Lipsius, in whose reconversion he played a leading part.

The interest of Baude's article is obvious. The friend of Sir Philip Sidney, of J.-A. de Thou, of Du Plessis Mornay, of the Chancellor Brulart de Silléry, is worth listening to on the position of the Essays in contemporary literature, and his own judgement is extremely perspicacious. Baude, however, is not the only member of the Parlement of Paris who has written of Montaigne.

[1] This accusation of vanity recurs constantly in various forms throughout the seventeenth century. Balzac is a good example (*Dissertations Critiques* 17). Baudius puts an unmerited construction on the statement of the essays : " Les gens qui me servent, il faut que je les appelle par le nom de leurs charges ou de leurs pays (i.e. *province*), car il m'est très malaisé de retenir des noms" (*Essais*, II, 17, p. 434 A). We need only refer to the Letters of Madame de Sevigné (e.g. 22 juillet, 1671) or to Molière (*Misanthrope*, II, 2, 4) and to the comedy writers in general to prove how common the practice was.

[2] *Disquisitionum Magicarum Libri Sex*, Louvain, 1599. See A. M. Boase, *Montaigne et la Sorcellerie. Humanisme et Renaissance* 1935.

An elder and more famous man, Etienne Pasquier, must be counted among the first learned admirers of the Essays. It was at the States of Blois, in the autumn of 1588, that Pasquier and Montaigne walked up and down the court of the *château* together. They had been previously acquainted, probably from 1581 or 1582, when Pasquier was a member of the special chamber sent to administer justice in Guienne and when Montaigne was Mayor of Bordeaux. Pasquier told the author that he should have consulted his friends before publishing his book, and fetching from his room a copy which he had with him, pointed out Montaigne's Gasconisms and other points which did not meet his approval. All this we learn from the letter to a friend which Pasquier wrote some years later, but which was only published in 1618.[1]

Pasquier is a warm admirer of the Essays and begins his letter by defending them against certain current criticisms. Montaigne's titles mislead. He brings enough which is to the point, replies Pasquier, and he adds most acutely : *c'est en quoi il s'est voulu de propos déliberé moquer de nous, et paravanture de lui-même par une liberté particulière qui lui était né avec lui.* It is just this same accent one hears in his speech as in his book. Montaigne's Gasconisms and his ' unaccustomed terms ' are then dealt with in much detail, and speaking of their conversation at Blois, Pasquier adds, a trifle piqued, that the Essays, none the less, never were corrected. Death, no doubt, anticipated Montaigne's intention, since the faithful Gournay tells the public that she received the manuscript exactly as it was to be printed.

Two points of interest emerge in the course of much detailed comment. Pasquier admits that he has never quite grasped what Montaigne meant by ' diversion ', and he seems to have thought the Third Book an inferior production of the author's old age. It is at least evident that he fails to recognize the superiority of the Book which Marie de Gournay rightly calls ' the consummation and perfection of the first two '. Like Scaliger, Du Puy, Balzac, Pascal, Huet, and many others, Pasquier seems to have found the *peinture du moi* too trivial—a stupid design excused by its execution.

In saying that he does not understand the meaning of ' diversion ', as used in the Essays, Pasquier has, unconsciously, explained just why it was so difficult for him, as for others, to excuse Montaigne's apparently trivial confidences and his digressions. Although Montaigne has explained the principle clearly

[1] *Lettres d'Etienne Pasquier* (1618), Livre 18, Letter 1 ; à Monsieur Pelgé, Conseiller du Roi et Maître en sa chambre des Comptes à Paris.

enough in his *De la Diversion*, it is not always realized how important (and how influential) it is. This cultivation, in every situation of crisis or distress, of a contrasted mental attitude to re-establish a harmony of passions and balance of mind, is what explains most of his alleged dilettantism. Even if Pasquier had remembered that the author's life was *intentionally* the subject of the later essays, there would still remain too much in them of what must seem trivial in his eyes just for lack of understanding the notion of ' diversion ' consciously employed as the very means to unity. Though as for that ' diversion ' which is a natural instinct (as Pascal saw),—or diversion *for variety's sake*— like most men of the Renaissance, he himself practised it.[1]

For Pasquier, as for Expilly and Lipsius, Montaigne is ' another Seneca '. His book is a *vrai séminaire de belles et véritables sentences*. Similarly his style, in spite of Gasconisms, is full of *beaux traits français et hardis* and of *belles pointes qui ne sont propres qu'à lui*. Montaigne then is Senecan (it may be said) both in style and thought.[2] He even appends, as a sample of our author, a selection of his maxims (mostly quoted incorrectly) over which he waxes strangely enthusiastic. Five out of thirteen are vaguely Stoical, and they are the most unoriginal of the lot. The limitations of his account are shown clearly by his strictures on the self-portraiture of the Third Book, by his admission that he doesn't understand ' diversion ', and lastly by his praise of the book as repertory of moral maxims. He is here very much the man of his time. It is hardly necessary to speak of the passion of the sixteenth and seventeenth centuries for *sentences*. In poetry each commonplace is printed in inverted commas in order that the eye may be drawn to it and that the mind may weigh it well. It long remained the form in which the ordinary mind preferred to receive philosophic ideas. Yet Pasquier's comments, (like those of Lipsius and like Expilly's Sonnet), are adequate for the Essays in the form in which he first read them. To the later development he is insufficiently sensitive. It was natural that La Croix du Maine should compare Montaigne with Plutarch, and that Pasquier should compare him with Seneca. Their names provide good parallels, high praise and sound criticism in so far as Montaigne was

[1] See a remarkable letter (VIII, i) to Pierre Pithou, parallel to Montaigne on old age. Published in 1586, it is a possible source rather than an echo of the Essays.

[2] See below, p. 119, note 1, for a comparison made by Théodore de Bèze, between the style of the Essays and the style of Lipsius—the latter often, as is well known, a caricature of Seneca.

formed by his constant reading of these authors and had begun by building his book from the spoils of theirs. Yet in so far as the critic's business is not merely to distinguish what is old—which is easy—but to appreciate and analyse what is new —which is difficult—these terms of comparison are disappointing and unsatisfactory.

We must note further, however, that in the Stoical view of Montaigne, another element, apart from the character of the ' first Essays ', has sometimes played its part. For in the circle of Montaigne's own friends the impression of Stoicism was strengthened by the admirable courage he showed in his attacks of nephritic colic. Thus Pierre de Brach, writing to inform Lipsius of the author's death, refers to Montaigne's conduct during an illness which overtook him in 1588 at a time when Brach was with him in Paris.

Les Médecins désespérant de sa vie et lui n'espérant que sa fin, je le vis, lorsque la mort l'avisagea de plus près, repousser de bien loin, en la méprisant, la frayeur qu'elle apporte. Quels beaux discours pour contenter l'oreille, quels beaux enseignements pour assagir l'âme, quelle résolue fermeté de courage pour assurer les peureux, déploya lors cet homme. Je n'ouïs jamais mieux dire ni mieux résolu à faire ce que, sur ce point, les philosophes ont dit, sans que la faiblesse de son corps n'eût rien rabattu de la vigueur de son âme. Il avait trompé la mort par son assurance, et la mort le trompa par sa convalescence.[1]

So too, Raemond writes :

Il soulait accointer la mort d'un visage ordinaire, s'en apprivoiser et s'en jouer, philosophant entre les extremités de la douleur, jusques à la mort, voire en la mort même.[2]

Such passages as these, for all their literary flavour, form a useful corrective to the idea which Montaigne, by insisting on his hopes of an easy and quiet death, later succeeded in creating in some too literal minds.[3]

[1] R. Dezeimeris : *P de Brach*, Vol. II, App. 1.
[2] *Erreur Populaire de la Papesse Jeanne*, 1594, p. 159.
[3] Perhaps even more salutary is this passage from the *Journal*, ' Sarà troppo grande dappocaggione e ischifiltà la mia, se tutto di ritrovandomi in caso di morte . . . e facendolami pui presso ogni ora, non m'ingegni si ch'io la possa di leggieri sopportare quanto prima ne sia sopraggiunto. Et in questo mezzo fia senno in pigliarsi allegramente il bene ch'a Dio piacerà di manderci. Non c'e altra medecina, altra regola e scienzia a schifare gli mali chenti e quali d'ogni canto e ad ogni ora soprastanno l'uomo, che risolversi a umanamente sofferirgli o animosamente finirgli '. cf. also *Essais*, II, 37, p. 578.

At his death, indeed, none were present but some of the family and a few country-gentlemen, his neighbours. Mindful of the example of his *intime frère et inviolable ami*, La Boëtie, Montaigne seems to have remembered scrupulously his obligations to his friends, and his servants.[1] He charged La Brousse, one of his brothers, with a message for his *fille d'alliance*. He remembered Pierre de Brach to the last—*ce qui me donne plus de regret de n'y avoir été, comme il disait avoir regret de n'avoir personne auprès de lui à qui déployer les dernières conceptions de son âme.* What were these last thoughts ? A final recommendation of the Essays to the friend whom he had chosen as one of his literary executors ? Some last psychological observation ? There were no fine speeches, however, at the end, for, says Pasquier, who has given us the only circumstantial account of Montaigne's death :

Il mourut dans sa maison de Montaigne, où lui tomba une esquinancie [quinsy] sur la langue, de telle façon qu'il demeura trois jours entiers, plein d'entendement, sans pouvoir parler. Au moyen duquel il était contraint d'avoir recours à sa plume pour faire entendre ses volontés. Et comme il sentit sa fin approcher, il pria, par un petit bulletin, sa femme de sémondre quelques gentils hommes, siens voisins, afin de prendre congé d'eux. Et arrivés qu'ils furent, il fit dire la Messe en sa chambre et comme le Prêtre était sur l'élévation du *Corpus Domini*, ce pauvre gentil homme s'élance le moins mal qu'il peut, les mains jointes : et, en ce dernier acte, rendit son esprit à Dieu—qui fut un beau miroir de l'intérieur de son âme.

What of Montaigne himself ? What did he think of the reception which greeted a book *consubstantiel à son auteur*. Did he find the world read his book as well as the free-lances, who took him captive, read his face ? Read him they did, even though Gascony thought it was a joke to see him in print. If Millanges was paid for his edition of 1580, printers beyond the Loire were ready to buy. Besides the second edition of Millanges (1582), there was that of Jean Richer (Paris) in 1587, and perhaps still others, if we may trust the word of La Croix du Maine.

But did Montaigne find they read him right ? We may find his answer in the Third Book and in the additions to the first two, published in 1588. He admits yielding to public opinion

[1] cf. Bernard Authomne : *Commentaires sur les Coutumes Générales de Bordeaux*, 1621, pp. 329, 330 : ' Feu Montaigne, auteur des Essais, sentant approcher la fin de ses jours, se leva du lit en chemise, prit sa robe de chambre, ouvrit son cabinet, fit approcher tous ses valets et autres légataires et leur paya les légats qu'il leur avait laisses, prévoyant la difficulté que feraient ses héritiers à les payer.'

by adding more and more examples and quotations to his text,
and he strengthened his statement on this point still further
before his death. *Je m'en charge de plus fort tous les jours, outre
ma proposition et ma forme première, sur la fantaisie du siècle et
les enhortements d'autrui.*[1] In a sense, no doubt, he enjoyed
embellishing his work with more parallels and instances,[2] but
this does not mean that he was blind, as has been often suggested,
to the possible harm he was doing to the book.

He accepted, then, the taste of the age for ' rich allegations '
and recognized that, in spite of his strange enterprise, a self-
portrait, the Essays were classed among the treasuries of the
anthologists.   After all what else *were* his earlier chapters but
marquetry work from Seneca and Plutarch.   Yet he was not
quite content, I think.   Does he not say, in a somewhat jocose
vein, of his *Vers de Virgile* (III, 5) :

Je m'ennuie que mes essais servent les dames de meuble commun
seulement et de meuble de salle. Ce chapitre me fera du cabinet.

In other words : You, dear ladies, see in my book one of these
short-cuts to classical knowledge, a repertory of moral maxims,
placed for general edification on the drawing-room table, but
not a bedside book, a *vade mecum*, as I should like to be.   He
was soon to find a strange exception in Marie de Gournay, who
recognized the merit of the Essays, as he himself says, alone in
her province of Picardy.

As for criticisms, they were not lacking, as we have seen,
but Montaigne, with a touch of Gascon obstinacy, insists that
his faults are part and parcel of himself.   It was enough that
he should recognize them, as in *Du Repentir* he recognized his
sins.   If adding examples was a point where he would yield,
correction was a word he did not like to hear.   Listen to his
defence, the perfect answer to some of the observations which
were made to him at Blois by Etienne Pasquier !

Je corrigerais bien une erreur accidentelle, dequoi je me suis plaint,
ainsi que je cours incessamment : mais les imperfections qui sont en
moi ordinaires et constantes, ce serait trahison de les ôter. Quand
on m'a dit ou que moi-même me suis dit : Tu es trop épais en figures.

---

[1] *Essais*, III, 12, p. 366, 7 B.C.   For his annoyance with those who
prized him simply as a stylist, see I, 40, p. 323 C.

[2] According to Mademoiselle de Gournay (*Préface*, 1617 and 1635), he
noted down ' ce qu'il trouvait par hasard dans les lectures qu'il faisait aux
intervalles de sa composition, puis il les rangeait dans son livre.'   This is
confirmed in part by Montaigne's Caesar and other books from his library
(see studies of Villey and Dezeimeris).

Voilà un mot du cru de Gascogne. Voilà une phrase dangereuse (je n'en refuis aucune de celles qui s'usent emmi les rues francaises : ceux qui veulent combattre l'usage par la grammaire se moquent). Voilà un discours ignorant.[1] Voilà un discours paradoxe.[2] En voilà un peu trop fol.[3] (1595 Tu te joues souvent : on estimera que tu dies à droit ce que tu dies à feinte.[4]) Oui, fais-je ; mais je corrige les fautes d'inadvertance non celles de coutume—Est ce pas ainsi que je parle partout ? me réprésente-je pas vivement ? suffit ! J'ai fait ce que j'ai voulu : tout le monde me reconnaît en mon livre et mon livre en moi.[5]

That is the point : to be recognized in his book for what he was, this was part of the realization of his personality. He here declares himself satisfied. Pasquier, and Camus (on the testimony of one who had known him personally) [6] are witnesses that his very speech and manner were as we see them in his book.

[1] cf. Scaliger.　　[2] e.g. The Apology.　　[3] e.g. *Des Vers de Virgile*.
[4] Perhaps Mademoiselle de Gournay (cf. below, p. 49).
[5] *Essais*, III, 5, p. 121 B.C.　　[6] See below, p. 115.

CHAPTER III

THE RECEPTION OF THE ESSAYS—III :
LA BELLE APOLOGIE

WE have seen Montaigne's Christian end, as reported by Pasquier. We must pursue further the question of whether the Essays appeared to its first readers a Christian book—whether that is, Montaigne's intentions and his own life being set aside, there was not matter, as Baudius said, for the inquisitors' pen in certain passages of the Essays. We shall see that, in one respect, at least, that which seemed most questionable to future generations, was precisely what appeared most admirable to some of the writers dealt with in this chapter —the fideism of Montaigne, and the various themes of the Apology : the misery and vanity of man, the uncertainty of knowledge and the intelligence of animals.

This last theme, still more than the other two, can be put to a variety of uses. In order to emphasize once more Montaigne's use of it in the first part of the Apology, let us turn first to a *Paradoxe sur les Bêtes Brutes*, published in 1586,[1] which may indeed have been partly composed before the Essays appeared, but seems to show the inspiration of the Apology. It is by Montaigne's friend, Etienne Pasquier.

We have already seen that Pasquier appears as a thorough fideist from the time of the Jesuit trial in 1564. And two of the very unoriginal maxims which he quotes from the Essays are chosen for their (indirect) connexion with fideism : *nous formons une vérité sur la consultation de nos cinq sens* ; in other words, the Aristotelian *nihil in intellectu quod non prius in sensibus*—the *tabula rasa* theory of knowledge. The other

---

[1] *Lettres* (1586), **XI**. *A Monsieur Turnebus le père, conseiller au Parlement de Paris.* It is presumably Odet de Turnèbe who is here referred to, who died in February 1581, and not his father, Adrien, the great scholar (died 1564). The letter as printed contains, however, a reference to the assassination of William of Orange in 1584, so that it is, at any rate in part, posterior to the publication of the Essays.

maxim is *Beaucoup savoir apporte occasion de plus douter*. This common-place is Pasquier's point of departure in the *Paradoxe*. It is doubtful whether reason is an advantage to man, for our reasoning is constantly distorted by the influence of the passions. Hence *nous batissons cette fille bâtarde, l'opinion* ; hence all philosophers have, to a greater or lesser degree, despaired of finding any certitude of knowledge. However this may be, says Pasquier, shelving the question, animals certainly do not lack reason. Here follows a long list of examples of their intelligent actions. Montaigne's credulity seems nothing compared with the apparent willingness of Pasquier to accept the incredible. As in Montaigne's case, it is impossible not to suspect a certain humorous indulgence in whimsicality. Note, however, that Pasquier puts his correspondent on his guard against imagining that from this paradox he would wish to ' form an atheism amongst us '. He writes simply *pour bannir de nous cette outre-cuidance et orgueil par lequel, nous nous donnans tous les autres animaux en proie, comme si nous fussions leurs Rois, nous sommes si misérables*. Note, further, that the conclusion of this letter offers a portrait of the man who is superior, not only to the beasts, but to the rest of men. Superior in intelligence, health and goods, he should be too unassuming to entertain anything contrary to the laws of his country, or to indulge in the imaginations of his own judgement. Traditionalist as he is politically, his religion is to praise God in all his creatures, for as much as he has given them certain blessings denied to man that he may profit by the abasement of his pride.

But this abasement of pride is not sought here in the interests of religion, except so far as the plea for broad religious views and for political conservatism are associated in the minds of the moderates or *politiques*. It is their ideal which Pasquier here puts forward and he uses the theme of human misery and imperfection, as Montaigne uses that of the relativity of custom, to lower the political and religious temperature of that age of heated passions.

A striking instance, however, of the use of a more emotional fideism, derived from the Essays, may be found in the works of Montaigne's life-long friend, Florimond de Raemond. Unlike that other intimate friend, Pierre de Brach,[1] Raemond, who

---

[1] Pierre de Brach (1549–160?) forms an additional link between Montaigne and Raemond. This friendship with Montaigne goes back to the days when Montaigne was still a *conseiller* at Bordeaux, like de Brach himself. We have seen him at Montaigne's bedside in Paris, and it was he who, with Mme de Montaigne, completed the initial process of tran-

succeeded to Montaigne's post as *conseiller* at the *Parlement* of
Bordeaux in 1570, is no *politique*, but remarkable among his
ultra-Catholic colleagues as a pillar of orthodoxy.[1] His self-
allotted task was the defence of Catholicism in a region where,
perhaps, more than anywhere in France, the schism had divided
house from house, and father against son. He is best known
for his unfinished *Histoire de l'Hérésie*. This work and his
previous books attacking the scurrilous myths of ' Pope Joan '
and the Pope as Antichrist have gained him the somewhat undeserved reputation of a fanatic. This is due perhaps to Bayle's
hasty acceptance of all the Protestant libels, but also to the
style of the *Histoire de l'Hérésie*, in which he often indulges in
would-be apocalyptic eloquence and a plethora of military metaphors. Where Raemond, however, is speaking, not from
hearsay, but from his own experience, he is level-headed and
comparatively moderate. The martyred heretics are not true
martyrs, of course, but their burning was a frightful error. He
recalls how first his father, and later he himself and his young
friends, as they came to witness such executions, were filled with
pity and admiration and could not believe that injustice had
not been done.[2]

Raemond speaks of Montaigne and quotes him frequently.[3]
The chief interest of these reminiscences is to show us the
scepticism of Montaigne turned into a weapon to be used against
the Protestants. Montaigne is the Pyrrhonist to whom Raemond
in his *Papesse Jeanne* refers with approval,[4] and the Apology is
for him the very essence of the Essays. He is as much of a
fideist as Montaigne, and he echoes the emotional attitude of

scribing the *copie de Bordeaux* after the author's death, preparatory to
the edition of 1595. It is interesting to note that two of Brach's best
sonnets are on the horrors of the civil war, a subject which (as he tells us
in a sonnet addressed to Montaigne) was suggested to him by the author
of the Essays as the most fitting subject of his pen, though it is one on
which he has rarely touched (see R. Dezeimeris, *Pierre de Brach*, 1861 ;
P. Bonnefons : *Les Amis de Montaigne*).

[1] Florimond de Raemond (1540–1601), born at Agen. He was the
editor of Montluc's *Commentaires* and the correspondent of Lipsius,
Pasquier and Du Plessis Mornay (see Tamizey de Larroque, *Florimond
de Raemond*, 1867 and A. M. Boase, *Montaigne annoté par Florimond de
Raemond, Revue du 16ᵐᵉ Siecle, 1928*).

[2] See also *L'Antichrist*, pp. 792–4, a remarkable passage, probably
referring to L'Hopital.

[3] The first anonymous editions of the *Erreur Populaire de la Papesse
Jeanne* (Bordeaux, 1587 and 1588) contain no references to, or reminiscences
of, Montaigne. The 1594 edition, to which I refer, is entirely rewritten.

[4] *Papesse Jeanne* (1594), p. 174.

the Essays again and again in a way which shows that he is not simply borrowing for the moment a convenient dialectic. Thus the beginning of *De l'Antichrist*, he says of God :

Ce grand ouvrier est mieux connu, s'il est aucunement [somewhat] ignoré, et de ses ouvrages ceux là portent mieux sa marque que nous entendons le moins. La grandeur des choses divines et célestes ne nous doit être mise en créance par la faiblesse de nos sens, autrement l'inégalité de notre entendement diversifierait la loi de Dieu et les moins capables seraient les moins informés de ce qu'il faut que nous croyons tous également d'une même facon. Le jugement de l'homme est si faible, qu'étant incapable de comprendre l'excellence et la grandeur des oeuvres de son facteur, il est le plus souvent réduit à désestimer les choses que son esprit veut goûter par raison humaine. Outil ondoyant, règle de plomb qui se plie comme on veut.

The following section of this same chapter is concerned with *Choses étranges dont nous ne savons la raison* and its conclusion refers us directly to the Apology and provides a mention of a passage of St. Gregory the Great which will be met with again in dealing with Charron :—

Qui nous fait si audacieux d'oser élever nos esprits, et, au dessus de leur portée, les guinder aux cieux, ramenant sous nos pieds les choses célestes pour en rechercher la raison . . . C'est lors, disait très bien Saint Grégoire, que nous parlons avec la plus grande éloquence des oeuvres de Dieu, quand l'étonnement et merveille d'icelles rend nos langues muettes. Et l'homme en parle mieux en se taisant, qu'il ne peut suffisamment expliquer en parlant. Mais laissons ce discours qu'on voit de tous points accomplis dans cette belle Apologie de Raimond Sebond, l'un des Essais de notre Montaigne.[1]

Again in the *Papesse Jeanne* an adaptation of one of the most famous pages of the *Belle Apologie* introduces Raemond's well-known *Regrets de la mort du seigneur de Montaigne*. The sequence of ideas is here very clear. The author describes a ceremony of the Papal induction symbolizing the transience of mundane glory. He speaks of vanity and death with the phrases of the Essays on his lips. This, he says, is Montaigne's subject —*Mais laissons cela à Michel de Montaigne*. Then it is that he expatiates on his friend's ' courageous and almost stoical philosophy ' and all his virtues. But if Montaigne, the man, is admired by his friend for his fortitude and his sage disquisitions on mortality, there can be no doubt that it is as a fideist and a force for toleration—I have already insisted on this connexion

[1] *De l'Antichrist*, pp. 20–21.

—that the Essays have influenced Raemond.[1] It is with Montaigne's words he insists that it is not for man to judge the limits of the possible, that self-flattery is the real mother of error, that *la plupart de nos disputes en religion sont grammairiennes.*[2] He goes out of his way to copy a phrase from the final recension of the Essays while this still lay in the hands of Brach or Madame de Montaigne—*fâcheuse maladie d'avoir telle opinion de soi qu'on se persuade qu'il ne se puisse rien croire au contraire.*[3]

It would be possible to quote passages on other subjects where Raemond is the faithful echo of his friend, but they do not permit any further indications as to Montaigne's influence. This much, however, is clear, that a large number of Raemond's general reflexions appear to come straight from the Essays. The two men must have been totally unlike in temperament, and on witchcraft their opinions differed considerably. It is clear that Raemond offers an interesting example of a Catholic whose piety and orthodoxy has never been doubted, and who shows himself a particular admirer of the Apology and the side of Montaigne which it represents. In his recent introduction to the new English translation of the Essays, Mr. J. M. Robertson says that the fact that Montaigne ' was not soon recognized as a philosophic force is the decisive proof of the completeness with which he had achieved his practical end, the undermining of active fanaticism, the lowering of men's blood pressures '.[4] This general statement seems to beg a number of questions, but I have no doubt that Robertson's phrase describes the influence of Montaigne on Raemond and that which Raemond, in spite of his occasional bellicosity, himself seems to have attempted to propagate among his fellow-citizens.

Within the circle of Montaigne's own acquaintance however, we may find a less favourable attitude to some of the views expressed in the Essays. These are the remarks of Antoine de

[1] It is not Raemond but his son, Abbé de la Frenade, who in his free Latin rendering of the *Papesse*, says France has lost a man, *quem nisi acerba mors extinxisset quos de stoica et Christiana Philosophia inceperat libros, perfecisset.* The father does not even mention Montaigne's books in this passage.

[2] *Papesse Jeanne*, pp. 225, 138 ; *Antichrist*, pp. 231, 232. This remark of Montaigne's (*Essais*, II, p. 266) is perhaps also echoed by Scaliger (*Scaligerana*, art. Grammatica) and by D'Aubigné (*Confession de Sancy*, ed. Reaume, p. 324).

[3] *Papesse Jeanne*, p. 316, *Réponse à un ministre de Béarn* ; *Essais*, I, 56, p. 406 c.

[4] *Essays of Montaigne*, tr. by E. J. Trechmann, Oxford University Press, 1927.

Laval, seigneur de Belair (1550–163 ?),[1] contained in his copy of the Essays.[2] Laval, who, besides being Geographer Royal, was also an eminent theological controversialist, evidently prided himself on his orthodoxy. And although he is often unjust, his marginal comments are also illuminating. It is perhaps mere professional caution that makes him deny indignantly that geographers imagine that all lands have now been discovered, and it is understandable that he should write of Montaigne's essay on suicide (II, 3) :

> Ceci n'a rien que de payen, directement contraire à la religion Chrétienne. Il était bon pour Sénèque et non pour nous.

Laval, however, sees a profession of deism, ' heretical and very dangerous ', in the passage of the Apology, in which Montaigne writes that, of all ' humane and ancient opinions ' on religion, the most plausible seems to him that which recognizes God as an ' incomprehensible power ', accepting in good part the homage rendered him ' under any name or in any form '. Dangerous perhaps, but Montaigne's statement is deliberately limited to ' humane and ancient opinions ', that is, to those which men would possess without Christian revelation and did possess before it ; nay, more, in its context, his remarks form part of a demonstration of the insufficiency of all such.[3] The ' indifferentism ' which Laval thinks he has here detected begins very noticeably to attract the attention of religious apologists in the last few years of the sixteenth century. Catholic apologists harp on an equivalence between the terms *politique* or moderate and atheist,[4] while in 1595 a Protestant, Laurent Pollot, in his *Dis-*

---

[1] See H. Faure, *Antoine de Laval and les Ecrivains Bourbonnais* 1870 : *Bulletin du Bibliophile*, 1898, p. 227 et seq. For Laval's note on the term *Essai*, see above, p. 3, and on Mlle de Gournay below, p. 61, note 1.

[2] *Les Essais* (ed. Courbet et Royer, Append.). The copy was in the possession of the late E. Courbet who published in his edition of the Essays (Courbet and Royer, V 252 et seq.) the extracts given here. The book which does not appear to have been sold with the rest of Courbet's library has so far eluded my attempts to trace it. Two remarks are therefore not misplaced (1) these extracts are probably incomplete, (2) Courbet does not mention the edition of this copy of the Essays. I am assuming that they were probably written between 1600 and 1620, but it is possible that Laval writes after the campaign of the next decade against the *Libertins* had begun. His place is nevertheless here as a member of an earlier generation.

[3] *Essais*, II, 12, p. 247, 8 A. The same passage is condemned by the Père Boucher in 1628, see below, p. 117.

[4] For example, *Atheomastix, sive adversus Religionis hostes universos (Politicos maxime) dissertatio* (1598). For an account of the terms employed to designate heretics or non-Christians, see Busson, *Pensée*

cours contre la Pluralité des Religions et de l'Athéisme, makes ' a courtier ' the representative of the doctrine that every man can be saved in his own religion.   The mere idea of tolerance smacks of religious indifference to many apologists of the sixteenth and seventeenth centuries, and it is not surprising to find Laval indignantly commenting on the impiety of Montaigne's relativism as expressed in the essay *Des Cannibales* (I, 31) :

il semble que nous n'avons d'autre mire de la raison et la vérité que l'exemple et idée des opinions et usances du pays où sommes.   Là est toujours la parfaite religion, la parfaite police, parfait et accompli usage de toutes choses.

Yet this theme is one of those used by fideists, such as Montaigne, to show the uncertainty of all natural laws and beliefs, and hence the necessity of faith.

Laval, however, is no fideist, and one corollary of his attitude may be found in another note on a passage of the Apology which follows closely on that already mentioned.   Two pages later Montaigne, developing his attack on anthropomorphism, says of the attribution to the gods of human imperfections, passions, relationships, human pleasures, deaths and buryings, *il faut que cela soit parti d'une merveilleuse ivresse de l'entendement humain.*[1] Laval's comment is at once unfair and illuminating :

Ces propositions tiennent une folle présomption en voulant avilir l'homme et ne m'étonne si cette Apologie est défendue sous peine d'anathème.[2]

We are here a long way from the *belle Apologie* !

It should be noted, first, that Laval's indignation seems to be, not on behalf of the Deity as blasphemously compared with the gods of Olympus, but on behalf of man and an anthropo-

Religieuse, Chap. I.   *Libertin* appears in the *free thinking* sense in La Noue, who adds, however, the adjective *spirituel* and describes them as *affranchis de l'Eglise, dociles à l'esprit*, but from R. Dupont (*Philosophie de l'Esprit*, 1602) without further qualification.   *Athée* and *déiste* are generally used quite indiscriminately.   *Esprit forts* is due to Charron (*Trois Vérités*).   For attempts at rational classification see below, p. 168.

[1] *Essais*, II, 12, p. 252 A.   The note of Courbet on this passage is doubly false.   The first Italian translation of the Essays was published in 1599, and though that of 1633 did not contain the Apology, this was published separately in the following year at the request of many readers who wished to possess the whole work.   The publisher complains, however, that his translation has not been a financial success.

[2] Laval presumably means he would not be surprised if the Apology *were* prohibited.   So far as I know, nothing of the kind was done until 1676 when the Essays as a whole were put on the Index.

centric view of the universe. Secondly, that, as an orthodox theologian, he had every justification for impugning Montaigne's complete rejection of anthropomorphism with regard to God, since that part of theology which deals with his nature and attributes was by the scholastics constructed precisely on such an analogy. The zeal with which Montaigne pursues the fallacy of anthropomorphism is an aspect of his thought which has been perhaps insufficiently stressed.

The anthropomorphic view of God's nature is closely associated with the anthropocentric view of the universe. Montaigne's ' cure of pyrrhonism ' is directed against anthropomorphism and anthropocentrism in the interests of religion and of anti-dogmatism, as well as of tolerance in a more general sense. Thus the one occasion on which Raemond criticizes an assertion of Montaigne, supplies an interesting contrast to the occasion of Laval's indignation. It is not *l'avilissement de l'homme* which makes him write in the margin : *Voici qui est bien hardi* ; but the reminiscence of Seneca's saying that man can surpass the gods themselves, since on occasion he can momentarily transcend his own nature, a reminiscence which is, of course, meant to be taken in a purely metaphorical sense.

These criticisms of the Geographer Royal serve to show how completely contemporaries, both of whom knew Montaigne personally, could differ in their attitude to the Essays. For Laval writes across the title of his copy, ' *J'ay cognu et fréquenté fort familièrement l'auteur.*' Indeed, we catch a glimpse of the two in each other's company in Laval's *Desseins des Professions Nobles et Publiques* (1605). This book consists of a series of imaginary lessons written for a son who died before its publication, and each lesson is followed by a short essay arising from what has preceded. Thus at the end of the ' lesson ' on Diplomacy, there is a treatise on ' *Les Lettres Missives* ', and we are told that it is the outcome of a discussion which took place at the table of ' *M. de Fresnes Forget, Sécrétaire d'Etat* ', where ' *Messieurs d'Evreux, de Montaigne, du Haillan, Paschal et autres* ' were present. Forget-Fresne wanted to know how it was that the learned pillars of the Universities wrote such bad letters, of which he showed them one, as an example, written by one of the first men of the kingdom in languages, philosophy and mathematics.[1]

---

[1] op. cit., p. 189a. Forget was the *rédacteur* of the Edict of Nantes, Du Haillan, the historian, from Bordeaux like Montaigne, and cousin to Pierre de Brach. Of Du Perron it is not necessary to speak here, if it is indeed he. He did not become bishop of Evreux until 1591, and there

The *Dessein des Professions Nobles* is a book on education. There is the usual reaction against pedantry, a recommendation of the direct method for teaching Latin,[1] and an insistence on the necessity of bringing the judgement of the pupil early into play. But Laval has nothing in common with our author. He disapproves of Aristotle's Ethics, of Seneca, of Epictetus and even of Plutarch as ethical teaching for the young. '*Ne sois pas si téméraire*, he writes, *de mêler avec l'étude des lettres saintes ce que les Profanes ont dit des Vertus Morales*' (p. 22*b*). It is still more remarkable that even as a stylist, Montaigne does not find favour in his eyes. The best authors of the language are, he says, Du Perron, Du Haillan, Du Vair and Marion.

The work of another amateur theologian, this time an advocate from Bordeaux, shows us that in 1595, the year of the definitive edition of Montaigne, the Essays were in the air, so to speak, in the author's own country. Jean de Champaignac,[2] whose *Traité de l'Immortalité de l'Ame* takes its arms against the Paduan fideists from St. Thomas himself, appears to conduct a detailed refutation of the first part of the Apology (the comparison of men and beasts), and yet his book is full of reminiscences of the Essays. Most of these, as M. Busson observes, come precisely from the Apology. When this rationalist has stated his case, the first objection he deals with is that of certain philosophers who, seeing the industry and marvellous actions of many animals, have attributed reason to them. This would mean that either the souls of both were incorruptible or both corruptible. Other ' wiser heads ', says Champaignac, have attributed these actions to the divine wisdom acting by means of natural instinct,[3] and he proceeds to explain away a vast number of examples of alleged

---

is reason to suppose that Laval is speaking of 1588 at which date he records having met our author. Charles de Paschal, Vicomte de Quente (1547–1625), was a diplomatist of some note, who published a book on his profession, the *Legatus* (1598). One of his minor works, a collection of prayers, is dedicated to Forget. The letter-writer seems likely to have been Jacques Pelletier.

[1] To be taught Latin in this way was not uncommon. Laval employed the method with his elder sons. The younger will not be taught in the same manner, simply because his father is too busy. We shall see that J. P. Camus also was taught in this way. What was singular in Montaigne's case was that he was taught Latin *before* French.

[2] *Physique Française avec un Bref Traité de l'Immortalité de l'Ame par M. Jean de Champaignac, Avocat au Parlement de Bordeaux et Maître de Requêtes de Mme la Princesse, sœur unique du Roi* (1595 Millanges, Bordeaux). Busson (*Les Sources du Rationalisme*, pp. 493–502) has dealt very fully with this author.

[3] *Traité*, p. 86 et seq.

reasoning by animals. Some of these examples lead me to believe that Etienne Pasquier's *Paradoxe* [1] is in his mind no less than the ' Apology for Raymond Sebond '.

Champaignac is no fideist, but like most men of his time, and unlike the official theology, he holds of God that :

Tout ainsi que le Soleil est le corps qui moins se peut voir, de même, encore que Dieu soit l'essence qui plus est intelligible pour sa constance invariable, c'est celle toutefois que nous entendons le moins.[2]

He repeats with approval the story of Hieron's saying that the more he thought of God the more incomprehensible he seemed. This is one of the stock sayings of all the Paduan school. He is exceptionally fond of considerations on the inconstancy of human nature, which has the one advantage for man that repentance is possible for him ; hence the difference between his fall and that of the angels.[3] Champaignac quotes Montaigne textually as to the importance of following received traditions in order to avoid the ' vast, vexed and flowing sea of human opinions '. These examples will serve to show that even if we cannot speak of influence, Champaignac and Montaigne have a good deal in common, and Busson has perhaps exaggerated the contrast between them. Their ' difference ' about animals is conducted with the utmost courtesy by Champaignac and I am not at all sure whether Montaigne is not numbered rather among the ' wiser heads ' by his opponent. Be this as it may, the book shows us how Montaigne was read with attention in his own province, and that the Apology was studied even by those who did not agree with its main views.

Apart from Raemond, Champaignac, (and Charron, who is to be studied later), Bordeaux can still offer us some interesting evidence on the reputation of Montaigne and on the views which seemed suspect to his contemporaries. The ground here is witchcraft. We have seen in Chapter I the discussion of spells and the purely psychological explanation offered by Montaigne in his essay ' On the Force of Imagination ' (I, 21), as also its condemnation by Delrio (see p. 23), but Montaigne also made a bold attack in a later essay (III, 11) on the belief in witches, and a noble plea for an end to persecution—' they have more need of hellebore than hemlock '. I have attempted to show elsewhere that Montaigne's own views coincide with the policy of no persecution, adopted for many years at Bordeaux during

[1] See above, pp. 30–31.   [2] *Traité*, p. 4.
[3] ib., p. 22, cf. p. 124 et seq.

the presidency of Jacques Benoît de Lagebâton, and that the essay *Des Boiteux* may have been written not only as a counter-blast to such treatises as these of Bodin (*La Démonomanie*, 1580) but as an effort to preserve the *status quo* within the jurisdiction of the Bordeaux Parlement.[1] It must, moreover, be repeated that, in contrast to modern popular belief, no one who has studied the subject denies the existence of witch-organizations all over Europe, the remains of an ancient Dianic cult with fertility rites probably dating from Neolithic times.[2] Modern opinion—with the exception of fundamentalists like Dr. Montagu Summers—would deny, of course, the supernatural powers firmly believed in not only by judges but by the devotees themselves of a pre-Christian deity whom they—again like their Christian judges—came to call the Devil. When these facts are understood the importance of bodily presence at the witches' ' coven ', becomes perfectly clear. It is implicit in some of Montaigne's remarks, although the basis of his attitude is the essential improbability of all the alleged supernatural *data* ; hence the criminal folly of persecution on largely worthless evidence : *Après tout, c'est mettre ses conjectures à bien haut prix que d'en faire cuire un homme tout vif.*

It is a melancholy fact that one of the factors which helped to make a *modus vivendi* between Catholics and Protestants durable, was the turning aside of the forces of religious fanaticism into a campaign of persecution against witches and witchcraft. It is no accident that the number of cases brought before the courts in France reaches its height under Henri IV and the years of the ensuing regency.[3] Florimond de Raemond appears to have been deeply shocked by the revelations made during such prosecutions. He had been *rapporteur* in at least one case, and is indignant that the Parlement of Bordeaux should have been accused, by Beza from his Genevan pulpit and by others unnamed, of not condemning witches to death. Elsewhere he writes sadly :

Il ne se passe jour que nos jugements n'en soient ensanglantés, et que nous ne revenions tristes dans nos maisons, épouvantés des choses hideuses et effroyables qu'elles confessent.[4]

Raemond appears to be full of prejudices against women. The

---

[1] A. M. Boase : *Montaigne et la Sorcellerie.* (*Humanisme Renaissance* 1935). Outside Bordeaux, see below, p. 246.
[2] Margaret Murray : *Witchcraft in Western Europe.*
[3] M. Foucault : *Les Procès de Sorcellerie devant les tribunaux séculiers,* 1907. Appendix.   [4] ib., p. 75.

subject of his *Papesse Jeanne* gives some opportunities which are made the most of. His animosity is nourished on something far more important than the traditional pleasantries of the so-called *esprit gaulois* or the virulence and smut of some of Régnier's contemporaries ; it is founded on theological prejudice reinforced by a preoccupation with witchcraft.[1] Raemond in his notes on the Essays—so far as we possess them to-day [2]—records no comment on Montaigne's complete incredulity on this subject. We have already seen that it was otherwise with Delrio. It is otherwise too with another councillor of Bordeaux, Pierre de Rostégui de Lancre (*c.* 1550–1630).[3] His attitude is that of a man disturbed and puzzled to find that an author so esteemed and so estimable should have doubted the bodily presence of witches at the ' coven ' or the possibility of producing impotence by means of a charm. Lancre is best known as the burner of the witches of Labourd, some six hundred of whom were done to death in the spring of 1609 by this painstaking magistrate in company with the President d'Espagnet, his eccentric colleague who escorted Mademoiselle de Gournay from Paris to Bordeaux in 1595. Two years earlier Lancre published his *Tableau de l'Inconstance et Instabilité de toutes choses, où il est montré qu'en Dieu seul gît la vraie Constance, à laquelle l'homme sage doit viser* (1607). So much does this title, this general theme delight him, that when he came to give an account of the witch trials of Labourd he called his book : *Tableau de l'Inconstance des Mauvais Anges et Démons* (1612).[4]

The first *Tableau*, though a good example of what, following Hulme,[5] I have called ' a critique of satisfaction ', is for the most part a tedious literary exercise. Although there are numerous

---

[1] See, in this connexion, the *Mallaeus Maleficarum*, I, 6.

[2] See A. M. Boase, *Montaigne annoté par F. de Raemond, Revue du 16ᵐᵉ Siecle, 1928.*

[3] He appears to have been at the (Jesuit) Collège de Clermont, travelled in Italy 1575 and 1600, was councillor at Bordeaux before 1583, when a *récusation* names him as an intimate friend of Camain, Montaigne's brother-in-law, who was later the residuary legatee of Charron. In 1625 he and his wife, who were childless, founded a house of ' Jesuitine nuns ' at Bordeaux, that is, of the order founded fifteen years before by Montaigne's own niece, Jeanne de Lestonnac (cf. *Archives de la Gironde,* XXIV, 176).

[4] The *Tableau de l'Inconstance and l'Instabilité* was republished in 1610. Lancre's other works are *Le Livre des Princes* (1616, see below, p. 116, note 3) : *L'Incrédulité et Mécréance du Sortilège pleinement convaincue* (1622) : *Du Sortilège* (1627, privately printed). In all these books, except the last, Montaigne is quoted.

[5] See Introduction, p. xxvi.

echoes of the Essays, none are particularly significant. The attitude of Lancre to Montaigne in his second *Tableau* and his *L'Incrédulité et Mécréance du Sortilège* presents a quite different interest. It gives also some idea of the respect in which our author was held in Bordeaux at the beginning of the seventeenth century. For Lancre is disturbed at the incredulity of Montaigne on this head, as he might well be with so much blood on his hands. In 1612 he is ' vexed and astonished ' to find Montaigne numbered by Delrio among heretical authors for his doubts as to the bodily presence of witches at the ' coven '. He evades the question of what Montaigne said, attempting to vouch for his orthodoxy by alleging his admiration for the great Jesuit theologian, Jean Maldonat.[1] He insinuates, therefore, that Montaigne did not really hold the witches' gatherings to be illusion, and consoles himself with the thought that Delrio does not call Montaigne a heretic, but says that this opinion is heretical. He admits, however, as we have said, that at Bordeaux the court for many years refused to prosecute.

Ten years later, he returns to the question of Delrio's condemnation of Montaigne for his incredulity as to spells producing impotence. This time Lancre's tactics are to show that Montaigne avoided any dogmatic opinion on this point, excused the ' liberty of his opinion ' and sought to escape responsibility by declaring his books were written only for his friends and relations. Here, however, Lancre's opinions are less clear. He sets out with the idea of excusing Montaigne, but his irritation and suspicion seem to end by getting the better of him.

Lancre liked to represent himself as a voice crying in the wilderness for a campaign of persecution, but statistics show there was nothing to be desired in the first quarter of the seventeenth century in this respect at Bordeaux or elsewhere. One sign of the extent to which demonology was accepted is seen in the attempts to make the existence of witches and of evil spirits a proof of the immortality of the soul. Champaignac, for instance, holds that the existence of evil *spirits* and their relations with man prove the *spiritual* nature of the human soul. The most impressive monument to this way of thinking is perhaps the work of Pierre Le Loyer, councillor at the Presidial Court of Angers. In 1586 he dedicated his *Quatre livres des Spectres ou Apparitions et visions et esprits, anges et démons se monstrant sensiblement aux hommes* to Catherine de Médicis. The book begins by refuting the Aristotelian, the Epicurean, and

---

[1] On their relations, see *art. cit.*

lastly the Sceptical denial of the existence of demons. Le Loyer's work was rewritten in a much-expanded form and republished in 1605, and again in 1608. M. Busson has suggested that the fuller treatment of the sceptical objections—the untrustworthiness of sense-perception—is due to an attempt to reply to Montaigne. I think the evidence is very inconclusive, but we shall meet precisely the same objections in a later writer, Jean de Silhon, and expressly directed against Montaigne.

If Le Loyer does not mention Montaigne, Delrio and Lancre remind us how important—and how *apparently* isolated—was Montaigne's scepticism in this matter. The Jesuit theologian, Théophile Raynaud—less well disposed than Lancre—does not hesitate to rank Montaigne and Pomponazzi [1] as the two most notable examples of heretical unbelief in witchcraft. Yet Montaigne was an author accessible to the general reader, while Pomponazzi's *De Incantationibus* was, like his other works, often hard to come by. None the less, the end for educated opinion began perhaps sooner than has been realized. A comparison of Naudé's statements in his *Apologie pour les grands personnages faussement soupçonnés de magie* (1625) and his *Mascurat* (1649) would show how much more absolute he dared to be after a lapse of twenty-four years, and Patin records only a few years later that the Parlement of Paris refuses to hear charges of witchcraft.[2] In 1672 Colbert forbids cognizance of such cases to the courts. If the suspicion of personal intrigue and injustice which hovered over many *causes célèbres*—such as those of Marthe Brossier, of Urbain Grandier, and the nuns of Louviers—the credulity of the witch-judges, such as Lancre, and the wild delation and state of panic produced in the general public, all played their part in this rapid evolution of opinion, it would be unwise to underestimate the importance of a book so popular as the Essays.

The authors so far dealt with in this chapter though diverse in interest have all been either friends or acquaintances of Montaigne or, like Champaignac and Lancre, men moving in the same parliamentary circles at Bordeaux. Further investigation fails, however, to show that Montaigne had any marked influence on the intellectual life of his native town in the years succeeding his death.[3] In order to complete our picture of

[1] *Théologie Naturelle* (1622), IX, p. 43. On Pomponazzi and Montaigne see Busson's edition of Pomponazzi's *De Incantationibus* (Rieder, 1930).

[2] ed. Reveillé Parise, II, 210 : see below, pp. 244-246, 249, 259.

[3] See, however, p. 396: and also p. 310, for a book written in 1623 by Charles de Gamaches, the second husband of Montaigne's daughter.

Montaigne's influence on his own generation, we must look further afield.

Let us take the strange poem *Gigantomachie ou combat de tous les arts et sciences avec la louange de l'âne* (1593), written by a Protestant, Paul Perrot de la Salle, the father of Perrot d'Ablancourt, the well-known translator of the seventeenth century.[1] The obvious source of this poem is the treatise of Cornelius Agrippa *De incertitudine Scientiarum*. For Agrippa, as for Montaigne, scepticism is the very foundation of faith. Perrot preaches a ' holy ignorance ' and places himself under the patronage of Socrates and St. Paul. The Protestant accent of the poem is rarely mistakeable, the general scheme follows Agrippa, but it is Montaigne who appears to supply the obvious source of many of the details.

In education, the loading of the child's mind with useless learning must give way to a simple knowledge of right and wrong.

> On lui apprendra, non ce que c'est que grammaire,
> Rhétorique, logique et l'art de savoir faire
> Des vers bien mesurés, ou de faire arguments.
> Mais d'être sobres, bons, adroits, humbles, prudents.

The schoolmaster with his birch-rod, and his school itself, is condemned, and Perrot advocates the country-walk, open-air and *leçons de choses* instead of books and libraries. After passing in review the disadvantages of various sciences from history to astronomy, he invites us to investigate the claims of the learned on behalf of ethics :

> Mais il est question de franchir plus avant
> Et de mettre contre eux encor la plume au vent
> Je veux couper chemin à leur œuvre morale
> Et payer les lecteurs d'une raison loyale.

All things are in a state of change, ideas of vice and virtue like the rest, and vary from place to place, and even from man to man. The very choice of good and evil depends on individual circumstances, and national custom.

> Athènes permettoit en mariage prendre
> Sa soeur, mais dedans Rome on n'osait l'entreprendre,
> Les femmes des Romains hantaient les cabarets
> Et c'était une chose honteuse entre les Grecs :

---

[1] The second edition, *Le Contr' Empire des Sciences* (1599), is here quoted. I am indebted to M. Busson for my knowledge of this book (see *Pensée Religieuse*, pp. 204–8. For Perrot d'Ablancourt, see below, p. 278).

Le Turc en a bon nombre, et cela nous est honte,
Entre nous qui faisons du mariage conte.
Chaque terre a son propre, et chacune Province
Ses coutumes, ses moeurs, son langage et son Prince :
Tel d'un vice est repris, tel est taché d'un autre,
Faisant chacun vertu du vice où il se vautre.

Is Perrot conscious of the possible significance of his own relativism ? He goes on at once to expound *naturam expelles furca* :

Ainsi n'est-il aisé avec l'art de gagner
Le dessus de nature, et contre elle enseigner
Car depuis que dans nous d'une course ordinaire
La coutume a pris pied, on n'y peut rien faire.

Unless the term ' nature ' is here used with irony—the irony with which Pascal suggest that what we call ' nature ' is only a more ancient custom—it is clear that Perrot's development is largely a literary exercise. It remains none the less significant because it is the earliest instance I have found of the use of this theme of the Essays, which plays so large a part in *libertin* literature of the seventeenth century.

The poem contains further passages inspired, it would seem, by the Essays, notably an attack on medicine and the medical profession which clearly derives from the essay *De la Ressemblance des Enfants aux Pères* (II, 37). It ends with a plea for tolerance, a direct attack on the theologians and their dogmatism, and finally a prayer for grace, for the voice of revelation, which recalls the final lines of the Apology :

Si l'homme à cette voix n'élève ses esprits
Encor ne sçait-il rien bien qu'il ait tout appris :
Cette voix est le but, la couronne et la lyce
De ceux aux quels est Dieu favorable et propice.

Even more than Raemond, Perrot de la Salle shows the devout use of that side of Montaigne whose later influence seemed most suspicious to the apologists, both Catholic and Protestant.

We are now in a position to review the literature dealt with up to this point and to draw some general conclusions as to the reception of the Essays by Montaigne's own contemporaries.

The ' first essays ' of 1580, with their obvious debt to Plutarch and still more to Seneca (together with Montaigne's character as a man), have obviously given their cue to many of the earliest critics. Montaigne, the Stoic—such is clearly the formula of

Expilly and Lipsius. For Pasquier, Montaigne is a second
Seneca, for La Croix du Maine, a second Plutarch. The latter,
however, like Expilly in his sonnet, Tabourot in his epigram,
and Van Veen in his *memoir*, shows the *picturesque* appeal of
the Self-Portrait, while its real importance is recognized by La
Motte Messémé and Pierre de L'Estoiie. On the other hand,
Pasquier, Scaliger and Du Puy—and even Baudius who notes
the subtlety of Montaigne's psychological analysis—show a
certain impatience with Montaigne's confidences. The style of
the Essays is admired in general. Baudius and Pasquier note
its richness in metaphor, its racy figures of speech ; but, on
the other hand, certain criticisms which will be again met throughout the seventeenth century, when different literary ideals have
come into fashion, are obviously already prevalent. The Essays
are said to be often confused in arrangement ; Montaigne indulges
in too many digressions ; his vocabulary is tainted with Gasconisms ; he is somewhat too outspoken on sex. We have
seen Montaigne's own defence under some of these heads. Both
Pasquier and Baudius tend to admit these criticisms and seek
to excuse Montaigne rather than to defend him. It is noticeable
also that Laval omits Montaigne's name from his list of the best
literary models. The expurgated edition of Simon Goulart bears
witness, not only to the scandal caused in some quarters by such
essays as *Des Vers de Virgile*, but to the desire for a Protestant
Montaigne. Its main importance, however, seems to be the proof
it affords of the undoubted success of the Essays. And, while
Montaigne himself admits his satisfaction with the way his book
has been received, he notes that it is hardly his own originality
that has gained him so wide a hearing.

The reflexion of the Essays in contemporary literature confirm to some extent this fact. But, although in the Miscellanies it is often the picturesque anecdote or the phrase which
is borrowed, we have seen that Montaigne's love of justice and
humanity, and his freedom from superstition bear some immediate fruit. This type of influence passes, in the case of La
Motte Messémé, from a consideration of special questions to a
more general influence on ethical ideas. In Expilly we have
an example of a new attitude towards savages inspired by the
Essays, while in L'Estoile the prevailing note of what is borrowed
may be summed up as the vanity of man.

In the present chapter, we have reviewed a number of authors
who reveal how controversial were certain important ideas of
Montaigne on religious subjects. The first part of the Apology,
the consideration of the intelligence of animals, is used as a

weapon against human presumption and human dogmatism by Pasquier, but refuted in form by Champaignac. The *Belle Apologie*, and, in particular, the emotional fideism which colours its arguments, is used by Raemond against Protestant dogmatism. It is an ethical relativism and a 'cure' of pyrrhonism, which, to Paul Perrot de la Salle, seem to be part of the spirit of true piety, while this same relativism of the Essays and their rejection of anthropomorphism seem highly dangerous to Laval. Finally, in one writer of Montaigne's own *milieu*, Lancre, and in one of his own relations, Delrio, we see another suspicion of heresy in the making : he does not believe in witches, or in the supernatural.

CHAPTER IV

MARIE DE GOURNAY—I : *LA FILLE D'ALLIANCE*

La vraie touche des Esprits, c'est l'examen d'un nouvel Autheur.
MARIE DE GOURNAY.

MARIE DE GOURNAY has already been mentioned. Her enthusiasm for the Essays, her meeting with her *père d'alliance*, her share in the publication of 1595, all this is common knowledge ; nor can one be familiar with the France of Richelieu without realizing that she became the victim of all the practical jokers of the literary world. For the stories of the ' *Soupe à la Grecque* ', the ' Three Racans ', or her interview with Richelieu, the reader may turn to Tallemant or the Memoirs of Marolles. All this clowning has prevented a serious examination of her ideas and of her personality, for she had a small stock of reasoned ideas which she set forth with considerable force and acumen, if, alas ! with little literary skill. ' *Les pointilles qui ne firent jamais un bon ouvrage ne le peuvent défaire* ' ; that is one of her admirable critical maxims. Yet, if minor defects cannot unmake a good work, they can and do prevent a mediocre one being read.

The facts of her life go far towards an explanation of the character of her writings. Marie le Jars de Gournay was born at Paris on the 6th of September 1565—the eldest child of Guillaume de Jars, Governor of the castles of Remy, Gournay and Moyenneville. Her father died while she was still very young, leaving his wife with six children. From the first Marie appears to have been athirst for knowledge. She taught herself Latin and even a little Greek, and when, towards 1585, the Essays fell by chance into her hands, her enthusiasm knew no bounds ; so much so, that her family were in danger of thinking her mad, until, as we have seen, some one produced Lipsius's letters and displayed his eulogy, which apparently reassured them and delighted her.

She next heard Montaigne was dead. This caused her much

48

sorrow ' *lui semblant que toute sa gloire, la félicité et l'espérance d'enrichissement de son ame, étaient fauchée en herbe, par la perte de la conversation et de la société qu'elle s'était promise d'un tel esprit* '.

She soon learnt, not only that this news was false, but that Montaigne himself had arrived in Paris, where she happened to be with her mother in the spring of 1588. She sent the great man a message, which brought him next day to pay a call on the Gournays. Montaigne must have found somewhat embarrassing the raptures of this romantic and learned young woman, whose beauty, as Marolles puts it, *était plus de l'esprit que du corps*. He appears, however, to have accepted the situation with good humour and to have had a real affection for his ' adopted daughter '—mingled with some sly chaff, if we may judge from one glimpse of their conversations together in Paris.

Mon père (she says) me voulant un jour faire déplaisir, me dit, qu'il estimait, qu'il y eût trente hommes en notre grande ville, où lors il était, aussi fort de tête que lui. L'un de mes arguments à le dédire, fut, s'il y eût eu quelqu'un, il fût venu le bienvienner,—et me plaît d'ajouter, idolâtrer ; et que tant de gens l'accueillaient pour un homme de bonne maison, de crédit et de qualité, nul pour Montaigne.

Montaigne visited ' his daughter's ' family at Gournay-sur-Aronde either once or twice in the course of this year, before the meeting of the States-General at Blois, where we have already seen him in conversation with Etienne Pasquier. The Essays of 1595 record a curious episode, at this date :

Quand je vins (says Montaigne) de ces fameux Etats de Blois, j'avais vu auparavant une fille de Picardie, pour témoigner l'ardeur de ses promesses, et aussi sa constance, se donner, du poinçon qu'elle portait en son poil (cheveux), quatre ou cinq bons coups dans le bras, qui lui faisaient craqueter la peau, et la saignaient bien à bon escient.

There can be little doubt that the girl was the romantic Mademoiselle de Gournay herself, and that this action was either a solemnization of the *traité d'alliance* to which she so constantly refers, between Montaigne and herself, or else the final argument and proof of an affection which had been met with a certain smiling scepticism. Montaigne was already at work adding to the Essays, though the 1588 edition had hardly been out more than a few months. A couple of the earliest additions of the *copie de Bordeaux* seem to have been dictated to Marie by the author himself, probably during one of his visits.[1]

The time at Gournay is likely to have passed quietly. *Vous me reprenez que je suis d'ordinaire trop taciturne*, says Marie, in the *Promenoir de Monsieur de Montaigne*.[2] This, her first published work, is a tale which she told him one day at Gournay, *sur le propos des tragiques accidents de l'amour récités par Plutarque*. When the visitor had left, she sat down to set it out in writing. Feeling some of the natural diffidence of the novice, she wrote for advice to Justus Lipsius. Had not the admiration for the Essays which she shared with him already saved her from ridicule? And since she had met Montaigne, he had exchanged letters with the scholar. He replied in his most fulsome vein : *Quid tu es qui ad me scribis ? Virgo ? sic facis fidem*. In return for this interest and admiration, she sent him, before the year was out, a copy of *un petit traité de l'alliance de mon père et moi*, but this Lipsius never received. Meantime, the *Promenoir* was finished on the 26th of November, and sent to Montaigne.

After the murders of Blois, the war made it increasingly hard to keep in touch with her celebrated friends, and thus opposed the ' progress of her soul '. It also forced her mother to borrow money, since many dues were left unpaid in those bad years. And when she died, in 1591, the family fortunes were in a poor way, property was sold, and the estate was divided. The third sister had just married the sieur de la Salle, a gentleman in the service of the Balagnys at Cambrai. The heroic Renée d'Amboise, wife of the marshal, took Madame de la Salle into her household. The independent Marie refused a similar offer. She assumed the responsibility of collecting the arrears of the family revenues, which she never succeeded in obtaining, while she had paid out the full share of her sisters and her two brothers.

In the meanwhile, Montaigne, too, had died (13th September 1592). He had kept up a correspondence with her, in spite of the difficulties of communication, and Marie at one time intended to publish these letters. On his death-bed he sent her a tender farewell by the hand of his brother, de la Brousse. Eight months later, she had not yet received it. She happened to write for the third time to Lipsius, from Cambrai, on 25th April 1593.

A month later she received a reply from Louvain : ·

---

[1] See Mario Schiff, *Mlle. de Gournay*, p. 6, and *Essais*, Edition Municipale, Vol. I, 153, 165.

[2] *Promenoir*, ed. 1594, p. 58.

Tuus pater iam est. Nuncio tibi, si nescis : renovo, si iam scis, periisse, quid dixi ? abiisse magnum illum virum : Montanum, inquam, nostrum ad alta et aethereos illos montes.[1]

She seems to have kept in mind the fact that her friendship with a man of Montaigne's age and health must in all likelihood be brought to an early termination. Yet she had hoped to see him again, and it must have been bitter to have been with the great man three short months or less, and to learn of her loss by what was, after all, a stranger's hand. ' *Elle fut si outrée ayant entendu la mort de Montaigne,*' says Raemond, ' *qu'elle fut presque réduite à en rendre l'ame.*' In the letter which she wrote to Lipsius from the château of Montaigne more than three years later, there is, in the words of M. Schiff, only the faint odour of long-dried tears.

Montaigne's wishes as to the posthumous publication of the Essays must remain, for the most part, conjecture. But it is clear that Marie had her part assigned her in this charge, and her claim is explicit in the privilege she obtained for her later folio edition (1635). Madame de Montaigne and Pierre de Brach sorted out the dead man's papers and arranged for a transcription of the copy of the Essays which had been left ready for the type-setter's hand.[2] This transcription [3] was sent to Paris, where Mademoiselle de Gournay supervised the printing of the folio volume which appeared in 1595.

The *Promenoir* had been published in the previous year, and, her task of editor acquitted, the *demoiselle* replied to an invitation from Madame de Montaigne to visit Guienne and to make the acquaintance of her ' father's ' relations.[4] It was in the company of the President d'Espagnet (see above, p. 41), that she travelled as far as Bordeaux. It is to him that she later addressed an interesting self-portrait in verse. D'Espagnet is even to-day an authority on natural magic for those who still dabble in such

---

[1] *J. Lipsii Epist. ad Belgas Cent.*, I, 15.

[2] See *Edition Municipale*, I, Introduction and App. I.

[3] It passed later into the famous library of Spanheim, if we may trust the statement of Moréri's dictionary.

[4] She was certainly encouraged into accepting by the fact that she wished to consult the original *copie de Bordeaux*. The remedying of some oversights, such as an omission of the author's *Au lecteur* and a couple of pages of one of the essays in the first book (which are actually corrected in a few copies of the 1595 edition by the insertion of pages), probably represent the results of this collation with the original (*Edition Municipale*, I, p. 462). They also make it clear that the *demoiselle* must accept full responsibility for a certain number of liberties which she took with the author's text (ib., p. 463).

matters, and it was, perhaps, he who started Mademoiselle de Gournay's interest in alchemy.[1]

She spent at least a year and a half in Gascony, and appears to have been on excellent terms with Montaigne's family and his friends. The respect of the family for her was obviously sincere, for later, when she was in financial straits, they apparently offered to help her : *et dix mille têtes en Gascogne le savent*. She wrote poems for Brach's *Tombeau d'Aimée*,[2] and for the *Tombeau du Sieur de Sponde*, a set of obituary verses collected by Florimond de Raemond. And, according to him, she had the intention of remaining in Guienne for the rest of her life.

From Montaigne she wrote two letters to Lipsius, which show the pains she took to secure for the public, not only of France but of other countries, the authentic text of the Essays. The second letter, accompanied by three copies, one for himself, one for the best publisher in Basle, the third for Strassburg, has already been mentioned. In the first she refers to the preface, written for the 1595 edition. She says that she repents of it and that she has cut it out of the copies she is sending to him. The volume sent to Lipsius contained, in fact, a short retractation in manuscript, similar to that which appeared from 1598 to 1617, but even more humble. I doubt, however, whether she ever really changed her mind. At any rate, she later repented of her repentance, for in 1617 the greater part of the original version is to be found, and in 1635 there are very few passages that were not there in 1595.

Marie must have left Montaigne at the beginning of 1597. In May, we find her in Belgium. She visited Antwerp and Brussels, where, as has been mentioned, she enjoyed something of an ovation, but, from this date onwards, we know far less of her life. She lived in Paris. Proud, poor, fiercely independent, she decided to live on her capital, write hard and attempt to merit a pension to support her old age. Unpractical and ingenuous, she seems pathetic and naïve in her constant begging

---

[1] D'Espagnet, whether because of, or in spite of, his researches, became a very rich man, according to his Bordelais compatriot, Jean d'Arrerac. The *demoiselle*, on the other hand, was later accused of having spent her patrimony in strange chemical experiments. This accusation she indignantly denies in her *Apologie à un Prélat* (*Avis*, p. 607). It may be noted that one of D'Espagnet's books contains a recipe for the preparation of talcum powder as a cosmetic in place of the harmful *blanc d'Espagne* then in use.

[2] See R. Dezeimeris, *Les Poèmes de Pierre de Brach*. Aimée (Anne Perrot) was de Brach's wife.

of favours from her patrons.[1]   She lost money by over-confidence in the goodness of others.   She lost a little, too—five hundred crowns, she carefully calculates—*par vanité de jeunesse*.   There were also those long-cherished experiments in alchemy.

The *demoiselle* kept producing a series of small treatises generally connected with some topical event.   Thus, in 1601, we have her *De l'éducation des Enfants de France (au temps de la première grossesse de la Reine)* : in 1608 her *Abrégé d'instruction pour le prince souverain.*   Two years later, there is the *Adieu de l'âme du roi de France et de Navarre à la Reine avec la défense des Pères Jésuites.*[2]   Marie had good reason to regret the king's death, for she had been recommended to his good graces and had been commanded to appear at Court, and it was his death which was the occasion of that first-class blunder, the *Défense des Pères Jésuites.*   For a woman—somewhat thin-skinned, in any case—to enter the lists on the most controversial subject of the moment, was a fearful imprudence.   She was roughly handled by the pamphleteers, and it was thus perhaps that the tradition of baiting her began.   Till the end of her life we find a double chorus of fantastic stories about the tricks played on her, and her eccentricities, and, on the other hand, the most hyperbolical praises of her learning.

It is possible to reconstruct from the *demoiselle's* dedications and from the people mentioned in her writings the circles in which she moved.   She had a pension from the king, but she seems to have outlived most of her protectors, or outlived their days of power, for she only died in 1645.   Tallemant, however, shows how the indefatigable Boisrobert procured her the graces of Richelieu.   In her rooms in the Rue de l'Arbre Sec, and later opposite the Oratorians in the Rue St. Honoré, she still held meetings of literary men, among them Marolles, who lived in the same house, the brothers Ogier, the brothers Habert, Colletet, Malleville, and La Mothe le Vayer, to whom she left her books

---

[1] Characteristically, she stuck to her coach for many years, for, as she says, it was due to her condition, and the streets of Paris were impossible for a woman of quality.   As characteristically, once she had given it up, she would not accept from Richelieu a special supplementary pension for its revival.

[2] This list should continue with the *Défense de la Poesie*, 1618 (and 1623).   *Versions de quelques pièces de Virgile*, 1619, *Echantillon de Virgile*, 1620.   *L'Egalité des Hommes et des Femmes*, 1622.   In 1624, appeared the incredible rearrangement of Ronsard's *Harangue de François de Guise* ; finally, in 1626, her collected works, *L'ombre de Mlle de Gournay.*   This was twice reprinted with a few additions under the title of *Avis et Présents* 1634 and 1641).   See M. Schiff, op. cit., App. A.

(all but a Ronsard, which went to L'Estoile, the son of the diarist). All these men, except the brothers Ogier, were among the early members of the Academy, and according to Marolles, it was in her house that the meetings which later blossomed out into this body first took place. This is just possible, but it is clear from Pelisson that it was at Conrart's house that the first and unofficial Academy had its beginning.[1]

Yet, though she knew a variety of celebrated people, whose letters she carefully preserved, Mademoiselle de Gournay was essentially an independent. Her ideas about style, though often misrepresented, were hardly those of the Academy, or, at least, of its more prominent members. Once it was set up, she seems to have welcomed an institution which could ' fix ' the language, but she was bitterly opposed to the way it developed its programme. L'écorcheuse Académie is what, according to Chapelain, she called it, and we shall see that her imaginary petitions in favour of le vieux langage français, as represented in St. Evremond's comedy and the Requête des Dictionnaires of Ménage, have a foundation in fact.

Chapelain himself evidently has a prejudice against her. He even accuses her of reprinting the Essays purely for her own profit, and attempting to strike too shrewd a bargain with the printer, Baudoin.[2] It seems, however, from a letter of Roland Desmarets (1594–1653), brother of the famous Jean Desmarets de St. Sorlin, that Chapelain was closely connected with a projected edition by the Elzevirs.[3] He is not, therefore, an entirely disinterested person, and although I would not wholly discount his accusation in this instance, her extraordinary generosity and goodness of heart are vouched for not only by such writers as Sorel and Costar,[4] whom her eccentricities amuse, but by her whole life.

---

[1] Histoire de L'Académie (ed. Livet, 1858), p. 56. They met primarily to hear the poems which Godeau, the cousin of Conrart, brought with him from Dreux. Conrart was, at one time, the next-door neighbour of the demoiselle, Rue de l'Arbre Sec, hence perhaps this confusion.

[2] Lettres (ed. Tamizey de Larroque), Vol. I, 93.

[3] R. Maresii Epistolarum, Lib II, (1655), I, 22, ad Joh. Capellano. It would be interesting to know the date of this letter, which, probably, however, is after 1640, as Chapelain could hardly fail to have discussed this matter in his correspondence, which we possess up to that year. It is very probable, nevertheless, that before this time he thought himself a better guardian of Montaigne's fame than the fille d'alliance (see below, p. 287). A letter of Conrart's (R. Kerviler : V. Conrart, p. 269) written in March 1645, recommends to the Elzevirs the publication of the Essais as a thoroughly safe venture.

[4] Costar writes : ' Je sais des actions d'elle que j'estime presque autant que tous ses ouvrages, et qui auraient eu beaucoup d'admirateurs, si elle avait eu plus de fortune et plus de rang dans le monde ' (Entretiens, p. 487).

With regard to Marie's character in a more general aspect, it is perhaps Roland Desmarets who seems best to hit the mark, when he writes : ' Others have been surprised at her learning. It was not that which I so much admired, but rather—for she was self-taught and, as I believe, had learnt late in life—it was that judgment which is particularly conspicuous in her writings '. It was true enough that she learnt her Latin, and whatever else she learnt, without a master. This, and the fact that she was that extreme rarity in her time, a professional writer, not a princess or a great lady dabbling in literature but an ordinary woman of good family, explains her cast of mind and many of her views. It explains her optimistic faith in education and, in part, the fervour of her enthusiasm for Montaigne. It is education which makes men good or bad, education which distinguishes the nobles from the people, education which makes the women of England and France superior to those of other countries. It is because she was self-taught, too, and a woman *unius libri*, that she so rapidly reached her full intellectual development. She is complete from the moment when she wrote the *Promenoir* and the Preface of 1595. In these two works we find indicated the themes which she was later to expand, in some cases even their very titles. It is this immobility, too, which explains the arrogant dogmatism of this curious disciple of Montaigne. It is not only true that she never repented of her Preface to the Essays, but we can be sure that, if any passage of other writings has been suppressed, the matter and often the very words will be found reproduced elsewhere.

Just because of her sensitiveness to ridicule, the earliest writings are the most illuminating. Take the earliest version of the *Promenoir* [1]—the story of the heroine's misfortunes need not detain us. It supplements the ' *Grief des Dames* ' and the ' *Egalité des Hommes et des Femmes* ' (1622), and as to Marie's feminism, it shows her exaggerated intellectualism applied to love. Nevertheless, the digressions of the *Promenoir* contain much good sense, and just the conception of love which a pre-destined old maid of considerable ability would inevitably develop as a shield to her self-respect. Her fundamental idea is that the reasonable life is the only way in which one can live consistently. It is as necessary, nay even more necessary, for women than for men. Order, moderation and consistency, she writes in Montaigne's words, are the only perfections to which

---

[1] This little book had some success. It was published in 1594, 1595, 1599, at Paris, and in 1607 at Rouen. There was also what was probably a pirated edition in 1598 (Chambéry : Molicier).

the vulgar cannot attain. ' *Nous appelons ordre en cet endroit une légitime, universelle, et correspondante disposition de nos jugements et de nos actions.*'

We find, of course, the spiritualized notion of love, usual in the then popular *Amours Tragiques*. But Marie transforms the idea of a union of minds by her conception of consistency. All true virtue must be conscious virtue, whereas men have decided that women's one virtue is *ignorer et souffrir*. If women were to read philosophy, they would know that continence is no commandment of reason but merely of the law. Yet they would still be continent because they would realize the importance of possessing their own souls. Mere prudence, failing any higher motive, would save them from falling victims to ' the pestilent disaster of depending on others '. Yet marriage is not scorned by Mademoiselle de Gournay. Only she would have us remember that an educated woman of any rank is more than a match for the most nobly born of men, and that the most important of all considerations is resemblance of character between those who wish to marry.[1]

Marie next turns upon her possible critics. What she puts forward is uncustomary, but great minds always seem eccentric simply because they follow reason instead of custom : *faire ce qu'on loue est la probité de ceux qui ne peuvent faire ce qu'il faut.* Why ! the *reductio ad absurdum* of the rôle which is given to women is the fact that, if Socrates had been a woman, he would have been considered the most scandalous in all Athens. It is not the least of Marie's original traits to have applied the familiar distinction of custom and reason (backed by Montaigne's ideal of consistency) to the subject of love and marriage.

Of course, one must expect gossip if one is going to be so uncompromising as she. Her ill-suppressed indignation at such gossip finds expression in a long digression on slander. The first Preface to the Essays contains a similar protest, and no less than three of her later *opuscules* are devoted to the same subject.[2] The earlier diatribes, in the *Promenoir* and the Preface, are incomprehensible, unless Marie had already been made to suffer. Unfortunately, hers was the sort of character which, by

---

[1] See also first edition of *Promenoir* (1594), p. 41*b*, suppressed later. ' Le vulgaire dit qu'une femme pour être chaste ne doit pas être si fine : vraiment c'est faire un peu trop peu d'honneur à la chasteté que de croire qu'elle ne puisse être trouvée belle que des aveugles. Au contraire il faut la subtiliser tant qu'on peut, afin que si chacun est assez méchant pour la vouloir tromper personne ne soit assez fin pour le pouvoir.'

[2] *De le médisance qui est la principale cause des duels* ; *De la moquerie* ; and *Des Broquards*.

opposition, becomes only more assured of its own qualities and opinions. She became embittered towards the end of her life, and Sorel records her terrible fits of rage against *la cabale*, the disciples of Malherbe, like Yvrande and Racan, who played poetical jokes on her, as well as disagreeing with her practical theories. It is only, however, when Marie loses her temper that she is readable ; it is only then that she writes good prose, though she is always capable of coining admirable phrases in the manner of her *père d'alliance* (or of Lipsius). She has an undeniable satirical vein. An excellent example of this is the ' *Grief des Dames* ', which is a supplement to Montaigne's *De l'Art de Conférer* (III, 8). The ' grievance ' is that men refuse to condescend to serious discussion with women. If they find themselves getting beaten, they have a whole series of tricks for turning the argument into mere banter.

The ' *Egalité des Hommes et des Femmes* ' is a more important contribution to early feminist literature. Marie's real originality lies in the fact that she does not try to demonstrate her contention by reasons, which, as she says, are always debatable, nor by examples, but by authority, and by the authority not only of the philosophers but of the Fathers of the Church and the Scriptures themselves. She begins with Socrates and Plato. In the Republic, women have the same functions and rights as men. Plutarch insists that the virtue of men and women is the same ; so, too, does Seneca. Even those who believe in a general inferiority admit exceptions. But any law which is not universally true does not belong to the necessary order of things. In this way various affirmations of Aristotle and Montaigne, *le tiers chef du triumvirat de la sagesse Humaine et Morale*, are cleverly turned to account. Erasmus and Castiglione are quoted. The Salic Law was merely made for military reasons, ' *les deux sexes étant faits non simplement, ni pour constituer une différence d'espèce, mais pour la seule propagation* '.

Odd as it may seem, Mademoiselle de Gournay shows some penetration in attempting to prove equality by theological authority.[1] It is a ' gageure ', of course, and she does not succeed in getting round the second chapter of Genesis, in spite of some sophistry. She dwells on such points as that all the ' Gentiles ' accepted the priesthood of women, that even among Christians they are allowed, under certain circumstances, to

---

[1] At the beginning of F. Loryots' *Fleurs des Secrets Moraux* (1614) the reader may find a similar attempt made by the Reine Margot (reprinted at the end of a recent reprint of Marguerite's *Mémoires* (*Collection des Chefs D'Œuvres Méconnus*).

administer Baptism. Yet she seems to have realized where the crux of the matter lay. Wherever one finds a deep-rooted prejudice against women, it is always justified on theological or religious grounds, a prejudice enormously strengthened, as Lecky says, by the store which was set by the Medieval Church on the celibacy of the priesthood. It was expedient, therefore, to insist on the inherent wickedness and inferiority of woman—woman, that ' desirable calamity '.[1] It is interesting to see the Abbé Bremond making excuses to-day for some of the heroes of his *Humanisme Dévot*, the Père Binet, for example, whose strictures on the weaker sex shock his urbanity.

With the great period of witch persecution from the end of the fifteenth century, a new association comes into play to counteract the Petrarchan and Platonic influences of the Italian Renaissance. We have seen signs of it in Raemond and Lancre. I could give an instance of it in a far more unexpected place. One of the Chevalier de Méré's letters is full of apparently rather stupid jokes about fairies. They are not silly, though in rather doubtful taste, if one sees that they depend on a mental hyphen—women-witches in a very literal and concrete sense. In the circle of the Hôtel de Rambouillet where women are idolized, the witch becomes a fairy, but the joke is incomprehensible if one does not see the theme on which it is a variation.

In speaking of the life of the salons, a phenomenon is mentioned which was more important historically than the purely rational feminism of Mademoiselle de Gournay, though the latter certainly goes deeper and helps us to understand what an original person this old maid was ; what ridicule inevitably

---

[1] Another point in the history of feminism to which anthropologists are now drawing attention, is the notion of menstruation as something unclean (see Fox, *Selene and Sex*, 1927). In the ' *Diverses leçons* ' of Louis Guyon de la Nauche (p. 554, et seq., ed. 1610), the author, a doctor, protests indignantly against the opinion of Aristotle and Albertus Magnus that menstrual blood was a deadly poison, ' Quelqu'un me pourrait dire que l'homme est bien net et non pas la femme. Je réponds qu'autant qu'est l'un que l'autre et qu'il n'y a aucune différence entr'eux sinon que du tempérament et que les parties que les hommes ont extérieurement, les femmes ont intérieurement '. Guyon, who nowhere else appears anything of a feminist, seems conscious of some of the significance of the subject. He insists on the relations of Jesus with women—His birth, His presence at Cana, His anointing by Mary Magdalene, and His healing the woman with an issue, His burial by women and His appearance to Mary in the Garden after His resurrection. See also J.-J. Bouchard, *Confessions* (ed. Gallimard), p. 70.

awaited her and provoked her passionate outbursts against *les médisants* ; what optimism and faith she had in the possibilities of education.

The Preface to the Essays [1] is meant to be a complete defence of Montaigne. Marie's enthusiasm can bear no restriction whatever. Yet her exhaustive treatment of other people's criticisms lends this Preface an additional interest. She begins with a long explanation of what she calls the cold reception of the book. We have seen that this opinion is difficult to accept, but Marie's remarks are well founded in some degree. For, she continues, the general public have always accepted what they admire on the authority of those whose greatness is already recognized ; their own unaided judgement is always the *contrepoil de la saine opinion*. Hence, the importance of Lipsius's letter. For the same reason, she would have liked to have published the letters which the Cardinal d'Ossat [2] wrote to Montaigne about his book, but Madame de Montaigne had searched for them in vain among her husband's papers.

The Essays have always served Marie as a test of the intelligence of others. She has asked people what they thought of the book, wishing to know what she should think of them. Alas ! judgement is, she says, *la chose de plus diverse mesure parmi les hommes, et leur perfection.* Virtue itself is founded on judgement ' *le seul jugement nous met en droite possession de Dieu* : *cela s'appelle l'ignorer et l'adorer en la foi* '.[3]

What are the criticisms levelled at the Essays ? First come questions of vocabulary. There are those who have disliked Montaigne's neologisms. Yet the novelty of his subject-matter, and the fact that no words exist in French for many of the author's notions, is sufficient excuse for him. On the other hand, she is confident that the Essays, as a book for all time, will help to fix the changeableness of the French language. In 1635, the accusation of too many Latinisms is associated with that of making new words. She repeats that Montaigne has only taken what was necessary, and, after all, nearly every single word of

---

[1] I have spoken of its three published forms and their relation to each other. It existed in some shape or another (see letter to Lipsius 1593) before Montaigne's death.

[2] It should be remembered that it was to D'Ossat that Montaigne was writing from Acque della Villa in 1581, when he fell into a *pensement si pénible de M. de La Boétie.*

[3] cf. Charron : *Trois Vérités,* I. 5.—' La vraie connaissance de Dieu est une parfaite ignorance de lui ; s'approcher de Dieu est le connaître lumière inaccessible et d'icelle être absorbé ', &c.

the language was originally Latin. Similarly, necessity excuses his Gasconisms.

Secondly, Montaigne has been accused of being too outspoken, if not of being obscene, in anatomizing love. His own reasons are the best reply ; the analysis of all human actions and passions is essentially his originality as a writer and the very purpose of his book. Self-knowledge is the necessary precondition of virtue ; nay, more—' *Toute vertu désire l'épreuve, comme tenant son essence même du contraste* ', and St. Paul himself is invoked as testifying to this conception of virtue, in which we recognize the influence of the earlier phase of Montaigne's thought and the echo of her own *Promenoir*.

Thirdly, there is alleged obscurity. This she refuses to admit, but in her letter to Lipsius in 1593, she says of the 1588 edition that she wishes it clearer in many places and that other things, capable of misinterpretation, had not been so abruptly said.[1] She wishes he had been kinder to those, like herself, who have goodwill but only moderate intelligence. The book is not one for novices ; it is *l'Alcoran des maîtres*, one of the first good books to take up, as it is the last to lay down.

In 1617, she adds a passage in reply to those who have said that Montaigne cannot treat his subjects at length. Plutarch, she says, often breaks off in the same way, and, indeed, many of the Essays are developed at great length. Besides—' *C'est le poids des conceptions qui fait valoir un Ouvrage* ', whether those conceptions are developed or not, and, indeed, a certain diversity is only another proof of the universality of Montaigne's mind.

The 1617 edition adds, too, a couple of pages on Baudius, who had dared, as we have seen, to accuse Montaigne of vanity and of an affectation of ignorance and lack of memory. What angers the *demoiselle* most is his insinuation that the Essays are not quite sound on religion. The first preface already dealt with this point, to which she really adds little, but the tables are turned on Baudius, a dubious Protestant, by means of a rather obvious *tu quoque*. She wishes us to take her word for it that, if the Essays themselves do not clear Montaigne from the imputation of impiety, she, who knew him better than any one, will guarantee his intentions. Yet even she admits that Mon-

---

[1] *Bulletin de Bibliophile* (loc. cit.) or Bonnefon : *Les Amis de Montaigne*, II, 339. In that letter we find, too, the first version of the ecstatic praise of the Essays which follows here in the Preface. ' Ce livre n'est pas l'entretien des apprentis : il s'appelle la leçon des maîtres. C'est le bréviaire des demi-dieux, le contre-poison de l'erreur, le hors-de-page des âmes, la résurrection de la vérité, l'ellébore du sens humain et l'esprit de la raison. . . .'

taigne may be more or less dangerous reading. His is a book for the wise. And who are the wise? Marie's answer is an attempt to combine one of her leading ideas, the identity of knowledge and virtue (hence the moral excellence of the philosophers) with Montaigne's notion of the two kinds of good believers, the ignorant and the really wise, the peasants and the philosophers. She makes the outrageous statement that ' no one would have found fault with the new religions if the great Montaigne had approved them ',[1] but, just because he was one of the really great, he provided a proof of his own proposition. The touchstone of true religion for her, as for her ' father ', is

la Sainte loi de nos Pères, leur tradition et leur autorité. Qui pourrait aussi supporter ces nouveaux Titans du siècle, ces écheleurs qui pensent arriver à connaître Dieu par leurs moyens et circonscrire lui, ses œuvres et leurs créances au limites de leurs moyens et de leur raison : ne voulans rien recevoir pour vrai, s'il ne leur semble vraisemblable ? Où toutes choses sont plus immenses et plus incroyables, là sont Dieu et ses faits plus entièrement : Trismégiste a côte appelant la Déité cercle dont le centre est partout et la circonférence nulle part.

This is one of the very few occasions on which the *demoiselle* speaks of religion. It shows a fideism with which we are now familiar, employed, as so often, against the Protestants, but it probably represents Marie's general attitude, modelled on that of her ' father '. The reader will have already noted that formula ' *L'ignorer et l'adorer en la foi* ' which we will meet again in Charron. Until we come to speak of him, we may also reserve comment on the familiar pseudo-geometrical description of God. With two exceptions, Marie never writes on any subject connected with religion. She is evidently pious, an admirer of Saint François de Sales, whom she often quotes and with whom she had corresponded, but it is, in fact, just because she accepts the same attitude as Montaigne that she feels herself completely free to develop her humanistic rationalism on ethical and political matters and to accept its results without a constant preoccupation with the question of how it all squares with the doctrines of the Church.

To return to the Preface, the next point dealt with is Montaigne's *peinture de lui-même*. It is particularly important since it makes it clear what originally so fascinated Mademoiselle de Gournay in the Essays. Montaigne was for her a practical guide

---

[1] Laval, who comments on the Preface to the Essays as well as on the Essays themselves, says very properly ' Que se peut-il dire de plus impie, inepte et impertinent ? ' Two other comments of his may be found along with this in the *Bulletin du Bibliophile*, 1878 (p. 2270 et seq.).

to life. His moral teaching sticks to the concrete, and he comes back constantly to his own experience, about which he is perfectly frank. She defends his most trivial confidences; only convention is against them and convention is an unreasonable master.

La vie même n'est qu'une contexture de pointilles. Il a vraiment raison de montrer comme il se gouvernait en l'amour, au devis, à la table, voire à la garde-robe : puisque tant d'hommes se sont perdus pour ne savoir se comporter à la table, au devis, en l'amour et en la garde-robe encore.

Reader, she says, you take a singular pleasure in learning about a great general or a great statesman. One must first be an *honnête homme* before one can be such as they, and that is what the Essays will teach you. There is some one who rails against Montaigne particularly for confessing openly his faults and errors, but surely dissimulation is the mother of all crime. It is a necessary act of courage to accuse oneself in public, and, as Montaigne says, one must see one's vice in order to confess it. *Après la Justice et la Confession de l'Eglise, chacun, au reste, se doit constituer Juge sur soi-même.*

Finally, there remains the question of Montaigne's borrowings. These are merely embellishments ; the substance is his own. In the later editions, Marie finds it sufficient to contrast the profound originality of Montaigne, *scrutateur universel de l'homme intérieur, et de plus, correcteur et fléau continuelle des erreurs communes*, with the writings of a Charron, *perpétuel copiste de celuici, réservé les licences où il s'emporte parfois.*[1]

In spite of some *boutades*, the Preface as a whole, is full of good sense, and provides a defence of Montaigne's self-portrait, the real centre of his book. Marie, however, makes the Essays too much the work of a moralist, too directly didactic in purpose. It is not that she does not realize to some extent the part which the Essays played in the organization of their author's life, for, as we shall see, the recognition and communication of personality is precisely what makes her set such store by friendship.

---

[1] Already, in 1595, there is a reference, naming no names, to those who steal wholesale from the Essays. We have seen some of them at work. There is only one other reference to Charron in Mademoiselle de Gournay's writings. Speaking of the new school, who polish their style instead of leaving it with the imperfect gracefulness of spontaneity, she says : ' *Passons, par comparaison, du langage à la substance : que ne préfèrent ces Messieurs aux Essais, la Sagesse de Charron, d'autant que cet ouvrier est dans une exacte méthode en la matière qu'il traite, cet autre à l'essor ?* ' (*Avis*, p. 286).

That is indeed one of the lines of defence of the *peinture du moi* in this Preface. But she had too much of a purely abstract rationalism in her to grasp fully the aesthetic tendencies of Montaigne's treatment of problems of conduct.

Now that the autograph copy of the Municipal Library of Bordeaux has been rightly recognized as the basis of the best text, Marie has been looked at somewhat askance as an editor. Yet given the code of the time, it must be agreed that she was a scrupulous and faithful one, at any rate so far as her first edition goes. A far graver charge is often brought against her last folio edition of the Essays, dedicated to Richelieu in 1635, where she has attempted to modernize some of the archaic expressions of Montaigne. How trifling her changes are may be judged from the fact that an essay of average length, chosen at random (III, 2) gives us the three corrections ; *dise* for *die*, *grande recepte* for *grand recette* and *plus libre* for *plus delivre*. But to do the *demoiselle* justice, it should be remembered that she has confessed the liberty she has taken with the Preface, and that from her own account of the matter she was forced to take action by the ' mercenary stationers '. She had intended a new edition for six or seven years, and without the help of *les Grands de France* she would never have got the printers to take the necessary risk, partly because the proofs needed such careful correction. *Leur même prière expresse m'a contrainte, non pas de changer, oui bien de rendre seulement moins fréquents en ce livre, trois ou quatres mots à travers champ, et de ranger la syntaxe d'autant de clauses.* She even confesses the suppression of the passage in her own praise, which people had pretended was the sole reason for her cult of Montaigne.

It is only fair that her defence should be stated, but it ought perhaps to be accepted with some reserve. Against her complaints of the niggardliness of the printers, Chapelain's accusation of her meanness towards the printer Baudoin must be remembered.[1] Nor can it be forgotten that thirteen years before she had conceived the project of reviving the waning reputation of Ronsard by publishing a *corrected* edition of some of his poems. She confided her project to Guillaume Colletet, who indignantly refused to have anything to do with the venture. Marie, nevertheless, published an arrangement of the ' *Harangue de François de Guise* ' (ed. Laumonier, V, p. 21), under the title of ' *Remerciment au Roi* '. She may, therefore, in the case of the Essays, be putting on the publishers' shoulders the responsibility for a proceeding which was likely to have a mixed

[1] See above, p. 54.

reception. It was a compromise, at any rate, unlikely to meet with the approval either of those who had a more scrupulous regard for the exact letter of an author's text or of those who, like Plassac-Méré and Mitton, proposed a complete re-writing of Montaigne.[1]

On the other hand, she had previously opposed any and every change in the manner of presentation. She opposed the ' Life ' which was first added in a Paris edition of 1608 (Nivelle). She was averse to adding marginal references to Montaigne's quotations. She opposed also the Index of Matters and the short analysis of Chapter-headings which appeared in the folio of 1635. The refusal to accept all these features makes it, in my eyes, sufficiently likely that she is speaking the truth in saying that she had retouched the text only under compulsion.

What can we learn from Mademoiselle de Gournay as to the popularity of the Essays ? Did she herself have any influence upon it ? It would be absurd to suggest that, because to many contemporaries she was a figure of fun, she actually threw discredit on Montaigne, though her stand for the *vieux langage français*, as it was popularly represented, must have drawn attention to the archaisms of the Essays. Racan, one of her chief persecutors, was evidently a reader of the Essays.[2] As for her friends, except La Mothe le Vayer and Marolles,[3] we have no means of judging as to whether they shared her cult.

Of the success of the Essays, she writes in 1601 :

Ce que ses écrits ont gagné de réputation publique jusqu'à ce jour, ce n'est pas par la meilleure de leurs parties, qui reste plus qu'à demi couverte, c'est par la moindre : comme exemples, histoires, et riches allégations : ces choses seulement les font rechercher du commun.[4]

In spite of a certain exaggeration, I think that our first two chapters have sufficiently justified the truth of these remarks. As far as quotations go, Montaigne himself confessed as much, and the way in which Montaigne was treated by the compilers of *Leçons* has already been seen. Yet the statement evidently underrates the intelligence of the ' common reader ', nor can we attach much importance to the irritation with critics of the Essays which appears in her later writings. Towards 1620, Marie has some astonishingly bitter reflections to make on those

---

[1] See below, pp. 302—305.   [2] Below, p. 110, 111.
[3] Below, pp. 260–276 ; pp. 277, 8 respectively.
[4] *Avis* (ed. 1641), p. 17.

who criticize Montaigne's style.[1]   Her outburst is probably only
a rather unjust reference to Pasquier, the second volume of
whose letters had appeared in 1618.   It is obvious, therefore,
that, since nothing short of her own enthusiasm would satisfy
Mademoiselle de Gournay, she is a thoroughly untrustworthy
guide in estimating the popularity or unpopularity of Montaigne.
It should be noticed that the criticisms referred to, seem to
deal with vocabulary and style, or else on the trivialities of the
peinture du moi.   She has nowhere added to her defence of
Montaigne's religion after the Preface of 1617, nor mentioned
those aspersions cast on the Essays, which find their expression
in the apologetics of Silhon (1626 and 1634) and Boucher (1628).[2]

[1] 'Dieu sait si ce mauvais ouvrage des Essais, ce sot discoureur et
parleur, s'il vous plait, est biffé de leur main !   Non seulement sur l'usage
de la Langue entière dont ils ne reçoivent que les deux tiers (chacun le
sait) mais encore sur trois Gasconnismes ou solécismes, bien que visiblement volontaires, sur autant d'autres mots hardis ou vieux, sur quelque
petit Latinisme ou quelque terme fort commun au Palais tel que peut
être un *ledit*, un *item*, un *icelui*' (*Avis*, p. 740).

[2] See below, p. 176, 7 (Boucher) ;   p. 179 ff. (Silhon).

CHAPTER V

MARIE DE GOURNAY II : IN MONTAIGNE'S FOOTSTEPS

' Il a tant jugé qu'il ne reste plus que juger après.'
MARIE DE GOURNAY.

AN examination of a few of Marie's later works, most of
them the pendants to one or other of the Essays, will
enable us to complete our portrait. Yet, despite her
modest intentions, Montaigne's outlook is often sensibly modified
in these supplementary Essays. Her programme is already
drawn up in 1595 and it may be completed from two later passages,
where she states a kind of *profession de foi*.

> Je tiens le parti de ceux qui jugent que le vice procède de sottise
> et conséquamment plus on approche de la haute suffisance, plus on
> s'éloigne de lui.

It is this Socratic maxim which Marie sets out to justify and
explain (anew) in her essay ' *Que l'Intégrité suit la vraie suffisance* ',
for the gist of it had already appeared in the Preface of 1595.
  She does not probably accept a rigorous dependence of virtue
on knowledge, but wishes to protest against the popular notion
that the cleverest people in the world are the most wicked, and
to show, not only that the really great man is always a philosopher, but that to be an *honnête homme* one must necessarily
be a man of letters—letters being for her, essentially, moral
philosophy. Idleness is repugnant to nature. When an Epaminondas or a Socrates have fulfilled their duty in life, they
cannot fill in their leisure moments profitably except with letters
and philosophy. Without letters, it is possible perhaps to
discharge the ordinary duties which are imposed by our profession and our walk in life, but to be the complete man is a
lesson to be learnt from the philosophers. And here is its analysis :

> la connaissance de nous mêmes, celle du bien et du mal et surtout
> en face du tyrannique aveuglement de la coutume,—cela s'appelle
> un entièr désabusement du monde : l'art de sentir la juste étendue

de notre clairvoyance, limiter la curiosité, retrancher les appétits vicieux, faire bouquer nos forces et nos volontés sous le joug des Lois et les droits d'Autrui, savoir en quelle occasion la vengeance est licite, jusqu'où la gratitude suffit, jusqu'à quel prix l'approbation publique est achetable ; juger des accidents humains parmi tant de faux lustres, et de fausses mesures de bien et de mal qu'elles représentent . . . savoir quand il est temps de croire et de douter, aimer, haïr, s'obliger et désobliger à propos, connaître sans passion ce qu'autrui nous doit et nous à lui ; et tant d'autres parties, en somme, requise à conduire la vie selon la condition juste et certaine.[1]

This is at once a declaration of Marie's philosophy and of Montaigne's, and, as originally stated in 1595, a literary programme which she afterwards carried out, at least, in part.

The good man, or even the great man, however, is not self-sufficient. He longs to communicate himself to those who are like him and have their friendship. *Etre inconnu, c'est aucunement n'être pas, car être se réfère à agir : et n'est point, ce semble, d'agir parfait vers qui n'est pas capable de le goûter.*[2] This is comparable to the insistence of the Essays on the need for recognition of the self by others, but Marie's chief point is that such recognition, in the form of friendship, is impossible except between those who are alike, and alike virtuous, since otherwise there is no basis for mutual admiration. Friendship is a giving of oneself, but ' *il faut bien prêter au vulgaire sa vertu mais il ne la faut donner qu'à la vertu même* '. Hence the subject of two more little Essays : ' *Que par nécessité les grands esprits et les gens de bien cherchent leurs semblables* ', and ' *L'Antipathie des Ames Hautes et Basses* '. They are conceived as pendants to Montaigne's ' On Friendship '. The argument of the latter takes its point of departure in the familiar notion that the wise man judges and acts by reason, the ' vulgar ' by custom and habit ; further, that the essential quality and perfection of *pertinence*, that is moral fitness, lies in the judgement of oneself and others. But only the morally fit can recognize the fitness in others. Just as only reason can recognize reason, so, only the good man, that is the reasonable man, can recognize his peers. Hence the war on custom and its inexhaustible variety, whereas reason and the reasonable attitude is unique.

It would be a mistake, however, to imagine that the reasoning outlined is the only foundation of this alleged antipathy. The notion of temperament, the pseudo-scientific theory of

[1] *Avis*, p. 266. This passage, which I quote according to the later text, occurs originally in a section of the Preface of 1595.
[2] *Préface* (1595).

humours, is certainly here at work.   The physical composition
of great souls is the natural cause of their being unable to reply
with repartee to those that mock them.[1]   So, too, it is most
exceptional to find great powers of memory ' *entre les gens de
jugement relevé* '.   Memory and judgement depend on different
temperaments.   We see here how these ' simplist ' explanations
of character, generally accepted at this time, influence even minds
not much preoccupied with them.   The hard and fast physical
basis given to differences of character supplies the background
of her theory of ' like to like '.

' *La seule noblesse* ', says Marie, ' *est l'intellectuelle* ' ;   the
appropriate virtue of the nobility (using the word in its ordinary
sense) is courage ;   but ' *si la vaillance n'est noble et magnanime
en un gentilhomme, la noblesse est un zéro* '.   In France men make,
as a rule, no distinction between mere fearlessness and true
courage ;   ' *Ils imaginent que tout ce qui porte quelque témoignage
de pouvoir, le porte aussi de valoir* '.   Hence they think it no ill
to offend the weak and attack the feeble.   They are still so much
under the false impression that nobility is purely a matter of
race, that they think no action can dishonour them.

If true nobility is a personal quality, it can be acquired ;
this is the refrain of her *L'Education des Enfants de France* and
the *Abrégé de l'Institution du Prince*.   The first of these essays
is frankly topical.   Written just before the birth of the future
Louis XIII, a great part of it is concerned with choosing a suitable tutor for the child.   She would like the choice of tutors
to be made by the Bishop of Poitiers, La Rocheposay (the friend
of the Abbé de St. Cyran).[2]   Montaigne would have been the
ideal man, or the Cardinal d'Ossat, but one is dead and the other
is forced to remain in Italy.   The qualities of this Mentor are
more likely to make him generally disliked than admired :   he
must be a man of reason, uninfluenced by passion or custom—
destined later to assume that difficult rôle of unofficial councillor
and friend, sketched by Montaigne in the last chapter of the
Essays.

Marie begins her *Abrégé* with a declaration of infinite faith
in the possibilities of education, though she is hardly so optimistic
later on.   Education makes the difference, such as it is, between

[1] *Avis*, p. 28.

[2] Henri Louis Chasteigner de la Rocheposay (1577–1651), pupil of
Joseph Scaliger, whose lifelong patron was his father, French Ambassador
in Rome from 1575–81 (see below, p. 148).   Louis d'Abain de la Rocheposay,
who welcomed the author of the Essays in Rome (1581) was, according to
the *Journal de Voyage*, '*fort ami de longue main de M. de Montaigne*'.

men and women, nobles and people. It is all-important even in the case of religion. Useless sciences must be dispensed with ; those really required are : ' *la morale théorique, qui comprend la Politique, et la Politique, l'Histoire* '. Moreover, letters in general, she repeats, are the only things which can occupy all the spare time of the Prince and save him from debauchery, but whatever he learns must be by his own wish, and he must enjoy learning it. He will be taught no Latin, unless by the method by which Montaigne was taught ; he must study the lives of great men—and so on, until we have a fairly complete résumé of what the Essays have already said.

As to the Prince's conduct once grown up, all her advice has one refrain ; he must make himself loved. She admits the same kind of compromise as Montaigne between what is right and what is useful. There is no such alternative, however, between being loved and being hated as Machiavelli has stated, ' *d'autant qu'il n'est aucune grandeur qu'un Prince dût acheter au prix des peines, des inquiétudes et gênes de l'esprit qu'il faut supporter ni des méchancetés qu'il faut faire pour régner par la terreur* '.[1] A king should aim at being great as a man rather than as a king ; it is the kingdom which invests him with his office for the public good. He must be obeyed no doubt, but it is shameful to be obeyed only by constraint. It is his absolute power, as much as flattery, intrigue and evil communications, which makes it hard for a king to be what he should. ' *Je sais qu'un grand personnage de ce temps* (Montaigne, perhaps) *prêche que la vertu est facile d'accès et d'usage : et je crois qu'il dit vrai pour les gens privés* ' ; it is not so for a king.

' *Des Vertus Vicieuses* ', another essay, finishes, too, in a minor key. How shall we judge whether actions are good ? Reason, is, by its very nature, equivocal, and we cannot know the results of our actions. It is by intention they must be judged. The general form of right intention is a sense of duty. We are usually led astray by inclination or utilitarian motives, and even an apparently good action done for these reasons is of no moral value. We cannot even count to ourselves as virtues the qualities we possess by birth and character, much less those of which we may even be unconscious. This train of thought is familiar, but what is striking is the way in which the statement of the problem lays stress on duty, intention and merit—the key-words, respectively, of legalist, ' rigorist ' and religious ethics—all of which are almost entirely absent from the Essays. Montaigne himself

[1] *Avis*, p. 230.

passed through such a phase and beyond it : concentration on motives and motives alone is the lesson which the Essays had taught Mademoiselle de Gournay.

Yet Marie's good sense makes her include among the ' false virtues ' those which, made with the best of intentions, lead, in fact, to disaster. So that there is a class of actions, after all, which must be judged by their results and not by their motives (a contradiction only to be reconciled by a distinction of ' good for itself ' and ' good as a means '). Marie's analysis breaks off, disheartened as it were, with an echo of her master's words :

> Quiconque retrancherait de l'homme toutes les vertus qu'il pratique par force, par intérêt, ou par inadvertance . . . logerait le genre humain plus près des bêtes que je n'ose dire.[1]

This ' rigorist ' consideration of conduct, its pessimistic conclusion and the inconsistency it contains, are seen in their true light, when we remember that, towards the end of the seventeenth century, Bernard de Mandeville (by exploiting this inconsistency in his ' Fable of the Bees ', and showing how action immoral from the intentional or rigorist point of view produces good and makes the world go round) exerted a considerable influence on ethical theory by showing how untenable any *purely* rigorist position must be. Critical analyses of intention, such as this little chapter of Marie de Gournay, and all the seventeenth-century interest in the passions form part of a current of psychological realism which in their obscure way prepare the arrival of Mandeville's bombshell.[2]

' *Des Vertus Vicieuses* ' seems to me one of the best things Marie has written. It is well constructed and to the point ; the argument has not to be extracted, as is often the case, from a conglomeration of examples, proverbs, and petulant outbursts against the age. Perhaps its pessimistic tone is the chief reason for this, since in reading *Les Avis* one realizes that the constant tirades against the slanderers, the scoffers, the courtiers and the writers of the new school, are primarily the result of the disappointed hopes and expectations of a particularly optimistic temperament. Here, for once, she accepted life as she really found it. More often she relieved her disillusion in the series of bitter diatribes which culminate in ' *Si la vengeance est licite* ', an attempt to justify by argument her wish to get her own back on her enemies. She believes that all punishment is by nature

---

[1] *Avis*, p. 323.   [2] See Introduction, p. xxxvii et seq.

vengeance, which is therefore recognized as a good thing in certain cases. Where the law can give no redress—certain kinds of calumny and libel are what she has in mind—one should be allowed to exercise a right to avenge oneself. She finds some difficulty in excluding duels from this liberty which she wishes to see recognized.[1]

A last word must be said of two chapters written round Montaigne's *Du Repentir* and *De la Prière*. *Des Fausses Dévotions*, largely built up of quotations from St. François de Sales, protests against hypocrisy, conscious or unconscious, and against the confusion of religious observance with true piety. A more interesting development of her views is to be found in '*L'Avis à quelques gens d'Eglise*' (1626). Her theme here is more especially the abuse of confession and the over-indulgence of confessors. It thus belongs to the series of controversies which centred first round J. P. Camus's *Directeur Spirituel Désintéressé* (1632), later round *La Fréquente Communion* of Arnauld, and which culminated in the *Lettres Provinciales*. It is to the Essays that Marie refers the reader for a proper definition of repentance : '*Le repentir est une absolue et constante dédite de notre volonté qui comprend une horreur de la faute commise, et conséquamment de la réitérér, en telle sorte que ni le repentant ne commettrait le mal, si c'était à refaire, ni ne le veut commettre à l'avenir.*' The critical point is the consideration of vices which have become habits : they are rare, she remarks with her habitual optimism. Absolution should be given wherever the sinner has promised a *dédite de la volonté*, even if he has been unable to accomplish it, as long as he has made progress at all. In the case of all the vices that proceed from opinion, however, and not from natural appetites, complete repentance is always immediately possible. St. Francis himself told her that if any of his penitents relapsed more than two or three times into any sin of importance, he would have sent them to confess themselves elsewhere. Until reformation, Marie says, Mass should be denied.

In these two chapters which concern the relation of the theory of the good life to its practice, Marie again insists on the unity of the two. Most of the virtues, those of good-heartedness and innocence, as she calls them, cannot be considered as possessed if they are ever lost.[2] But besides the recurrence once again

---

[1] *Avis*, esp. pp. 123–25. This essay also contains some interesting justification of vengeance on utilitarian grounds. The expressions used in *L'Ombre* (the first edition of the *Avis*) are far stronger as to utilitarian basis of *all* laws (cf. p. 296).

[2] *Avis*, p. 114. Note the influence of Stoicism, possibly Lipsius.

of this rigid Virtue-equals-Knowledge formula, there is Marie's insistence on the ' inwardness ' of religion. It is to be noticed, therefore, that her hero among the great Churchmen is St. François de Sales, who constantly reappears in her pages.

Apart from the last two works, the reader may have been struck by the purely ' profane ' character of Marie's writings. The tragic sense of life, the reflection on the vanity of man, and above all the vanity of reason, are hardly ever to be found. Mademoiselle de Gournay's is a purely rationalistic humanism. It is apt, however, to be forgotten that the strict and the original sense of the term ' humane ', as in ' humane letters ', is ' humane ' as opposed to religious, profane as opposed to sacred. Humanism, then, in the strict sense, is very clearly bound up with fideism and complete divorce of faith and reason. I have carefully quoted most of Mademoiselle de Gournay's sayings about religion. The reader will have noticed the formula given in the Preface of 1595—' Ignorer Dieu et l'adorer dans la foi '. It is just this attitude, and the complete separation of the spheres of faith and reason which goes with it, that leaves her free to develop her rationalism, which is also humanist in the broader sense, that other sense which may be defined as the maximum development of all man's capabilities. This notion, in a certain form, we have seen to be the very centre of Marie's philosophy of life. If the good man does not cultivate letters, he leaves a whole side of his nature, and hours of his spare time, lying idle and unused.

And as to ' letters ' themselves, in the sense of literary criticism, what are Mademoiselle de Gournay's principles ?

Le parler est exactement une image de l'esprit de sorte qu'il est ferme et solide, ou lâche et mol ; il fait voir à quel de ces deux points l'esprit se chausse ; et l'esprit étant après une image des mœurs.[1]

This fundamental maxim should be kept in mind ; it shows us the articulation between her other ideas and her aesthetic. Just as she will hardly admit a distinction between knowledge and virtue, she insists here on the essential connexion between matter and form or expression ; and with more justification. The tendency of her contemporaries was notably towards a consideration of manner alone. Her influence might have been a happy one, had she not been a figure of fun and the uncompromising representative of the linguistic theories of the Pléiade. She represents those theories, however, with more good sense than she has been credited with. French must be enriched, no doubt, as Du Bellay recommends, by provignement, but it must also

[1] Avis, p. 447.

be fixed. One of her claims for Montaigne is that his book will help to ' fix ' the language. As for the dialects, arguing with good sense that a rhyme is for the ear and not for the eye, she accepts the pronunciation of Paris alone, where the people have more or less the same way of speaking as the court. This is exactly the position of her enemy, Malherbe, towards language in general.[1]

The two authorities on language are custom ' *contre lequel je guerroie partout ailleurs à feu et à sang* ' and the great writers of the language, such as Ronsard, Du Bellay, Du Bartas, Desportes, Du Vair, Du Perron, D'Ossat and Montaigne. What she opposes are the attempts of the new school to ' purge ' the language. They wish to kill something living. ' *Vieux mot est celui de la vieillesse duquel nous sommes averti par la cessation et le silence de l'usage, non par l'avis de nos voisins.*' [2] A language must evolve, she admits, but it would be particularly regrettable if the writers of the greatest century France has yet known should become unreadable. The mass of rules and exceptions, the affected prudery of the ' new school ' [3] is merely absurd. In *La Version des Poètes Anciens* she makes an admirably reasoned defence of the banished words.

The value of a piece of writing is like that of good wine *en son esprit et en sa vigueur*. Since expressiveness is one of the essential criteria, Marie permits herself to find that French is sometimes a little bald. She would like to see it enriched by more metaphors and metaphorical forms of speech. The new school, however, are on the opposite tack ; they are out to suppress expressive terms both old *and* new, all those strong phrases and short pithy words *qui fortifient à toute heure une clause en la reserrant, surtout en la Poésie.*[4] They involve themselves in contradictions, for, according to them, French is at once

---

[1] ' Quand on lui demandait son avis de quelque mot français, il renvoyait ordinairement aux crocheteurs du port et disait que c'était ses maîtres pour le langage.' *Vie de Malherbe*, by Racan (cf. *Essais*, I, 26, pp. 218 and 231. ' Peusse je ne me servir que de ceux (des mots) qui servent aux halles à Paris ! ')

[2] *Avis*, p. 432.

[3] Whenever Mademoiselle de Gournay speaks of the *cabale, les douillets les femmes, les pédagoguesses poupines*, she names no names. She admires Malherbe, though not his rules. Gombaud and Malleville were her friends. She naturally quotes not only Théophile and Régnier as those who are good poets, *in spite* of the rules, but also Des Yveteaux, Lingendes, Motin, Des Marets, nor can we say that St. Amand, Boisrobert or even Racan, her ' pests ', bother much about the Malherbian poetics. I think her real attack is on the *poètes de salon* such as Voiture and Godeau.

[4] *Avis*, p. 447.

too grave a tongue to admit of the use of diminutives, and too weak for the epical style. At the same time as they cut down the vocabulary, they fill up their measure with dross ' by the superstitious usage of a cloud of particles ',

au lieu qu'il le faudrait accourcir au possible : car l'excellence et la vigueur d'un dialecte consistent, entre autre choses, en la brièveté, tandis que le nôtre, français, est des plus babillards.

A rigid and religious avoidance of hiatus is, to her mind, yet another mistake. But listen finally to this admirable passage on style.

Pour conclure, il faut casser un noyau avec effort, il faut briser un os et mordre vertement une pomme, non pas les lécher ou morciller doucement, qui veut en extraire l'amande, la moelle et la bonne substance qu'ils recèlent. Ainsi faut-il mettre une Langue sous presse pour en tirer le suc et les délices : de facon que ceux, en usant d'autre sorte, parlent superficiellement et sèchement, alors qu'ils croient parler doucement. . . . Que d'autres y cherchent, s'ils veulent, le lait et le miel, nous y cherchons ce qui s'appelle l'esprit et la vie, la vie, dirai-je avec raison, puisque toute Langue qui manque en son débit de ce rayon divin, celeste, qu'on appèlle puissante dexterité, souple, agile, afilée, est morte.

Or this on obscurity :

' Je ne l'entends pas ' O Dieu ! si la mesure du prix d'un écrivain dépend de la facilité de l'intelligence, que deviendront Aristote et Platon . . . ?

Her real grievance with the followers of Malherbe is that their poetic is *purely* a matter of technique and grammar. In this they cannot even call the great names in criticism to their side. It is not the tendency but its exaggeration which she blames. Its representatives lay down the law with such dogmatism, maintaining, not only that all that does not accommodate itself to their rules is bad, but that all that does so is good. She appreciates much of their work but not their theories.

So far we may find Mademoiselle de Gournay's ideas far sounder than those of her opponents. If they had found more favour, French poetry of the seventeenth century might have more of the virtues of the English Metaphysicals or of Góngora —force and pith instead of a rather empty gracefulness, and real conceits (for that is what she really means by metaphors) instead of mere *pointes*.[1] Next to expressiveness she believes

[1] The Abbé Bremond has shown in the first volume of his *Histoire du Sentiment Religieux* that there are still some admirable things to be discovered among the immense mass of the religious poetry of this period,

in the absolute value of originality, and, by reason of her insistence on the indivisibility of form and matter, we find her stating in a way far beyond her time the essential uniqueness of anything which is supremely well said.[1] It is thus evident that the seventeenth-century notion of literary discipline could have little meaning for her. She could not see its advantages. It is here that she errs, not when she attacks the details of the *cabale's* programme, where, as we have seen, she certainly strikes home. Genius, according to her, cannot tolerate this slavery of rules. Loss of liberty means loss of power and inspiration. One cannot ' invent ' in fetters, she imagines. She goes further : a few defects, even a certain negligence, look well. In this fallacy, as in her most acute critical sayings, we recognize once more the influence of the master.

Mademoiselle de Gournay's ideas on writing, on poetry and on the language have perhaps little historical importance. She is, in the phrase of Lanson, *attardée et égarée !* Yet it is a mistake to judge matters so entirely from the point of view of posterity. There is no doubt she belonged by temperament, by education, by sympathy to the century that was past. Had she been taken more seriously, however, she might have had a salutary effect on her own. It should not be supposed, however, that Marie's well-founded protests against the exaggerations of the purists were not echoed by other writers. Yet it is not until 1638 and the scandalous pulling to pieces of the *Cid* that Marie's friend, La Mothe le Vayer, takes up cudgels in public against these tendencies on much the same lines as the *demoiselle.* It is not until 1650 that Scipion Dupleix seconds these criticisms with his *Liberté de la Langue Française.* Marie's *Défense de la Poésie* had, on the other hand, appeared as early as 1618 and was reprinted in 1623 and again republished with her other critical writings in first edition of her collected works in 1626. She perhaps cried ' wolf ' before the real wolf was there.

Apart from Charron, Mademoiselle de Gournay is the most authentic disciple of Montaigne whom we shall discover in the period under view. It has seemed unnecessary to draw the attention of the reader to her constant echoing of Montaigne's

poetry which has more in common with Crashaw than with Malherbe, Théophile, and their successors. I am thinking particularly of La Cépède and Martial de Brives. Mademoiselle de Gournay gives us the ' theory ', moreover, of a poetical school or manner which held the field for a few years at the turn of the century. See my article : *Then Malherbe Came* (*Criterion*, 1931).

[1] *Avis*, p. 83 : ' La parfaite excellence ne se peut loger qu' avec la particularité.'

doctrine. At every turn, as she confesses, she finds herself upon his track. The elements are almost invariably taken from the Essays ; the arrangement and the resulting attitude are often entirely her own. In some respects they are an epitome of the tendencies of the Renaissance in general. Montaigne, it has been said, ' wears his humanism with a difference '. He lacks the intellectual and the aristocratic prejudice of his age to an extraordinary extent. Both of them reappear strongly accentuated in his *fille d'alliance*. There is hardly a word against pedantry in her writings, except when she levels this charge against the followers of Malherbe. She had the exaggerated respect for learning and culture and the all too sanguine hopes of education that were more characteristic of the Renaissance than of Montaigne.

He was an individualist because he was a sceptic. His critique of custom and of authority drove him in upon himself at the same time as his critique of reason paradoxically saved his faith. The dogmatic temperament of his disciple accommodates itself to the formulas of the widespread fideism of the days of her youth, and allows her to keep Montaigne's respect for the individual, and the free exercise of the individual judgement, unfettered within its limited sphere. What she could not have was his preoccupation with introspection, though there are traces of what he had taught her in her insistence on the importance of consciousness and self-consciousness. Even under more favourable circumstances she could never have given us a portrait of herself. She made that pretension by the excellent title of the first edition of her collected works : *L'Ombre de Mademoiselle de Gournay—L'homme est l'ombre d'un songe, et son œuvre est son ombre*. She attempted in her *Peinture de Mœurs* to put it into practice. It is not successful. For one thing, like all she ever said of herself, it is a defence and, secondly, it is purely moral. To succeed in the *peinture du moi* it is necessary to add the subtle balance of scientific observation and that rather passive contemplation of life, by its nature aesthetic, which go to make up the physiognomy of Montaigne.

CHAPTER VI

PIERRE CHARRON—I

*Empêcher la liberté de l'esprit l'on ne le saurait ; le vouloir faire c'est
la plus grande tyrannie qui puisse être. Le Sage s'en gardera bien active-
ment et passivement, se maintiendra en sa liberté et ne troublera celle d'autrui.*

PIERRE CHARRON

IT was the second of July, 1586. The army of the League,
under the Duke de Mayenne, lay round the little town of
Castillon-sur-Dordogne, from behind whose flimsy walls the
Protestants were putting up a brave fight. The sound of the
besieging cannon must have been audible five miles up the valley
when Montaigne presented to Pierre Charron, the well-known
preacher from Bordeaux, a small octavo volume from the circular
shelves of his library : *Il Catechismo o vera institutione christiana
di M. Bernardino Ochino da Siena—Liber prohibitus.*[1]

Such is the first and the last occasion on which we catch a
glimpse of the two face to face. That the book which stands
witness to the friendship of these men, whose religion or irreligion
has been discussed ever since, should be the work of one of the
most advanced minds of the Reformation, seems at first sight
a most significant fact. Ochino's catechism, however, differs
but little from the similar writings of Luther or Calvin, apart
from its curiously Cartesian opening and its insistence on the
universality of moral law. The last point may be kept in
mind ; otherwise this gift can hardly be said to shed any light
on Montaigne or his disciple. Charron's friend, La Rochemaillet,
is the authority for what other scanty information we possess
as to their relations. Charron's intimacy with Montaigne is
dated from about 1589, his admiration for the Essays mentioned,
and La Rochemaillet adds that their author, dying without male
descent, granted permission to the priest to bear his arms. Be

---

[1] Bâle, 1561. For a description of this book see *Revue Hist. Litt. de
la France*, 1895, p. 354.

77

this as it may, it seems that Charron, who never acknowledged
in print his enormous debt to Montaigne, intended to make
some amends for this omission by his will, which bequeathed
to Montaigne's own sister, Léonor de Camain, and her husband
the major part of his not inconsiderable fortune.[1]

Charron's life is not within the scope of this chapter.[2]   To
seek an explanation of what is unorthodox in his writings by
an attack on his life or an attempt to make him out other than
a pious, honest, capable ecclesiastic is misguided and fruitless,
and it is not until long after his death that some vague insinua-
tions against his conduct are to be found.[3]

Charron, though it might not be recognized from a superficial examination of his writings, was a man of violent passions.
Physically robust, red-faced, white-haired, he died of apoplexy
in a Paris street at the age of sixty-two.   He was one of those
who, after the assassinations at Blois, were swept into the League
by a wave of indignation.   He is an optimist who for months
goes on hoping against all appearances that he will be admitted
at forty-seven into a monastic order with the strictest of rules ;
who expects to finish in three months a work—La Sagesse—
which takes him nearly three years, and who constantly, and
up to the end, underestimates the strength of the opposition
which that work has aroused.

Charron was a fighter and his writings are often polemical,
a fact which no doubt partly explains why he was content with
a mere rearrangement of other men's views.   Owing to this
manner of composition, a host of incompatible opinions here
rub shoulders.   It is notoriously hard to pin down the elusive
Montaigne, but sheer inconsistency makes it almost as difficult
to determine the real views of Charron, in spite of all his method.
The ' tiring divisions ' of Charron's great work, as Pascal called
them, have, however, a very real importance as indications of
the weight which is to be attached to his various assertions and
as guides in an edifice of which a truer idea can sometimes be

---

[1] It is this same Camain who has been already mentioned as an
intimate friend of Pierre de Lancre (above, p. 41, note 3).

[2] See J. B. Sabrié, Pierre Charron, 1913.

[3] They are made by one who may have been in a position to be a
judge of his conduct, but who was clearly no impartial one (cf. Scipion
Dupleix, La Liberté de la Langue Française, 1651, p. 126).   Charles Sorel
(Bibliothèque Française) suspects a quarrel between the two men.   As for
the ' mad-dog Garasse ', as Carlyle called him, we may be sure his calumny
would have been made in less general terms, if he, with all the Jesuits
of Bordeaux at his back, could have laid any definite charge at Charron's
door.   See, too, Mersenne, L'Impiété des Déistes, Pt. I, p. 183.

obtained by looking at the disposition of the whole rather than at the borrowed bricks of which it is built.

Charron's first published work affords an opportunity of dealing with the author's fideism. The Essays are already not infrequently quoted here ; but although both may be regarded as disciples in common of the Paduan school, it seems likely that, without the encouragement of his senior, Charron would probably have adopted less pronounced views. *Les Trois Vérités* (1593) was written as an answer to Du Plessis Mornay's *De la Vérité de la Religion Chrétienne* (1581), but only the third Truth is directed against the Reformers, or, as the author declares, to proving that ' of all creeds the Roman Catholic is the best '. The first proves the existence of God, and the second deals with the religion in general ' or the duty of man towards God in this world '.

Charron goes quite as far as Montaigne in his separation of the spheres of faith and reason. Yet his attitude comprises some interesting elements foreign to the Essays. One of these is the way in which Charron links up mysticism and fideism. God is unprovable and unknowable because infinite ; hence the constant danger of all human attempts to conceive God is their anthropomorphism. God can only be conceived by a kind of mystical adoration. Here we find all the favourite comparisons of mystical theology : God, the great silence, the abyss, to be conceived by negation, the ' deep but dazzling darkness '. Charron refers us at large to the pseudo-Dionysius, St. Gregory and Augustine. He returns later to this vague mysticism in his *Discours de la Divinité*, where anthropomorphism is again severely dealt with.[1] Charron does indeed enumerate the probable proofs of God's existence, but frankly admits their insufficiency. A certain prominence is given to such considerations as conscience, and Godhead as the type of virtue and goodness.[2] The existence of demons and the phenomena of possession are also brought forward as guarantees for the existence of invisible spiritual powers.[3]

A fideism, which corresponds closely to that of Montaigne is also represented in the *Trois Vérités*. The last chapter indeed of the Second Truth reads like a pastiche of the Essays. Its conclusions are worth reproducing, for they state very clearly the nuance of Charron's position and some of his motives for adopting it.

---

[1] loc. cit, §§ 8, 9, 11, and anthropomorphism, § 14.
[2] Chaps. 6 and 8. [3] Compare Silhon, below, p. 177, 178.

There are two sources of truth, faith or reason ; faith is more perfect however.

Ce sont deux mains et deux moyens d'appréhender et recevoir une chose, la raison et l'autorité, auxquelles répondent la science et la foi : celle-là est pour l'homme, celle-ci pour le Chrétien : celle-là est en perpétuelle agitation et incertitude, celle-ci, plus noble, est à recoi et en sûreté.

By reason, only those articles of religion can be proved which are least specifically Christian. Now all the articles of the Christian religion are equally important (*égaux en créance non pas en intelligence*). Hence to believe without the aid of reason is more profoundly Christian ; faith alone is preferable everywhere within the sphere of religion, since, if admitted, reason can only supply doubtful arguments on certain points. Christianity demands total self-renunciation, and, because this ideal is difficult, it has always been torn by sects. Not only the flesh but reason often rebels : *le croire force l'homme supérieur ; le faire contriste l'inférieur*.[1] And Charron goes on to quote that favourite refrain of the Essays :

La raison, un outil ondoyant, règle de plomb, pliant, changeant, mal assuré. L'on ne saurait tant alléguer de raisons pour une part, que l'on n'en trouve autant ou plus pour l'autre.[2]

Already in this book, in spite of once using ' pyrrhonism ' as a term of condemnation, Charron adopts much the same attitude as the scepticism of the Apology. If he seems to admit two ways, faith or reason, of which the former is however more perfect, so too, Montaigne, in the Apology, reminds the noble lady for whom he writes that perhaps she would be better to *maintenir son Sebond par la forme ordinaire d'argumenter*.

In *La Sagesse* Charron is at once a more pronounced rationalist and a more pronounced fideist than in his other writings : more fideist, partly because it is easier for the philosopher to insist on the existence of two water-tight compartments than for the theologian to put this thesis into practice ; more rationalist, because this book is chiefly concerned with ethics and in this sphere Charron is indeed a rationalist.

---

[1] *Troisième Vérité*, p. 134. Note how Charron neatly turns to account the familiar finalist argument : man has a natural desire for certain knowledge of the external world and himself, hence it is legitimate to believe God has given him means of satisfying it. No, says Charron, he is given this appetite, *whose essential quality is that it cannot be satisfied*, in order to raise his mind to God (*Discours Chrétiens*, I, § 5).

[2] ib., p. 152.

It is well to notice his insistence on the aspect of fideism as a preparation for the religious state of mind, not merely as a preliminary penance (as in the formula already quoted), but as a method for converting the heathen. In one of the additions to the second edition of La Sagesse, where he is defending his surséance de jugement against the imputation of religious indifference, he suddenly carries the war into the enemies' camp, and having called on mystical theology for corroboration, he writes

Donc il sémble que pour planter et établir la Chrétienté en un peuple mécréant et infidèle, serait une très belle méthode de commencer par ces propositions et persuasions : que tout le savoir du monde n'est que vanité et mensonge . . . que Dieu a bien créé l'homme pour connaître la vérité, mais qu'il ne la peut connaître de soi ni par aucun moyen humain. . . .[1]

This method is equally useful for preserving one's faith, and consists in employing what has been called in connexion with Montaigne a ' critique of satisfaction '. Yet the first chapters of La Sagesse on human vanity, misery and presumption—derived mainly from the Essays—have not primarily this religious end in view, any more than Charron's ' critique of reason ' has the intention of maintaining a real philosophical scepticism. The function of these first chapters is to help the reader to realize his own misery, human and personal, in order that he may realize the real starting-point of psychology and ethics, self-knowledge. This can be seen clearly enough, if the book is looked at as a whole.

The sweeping nature of Charron's attack on human presumption, of his affirmation of human misery, has also perhaps another side. The ' Ecclesiastes touch ' is certainly often connected in the Essays with fideism ; it is also sometimes inspired by a re-action against fanaticism and intolerance. That is, it is sometimes used, as in the Apology, with some ulterior end in view, but it is far more often, and more fundamentally, a spontaneous attitude, a tragic sense of life. When Charron concentrates the essence of this side of Montaigne in the first pages of his manual, we are conscious that this attitude, natural or not, is chosen with a purpose, just as we are conscious of special pleading in Pascal's variations on the same themes of Montaigne, which we should have felt even more clearly had the Pensées ever gone beyond the note-book stage. Why then does Charron begin with this sweeping indictment, which evidently met with some

[1] La Sagesse, II, 2, § 6 B (i.e. 2nd edition).

disapproval of the kind we have seen directed against Montaigne by Antoine de Laval,[1] and which caused him to transpose this section of *La Sagesse* to a less prominent position in the middle of the first book ? His object here is clearly neither to convert China nor confirm Christendom. In effect, is it not true that one of the most important contentions of his book is to be the necessity of distinguishing morality and religion ? Yet Charron is naturally concerned to make it clear that the good life, even according to the law of nature, much more according to the law of Christ, is an impossibility without the grace of God.[2] But in spite of his orthodox protestations, grace plays little or no part in his system of ethics. How could it be stressed ? I think that Charron hoped, by this preliminary discourse, to make his readers feel he was not oblivious to the fact of original sin. He does so, as a philosopher, by developing the familiar theme of human imperfection. How much in keeping with contemporary Christian feeling most of this section is, may be seen by reference to Du Plessis Mornay's *Discours de la Vie et de la Mort* (1576) or P. Du Moulin's *Héraclite ou de la Vanité et Misère de la Vie Humaine* (1608).[3]

This opening must be regarded then mainly as a justification for the treatise on ' wisdom ' which is to follow, pointing out the importance and the urgency of the task, and its necessary starting-point in self-knowledge. This γνῶθι σεαυτόν, as Charron appears to be only confusedly aware, is the one principle which is capable of making good sense of the many apparent contradictions of his book. But these chapters also form, to some extent, a corrective to the moral optimism of the rest of the work. They prepare the reader for the mitigated scepticism later recommended to the Sage, by presenting it, first of all, in a form familiar to contemporaries—the bankruptcy of reason appearing as an element in a description of man's condition, where the leading thought is that of self-renunciation and self-condemnation as the first essential of piety. The bankruptcy of reason is later seen not to extend in so absolute a degree to the sphere of ethics.

[1] See above, p. 36, also Garasse : *Somme*, p. 89.
[2] An annotated copy of Samson Lennard's translation of Charron (*Of Wisdome*, 2nd ed., 1615 ?) in the British Museum (8403, i. 8) shows very clearly how much an anonymous Englishman of learning and piety, reading the book towards 1660 with evident sympathy for the most part, amends most of Charron's passages on Grace, which seem to him to savour of Pelagianism.
[3] It is immaterial that these two writers are Protestants. For Catholic books of the same type see Introduction, p. xxvii.

The section immediately following these first eight chapters gives a comparison of man and the animals (also transposed in the second edition). The direct debt to Montaigne might be easily exaggerated, and poor humanity fares better here than in the Apology. The purpose of the section is that of a transition to the physiological and psychological analysis which is to follow, made by placing man in his true position in the universe as an animal, though a privileged one. Otherwise, man, for lack of recognizing that his fellow-creatures are also truly God's children too, *vient à en abuser et exercer cruauté, chose qui rejaillit contre le Maître commun et Universel qui les a faites*. The analysis which follows begins in the first edition with an anatomical description of man, of the beauty of his body, passing on to chapters on the senses, the 'sensitive soul' and finally the 'rational soul'. This order was also subsequently reversed, so that, in the second edition, this 'consideration of man with the animals' no longer forms the link it was originally intended to be, and the clarity of the underlying reasoning has suffered. It must be added that there are grounds for thinking that Charron's attribution of reasoning powers to animals was not quite so flattering to them in his eyes as some of his detractors appear to have imagined ; for to set down their actions to instinct is to flatter them still more, since instinct appears to him a more direct mode of the action of God.[1]

One of the most capital affirmations of *La Sagesse* is Charron's division of morality and religion. This must not only be brought into relation with the circumstances under which Charron was writing, the disappearance of any moral code as a consequence of the religious wars ; it must not only be seen as an important recognition of the nature of ethics, but it must be recognized also as having considerable bearings on Charron's views on the character and function of religion itself. Charron's fideism is not merely a confession of the inadequacy of logical argument to establish the articles of religious belief, it is an affirmation about the nature of such belief itself. For him, it is something essentially passive, entirely dependent on an act of God's grace. What is supernatural is concentrated in the intellectual sphere, what is 'natural' in the moral sphere. Metaphysical truths are attained by some intuitive, non-discursive process akin to divine illumination, just as 'invention '—that is both artistic and scientific invention—is, when genuine, a revelation from

[1] *La Sagesse*, I, 8, § 7. For the importance of this point in connexion with Descartes, see below, pp. 228–232.

God.[1] Yet the understanding is a faculty which naturally seeks those truths which it cannot attain except by imposition from above and by renunciation of its own forces. The characteristic operation and function of the intellect is just the dialectic process of weighing this reason against that, without presuming to arrive at any final conclusion. This then is what appears to be at the bottom of Charron's mind when he recommends his sage to judge of all things and to decide of nothing : *les oppositions et les contradictions raisonnées sont les vrais moyens d'exercer cet office de juge.*[2]

In his chapter on true piety (II, 5) Charron wishes to insist on the irrational character of religion, and on its inevitable descent to mere superstition, whenever faith is not really ' from God '. He is eager to bring out this inevitability and attempts to do so by a historical survey of the universal characteristic of all religions—their irrationality. They are all *étranges au sens commun*. The remarkable lack of sufficient guarding clauses relative to Christianity in the first edition is here due perhaps to the fact that the mere articles of Christian belief, without that genuine belief which is the product of grace, seem to him simply on a par with the articles of any other religion. It is due also to the idea that some of the outer forms of Christian life may be defended from the charge of absolute superstition by showing that they are common and essential to all forms of religion : although, at the same time, just because they are common to all religions, they are less important than those features peculiar to Christianity.[3] The lack of cautionary statements of this kind, shown by Charron in general, is, however, to be put down rather to the fact that he cannot conceive that, even if there are those who disagree with him, they should suspect him of an attack on religion, priest as he is and proud of his priesthood.[4] It is also due to the fact that Charron is merely summing up the words of another writer, namely Montaigne in the Apology.[5]

[1] I, 16, especially §§ 12, 13. The passage suggests, however, that Charron was no sceptic of the results of empirical science (end of § 13).

[2] op. cit., II, 2, § 4 B (2nd edition).

[3] cf. *Essais*, II, 12, pp. 248, 249.

[4] An excellent note might be written on the priestly traits of the ideal sage imagined by this man who directed that he was to be buried in full canonicals ' as if about to celebrate the Holy Sacrifice of Mass '. Note the phraseology of the following sentences making clear the opposition of ' profane ' and ' sacred ' : ' C'est à faire aux *profanes* et aux bêtes de se laisser mener comme des buffles. . . . Qu'aura le *sage et sacré* par dessus le *profane* s'il faut qu'il ait son esprit, sa principale et héroique pièce, esclave du commun.'

[5] See especially *Essais*, II, 12, pp. 154, 155, 230, 248 et seq.

It is in a kind of pulpit-style,—if the words are those of the Essays [1]—that after insisting on divine inspiration as the one character of true belief, Charron goes on to ask in a rhetorical question : how can we Christians pretend to have real faith, how can we pretend to believe the immortality of soul,[2] as all over the world men confess it, while we lead the lives we do ? What signs are there of the working of God in us ?

Si elle (la religion) tenait et était plantée par une attache divine, chose du monde ne nous pourrait ébranler, telle attache ne se romprait pas si aisément, s'il y avait de la touche et du rayon de la divinité, il paraîtrait partout et l'on produirait des effets qui s'en sentirait.[3]

We believe that we believe, we would fain have others believe that we believe ; but do we really ? In a sermon, or as an exhortation such as they represent in their context in the Essays, these questions might pass for ' current divinity '. If one comprehends the full extent to which Charron's theory of belief is anti-rational, this paragraph, which prefaces an attack on superstition, is seen in its true light and need excite no surprise, but as a reasoned statement of fact, following on a bold piece of comparative theology, it is little wonder that these pages were regarded by many people with extreme suspicion.

It is not merely the tendency of man to misunderstand and degrade religion which causes Charron to devote himself to an attack on superstition. It is his dialectical method, ' reasoned contrasts ', and even his own pugnaciousness, which, in its turn, causes him to attack from the outset of his book the three ' plagues ' of men, superstition, formalism and pedantry. Each of the three will be found to represent an intellectual error which has as its result a false view of ethics. The superstitious man is he who has an unworthy and anthropomorphic idea of God. Since he thinks meanly of God, his religion reduces itself to the

---

[1] *Essais*, II, 12, pp. 150–4. Most of this chapter of *La Sagesse* (II, 5) is derived from these pages, often word for word. The difference is in the spirit in which Montaigne writes. The main preoccupation, the struggle of Catholic and Protestant, the scandal and the indignation it arouses, are replaced in Charron by a more generalized philosophical statement, which hardly reflects the religious schism of the time in any way.

[2] cf. I, 14, § 15 and II, 5, § 8. A comparison of these two passages on the immortality of the soul will demonstrate admirably the honest intentions of Charron, his desire for accuracy and his lack of tact. A parenthesis introduced in order to facilitate a cross-reference given in the margin will be seen to have caused an ambiguity which Garasse and others were only too ready to misinterpret. Charron's remarks can be exactly paralleled in the Essays (II, 12, pp. 300, 301, 302).

[3] *La Sagesse*, II, 5, § 8.

practice of magic. The danger of the one point at which the superstitious man has got beyond the magical stage of religion is indicated. He thinks the intention of pleasing God can sanctify all he does. Charron—his intellectualism not here at fault—remarks that this goodwill, without some adequate and non-anthropomorphic conception of God, is bound to lead men astray. Moreover, owing to this magical conception of religion, the superstitious man has no notion of morality apart from pious practices for the propitiation of a God he fears.

The ' formalist ', at the other extreme, completely disregards motives. He considers that compliance with mere external forms and usages is morality and has no conception of any guide to conduct except conformity with local law and custom, which he fails to control by ' the law of nature, that is, the universal equity and reason which lightens each one of us '.[1] The formalist's intellectual error may be said to be his lack of recognition of this law, the true foundation of morality.

The third plague are the pedants. The pedant is largely the victim of false psychology. Knowledge is for him a matter of memory, which he exploits at the expense of judgement. But, according to Huarte's theory of the temperaments, which Charron adopts, these two faculties are incompatible in any high degree. This is the fundamental cause of bad education.[2] Knowledge acquired in this manner is left by the pedant completely out of relation with life.

The influence of the Essays on Charron's conception of the formalist [3] and the pedant is obvious. The analysis of *pédantisme* supplies an excellent example of just where Charron's strength lies : the reduction of other people's views to a rigorous syllogistic expression, which may considerably modify them—and whose very rigour often reveals, as in this matter of memory and judgement, how many questions they beg—but which cannot fail to stick in the reader's mind. The attack on the pedant is obviously very characteristic of this period, but the actuality of Charron's attack on superstition and its importance is no less so, coming as it does at the end of forty years of religious strife and fanaticism, which had produced no worse result than this complete confusion of piety and morality.

There is one trait which these three enemies of Charron

---

[1] *La Sagesse*, II, 3, § 4 A.
[2] ib., I, 15, § 4 et seq., especially § 8 ; III, 14, § 13 et seq.
[3] cf. especially *Essais*, III, 12, pp. 371, 372 (criticism of *la preud'homie scholastique*).

possess in common, their dogmatism. This vice is attacked in *La Sagesse* under various forms, not the least interesting object of attack being the Scholastic philosophers.[1] The presumption at the root of dogmatism has three degrees : credulity, obstinacy in what has been lightly believed, and, thirdly, the attempt to impose this belief on others either by forbidding the discussion of certain principles or authorities or by an appeal to some alleged miraculous event ; *où le moyen ordinaire faut, on y ajoute le commandement, la force, le fer, le feu.*[2]

Where may we look for those who are free from this vice of dogmatism ? The answer may be found on turning to one of Charron's many divisions of mankind, borrowed from Montaigne's ' three states of man ' or the notion of ' pastoral wisdom '.[3] The peasants and the philosophers, who have returned, like Socrates, to a state of informed ignorance, knowing that they know nothing, these are the two kinds of true believers. Those in between, the semi-learned, are the seat of trouble in the world, just as it is in the middle region of the air that the tempests rage. There too, as Charron quaintly adds, the meteors are formed.[4]

Charron returns again and again to this triple division of mankind. His attempts at developing it, however, seem rather confused, and it appears that in practice these distinctions are a matter of degree. It is from the point of view of the relative excellence of the classes that the difference between Charron's use of this theme and Montaigne's use is clearest. There is little suggestion in *La Sagesse* that the simple folk are somehow comparable to the real philosophers.[5] Socially they are both submissive, just as their humility makes them capable of receiving religion as it should be received—from above. But the *Ethériens* are *plutôt démons qu'hommes* [6] and a society of them alone is as inconceivable as a society of only the vulgar would be.[7] For Montaigne, the peasants and philosophers are not only alike

---

[1] cf. II, 2, § 3 : ' *Les dogmatistes et affirmatifs qui sont venus depuis* ', &c. See also I, 7, §§ 6–9 and II, 1, § 11. [2] I, 7, § 9.

[3] See above, p. xxxi and R. Berthelot : *Revue de Métaphysique et Morale*, 1924. *La Sagesse de Shakespeare.*

[4] cf. *La Sagesse* (I, 16, § 4 ; I, 31) ; II, Preface and *Essais* (I, 54, pp. 397, 398; II, 17, pp. 417, 447 ; III, 10, p. 317; II, 10, p. 117, &c.). For the *meteors*, see below, p. 129, note 1.

[5] See, however, *La Sagesse*, II, 3, § 6.

[6] The expression (cf. the *daimon* of Socrates) should be linked with Charron's idea of personal revelation or true ' invention '. See below, pp. 214–220, on Descartes.

[7] cf. *Essais*, II, 20, pp. 465, 466, where Montaigne, more faithful to truth than to himself, points out that the best minds are too perspicacious to succeed in the business of life.

good believers but their ' virtue ', the virtue of Socrates and of his own Gascon peasants, achieves the same ' follow nature ', an ideal of harmony and spontaneity not of conflict. The considerations of spontaneity, ease and grace have their place in Charron's ideal, but in *La Sagesse* this triple distinction is purely a distinction of degrees and types of *intelligence*. It is intellectual, not moral.

These *raisonneurs*, the dogmatists of the middle class, are those who always accept the opinions of the majority, thinking it is not permitted to search for truth ; indeed utility matters more to them than truth.[1] The most able among them govern the world. With them are contrasted the real thinkers, the inquirers, who know how to doubt and the uses of doubt. Note that Charron in no way contradicts the fideist side of his triple division. It might seem that the disputers are those who do *not* accept current opinions. His answer would be that the majority in one age or place is not the majority in another. Whenever, or if ever, something truly universal is found, Charron would call this natural, that is, divinely instituted. Since, however, he distinguishes, and is logically justified in distinguishing, that universality from the mere consensus of opinion of a few thousand men during a certain period, ample room for the dissensions of the dogmatists obviously remains.

So too, one might think that Charron, the fideist, would hold that it was not permitted to try and reason out the truth. No, the search is a duty ; the opposition of reasons to each other is the characteristic process of the human intellect. But it is in the nature of this process that one should not arrive at results, or, at best, only at provisional ones, such as Charron certainly believes can be attained in ethics and psychology if not in the physical sciences, on which he is generally silent. And the fact that we can arrive at no permanent results, no ultimate necessary truths, will make us the more ready to receive religion in the spirit we should. Therefore for happiness' sake—to put it no higher—one must learn to doubt with pleasure, and to decide, where decision is possible, by rational argument. Hence the *universelle liberté d'esprit*, the *juger de tout*, which are the preparation for *la vraie preud'homie*.

In the preface to the Second Book Charron adds some more details on the Three States. He notes two types, both of the first class, and he dubs them Democritus and Heraclitus. They are both true sages, but the former type, who laugh at this empty

---

[1] cf. Julien Benda's *Trahison des Clercs* (1925).

world, ' have not enough goodness of heart nor enough charity '. The others, the Heracliteans, fear the opposition of the world and speak their minds only darkly and *à demi-bouche*. I confess I am unable to guess to which class Montaigne, for instance, himself belongs. ' I, writes Charron, come after them and below them : but I say in good faith what I think and believe both plainly and clearly.' He fully expects the attacks of the ' middle story ', but he hopes for the approval of the *simples et débonnaires, et les Ethériens et sublimes*. In spite of the prominence of the Three States in *La Sagesse*, Charron generally thinks along the lines of the common humanist intellectualism with its division of the vulgar and the wise.

The reader will remember the poetical background given by Montaigne to this train of thought, and his quotation of the Georgics :

O fortunatos nimium, sua si bona norint,
Agricolas !

In a chapter on ' rustic and town life ' Charron writes : ' The celestial fire which is within us desireth not at all to be shut up, but loveth the open air and the fields, wherefore, saith Columella, country-life is cousin (*consanguinea*) to wisdom, for that it cannot be without fair, free thoughts and meditations.' [1] This reflection is not however linked up with the Three States. The reference to Columella's Treatise on Agriculture and Virgil should remind us that there is a philosophical as well as a poetical side to the development of ' pastoral ' literature, which, though not unknown in the Middle Ages, first enjoys such enormous success at the Renaissance.

One last and most important fact must be recalled in connexion with this division of three types. The theory of temperaments is brought forward as its chief cause, and indeed all fundamental differences of human character are referred by Charron to the ' humours ', that is, to the alleged combination of certain elements in the body.[2] The full significance of the theory of the four temperaments as developed in the sixteenth and seventeenth centuries and the special use which Charron makes of it, will be seen later.

[1] *La Sagesse*, I, 52.   [2] ib., I, 39, § 1.

CHAPTER VII

PIERRE CHARRON—II.

Les hommes sont naturellement bons et ne suivent le mal que pour le profit ou le plaisir.

Pierre Charron.

IT is a commonplace to say that the Renaissance opened men's eyes, ears and minds. One fact, the most important of all psychologically, does not always receive its proper prominence, a new consciousness of the diversity and variety of life. At certain moments of human history, when this same richness of life is too chaotic and the mind takes fright, the characteristic results appear to be such phenomena as Gnosticism, and the asceticism of the Dark Ages. Their counterpart is a geometrical art (e.g. Byzantine or Celtic). The Renaissance man however did not take fright. For those who keep their heads, there are various reactions to this consciousness of infinite diversity. First the lyrical attitude, the most childish and least sophisticated of them, which is content to express its wonder at this richness. Perhaps this is the typical reaction of the age in question. There are also others ; first, perhaps, a certain religious nuance of the lyrical attitude, a *Benedicite omnia opera.* Bremond has drawn attention to this in his *Humanisme Dévot.*

Two others might be called the theological, and the scientific attitudes. By the theological, I mean the finalist explanation and co-ordination of natural phenomena. We shall see later by what subtle methods Descartes strove to destroy the theological assumptions on which such an ideal must rest. The compromise adopted in the *Méditations* and the *Principia*, was the denial that we can understand anything of God's nature or his ends, because he is infinite.[1] The widespread fideist affirmations of the incomprehensibility of God, while they do not repose on any views about the nature of the infinite or the eternal verities, tend to discredit finalism. There is, moreover, an important

---

[1] *Principia*, I, §§ 19, 26, 27.

connexion between this theological attitude to nature, anthropomorphism, and what might be called anthropocentrism. Instead of referring a set of phenomena for their explanation to God's perfection and the perfection of his creation, they are referred, by a kind of short-circuit, to the convenience and service of man. Lastly, empiricist co-ordination of the diversity of experience, the method which has made the advance of modern science possible, is too familiar to need characterizing.

It must, however, be kept in mind that among other forms of this diversity were a new variety of opinions, of customs, of social conditions from different countries. Here, in particular, may be distinguished an attitude unlike the others mentioned, which are all purely philosophical—*des attitudes de clerc*, as M. Benda would say. This last attitude is the exploitation of any diversity in view of some ulterior end. The most general end, to which this exploitation of a chaotic variety can be applied, is such as to keep it still, in fact, a disinterested, ' clerical ' attitude, that is the encouragement of the critical spirit. For this and its counterpart, tolerance, are truly not the mere sign but rather the essence of civilization itself. Such purposes as the encouragement of toleration, liberty of thought and conscience, are, however, sometimes less purely philosophic. The critical spirit is the chief weapon of liberalism, the grand instrument of attack on any received order of things, religious, social or intellectual, which is content to imagine itself unique and inevitable simply because received without discussion or reflection.

This last attitude, as also the first, the lyrical, is characteristic of the Essays. A great part of Montaigne's scepticism is a thinly disguised and sorely needed argument for tolerance and the critical spirit in every sphere. This is particularly true of all the many essays which touch on the diversity of custom. The importance of books of travel in the same connexion has only recently attracted the attention it deserves,[1] and it will be seen what use La Mothe le Vayer makes of the procedure of Montaigne (or perhaps more truly of Sextus Empiricus) and his utilization of the traveller's tale in preparing some of his lists of strange diversities. This same method of attack as an argument against innate ideas may be found in the first book of Locke's Essay.

Yet Montaigne's use of the principle of contradiction is not merely a plea for the critical spirit. For one may truly speak of a relativism with regard to the Essays. And here perhaps

[1] See especially Geoffrey Atkinson, *Les Relations de Voyage du XVII*e* Siècle.*

an interesting distinction between master and disciple imposes itself. Charron conceives the antinomy as the characteristic process of reason ; he also conceives human nature as essentially a dualism of mind and body. He shows, further, an inconsistency of a curious kind in identifying all that is evil now with the body,[1] now with the spirit (*l'esprit*). This inconsistency not only illustrates the Christian theme of the double nature of man, but also sheds a strong light on the cross-currents created by fideism on the one hand (mistrust of reason, evil as grounded in intellectual error), and the more usual notion of original sin (carnal temptations as type of evil) [2] on the other hand. What is to some extent a resolvent principle between these two trends of thought is supplied here by Charron's treatment of the passions, for to these are attributed the corruption of the understanding by the imagination and the senses. This corruption, however, is considered more often as the cause either of error or of unhappiness than of vice.

Apart from such inconsistencies, however, Charron delights in a method of exposition by contrasts, based on his notion of the function of antinomies. Yet I do not think that he conceives the principle of contradiction as inherent in the nature of things, but merely as peculiar to the nature of man, while Montaigne seems to suppose a *real* ' doubleness ', not merely as perceived by the mind but as actually existing in the world of things. It is clear, however, that we may fairly represent Charron's ' scepticism ' as founded on a certain view of the nature and limitations of reason and closely connected with his fideism, and we might say that the use of this position as a weapon against dogmatism and narrow-mindedness naturally follows from it.

It remains to be shown how this scepticism is linked up with Charron's ethical system, his ideal of ' wisdom ', which he defines as being neither a certain level of intellectual knowledge nor a mere non-moral discretion in the affairs of life.

This connexion is set forth in the chapter on *Universelle et*

---

[1] Note in spite of this, the attack on asceticism (II, 6, § 2).

[2] cf. such texts as the following : ' *Tout ce qu'il y a de mal, non seulement en l'homme, mais au monde, est forgé et produit par l'esprit* ' (I, 2, § 2) ; ' *L'esprit . . . parcelle, scintille, image de la Divinité ne respire que le bien et le Ciel où il tend toujours, la chair, au contraire . . . tend toujours au mal et à la matière . . .*' (I, 9, § 2). A glorification of the body and a eulogy of health and physical beauty follow immediately on this last passage (I, 10, 11). The best Catholic thought has generally insisted on the purely negative character of evil. For a strong expression of such a view and an interesting contribution to Christian Ethics made about this time, see J. Bodin, *Paradoxe sur la Vertu* (written 1591).

pleine liberté d'esprit. The sage is to cultivate a state of mind, not only identified with the suspense of judgement of the Sceptics or the indifference of the Academy, but akin to Aristotle's magnanimity or the *Nil Admirari* of the Stoics. This is simply a tranquillity of mind which cannot be attained until a man is content, like the ancient philosophers and unlike the scholastics, to admit he does not possess any certain knowledge. The ancients who have appeared dogmatic were not so at heart, like those others who would rather be contradicted in the most insulting terms than ignored. The point here is not whether the claim to know things with certainty is justified, but that the dogmatic attitude is bound to lead to stubborn refusal to recognize errors, and what is worse, a hot-headed contentiousness, which makes a man the prey of his passions and is thus incompatible with happiness.

This suspense of judgement then is just the critical spirit already mentioned, and the second point of Charron's chapter concerns that attitude to diversity characterized as exploitation of difference. A consideration of all the beliefs, opinions, customs and laws of different times and countries is what he calls the ' universal spirit '. The third point of this ' liberty of mind ' —which he insists is only of mind and does not imply any lack of conformity with received customs—is ' liberty of will '. Under this heading the exaggerated value set upon self-sacrifice and zeal is criticized. Here we have the polemical Charron once more, yet his attacks are always part of the development of a positive idea ; in this case, it is all that Montaigne sums up in his essay : *De Ménager sa volonté* (III, 10). Current morality demands complete self-sacrifice in any public cause, good or bad ; if this is not shown, one is accused of lack of charity. Anyone who only supports a cause with moderation is also condemned. But this indiscreet zeal destroys all peace of mind by worry ; it helps rather than hinders in the conduct of affairs ; it corrupts the judgement and destroys all fair-mindedness. A man must know what he owes to the public weal, but that involves also the knowledge that he does not owe all. To confound the responsibilities of office with those of the individual is absurd.

Charron has made some rearrangements of this important chapter in his second edition, but the alterations underline what is fundamental. The sage is to ' judge of everything ' : that is, examine everything in a spirit of inquiry, not decision (Christian doctrine always excepted). To hinder intellectual liberty is, first, impossible ; secondly, the greatest tyranny imaginable, and one the sage should resist. The sage has ' indifference of taste ' (this is simply suspense of judgement under a new name). Charron accepts the charge of scepticism and shows its use even in religion.[1] Finally, speaking of the ' universal spirit ', he adds the various characters of men to his list of diversities to be studied.

To sum up, Charron recommends a preliminary ' cure ' of vulgar errors, combined with the abandonment of dogmatism and zeal, since these foment the passions. It is almost true to say that the ' cure ' of the passions is the general head under which the cultivation of this mental freedom is a subsection. The descriptive psychology and the vague Stoicism which Charron has borrowed from Du Vair [2] to build up the part of *La Sagesse* which deals with the passions, call for no special comment. His *traité des passions* resembles a host of others written at this time. Yet the various remedies suggested for the passions are worth noting.[3] The first, insensibility, is bad and is rejected ; Charron calls it a ' spiritual leprosy '.[4] The second remedy, the dominating passion, is also non-moral : for one passion must dominate inevitably, just as one of the humours must dominate the temperament. The third is approved ; this is Montaigne's ' diversion '. The fourth and last is *vive vertu, résolution et fermeté d'âme*, a noble impassiveness. Here reason masters the passions by knowing them and judging of their power (compare Spinoza).

Having examined this preliminary ' cure ' of passion and prejudice we must next attempt to analyse Charron's description of *la vraie preud'homie*.

Involuntary action or lack of temptation cannot give rise to any truly moral conduct ; intention is the only means of judging what is moral in our own or other people's conduct.[5] The current ethical ideal is something purely external, a slavery to every kind of formalism. Not only the customs, forms, and religions which men observe, differ from place to place, but their disagreement in one place, not only in a similar but even in identically the same instance, shows how contingent and fortuitous this formalist morality is. The most difficult life to lead

---

[1] cf. *La Sagesse*, II, 6, § 2.

[2] On Du Vair, see below, p. 108, note 4.

[3] cf. *La Sagesse*, II, 1, §§ 5–11.

[4] *Essais*, III, 10, p. 310. Montaigne uses the expression for a blissful ignorance, and remarks it constitutes a good fortune philosophy does not despise.

[5] Charron's criticism of the Superstitious—that they think intention excuses everything [I, 6, § 13]—is not necessarily discrepant with this assertion. He might put it that intention is a necessary yet not a sufficient consideration in both practical and theoretical ethics.

is that of the private individual. Strong temptations, opportunities to commit the more obvious crimes, rarely come his way.
Forms and ceremonies touch him only at certain points of his
life. It is necessary to find a rule of life that goes behind these
popular guides, a principle that applies generally to any and
every man.

This principle of ethics is the law of nature, the light of natural
reason, ' *un éclair et rayon de la divinité, une défluxion et dépend-
ance de la loi éternelle et divine* '. By acting according to this
natural light man acts at once according to God and his own
nature, since this natural reason and equity is what is most noble
in him. God and Nature are in the universe as a king in his
state and as the fundamental law which governs that state.
Nature is at once the mistress who enjoins *preud'homie* upon us,
and the law which instructs us in its provisions.

Toutes les tables de droit, et les deux de Moïse, et les douze des
Grecs, et toutes les bonnes loix du monde, ne sont que des copies et
des extraits produits en jugement contre toi qui tient caché l'original
et feint ne savoir que c'est.[1]

This reference to ' good laws ' is a characteristic piece of question-
begging, but the general conception of Charron is familiar enough.
The existence of an innate moral law is one of his profoundest
convictions, and in what is perhaps the one intimate utterance
of the book, the prayer for grace and for the benediction of his
book which comes towards the close of this chapter, he speaks
again of *l'obligation et instruction que m'en avez donné en la Loi
de Nature qu'avez planté en moi.*[2] The lyrical glorification of
Nature, the rationalist tendencies of the day, the revival of the
Stoical ideal of ' follow Nature ' are all aspects of Renaissance
thought which seem to be included in this notion of the law of
Nature. It is well to remember, however, not only the prominence accorded by Justinian and the Roman jurists of the Empire
to *jus naturale*, law based on natural reason, and the influence
which this and its practical synonym, *jus gentium*, exercised
both on ethical speculation and on the formation of modern
international law, but also to be reminded of the Church's traditional attitude to natural law during the Middle Ages. ' What
the canonists and schoolmen added to the classical Roman theory
was the identification of the law of nature with the law of God
revealed in human reason.' Hence the authority given to philo-

[1] *La Sagesse*, II, 3, § 4 A and B.
[2] ib., II, 3, § 16 B. Notice ' *agréer mon désir, mon essai, mon petit
œuvre* ', i.e. *La Sagesse.*

sophers of antiquity like Aristotle whose writings formed a natural revelation granted to reason.[1]

'The Laws of Ecclesiastical Polity', of Hooker (1594)—the last man before modern times, says Sir Frederick Pollock, to treat the question with the scholastic tradition behind him—suffice to show the Broad-Church rationalism which this law-of-nature-law-of-reason line of thought involves.[2] Now from whence Charron derived his not very original conception does not concern us here, though his own legal training should not be forgotten, but the mention of Hooker and the character of his work serve to focus the attention on what is perhaps sufficiently evident : the inconsistency of this notion of reason as something divine and infallible with what has been said elsewhere by Charron of the characteristic imperfection of the intellectual processes of the human mind. What is worse, we have here to grapple not only with a direct contradiction between this and other parts of La Sagesse, but in this very chapter the author goes on, after stating that the law of nature, or conscience, is eternal, innate, inviolable, ineffaceable, to assert that it has been totally lost.

Universality is the only mark or criterion of what is natural, and we can point to no single law or usage which has not been or is not contradicted somewhere in the world.[3] It has been lost, thanks to a formalism, which has confounded all our notions of right and wrong,

Certes il ne reste plus aucune image ni trace de nature en nous, il la faut aller chercher aux bêtes, où cet esprit brouillon et inquiet, ce vif argent, ni l'art, ni la belle cérémonie ne l'ont pu altérer, elles l'ont pure et entière, sinon qu'elle soit corrompue par notre hantise et contagion, comme elle est aucunement.[4]

The perfection of man in this world, he continues, immediately, is to 'follow nature, that is reason '.

How are all these statements to be reconciled ? Reason is the constituent principle of the law of nature, of man's nature ; that is, reason is of the very essence of man and also of the essence of God, yet so corrupted as to be totally lost. Some such law may be seen more plainly in beasts than in men. There,

---

[1] Henry Maine : *Ancient Law* (Pollock's edition, pp. 73–8, 114 et seq.).

[2] Note that the personal controversy which gave birth to this work partly concerned Hooker's assertion that what was known by the light of reason was *more evident*, if *less certain*, than what was seen by the illumination of grace.

[3] *La Sagesse*, II, 3, § 8.

[4] ib., § 9.

an inner law of nature may be recognized, but I do not think Charron really imagines that this law is ' of reason ', except by analogy, in spite of his remarks elsewhere on processes of animal thought. For it is just in its non-rational character that the law of animal nature seems universal and unerring. It may be recognized, in fact, just in so far as it is clearly universal. Thus, with man, Charron's problem may be put, from its empirical aspect, in the following way : the law of man's nature is by definition what is common to all, for mankind is one race, yet to find what is literally common to all is quite impossible.

One way out of this problem is supplied by Christian doctrine, by calling in the supernatural, but the thought of both Montaigne and Charron, when they are being most honest with themselves, commits them to a humanist ethic, not in the sense that this will eventually show itself incompatible with the notions of original sin and grace, but, as Charron would put it, that its truth should be evident to all men, whether Christian or heathen. The logical value of universality is confused and confounded everywhere in the thought of the Renaissance and early Post-Renaissance thinkers with all the vague metaphysical prestige, the superior truth and reality claimed for what is universal. Hence, no doubt, so much in Montaigne and his followers which concerns animals and savages. Yet the solution of this problem must be sought, in so far as it is solved in *La Sagesse*, where Montaigne sought and found it : at the other extreme, on the individual plane, through the personal life.

It has often been said that *La Sagesse* leaves out the best part of the Essays, Montaigne's delightful self-portrait, yet the philosophical significance of that portrait did not wholly escape Charron. The *maîtresse forme* is the one fixed point in Montaigne's relativistic universe. But even to know this fixed element in the individual is, he believed, only possible by an effort of continuous introspection and reflection on past experience, and it is only when truly known that the contradictions, not only of the individual organism, but all those other antinomies which the human mind perceives outside itself, fall into some order, and a harmony both intellectual and moral can be achieved.

According to the formula of M. Fernandez, the problem is the unifying of the incoherent *moi* by some intrinsic principle. In other words, man possesses already a ' soul ' and yet, in some sense, must gain it—gain it not, as Christianity has misinterpreted Christ, in a hereafter, but here and now in this present life. This idea of self-salvation, of salvation as a conquest, has only in modern times emerged from the trappings of religious dogma, but was it not partly this that the men of the Renaissance meant when they spoke of the conflict of reason and custom, seeing the search for one's personality as ' the necessity of becoming an individual by resisting the pull of the crowd ' ?   But when it is stated thus as the conflict of reason and custom, a further difficulty confronts us.   The current Aristotelean definition of man is an ' animal with reason '.   If reason is the quality which distinguishes man from the animals (and we have seen the doubts of Montaigne and Charron on this point), it is a principle not of differentiation but of resemblance between individual men.   For right reason, the ' essence ' and the ' perfection ' of human nature, leads us to an identity of views, and it is in organic life, in so far as we are bodies, that we differ from one another.

We can now understand the problems among which Charron is groping his way, when he states that man's ' reason ', or his ' rational soul '—to use the School term which more accurately reflects his meaning—is indeed an emanation of the Divine nature and so bears the imprint of divine law ; yet that some process must happen to it, which cannot be summed up either as its liberation from error, prejudice and convention, or as a perfected control over the passions and the temperament, but rather as a bringing into harmony of all the factors in life in order that the individual may truly function as a whole.

The value of Charron's treatment of this question lies, first, in his effort to develop a humanist ideal, and not a religious one, which would have left this world overshadowed by a world-to-come and postpone the realization of that ideal until hereafter.   Its value exists, further, just in so far as considerations relative to personality have been brought into play in the search for this ideal. Its weakness lies partly in a knowledge greatly inferior to that of Montaigne as to what exactly is involved in personality, partly in a couple of traits which are themselves causes of that inferior knowledge :   Charron's intellectualism and the Christian background of his thought.   This semi-divine Reason or Conscience is obviously something far wider than the discursive ratiocination to which Charron denies the possibility of knowing any metaphysical truth, but he not only uses the same term but quite plainly confounds the two.   He remains consistently fideist in his metaphysics and religion, rationalist in his ethics.[1]   More important still is his hypostasis of the Law of Nature, and the

---

[1] Note that in spite of fideism Charron holds to some vague notion of innate ideas [I, 15, § 10, 11].

constitution, one might almost say, of Nature into a fourth member of the Trinity. Charron's imagination is moved and his religious instincts aroused by the conception of universal law.[1] But it is only psychologically and in the psychology of the individual that his views on natural law and reason can be construed into consistent sense.

In dealing with the Essays it has been seen how their actual composition was part of the organization of the author's personality. Charron's book, on the other hand, stands so much apart from him that its arrangement indeed is all that is really his. One aspect of the Essays is as a practical example of the organization of a personality; *La Sagesse* is a purely formal treatise. If these differences are borne in mind, it can be shown that the consideration of personality, the one way out of the dilemma just propounded, plays no inconsiderable part in the scheme of *La Sagesse*.

The primary object of the first chapters is to point out the importance of self-knowledge. This is, however, only the starting-point of Charron's observations on the subject. The second condition of true *preud'homie*, after the recognition of a moral law, is, *Avoir un but et train de vie certain* (*La Sagesse*, II, 4). The chapter insists on the importance of taking individual nature into account. Wisdom cannot be harmonious or ' sweet '—a favourite adjective of his—without doing so. This chapter, though it shows the importance of personality, makes the mistake of imagining that the then immensely popular theory of temperament was a highroad to the discovery of the *maîtresse forme*. As a help to a harmonious life, even merely as an attempt to stress the importance of fact and circumstance to ideals, it is, of course, already of great value. Temperament, climate and profession are the chief heads under which this choice of way of life is ranged. It has already been seen how Montaigne's notion of the Three States of man is given a physical basis in temperament by Charron. That is, a ' simplist ' type-psychology is allowed to take the place of a truly individual psychology. But to do the book justice it must be borne in mind how many of the penetrating first-hand observations of the Essays have

---

[1] The enormous seventeenth-century interest in Natural Law, which formed the basis of most of the serious ethical discussion of the time, may be indicated by noticing the different angles from which it was approached : that of Selden (1640), legist and orientalist ; of Puffendorf (1672), legist ; the inductive philosophical approach of Hobbes (1650), and lastly the metaphysical treatment of the Christian Platonist, Yves de Paris (1658). (For a bibliography of the subject, see George Winhold, *Notitia Scriptorum Juris Naturae*, Leipzig, 1723).

been here reproduced. The weight, however, which Charron attaches to these considerations can only be fully understood when this chapter on *Avoir un but et train de vie certain* is seen together with the first book of *La Sagesse*,[1] no less than half of which is devoted to this question of the diversity of human conditions. Conversely the large place these chapters of the first book fill cannot be understood except by reading them with the fourth of the second book.

As far as race and climate are concerned—a part of this work borrowed from Bodin's *Republic*—nothing need be said here.[2] The theory of temperament, which Charron has derived from Huarte's *Examen*, enjoyed prodigious influence in the sixteenth and seventeenth centuries, and is generally completely ignored to-day except in so far as it is reflected in the comedy of humours, and the *Characters* of Overbury, Earl and La Bruyère. It is as much a feature of the seventeenth century as astrology was of the Italian Renaissance. The Aristotelian theory of humours, adopted by Galen, formed the basis of medical practice down to the eighteenth century. In the hands of certain sixteenth- and seventeenth-century writers, chief among them Juan Huarte, a Navarrese doctor who published in 1573 his *Examen de Ingenios*,[3] it aimed at a complete classification of human types to be used as a practical guide to a choice of profession and cultivation of aptitudes. Modern psychology is far from regarding this classification of human types as unfounded. As a modern text-book has it : ' Recent work on the internal secretions or hormones, though still in its initial stages, makes it probable that not only physique, but character also, is closely dependent on what is known as the endocrine balance '.[4] The inferences of Huarte and his contemporaries were not wrong-headed but overhasty.

Huarte's book and its system had an enormous success, and was not alone in its line.[5] The theorists of the seventeenth century,

---

[1] See especially I, 15, §§ 4–10, I, 36–53.

[2] See Busson, *Rationalisme*, pp. 457, 547, 548.

[3] Huarte was thrice translated into French ; by Gabriel Chappuys, 1580, republished 1598, 1607, 1619, 1632, &c. ; by Vion d'Alibray, 1645, and by Savinien d'Aliquié, 1672.

[4] C. K. Ogden : *The ABC of Psychology*, 1929, pp. 263, 264. See also General Smuts, *Holism and Evolution*, on the demand for a science of ' Personology '.

[5] It will be enough to mention along with it Garzoni's immensely popular *Piazza universale di tutte le professione del mondo* (1585) and Antonio Zara's *Anatomia ingeniorum* (1615). Barclay in his *Icon Animarum* (1619) combines this classification, as Charron does, with the notion of the influence of climate and race, given so much prominence by Bodin

a political age, avid of scientific results which were of practical value, seized upon this ' simplist ' physiology masquerading as a science of the psychology of character, and claimed it as a guide to judge men by. The notion, in its extremer forms completely determinist and materialist, was difficult to reconcile with theological doctrines of the spirituality of the soul, but it appears to have caused no great scandal owing perhaps to its Aristotelian origin. Guibelet's *Examen de l'Examen des Esprits* (1631), which attacks Huarte from the theological point of view, only does so with the greatest caution.[1]

The collection of the questions treated at the public debates of the *Bureau d'Adresse*,[2] are an invaluable repertory of current opinions under Louis XIII. They give a good idea of the seriousness with which this classification by humours was taken, and the number of questions in which it was made to play a part. It is prominent, too, in many of the Treatises on the Passions, and in the description of individuals one is constantly meeting with this kind of statement : *la couleur de ses cheveux et de son visage montrait le juste temperament de cette mélancolie que les philosophes appellent sage et ingénieuse.*[3] Mademoiselle de Gournay founded her notion of the antipathy of the generous-souled and the vulgar (at least in part) on the physical incompatibility of their temperaments.[4] Finally, the works of one of the first members of the Academy, the doctor, Marin Cureau de la Chambre,[5] will give us some idea of the exaggerated psycho-physical parallelism which was apparently ruined by Descartes' clear division of mind and matter.

La Chambre's *Caractères des Passions* (in 5 volumes), his ' *Principes de la Chiromancie* ' and ' *Secrets de la Physionomie* ' are all parts of one vast unfinished plan with the general title of ' *L'Art de Connaître les Hommes* '. It will be sufficient to

in the Sixth Book of the *Republic*. For some of the more amazing metamorphoses of the theory of humours, especially in Germany, the reader may be referred to Karl Borinski's ' *Gracian und die Hof Literatur in Deutschland* '.

[1] See, however, Fr. de Gravelle, Sieur d'Arpeutigny (*Abrégé de philosophie*, 1601, p. 81), who is astonished that the inquisition has not condemned Huarte for maintaining that temperament has an influence on the ' rational soul '.

[2] *Recueil Général des Questions Traitées és Conférences du Bureau d'Adresse*, 1638–1660, especially I, 237, II, 566.

[3] Pellisson: *Hist. de l'Académie*, I, 164. From a funeral oration on the Academician Bardin.

[4] See above, pp. 67, 68.

[5] See R. Kerviler, *Marin Cureau de la Chambre*, 1877, and see below, p. 193.

quote his five general rules from the beginning of the first-named book : (1) Those who have the physical appearance which accompanies a certain passion are by nature subject to that passion, (2) Those who physically resemble an animal have the same character as that animal, (3) Those who have something of feminine beauty are effeminate ; and so with manly beauty, (4) Those who resemble a certain racial type have the character of that race. (5) The last rule is called ' syllogistic '. The author's example is more lucid than his explanations :

Ainsi quand on sait qu'un homme est timide, on peut assurer qu'il a l'inclination à l'avarice, qu'il est artificieux et dissimulé, qu'il a accoutumé de parler avec douceur et soumission, qu'il est soupçonneux, incrédule, mauvais ami et autres semblables. Et bien qu'on ne remarque point de signes particuliers de toutes ces dernières qualités, on ne laisse pas de juger qu'elles s'y trouvent parce que l'on a connu le principe d'où elles prennent l'origine.[1]

Now, though Montaigne himself was always talking about his ' humours ', his use of the term is as vague as our own to-day. He insists indeed on the close dependence of body and soul as parts of a single human organism, but he recognizes that the dependence is mutual. That of these theorists is one-sided, since it attempts to explain the bent of the mind by the constitution of the body. Worse still, they explain the latter by qualities, which, at least as then regarded, were entirely fictitious. There was, as already indicated, a deep-seated reason for this one-sidedness. In so far as the universal character of the spiritual faculties was insisted on, it was impossible to ascribe individuation except to what was corporeal. The term ' Soul ', however vague, has a connotation which involves some notion of individuality, while the term ' Reason ' has not.

Thus Charron himself helped to popularize a theory which, it may be suspected, diminished curiosity in individual psychology by its pretension to answer all such questions, and which was inimical to introspection by reason of its tendency to phenomenalism—all that seems outwardly *is* inwardly. Nevertheless, since Charron has grounded his insistence on the importance of temperament, of profession, race, age and station in life on an ideal of harmonious personal development, he has been even here more faithful to his master than is generally supposed. That he should, however, have offered, as a step and as a help towards this personal life, observations drawn from a type-psychology of insufficient scientific worth—so rigid that it

[1] *Caractères des Passions*, 1648 : Avis nécessaire au lecteur.

affirmed, for example, that great judgement and great memory would never be found together—was certainly a misfortune. Not only did it mean the substitution of shallow, abstract generalizations for the subtle, concrete and truly individual method of Montaigne's introspection, but something in the nature of that introspection was the only method of escape from the clear dilemma of the inner law, which is in each man and has yet to be found.

Comment has only been made in this chapter on the most important aspects of *La Sagesse*. It is preferable to deal with these thoroughly rather than attempt a complete but perfunctory analysis of the whole. One point has, I think, emerged, the fidelity of Charron to Montaigne in almost all essentials. This fidelity has often been denied. For some *La Sagesse* is far less bold than the Essays. It is only possible to subscribe to this assertion in so far as Montaigne's relativism is possibly ontological and Charron's merely psychological. According to others, Charron is far bolder. This Busson maintains only as regards the claim that ethics are independent of religion.[1] Yet this is implicit in Montaigne. It is true rather that Charron's systematic method simply revealed more clearly than the delightful divagations of the Essays that the thought there contained was at variance with current religious ideas. Yet since this is so, it remains somewhat astonishing that many seventeenth-century writers should, in attacking Charron, have made a practice of studiously ignoring the source of his ideas, or of expressly excepting the Essays from their censure. Their reasons for doing so may be left for investigation in another chapter. The effect, then, of *La Sagesse* was to increase the dissemination and intensify the influence of the Essays. Their ideas are the same ideas in the main, but we may yet find it possible to draw some inferences as to the cup in which different classes of readers preferred to drink their draught.

[1] *Sources du Rationalisme*, p. 456.

CHAPTER VIII

THE NEW AGE

W HAT was the size and nature of the public who read the Essays in the seventeenth century ? Towards its close, when new impressions had ceased to appear and the book was on the Index, Huet, Bishop of Avranches, was to write of Montaigne :

. . . Son esprit libre, son style varié et ses expressions métaphoriques lui ont principalement mérité cette grande vogue, dans laquelle il a été pendant plus d'un siecle, et où il est encore aujourd'hui: car c'est, pour le bien dire, le Bréviaire des honnêtes paresseux et des ignorants studieux qui veulent s'enfariner de quelque connaissance du monde et de quelque teinture de lettres. A peine trouveriez-vous un gentilhomme de campagne qui veuille se distinguer des preneurs de lièvres sans un Montaigne sur sa cheminée.[1]

But the book was already a classic, was already to be found in the country-houses—even in the ' Horseback Halls ' of France —at the very outset of the century.

Michel de Marolles (1600–81), in a delightful description of his own childhood spent in the depths of Touraine, gives us, under the rubric ' bibliothèque de campagne ', a list of the few books which formed the household library about 1607. Here we have Homer in De Certon's translation, Ovid's *Metamorphoses* in that of François Habert, Ronsard, Du Bartas, Robert Garnier, Amyot's Plutarch, Du Haillan's History, Amadis of Gaul, the pious works of Grenada, and the Essays of Michel de Montaigne.[2] Henri de Campion, born just over a decade later, tells us how under his uncle, a country gentleman of Normandy, he was brought up on three authors, Plutarch, Seneca and Montaigne, of whom the two latter are still his favourites.[3] Thus we are

[1] *Huetiana*, Art. VI. For Huet on the Essays see p. 426. For a discussion of the phrase, *Bréviaire des honnetes gens*, &c., see below, p. 116, note 3.
[2] Michel de Marolles : *Mémoires*, 1656, folio p. 9.
[3] Henri de Campion : *Mémoires* (Bib. Elzevir), pp. 5, 6.

already justified in saying that Montaigne had become a stan-
dard author, read by even those whose reading was not wide.
He was, from the very beginning of the century, a classic to be
placed alongside the classics of antiquity. This makes it often
hard to know how far what have become current ideas are really
consciously the echo of the Essays ; similarly, to-day many of
the ideas of Nietzsche or Bergson form part of the mental equip-
ment of those who are not directly acquainted with their writings.

The height of Montaigne's popularity ought by rights to come
in the first twenty-five years of the seventeenth century, the
time when the Essays were not yet old-fashioned but already
commanded a very wide public. These years, however, are not
rich in the sort of publications where one would most readily
expect to find echoes of the Gascon sage. Most of the prose
then written or published is concerned with political or theological dispute. Up till 1669 a new impression every two or
three years shows the continuous demand for copies. The
popularity of the book seems to be further indicated by the
eagerness of several publishers to share in each edition as a profitable venture. This must be true of the octavos and the less
numerous quartos, but the sharing of folios probably indicated,
on the other hand, a desire to avoid the risk which the growing
unpopularity of these unwieldy books involved. Both the Essays
and La Sagesse were, at least in any small size, among the safest
investments for the printers down to the middle of the century.[1]
It is impossible to estimate accurately the real number of independent editions of the Essays, except by the investigation of
each issue under a different printer's name, owing to the fact
that editions of the same or adjacent years under the names of
various houses of Paris, Rouen, Lyon, &c., rarely differ except
in the lower half of the title-page. Their total number, however, must be about thirty-five.

Since La Sagesse is, in the main, a faithful adaptation of the
Essays, the editions of Charron are germane to our subject by
their aid in the distribution of Montaigne's views. Making
allowance for those editions shared as described above, La Sagesse
appears twenty-five times between 1601 and 1672. From then
nothing until 1768 : pour servir de suite aux essais de Montaigne.
To La Sagesse must be added Charron's own summary and
defence, the Petit Traité de Sagesse which went through twelve
editions from 1606 to 1645. Both of these books appear at
regular intervals of two to four years. The peak of Charron's

---

[1] V. Conrart : Correspondance (Kerviler 1881), p. 268, Letter to A.
Rivet, 18 March 1645 and Patin Lettres (ed. Triaire), I, p. 249.

popularity is doubtless in the 1620's. In the three succeeding years—1621, 1622, 1623—new impressions of *La Sagesse* are printed. This is the very moment when the theologians, like Garasse and Mersenne, are attacking Charron. Another edition of both the *Petit Traité* and the larger book appears in 1625, and if there is thenceforth a short cessation for five years, Charron's theological works still appear during that period.

Yet, setting aside Mademoiselle de Gournay, Charron, and J.-P. Camus (to be studied in our next chapter), the first twenty years of the century reveal Montaigne's influence in a great diversity of writers. Even the pamphlets of the time might be searched not without profit, as is revealed by Louis Godet's *Apologie des Jeunes Avocats* (1613).[1] Godet, having complained of the unnecessary complexity of French jurisprudence with its multitude of local codes, ends with some general reflections on life, partly in verse :

> Bienheureux qui n'a connaissance
> Ni du bien ni du mal ;
> Etant en état d'innocence
> Il vit ainsi qu'un animal
> Qui par l'instinct de la Nature
> Est tout seulement poussé . . .
> Et par trop vaine est la créance
> Qui nous fait ainsi cajoler,
> Que l'homme a beaucoup d'avantage,
> Etant doué de la raison :
> Il n'est que d'être du tout sage
> Ou de vivre ainsi qu'un oison.

Cette connaissance trop profonde est toujours accompagnée de quelque fâcherie, et le tout simple manouvrier qui, ne pensant qu'à son ouvrage, ne reconnaît les piperies du monde, a plus de contentement que le plus grand Philosophe lequel en fin de compte est contrainte de tendre les mains et confesser qu'il ne sait du tout rien, et que rien n'est certain que l'incertitude même, et principalement en la Jurisprudence, pour laquelle notre vie est par trop courte et toutes définitions trop hasardeuses.

La Philosophie Soldade (1604), by Vital d'Audiguier (*c.* 1569–1624), the translator of Cervantes' *Novelas*, is little more than a pamphlet—but again a philosophical pamphlet ! Audiguier's philosophy is Senecan in tone, but the influence of Montaigne is seen both in thought and in style—so much so that some of its pages have the air of a pastiche :

[1] *Apologie des Jeunes Avocats avec la Recommandation de la Poésie et de la Nouvelle Jurisprudence.* Chalons.

Nous avons assez vécu pour les autres. . . . Apprenons à savoir qu'est c'est du repos et nous confesserons que la plus grande partie du monde est de savoir être à soi. Ceci ne veut pas dire qu'on ne doive être bon pour les autres ; mais il s'entend que toutes les autres choses doivent être postposees au bien de l'âme : et tant de vaines affections que tyrannisent notre repos résolues à cette seule. Toute la gloire du monde ne vaut pas qu'un homme d'entendement étende seulement le doigt pour se l'acquérir. Gravons nous cela dans le cœur et pensons que c'est la plus riche devise que nous y sussions jamais mettre.

Audiguier's essay is followed by an amusing ' manifesto ' in which he poses as an ' enemy of the world ' (a phrase which has no religious nuance) and which ends with the Socratic declaration : *Ma science de ne rien savoir, ma présomption de la connaître : hors de là je n'en sais point.* Audiguier quotes or paraphrases the Essays again in a defence of duelling (1607) and in his *Libres Discours* (1609). His fideist tendencies are perhaps also shown in his translation of the *Novelas*, where he protests that Cervantes has too often mixed ' the sacred and the profane ', and where he suppresses numerous references to God and Heaven. By contrast it is worth noting that the rival translator of Cervantes, François Rosset (1570–1619), is one of the earliest writers to imply that Montaigne's day is over and that his work has been overestimated. He refers in his *Amants Volages du Temps* (1617) to ' *les Essais de Montaigne, qui pour lors avaient plus de vogue qu'un bon livre* '.

Rosset may say what he will, but, in spite of the views of a few purists, it would be hard to exaggerate the vogue of Montaigne during these years. We shall see in a later chapter how the Essays were utilized by writers on education and on *honnêteté*, we may also see him quoted in the novels of the period. John Barclay, whose *Argenis* (1621) was the most serious rival to the *Astrée* until the arrival of La Calprenàde and Gomberville, founds upon the Essays a long discussion on the diversity of custom— even down to the wearing of clothes—and makes the King (Henri IV ?) repeat Montaigne himself on the subject of boorish provincialism : *car il n'y a point d'injustice plus grande que de condamner les choses que nous ne faisons pas ou que nous n'avons point vues, principalement lorsque des nations entières y condescendent.*[1] De Lannel, too, in his *Roman Satirique* (1624) refers to Montaigne (p. 604). On the other hand, it is Charron whom Sorel generally quotes rather than Montaigne. There are allusions,

---

[1] I, 16 (French translation). On Barclay, above, p. 100, note 5.

both serious and comic, to him in *Le Berger Extravagant* (1622) and in *Francion*.[1]

M. Busson has pointed out a remarkable instance of the use to which Montagathe, the author of a pious romance, *Uranie*, published in 1625, has put the fideism of Montaigne. One of the episodes is concerned to defend the notion of Providence. The Sea nymphs, who have watched his hero and heroine drown, reply to the author's impious questioning of God's wisdom with a paraphrase of the Apology :

Comment comprendras-tu celui qui est du tout incompréhensible ? . . . Ne sais tu pas que cet Estre suprême se connaît mieux en ne se connaissant pas ? . . . Sois modeste et tempéré en tes recherches et te souviens que la science et le désir de savoir ont leur excès en ceci . . . il faut seulement croire quand il est question du Ciel. . . .[2]

In the case of J.-P. Camus, the great purveyor of the pious novel, we shall see there are special reasons for an absence of Montaigne's ideas, but in numerous other works of piety, we can see how acceptable the Essays seemed to the *bien pensant* mind. The *Impiété Combattue par les Infidèles* (1608) of Rebreviettes d'Escoeuvres quotes ' our Montaigne ' with obvious gusto (p. 144) ; the monk, Polycarpe de La Rivière, after transcribing, in his *Angélique : Des Excellences de l'Ame* (1626), the maxims of the Essays on education and on *l'ignorance qui se sait, qui se juge*, appeals to him by name in favour of a more generous view of female chastity.[3] And Etienne Binet in his *Consolation et Rejouissance pour les Malades* (1620) reprints the essay *De la Force de l'Imagination* which seemed so heretical to Delrio and Lancre.

To complete this sketch of Montaigne's position, we should do well to consider the poets. What of Malherbe himself ? His poetic ideal, so Roman, so monumental or *inscriptive* in tendency, is doubled by an equally characteristic Roman Stoicism in the temper of his mind. It is not for nothing that he was the translator of Seneca, and the friend and admirer of Guillaume Du Vair.[4] Yet a different side of him appears, too, above all in

[1] On Sorel, see below, p. 299. *Berger Extravagant*, p. 414, *Francion*, p. 170.

[2] op. cit. p. 133. See also p. 728 on the incomprehensibility of God (Busson, *Pensée Religieuse*, p. 185).

[3] op. cit. p. 707. This appeal to Montaigne is taken from Marandé's *Le Jugement des actions humaines* (see below, p. 200, note 4).

[4] Du Vair's *De la Constance* (1594) appears at first sight to contain certain passages deriving from the Essays. This work, however, is the mere rewriting in a more dramatic form of the same author's *Sainte Philosophie*, his *Philosophie Morale des Stoiques* and his translation

the more intimate utterances of the tyrant of words and syllables, who is said to have remarked that Montaigne needed translation.[1] Take, for instance, one of the most charming letters to Balzac,[2] in which he consoles him for the attacks of the Abbé de Croisilles :

Ne savez-vous pas que la diversité des opinions est aussi naturelle qui la différence des visages, et que vouloir que ce qui vous plaît ou déplaît plaise ou déplaise à tout le monde, c'est passer des limites où il semble que Dieu même ait commandé à sa toute puissance de s'arrêter. Quelle absurdité seroit-ce qu'aux jugements qui font les cours souveraines de nos biens et de nos vies les avis fussent libres, et qu'ils ne fussent pas en chose dont toute la recommandation est de s'exprimer avec quelque grâce. . . . Non, non, il est de l'applaudissement universel comme de la quadrature du cercle, du mouvement perpetuel et telles autres chimères : tout le monde le cherche et personne ne le trouve.

It is possible to doubt the inspiration of this passage, but what about the end of this letter, which is the summing up of the philosophy of the poet who was somewhat unjustly called *Le père La Luxure* ?

Je n'ai, grâce a Dieu, de quoi murmurer contre la constitution que la nature m'avait donnée. Elle était si bonne qu'en l'âge de soixante et dix ans je ne sais ce que c'est d'une seule des incommodités dont les hommes sont ordinairement assaillis en la vieillesse. . . . Mais quoi ! pource qui je ne suis point mal serais-je si peu judicieux que je me fisse accroire que je suis bien ? Je ne sais quel est le sentiment des autres : mais je ne me contente pas à si bon marché. L'indolence est le souhait de ceux que la goutte, la gravelle, la pierre ou quelque semblable indisposition mettent une fois le mois à la torture. Le mien ne s'arrête point à la privation de la douleur, il va aux delices ; et non pas à toutes (car je ne confonds point l'or avec le cuivre) mais à celles que nous font goûter les femmes en la douceur incomparable de leur communication. Toutes choses à la verite sont admirables en elles : et Dieu, qui s'est repenti d'avoir fait . . . l'homme, ne s'est jamais repenti d'avoir fait la femme. . . .[3]

of Epictetus, and, if these books are consulted, it will be realized that, with the possible exception of two passages, Du Vair owes nothing to Montaigne. Such a comparison also shows how completely distinct in feeling and in style is the Stoical current.

[1] *Bib. Nat.*, Nouv. Acq., Fr. 4333. Anon (towards 1670) ' Montaigne est en vogue à present . . . Malherbe disoit qu'il fallait le traduire '.

[2] *Œuvres* (ed Lalanne), IV, pp. 89–97.

[3] The rest, too, is worth quoting : ' Mais ce que j'en estime le plus, c'est que de tout ce que nous possédons, elles sont seules qui prennent plaisir à être possédées. Allons-nous vers eux, elles font aussitôt la moitié du chemin. Leur disons-nous : Mon cœur ', elles nous répondent

Elsewhere, too, Malherbe's reflections on life seem to ring the changes on Montaigne's formulae :

La force et la prudence sont de puissantes machines : mais si le destin n'est avec elles, une chenevotte et cela est tout un (IV, 54). Qu'on die ce qu'on voudra de la prudence humaine, je ne la veux pas exclure de l'entremise de nos affaires, quand ce ne serait que de peur de trop autoriser la nonchalance : mais pour ce qui est des évènements, il faudrait d'autres exemples que ceux que j'ai vus jusqu'à cette heure pour me faire croire qu'elle y ait aucune jurisdiction. Qui est heureux, il ira aux Indes sur une claie : qui est malheureux, quand il serait dans le meilleur vaisseau du monde, il aura de la peine à traverser de Calais à Douvres, sans courir fortune de se noyer (IV, 73).

When we note certain indications in Racan's *Life*, Malherbe's contempt for learning, his insistence on the importance of ethics rather than religion,[1] his death-bed confession obtained unwillingly for conformity's sake, his remark, finally, that *le bon sens* has nothing to do with religion, then I think we may put him down as one of those latitudinarians on whom the Essays had (as we shall see) so immense an influence.[2]

The admiration of Racan, Malherbe's favourite disciple, for the Essays must also be noted. Honoré de Bueil, Marquis de Racan (1589–1670), was a man of some originality of mind and real poetic talent. His pose was ignorance and laziness, though it may be doubted whether he was either as ignorant or as lazy as he liked his friends to think.

Racan's philosophy is Montaigne's. The harangue he made to the Academy on the ninth of July 1635, ' Against the Sciences ', is mostly a serving-up of certain ideas from the Apology. His letters are full of echoes of the Essays.

" Mon âme ". Leur-demandons-nous un baiser, elles se collent sur notre bouche. Leur tendons-nous les bras, les voilà pendues à notre col. Que si nous les voulons voir avec plus de privauté, y a-il peril ni si grand ni si présent où elles ne se précipitent pour satisfaire à notre désir (p. 96). See, however, his praise of the reserve of women *en une affaire où il y va de l'honneur et de la vie* (p. 32). These passages offer the exact parallel to Montaigne's opinions in the *Vers de Virgile* and elsewhere.

[1] Notice, too, how Malherbe's defence of tradition, of conservatism in the formula : ' the religion of *les honnêtes gens* is that of their king ' has its echo in Balzac, who declared that his religion was that of his mother and his nurse (*Lettres*, I, 14) or the story told of Descartes by J. du Bois—' *Je suis de la religion de mon roi. . . . Et de la religion de ma nourrice.*'

[2] See also III, p. 343 (treatises on civility), p. 369 (rois et crocheteurs) ; IV, 79 (*Cette vie est une pure sottise*).

Je me suis résolu d'écrire sans préparation tout ce qui me viendra en la pensée, en prose et en vers, à l'exemple de mon cher ami, Montaigne. Je le veux imiter en toute chose, fors à mettre le titre et ne pas dire un mot du sujet que l'on s'était proposé à traiter.[1]

From Montaigne Racan learnt how to speak of himself with a good grace. He believes in the irreductability of individual character, hates doctors and smiles at ambition, the more since he himself was once a prey to it.[2] We may find in his work the reflection of the ' happy savage ' idea.[3]

In religion he follows *le prône de notre curé*. His letter to M. Armilly on the death of an atheist is full of echoes of Montaigne. Finally one passage showing his fideism may be quoted :

Cette stupidité que je reconnaissais de moi me fit résoudre à me tenir aveuglément en la créance que j'avais apprise de ma mère et de ma nourrice, sans m'alambiquer l'esprit de toutes les opinions nouvelles qui sont contestées entre les jansénistes et les molinistes. J'ai fait ce que j'ai pu pour les ignorer. . . . Le paradis était ouvert plus de quinze cents ans devant que Jansenius et Molina vinrent au monde : puis que l'on s'était bien passé jusqu'à present de savoir ces diverses opinions de la grâce, l'on s'en passerait bien encore, et je dirais volontiers au sujet de ces propositions nouvelles, ce que disait Théophile :

Quelque nouveau salut qu'on prêche en l'univers
Qu'on ne redoute point ni mon bras ni mon vers.

The questions at issue seem to him unimportant, for like his friend Coëffeteau, Bishop of Marseilles, and Malherbe, he holds that *bien vivre est bien servir Dieu*

et crois que cette justice et cette bonté infinie qui daigne prendre soin de nous dispenser après cette vie les peines et les récompenses ne nous condamne point comme un juge *a quo* sur un petit manque de la forme.[4]

A study of Racan's best poetry, his very free paraphrases of the Psalms, would reveal certain utterances which echo the ideas of the Essays pretty closely. Thus Racan adds to his rendering of *Coeli enarrant* (the 18th Psalm), two ideas completely absent from the original : the disinterestedness of true

[1] Racan : *Œuvres* (bib. Elzévirienne), I, p. 309 to Chapelain, Conrart and Ménage.

[2] cf. *Bergeries : Epître á Malherbe*, and letter quoted above.

[3] ib., I, p. 189, ' *Stances pour un Americain dansant dans un ballet* ' (take as contrast the sonnet of Arbaud Porchère, another Academician, *Sur la découverte du nouveau monde—Rimes* (ed. 1855), p. 57).

[4] *Œuvres*, I, 332 et seq. (see also Racan's letter in *Recueil*, published by Faret in 1627).

devotion (cf. Charron on *La vraie preudhomie*) [1] and again the powerlessness of reason.

Another poet of the early seventeenth century—to my mind the equal of either Malherbe or Racan—the ill-fated Étienne Durand (1585–1618)—supplies us with a perfect example of the poetical rendering of one of Montaigne's favourite themes in his *Stances à l'Inconstance* :

> . . . Notre esprit n'est que vent et comme un vent volage
> Ce qu'il nomme constance est un branle rétif :
> Ce qu'il pense aujourd'hui demain n'est qu'un ombrage
> Le passé n'est plus rien, le futur un nuage,
> Et ce qu'il tient présent il le sent fugitif.
>
> Je peindrais volontiers mes légères pensées
> Mais déjà, le pensant, mon penser est changé ;
> Ce que je tiens m'échappe, et les choses passées
> Toujours par le présent se tiennent effacées,
> Tant à ce changement mon esprit est rangé . . .[2]

Those who read this little-known poet of genius will perhaps feel that in Durand's *Stances à l'Amour*, some of the images or ideas might also be traced back to the Essays.

Such instances of poetical borrowings could doubtless be multiplied, but it will suffice for our purpose to turn to a type of poetry, which is definitely philosophical. It has been seen already how widespread is Montaigne's type of emotional fideism, with its meditation on mortality, on the vanity and ignorance of man, on universal change. One of the places in which this may be found most often is in the *Quatrain moral*. Gnomic poetry enjoyed great favour from the end of the sixteenth century almost down to the time of the Fronde. It is only necessary to consult Guillaume Colletet's *Traité de la Poésie Morale* (1658) to realize how much of it there was. The names of Pibrac and the Conseiller Matthieu are known to every one, if only from a reference in Molière's *Cocu Imaginaire*. Pibrac, however, writing before the Essays, lies outside our subject, and is definitely anti-fideist.

If we take Matthieu's *Tablettes* (1610 and 1620), the *Quatrains* of Antoine Favre, the father of Vaugelas, and the anonymous *Quatrains de la Vanité du Monde*, all of which were frequently reprinted in a single volume with Pibrac, a fair notion of this literature may be obtained. Matthieu is Senecan. Death and

---

[1] See below, p. 133 and H. Bremond, *La Querelle du Pur Amour*, 1933.
[2] *Méditations d' E.D.*, 1612 (republished from only known copy by F. Lachevre : *Le Livre d'Amour d'Etienne Durand* (1907).

change—since all change leads to death—are his subjects. There is much here that partakes of the nature of a ' critique of satisfaction ', but it is almost impossible to make *rapprochements* with the ideas of Montaigne ; much less can we speak of influence. Favre is purely Christian. To use the distinction employed in the titles of this gnomic *genre*, his verses are ' spiritual ' not ' moral '. The third and anonymous author, inspired to some extent by Ecclesiastes, succeeds in bringing together a remarkable number of ideas with which we are already familiar, in the space of seventy-four four-line verses. Nothing exists in the mind but what has been in the senses ; sense-perception is fallible, therefore knowledge is uncertain : all authority for knowledge is merely human : climate, by its action on humours of men is an instrument of universal change : all these are represented, and ' All is vanity, all is flux ' is conveyed in a number of images, some of which seem to have been stolen and condensed in those stanzas of J.-P. Camus which close the tenth volume of his *Diversités* (see below).

Even with the anonymous author, it is going too far to speak of an influence of the Essays. These ideas are common to Montaigne and Renaissance Humanism in general. On the evidence of a dozen examples of *quatrains* from 1587 to 1658, it is fair to say that most of this literature is purely and exclusively Christian as opposed to humanist in its inspiration. Two examples, however, of the influence of Montaigne and also Charron on authors of this kind may be found among the latest and the most ambitious collections of *quatrains* : the *Sentiments Universels* of Pierre Forget de la Picardière and the *Sentiments Chrétiens, Politiques et Moraux* of Antoine Garaby de la Luzerne. The former was first published only in 1630, the latter in 1642, and, since their interest differs considerably from the collections mentioned above, they, as also the famous *Quatrains du Déiste*, will be discussed in connexion with Régnier, Théophile and other satirists.

Up till now we have been mainly concerned in this chapter with writers who belong to what Bremond has called *L'Humanisme Dévot*. As a typical example of this feature of the Counter-Reformation we shall turn to J.-P. Camus, bishop of Belley. In order to show, however, how a less devout humanism explains the estrangement of many good Catholics from the Essays, it is necessary to study thereafter the verse satires which are such a feature of the first half of the seventeenth century in France. Only thus do the attacks of Garasse and Silhon become comprehensible.

CHAPTER IX

JEAN PIERRE CAMUS—I : *LE BRÉVIAIRE DES GENTILSHOMMES*

' Il a été un temps que ce livre m'était journellement en pratique, comme Tertullien à Saint Cyprien : oui, Achante, lorsque je professais une autre robe que celle à laquelle je me suis finalement attaché.'

J. P. CAMUS.

READERS of Sainte Beuve will remember Jean Pierre Camus, bishop of Belley and bosom-friend of St. François de Sales, as *l'Elisée un peu folâtre de ce radieux Elie, toujours mené par la fleurette, par le son, par le calembour.*[1] One of the sisters of Port-Royal found the reading of his novels disturbing to her spirit of devotion. Perhaps the Abbé Bremond [2] does more justice to his real qualities, when he says that here was the man who might have given France a worthy translation of the Bible. Camus himself calls St. François de Sales his Elijah, but there was an earlier prophet in his life— one, he says, who was to him as Tertullian to St. Cyprian, and whose *ipse dixit* was for ever on his lips, a singular Tertullian— Michel de Montaigne. For at least a dozen years the Essays were his favourite reading, and the eleven volumes of the *Diversités* (1609–18) bear, on a very handsome proportion of their twelve thousand odd pages, the marks of his youthful enthusiasm. Still more important is the appreciation of Montaigne which Camus wrote to a friend at the moment when he had decided that he would have to give up reading him. As a piece of writing it is among his best efforts. As a piece of literary criticism, it shows more insight than many famous writers on Montaigne have shown since. For Montaigne was still almost a contemporary, though his young admirer was born four years after the

---

[1] The ' mad dog Garasse ' is, for Sainte Beuve, *une plume assez dans le genre de Camus.* (*Histoire du Port Royal*, ed. 1860, II, p. 241 (and I, 255 ; II, 311.)

[2] H. Bremond : *Histoire du Sentiment Religieux en France*, Vol. I, L'Humanisme Dévot.

'first Essays' appeared. And Camus has at least some inside knowledge of Montaigne as a man. It is not without interest to hear him say :

Un galant homme qui a vu cet auteur et conféré avec lui souvent m'a dit qu'il parlait tout de même qu'il écrit d'une façon brusque, avec des clauses serrées, et persuadait vivement et puissammant ce qu'il voulait, en termes fort clairs, expressifs and énergiques :

or to hear perhaps the same friend vouch for the truth of Montaigne's self-portrait, *livre uniforme à son auteur*. Add to this the fullness of treatment which Camus gives to his subject and the interesting form it takes (of *personal* reasons against a devotion to the Essays), and it will be seen that this letter, printed in a volume of the *Diversités*, is capital as a historical document for the cult of Montaigne.

Camus was born on the 3rd of November 1584. His father, governor of Etampes, came of a family distinguished in the magistrature and at the Bar. He was brought up with a large family of brothers and sisters, fifteen all told, and he learnt his Latin, like Montaigne, by the direct method. His father was later induced to send him to school much against the advice of his tutor, but there they continued the same method together.[1] He then studied Jurisprudence and was a doctor of laws by the time he was eighteen.

About 1605 Camus appears to have suddenly decided to take orders. In one of his letters he refuses to divulge the motives of his vocation, which, he insinuates, were *domestiques et privées*.[2] The family decided that the young man should enjoy a good ecclesiastical post, failing a temporal one, and in 1608 Henri IV was induced to appoint him to the diocese of Belley which had been four years vacant. Camus, who owed this honour in part to his budding reputation as a preacher, was installed and consecrated on the 30th of August 1609 at the age of twenty-five by St. François de Sales, henceforth his intimate friend and adviser.

Monsieur de Belley, *un des hommes de France qui a le plus fait*

---

[1] *Diversités*, VI, 390 et seq. Camus tells us he has adopted the same method with a young brother he has with him at Belley.

[2] The suggested identification of Camus with the character of one of his novels, *Alexis*, is extremely doubtful, and, even though some part of the romantic story which is told there of the hero's conversion and persecution by his family may be true, there is much which is incompatible with what may be deduced from the *Diversités*. See F. Rousseau, *Revue des Études Historiques*, Jan.–Mars 1925.

de volumes,[1] was a precocious youth.   He tells us how he excused
his *avortons nés avant terme* to St. François.   These early writings
are to be found in his *Diversités*.   Turn to the eighth volume,
published in 1613, and containing a selection of his personal
correspondence.   Five letters are addressed to a certain Achante.[2]
Camus blames Achante for his affectation.   He has received from
him a letter about the death of a friend, which he finds too well
written to be a genuine expression of grief, and he wonders
whether, since Achante has borrowed from the Essays, he re-
sembled Montaigne in his affection for his dead friend.   As for
borrowing—' nourishing oneself '—he approves of it as a general
method, and particularly the imitation of Montaigne.   *Je suis
partial à celui-là non pour l'imiter, car je ne saurais d'autant
que mon naturel m'aliène de son style, mais pour l'admirer.*
The third letter is a development of this remark and tells us
why he, Camus, a priest and bishop, should not imitate Montaigne and why Achante, who is a soldier and a courtier, should.
Had Camus worn a sword himself, he would have followed Montaigne in all things.   He is the *bréviaire des gentilshommes*,[3] a

[1] Tallemant : *Historiettes* (ed. Paris), IV, 148.   The Catalogue of the
Bibliothèque Nationale credits Camus with close on 200 volumes.   He
composed thirty-five volumes of novels between 1620 and 1630.

[2] The first of these letters (*Diversités*, VIII, p. 405) was written in 1610
or 1611.   Who is Achante ?   In Camus' earliest novel, *La Mémoire de
Darie* (1619), which represents the story of the marriage of the brother
of St. François and the daughter of Sainte Chantal, the husband of the
latter, the baron de Chantal, appears under the name of Achante.   He
was, however, killed in a shooting accident in 1600.   His son, Celse
Bénigne de Rabutin, the father of Madame de Sevigné, might seem a
possibility.   He was, however, born in 1596.   Now the last letter to
Achante entitled *Vaine Poursuite d'Affaires*, which for purposes of argument we may date just before publication in 1613 (op. cit., p. 465), refers
to a useless visit to the Court made by Achante.   The terms in which
this is spoken of are certainly vague, but they hardly suit the hypothesis
that the recipient was only seventeen years old.

[3] The Cardinal Du Perron is said to have called the Essays ' le Bréviaire
des Courtisans '.   This remark is not in the *Perroniana*, though it may
be hidden, unindexed somewhere in the three large folio volumes of his
works.   The earliest reference to it I have found is in the *Honnête Garçon*
of F. de Grenailles (1642) p. 188.   Lancre makes a reference to this
remark of Camus in his *Livre des Princes* (1616, p. 281) : ' quelqu'un a
dit des Essais du Sieur de Montaigne, que c'était le Bréviaire des Gentilshommes, dans lequel il trouvait toujours des grâces nouvelles : je ne sais
s'il entend le louer par là.   Car s'il veut dire qu'il est aussi ordinaire
aux Gentilshommes que leur bréviaire, il s'en trouve fort peu faisans
profession d'armes qui l'ayent en main ni qui y daignent seulement
jeter les yeux : néanmoins je veux croire qu'il ne l'a dit en mauvaise
part '.   (Montaigne himself had said of Amyot : ' C'est notre bréviaire '
(*Essais*, II, 4, p. 45).)   On this incomplete evidence, we should do better

man learned in the art of living.   He has read and re-read him, always to find new beauties.   He is all pith, every word counts. ' A pity,' says Camus, almost too characteristically, ' he has not written more.'   Yet Montaigne's manner, free and involved, with its constant digressions is the style for a gentleman writing, as he was, for his own pleasure.   It will not do for a bishop, above all, for a man who is by nature an imitator.   Why, as he writes of Montaigne, he instinctively imitates his style !   It has crept into his writing in the past, and it is for this *literary* reason he has made up his mind to give up reading—except occasionally —*cette douce et contagieuse Syrène.*

Achante, however, he says, cannot do better than imitate Montaigne, the model of that negligence and learned ignorance which becomes a gentleman.   He has a few Gasconisms, it is true, and he often coins words, but with such success that he ought rather to be praised than blamed for doing so.   Montaigne's manner, however, makes him a hard nut to crack, and it is not easy to extract the real marrow of his book.   ' I laugh,' Camus says, with perhaps a malicious reference to Mademoiselle de Gournay, ' to hear any woman assume a well-informed-ness on this subject.   He has no nourishment for such feeble jaws.'

In the matter of quotations Montaigne is a master, but here again Camus finds it impossible to adopt his method.   He condemns the fashion of the day in cramming the margins with references and quotation in the original tongue, while only using translations in the text itself ; for variety should be the ideal aimed at.   Achante should quote as Montaigne does, from memory, often ignorant of the source of his quotation.   Let him put it in Latin when it so enters his head, for if pedantry brought in this affected precision of learning, the courtier's affectation of ignorance is no better.

The second reason which Camus gives for not imitating the Essays is Montaigne's brevity.   This soldierly terseness is suited to the man and the robe, and thus also to Achante.   For himself, he would not altogether despair of approaching this difficult ideal, but he has no wish to, not from any dislike but simply from necessity.   In a man who must preach almost every day of his life this concise style would be difficult in delivery. It would be actually injurious to the clearness of his meaning.

to set down the *bréviaire des courtisans* as a variant on Camus, until some reference to Du Perron earlier than that of Grenailles comes to hand.
   Jean Puget de la Serre's *Le Bréviaire des Courtisans* (Brussels, 1630), a bad piece of pious eloquence, has no connexion with the Essays.

Nor is it in his genius to be brief, and to affect what was natural in Montaigne would be unnatural in him.

Thirdly, as a priest he must avoid all unseemliness of language. He is inclined to think Montaigne a little too free of speech, yet he adds, ' it is with such a manner that he is always as good as forgiven in advance ' *Il rebrasse le haillon de la sotte honte bien haut*,[1] but it is in order that we may blush for our vices, nor does he ever spare himself. When Montaigne's condition is considered, he seems to Camus amply justified, nor would Montaigne's licence ever prevent him from reading the Essays, even though he may not imitate him.

It is however the danger of speaking too much of himself which induced him in the end to give up reading Montaigne, for this infection had crept even into his earlier Discourses. Yet this again is no reflection on the author, ' for he is the subject of his book, not I of mine '. ' *Je désire me former, non me réciter, et m'instruire en enseignant autrui, non pas me représenter.*' This self-representation is indeed a unique quality in Montaigne— ' this pilgrim ', as he quaintly calls him.[2] None has equalled him and none preceded him, and none are likely to follow him. He is the ' Phoenix of this Matter ', recording, as he does, a private life ; not his acts but himself, his character, virtues and vices are his subject. He has no vanity in this and shows himself as he is and not as he might be. ' But why should we believe him speaking of himself ? ' asks an imaginary objector. ' Why not ? ' replies Camus ! ' It is a popular error to believe a third person speaking of another, rather than a man speaking of himself.' His one design was to study himself. His art is that of taking his own pulse, and indeed

le plus propre office et emploi de l'homme est se connaître soi-même nettement et sans flatterie : qui est le plus haut point de la saine Philosophie et le plus haut étage de la sapience selon Socrate, Socrate pour cela jugé par l'Oracle pour le plus sage de son temps. Et il est, ce me semble, arrivé bien proche du but de son entreprise, s'il eût voulu avancer d'un pas dans sa réformation.

What then was this one point ? Camus defends his author from the charges of Epicureanism and Atheism. His enthusiastic review has been so complete that one is left wondering whether he at bottom thinks Montaigne was not quite orthodox in his religion, or whether, as is indeed more likely, he refers to *cette imperfection d'être enclin à l'amour* ; for he seems most indignant with the more serious accusations against Montaigne.

[1] cf. *Essais*, III, 5, p. 84.
[2] See *Dict. Académie : pèlerin :* homme fin, gaillard, bon apôtre.

Free of tongue, he exclaims, how should that make him an Epicurean, still less an Atheist? He was of a sensual nature, if you like, a man ' who liked to live and feel himself alive ', but there are no signs that *that* ever made him forget his duty to God or his neighbour. He praises Epicurus, you say. So does Seneca. Epicurus has suffered much from the attacks of ignorance. The letter he wrote on his dying day to Hermarchus is enough to show the quality of his virtue. But he says virtue lies in pleasure! There is, says Camus, echoing his beloved Montaigne, as much and more pleasure in virtue than in vice. Is any willing act done without pleasure, not only eating, drinking, sleeping, but thinking, praying, reasoning? Is there not pleasure even in weeping, in sadness and in the tortures of martyrdom? This is a mere verbal prejudice, and to scan Montaigne closely he seems rather something of a Stoic. His resolutions against death, poverty and pain are taken from stoical arguments. Even his style smacks of the Stoic.[1] But had he been still more sensual, how many men in his walk of life whose most serious occupations are hunting, dancing, and making love, leave the world to acquire by study a true and solid virtue and to secure themselves against the strokes of fortune?[2]

As for those who call him *athée couvert*, they are either totally ignorant or malicious. Everywhere he protests his piety and defends the true religion, to which he is always respectful. If he does not treat such questions deeply, it is because it is not his affair. ' What then is the object of the Apology? ' so he has been asked by one of Montaigne's critics. Not what you think, says Camus; he had more conscience and fear of God than you imagine.

C'était un auteur qu'il avait traduit en Français, et qui, ayant été diversement reçu par les mains des hommes, l'obligea à le défendre contre ceux qui condamnaient cette Théologie Naturelle, comme la foi ne dépendant pas des preuves ni arguments de l'esprit humain, ce qu'il avoue ingénuement. Mais il montre qu'encore après la foi la raison humaine, comme la servante après la maîtresse, peut apporter quelque lumière.

---

[1] Cf. *Diversités* VIII., pp. 439, 440. ' Pauvre jugement, à mon gré, sur ce livre, celui de Bèze, ainsi que m'a dit l'avoir entendu de sa bouche un brave et docte Comte de nos montagnes Savoysiennes, savoir que le Montaigne avait corrompu la langue française, comme Lipsius, ce grand homme en toute littérature . . . avait gâté la Latine.' Lipsius modelled himself on Seneca.

[2] In praising the Essay on ' Some Verses of Virgil ', he remarks curiously that Montaigne is something of a Platonist in general and in particular in that Essay in his treatment of love.

' Granted, but he says animals have reason,' replies the objector. A fine argument, says Camus, to pretend that because Montaigne, following Plutarch, has shown how nearly some operations of instinct among the beasts approach human reason, *therefore*, he is an Atheist.

— De plus, il semble qu'il nous veut abrutir et ôter la raison.

— Nullement, mais il empoigne ce lieu commun de la philosophie, où les misères de l'homme tant corporelles que spirituelles sont dépeintes, et montre que nous abusons tellement de notre raison qu'au lieu de nous en servir en bien, elle nous sert d'un outil de dépravation. . . . Tirez de là, pour voir, un argument qu'il soit Athée.

— Enfin il a ce but principal de prouver qu'avec la seule lumière naturelle, nous pouvons encore venir à la reconnaissance d'une divinité.

— Et concluez de la qu'il soit Athée ! De vrai qu'il en parle fort ambiguement, obscurément et par ambages en tout ce discours, il le faut avouer, mais c'était plus par crainte de définir rien contraire à la créance de l'Eglise que pour désir qu'il eut d'avancer rien de nouveau ni de violer aucune opinion particulière.[1]

This last part of Camus' defence of the Apology may seem a trifle obscure. That is because he makes the imaginary critic change his ground. The second objection, that Montaigne assumes that by reason one can recognize the existence of a Divinity, is only comprehensible from an extreme fideist point of view. While the first, that Montaigne has the impiety to be a sceptic, is, on the other hand, a rationalistic objection. To that kind of remark Camus has a ready reply, but he evades the issue on the second count and merely alleges the confusion and the reserve of Montaigne's work. Camus obviously, however, understands the Apology pretty thoroughly, for he had himself imitated it a few years before, and he held the same views even in 1618 and 1619, as we shall see.

The most general virtue of the Letter is its complete sympathy. Camus puts himself unreservedly in the shoes of the author he is criticizing. He justifies Montaigne by Montaigne's circumstances and intentions. He couples his enthusiasm with a detachment due to the conditions under which he was writing. He is, to some extent, an excellent critic by the mere accident of having had to see clearly the reasons for which he must abandon the reading of his *auteur familier*. Yet he understood, far better than even Mademoiselle de Gournay, that Montaigne's study of himself was really the centre of the book, and this is the immense superiority of both of them over most of the more

[1] ib., pp. 453, 454.

serious critics of the Essays from Pasquier to Malebranche, though the ' conceit ' of a ' portrait of the author ' had, as we know, caught the imagination of many readers from the first. For Camus, however, the point of departure of the Essays is the retreat of the author from the world that *he may order his life*, and arm himself against misfortune. He sees the Essays definitely as part of a discipline to which the author subjected himself, and it is round the man and his condition that all his other qualities are grouped. The great virtue of this appreciation is the insistence on the fundamental originality and unique achievement of Montaigne. In this study of himself he is like Socrates (' esteemed for this the wisest of his time ') ; like Socrates, too, in his spirit of inquiry and his aversion for coming to conclusions. As a psychologist he is ' the mirror of all the world ', a moralist who persuades by showing us vice not merely as ugly but as ridiculous and unworthy of any ' well-born soul ', and virtue as not more necessary than it is pleasurable.

On the other hand, it is doubtful whether Camus realized the importance of Montaigne's principle of the *maîtresse forme*, which every man must search out for himself. In this letter to Achante he is recommending all the time to his friend the *imitation* of Montaigne,[1] and among his own reasons for not imitating Montaigne he only once mentions his own character ; elsewhere it is simply his social position, his office as priest and bishop. And how far, in practice, Camus was from having learnt not to indulge his own imitative bent is illustrated by the story which he tells against himself. How, about this time, during his first years at Belley, he abandoned his natural vivacity of style and delivery to the consternation of his flock, in order to imitate in the pulpit the ponderous slowness of his friend St. François.

[1] It should be remembered, however, that this imitation is recommended as a *cure* for Achante's preciosity.

CHAPTER X

JEAN PIERRE CAMUS—II : *L'HUMANISME DÉVOT*

IN the *Diversités*,[1] Camus presents himself as the *natural* disciple of Montaigne and a *natural* composer of miscellanies. He gives us a list of thirty possible names which he might have chosen for his book (that of Essays amongst them), and states his method with a definite echo of Montaigne :

> Je prends les premiers sujets qui me viennent en tête et crois que j'irai tant qu'il y a d'encre et du papier au monde, aussi ne veux-je faire que ce livre en toute ma vie, sa grandeur c'est à Dieu de la mesurer, lequel sait les jours et moments de ma vie. Pour dire vrai ce n'est pas ici la leçon d'autrui, je ne suis pas assez savant maître : c'est la mienne.

Such is the author's own account of these volumes. They are, for the most part, a series of *pastiches*. Camus may write about the Kabbala, mathematics, or the attributes of God, and the reminiscences of Montaigne may therefore cease for fifty pages or so ; but as soon as he returns to any subject more within the sphere of the Essays, their phrases are once more on his lips. His chapters mostly resemble the earlier marquetry work of the Essays. The author is not an old man writing from the fullness of his experience, and their substance is supplied by the wholesale pillage of Seneca, Plutarch, and other authors, both ancient and modern, among whom ranks not least Montaigne, ' who of all our modern writers has most nearly matched antiquity'. Even when Camus is expressing some entirely different opinion from that of Montaigne, he will use Montaigne's words if he can, nor is there much difference in this respect between the first and last volumes of this collection. Camus was to renounce his youthful enthusiasm for the Essays in very different terms from those of his letter to Achante, and little trace of Montaigne can be found in his later writings, but there is no indication of this

[1] *Les Diversités de Messire Jean Pierre Camus, évèque et seigneur de Belley*, XI vols., 1609–18.

change in the *Diversités*. Even the *Traité des Passions* (Vol. IX), written with the help and advice of St. François, contains much that comes from Montaigne. Yet I am much inclined to think, from certain passages of Camus' *Esprit de Saint François*, that it was the saint, his Elijah, who weaned him from the Essays ; it is a process of which we have no record, but from 1616 onwards the *Homélies*, his chief compositions during the next five years, show only the rarest traces of Montaigne, and that mostly in their phraseology.

Before going further it will be as well to say a word about the style of the *Diversités*. Quotation may give the impression that this style is closely modelled on that of Montaigne. The reader should, however, be put on his guard. In spite of his Montaignesque phraseology and ideas, his own manner (in itself very varied) is always different from that of the Essays. He is himself perfectly conscious of this.

Je dis donc que le style doux, équable et modestement étendu revienne plus à mon humeur, si ne laissé-je de goûter, savourer et admirer grandement la vivacité, énergie de langage serré et pressant des Essais.

Indeed this is the one point in his criticism of that book, where he does seem to realize the irreductibility of differences of character.

Their great difference is better stated in terms of *speed*, that fundamental quality of style which determines the organization of sentences and periods. The typical movement of Montaigne is very slow, but not invariably : in the Apology, for instance, as if conscious of the immense length of the chapter, Montaigne often seems almost to hurry along. Yet, particularly in the mature style of the Third Book, there can be no doubt of this slowness ; sometimes measured like the Elizabethan blank verse which it resembles in its ' macroscopic ' effect and its emotional resonance, more often its speed is not the slowness of articulation, but a matter of ' rests ' between sentences. It is like a conversation where the author's active mind waits a moment, every now and then, for the reader's assent, reflecting meanwhile on what has been said, ready to go on again with some restrictive or complementary clause, his thought always turning back and growing out of itself. Montaigne shows himself well aware of this dependence of his style on the pause, when he writes in his manuscript instructions to the printer : ' *C'est un langage coupé qu'il n'y espargne les pouincts et lettres majuscules* '.[1]

---

[1] *Essais*, Edition Municipale I, Appendix I.

Camus invariably fills out any remark he may take from Montaigne to make it fit his flowing and rapid style. The Bishop of Belley spoke [1] and wrote at a prodigious speed. In the last chapter of the second volume of the *Diversités*, he tells us, near the end, that he has written up to that point within two hours. This represents, roughly, over 2,200 words an hour, and Camus never tires of telling us—with Montaigne again—that he never corrects, though he may add.[2]

The title which the Abbé Bremond has given to the first volume of his *Histoire littéraire du sentiment religieux—l'humanisme dévot*, exactly fits the general tendency of Camus' ideas, though Bremond has not drawn on these early works. Again and again he takes up some theme of the Essays and transforms it by adding a definitely Christian turn which was absent from the original. Suppose Camus begins a chapter *Des Choses Frivoles* with the opening of Montaigne's essay ' On Vain Subtleties ', the conclusion is not the feebleness of man's judgement but the lesson that the devil avails himself of such subtleties.[3] Unlike Montaigne, he approves of Spurina's self-mutilation.[4] If he writes on ' Self Knowledge ',[5] that knowledge is the nature of man interpreted according to Christian doctrine ; man should endeavour to bring home to himself the vileness of the flesh rather than the greatness of the soul. In another chapter, *De suivre son naturel*,[6] he speaks of Nature with a capital and interpreted according to the Church, rather than individual character. But he goes on to admit how impossible it is to succeed in a profession for which one is not suited, and adds the lesson of tolerance : do not let us measure others by ourselves, *comme si la nature n'avait pas mille millions de visages, sa plus admirable production consistant en sa variété.*

In spite of his Greco-Latin erudition, in spite of the impression of general curiosity and open-mindedness which he gives, Camus is thoroughly Christian in his ideas. It is needless to mention all the commonplaces of Renaissance philosophizing which he takes over more or less superficially from the Essays —the tyranny of custom, the wisdom of Nature, the wise man's consolations against misfortune, which are, of course, a salutary mortification to the Christian.

[1] *Esprit de S. François*, I, § 20.
[2] Again his *Paracelse à Monsieur le Grand* (Vol. VIII) represents three days' work under pressure of time (about 20,000 words). ' *Il faisait un petit roman en une nuit*,' says Tallemant of him later, ' *et il en a fait beaucoup.*' [3] *Diversités*, II, 456.
[4] ib., II, livre 9, chap. 5 (*Essais*, II, 32, pp. 541, 542).
[5] ib., I, p. 33*b*.   [6] ib., VII, livre 26, chap. 6.

On social abuses Camus has some of the outspokenness which represent one side of the influence of the Essays.[1] He writes in strong terms (timidity was never his failing) not only against sale of office, a subject on which he preached three homilies to the States-General in 1614, but also against unequal taxation, and the brutal treatment of lunatics. He is certainly, however, a believer in witchcraft and spells, and is warm in his praise of Delrio.

His general views on ethics reduce themselves more or less to a ' cure ' of the passions, after the manner of the earlier Montaigne. In his *Traité des Passions* whose purpose is *de dresser ces ressorts à la vie spirituelle*, the one element which comes from the Essays and is Montaigne's own, is his insistence on the use of ' diversion ', that term which Pasquier failed to understand.

What belongs also specifically to Montaigne and reappears here is a recurring reflexion on the diversity of things, coupled with that preoccupation with contrary qualities as complementary to each other, which is so characteristic of the Essays. With Montaigne this notion, starting as a mere commonplace or a poetical trope, eventually blossoms out into a kind of philosophical antinomianism. We can see it, in the *Diversités*, dropping back again to a mere metaphor, yet with the imprint of the Essays coming out very clearly in its expression :

Comme la douleur et la volupté, la peine, la récompense, l'épine et la rose, la pointure et le miel, choses très différentes, sont inséparablement collées ensemble par je ne sais quelle concaténation naturelle : ainsi sont l'espérance, fille ainée de la cupidité, et la crainte.[2]

The enumeration seems unnecessary to enforce so banal a conclusion.[3]

The *Omnia Vanitas* side of the Essays appeals strongly to Camus. He, too, has given us an ' Apology ', the *Essai Sceptique à Monsieur Tambonneau de Courcelles*,[4]—the only chapter of the *Diversités* which bears the title of essay. A dedicatory letter shows that this *essai de son art universel* was originally given in 1603 or 1604 as an extempore lecture and that it is one of the earliest of the writings printed in these volumes. He apologizes for placing work of his youth among the contents of

---

[1] See above, pp. 6, 7, 14. [2] ib., I, p. 333*b*.
[3] Take again this from a passage on living and dying well (VIII, p. 303) :
Chose étrange que les contraires naissent l'un de l'autre et que deux routes si diverses arrivent à pareil but : ainsi la meilleure arme est celle qui replie sa pointe à sa garde et le cercle s'arrondit recourbant ses deux bouts.
[4] ib., IV, livre 15, chap. 3.

these volumes written five years later, and warns the reader, lest he should think some parts of it a little too free, that it was written before he intended to become a priest.

J'étais lors [he tells us] tout frais émoulu de la boutique de l'Empyrique Sextus, de sorte que la tête pleine de ses maximes, je me proposai ce problème bizarre de l'opinion, de la vérité, de l'indifférence, ainsi l'avais-je premièrement baptisé, comme vous savez.

It may be true that the *Essai Sceptique* is directly indebted for its plan and its general arrangement to the *Hyptotyposes*, but it is equally certain that Camus has pillaged (often almost textually) a great part of the Apology. It would be hard to find a dozen pages which do not contain almost as many reminiscences of Montaigne. Indeed it is with a phrase from his familiar author that he begins :

Si l'étrangeté ne me sauve, je ne sors point à mon avantage de ce dessein farouche et téméraire que j'entreprends . . . : Que tout ce que nous jugeons est faux : et puis vrai : pour établir enfin l'indifférence des Sceptiques.

Camus leads off his attack where Montaigne finishes—by dealing with the illusions of the senses. From this we pass to the imagination, to the understanding, and wind up with a lengthy examination of all the sciences in turn. Thus the thesis is considered as proved ; not, however, as the author promised, the actual falsity of human knowledge, but rather its fallaciousness. This part of the argument occupies more than two-thirds of the essay. The antithesis is dealt with quite briefly, and with evidently less consciousness of paradox and special pleading than in the first part. The conclusion begins with a short account of Pyrrho and the Pyrrhonists and proceeds to yet another examination of the different provinces of knowledge, with a view to showing, not their fallibility or certitude, but their uselessness and vanity. This is fortunately cut short by referring the reader back to the first part which, the author implies, is substantially true.

Camus is as determined a fideist as Montaigne or Charron, though less sceptical than the first, and more given to the emotional side of the *vanitas* theme than the second. Camus disapproves of the scholastics. Theology is better without such a servant as philosophy. The affirmations of the *Essai Sceptique* are categorical :

Il n'y a aucuns principes au monde que ce qu'il a plu à Dieu de révéler, comme la foi et la science qui en traite, laquelle pour être sur-humaine, j'ôte toujours de ces termes.

C'est sur cette base (la foi ancienne) que notre Théologie étant droitement fondée, ne peut errer, et par conséquent est-ce science : mais se démentant de cette ferme assiette pour donner liberté aux fonctions de l'esprit humain de courir à sa poste, c'est ce qui engendre les erreurs et ce qui fait tomber en opinion ce qui auparavant était très assurée science, et ne semble-il point que sous le nom de Scholastique on la traite un peu trop philosophiquement et qu'on ne licentie un peu trop la raison humaine ? Les Docteurs sont prou sages pour y aviser, mais je penserais qu'il serait dangereux que la raison ne prît quelque authorité parmi ces disputes : nous venons de voir les inconvenients où sont précipités de cette façon les hérésiarches, &c.[1]

In spite of the fact that Camus is arguing here the first part of his paradox (that all is uncertain), we can accept the above as his real opinion, not only at the time he wrote, but also at the time he published, for he reaffirms it again and again in the *Diversités*. All heresy derives from reason. Nor is he merely moved by the dogmatism of the Protestants. We may supplement the *Diversités* by some even clearer passages of the earlier Homilies. In a volume published in 1616 we may note his precise views on belief in the existence of God and the immortality of the soul. The latter is believed rather than known ; of the former he says :

J'avoue avec Cicéron, que l'instinct de Nature dicte aux plus sauvages nations qu'il est un Dieu, la lumière naturelle va bien jusques là : mais quel est ce Dieu, nous demeurons tous en ce point : de là tant de fausses créances qui ont régentés les cerveaux de l'antiquité.[2]

Camus stands here more or less on the same ground as Montaigne or Charron, and many other apologists at the beginning of the seventeenth century accept much the same view.[3] It is perhaps worth noting that Camus, at the time he wrote the *Essai Sceptique*, seems to hold the supposed Aristotelian principle of all knowledge through the senses,[4] though later, and even at this time, he appears elsewhere as a vague Platonist. The fact of the matter is that at the time of writing the *Diversités* and the earlier Homilies he had little philosophical or theological training. What is far more important than his fideism on points of dogma is the emotional attitude to faith and reason, found also in Montaigne himself.

[1] ib., IV (ed. 1620), pp. 284, 294.
[2] *Homélies Festives*, p. 293.
[3] See Busson, *Pensée Religieuse*, passim.
[4] *Diversités*, IV, 247 (compare Marandé below, p. 197).

I have already said that the conclusion of the *Essai Sceptique* is not the falsity of the sciences but their vanity. According to the ingenious formula of this chapter : *nous resemblons a ceux qui songent qu'ils songent : si est-ce qu'ils rêvent.*[1] The constant refrain which here and elsewhere typifies his attitude to reason is that of Montaigne :

Certes, c'est un outil et engin merveilleusement souple et maniable que l'humaine fantaisie, et selon la mauvaise inclination de notre perverse et corrompue nature ployable et contournable plutôt à mal qu'à bien.

If the term ' critique of satisfaction ' can be applied to Montaigne, with Camus its chief form is certainly a ' critique of reason ' (in a non-Kantian sense). The more general attitude may be seen also in the set of verses which close the tenth tome of the *Diversités*, the last volume Camus had the intention of publishing.[2]

The rejection of any claim or wish to verify what is believed, which is the psychological reality of fideism, may encourage a vague mysticism as we have noticed in certain passages of Charron. We find this too in one of the *Homélies Dominicales* (1616). Camus refers us to the same text of the pseudo-Denys as Charron does :

La foi est cette sainte noirceur, *Sancta Caligo*, dont parle St. Denis Aréopagite, où Dieu se plaît d'être admiré avec silence.[3]

But even here he makes it pretty clear that he is not really a sceptic of reason in ' natural philosophy ' any more than Montaigne or Charron were.

One last characteristic, and again fideist, notion of the Essays must be mentioned. This is the theme of ' Pastoral Wisdom ' or the ' Three States of Man '. We have already seen the prominence which Charron gives to this idea. Camus too returns to

[1] ib., p. 352.
[2] ib., I, p. 430b ; II, p. 25. cf. also IV, pp. 219, 220 ; VII, livre 24, chap. 3, &c. (Compare *Essais*, I, 25, p. 180 : II, 12, pp. 283, 309, 318 ; II, 17, p. 429, &c.) Villey suggests some parallels which, on verification, are no parallels. These are Montaigne's own expressions. It is worth noting that in the *Comédie des Académiciens* (Act III, Scene 3), when Sérizay mocks at Mlle de Gournay, Saint Evremond makes him begin :

Tout ainsi que l'esprit est vague et *contournable*
De même le discours doit être variable.
(his italics).

Perhaps more than verbal satire is intended. The words *alongeable* and *contournable* were invented by Montaigne (J. Coppin : *Étude sur la Grammaire et le Vocabulaire de Montaigne*, 1925, p. 94 et seq.).
[3] loc. cit., p. 76.

it again and again, and, curiously enough, he seems on one occasion to echo Charron rather than Montaigne.[1] No mention of Charron, however, is to be found in these volumes, and, so far as I can judge, no other reminiscence of *La Sagesse* ; the parallel, therefore, is perhaps merely fortuitous.

Had Camus read *La Sagesse* ? A young man of omnivorous literary tastes can hardly have avoided doing so. It was not till 1606 that *La Sagesse* was placed on the Index ; it was not until about then that Camus had any intention of entering the Church.[2] However, the fact that Camus, whose allusiveness and outspokenness on every subject is remarkable, should never have mentioned Charron as a base copyist of his idol, Montaigne, is rather extraordinary. If Charron was on the Index, he had not the reputation which Garasse strove to give him fifteen years later. In 1623 Father Nicolas Caussin, another Jesuit, confessor to the King, was not ashamed to utilize Charron in his popular *Cour Sainte*.[3] Even in 1626 Silhon adds a special note of apology to his errata slip for anything offensive he may have said about this author. Charron would have provided Camus with the Essays rearranged so as to avoid the four objections he puts forward to his friend as reasons for giving up reading Montaigne. Is Charron not methodical, clear and impersonal ? His language, could not possibly shock any one—except perhaps the prejudiced Garasse. Camus, doubtless, must have known *La Sagesse*, but considered it wiser, among other reasons, because of his admiration for Montaigne, not to underline the connexion of the Essays with that other even more controversial work. I have mentioned the worthy bishop's fondness for this notion of the ' Three States ', however, simply to give a further example of the connexion of his fideism with that of Montaigne. It was this side of the Essays which was most clearly reflected in the *Diversités*—the constant refrain of the impotence of reason, that double-edged weapon, and, lastly, the insistence on the two kinds of true believers.

At the time of his letter to Achante, Camus resolves, unwillingly, to wean himself from the Essays, while admiring them

---

[1] Montaigne indeed when writing on this point says : *La moyenne région loge les tempêtes* (*Essais*, III, 10, p. 317 B). We have seen (p. 87) the development of this expression by the addition of an *en laquelle se forment tous les météores* (*Sagesse*, I, 39). This comparison we find once more in the *Diversités*. Charron describes the higher region of the air as *sereine, claire, nette, et paisible*. Camus as *calme, net, serein* (*Diversités*, III, 1. II, 8.)

[2] Charron's conclusion that Immortality was doubtful on rational grounds had been censured by the Sorbonne in 1603.

[3] See below, p. 186.

as much as ever.   In his *Pétronille*, a novel published in 1626, we find the following passage :

Et je confesse encore ici franchement que dans mes *Diversités* et mes *Homélies* je n'y ai eu aucun soin de la diction ni du style, me contentant d'exprimer en quelque façon que ce fût mes conceptions, et que, s'il y a des mots étrangers ou barbares, je veux dire qui ne soient pas du plus pur air François sous lequel je suis né, ils me sont arrivés par contagion de la lecture des Essais de Montaigne, livre qui m'était autant en délices durant ma jeunesse qu'il m'est maintenant à dégoût.[1]

Six years later he repeats almost the same words in his *Voyageur Inconnu*,[2] where in the same breath he speaks with admiration of the eloquence of Du Vair, who, if I am not mistaken, is referred to with scorn in one of the racy digressions of the letter to Achante.   The first of these two texts leaves little doubt as to his distaste not only for Montaigne's style but for Montaigne's doctrine, and I question whether there are more than a dozen lines in the two stout volumes of his *Alexis* and the two thousand pages of the *Esprit de Saint François de Sales* (1639–41) which bear the vaguest trace of the author who was once his master ; nay more, in the latter, speaking of those profane writers, Plutarch and Seneca, by whom he set too much store in his youth, he seems purposely to avoid the very mention of Montaigne's name.[3]   It is useless to search the later productions of Camus for any direct reflexion of the Essays.   It even seems doubtful whether any permanent influence of Montaigne on him can be shown, apart from a certain fondness for pithy phrase.

In 1619 Camus published his first novel, *La Mémoire de Darie*, to be followed by a host of others.   They form part of the St. François' programme, the religious welfare of the laity ; in this case, the provision of good light literature for those who are still ' in the world '.   He was encouraged to this enterprise by St. François himself who henceforth dominates his life.[4]   Attempts

---

[1] *Pétronille, accident pitoyable de nos jours, cause d'une vocation religieuse*, p. 444.

[2] p. 90.

[3] A reference to the *Diversités* by Naudé, in the *Mascurat* (pp. 164, 165), makes it clear that these volumes were rather an embarrassment to him in later life.

[4] In 1628, six years after St. François' death, he gave up his see.   Shortly after he began his ill-fated attack on the mendicant friars, whose disorders had already given him much trouble at Belley.   In 1631 he published his *Directeur Spirituel Désintéressé*, which gave him even more enemies by its attack on regulars who acted as confessors.   In spite of Richelieu's

have been made to attribute to Camus a semi-Pelagianism, which, so the accusation runs, he has attempted to foist on his 'Elijah' in the *Esprit de Saint François*. The Abbé Bremond replies to this charge by pointing out that St. François was a semi-Pelagian himself.[1] It is not only, however, the *Esprit* which Camus intends as an account of the teaching of St. François. Apart from his novels, sermons and pamphlets, those books, in which we might look for some connected account of his ideas on religion or ethics, are all 'selon la doctrine de S. François de Sales' :—*L'Acheminement à la Dévotion Civile* (1625), *Le Vrai Directeur Spirituel Désintéressé* (1631), *La Syndérèse* (1629), *De l'Unité Vertueuse* (1630), &c. Their very titles exemplify the nature of the task which St. François and his disciple set themselves—not the defence of the Church, but the organization of the Christian life within that body, especially for laymen, which is just what Camus means by 'civil devotion'. Both bishops are great Churchmen by their practical work in the care of souls. The great bulk of the writings of St. François himself consists of his letters of direction and the transcription of his spoken admonishments to those under his guidance. It is, therefore, useless to ask whether Camus was a fideist in later life or what his opinions on many points of dogma may have been, unless one is prepared to sift the immense body of his writings for incidental remarks.

The real interest of this part of the work of St. François and of Camus is their psychological insight and their interest in character. A greater attention to the spiritual welfare of the ordinary men and women, brings necessarily with it the consideration of how, in the immense variety of its temporal occupations and circumstances, the lay world can best serve God. Hence the insistence of St. François on the inner life, his interest in the problems of the individual ; and it is this interest and this insight into individual psychology, together with his advocacy of the more cheerful side of Christianity, *eutrapélie*—the virtue of

attempts to stifle him, Camus carried on a war of pamphlets for four or five years. After living a life of ascetic retirement at the Hospital of the Incurables at Paris, he became the Vicar-General of the Bishop of Rouen, and it was as such that he had to deal in 1649 with the unfortunate affair of Jacques Forton de St. Ange, a theological rationalist, accused of heresy by Pascal. A few months before his death in 1651 Camus was induced to accept the see of Arras, where, however, he was never installed. It is hardly necessary to speak of the trumped-up story of the Conference of Bourgfontaine, in which he was later said to have taken part.

[1] H. Bremond : *L'Humanisme Dévot*, p. 526 et seq.

' joyous conversation '—which have sometimes caused the author of the *Philothée* to be spoken of as a follower of Montaigne.[1]

St. François, it is true, has quoted Montaigne in his *Controverses*, where indeed he shares, with Commines and Erasmus, the distinction of being the only profane author whose witness is called upon.[2] This early work was written during St. François' mission in Chablais in 1595–6. It was directed against the Protestants, and it is not perhaps to be forgotten that in that same year appeared the curious Calvinist edition of the Essays from the press of Fr. Le Febvre in Lyon. This is the only book, his first, in which St. François mentions Montaigne, and not even there do the Essays seem to have had the slightest influence on him.[3] Their vague resemblance is one of character, and if the great saint shows such a knowledge of the human heart, its scruples, doubts and reflexive movements, it is from his own genius and his unrivalled experience as a spiritual director that this knowledge comes. So that when Bremond notes on the part of Camus a more profound and closer psychological analysis than that of his master—who is sometimes indeed a shade too poetical—one may hesitate to attribute this fact (of which I have yet to be convinced) to his having sat at the feet of his Gascon ' Tertullian '. For there is precious little psychology to be found in the *Diversités*. It is dangerous to be affirmative with such a versatile man as the Bishop of Belley, but, at least, those later works of his which I have named derive wholly from St. François, and there is certainly nothing of Montaigne in them. His novels, too, show not the slightest gift for characterization ; their greatest virtue indeed seems to lie in the turn for picturesque description which they occasionally display.

One has only to look at Camus' *De l' Unité Vertueuse* to see how little in common with the Essays—or with the Stoical discussions on the unity of virtue—his concern for the individual possesses. The idea here is that people should choose one appropriate virtue which, if properly practised, will lead *ipso facto* to the practice of all. The choice of this virtue might seem to bear a superficial likeness to Montaigne's notion of the *maîtresse forme*, but the methods advocated exclude all real likeness. Alternatives are offered as to a means of choice, by lot, by advice

---

[1] For example : Joachim Merlant : *De Montaigne à Vauvenargues*, 1914.
[2] St. François de Sales : *Œuvres* (ed. Annecy), I, pp. 180, 182, 186, 328.
[3] St. François is a rationalist, in spite of a remark (I, p. 146) which might be wrongly interpreted. Notice an express contradiction of the fideist views on reason (ib., pp. 330–2), and a taking to task of Luther for preaching the *passiveness* of belief.

of a confessor, by what is most in keeping with one's walk in life, by awaiting inspiration, or, finally, by selecting a virtue which is the opposite of one's greatest imperfection. The third of these is the only consideration which would have been entertained by Montaigne.

So much for the concern of St. François or of Camus with the individual. It is not merely that the differences which they consider are mostly social and occupational, but it is the whole ' rigorist ' ethical position that they represent which must be contrasted with that of Montaigne. It is just in so far as the ' Salesians ' have occupied themselves with the psychological analysis of motivation that they have perhaps prepared the way for the modification of strictly rigorist ethics. The impression of a less ascetical Christianity which is given by ' devout humanism ' comes partly from the fact that they have attempted to incorporate the humanist notion of the goodness of the passions into their Christianity. Camus writes indignantly in his *Traité des Passions* that the man in the street takes the word ' passion ' as the equivalent of vice. St. François introduces as a safeguard a distinction between ' passions ' and ' affections '. They recognize, perhaps, the psychological truth that nothing is done except by desire (the will being simply a dominant desire), just as a realist like Montaigne does, but here the resemblance ceases. Montaigne rejects the virtue-conflict position because he is a utilitarian. They insist on it because of their notion of merit, and also because their ideal is the love of God, ' pure love ', an unselfish passion, but still a passion. It is against this sophisticated coping-stone of what is in many respects a true psychological substructure that a part, at least, of the orthodox attacks of a Bossuet will be directed. For, from the strictly rigorist point of view no act determined by the passions, that is, corrupt human nature, can have a moral motivation. Hence the Jansenist insistence on what is no doubt the orthodox doctrine, that no action is good unless sanctified by God's especial grace.

Camus himself made a striking defence of the doctrine of ' pure love ' in his *Caritée* (1640). Readers of the Abbé Bremond's masterpiece will remember the plate which shows Charity setting fire to Heaven and pouring water on the flames of Hell.[1] In this emphasis on disinterestedness it is possible to see a certain parallel to Charron's praise of *la vraie preudhomie*, of virtue as its own reward. I do not think that it is possible to press this

[1] The engraving of A. de Bosse, borrowed from Jérémie Drexelius, bore the legend : *La Vraie charité C'est d'aimer Dieu pour Dieu* (H. Bremond : op. cit., I, pp. 184–6, and *La Querelle du Pur Amour*, 1933).

resemblance very far. It is true, however, that the whole
Pelagian temper of the Jesuits and of the 'Salesians,' tending
to a greater confidence in human nature, and hence doubtless,
potentially, to a humanistic ethics, was condemned by Jansenism just because of such possible implications.   Jansen himself,
a compatriot of Lipsius (who became the darling of the Jesuits),
definitely condemns Pelagianism for its Stoical tendencies, that
is, for its claim that the human will is not utterly corrupted.

The Pelagianism of St. François and his disciple, however,
does not bear the mark of Montaigne's influence as does the
Christian Epicureanism of Gassendi, Sorbière and Sarasin.   It
represents, however, a current in the religious thought of the
century which is, at least, as important as that of Jansenism.

In Camus himself, so typical of the more expansive side of
the Counter-reformation, we see that the influence of the Essays,
great as it was, is but short-lived, that his renunciation is formal,
his disgust affirmed less than two years after he had taken up
the defence of Théophile de Viau in one of his novels.[1]   And
even when that influence was at its height, a definitely Christian
turn is given to Montaigne's thought at the hands of Camus.

[1] See F. Lachèvre, *Théophile de Viau*, p. 131, and F. Rousseau, *Rev.
Questions Historiques*, 1923.

CHAPTER XI

LES DEMI-SAVANTS—I

Vous n'avez pas sitôt dit que c'est un Poète, qu'il semble que'ce soit une conclusion certaine et infaillible que c'est un débauché et un esprit libertin.
GUILLAUME COLLETET

IT has been said with some reason that Régnier's ' philosophy ' is that of the Essays.[1] When, as here, it is a question of the mere elaboration of some of the current themes of Humanism, it is wise to speak guardedly of possible influence. Yet these themes are those which are particularly, if not peculiarly, Montaigne's own. They may well be summed up under the titles of two of Régnier's satires : *Le Goût Particulier décide de Tout* (V) and *La Folie est Générale* (XIV).

The first of these two Satires, addressed to the poet, Bertaut, has as its theme : ' No one can please everybody, neither you nor I, Bertaut, for tastes differ.' But Régnier is chiefly concerned to show how much more than mere tastes stand in contradiction.

> Tout, suivant l'intellect, change d'ordre et de rang :
> Les Mores aujourd'hui peignent le diable blanc.

Many blame the author's way of life. He knows he is a little too fond of his pleasures and that he wastes his time. Yet so does Bertaut in despising the world and seeking literary immortality. Such contrasts as these are superficial, but even the perception of physical qualities depends on our organs. What of the jaundiced eye, the bilious tongue ?

Nor is this all :

> Charnellement se joindre avec sa parenté
> En France, c'est inceste, en Perse charité.
> Tellement qu'à tout prendre en ce monde où nous sommes
> Et le bien et le mal dépend du goût des hommes.[2]

[1] See, e.g., J. Vianey, *Mathurin Régnier.*
[2] cf. *Essais*, I, p. 14, Title and beginning.

135

This diversity does not vex him. What does do so is the prejudice involved in most praise or blame. He is a law-abiding
citizen, and yet he is found fault with for his amorousness which
is due to his temperament and his age. One cannot have it both
ways, for it is this same warm temperament that makes him a
poet. Each time of life has its inevitable qualities and defects ;
old age is at once the talkative and the censorious age. And
in spite of their lectures, these grey-beards confound virtue and
vice, and have no real esteem for morality, simply because their
criteria are self-interest or mere imitation, instead of motives :

> Et c'est ce qui nous porte à cette indifférence,
> Qu'ensemble l'on confond le vice et la vertu,
> Et qu'on l'estime moins qu'on estime un fétu.[1]

Of what matter, is it, Régnier continues, to do good or ill
if an arbitrary judgement, whether favourable or unfavourable,
is all we can expect upon it, so that no action has any more its
true quality. The poet here appears to have fallen into almost
as gross a fallacy as those he pillories above ; for, having used
chacun son goût as a personal defence, he proceeds to contrast the
virtue of former days, modelled on ' nature ', with the lax modern
formula of acting according to times and circumstances. He ends :

> laissons là le monde et ses humeurs :
> Et si selon son goût un chacun en peut dire,
> Mon goût sera, Bertaut, de n'en faire que rire.

One cannot take Régnier very seriously as a ' relativist ', but
what is important are not his conclusions, but his considerations.
We have already seen the significance of the line of thought
represented here by ' incest in France, charity in Persia ',[2] of
the insistence on the influence of temperament, and we know
also where to place the Democritan philosophy of laughter and
disdain. It is precisely this philosophy which makes Régnier
connect dogmatism with the weakness of the human intellect.

> L'homme le plus parfait a manque de cervelle :
> Et de ce grand défaut vient l'imbécillité
> Qui rend l'homme hautain, insolent, effronté,
> Et selon le sujet qu'à l'œil il se propose
> Suivant son appétit, il juge toute chose.

[1] Compare this with the attacks of Charron on the ' formalists '.
[2] See passages of La Luzerne and other authors dealt with in the next
chapter for imitations of this verse. Régnier's maxims are often quoted
(e.g. Renaudot : *Recueil Général des Questions . . . du Bureau d'Adresse*,
II, p. 431 . . . ' Mais les uns trouvent la raison où les autres n'en trouvent
point. D'où Régnier dit plaisamment en ses Satires que chacun a la
sienne ').

So we return in Satire IX to the subject of tastes once more. A dominating passion is the only reason men know.

> De là vient que chacun, même en son défaut
> Pense avoir de l'esprit autant qu'il lui en faut
> Aussi rien n'est parti si bien par la nature
> Que le sens, car chacun en a sa fourniture.

Such at least is the delusion of most people, but perhaps there is a way out for those who are intelligent enough to have a little self-distrust—namely, the comparative method, the examination of the lives of the great men of the past. (Régnier appears here to accept the imitation rejected in Satire V.) Tradition seems to him a guiding principle whether in religion or in poetry : he couples Calvin with Malherbe. If Vergil, Tasso and Ronsard are all to be written down asses : *Allons comme eux aux champs, et mangeons des chardons.* The satirist's business, however, is chiefly a different kind of observation : to note the foibles of others, not forgetting his own. For the rest :

> Or ignorant de tout, de tout je me veux rire.
> Faire de mon humeur moi-même une satire :
> N'estimer rien de vrai, qu'au goût il ne soit tel ;
> Vivre : et comme Chrétien adorer l'Immortel.

All these themes reappear in *La Folie est Générale* (XIV), but the point insisted on there is that each man by his inclinations is the maker of his own fortune. Character as the reality of fate is perhaps Régnier's profoundest theme. He harks back again to the notion that every man, even the famous simpleton Cousin, has his ' reason ', which is no reason for another man ; even the animals have their ' reason '. Why then go against other people's opinions ? Régnier admits that he appreciates the ideal of Stoicism—a certain *nil admirari*. Yet, like Montaigne, he decides there is a humbler philosophy which suits him better (Satire XV) :

> Pour ceux qui n'ont l'esprit si fort ni si trempé,
> Afin de n'être point de soi-même trompé,
> Chacun se doit connaître : et par un exercise,
> Cultivant sa vertu, déraciner son vice . . .
> Mais puisque tout le monde est aveugle en son fait,
> Et que dessous la lune il n'est rien de parfait,
> Sans plus se contrôler, quand à moi, je conseille
> Qu'un chacun doucement s'excuse à la pareille.
> Laissons ce qu'en rêvant ces vieux fous ont écrit,
> Tant de philosophie embarrasse l'esprit,
> Qui se contraint au monde, il ne vit qu'en torture
> Nous ne pouvons faillir suivant notre nature.

Régnier's general ideas are doubtless neither very original
nor profound, but they are substantially those of the Essays.
With two important exceptions they are also the stock themes of
the other satirists of the seventeenth century, many of them
perhaps intellectually, if not artistically, Régnier's superiors,
and they show even more clearly how much they have nourished
themselves on Montaigne and Charron.

One of these exceptions is the criticism of social abuses.   It
has probably not yet been fully realized that one of the best
places to look for free-speech and an unvarnished reflexion of
contemporary opinion on a host of subjects, in that age which
saw the rise of a centralized absolutism, is the Satire.   Even
when allowances have been made for the fact that hypocrisy
and venality are the great satirical subjects of all time, the constant recurrence of these two subjects in this period represents
a protest against very real abuses : the immense amount of hum-
bug which was the inevitable by-product of the religious revival,
and the growing dissatisfaction with the sale of offices, which,
so far as justice was concerned, was made worse by the com-
plications of hundreds of different local codes.[1]   Quite apart from
such subjects, there are a fair number of anti-war satires, most
of which fall short of what would to-day be called pacificism ;
there are also many references to the misery of the people and to
the burden of the *taille*.   The common notion that La Bruyère's
grim picture of certain *animaux farouches* is the one appearance
of the peasant in the literature of the age, is hardly borne out
by a study of the satirists.[2]

The other feature which is only faintly reflected in Régnier
and concerns us more closely is the satire on the pride, misery
and folly of man.   The title indeed of one of the poems of Régnier
(*La folie est générale*) indicates sufficiently one of these themes,
but his verses hardly bear out the title so well as other passages
of his works.   Perhaps the best known of all those Satires in
this vein is the eighth of Boileau :

De tous les animaux qui s'élèvent dans l'air,
Qui marchent sur la terre, ou nagent dans la mer,
De Paris au Pérou, du Japon jusqu'à Rome,
Le plus sot animal, à mon avis, est l'homme.[3]

[1] See J. de la Fons, *Le Dauphin*, 1608, VI (Du trop de loix) ; Du
Camp d'Orgas, *Reflexions*, 1689, p. 50, &c., &c.
[2] cf. also François Maynard : *Poésies* (ed. Cohen, p. 287). *Pour
Monsieur le Cardinal Mazarin* : ' . . . le peuple est pâle et de faim et
d'effroy Et dans les champs broute comme les bêtes.'
[3] See below, pp. 395, 396.

From Régnier we may pass straight to Théophile, for Cicognes, d'Esternod, Berthelot and Auvray have little interest for the history of ideas. With the famous prosecution of Théophile we are not directly concerned. An impartial reader of the documents published by M. Lachèvre,[1] will rapidly convince himself that obscenity and probably personal intrigue have as much to do with the case as Théophile's alleged anti-religious opinions. He was no doubt a deist of sorts, but the examination of his works undertaken by his inquisitors reveals little which from this point of view could be conclusively shown as heretical except to the prejudiced eye of an over-ingenious judge. He had no philosophical training. We see him asking advice about the elementary text-books in the very last year of his life.[2] Abstruse speculations as to the origin of the world do not interest him and he resents the dogmatism of his friend Desbarreaux, *l'illustre débauché*, about such matters. Even astronomy, which appears to him the most certain of the physical sciences, remains very obscure. The ideas expressed by Théophile, either in prose or verse, concern man and man alone, except for his conception of 'Nature'—that ambiguous term which may perhaps find some elucidation in the course of our enquiry.

When Mairet edited the letters of Théophile in 1641, he declared in his preface that for force of imagination, vivacity of mind and beauty of concise style Théophile and Montaigne were 'the two Senecas of our age and our tongue'. Théophile himself says more truly elsewhere that he cannot imagine two characters more different than his own and Seneca's. Could he have said the same of Montaigne? There is much in Théophile's verse, and more in his prose, which suggests that he had studied the Essays to some purpose. There are other influences, however, which partly coincide with that of Montaigne : there is, above all, that of Régnier. This is especially clear in the *Satire première*, which may be compared with Régnier's *Goût particulier de tout* (V).

It begins with a comparison of man and the animals, intended to disillusion human pride ; the animal does not suffer from all the disadvantages which arise from different and contradictory humours of men. So we come back once again to the question of temperament and its place in life.

> Ce que veut mon caprice à ta raison déplaît
> Ce que tu trouves beau, mon œil le trouve laid.
> Un même train de vie au plus constant n'agrée
> La profane nous fâche autant que la sacrée.

[1] *Le Procès de Théophile.*   [2] *Œuvres* (bib. Elzévirienne), II, p. 428.

There is a time when every one is the contrary of what is most characteristic of him. So both reason and humour differ in the same person.[1] Each age of life has its characteristic passion and inclinations, even old age, which for Théophile is the age of envy ; for it is envy of desires and pleasures no longer theirs that make old men censorious. *J'approuve qu'un chacun suive en tout la nature* : that is the road to happiness, to happiness even in misfortune. It is wrong to blame a man for following his tastes. Let him be whole-hearted in his dominating passion, whether it is money-getting, ambition, war, hunting, or love. The notion is amoral, but in the idea of whole-heartedness as a necessity to happiness, Théophile has got hold of one of the conditions of *personality*. The attitude is a reaction from the idea of conflict and an abstract universal ideal, things deemed essential to morality and overstressed by Christian ethics. The end of the satire completes the expression of this view ; to follow one's bent, one's individual nature, this is *bonnes mœurs*. The great source of vice is imitation of others :

> Celui qui de nature, et de l'amour des Cieux,
> Entrant en la lumière est né moins vicieux,
> Lorsque plus son génie aux vertus le convie,
> Il force sa nature et fait toute autre vie . . .
>
> Car l'imitation rompt notre bonne trame
> Et toujours chez autrui fait demeurer notre âme.[2]

This condemnation of imitation has also, as with Régnier, its literary side : it is the most familiar aspect of Théophile for many students of French literature :

> Imite qui voudra les merveilles d'autrui
> Malherbe a très bien fait, mais il a fait pour lui.

It has not been represented sufficiently as the application of a general principle.

Most of the leading ideas of Théophile have been already seen in this satire. ' Follow one's individual nature ' is sometimes represented as right because it makes happy, sometimes as making happy and therefore right ; but Théophile at least distinguishes merit or virtue, to which he makes no claim, from

---

[1] cf. *Œuvres* I, p. 224.

[2] ib., (ed. cit.), I, pp. 240, 241. (cf. perhaps *Essais*, I, p. 311 ; II, pp. 398–400 : and especially III, p. 229) : the whole passage seems a development of the views of Montaigne, or perhaps Charron, with whom the notion of a celestial fire inspiring reason in its natural purity is more characteristic.

what is just the luck of possessing ' *une âme bien née* '. Again in one of his letters Théophile giving the lie to a ' foolish friend ', who has quoted him the proverb, ' Everyman is blind in his own affairs ', declares his faith in introspection, which he opposes to the life by example.[1] In so far as ' follow nature ' means ' avoid conflict where possible ', the idea of the benefit of yielding somewhat to adversity seems almost as dear to him as the similar idea of ' diversion ' is to Montaigne.

The *Histoire Comique*, however, an unfinished work, which would doubtless have constituted a kind of autobiography, shows the influence of Montaigne more than anything Théophile wrote, and completes and corroborates the account given of his ideas, as expressed in the poems and letters. It is assuredly Montaigne who taught Théophile to excuse his digressions with such good grace. But that is not all. Take chapter two :

Ce jour là comme le ciel fut serein, mon esprit se trouva gai ; la disposition de l'air se communique à mon humeur ; quelque discours qui s'oppose à cette nécessité, le tempérament du corps force les mouvements de l'âme. Quand il pleut je suis assoupi et presque chagrin, lors qu'il fait beau, je trouve toute sorte d'objets plus agréables . . . je connais qu'au changement du climat mes inclinations s'altèrent : si c'est un défaut, il est de la nature et non pas de mon naturel. . . .

Ce qui ne me touche . . . ni le corps ni l'âme ne me donne point de douleur ; je me porte, Dieu merci, assez bien de l'un et de l'autre. . . .

Je ne résiste point par philosophie aux atteintes du malheur : car c'est accroître son injure, et tout le combat que le discours fait contre la tristesse la rengrege sans doute et la prolonge.

Or again :

Je me sais facilement accommoder à toute diversité de vivres et d'habillements : les climats et les hommes me sont indifférents.

There is more a pose of detachment here than in Montaigne ; yet what Théophile praises and demands is a controlled indulgence in emotion and an appreciation of types of beauty, which again suggests the attitude of the Essays :

Il faut avoir de la passion non seulement pour les hommes de vertu, pour les belles femmes, mais aussi pour toute sorte de belles choses.[2] J'aime un beau jour, des fontaines claires, l'aspect des

---

[1] *Œuvres*, I, p. 216; ib., II, p. 326. (cf. pp. 189, 190 below, on Chanet.)

[2] cf. ib., II, p. 205 : ' Le Ciel nous donne la beauté Pour une marque de sa grâce ', &c. (perhaps *Essais*, II, 17, p. 419 and especially III, 12, pp. 369, 370, 371).

montagnes . . . j'aime encore tout ce qui touche plus particulièrement les sens ; la musique, les fleurs, les beaux habits, la chasse, les
beaux chevaux, les bonnes odeurs, la bonne chère, mais à tout cela,
mon désir ne s'attache que pour se plaire et non point pour se travailler ;
lorsque l'un ou l'autre de ces divertissements occupent entièrement
une âme, cela passe d'affection en fureur et brutalité : la passion la
plus forte que je puisse avoir ne m'engage jamais au point de ne la
pouvoir quitter dans un jour.

The suggestion of control by an eclecticism of tastes, by a certain
comprehensiveness, is far nearer the Essays than the views of
the *Satire Première* on the dominating passion, or the Christian
epicureanism of the Ode :

> Heureux tandis qu'il est vivant,
> Celui qui va toujours suivant
> Le grand maître de l'Univers,
> Dont il se croit la créature . . .[1]

This last ode, in spite of its end—*Jésus Christ est sa seule foi*
—raises the question of Théophile's religious opinions. It is not
fair to discount all his protestations of orthodoxy, although they
were indeed largely made to save his neck, but his real creed
was clearly a short one. There are indications that there
were certain Christian doctrines which he could not swallow :
one of these was creation *ex nihilo*, the other a Providence
constantly interfering in mundane affairs. Nature, which had
a rich psychological meaning for him, represented also, and
perhaps primarily, the immanent power (whatever the relation
of that concept to God[2]), which ordered the affairs of the
created world, and in this concept that of Providence was merged.
  It is probable, on the whole, that Théophile's ' follow one's
bent ', and ' avoid conflict ' become for him fundamental principles in virtue of some hypostasis of nature as a kind of demi-
urge. Did this idea come to him from the unfortunate Vanini,
the author of *De Admirandis Naturae Reginae Deaeque Mortalium
Arcanis*, burnt at Toulouse in 1619 ? The doctrinal ideas of the
group of *libertins* of which Théophile was a member must rather
be gathered from Desbarreaux and the author of the *Quatrains
du Déiste*. So far as Théophile's works go—and his permanent
importance is through those works, immensely popular as they

---

[1] *Œuvres*, I, p. 190.
[2] Compare the comment of Théophile's ardent admirer, the Chevalier
de Méré, on the poet's assertion : *la fortune ne doit rien aux sages et Dieu
leur a assez donné* :—*Il avait accoutumé à dire la Nature* (R. H. L., 1923,
Cahier du Chevalier de Méré), pp. 47–52.

were—it is only on his psychological and ethical ideas that any adequate judgement can be formed. There Montaigne's influence was certainly far from negligible on a poet, who appears from so many points of view a kind of seventeenth-century Oscar Wilde, brilliant, influential, persecuted, probably homosexual, unstable, possessing to the end the charm and the limitations of a certain immaturity. The study of Théophile also makes it increasingly clear how Montaigne was bound to become a suspect in the eyes of those who represented Christian ethics.

Two other poets help to complete our picture of the influence of the Essays on the satirists in the sixteen-twenties. The first of these, Robert Angot de l'Epéronnière, born at Caen about 1581, is the avowed disciple of Charron. The *Exercises de ce Temps* (1617) possess by reason of their picturesque vivacity a certain originality, to which Angot made no claim, as M. Lachèvre has shown. He writes in order to paraphrase, *pour s'exercer.* His choice of models includes Charron and Montaigne. Interesting passages inspired by the former occur in the first edition, while the Essays are drawn on in two Satires added in the editions of 1626 and 1631.

The ninth of Angot's satires (*Le Débauché*) begins with a long paraphrase of the opening chapter of *La Sagesse* on the necessity of self-knowledge as the beginning of all wisdom, even the knowledge of God. Unfortunately *chacun voit un autre et de chez soi s'étrange* ; we thus make demi-gods of ourselves. The fourth, a satire on pilgrimages, containing descriptive passages which make one think of the elder Breughel or of Jan Steen, starts with a close paraphrase of Charron's chapter : *Étudier à la vraie pitié*, an essay in comparative religion with curiously equivocal suggestions as to the influence of climate, and the efficacy and value of practices of piety :

> C'est une chose étrange dans la nature humaine
> De voir que les mortels se donnent tant de peine
> A choisir à leur goût une Religion
> Plutôt par vanité que par dévotion,
> L'entendement de l'homme enivré d'imposture,
> Se formant au dedans des vœux à l'avanture :
> Or le nombre excessif de ces Religions,
> Dissemblables en soi par tant de nations,
> Dans un même climat qui prirent leur naissance,
> Tiennent pareil progrès, ont même connaissance.
> Chacune a sa créance et les points de sa loi
> Qu'elle fait observer pour articles de Foi,

> Ses mystères sacrés, ses Fêtes, ses Miracles,
> Ses prophètes, ses saints, ses jeûnes, ses oracles ;
> Toutes nous vont prêchant qu'il faut adorer Dieu,
> Qu'il s'appaise et fléchit, le servant en tout lieu
> Par prières, présents, vœux et pélerinages,
> Nous étant présent sous diverses images.
> Soyons donc pélerins . . .[1]

Angot writes ostensibly only against the hypocritical spirit in which most pilgrimages are undertaken and the abuses they often involve.

The apparent ambiguity of the passage of Charron here paraphrased has already been explained (p. 84). Whether Angot himself is as well-intentioned as Charron towards religion remains doubtful. No hostility is shown, and his unassuming naturalism may have squared in his mind with traditional religion, but there are a couple of passages which seem to imply that he expected no immortality of the soul.[2] The evidence, however, as with Théophile, is enough to establish a certain attitude of critical detachment towards Christianity, of tolerance, and, along with it, a secular philosophy of life.

It is in *Le Cours* (1631) that Angot's humanism more directly reveals its connexion with Montaigne. Society, full of vanity and change, is the true portrait of human nature, a book or a mirror in which one sees the self-worship of men.

> Plusieurs vont formant l'homme, et moi je le récite :
> Je le peins mal formé, tel qu'il est, je l'incite
> A faire son devoir, et s'il se pouvait mieux
> Je le présenterais pour l'objet de nos yeux :
> Mais mèshui c'en est fait, et Nature est forcée,
> Cuidant le façonner d'une artiste pensée,
> C'est un objet volage et plein de changement,
> Un sable sans arrêt qui roule à tout moment :
> Le monde est inconstant, ici-bas tout change,
> Aujourd'hui l'homme est bête, et demain c'est un Ange,
> Tout y meut, tout agit d'un mouvement divers
> Depuis le haut du Ciel jusqu'au profond des mers,
> La constance en effet n'étant pas autre chose
> Qu'un branle languissant qui jamais se repose,
> Nul objet n'est certain, mais trouble et chancelant,
> D'ivresse naturelle il se vire en roulant.[3]

---

[1] *Exercises de ce Temps* (Textes Français Modernes, 1924), p. 29.

[2] ib., p. 115 : ' Car on dort long temps ', &c. ; p. 137 : ' Et quittant tout au monde ', &c.

[3] ib., pp. 131, 132 (*Essais*, III, 2, pp. 26, 27. Ange ou bête, cf. III, 2, p. 29; III, 13, p. 449.)

Here then is a well-known page of the Essays arranged in verse : the Heraclitean side of Montaigne without any of the familiar religious *arrière-pensée*. It only remains to quote another passage in which Angot describes his way of life and affirms his admiration for *La Sagesse* and the Essays. Others live constrained by the conduct their passions demand of them :

> Pour moi je n'aime rien tant que cette liberté,
> La Reine de mon cœur, unique Déité,
> Et passe heureusement le courant de ma vie
> Evitant les sources de la mélancolie,
> Je suis toujours gaillard, sain, dispos et joyeux
> De l'or ou de l'argent nullement soucieux
> Je noye les ennuis quand je bois à plein verre . . .
> Après avoir bien bu je chante une chanson,
> Toujours auprès de moi on voit dessus ma table
> Charron le Philosophe, et Montaigne admirable
> Qui ne me cèlent rien m'étant toujours ouverts . . .
> Hé ! vain ambitieux, Avare insatiable,
> Tes Etats, tes Trésors te rendent misérable ;
> Pauvres dans la richesse, hé ne savez vous pas
> Que ce n'est rien qu'horreur l'inopiné trépas ?
> Et qu'un jour agités de quelque maladie
> La Parque coupera le fil de votre vie,
> Car dedans les grandeurs vous et moi nous mourrons
> Et quittant tout au monde, éloignés nous irons
> Dormir sans réveiller dans une fosse obscure,
> Comme l'a décrêté la divine Nature.[1]

Angot's last satire, *Le Content* (XIV), repeats what one might call this simple creed of Horatian Epicureanism.

This poet, more superficial than Régnier or Théophile, is also more clearly pagan. He has deserved our attention not only because he represents the naturalism which was called *libertinage* at that time, and because he represents a type of mind which writers of the time unkindly, but not unjustly, referred to as that of the *demi-savant*,[2] whose irreligion is a commonplace of the century, but because he also makes the pretension of having Charron and Montaigne as his masters, a pretension which will be seen to figure elsewhere as an accusation against these authors.

The paraphrases of Angot, interesting as they are, do not

---

[1] Op. cit. pp. 136, 137 (see also p. 135 : ' Les actions des grands ', &c., compare with *Essais*, I, 42, p. 331, or possibly Seneca, Ep. 76, § 31, 2).

[2] This term of opprobrium is bandied about by every one, of course. Angot himself uses it (Sat. X, p. 101 and end).

perhaps demonstrate a deep influence so clearly as the less direct reminiscences found in the satires of Du Lorens. Du Lorens[1] does not mention Montaigne by name ; but he mentions Charron, perhaps with a detached smile, for that is part of his prudent pose, assumed whenever some heterodox opinion as to religious freedom has just been explained with obvious zest and cogency. It is chiefly by the number of themes which he echoes that Du Lorens shows himself clearly a disciple of Montaigne and Charron (and perhaps more of the latter) ; for most of his ideas taken separately might appear merely typical of humanism in general. Here we find ' follow nature ',[2] ' life's a comedy ', ' suspense of judgement is the acme of wisdom ',

> Qui gît à se montrer bénin à l'entretien,
> À bien juger de tout et ne juger de rien.[3]

A favourite and constant refrain is *autant d'humains, autant de jugements*. It is precisely a failure to recognize this essential diversity which makes men presumptuous dogmatists :

> La plupart des Docteurs tiennent que l'homme à l'homme
> Est aussi ressemblant que la pomme à la pomme.
> Que le chien est au chien, le cheval au cheval,
> Et delà, de par Dieu, procède tout le mal,
> Tout l'inconvénient, car c'est cette créance,
> Qui des cœurs insolents bannit la révérence . . .[4]

It is worth noticing that there are two rather inconsistent inferences which are both on occasion drawn from this kind of opinion. On the one hand, this diversity of human nature, as contrasted with the uniformity of animal life, is conceived as due to the loss of some regulating principle by mankind and so connected with original sin. Yet since it makes room for a reverence for the supra-rational, thought of as based on doubt or suspense of judgement, this very loss is a condition of religion on the prevalent fideist view. These two lines of thought are constantly present in seventeenth-century humanism, yet I recall no attempt at their reconciliation.

---

[1] Jacques du Lorens, born at Châteauneuf about 1583, died in 1650 at Chartres, where he was a magistrate. His *Satires*, to which Boileau owed not a little, first appeared in 1624. This edition will be quoted unless otherwise stated ; those of 1633 and 1646 differ considerably in their details.
[2] *Satires* (1624), p. 41.
[3] ib., p. 68, cf. *Sagesse*, II, 2 (2nd ed.).   [4] ib., p. 109.

Diversity again suggests familiar questions as to the validity of reason and the objectivity of good and evil :

> Donques la raison est un bâton à deux bouts
> Dont se jouent ici-bas les Sages et les fous,
> Or la Nature entre eux fit un joli partage ;
> Le Sage se croit fou et le fou se croit sage.
> Si le bien et le mal gît en l'opinion,
> On voit de quel côté tombe la lésion . . .
> Le vrai Sage pourtant doit sentir ce qu'il est.[1]

Perhaps it is Plato, for whom Du Lorens professes an admiration, Plato who teaches *le moyen de rire et de se voir*, from whom he also derives some of his preoccupation with self-knowledge and the interdependence of pleasure and pain, but the attacks on pedantry and pedants seem to betray pretty clearly another favourite author. We see the tutor at Du Lorens' table who is ruining his son's judgement and making him argumentative.[2] Pedants are always rigid and unadaptable, parochial ; they do not understand that the wise man knows his shirt from his skin, conforms to use and custom without attributing any positive value to his conformity.[3]

The ideas of Du Lorens, in general, are, then, pretty similar to those of *La Sagesse*. Let us now examine his attitude to religion. We shall find here an even closer resemblance. His satires are mostly concerned with various aspects of this subject : hypocrisy and venality, superstition, toleration and liberty of speech.

Book I, Satire VII, addressed to the dissolute Valençay, Bishop of Chartres and later of Rheims, is entirely concerned with religion. The attitude of Du Lorens seems to be at bottom the advocacy of a very Broad Church Christianity. Every one wants their own say nowadays in religious matters ; the presumption of individual judgement is to be found even among

---

[1] *Satires*, p. 150.

[2] ib.pp. 169, 170. cf. Annibal de Lortigues (*Les Poèmes Divers*, 1617). His *Invective contre un Pédant*, refers us directly to Charron.

[3]   Otez-moi ces Pédants qui n'ont qu'une posture,
      Qui rélèvent si fort de leur sotte nature,
      Qu'ils ne veulent en rien diminuer ses droits,
      Qui n'ont jamais appris à rien dissimuler,
      Moins qu'avecque les loups toujours il faut hurler
      Et qu'un train si réglé ne convient qu'à la bête
      Non à l'homme qui a la raison dans la tête,
      Qui doit s'accommoder aux lieux et aux saisons
      Imitant le Soleil . . .

(pp. 68, 118).

the ignorant. The arguments of the indifferentists in religion are explained at length.[1] Although Du Lorens ends a remarkable passage with a metaphorical raising of his hands *Je vous laisse à penser où nous sommes réduits*, what are ostensibly his own views do not seem to differ very much from the attitude of the *braves du temps*. Elsewhere, however, (*Satires* II, 6) he protests his orthodoxy even to the point of hell-fire and indulgences. His complete sincerity must be questioned, but it is important to notice the first of these articles. That Eternal damnation was one of the most questioned tenets of traditional Christianity at this time will be seen again and again both by its rejection or by its explicit acceptance, which implies how hard it was for the intelligent man to swallow even in the seventeenth century. Already little boys were disposed to put hell-fire among the fables of their elders. Tristan L'Hermite tells us in the *Page Disgracié* how he called in doubt at an early age a vivid description of the lower regions given him by his reverend uncle, the Archbishop of Lyons.

To return to the Seventh Satire, Du Lorens argues that one must anyhow live at peace with heretics, for one can't get rid of them. Religious wars are horrible. Here is a bitter thumb-nail sketch of a warlike bishop in his armour.[2] Only God's grace can effect conversions. Controversy may be left to Cardinal Bellarmin and James of England. Du Lorens then makes a strong plea for a toleration which goes almost as far as

[1] *Satires*, p. 47 :
    Si la religion va suivant la police,
    Si chacun la mesure à l'aune du caprice,
    (Comme dit un quidam) pourquoi ne ferait-on
    Dedans un même lieu le Prêche et le Sermon ?
    Les braves de ce temps aiment l'indifférence
    Et croyent pouvoir tout en bonne conscience ;
    Disent qu'il faut tout voir, ne s'offenser de rien,
    Que les Religions visent toutes au bien,
    Que Dieu comme un grand Roi nourrit les controverses
    Pour se faire honorer en manières diverses ;
    Pourvu que l'on accorde un devoir principal
    De croire en Jésus Christ, qu'il n'y a plus de mal
    Pour être en différend sur quelque point d'histoire,
    S'il est ou s'il n'est pas de feu du Purgatoire
    S'il faut prier les Saints d'intercéder pour nous
    D'autant que le Seigneur en peut être jaloux.
(cf. *Essais*, II, 12, pp. 247, 248.)
    [2] This *Horace Chrétien*, as he is here called, is perhaps the Bishop of Poitiers, La Rocheposay, defended by the paradoxical St. Cyran for his appearance in battle against Condé in 1615. For Mademoiselle de Gournay's opinion of him, see above, p. 68.

Deism, and which is partly backed with the authority of Charron :

> Si les Religions ainsi que les frimas
> Procèdent d'influence et suivant les climats,
> Comme on dit qu'un chanoine a mis en sa Sagesse,
> Pourquoi ne vivrons nous en extrême paresse,
> Les recevants ainsi que la pluie et le vent
> Et sans se soucier quel bout va le devant ?

Up to this point it is conceivable to take Du Lorens' words as a subtle manner of casting ridicule on the notion of climate as explaining adequately the variety of religion—although indeed other passages make this unlikely—but there can be no doubt of his meaning in the lines that follow :

> Si du père défunt, sans chercher davantage,
> Le bon fils prend la foi, comme il prend l'héritage,
> Si le pur don du Ciel il la faut estimer,
> Qui n'est que personnel,—nous faut-il animer ?
> Et avons nous pouvoir, pauvres fols que nous sommes,
> D'en faire part à force à tous les autres hommes ? . . . [1]

Beliefs cannot be changed except by consent. Whatever I think

> Je garderai toujours en mon entendement
> Que vous n'y pouvez rien sans mon consentement
> Trop libre est ma pensée, mon imaginative
> Des volontés d'autrui ne peut être captive,
> Tous les hommes jadis pour leurs commodités,
> Par crainte ou par amour ont fait des déités ;
> Les rats et les souris ont trouvé révérence
> Chez les Egyptiens pères de la science.

Matter for dispute will always remain. Any single page of the Bible will provide a controversy with the *savants libertins*. What he desires is a compromise with the Protestants, banishing the abuses of the Church.

Du Lorens is a Catholic but a humanist, who like all real humanists accepts the inescapable nature of the individual judgement everywhere except in religion, but cannot avoid *half* accepting it there also. In 1633 he expresses his gratitude to the king for the (partial ?) freedom of speech granted to his subjects : *de dire leurs avis des choses d'ici-bas.* It is at least a safety-valve for explosive matter. In 1646 he admits his admiration for *bizarrerie* everywhere except in religion to a friend who thinks

---

[1] *Satires*, p. 52 (cf. *Sagesse*, II, 5, § 1).

of turning Protestant, and in his self-portrait, full of a certain familiar Senecan stoicism, he says :

> je suis peu dévot
> Non que, grâces à Dieu, je sente le fagot,

yet none the less temperament—and an independent one has its disadvantages—does have its influence here too, it is implied, and on the whole of life.

CHAPTER XII

LES DEMI-SAVANTS—II

Les demi-sages et les demi-savants . . . Vous connaissez ces sortes de gens, qui ont lu Montaigne et Charron et qui ont ouï parler de Cardan et de Pomponace.

GUEZ DE BALZAC

IT is well at this point to be quite clear as to the real matters at issue between the Church and the French Deists of the seventeenth century, even though the most undoubted representative of the latter may perhaps only have an indirect connexion with Montaigne. Let us take the *Quatrains du Déiste*,[1] probably written about 1620, which, after circulating in manuscript, were refuted in form by the Père Mersenne four years later. They are attributed, on rather scanty evidence, to a certain Claude Bélurgey, professor of Philosophy at the Collège de Navarre,[2] and reveal what it was that the Deists (the appellation is self-chosen by the anonymous author) most strongly objected to in traditional religion. This is almost the only authentic document for the opinions of Deists in the first half of the seventeenth century, the most important piece of writing of this kind between Bodin's *Colloquium*[3] and Cyrano's *Histoire Comique de la Lune*, and it must be insisted that, except perhaps to Roman Catholics, the opinions expressed do not seem entirely incompatible with Christianity, and I fancy many modern Chris-

---

[1] F. Lachèvre : *Procès de Théophile*, Vol. II, Appendix.

[2] The evidence appears to be Mersenne's statement that they were written by a celebrated Dialectician who had taught his subject for thirty years (*Questiones* : Preface), and from the description of Bélurgey's alleged beliefs in Patin's Letters (ed. Reveillé-Parise, II, 478). See Lachèvre, R.H.L., 1919.

[3] Busson (*Pensée Religieuse*, pp. 94–105) is of the opinion that the *Colloquium*, the extant version of the famous *De Tribus Impostoribus* (which he dates from some time in the middle of the seventeenth century), and the *Quatrains* all derive from some earlier work now lost. He further emphasizes the *popular* character of the *Quatrains*, which, as I show, are partly inspired by *La Sagesse*.

tians would subscribe to almost all the author says.   In distinction to Herbert and Grotius, he is, however, what Sir Leslie Stephen would have called a Critical rather than a Constructive Deist.

The attack is directed against the anthropomorphic conception of an avenging God and against asceticism.   The main points of the very able argumentation may be summarized as follows :

That God is good, the Bigot (so the author dubs his opponent) will admit, and he cannot command us to love our enemies and himself hate them.   The ignorance of the bigot is excusable if he supposes God to punish the wicked after death for a limited time, but not if he supposes their punishment to endure for ever. It is a foolish objection to say God must be cruel to be just, and a contradiction to think that the love of God towards men can cease.   The bigot's conception of divine punishment involves him in hopeless difficulties.   Can God be offended at what he himself wills ? [1]   It is unnecessary to go into the discussion, which here follow, on free-will and foreknowledge, though this argument may be noted ; if God rules the world by the ' laws of the world ', why does the bigot wish to impose his opinions on every nation ?   The conclusion of this section (quatrain 49) is that there is no such place as hell nor any punishment after this life.

Traditional religion has a purely political origin.   It is worse to think unworthily of God than to deny him altogether :

> Il n'est pas moins mauvais de nier simplement
> Une Divinité, que de la croire telle,
> Qu'elle tire de l'heur et du contentement
> A nous faire souffrir une peine immortelle.

> Qui est l'homme bigot lequel n'aimât trop mieux
> Etre nié des siens par leur ingratitude
> Que d'en être avoué et dépeint furieux,
> Cruel, impitoyable et plein d'inquiétude.[2]

It is unworthy to think of God as angry because the animal in us adds to the ills of our common lot.   Does not the bigot make God punish uselessly, if for eternity, and if to us it is recommended to forgive, how can God himself fail to do so ?   God must have formed us for his ends ; he is our father and we ought to believe

> Que nous parviendrons tous au repos limité
> Par son divin amour pour notre meilleur être.[3]

[1] cf. *Essais*, II, 12, pp. 257, 296 (on punishment).
[2] Quatrains 59, 60.   These lines are clearly inspired by *La Sagesse*, I, VIII, § 2 : ' Il y a plusieurs hommes ', &c.
[3] ib., No. 75 (an agnostic attitude to a future life is also conveyed by the last line of this poem).

And suppose we eventually do end in nothingness, was it not from thence that he created us ?

As for those who torture themselves as penance for the faults of their lives, how do they think God can delight in such mad agitation ? [1] Self-punishment, according to the law, is no punishment, and it is ridiculous to invent new misfortunes for ourselves. And if God does choose to punish us through evil spirits, the ministers of his justice, why should men usurp this office and God's authority ? Asceticism is a refusal of the dishes of life's banquet, and if one may hope for the pleasures of eternal life, why may we not enjoy the former here and now, while waiting for the latter hereafter ?

The bigot does good in the hope of reward, and avoids ill through fear of punishment. His is the only form of ignorance which has sworn loyalty to its own traditional errors. The Deist's virtue is disinterested, and the principles of his life are the worship of God and ' do as you would be done by '. He is the only observer of true religion, and although the Atheist is wrong in denying God and the divine government of the universe, his blasphemy is not so great as that of the bigot's blasphemy in his opinion of divine justice.

This criticism of Christianity is thus made in the name of a moral ideal claimed as superior to that of Christianity, and of a less anthropomorphic and more worthy conception of God. The parallel with the Essays, and their systematic restatement in *La Sagesse*, is then clear. There a criticism, partly implicit, partly explicit, of current Christian doctrine and Christian living is made from these same two starting-points. Yet both these authors would have rejected many of the implications of the Deist poem, and so would the majority of their disciples. The anonymous author is an out-and-out rationalist, whereas Montaigne and most of his followers were trying at once to be rationalists in ethics and fideists in religion. This poem thus permits us to make certain useful contrasts, while the common starting-point enables us to place most of the so-called *libertins* somewhere along a line which, logically, leads we now know whither.

Many of the most undoubted *esprits forts*, however, are not rationalists like the author of the *Quatrains du Déiste*. The best poems of Desbarreaux (1599–1673), the friend of Théophile, for example, are composed on the themes of the fideist ideology : the presumption and misery of man ; the uselessness, nay more,

[1] cf. perhaps *La Sagesse*, II, 6, § 5.

the crimes of reason, the happiness of animals, and lastly, ' life's a dream '. This sometimes brilliant poet was a man of most unstable character and, as all observers agree, always dogmatically absolute in dispute in spite of his frequent changes of opinion. The themes of fideism seem to have gratified his impulse for self-humiliation and, no doubt, this facilitated his final conversion.

It is impossible to read many passages from Desbarreaux's sonnets without being reminded of the Essays, but the influence is too vague, the themes already too familiar to detain us in spite of the merit of the expression.   One sonnet will suffice : *La vie est un songe.*

> Tout n'est plein ici-bas que de vaine apparence,
> Ce qu'on donne à sagesse est conduit par le sort,
> L'on monte et l'on descend avec pareil effort
> Sans jamais rencontrer l'état de consistance.
>
> Que veiller et dormir ont peu de différence.
> Grand maître en l'art d'aimer, tu te trompes bien fort
> En nommant le sommeil l'image de la mort,
> La vie et le sommeil ont plus de ressemblance.
>
> Comme on rêve en son lit, rêver en sa maison,
> Espérer sans succès, et craindre sans raison,
> Passer et repasser de l'une à l'autre envie,
>
> Travailler avec peine et travailler sans fruit,—
> Le dirai-je, mortels, qu'est ce que cette vie ?
> C'est un songe qui dure un peu plus qu'une nuit.[1]

Jean Dehénault (*c.* 1611–82), another free-thinking poet of merit, one of the numerous translators of Lucretius, writes of reason in this same vein.   His chief themes, like those of Desbarreaux are the mortality of the soul, the folly of ambition [2] and a thorough-going hedonism.[3]

Passing on to another collection of *Quatrains*, the *Sentiments*

---

[1] *Poèmes Libertins* (ed. Lachèvre), p. 248 ; see also pp. 243, 244, 251.
[2] cf. Desbarreaux : *On ne foute point dedans la gloire*, &c.
[3] See F. Lachèvre, *Les Œuvres de Jean Dehénault*, 1922, p. 45.
  Notre raison n'est rien, ou n'est rien de solide,
  Etre sage est un bien que nul ne s'est donné
  Et ce n'est proprement qu'être heureusement né.
  Quel que soit l'homme enfin, il est ce qu'il doit être
  Et la nature en lui ne s'est point fait un maître.

Universels of Pierre Forget, Sieur de Beauvais et de la Picardière,[1] we shall now see these, as also the writings of Garaby de La Luzerne, as the expression of what might be called a liberal Catholicism, an attitude differing at once from the deist tenets just examined, although presenting many points of resemblance, and also from the ' pious humanism ' of Jean Camus. Here is his own statement of his position :

> Entre le zèle scrupuleux
> Et l'esprit de libertinage,
> Je suis en doute qui des deux
> Offense le Ciel davantage.
>
> L'un et l'autre tombe en un vice
> Qui blesse la Divinité,
> Car l'un méprise sa Justice.
> L'autre mécroit de sa bonté.

On simple, everyday matters half the pious people one meets are unable to decide anything except after interminable discussion. It is the cold, slow temperament which makes these people at once prudent and vacillating even where choice appears most clear. Forget appears to be thinking of the state of mind produced by an exaggerated preoccupation with responsibility and personal salvation ; for he goes on to tax the devout with dogmatism, on the other hand, about what they take to be matters of fact. They are incapable of appreciating any one else's point of view and think they ' apprehend like angels ', while in danger of falling into the angels' sin. The vice of not knowing how to discuss a difference of opinion calmly is condemned over and over again in these *quatrains*.

The characteristic features of fideism appear in Forget's insistence on the proper way to think of God :

> Il faut que ton cœur le regarde
> Comme tes yeux font le soleil . . .
> N'épluche point en son essence
> Ni l'Eternel ni l'Infini . . .
>
> Cesse de vouloir aspirer
> Où la terre ne peut atteindre ;
> Connaître Dieu, c'est l'adorer,
> Se soumettre, espérer et craindre.

[1] The author, who died in 1638, was a diplomatist, charged with several missions in Germany and in Turkey. The *Sentiments Universels* appeared in 1630 (folio) ; 1636 (4°) ; and the edition of 1646 (12°), for which the privilege was given to the author's brother, a Canon of Tours, is called the fourth on the title-page. I quote from it.

His being can only be expressed by negatives. Man's true science is a Socratic ignorance. Man acts the part of lord and master over the other animals, as if he did not know how little his destiny differs from theirs, while they enjoy many privileges we shall never have.

> Nous sommes tous par le trépas
> Convertis en la même cendre.

We trample on their innocence, in which they serve God without offence. Man boasts of reason : it is, however, the principle which makes him a prisoner, and which, ill-followed, causes all his misery. Reason, too, has a purely individual authority, but individualism is an arch-heretical principle in religion :

> Mais au fait des divines Loix,
> Où manque la parole écrite,
> Les siècles et le plus de voix
> T'y doivent servir de conduite.

Elsewhere there is the written word of God and the Church its interpreter.

Forget argues in an odd way for the acceptance of all that the Church teaches and observes—even purgatory, saint-worship and indulgences. Nothing is wrong, he says, which God has not expressly forbidden, and it is not forbidden, and therefore cannot be wrong, to accept the authority of the Church. This rejection of the individual judgement will be found to conflict with some of his ideas on ethics, and this submission seems partly conditioned by a very strong dislike of the Protestants.[1]

Piety is, of course, of no worth apart from *les devoirs d'un homme de bien*. Forget's position as regards ethics is revealed by two definitions. Fortune is really ' to act appropriately ' : the goddess Fortune of the ignorant is Nature, the origin of all change. Here, then, are our two old friends ' follow Nature ' and ' act appropriately ' identified. The difficulty is to know what really is natural.[2] Temperament limits, but does not determine, choice of action. Differences of feelings and tastes are enormous and render it necessary for each man to judge for himself (except presumably in religion). Knowledge of good and evil, as far as the individual is concerned, is independent of all revelation, yet Forget also says there is no real virtue without grace : Socrates and Cato were only groping in the dark. Duty, too, is later defined in terms of God's will.

Among much practical advice, one or two leading ideas

[1] *Sentiments Universels*, pp. 153-7.   [2] ib., pp. 3, 4.

emerge. There is no real evil except constraint. Though Forget believes in the possibility of complete voluntary control of the passions, constraint is also to be avoided by adaptation. The notion of harmony of character is reproduced from *La Sagesse* :

> Le Sage Mondain s'accommode
> Tant aux lieux qu'aux Esprits divers . . .
>
> Et toute action qui se gêne
> Dans l'effort d'un soin continu
> Ressent son esclave à la chaîne
> Plus que son esprit ingénu.
>
> N'espère point d'avoir jamais
> De grâce en nulle compagnie,
> Si jamais tu dis ou tu fais
> Rien qui répugne à ton Génie.[1]

Are such considerations intended as more than aesthetic ? Yes, for the author goes on to explain that reason by habit or heredity produces goodness, custom makes seemliness (*bienséance*) and nature makes beauty, and for him as we have seen, the concept of ' nature ' means ' act appropriately '. Reason, conformity to custom, and conformity to individual nature all have their place in the good life. He insists in various ways that the moral ideal is a personal one, and that the individual must recognize and accept his own limitations. There is no universal excellence of mind, and every virtue has its shadow counterpart.[2] It is on these lines that the harmony-in-diversity of the Universe is to be accounted for. Finally

> C'est un coup de vertu suprême
> Se connaître et se modérer,
> Et savoir prendre chez soi-même
> La règle pour se mesurer.[3]

The *Sentiments Universels* express the views of a latitudinarian humanist, strongly influenced by the Essays, and yet determined to remain an orthodox Catholic. This, which was indeed the position of Montaigne himself and of Charron, is rendered possible by their fideism. The gnomic verse form renders glaring some of its inconsistencies, as maintained by Forget.

Antoine Garaby de La Luzerne (1617–79), a man somewhat

---

[1] *Sentiments Universels*, p. 35 (cf. Charron, II, 4, § 3 and La Rochefoucauld, below, p. 346.
[2] ib., 36, et seq.   [3] ib., pp. 57, 58.

younger than any yet dealt with here, supplies a most complete
example of the well-digested influence of Montaigne and of
Charron.[1] His *Essais poétiques* (1638) contain a number of
excellent satires, among which may be noted the first, a typical
effusion on the ' infirmity of man ', and the second, a satire on
' ignorant censors', among whose unfair judgements are that

> Charron est trop hardi, Montaigne est trop volage.
> Trop de sujets divers y tiennent même page.

The most trenchant and amusing onslaught, however, is on the
country gentry.   There is also an attack on religious hypocrisy,
which, like most of these satires, was considerably revised.[2]   La
Luzerne's only other published work is a collection of quatrains,
to which he later added a prose commentary.[3]

The first pages are concerned with religion, which must not
be either attacked or defended by reasoning.   Questions lead
to doubt, and doubt to unbelief.   The supernatural, however,
must be kept in its place ; it is as wrong to attribute everything
to ' secondary causes ' as to see everywhere the direct action of
God.

La Luzerne doubts whether any real Atheists exist, and he
is sure there are arguments for the existence of Him whom all
the centuries have worshipped, though for the most part under
various disguises.   God is incomprehensible, to be conceived (if
at all) by negative propositions, as he writes elsewhere in a letter :

Quoique libertin au jugement des cafards, on me verra toujours le
genouil en terre et les mains élevées vers le Ciel pour adorer cet
Être suprême que nous devons reconnaître et que nous ne pouvons
connaître.[4]

Superstitiously to conceive God subject to human passions
is almost as blasphemous as to deny Him altogether.   All
religions are contrary to common sense, either ludicrously below
its level, as in the worship of almost every kind of creature, or

[1] Born near Coutances, he studied at Caen, and formed one of a distinguished literary circle in that town which included Huet, later Bishop
of Avranches, his own cousin Moisant de Brieux, the poet Des Yveteaux
and Jean Lemyère de Basly.   He was also a friend of Chapelain, Ménage,
and many of the learned men who met under the roof of the Du Puy
brothers, the king's librarians.

[2] *Satires Inédites*, Rouen, 1888.   For *Le Pharisien du Temps*, see
below, p. 162.

[3] *Sentiments Chrétiens, Moraux et Politiques*, 1641 (and 1642).   *Sentiments*, &c., . . . *Maximes d'Etat et de Religion, illustrées de paragraphes
selon l'ordre des Quatrains*, 1654.

[4] *Satires Inédites*, p. xxxv.

else above it. This strange variety of belief is itself a proof of human infirmity. Yet each religion claims to be true to the exclusion of all the others although ' the most important, most debated, least evident and yet most boldly determined thing in the world is the true service of the divinity '.[1] So too, echoing Charron, he says that a belief in immortality, though universally received, useful and probable, is known only by faith. The proper motive for God's service has nothing to do with a fear of damnation ; yet the question of personal salvation, of the state of grace at the moment of death, seems to have preoccupied the author in writing his *Sentiments*. The prick of conscience in this life seems to presage the vengeance of God in a hereafter. God is not praised by the wicked here, nor by those in hell-fire, for their despair makes them disown Him, but He *is* praised in purgatory.[2] In 1651, however, La Luzerne writes to his friend, Hallay :

La miséricorde de Dieu ne doit rien à sa justice. Il ne nous a point fait pour nous perdre. C'est là tout le sujet de mon raisonnement.

When it comes to any question other than religion, reason is the principle involved :

La raison est le seul juge de nos différends en toute matière que de la Religion. Pour savoir si tout ce qui se qualifie raison l'est à juste titre, il faut voir s'il se rapporte à la nature.

Learned authority counts for nothing against reason. In matters of conduct, conscience is always to be consulted : *C'est cette seule justice humaine dont aucun ne saurait décliner la jurisdiction.* A worldly sage is any angel's equal in knowledge of what virtue is, but in its practice often the feeblest of men : hence a number of allusions to conditions of grace. La Luzerne's is, on the whole, a humanist ethics : One must be a good man *parce que la loi de son être et de l'univers le requiert.*[3] It is more important than piety, even in God's sight, who looks first to see whether *tu es homme de bien moral premier que traître Chrétien.*
Virtue lies above all, in a harmony of the passions :

> Ce que la musique est aux tons
> D'une agréable symphonie
> La vertu l'est aux passions
> Dont elle cherche l'harmonie.

Not only must they not be suppressed but their variety is to

---

[1] *Sentiments* (ed. 1654) p. 11.   [2] ib. (ed. 1642), p. 58.
[3] ib. (ed. 1654), pp. 45, 154 ; (ed. 1642), pp. 92, 93.

be cultivated, especially since temperaments differ. Virtues do depend on physical conditions, and many are incompatible with each other : *grand argument de notre faiblesse.* He recommends what Montaigne calls diversion rather than asceticism, which is the great error of the weak, due to their failure to distinguish between different kinds of pleasure.[1] Taking up the opinion of Charron, notorious at the time, on the subject of clothes, he insists that the shame which many would feel to go naked is not natural, for the body, ' being a work of God, has nothing nasty or reproachable about it '.

An unpublished poem of La Luzerne, *Préjugés de bon sens,* emphasizes some of these ideas :

> Je vois que la vertu ne s'estime chez l'homme
> Qu'au prix des ses humeurs.

Chastity is very differently esteemed in various countries. He echoes Régnier : ' what is incest in France is not so in Persia '. Filial piety may take the form of killing one's aged parents. Every one has his reasons and the individual's judgement must not be disputed.

Turning to the relations of the wise man and society in which he lives, the debt to Montaigne is very evident. Man is not born only for the State : *Prêtons nous aux autres, demeurons en propre à nous-mêmes.* On the other hand, La Luzerne blames his friend Des Yveteaux for neglecting his social duties.[2] He frequently recommends mere conformity to custom, failing real adaptation. This is the idea which under the name of *morale provisoire* many writers have been hasty enough to imagine peculiar to Descartes.

Les plus belles âmes sont les universelles et s'accommodent à tout. Le Sage fait comme les autres, au moins, pour l'extérieur.[3]

The usual corollaries of this attitude—cosmopolitanism and tolerance—have considerable stress laid on them. The instinctive love of one's country is indeed rather astonishing. Is not every man a citizen of the world ? [4] As for the ' barbarousness ' of those nations who go naked, ' you call them barbarous because they do not suit your notion ; but there lies the crux of the whole debate '.

---

[1] *Sentiments,* (1654), p. 100.
[2] ib. (1654), p. 165, Bib. Nat. MS. N.A.F. 330.   The MS. poem is a reply to Des Yveteaux's famous sonnet, and ends : ' Et se tirer du jeu, c'est quitter la partie.'   On Des Yveteaux, see below, p. 310.
[3] ib. (1654), p. 127 (cf. *Essais,* II, 17, p. 436).   [4] ib., p. 78.

In his anxiety to impress this lesson of broad-mindedness on the reader, La Luzerne turns back to the same theme of human folly, so often associated, both by him and others, with fideism.— ' The world's an ass ; why build asylums ? ' The theme of folly tempers his ethical rationalism. Readiness for misfortune is, no doubt, the justification of wisdom, but the instinctive courage which a mere peasant can show in the face of death, impresses him even as it impressed Montaigne.[1] Nay more :

tout ce que peuvent faire les plus grands philosophes qui étudient la nature est d'arriver avec grand travail et difficulté à ce point d'apathie où les brutes se trouvent d'elles-mêmes toutes portées.[2]

So we end with the folly of human occupations and preoccupations : the curiosity of the alchemists, the attainment of posthumous fame,[3] the plans of old age, and worse still, the ambitions of princes.

> Quelle plus injuste manie !
>   Bouleverser les nations,
> Pour établir la tyrannie
> De nos vaines prétentions ?

> Rien n'est si peu sage que l'homme ;
>   Noé fit le fol en buvant,
> Adam en mangeant la pomme
> Et moi, possible, en écrivant.

Nous avons commencé ce livre par le discours de la Sagesse, l'Amour et la crainte de Dieu : nous le clorrons par ce théorème général de la folie des hommes et de la mienne propre. Je suis homme et partant sujet à extravaguer. Je suis homme, et comme tel inséparable de ces cinq ; vanité, faiblesse, inconstance, misère, présomption. *Nihil superbius homine ac miserius* au discours de Pline qui est bien vrai.[4]

La Luzerne is also an admirer of Machiavelli—*le bon citoyen Macchiavel*, as he calls him—and the *Sentiments* contain a great number of political maxims, many of which testify to this

---

[1] *Sentiments*, pp. 58, 116. See *Satires Inédites*. Introduction, p. xlvii, a noble and eloquent letter written in 1666 asking that the peasants of his fief should be temporarily excused from the *taille* : also his satire, *Le Noble Campagnard* and *Sentiments*, pp. 166, 167, on humanity and thoughtfulness towards those of inferior station.

[2] *Satires Inédites*, p. xxxiv.

[3] *Sentiments* (1654), p. 198 : ' Possible parle-t-on de nous maintenant à cinquante lieues d'ici ; nous n'en sentons rien ; aussi peu ferons nous quand nous serons morts.'

[4] ib., pp. 202, 205 to end.

admiration.[1] If some savour of *real-politik*, most succeed as shrewdly as the Essays in showing that honesty is *generally* the best policy.

Did space permit, one might draw attention to yet other ideas of this attractive personality. It must suffice to mention a satire (*Le Pharisien du Temps*) written about 1670, which shows the exasperation of the liberal-minded with the quarrels and intrigues of the devout. The *Cabale des Dévots* or *Compagnie du Saint Sacrement* comes in for some shrewd blows, especially for their brutal and short-sighted methods in dealing with prostitutes.[2] The Jansenists are palpably referred to as a *secte androgyne*. References are made to the indulgence of some confessors, to the abuse of ' mental prayer ', the abandoning of old saints for new. This attack is less remarkable, however, coming, as it does, after the final success of *Tartuffe*.

There can be no doubt about La Luzerne's regard not only for religion, but for Christianity; in this he differs from such writers as Angot, Théophile, and even Du Lorens, and is only the more truly Montaigne's and Charron's disciple. Nevertheless, in his tendency to make ethics ultimately independent of religion, in rationalist independence and regard for toleration as well as in his fideism, he is of the same line of descent from our author as the other writers dealt with in this chapter.

Taking them all together, including Bélurgey (if he be the author of the Deist poem) and Desbarreaux, we have a pretty fair idea of all the various shades of opinion which the seventeenth-century would have called *libertinage*, that is ' free thought ' which its enemies sought to identify with ' free living ', and which they suggested was the danger of the semi-learned—*les demi-savants*. We have seen what part the ideas of the Essays, either directly or as rendered by Charron, have obviously played in the intellectual life of these various poets or poetical moralists. The attacks of Catholic apologists on Montaigne and Charron begin at the time of Théophile's trial in the early sixteen-twenties. The reader is now in a position to understand that attack, or that counter-attack, as it was from the point of view of those apologists.

Common to most of the authors studied in this chapter is their distinction of religion and ethics. They are preparing the way for a *morale laique*, which is not exactly the abstract rational-

---

[1] *Sentiments* (ed. 1654), pp. 18, 20, 21, 23–5, 32, 37–41, 50, 51 ; (ed. 1654) pp. 27–52, 65–7, 70.
[2] See Raoul Allier, *La Cabale des Dévots*.

ism of the *philosophes*. There is an insistence on a pluralism of ethical values, on harmonious development as a question of personal adaptation, conflict having in itself no positive value. There is a consciousness of the difficulty of seeing what human nature is universally, a keen awareness of the limitations of reason, which precludes these humanists from the optimism of the rationalistic eighteenth century and encourages them in the attitude of external conservatism and conformity with which they prudently accompany their advocacy of tolerance in every sphere of life. Where they criticize Christian doctrine, they do so in the interests of true religion and in the name of Christianity. Their several debts to Montaigne and Charron have been shown in detail. It is with Molière, La Fontaine and certain lesser writers that this chapter should end. They, however, come after the revival of a Christian Epicurianism by Gassendi and involve some reference to his views, and after much of the writing on *honnetêté*, which is so important in a discussion of Molière. Since we have learnt enough to understand the attacks of numerous apologists on Montaigne and Charron, we may safely relegate them to a later chapter.

CHAPTER XIII

COUNTER-ATTACK—I : GARASSE, MERSENNE, BOUCHER

Il est bon au reste d'avertir ici en passant que les Écrivains qui ont le plus décrié Montaigne, le louent malgré eux en quelques endroits et le pillent en d'autres.

SEGRAISIANA

TACTICS—such is the note which must be emphasized in the first phase of the campaign against Montaigne and Charron. It will be convenient, therefore, to begin with the least prudent of these numerous apologists, François Garasse.[1] His references to Montaigne are apparently full of respect for an illustrious author and a good man, but when we examine closely his attack on Charron, clear-sighted and yet grossly unfair, we are forced to the conclusion that what these references imply is a wish to use the name of Montaigne as yet another stick with which to beat Charron. His objection to Charron is so strong, partly, because of the popularity of *La Sagesse*, and still more because many actually think of him as a pious author.[2] But his forbearance with regard to the Essays is not the reflection of his own private opinion, but merely a tribute to Montaigne's reputation, solider than that of Charron.

Note, first, the form this tribute takes in *La Recherche des Recherches* (1622), a violent attack on Etienne Pasquier. Pasquier's real offence was his enmity to the Jesuits, but no consideration, however far-fetched, which can put his adversary in an unfavourable light, is neglected by Garasse. Pasquier's letter containing an appreciation of the Essays is much too good an

---

[1] Garasse, born at Angoulême in 1585, entered the Society of Jesus in 1601 and became first known as a preacher. The Jesuits finally imposed silence on their fiery defender, who died in 1631 nobly tending the sick in the plague-ridden town of Poitiers.

[2] See *Doctrine Curieuse des Beaux Esprits de ce Temps*, 1624, p. 1015 : ' Pour Charron je suis marri que je n'en puisse faire un plus favorable jugement . . . &c. (cf. also p. 274).

occasion to be lost.[1] Montaigne's self-portrait was criticized as being rather presumptuous and boastful. What ! cries Garasse, he sullies the memory of his professed friend, and he himself provides a far worse example of the same faults ! In spite of the praise of the Essays, and of Montaigne himself which Garasse adds,[2] there is too obvious an end in view for any conclusion to be possible as to his real opinion. Two years later, in the *Doctrine Curieuse*, Montaigne finds himself compared with Homer. But in what ambiguous terms !

Les uns l'ont élevé jusques au Ciel, et l'ont appelé ὕλην τῶν θείων νοημάτων, la forêt ou taillis des divines conceptions, et d'autres l'ont ravalé jusques aux enfers, et l'ont appelé βάναυσον ἔλεγχον, l'enclume et la boutique de toutes les répréhensions du monde . . .[3]

When we note the absurd invective against Homer and Virgil which Garasse published in 1625, it would be too much to say that this comparison implies any admiration for the Essays. Montaigne's sincerity is vouched for in the *Somme Théologique*, it is true, but at the expense of Charron [4] ; and the dissociation of the two authors is obviously made more from a desire to discredit Charron than to justify his master.

Mersenne, on the other hand, nowhere mentions the Essays, and in his attacks on Charron he adopts a moderate tone, which again reflects a respect for a general opinion which he is far from sharing.[5] Silhon, again, provides a good example of the esteem in which Charron was held. He makes some bitter remarks in his *Deux Vérités* about Charron's opinion that the immortality of the soul was not capable of proof.[6] Before the book went to press, representations were evidently made to him which resulted in the following note being added to the *errata* slip :

---

[1] See above, pp. 23–25. *Recherche des Recherches*, V, § 4.

[2] ib., V, § 13, pp. 950 et seq.

[3] *La Doctrine Curieuse des Beaux Esprits de ce Temps*, 1624. Other references to Montaigne, pp. 121, 976.

[4] . . . Il n'y a lecteur sensé qui ne voie fort bien—lisant ces discours— et qui ne die que Charron n'est ni Aristote, ni S. Thomas, ni Sénèque, mais bien que c'est un Michel de Montaigne dévalisé, et mis en mauvaise posture, faisant dire à son Maître ce qu'il ne pensa jamais. (*La Somme Théologique des Vérités Capitales de la Religion Chrétienne*, 1625, pp. 663, 664.)

[5] *Impiéte des Déistes*, Part I, p. 196 . . . suis content d'excuser Charron (par une supposition prétendue qu'il n'ait point eu de mauvaise intention : nous supposons bien des choses impossibles).

[6] *Les Deux Vérités* : *L'une de Dieu et de sa Providence* : *L'autre de l'Immortalité de l'âme* (1626), p. 254.

Quelques gens d'honneur ont trouvé mauvais de ce que je blâme un peu Charron en mon Introduction de la Seconde Vérité, j'en ai été marri et ne désirant que personne se blesse dans mes écrits, j'en eusse ôté l'occasion s'il eut été en mon pouvoir.

Silhon indulges in a good deal of detailed criticism of Montaigne (*troublefête quoique Catholique*) in all his works, but he never associates the two writers. Furthermore, the Abbé de Saint Cyran himself in attacking the *Somme théologique* of Garasse undertakes a lengthy justification of Charron ; as also does another of Garasse's opponents, François Ogier.[1] The Père Boucher, however, attacks both authors together in his *Triomphes de la Religion Chrétienne* (1628), and Charles Cotin in 1629 says the *forts esprits* read Montaigne and Charron without understanding them.[2]

The *Doctrine Curieuse* of Garasse is an attempt to show that the maxims of the *libertins* or free-thinkers are absurd. It begins, therefore, with a table of these maxims. The first attack is on the division of minds into different classes by the writers on temperament, for they say that only a superior mind is capable of the doctrine of the *beaux esprits*. Huarte and Barclay (*Icon Animarum*) are taken to task for the 'impiety' of attempting to enumerate and classify scientifically the diversity of human character. The triple distinctions of Cardan, of Charron and Vanini are then examined. Garasse particularly resents the idea of the influence of climate on character. His inaccurate account of Charron distinguishes (1) the popular mind or the 'ordinary Christian', (2) those who are capable of perceiving the superstition of the vulgar, but have not the strength to break with received ideas, and (3) the *esprits écartés*, who are according to him *toujours égarés hérétiques et brouillons*. These attempts at classification are easy game for Garasse. It is evident that, in his interpretation of Charron's adaptation of Montaigne, no traces of the original comparison of the first and the last class remains.
The *beaux esprits*, Atheists and Deists, are for Garasse 'new dogmatists'. Even apart from those who think belief in God a necessity only in a political sense, the others hold faith a servitude to be made as light as possible, with a minimum of the supernatural. They wish to choose their articles of faith,

---

[1] St. Cyran (*Somme des Faussetés contenues dans La Somme Théologique* . . . Pt. II), and le Prieur François Ogier : *Jugement et Censure* . . . 1623.
[2] Charles Cotin : *Discours à Théopompe sur les Forts Esprits de Ce Temps*, p. 7. See also Cotin, *Traité de l'Immortalité*, Chap. X, pp. 120–31.

like the Protestants. Not only do the free-thinkers want to cut out the supernatural, thus destroying the essence of faith, but they dislike all the severer doctrine of the Bible.

The question of eternal punishment and pagan virtue come up, naturally enough. Garasse knows that some eminent Fathers of the Church can be quoted against him on the second point. He treats the question openly, and his counter-objection is thoroughly sound from his point of view : these Fathers were Platonists, they identified the Logos (reason) and the Holy Ghost, and believed that an implicit faith was granted to many pagans. Garasse is at particular pains to gain his point here, just because it is the independence of morality which rightly appears to him to be the issue.

The *beaux esprits* believe that Nature is the one power active in the world. This involves a fatalism which encourages them in self-indulgence of the grossest kind. Garasse, least of all these Catholic apologists, cannot resist the assumption that all his adversaries are evil-livers. But the conception of Nature encourages such indulgence, apart from fatalism, for they hold :

> Que la Nature ayant non seulement permis, mais encore commandé aux bêtes et choses insensibles de prendre leur repos et leur contentement en l'exercice de leurs facultés et puissances, que nous qui sommes hommes et les maîtres du logis, ne devons pas être de pire condition que nos valets, et par cette règle que nous ne devons refuser . . . à nos sens rien qu'ils désireront en l'exercice de leurs facultés naturelles, et faire au contraire, c'est se défaire soi-même, commander tyranniquement, et démentir la Nature.[1]

To condemn entirely such a view, as Garasse does, is to condemn humanism in general (or ' naturalism ' [2] as he calls it) and Aristotle in particular.

A good analysis of the term ' Nature ' is given. Three senses are distinguished : (1) the predetermined law of God, (2) the inherent nature of any species, and (3) the special characteristics of individual creatures. He claims that the third only is the sense of the ' Atheists '. Bearing the writers of our last chapter in mind, it seems doubtful whether this is quite accurate even in the case of Théophile, although it is the sense which interests us most in connexion with the Essays. Garasse also notes the use of the word in the meaning of a gift, a talent or *daimon* (cf. Goethe's *Eine Natur*, a real individual). To suggest that animals are perhaps happier than men is apparently impious, because it is to leave immortality out of account. The

---

[1] op. cit., pp. 676, 677.   [2] See above, p. xxxii.

argument does not occur to Garasse that man, since the fall, has lost an innocence that animals have, and that the possibility of future felicity is not the same as present happiness.

In the seventh section of the *Doctrine Curieuse*, objection is taken not only to the assertion that immortality is unprovable, but also to the statement that it has no necessary connexion with the existence of God, and that there are no such things as angels or devils. The book ends with the ' library ' of the *beaux esprits* : Pomponazzi (whom he hasn't read) [1] Paracelsus and Machiavelli. These are the most dangerous. Paracelsus encourages an overweening curiosity. To these Cardan, Charron and Vanini are added. Of Rabelais it is impossible to read a page without mortally offending God (he has only read extracts given by Pasquier).[2]

In the *Doctrine Curieuse* we have the reaction of a zealous Catholic of average intelligence towards the whole complex of humanist ideas, many of them not necessarily incompatible with a liberal Catholicism, as seen in La Luzerne, for example. In the *Somme Théologique* (1625) we have an attempt to establish the ' capital truths ' of Christianity against all those whom the author groups under the name of *Athées* and *Athées couverts*. These he classified under various heads. Besides those (*furieux ou enragés*) who hold that God is not, or is bad, and those who profane religion by flippancy, there is the *libertin*, a kind of Epicurean, the Pyrrhonist and the *Athée brutal et mélancolique*, who represents what Garasse calls le *Diogénisme dans le Christianisme*. Charron is of the last type, which is always melancholic by temperament, stoical and dogmatic.

This dogmatism or rationalism is not very apparent from what Garasse has to say about his chosen enemy. It is the principle of ' conscientious ignorance ' which seems to him the source of all that is most poisonous in *La Sagesse*. Garasse derives from this both Charron's dislike of anthropomorphism, whether of thought or plastic representation and symbolism, and also his other criticisms of superstition. He objects to Charron's abasement of man, which is attributed to personal vanity and a wish to make human beings into beasts and withdraw them from religion. The demand for suspense of judgement is made

---

[1] Some of Pomponazzi's works were very difficult to procure at this date. Silhon says he was unable to find a copy of his *De l'Immortalité*.

[2] cf. *Borboniana*, LXVIII. ' J'ai eu longtemps un Rabelais : mais il n'était pas à moi, l'etait celui de Monsieur Guyet, qu'il avait laissé en mon étude. Il se confessait tous les ans qu'il avait un Rabelais qui n'était pas chez lui : et moi je me confessais d'en avoir un que n'était pas à moi.'

in the name of a peace of mind which is as psychologically unattainable as it is undesirable.

What is interesting is the fact that, in spite of the not uncertain voice which Garasse raises against the Pyrrhonists—under which name he includes every form of indifferentism—in spite of all his jibes at those who do not think Theism and Immortality evident and provable truths, his own assurance seems to fail when he has to approach these two fundamental articles. On the question of the existence of God, he writes :

> J'entre d'abord dans une question bien chatouilleuse, qui a sa face et son revers comme une médaille, et qui peut avec indifférence de louange et de blâme soutenir le pour et le contre, voire dirai-je, que si les Athéistes couverts de notre siècle n'abusaient de cette religieuse ignorance de la Divinité qu'ils tâchent d'introduire, je pencherais quasi de leur côté et dirais qu'il vaut mieux se tenir dans une simple ignorance de Dieu que d'éplucher trop curieusement ses secrets.[1]

So, too, at the conclusion of all his argumentation on this matter he admits there is no clear rational demonstration of God's existence, only a strong presumption *a posteriori*.[2] Yet Garasse found his *Somme* censured by the Sorbonne for quite another reason, not for fideism, but for holding, with the Christian optimism typical of the Society, *qu'il ne faut user que de la lumière de la raison pour être Chrétien '*.

Lastly Garasse holds that the diversity of the universe, the complexity of all structure, the difference of men's faces, and even the variety of inclinations which incline men to various states of life—as scavengers, hangmen, or galley-slaves—all this is inexplicable except through God.[3] Such is his answer to the first stammerings of empirical science.

It is impossible to leave Garasse without further mention of St. Cyran's defence of Charron. It was, in a sense, this work which opened the battle between Jesuits and Jansenists, and made Bayle observe that Garasse was the Helen of their war. *La Somme des Fautes et Faussetés contenues dans la Somme Théologique du Père François Garasse* consists of three massive quarto volumes launched at the unfortunate Jesuit's head in November 1626, and couched throughout (with the exception of a dedication to Richelieu) in the form of a letter or objurgation to his victim. The first tome reveals the misinterpretations and misrepresentations of the Fathers of the Church committed in the *Somme Thélogique*, the third its author's misquotations of Scripture, the second deals similarly with certain Scholastic

---

[1] *Somme*, p. 81.   [2] ib., p. 106.   [3] ib., pp. 167–75.

philosophers, but the whole of the second half of it is devoted to Charron. And St. Cyran makes a point of drawing Richelieu's attention to this vindication of a man grossly calumniated, whose *Trois Vérités* the Cardinal du Perron and other Churchmen have held in the highest esteem.

St. Cyran had never read Charron before he examined the *Somme Théologique*, but was so struck by the unfairness of Garasse that he at once bought his works. He chooses nine or ten of the most glaring blunders of Garasse for exposure, and ends with a threat of more to follow should his adversary fail to retract. Certain of these points—a misprint of Charron exploited, or a truncated quotation—need not detain us. Nor even the correction administered to Garasse on the subject of shame. Nothing is *naturally* shameful, and only man's sin has created shame, as Charron himself noted, says St. Cyran, while Charron's language, far from being ' immodest ', compares favourably not only with that of Garasse, but with that of St. Augustine himself !

More significant is the defence of Charron's remark (in the *Discours Chrétiens*), that it is dangerous to speak too much of God's judgements ' according to human laws and human conditions ', and, above all, St. Cyran's comment on Charron's exclamation : *Qu'est ce qui découvre la faiblesse humaine plus que la religion ?* Such a reflexion is so far from being ' atheistic ', that the greatest Doctors of the Church, ancient and modern, are constantly repeating it. Nor is this error of Garasse a mere trifle, but essential to religion : *La religion fait sentir à l'homme son mal et le fait courir à Dieu.* St. Cyran here goes straight to that side of Charron's philosophy which, with his own Augustinian conviction of *le néant humain*, he saw to be truly Christian, whereas for the semi-Pelagian Jesuit the ' abasement of man ' is precisely that which most of all renders *La Sagesse* dangerous.

There will be occasion later to speak of an apologetic work of Father Boucher, published in 1622, and we may note a sermon of Father Binet printed in 1620, which strongly attacks indifferentism in religion as equivalent to atheism and represents it as fashionable.[1] Despite these two works, Mersenne's [2] *Quaes-*

---

[1] E. Binet : *Question de ce Temps* : A savoir si chacun se peut sauver en sa religion . . . (*Œuvres Spirituelles*, 1620). See also Moyse Amyraut, *Traité des Religions contre ceux qui les estiment toutes indifférentes*, 1631.

[2] Father Marin Mersenne (1588–1648), of the order of Minims, is best known for his friendship with Descartes. The publication of his *Correspondance* now in progress (Vol. I, 1933) is of immense interest for the history of the sciences, of philosophy and the religious controversies of the first half of the seventeenth century.

tiones celeberrimae in Genesim (February 1623) mark a date in the struggle against the *libertins*. The *Impiété des Déistes* (1624) and the *Vérité des Sciences* (1625) are only the development of certain parts of this immense folio volume. Far the most violent of his books, most of it is an attack on physicists who maintained the eternity of the world and other Averroist theses, and does not concern us here. One chapter, however, deals with Atheism, and it is there that the author gives his famous estimate that there were fifty thousand atheists in Paris. He evidently is inclined to suggest they are a secret society. Their favourite authors are Bonaventure des Periers, Cardan, Machiavelli and Charron.[1] This chapter was suppressed in almost all copies of the edition, and was replaced by another headed : *Deistorum Impietas*. The Deists believe in God but not in his Providence. They claim to be rationalists. But we, too, are rationalists, replies Mersenne with indignation. This revised chapter seems to rest on more solid information than the version suppressed. In the interval Mersenne had probably had time to study the Deist poem, which he mentions in his Preface.[2]

In *L'Impiété des Déistes* he elaborates his attack on the Deists. This new sect propagates a more venomous doctrine than atheism ; for their name deceives the simple-minded and enables them to sap the foundations of Catholicism. Mersenne cannot resist the temptation of showing how, in his opinion, Protestantism is the source of Deism. For him, like the other apologists of the time, all Christian doctrine seems undermined by any criticism of asceticism or of eternal punishment, and he returns anew to the question of divine justice in the *Vérité des Sciences*. Mersenne appears horror-struck that Pastor Du Moulin should have suggested that Christ was one who died to save *even* his enemies ; that Du Moulin should object to ' self-maceration ' ; that he should believe with many Protestants, that every man can be saved in his own religion.

Mersenne admits, however, that Deists will receive the Eucharist and that many others of them are Catholics at heart. Their opinions are dealt with as derived from four sources : *Les Quatrains du Déiste*, which gains the honour of a formal refutation, Charron, Cardan and Bruno. Most of the first part of the book is taken up by a discussion on ' moral goodness ', which, after much splitting of hairs, arrives at the commonplace conclusion that the moral life is life according to right reason. Further on, the usual objection is made to the Stoical ' live according

---

[1] op. cit., p. 671.   [2] See above, pp. 151–153.

to nature' as a characteristic maxim of the *libertins* : for by them it is to be understood of individual nature and reduces itself to mere gratification of impulse.[1] Mersenne here appears a thorough-going rationalist, who even has pretensions to prove the doctrine of the Trinity,[2] and it is chiefly the rationalist side of irreligion which he examines.   The Sceptics are intentionally left over until his next volume.   The criticism of Charron, however, seems to cover some of this ground, and a preliminary chapter, proving ' the excellence of man ', is obviously a reply to the opening chapters of *La Sagesse*.   Mersenne notes with gratification that Charron professes to exclude religion from his ' pyrrhonism '.

It has already been shown that Mersenne's opinion of *La Sagesse* was profoundly hostile beneath a veneer of respect. But his discussion of the variety of ways in which the book is regarded is worth noting.   Some think it is *séminaire d'irreligion*, others merely that it is dangerous if not read with care ; but there are also many who think it the best of all books for its concise, nervous style and its abundance of maxims :

> Ceux là sont ordinairement libertins et se moquent des cérémonies l'Église, marris de ce qu'il leur faut garder ses ordonnances sur peine d'être déclarés hérétiques.

Yet he admits that, besides these, there are many wise and judicious people who see no harm in the book, if properly understood.[3] He makes the interesting remark that he himself has often longed for a really Christian Book of Wisdom which would show that the Catholic faith and religion are in no way repugnant to the best imaginable state of society, and that they do not let or hinder subtlety of mind, scientific investigation or reasonable pleasures.   Mersenne ends the second part of this book (chiefly concerned with Bruno's conception of a universal soul) on his favourite note that so much speculation and so many philosophies are perfectly compatible with Catholicism, which does not interfere with them.   To suppose a universal vegetative soul of the world, for example, is not an impious opinion.   This conciliatory tone stands to Mersenne's credit, for he is writing in the very year when Sorbonne and Parlement condemned no less than fourteen theses on physical questions on the sole ground that they were contrary to Aristotle.[4]

In the *La Vérité des Sciences contre les Sceptiques et Pyrrhoniens*

---

[1] *Impiété*, Part II, p. 420 et seq.   [2] ib., Part II, pp. 114, 115.
[3] ib., Part I, pp. 183, 195.
[4] For an account of these ' Alchemist' theses see Busson, *Pensée Religieuse*, pp. 229 et seq.

one might expect to find some observations on the Essays, or, at least, signs of some familiarity with them. This is not so, however. Three speakers appear in these dialogues : the Sceptic, the Alchemist and the Christian philosopher. The Alchemist represents natural and experimental philosophy. Criticism of his views, as well as those of the Sceptic, enable the author to make his own position clear.

The Sceptics are free-thinkers who ' confining all human knowledge to the limitations of sense and the outward appearance of things, unworthily debase us to the vilest of conditions '. The usual arguments as to the uncertainty of knowledge are stated forcibly enough by the Sceptic ; language is said to be purely conventional, and ethics a question of ' go as you please '. The Alchemist defends his science, which is experimental not speculative, maintains the validity of proof by general consent, and concludes that the one truth contained in Scepticism is merely that little is known to man. The Christian Philosopher then replies to both. Apart from experiment, there are self-evident rational principles such as the law of contradiction. The foundation of ethics is the conservation of the rational part of our nature, or, with more certitude, the commandments of God. The foundation of religion is not general consent but its conformity with reason and with the greatness of God.[1] Names of things are appropriate in direct proportion to their onomatopeia. Rationalism has its limits, however. The attempt of some Alchemists to ' explain ' the mysteries of religion by chemical analogies is to be condemned. After an examination of Aristotle's errors in physics and a refutation of the ten sceptical rules of Sextus,[2] the book ends with a discussion of the syllogism.

Since there are at any rate some self-evident truths, the Sceptic is wrong in denying that the premise of a syllogism can ever be proved. Mersenne makes a statement which amounts more or less to the Cartesian notion of the absolute validity of what is *clearly* conceived by reason. Proceeding to examine the inductive method advocated by Bacon, whom he describes elsewhere as the ' ape of Pyrrhonism ', he maintains that it is impossible to know the nature or substance of individual things, since the senses only perceive accidents, and all understanding comes through sense experience. Hence Bacon's experimental method seems to him without value.[3]

[1] *Vérité des Sciences*, p. 67.
[2] The *Hypotyposes* had just been republished (1621) in H. Estienne's translation.
[3] *Vérité des Sciences*, p. 222 et seq.

Bacon, and our old friends Democritus and Heraclitus are all sceptics, yet if one turns to another book of Mersenne where he has no axe to grind, one cannot help feeling that this defender of reason himself makes but modest claims for human knowledge. Already, after reading his *Vérités des Sciences*, Pierre Leloyer (see above, p. 42) writes to him : *Je vois qu'êtes sectateur de la seconde Académie et de Carnéade, lequel de quelque chose proposée et mise en dispute, estimoit qu'on pouvoit discepter probablement,*[1] and in his *Questions* (1634) not only admits that ignorance and learning are extremes that meet, but that :

nous n'aurons jamais autre science que celle des effets extérieurs, sans en pouvoir pénétrer les raisons et sans savoir la manière dont elle (nature) agit, jusques à ce qu'il plaît à Dieu de nous délivrer de cette misère.[2]

Galileo's astronomy is treated at length in this collection of scientific essays, and Mersenne obviously approves his conclusions, though, writing two years after the condemnation, he has not the courage to say so. Hence, in part, Mersenne's suspense of judgement in this matter, shared by many other men of the time. Revelation is the only answer to such questions, and doubts are expressed as to whether physics can ever be properly called a science. It is not an encouraging conclusion for this ardent scientific investigator and credulous soul, of whom Gassendi said slyly, ' in him there is no guile '.

With Mersenne's views on philosophy and religion those of Silhon may be usefully compared and contrasted, but before dealing with this eclectic, who came under the influence of his friend Descartes and also of the revival of Platonism, it will be well to devote a little attention to an older man, Father Boucher, a Franciscan.

Jean Boucher, born at Besançon, presents several points of interest. His first book is the record of a voyage in the East undertaken in 1610 or 1611, *Le Bouquet Sacré*. The following passage from it is not perhaps without significance :

Ils (*the Mohammedans*) disent que Dieu donna au commencement du monde une loi naturelle à l'homme, laquelle lui donne des règles suffisantes de vertu : mais l'homme l'ayant oublié, Dieu lui envoya celle de Moïse, mêlée de douceur et de rigueur, et voyant que l'homme

[1] *Correspondance*, I, p. 521.
[2] *Questions Théologiques, Physiques, Morales et Mathématiques*, 1634, p. 11.

se plaignait de la rigueur de cette loi, il envoya Jésus Christ, grand prophète, pour lui en donner une qui était tout pleine de douceur . . .[1]

Man having abused this law for six hundred years, then came Mahomet with his severer law and his fire and sword.

Boucher's evident interest in the concept of the law of Nature was perhaps stimulated by his travels, and it plays a considerable part in his *Mariage de la Vertu avec la Religion sur cette question : Savoir si la Prud'hommie est estimable hors la Religion* (1622). This book is remarkable for the moderate tone adopted in attacking the free-thinkers to whom it is dedicated. Its title shows that it deals with the root of the matter.

Boucher begins by pointing out that, although faith and reason are not contradictory, only persuasive proofs, not demonstrations, of the articles of faith can be given, nor can philosophic truths disprove any article of faith. Unlike the other writers hitherto mentioned in this chapter, he presupposes an honest love of virtue in his adversaries and does not make the gratuitous assumption that, because they are heretics, they must all be rakes. He also presupposes that they believe in the immortality of the soul, though this has no bearing on his argumentation. By religion is not to be understood a multitude of superstitious observances which the Church is forced to tolerate nor the vast hypocrisy prevailing among even the clergy.[2] Religion is the knowledge of God and how to adore and serve Him.

Boucher's main thesis is that virtue and religion are mutually dependent on each other for their value. His remarks on the disinterestedness of virtue,[3] and on duty require no comment. Natural law is an *échantillon de cette Loi éternelle par laquelle l'homme sait se gouverner et conduire droitement et justement*. It consists in a natural instinct to know, love and serve God, to know the truth of all things, and to do nothing to others except what one would have them do to oneself, and in an instinct of self-preservation, propagation, parental affection and love of one's neighbour. Since the Fall, all these articles have been abandoned in one way, or in some place or other, but their principle, founded on natural reason, is not extinct in human nature though generally merely theoretical. Only religion can re-establish its practice. This naturally leads on to the question of salvation; when and where can the

---

[1] *Le Bouquet Sacré ou Voyage en Egipte* . . . (1613 ?). References to Mohammedans occur in Boucher's other works.

[2] *Mariage Aux Libertins*, II.

[3] Boucher notes that no threat of punishment can stop or hinder the committing of crime (ib., p. 41.)

observance of the Law of Nature suffice to save a man ?   He gives in its usual form the answer of all but the most rigorous : everywhere before Moses, everywhere after Moses except for the Jews, everywhere to-day where a knowledge of Christianity is impossible.

But just as it is evident that to-day a knowledge of God adequate for salvation is impossible by the light of reason alone, so the rational foundation of ethics in natural law is insufficient to produce the good works necessary for salvation, or even for the proper exercise of the moral virtues.   The existence and goodness of God are indeed known rationally, but only to metaphysicians.   The authority of the Scriptures is necessary to the ordinary man.   Thus the free-thinkers attacked here are rationalists who ask why God should demand belief in what is beyond reason.   The usual answer as to human presumption is given. The author finally reproaches the *libertins* for adopting a completely negative attitude towards the whole traditional legacy of human knowledge.

Boucher's treatment of the Law of Nature may be usefully compared with that of Charron, and serves to keep before us an increasingly important aspect of seventeenth-century ethics.[1] His other apologetic work, *Les Triomphes de la Religion Chrétienne* (1628), is interesting for its attack on the Essays and *La Sagesse* and for the fact that a good deal of it is devoted to showing that all human sciences are uncertain.   Here Boucher uses the method and almost, it sometimes seems, the phrases of Montaigne himself.   This is, of course, the obvious manner of refuting Deism or natural religion, which is what the author is attempting to do.   Thus the one point on which Montaigne is attacked in person is his approval ' among all humane and ancient opinions ' of the view that God has always accepted any form of honour and reverence paid to Him on the foundation of a worthy conception of His nature.[2]   Boucher thinks this impious assertion is well enough countered by Montaigne's own comments on human sacrifice only a few pages further on in the Apology, that is to say, Montaigne admits such service to be blasphemous, but both writers shirk the real question : what is a *worthy* conception ?

Continuing his observations to the adversary, Typhon, *Maître des Déistes*, Boucher writes of Montaigne :

[1] Notice how the final section of what is intended as a popular work, making a special appeal to women, the *Philosophe François* of Cerisiers, almoner to Gaston of Orleans (1643), is devoted to Natural Law.

[2] *Les Triomphes de la Religion.*   Question 58.   See above, p. 35.

Vous avez bien raison d'appeler cet auteur une mer de conceptions, car c'est vraiment une mer, mais pleine de bancs et d'écueils, où plusieurs faibles esprits et ignorants, malassurés en leur créance font naufrage et vont échouer leurs vaisseaux. Le Sieur de Montaigne a malmené la Religion, Charron, son disciple, ne lui a pas donné un plus doux traitement au second livre, chapître 5 de sa Sagesse où il dit ces paroles :

> Toutes les Religions croyent que le principal et plus plaisant service à Dieu et puissant moyen de l'appaiser et pratiquer sa bonne grace, c'est se donner de la peine, se tailler, imposer et charger de forces besognes difficiles et douloureuses . . . et encore plus aux fausses qu'aux vraies, au Mahumatisme qu'au Christianisme . . . suivant cette opinion de quelle nature doit être Dieu ?

With Boucher it is once more the attack on asceticism for which Montaigne and Charron are most severely blamed. Charron is also particularly censured for comparing Christianity in any way with other religions. The pages devoted to the Essays and *La Sagesse* end thus :

> Or je ne me suis émancipé d'écrire ces choses pour ravir l'honneur que ces deux beaux esprits, Montaigne et Charron, ont mérité, . . . mais c'est pour avertir ceux qui les liront désormais de prendre garde de sucer, en n'y pensant, un doux vénin qu'ils ont glissé par inadvertance (ainsi que je crois) dans leurs livres, mêlés de plusieurs propositions trop hardies et dangereuses. . . . Le livre du Sieur de Montaigne est comme un plat d'Ecrevisses, où ce qu'il y a de nourrissant est vraiment friand et délicat mais il y a plus à éplucher qu'à manger, et celui de Charron est semblable à un beau pré bien fleuri : mais gardez vous, enfants, car le serpent vénéneux est caché parmi l'herbe.

These two authors are again taken to task jointly for holding immortality to be the most doubtful question in all human knowledge. That they add at the same time that it is universally and usefully received, appears to Boucher the more pernicious since it implies there is no foundation whatever for it in reason.[1] Boucher makes this truth the consequence of a belief in divine Providence. He admits that knowledge of the soul is even more obscure than knowledge of God ; and a feeling of uncertainty, as to how far his arguments on Immortality will go, is betrayed by his appeal to the notion of a tradition reaching back to Adam, who had presumably a clear and direct knowledge of his soul.[2]

The influence of fideism on Boucher is marked and he is surely the mere echo of Montaigne when he writes in reply to the query whether rational religion is not enough :

[1] *Les Triomphes de la Religion*, Livre VI, i.   [2] ib., p. 713.

Davantage l'entendement humain s'enveloppe et s'embarrasse dans une confusion de fantaisies, d'opinions, et d'imaginations, non seulement en la diversité des objets qui se présentent à lui, mais encore sur un même sujet. . . . Cette raison est comme une épée à deux mains, faisant divers jugement sur un même sujet. Toutes choses (dit Héraclite) portent en elles les visages qu'on y veut trouver, et tout est vrai à chacun ce qui lui semble être véritable selon son imagination. Nul ne peut donner une raison si forte sur un sujet qu'un autre n'en puisse controuver une contraire aussi forte en apparence que la précédente.

And so on for a couple of folio pages. Reason is a *touche pleine d'erreur et de manquement*, nature, in Plato's words, an enigmatic poem ; and therefore, he concludes, knowledge of God by reason only is uncertain.[1] Boucher has the same purely *passive* notion of faith as many who lean more evidently to fideism. That there are people who have not faith, that there are genuine free-thinkers, should not astonish anyone :

car la Foi n'est pas un bien que nous puissions acquérir ni conserver par nos propres Forces c'est un pur présent et pur don de la liberalité de Dieu. . . .[2]

Science depends on sense-experience, which is fallible ; reason is a Proteus, and man's typical act self-deception ; every human judgement seems distorted by circumstances. Boucher develops these considerations in pages which seem sometimes strangely familiar to the student of the Essays.[3]

Whether Montaigne had any real influence here or not, *Les Triomphes de la Religion* is an excellent example of the fideism of even the apologists who attack Montaigne and Charron. These authors are not attacked in Boucher for their scepticism. Charron is not attacked primarily for his scepticism by Garasse. Both these authors have fideist leanings themselves. With Mersenne, Charron's ' pyrrhonism ' is a definite and important charge ; with Silhon, who has come under other influences, scepticism becomes the great accusation against both authors, and the attack is levelled (quite naturally) at Montaigne far more than at Charron.

[1] *Les Triomphes de la Religion*, pp. 99, 100. cf. p. 119 : ' Et ce qui est estimé aujourd'hui honneur et vertu dans le monde,' &c.
[2] ib., p. 145.   [3] ib., pp. 147, 149–51 (119, 291).

CHAPTER XIV

COUNTER-ATTACK II: SILHON AND CHANET

JEAN DE SILHON, a Gascon born near Nérac, begins his first book, *Les Deux Vérités* (1626), by demolishing *une opinion reçue même parmi quelques Chrétiens : Qu'il n'y a science de rien et qu'il est permis de douter de tout.* Montaigne appears on the scene almost at once. His infinite regress of doubt is interpreted as a reaction against the vanity of intellectual pretensions : but, this critic asks, is it not as vain and as vainglorious to 'suppose human understanding to be capable of an infinite series of acts'? Belief is natural to man, and religion common to all ages.

Silhon proceeds to develop the usual proofs of God's existence, relying chiefly on the alleged necessary assumption of a first cause. Each separate part of creation is examined in turn from this point of view. Silhon then sets out to prove the existence of angels, for their intellectual nature appears to him to afford a proof that the origin of their creation must be spiritual. He concludes the existence of good spirits from the existence of evil ones, which seems clear to him from the evidence of witches and sorcerers. Here Montaigne again crosses Silhon's path, for he has ascribed all that concerns the witch's ' coven ' to the force of a morbid imagination and Delrio's criticism of the Essays is quoted with approval by him (above p. 23). The crux of the matter is, however, the bodily presence of witches at the ' coven ', a question of fact, for which the evidence is circumstantial. Even Montaigne does not give his opinion affirmatively, but, as is usual with him, in the form of a doubt :

> On peut dire pour sa défense qu'on ne peut justement censurer celui qui soumet si religieusement ses pensées, ses écrits et ses actions à la censure de l'Eglise Catholique, Apostolique et Romaine.[1]

Silhon thinks that such men as Montaigne would be less prejudiced if they remembered the ingenuity of the devil as shown

---

[1] *Deux Vérités*, pp. 183–6.

in the idolatrous practices of the inhabitants of the New World. For himself, he is persuaded of the possibility of copulation with evil spirits, and of possession by them ! It is hardly surprising that he holds them to be at least as powerful as angels.

In a letter written a few months after the publication of the *Deux Vérités*, and in which he exposes the plan of an apologetical work never carried out,[1] Silhon announces his intention of criticizing ' the extravagant force which Cardan, Pomponazzi and Vaninus attribute to the imagination ', not for any reason connected with the argument outlined above, but because such considerations ' might dim the splendour of the supernatural actions of Jesus Christ and his saints '. It should be noticed that criticism of Montaigne or any other writer's opinions either on witchcraft or on the force of the imagination is entirely absent from Silhon's later works.

The author considers his first Truth (theism) demonstrated, although, in fact, these chapters abound in arguments which beg the whole question. Yet, in spite of beginning his second ' Truth ' with a condemnation of Charron for holding immortality to be the most universally received and least proved of beliefs, in spite of asserting that on it depend all individual and social morality, Silhon holds this tenet, apart from revelation, ' to be not without some remnant of doubt '.

It is obvious, he says, that it is within God's power to make our souls immortal, and equally possible for Him to make the souls of animals immortal. But animal life is entirely bound up in the body ; whereas so far as the human soul is concerned

si en elle même et sans ses organes elle a une vertu et force d'agir plus noble qu'avec, il faut avouer que Dieu le conservera faisant des actions plus dignes de sa condition.

Silhon holds the functioning of the intellect to be independent of the well-being of the body, and adopts a psychology which is clearly due to Platonist influence. He invokes the proceedings of the Fifth Lateran Council to support a claim that man is literally angel and animal. The ' rational soul ' is not merely the form of the body ; but also in itself a creature of the same order as the angels and hence dependent on bodily organism only in the sense that an eye, if it *does* look through a window, is dependent on the cleanness of the glass.[2]

This line of argument is then dropped to follow up another,

[1] N. Faret : *Recueil de Lettres Nouvelles*, 1627, p. 469.
[2] ib., pp. 288, 290, 380, 381, 385. See E. Gilson, *Études de philosophie* : *L'Innéisme Cartésien et la Théologie*.

in which Montaigne again becomes prominent. This time Silhon is the debtor of the Essays. That the goodness of God implies the immortality of the human soul is shown by a comparison of men and beasts (*Discours III*). If man has no other destiny he is far more miserable than they. A good deal of this comparison, especially as far as the misery of human life is concerned, seems to be derived from Montaigne and Charron.[1] Some of it is familiar in another way as the source of some of Pascal's best-known thoughts on war and social injustice:[2] *Véritablement c'est le faîte de la gloire du monde que de savoir tuer avec justice, etc.* Silhon here expresses himself on the ways of those in authority and on the ills of society in a very different tone from that of his later writings, such as *Le Ministre d'Etat.* Civil government is founded on a contract involving restraint of liberty—lest worse befall. The echo of the Essays is heard: justice is imperfect, for it only punishes;[3] all the glory of the world will not soothe the pains of megrim or of gout. Property is an ill from which the Apostles purged the first Christians; as its guardian, men must needs have laws, law-suits and magistrates,

qui se font encore remercier pour les avoir dépouillés un peu plus civilement et en lieu plus honorable qu'au milieu d'un bois.[4]

Not only the goodness of God but his wisdom and justice imply immortality, since the world was created for man.[5] Silhon objects strongly to the view that virtue is its own reward: on the contrary, it is in itself *sans goût de plaisir.* It is hardly necessary to comment on the contrast with the favourite notion of the Essays and of Charron that virtue and pleasure are closely bound up with each other.

The author next discusses faith and reason, making a distinction between divine faith and human faith. The latter is dependent on sensory experience, and must necessarily precede the former. Human faith means the persuasion that the historical side of Christianity, the documents for the life of Christ, for example, or his miracles, make good their claim to manifest the hand of God. Silhon introduces at this point the first sketch of the famous 'wager', later taken over by Pascal: Christian doctrine says one is obliged to believe on pain of

---

[1] *Deux Vérités*, p. 331.
[2] See Ernest Jovy, *Pascal et Silhon*, 1927 (and *Essais*, III, 5, p. 126).
[3] *Deux Vérités*, p. 344.   [4] ib., p. 348.
[5] ib., pp. 355 and 81 (Silhon does not accept Copernicus, see p. 65).

eternal damnation, hence mere prudence gives us the will to believe and to force the understanding.[1]

If, however, human faith depends largely on miracles, the certitude of sense-perception becomes of capital importance.

D'où vous pouvez juger combien est téméraire l'opinion de Montaigne (et de quelques autres troublefêtes, quoique Catholiques) qui dit que nous ne pouvons nous assurer de rien que de ce que Dieu nous a révélé. Certes si cela est vrai nous ne pouvons pas nous assurer de cela même, car si cette foi humaine dont nous venons de parler est trompeuse, et si tous ces effets que les Juifs ont connu et tous les peuples de la terre par leur propre expérience pouvaient être des illusions, s'en est fait de la Religion Chrétienne, puisqu'on lui dérobe son pied et son fondement.

He thinks, however, that ignorance may excuse those who advance such opinions without seeing the desperate consequences which they involve.

If prudence urges us to ' human faith ', as suggested, eternal punishment also becomes a doctrine of special importance. Silhon's next chapter is entitled, *La Justice de Dieu montrée en la peine des damnés, et que les Payens ont mérité cette peine, encore qu'ils l'ayent ignorée, et même si peut-être ils ont été sauvés.* The argumentation is as feeble as it usually is on this subject, and the author honestly admits he has never found any satisfactory explanation about hell or purgatory.[2] The notion of *continuous creation*, derived from Plato's *Timaeus*, which enjoyed such fortune with Descartes and the Cartesians, is here introduced. It is used to back up the argument that, since God's benefits and rewards have continuous and infinite duration, so too his punishments must be eternal.[3] Silhon seems conscious that to suppose that the pagans are all damned does not quite square with the notion of a merciful God. Even the felicity of those who are saved is purely gratuitous on the part of the Deity, but only those pagans who transgressed the Law of Nature committed mortal sin, so there may be some hope for them. It ought not to surprise us, however, if hell is crowded : *Chaque particulier a pu se damner ; pourquoi pas tous ?* [4]

Montaigne and his opinions enter this book in three ways. His scepticism is rejected as a general position ; it is rejected more particularly with regard to witches. Lastly the Essays supply, if not the inspiration, at least some of the details of a

---

[1] *Deux Vérités*, p. 425 et seq.   [2] ib., p. 440.
[3] ib., p. 462 et seq.   [4] ib., p. 478 ; also p. 270.

comparison of human and animal life, which forms an important part of Silhon's argumentation.

De l'Immortalité de l'Ame (1634) is, in part, a mere rewriting of Silhon's earlier work. He had come under the influence of Balzac, and a comparison of much of this book with *Les Deux Vérités* will certainly profit the student of French prose style. The author begins with a short discussion on Plato and Aristotle. He objects to the neo-Platonism which is brought into the treatment of the mystic life by fashionable theology,[1] but so far as the immortality of the soul is concerned Plato is preferable to Aristotle. Silhon, a true eclectic,[2] tries to show that both philosophers are really agreed about the relations of body and soul. He condemns the temperamental psychology of Huarte, as leading obviously to the rejection of immortality, a consequence which Huarte's real master, Galen, accepted.[3] He adds that he has been blamed for writing in defence of the foundations of religion. The significance of this common objection to apologetics has been discussed. Silhon writes in the same year as Yves de Paris who replies to a similar objection, the year after Marandé's *Théologien François* was disapproved of on principle by the Assembly of Clergy.[4] Silence is, in certain quarters, the order of the day. Silhon replies that the more Christians avoid such a defence of their beliefs, the more their adversaries think they are afraid of their weakness :

Ils pensent que si nous avons pour nous le temps et la coutume, ils ont pour eux la raison et le consentement des plus sages. Il faudrait les détromper et les guérir de cette vanité, ce qui n'est pas impossible.[5]

He claims to make a ' moral demonstration ' of Immortality, by which he means that, although none of his arguments are perhaps conclusive by themselves, they are so all taken together.[6] The second chapter of *De l'Immortalité* contains another *réfutation du Pyrrhonisme et des raisons que Montaigne apporte pour l'établir.* It is unnecessary to go over the same ground, but it may be noted that Silhon insists at greater length that

---

[1] cf. Espinas : *Pour l'Histoire du Cartésianisme* (Rev. de Métaphysique et Morale, 1906, p. 266 et seq.).

[2] cf. *Deux Vérités*, pp. 38–40 (*universalia post rem*), 109, 267.

[3] Silhon attaches elsewhere considerable importance to temperament. See *De la Certitude des Connaissances*, pp. 161, 162 : *Le Ministre d'Etat*, pp. 194 et seq., 218.

[4] See above, pp. xix, xx, xxi.

[5] *De l'Immortalité*, p. 64. See above, pp. xxii–xxiv. Also Petrus Firmianus : *Genius Saeculi*, e.g. p. 226.

[6] ib., p. 871.

Montaigne was not really so anxious to defend scepticism as to burst the bubble of intellectual vanity. He does not again use Montaigne's comparison of man and the animals in his argumentation, but he examines what he now takes to be the essence of it, namely that animals have reason : *Voilà le grand argument de Montaigne et ses sectateurs et la meilleure pièce de leur batterie.* Even if Montaigne was right, this would mean not that man was mortal but that animals were immortal. Here again his intention was only to humble the vanity of man, but his paradoxes are pernicious and dangerous in spite of his good intentions.[1]

Two points should be noticed incidentally about this book. A sketch of Descartes' *Cogito* here appears three years before the ' Discourse on Method '. Silhon employs it as a final argument against Montaigne's scepticism, and indicates that from it a proof of God's existence may be drawn.[2] Note also that he insists on gratitude as the basis of morality, which is essentially founded on reason.

Silhon is still, in 1634, a precursor, but his third book [3] against Montaigne, written much later and published only in 1661, presents no new interest. The argumentation is lengthier and often clearer. Montaigne is now *the* enemy :

J'ai donc choisi cet Auteur pour le combattre, comme un Auteur de grand nom, et dont les Ecrits ont été recueillis avec honneur dedans et dehors le Royaume. Je ne prétends pas pourtant de diminuer par là le prix de ce qu'il y a de bon dans son livre où il y a plusieurs bonnes choses, sans parler de la noblesse et la force de son style.[4]

Silhon's own position here emerges more clearly in some respects from his renewed examination of the claims of scepticism. He rejects the notion of sense-experience as the only source of knowledge for some kind of *innéisme*. He seems to believe that the first principles of Metaphysics ' *viennent à s'éclore dans l'entendement de sa seule lumière et sans l'influence médiate ou immédiate d'aucun objet sensible* '.

The second section of this work is devoted to Ethics. Self-interest is necessary to man ; it is *le lien de la vie civile et l'âme de l'économique* ; not only that, but He who wishes to be loved for His own sake also permits us to love Him for our own. Duties are founded on the principle of gratitude and vengeance. *Le droit des gens* is the authority to which the individual may here appeal from his personal prejudice. Silhon's treatment of

---

[1] *De l'Immortalité*, pp. 440 et seq., 486 et seq.
[2] ib., pp. 178, 179, 245–8.   [3] *De la Certitude des Connaissances Humaines.*
[4] *De la Certitude*, p. 9.

the virtues has no interest, except what appear to be a few reminiscences of the Essays.[1] His preoccupation with social morality should be noted.

A continuation of Silhon's *Ministre d'Etat* (1631), a treatise of political and historical reflexions which does not concern us here, forms part of *De la Certitude des Connaissances*. The book ends with a section on ' moral demonstration ', which develops at considerable length what was briefly treated in the *Immortalité de l'Ame*. This section shows very clearly how far even a theologian like Silhon—almost a Cartesian [2]—is from claiming to be able to prove directly the immortality of the soul. He says, for example, that the human soul has not in itself any principle which would make it eternal any more than a fly has : it is entirely a question of God's will. That will, again, is only to be known by the scriptural revelation and the miracles which are signs of its divine origin.[3]

Silhon, though he does not entirely escape the influence of fideism is far less a fideist than the other apologists studied in the last chapter. He differs from them also, however, in the clearness with which he sees the danger of Montaigne's scepticism as regards sense-perception and his attribution of reasoning powers to animals.

It would be possible to add to the writers mentioned here other apologists who direct their criticism against Montaigne and Charron as Pyrrhonists, and, from Silhon onwards, the question of the reasoning of animals is constantly linked with the question of immortality and with the names of Montaigne and Charron—by Scipion Du Pleix in 1626, by J. Bogot in 1644, by Charles Cotin in 1646, by Sir Kenelm Digby (who falls outside our field) in 1651, by Jean Claude Petitot in 1656.[4] Campanella devotes a section of his *Atheismus Triomphatus* (1636) to the subject, and the one passage where Descartes has mentioned our two authors by name is concerned with this, the nature of animals. We must, however, reserve the question of the influence of Montaigne or Charron on Descartes for a later chapter.

Like Boucher, Silhon, though hostile to Montaigne on the

[1] e.g., ib., pp. 139–142.

[2] Apart from the *Cogito, création continue,* relation of body and soul, note a passage on the conversion of the steps of discursive proof into a single intuition (*De la Certitude,* Livre I, 1). Cf. *Rev. de Mét. et Mor.,* 1906, pp. 266 et seq.).

[3] ib., p. 558.

[4] See Busson, *Pensée Religieuse,* pp. 189–96, to whom I am indebted for some of these references.

whole, certainly owes something to the Essays. The very reaction of both men shows the impression the book made on them. It would be possible to name other ecclesiastical writers, their contemporaries, who borrow without any apparent reaction. *La Cour Sainte* (1624) of the King's Confessor, the Jesuit Nicolas Caussin, a work of considerable popularity, translated in its time into five European languages, contains what is in effect an attenuated adaptation of the second book of *La Sagesse*.[1] *La Dévotion Aisée* (1656) of Pierre Le Moine, another Jesuit, is indebted to Montaigne for a number of its most remarkable passages.[2] Such examples could doubtless be multiplied.

Finally, one last attack, ostensibly on Charron, but also on Montaigne must be mentioned. Pierre Chanet was a doctor of medicine at La Rochelle, a Protestant, whose *Considérations sur La Sagesse de Charron* were first printed anonymously at Paris in 1643 by the good offices of Gui Patin.[3] The book enjoyed some success for it was reprinted in the following year with the author's name, and again in 1662. The wish to avoid direct reference to the name of Montaigne, and to concentrate attention on Charron is still obvious. There can, however, be no doubt that Chanet is really attacking one as much as the other, for he explains that the order of his chapters has been dictated by the plan of the Apology for Raymond de Sebond. And while specially asking the reader to note that Charron's opinions are all ' literally and accurately transcribed ', he adds that he has many reasons for wishing to avoid mentioning the names of those to whom he is indebted.[4]

[1] op. cit., Livre III, § 7 et seq. (Douze maximes de Sagesse). Caussin says these are derived from Pico della Mirandola's *Vita Spiritualis*. This is not so. Cf. also III, § 27, &c.

[2] op. cit., pp. 3, 60, 117, 281. Le Moine comes in for some hard, not to say unfair, treatment in the Ninth, Tenth and Eleventh *Provinciales*.

[3] Patin : *Lettres* (ed. Réveillé Parize), I, 288. ' J'ai fait ici imprimer depuis peu un livre françois intitulé *Considérations*. . . . L'auteur en est inconnu *aut saltem non vult nominari* ; un temps viendra qu'il parlera.' (19 juin 1645) : again : '. . . Il est âgé d'environ quarante ans : il est fort savant, sanguin, mélancolique, qui a fort voyagé : il est fils d'un ministre de Marans qui est encore vivant ', &c. (17 août '43), also 3 March '56.

[4] In the preface to the first anonymous edition, according to which the book must have been written towards 1630, the author says he expects the disapproval of ' *ceux qui prennent Charron pour Socrate et l'Apologie de Raymond Sebond pour l'Évangile* ' (perhaps especially Naudé : see below, p. 243). The preface to the second edition under Chanet's own name changes the sentence *in order not to introduce Montaigne at all*.

The real interest of Chanet's book is that it is not written from a theological point of view, except in so far as such considerations dominate the whole thought of the time. It involves a certain amount of philosophical reasoning, though logical fallacies abound on almost every page. It is the reaction of seventeenth-century ' common sense ' to all that appeared paradoxical in Montaigne and Charron. ' Common sense ' is the body of opinions which an age accepts as evident, but whose evidence is almost entirely reducible to mere familiarity. Its attitude to paradox is the jeer. This book is most illuminating as the rationalization of these jeers, though some of it is sound enough criticism, and some even shows how Chanet himself and the age had moved towards Montaigne's point of view.

The first chapter sets out to show that the world was made for man.

Il n'y a que Charron et fort peu d'autres, qui nous veulent disputer ce privilège, soutenant que les plus chétifs animaux, par exemple les oisons, en peuvent dire autant, et peut être plus justement, et plus constamment.

Montaigne's satirical *boutade* which imagines the gander supposing himself the ' darling of nature ' is treated to a solemn refutation, and Chanet's jokes about ganders echo through three-score pages. He seems, on the contrary, to believe that the movements of the stars have been specially instituted to provide an occupation for astronomers ! After an ingenious attempt to explain the usefulness to mankind of vipers and poisonous insects, we arrive at the old question : would the attribution of reason to animals invalidate a belief in immortality ?

To establish that animals reason, only implies that either they and we are both mortal or both immortal. If he were forced to such alternatives, the author would prefer the former, but the belief is not in doubt, though ' without physical proofs '. The theological side of the question being disposed of, Chanet proceeds to analyse and interpret the terms ' reason ' and ' instinct '. Instinct is the direct, yet not miraculous, action of the Deity. Although the most marvellous actions of animals are ascribed to instinct, Chanet has no leanings to the Cartesian view of animals as machines (unknown when his book was first written), and he accepts the Aristotelian psychology of rational and sensitive souls. According to that psychology the higher includes the lower, and instinct has therefore its place somewhere in human life. ' Instinct ' appears to be responsible for the fall of solids towards the centre of the earth (p. 77), and for muscular reflexes, though not for actions of the sensitive and vegetative soul conditioned by the objects of perception.

Chanet first defines reason as the power of reflecting on the results of ratiocination, and of reflecting on reflexion *ad infinitum* (pp. 49, 50). In a second definition it appears as the ' faculty of proving one thing by something else different ', but his real thought, as seen in Chapter VII, is of reason as itself the definition, logically, and the ' essence ', ontologically, of man.[1] From this then almost unquestioned principle Chanet produces his crowning argument against the view that animals reason.   If they did, they would have knowledge of God *puisque qu'il se manifeste si fort par ses effets que c'est des plus aisées connaissances que nous puissions avoir*.   There are those, however, who claim that the elephant is a religious animal.   Here is Chanet's reply :

Mais à parler sérieusement en ces matières si importantes, je demande à ces auteurs que c'est qu'ils appellent la connaissance de Dieu. Est-ce l'action par laquelle nous connaissons Dieu, et la science qui nous en reste, ou bien la faculté de notre âme, par laquelle nous le connaissons ? Ils seraient trop impertinents, s'ils disent qu'une action ou une habitude fût notre différence spécifique. Car en ce cas les enfants ne seraient point hommes et n'en aurait point les propriétés. Nous mêmes cesserions d'être hommes toutes les fois que nous n'appliquerions pas notre esprit à connaître Dieu.[2]

The confusion of thought is not uninstructive.   This identification of reason and of knowledge of God rests at bottom on the very familiar, though unorthodox, conception, which the Stoical current did much to propagate, of the ' rational soul ' as a part of the divine nature.   It is this notion (underlying the theory of natural law), which finds its place in the second part of this book.   Here Chanet sets out to show the veracity of sense-experience, and that laws, customs and institutions do not all rest on *l'opinion, qui ne fait pas, comme veut Charron, toutes nos inclinations et toute notre morale*.

Charron pretends that his book is written in order to ' teach us to know ourselves ', and yet most of it is spent in establishing the uncertainty of knowledge.   After dealing with hallucination, and making the usual point about the normal functioning

----

[1] For the immense significance of this view, see L. Rougier, *Les Paralogismes du Rationalisme* and also *La Mystique Démocratique*.

[2] Chanet's idea of the limitations of knowledge is probably more truly reflected by this assertion : ' the knowledge of man which extends to that of effects and only of a few causes, is sufficient for him to attain unto his end which is God ' (cf. *Essais*, III, 11, p. 326).

of the organism, Chanet goes on to maintain that ' reason does not contradict itself ' (Chapter V). To hold the contrary is to deny the law of contradiction. Examples from Charron are quoted, which, of course, really show that there are a multitude of cases where the logical principle of contradiction is not involved at all ; such as Plato refusing to wear a rich robe for one reason, Aristippus accepting it for another : the examples are all concerned with conduct and choice. Chanet seems to imagine he has refuted the whole case of his adversaries by giving his own resolution of half a dozen dilemmas of this order.

The third chapter, however, *Que ce n'est point une témérité aux hommes de préférer leur propre jugement à celui de tous les autres* exposes a perfectly genuine absurdity from which neither Montaigne nor Charron can be entirely acquitted. Chanet accuses his adversaries of saying that *because* truth is unattainable, *no one* should trust their own judgement, and that hence opinion and prejudice must rule the world. This is to put a finger very accurately on the discrepancy between the individualism of the Essays—and even of Charron—and their conservatism, their insistence on conformity with the way of the world. Of course, the explanation is that the scepticism of Montaigne is to some extent a reaction, an attitude adopted *in view of* an end, namely, tolerance. It is precisely the unconstructive prudence of this attitude that most distinguishes Montaigne, Charron and their disciples from the eighteenth-century *philosophe* and the modern liberal.

Chanet recognizes that this mistrust of one's own opinion is primarily a reaction against dogmatism, although previously he protests indignantly against the favourite intellectualist maxim of humanism, that the vulgar are always wrong.[1] He admits that every one thinks he possesses common sense (*le bon sens*), but, because this is obviously false, it does not follow that no one possesses common sense. There are occasions when it is obviously not rash to maintain our opinion against the opposition of everybody else in the world ; if, for example, I and they disagree about my health or my identity.

The next chapter resolves itself into a discussion of the theory of temperament. Chanet does not admit that judgement and memory are never found together in any eminent degree.[2] It will be remembered how Charron adopts this idea from Huarte and how he applies it to the Pedants, and how even Montaigne, especially in speaking of himself, is fond of contrasting memory and judgement, and how amused he is to find that the country

[1] ib., pp. 149, 150.   [2] ib. II, 4.

folk confuse the two.[1]   Chanet does not seem, at first, to dispute
the influence of the humours, but he denies Huarte's deductions
and opposes to him the authority of Galen and Averrhoès.   Later
he appears to hold that the understanding is entirely independent
of the bodily organism,[2] and hence judgement, being not a faculty
but a habit of the understanding, cannot be influenced in any
way by the physical condition of the organism, but only by
some incompatible habit of the understanding.   Besides, he
adds, the theory as interpreted by Huarte and Charron involves
its own converse : that those who had no judgement (dependent
on a ' dry humour ') would necessarily have a good memory
(dependent on a ' moist ' one) : and this is obviously not so.

This question of the individual judgement *contra mundum*
is continued in the sixth chapter (*De la Connaissance de Soi
même*).   It is interesting to see the real agreement of Chanet
and ' our adversaries ', as he always calls them, on the value
of the individual's judgements on himself, though he has plenty
of other criticisms to make.   To study human defects, as Charron
does, is not sufficient to make a man follow virtue ; he must
recognize its nature and its beauty, and that he is really capable
of it.   The ancient oracle was right to pronounce its ' know
thyself ', for, as the pagans did not know God, they themselves
were the properest objects of their own contemplation, particularly since the power and providence of God is manifested more
evidently in man than in the rest of creation.   But to-day, writes
Chanet, we have almost reached the limits of science.   It is false
to say, as Charron and Montaigne do, that man is the least-
known object of philosophy either with respect to his mind or
his body.

Charron is right, however, in saying that ' each of us knows
himself better than he is known by all the rest of the world '.
The proverb to the contrary is absurd.[3]   Chanet does not believe
that intelligent people are blind to their main defects, but only
to their foibles.   And he almost quotes the Essays themselves :

Il n'y a que vous qui sachiez si vous êtes juste, si vous êtes tem-
pérant, si vous êtes véritablement homme de bien, ou si vous êtes
un hypocrite.[4]

Why then do so many neither convert themselves nor mend their

---

[1] See above, pp. 86, 87, 99–103 et seq. ; *Essais*, I, p. 39; II, 17,
p. 432 et seq. ; III, 9, pp. 239, 240.
[2] ib., p. 337 et seq.   [3] Compare Théophile, above, p. 141.
[4] ib., p. 353.

ways ?   Chanet makes a physician's reply : all common ailments
are not curable.

Les inclinations que nous avons de naissance sont si fortes et la
coutume nous en rend quelques unes si familières qu'à moins que de
vivre dans une contrainte perpétuelle, il nous est impossible de ne
les faire pas paraître . . .   J'ajouterai pour la fin, qu'il y a beaucoup
d'hommes qui aiment leurs défauts, et les doivent aimer pour ce qu'ils
les aident à les faire valoir et les font parvenir à leur fin principale.[1]

In an amusing digression he defends authors from the legendary
charge of vanity.   The most able are least contented with themselves.   They are more conscious than any one else of the
qualities and defects of their work.

En effet, il n'y a que l'auteur même qui puisse bien juger de son
ouvrage.   Un autre ira inconsidérément condamner un livre à cause
qu'il en aura lu les plus belles pensées ailleurs.   Mais l'auteur n'en
estimera moins son livre pour ce qu'en conscience il saura bien que
ses pensées ne sont pas dérobées . . .   Que si vous remarquez des
fautes dans un livre, ne pensez pas qu'elles soient toutes inconnues
à son auteur, mais plutôt assurez vous qu'il y voit plus de contradictions, et que pour certaines raisons il y laisse d'autres fautes qu'il
connaît que tous les critiques du monde n'en sauraient deviner.[2]

The words an author uses, since words mean just what we make
them, have more meaning for him than for any one else.
    It is surely significant that this defence of the individual
judgement should develop in Chanet's hands into a disquisition
on literature which shows such leanings to subjectivity.   Individualism, subjectivism and a belief in the power of introspection
are all tendencies in the same direction.   The solipsistic idealism,
which starts in the modern world with Descartes and reaches
its height with Kant, is the philosophical foundation which does
not yet underlie such views as these of Chanet.
    This book ends with an examination of Charron's opinions
on the Law of Nature.   Some of Chanet's remarks are well worth
noting, for he is bent on criticism, and very fair criticism, the
best in his book.
    All that Charron says is vitiated by his failure to distinguish
between Nature considered as an exterior power, which exercises
influence over us, and the nature of man, which he himself
declares to be the *ressort intime* of Wisdom.   Also having made
this nature his cardinal principle, he does his best to show that
it is rendered unrecognizable by the action of custom, while

[1] ib., pp. 356, 357.   [2] ib., p. 360.

holding that it is still visible in animals and savages. There
is a still more manifest contradiction in Charron's habit of talking as if to ' live according to Nature ' were equivalent to ' living
according to reason ', while saying that our nature has been
destroyed and deformed *by* reason. He wants to put us poor
mortals on the right path by setting us to study philosophy, one
of the sciences which he specially condemns. All these inconsistencies are the results of his borrowings. Chanet pursues his
advantage by enlarging on one or two absurdities which follow
from Charron's assertions. Since reason is the ' real ' definition
of man, how can Nature, taken as the same thing as reason, be
in animals and not in man, particularly since it has been shown
that animals do not reason ? If Nature is not a mere abstraction, it must be either God's providence or the particular and
specific nature of each species of creature. But their specific
natures are often incompatible. It is thus absurd to ask men to
imitate beasts in general. Again, if man's nature *is* reason, it
can hardly be said that the sciences pervert human nature, since
theology, jurisprudence and moral philosophy contribute directly
to make our actions conformable to reason.[1]

Chanet devotes a whole chapter to Charron's claim that any
law which can be said to be natural must be received universally
by all men.[2] He is under the significant delusion that Charron
makes this exorbitant demand for genuine universality in order
to ruin the whole notion of ' natural truths ' or ' natural laws '
and to clear a way for the view that all things seem equally just
and equitable according to Nature and that opinion only decides
between them. He would ask whether this notion itself is
' natural ' ; for it certainly is not received universally. Some
think that the sun turns round the earth, others think the contrary, but in spite of this disagreement one of these views is
true, *and hence natural* (*sic*). Because there is not one single
stature for all men, it does not follow that there is no natural
one. Besides, if there are no undisputed opinions in physics,
there are truly universal opinions in ethics, and this ruins Charron's case, for on his own principles these are natural and not
mere matter of opinion. There are ' laws which have been
universally recognized as just and practised by all the peoples
of the earth '. Justice may be a ' habit ' which can be acquired,
but that does not prevent it being natural, if only potentially so.
Also, since the end of any object necessarily precedes that
object, Justice is independent of and anterior to the human will.

[1] *Considérations*, p. 367 et seq.   [2] Livre II, chap. 7.

Chief among such universal laws mentioned is the maxim, ' do as you would be done by '. Chanet maintains that the Ten Commandments are universally recognized. If there are nations where it is deemed right to kill one's parents, this is only an interesting though mistaken interpretation of the fourth commandment of Moses, ' honour thy father and mother ' . . . ! Finally, an attempt is made to show against the opinion of Charron, that to wear clothes, to practise monogamy, and to bury the dead and not burn them, are ' natural ' practices, and that nakedness, polygamy (or polyandry) and cremation are unnatural.[1]

Another doctor, to whom reference has already been made (p. 101), Marin Cureau de la Chambre, a member of the Academy, replied to Chanet, defending the rationality of animals in his *Caractères des Passions* (Vol. II). Chanet in his turn wrote *De l'Instinct et de la Connaissance des Animaux* (1646), and La Chambre in 1648 his *Traité de la Connaissance des Animaux*. These books have no interest from the point of view of the Essays, except in so far as they testify to the popularity of the problem and the importance attached to it. La Chambre's thesis is not that of Montaigne. He holds that animals *reason* but have no *general ideas*. It may be noted, however, that in the second edition of his treatise (1662), he prides himself on having had his name placed alongside the ' great man ' whom Chanet has attacked, and says he will never be ashamed to see his name coupled with theirs.

Chanet's criticism of *La Sagesse* and the Essays, with all its mixture of good sense and false reasoning, forms a useful pendant to the criticisms of the various apologists. On the whole, the same features of Montaigne and Charron are attacked ; the abasement of man, rationality of animals, scepticism, and relativity of laws and customs.

In the second half of the seventeenth century a renewed attack on Montaigne is made, beginning with Pascal and the publication of the Logic of Port Royal. Charron seldom appears worthy of mention, and the general literary reputation of Montaigne is evidently rather changed. With the regard to apologists already mentioned, it will be enough to bear three points in mind. Montaigne and Charron are blamed for hesitating to admit that certain fundamental religious dogmas were capable of proof, but, in spite of this, similar misgivings are to

[1] See *La Sagesse*, I, 14, I, 42, § 10.

be detected in these critics themselves.[1]   The importance of the division of religion and ethics, maintained implicitly by Montaigne, explicitly by Charron, is realized and is opposed.   Yet reason or the Law of Nature, separately or conjointly, are recognized as the fundamental principles of ethics by these apologists. So far there is a certain agreement (at all events with Charron). The originality of Montaigne is just his insistence on the individuality of this reason, this ' nature ', and even on a plurality of values.   This tendency is utterly condemned as equivalent to a denial of any objectivity of value, and a recommendation to self-indulgence.   Lastly justice is done, on the whole, whether sincerely or *pro forma*, to the intentions of our two authors, but the paramount influence of their ideas on free-thinkers is never called in doubt.

[1] For criticism of such leanings to fideism see Antoine Sirmond, S.J. *De Immortalitate Animae Demonstratio physica et Aristotelica Adversus Pomponatium et asseclas*, 1635 (in French 1637).   The Preface appears to attack Silhon.   Also Petrus Firmianus (Zacharie de Lisieux) : *Genius Saeculi*, 1656, pp. 105, 167, 179 et seq., 246 et seq. (especially on Charron, pp. 255, 259).

CHAPTER XV

LÉONARD MARANDÉ

THE influence of the Essays was exercised on people of more considerable intellectual calibre than the satirical poets, country gentlemen, or provincial magistrates. At the time of Théophile's trial, in 1624, at the moment when Garasse and Mersenne were raising a hue and cry about *La Sagesse*, another less ambitious attempt to rewrite the essence of Montaigne, was published by Léonard Marandé under the title of *Le Jugement des Actions Humaines*.[1]

Of Marandé little is known. He appears to have been a young man when he printed the above-mentioned, his first work.[2] From the preface to his Latin novel *Ariades* we learn that he has been private secretary to the French Ambassador in England and in Venice.[3] It was not apparently due to his sojourn in England that he found in 1629 an English translator, J. Reynolds ; for the latter remarks in his dedication to the Earl of Dorset that the author's is ' a name that I more honour than know.' Marandé must have taken orders about this time and was later one of the King's Almoners. In 1631 he presented his *Théologien François* to the Assembly of Clergy who refused this homage (see Introduction), but voted a sum of money to the author. A second edition of the *Jugement des Actions Humaines* appeared in 1635 with important additions. Marandé's later works, mostly theological manuals or pamphlets against the Jansenists, have no interest for the purpose of this study.[4]

[1] *Le Jugement des Actions Humaines par Léonard Marandé, Parisien*, 1624, 8° (dedicated to Richelieu) : Second Edition, 1635.

[2] ib., p. 210.

[3] *Ariades*, 1629 and *Abrégé de l'Histoire d'Ariades*, par L.S.D.M. 12°.

[4] Among these works are : *Les Antiquités de l'Eglise* (1636) ; *Abrégé de toute la Philosophie* (1642 ? and reprints, a manual for students) ; *Les Inconvénients du Jansénisme* (1654) ; *Réponse à la Seconde Lettre de Monsieur Arnauld* (1655) ; *Réponse à l'Ecrit que Monsieur Arnauld a fait présenter aux Docteurs* (1655) ; *La Clef de St. Thomas sur toute sa*

Le Jugement des Actions Humaines, recommended by Naudé in his *Bibliothèque politique* and by Sorel in the *Bibliothèque Française*, consists of six discourses with a number of subdivisions. The first of these on the Vanity of man, the second on Sense-perception, the third on Opinion, and the last on Moral Virtue, while not without some quite original development of Montaigne's ideas, are built up out of passages adopted from the Essays and reminiscences of them. In the other two chapters, on the passions and felicity, the influence of Montaigne is negligible.

Marandé's remarks on human vanity need no detailed analysis. The reader knows what ideas to expect in this context. A longish quotation is enough to show the tone and the literary value ; the more appropriately since it touches on ' diversion ', a notion of Montaigne which specially appeals to this disciple and imitator :

Le plus sage que fait-il autre chose que gauchir en toutes ses actions ? S'il frappe au but de la constance c'est par voies indirectes : il ne vise jamais où il donne . . . Et de vrai, s'il ne peut vaincre ses vices, il se transforme comme cet Achélois pour se dérober d'entre les bras de ses ennemis, et tâche ainsi en connivant de leur échapper. S'il n'en peut étouffer la semence en son sein, il s'efforce d'en changer des fruits par la greffe de quelque différente passion, qu'il ente sur le pied et sur la tige de celle-ci. C'est ainsi qu'il trouve moyen de perdre la pensée d'un ressouvenir fâcheux et déplaisant en la presse de quelques autres pensées et divertissements, où elle perd sa trace, s'égaie et se fourvoie de nous insensiblement, pour montrer que l'inconstance fait sonner assez haut la jurisdiction qu'elle a sur nos cœurs, voire, dans les mouvements plus intérieurs et plus secrets de notre âme. Peu de chose nous arrête, et chose de moindre valeur nous en divertit. L'apparence des choses nous déçoit et nous touche autant et plus que la vérité même. Les plaintes d'une Ariadne, que nous savons être fabuleuses et inventées à plaisir, tirent quasi les larmes de nos yeux. L'action feinte d'un comédien nous donne du frissonnement ; et la robe de César fait naître plus de regret et de sédition dans le cœur des Romains que sa mort toute fraîche encore et toute sanglante n'avait su faire.[1]

The ' wisdom of man is but folly '. Even were we capable of true wisdom, that wisdom would still be at the mercy of a frenzy, a fever or a fit. Virtue lies in order and moderation, and yet,

---

Somme (1688-9) ; and *Le Philosophe Chrétien* (? mentioned by P. Forton de St. Ange : *Conduite du Jugement Naturel*).

Marandé's brother was a friend of Boisrobert and in service of Abel Servien, the diplomatist (Boisrobert : *Epîtres* : Série II. Dernière épitre).

[1] *Jugement des Actions Humaines*, pp. 21-3.

as all the ancients held, *les plus belles âmes sont celles qui ont le plus de variété.*

Marandé's critique of sense-perception begins by establishing the interdependence of body and mind. All knowledge comes through the senses—diversified forms of the sense of touch—but none the less the mind contains *les intelligences et les vives images de la Divinité.*[1] Perception is shown not to be purely passive by the difference of intensity of sensation felt by similarly placed observers. Not only are the senses unable to discover the ' essences ' of objects, but sensation is already altered and changed before it can reach the understanding. Even unanimity about sense-experience would only permit us to establish a science of our ignorance, not of the world of objects. Through the *phantasmata* (*espèces*) we know only the images of things, and the more intelligible they become the further removed they are from the objects in themselves. Just as the sun makes visible the beauty, not the nature, of visible things, so in general the senses permit us to admire creation as it were an enigmatic poem, according to the expression of Plato. Science belongs to God only ; there can be no principles unless God has revealed them and hence no science.[2] From the evidence of the senses there is no appeal, even in mathematics, and yet how unsatisfactory is the knowledge they appear to give.

The critique, which follows, of various sciences, and the results they have attained, is reminiscent of the corresponding part of the Apology. Everywhere sets of contradictions are apprehended by reason, *si nous appelons raison cette apparence de discours qu'un chacun se forge en l'esprit selon sa suffisance.* As for following opinion,

Si le Sophiste et celui qui contrôle tout [i.e. the dogmatist] savait aussi bien rire de soi-même comme les autres, je trouverais son parti le plus fort. Mais de croire les apparences dont on ne peut se défendre : c'est trop grande simplicité.[3]

Not only the Sceptics but all the sects of the philosophers have made profession of knowing nothing *et se sont penchés de ce côté là comme le plus doux chevet pour reposer une tête bien faite.* The animals are superior to us in a certain intuitive knowledge. However their minds work, this knowledge is more noble and more absolute than our discursive reason. ' True science or truth itself is a stillness of the mind ', like the knowledge of angels, and without ratiocination.[4] Yet man has some knowledge of

[1] ib., p. 44.   [2] ib., p. 59.   cf. also p. 253.
[3] ib., pp. 75, 76.   [4] ib., p. 91.

himself *et de ceux qu'il fréquente*, which, however, he despises, and esteems only the authority and book-learning of others, who are, or were, but men like himself. If he examined *their* private lives, would he be so imposed upon ?

Like all these sceptics and fideists from Montaigne to Pascal, Marandé thus argues the infirmity of man largely because his conception of the conditions of knowledge demands too much, because he starts from the ideal of an *a priori* rationalism ' which is exorbitant ·because contradictory '.[1] Where action and the practical reason are concerned, it is less easy to demand the same exaggerated standards of proof, less easy also to remain satisfied with the passive attitude of Faith as these fideists understand it. Such a feeling of dependence on Grace, such a waiting for its supernatural action, is hard to attain even for a Jansenist. And this, no doubt, goes far to explain the attitude of so many of these writers who are fideists in religion and metaphysics, yet rationalists in ethics. They are really rationalists all through, but disheartened because they have asked too much.

Thus in the next chapter following this critique of human knowledge, Marandé, taking up cudgels against authority and tradition, proceeds to establish that : *Retrancher la liberté du jugement est ravir au Soleil sa lumière et priver l'homme de son plus bel ornement.*[2] He holds

qu'il vaut mieux s'essayer et être assuré de son impuissance plutôt par son propre savoir que sur le crédit et autorité d'autrui. Nos actions sont de si peu de conséquence que, si en leur perte elles y enveloppent encores celle de notre temps, nous devons avoir moins de regret de les employer dans cette recherche curieuse que de les consommer encore plus inutilement dans la vanité des choses où nous nous sentons traîner par le courant de l'eau, je veux dire, par l'Erreur et l'Opinion.

Yet few, he admits, are fit safely to free themselves thus from tradition[3], for the rationalistic approach to religion generally ends in the position of euhemerism, and if a man's speculations seem contrary to religion, he can be sure he is wrong. Religion is, then, excepted from this liberty of speculation, but there is room enough elsewhere for us to use our wits, namely, in a critique of the false pleasures and unnatural desires which govern the actions of men.

There is ambition, for example, which deceives us with the prestige of office. Those placed in authority fail to keep what

---

[1] See L. Rougier, *Les Paralogismes du Rationalisme*, 1920, pp. 132, 133, 310 et seq.
[2] *Discours III*, § 1.   [3] cf. Descartes, below, p. 222.

Montaigne calls an *arriére boutique toute franche, toute sienne.*
They have to put up with the consequences of prominence. Can
kings have any real pleasures, since what is pleasure if unshared ?
They are deceived by flattery : but every one is in the same
condition there, for who can flatter a king so well as we all flatter
ourselves ? The vulgar, it might seem, should be in a better
position to be critical and self-critical. They are so little so,
that the first necessity is to avoid their prejudices. Environment and heredity have made our customs and usages seem so
natural that we condemn all others as barbarous.

We should endeavour to be impartial and cosmopolitan :

> Il faut produire de telles actions que le service qu'elles rendent
> à notre patrie rejaillissent sur toute la terre.[1]

Hence reason must be our only guide, remarks the author, with
an inconsequence which I have tried to explain. By reason alone
can we free ourselves to some extent from this slavery of custom
and prestige, and, though pain is the one real evil, even pain is
feared with exaggeration. It is almost impossible to escape all
the prejudices of vulgar opinion ; the sage should be content to
conform outwardly, if only he can free his mind.

To this ' cure ' from the ' idols ' of opinion and custom,
Marandé adds the section on the passions which is almost *de rigueur* in this kind of book. Here the treatment is banal, with
some debt perhaps to Du Vair. Marandé will not admit that
the passions are indifferent ; they are uncontrollable and must
be stifled. Something, however, in favour of almost every one
of them is discovered, when they are dealt with in detail. There
is a good deal of picturesque psychological description more
ingenious than convincing.[2] More original is the discussion of
felicity which follows. Felicity, is generally considered, says
Marandé, under two heads, active and contemplative. The
latter is more divine, but quite impossible to attain in this world.
Active felicity is *un parfait repos de l'esprit dans l'usage des biens
qu'il trouve autour de lui.* Contemplation may add to the happiness of life, but is more apt to bring the restlessness of doubt
and curiosity. The immediate end of any action is always
pleasure, but felicity depends on moral goodness.

It is, however, the last chapter of Marandé's book which is
most interesting and sets all that precedes in its proper perspective. *C'est assez faire du philosophe : il faut un peu faire de
l'homme à son tour.* The moral ideal described so far, where the

---

[1] ib., pp. 132, 133. [2] e.g. p. 210 et seq.

passions are stifled and goodness and felicity are inseparable, is that of ' heroic virtue '. It is for those ' of the first class ' like Socrates, not for most men. For the rest of us the cultivation of ' moral virtue ' or temperance is more appropriate. Its characteristic proceeding in the trials of life is *le divertissement*. This section of Marandé's book is simply a development of Montaigne's ' diversion '. It forms a strange contrast with Pascal's treatment of the same themes ; not only in the general attitude adopted but in the considerations involved, for the author insists on its physiological basis. It is the concentration of the ' vital spirits ' round the heart or in the brain which makes the poignancy of pain. They must be dissipated.

Ainsi cette puissance divisée s'affaiblit de sorte que le premier objet capable d'échauffer et de toucher vivement notre pensée s'empare aisément de la place.[1]

Any ill, any subject of sorrow, becomes an obsession which absorbs the attention of the mind, and every obsession destroys well-being because it deprives the other parts of the body of the presence of the vital spirits.[2]

Enfin comme les poisons sont employés utilement en nos médecines, les Passions, vrais poisons de l'âme, servent à la guérison de ses troubles, lesquels ne se peuvent appaiser plus promptement que par l'effort d'une Passion contraire. Voilà les armes dont *notre* Vertu se couvre.[3]

True felicity, in fact, depends on achieving a harmony of the lower and higher nature of man. Temperance, itself the very condition of pleasure, *nous porte dans le sein de la volupté non pour s'y engager notre âme, mais pour s'y agréer : non pour s'y perdre mais pour s'y trouver.* Continence and temperance are contrasted : the latter gains victories, the former steals them : it is only appropriate to women.[4] For a philosopher moderate indulgence in every field is to be recommended. It is absurd, however, to imagine that virtue can indifferently cure all human ills. Philosophy, particularly that of the Stoics, claims far too

---

[1] ib., p. 329.
[2] Marandé alludes to the concentration of the ' spirits ' in artistic creation, and the insensibility to pain, &c., sometimes consequent from it. He does not explain satisfactorily how this analogy can do anything but weaken his physiological argument.
[3] ib., VI, § 1 (end).
[4] At this point Marandé makes his one direct reference to Montaigne, and pays him a compliment by an allusion to the title of his (Marandé's) book : ' Montaigne, cet excellent juge des actions humaines ' (ib., p. 343).

much in this respect. A philosopher suffers from gout as much as a peasant, probably more.

Cette stupide ignorance qui donne un je ne sais quelle sorte de patience aux maux présents et nonchalance aux sinistres accidents futurs, n'était-il pas plus avantageuse à l'humaine Nature ? . . . La Nature nous avait mis en un degré bien sûr ; il fallait y demeurer, nous ne pouvions tomber de là, parce que c'était la plus basse marche.[1]

All philosophy is indeed, as it were, a tree under which some incomplete shelter may be found in a storm. It can uncloud our minds from prejudice, but it cannot protect us from pain.

The author is thus led to make this distinction : the mind alone is judge of truth or error, the senses alone of pain or pleasure —*and hence of value*. These are the two kinds of human judgement which remain always *quoad nos* (*quant à nous*) ; for God alone has knowledge of essences. The mind usurps the office of the senses and the senses that of the mind. We dare not embrace the good without the sanction of reason :

Si quelque chatouillement leur donne [aux sens] un movement contraire à celui de la Raison, elle a aussitôt le bâton levé . . . Ils se pouvaient bien passer d'elle et du fruit de cette méditation qui la rend si recommandable : joyau precieux à la vérité et plus nécessaire à cette petite république pour l'ornement et la bienséance que pour la nécessité absolue.

For what is necessary after this manner is universal and equal in all   Plato was no *more* a man than a street-porter is. Hence reason—not being equal in all men—is merely one of the accidents of man's nature. This rejection of reason as the essence of man, which is at the basis of the Aristotelian, the Scholastic and the Cartesian rationalism, and whose political consequence is democracy, should be duly noted.[2]

The senses deny such truths as the existence of any infinity and also the immortality of the soul, but the false goods forged by the mind are even more pernicious. Good may be defined as ' an object favorable to the inclination of the touch '. ' Granted that the felicity of man lies in virtue, (which is not true, speaking absolutely), I maintain against the Stoics that felicity is incompatible with pain ' : so Marandé proceeds. The thesis of the Stoics is false because the perfect state of man—the end to which he tends—must be one satisfactory both to mind and body. Nay more, the body *doit avoir la meilleure part en la félicité puis-*

[1] ib., pp. 358, 359.
[2] See Rougier, op. cit. Introduction. Contrast Chanet above, pp. 187, 188.

qu'il est la vraie touche du bien et du mal.   It is obvious that continuous pain ends by incapacitating the faculties of the mind.

La raison est un effet matériel et corporel lequel a sa racine dans l'âme, et qui ne peut se perfectionner que par le bénéfice des organes et la rencontre médiocre des esprits du sang subtilisés.[1]

A pleasant place, a fine day, he adds, echoing the Essays, clears the judgement, soothes the mind, banishes melancholy and makes our reason more manly and vigorous, *en bref il nous rend plus honnêtes gens.*[2]   If the reason, of which the Stoics boast so much, is ruined, where then lies their felicity?

We thus reach Marandé's conclusion : *La vie de l'homme est une harmonie composée de tant de tons différents, qu'il est bien malaisé que la vertu les tienne toujours d'accord.*   This last section is in part a general defence of the author's position as regards ethics. ' To promise more than one can, is the part of an ignoramus.   To hope for more than one ought is the part of a novice : To hope and to promise oneself possibilities, is the part of a man of experience.'   He applies this to his own contrast of heroic and moral virtue.   His is a modest ideal, but not an empty one. He does not, however, attempt to face the charge of hedonism. It does not cross his mind, for he is frankly eudaemonist.   The ordinary idea of happiness is an exaggerated one ; hence disappointment with a virtue which is supposed to be inseparable from it, honoured by everyone, but with lip-service only.   Besides, the ideal of stifling the passions renders those who are *vides et déchargés de passions* particularly subject to vanities. So Marandé ends his book as he began it on the favourite note of vanity :

Enfin quelque avantage que nous puissions donner à notre semblable, quelque honneur que nous y puissions rendre :

l'homme n'est rien qu'un songe
Qui de songes menteurs se repaît et se ronge,
En son plus ferme état n'ayant rien de constant,
Une ombre que le jour dissipe à sa venue,
Un éclair allumé dans le sein de la nue
Dont l'être et le non-être ont presque un même instant.

Le Jugement des Actions Humaines is certainly a notable attempt to extract a methodical philosophy from the pages of the Essays.   It must here suffice to draw attention to three points.

---

[1] *Jugement*, p. 386,
[2] ib., p. 387. Compare Théophile (above, p. 141).

There can be no doubt of the author's religious convictions. His critique of sense-experience and of reason, and his exploitation of the theme of vanity are certainly accompanied by a belief in a metaphysical realm of essences which are in God or are God, for on this point Marandé appears to hover on the borders of a certain Platonism. At all events, his book helps to make clear once more that there was nothing in the Essays which to many men of that age appeared necessarily incompatible with Christianity. If some doubt remains as to the sincerity of Charron, I do not think any reader of Marandé can suspect him in the same way.[1]

The second point of interest is the way in which, by his distinction of heroic and moral virtue, he succeeds in setting up—inspired by the Essays—a view of ethics ultimately hedonist and utilitarian, as a kind of ' sous-morale ', alongside the rather conventional ideals of a Christianized Stoicism. Here we seem to have another pluralism of values, differing from that seen in Régnier and Théophile. In effect, however, heroic virtue is implicitly rejected not only as an impossible ideal for almost all men, but as in itself of doubtful validity. Marandé's insistence on harmony rather than conflict and on *divertissement* distinguish his hedonism from that of Gassendi, whose historical importance is, of course, incomparably greater.

Thirdly, it must be noted that Marandé has made use of ' all is vanity, all is doubt ' after a manner now familiar to us, in the second edition of his book (1635) where he has added a chapter on the movement of the Earth and another on Astrology. He wishes to undermine the dogmatism of the opponents of

[1] Another striking example of the influence of the Essays on a deeply religious mind may be briefly mentioned at this point. In 1625 a Protestant refugee, Jonathan de St. Sernin, cooped up in his room in a London lodging-house for fear of the plague which then raged in the city, set pen to paper in a modest literary venture : he began a commentary on the Essays. The result appeared in the following year : *Essais : et Observations sur les Essais du Seigneur de Montaigne* (Ed. Allde, Londres, 12°). The most remarkable thing about this little book is the pious and Biblical turn given to Montaigne's remarks. St. Sernin's own essays are two in number : *De la Science* shows (after Montaigne) the uselessness of intellectual pursuits. Faith is the mother of all the virtues. The second essay criticizes the Aristotelian definition of virtue as a ' habit consisting in a mean '. It is not a habit, because what is habitual must happen always and without exception. Virtue depends on faith (*celui qui a la foi une fois ne la peut perdre, mais c'est qu'elle n'opère pas toujours*). St. Sernin appears to have been in part moved to write by Montaigne's notion of diversion ; *séquestrant et divertissant mes pensées de ce mal pestiféré et de l'appréhension de la mort avec les ardentes prières que j'ai faites à Dieu.*

Copernicus and Galileo, and disguise his own convictions under an affectation of detachment. Hence the strange circumlocution of some of the title headings.[1] Hence also his adoption of the personal digression after the style of the Essays, and its utilization as an indirect reproach to dogmatism.[2] But Marandé garnishes these chapters with further reflections of this kind for another reason, namely, because he sees clearly enough that the conviction of those who think the Earth must be at the centre of the universe comes largely from their anthropocentrism, at which he takes every opportunity of jeering :

> Qui voudrait persuader à l'homme, dont la vie n'est qu'un pélérinage sur la terre, qu'il est immobile comme une plante et que les pays nouveaux qu'il découvre en voyageant ne forment qu'une teinture de tapisserie qu'on lui déploye pièce à pièce, n'aurait pas meilleure raison que celui qui nous allégue que pour bien philosopher, il fallait que l'univers se promenât autour de nous.[3]

Why ! these people draw an argument from astrology ![4] The stars are placed in heaven for the service of man. If the Earth is not the centre of the universe, so they argue, it could not receive their influence.[5]

> A leur compte le Soleil et tout les Astres qui marchent si fièrement sur nos têtes, ne se lèvent que pour se rendre compagnons de notre travail, et ne se couchent que pour ne point troubler notre repos :

[1] La vanité et la faiblesse de l'homme ne paraissent point avec plus de pompe et d'éclat que dans l'ordre de nos raisonnements que nous appelons raison (VII, § 1).

La science de l'homme est un colosse orgueilleux enflé du vent de nos opinions, et qui en sa superbe démarche ne peut souffrir la moindre piqûre qu'il ne tombe en langueur, ne se sèche et ne se réduit en fumée (§ 2).

La science de l'homme est si faible qu'elle ne peut garantir ses plus fermes propositions, &c., &c. (§ 7).

[2] . . . Si on avait voulu établir le mouvement de la terre avec autant d'assurance et de certitude, qu'on a pensé faire celui du premier mobile, peut-être aurais-je pris le parti contraire, tant j'ai de répugnance à supporter l'orgueil de nos raisonnements. Je ne vois rien qui nous sièze mieux que le doute et l'incertitude ; il n'est pas que je ne fasse quelque fois du têtu et de l'assuré mais pour le moins je ne demeure pas longtemps en mon opiniâtreté. Je reprends volontiers mon assiette ordinaire et considère après ce que j'ai fait comme une chose qui n'est plus à moi, puisqu'il tient si peu à mes sentiments qu'il ne me ressouvient plus qu'elle ait fait partie de moi-même, au moins de mes pensées et de mes raisonnements . . . (ib. (1635), pp. 655–60).

[3] ib., p. 544.

[4] Probable allusion to the astrological arguments of J. B. Morin, *De Telluris Motu vel Quiete*, 1631.

[5] *Jugement*, p. 532.

et ces étoiles innombrables n'habitent ce grand pourpris que comme des fleurs inutiles pour le seul divertissement de notre vue, et néanmoins la plus petite d'entre elles, se dit on, est hors de comparaison plus grande que le monde que nous habitons.[1]

The fact is, argues Marandé, that we only receive the service and utility of things in general by accident, because each thing is seeking its own good, its own service.[2]

Finally, speaking of matter, the substance of all physical things, he observes :

Qui veut élever sa pensée dans le secret de cette méditation reconnaît facilement que toutes les créatures ne sont pas moins nobles les unes que les autres, ce que nous réservons pour une autre fois.[3]

A few notes on the author's constructive views must suffice. Scriptural authority is alleged by both sides and may be left out of the question. Superficially, no doubt, the Copernican theory may seem improbable, but it has already many eminent names behind it, and simple inspection of external appearances is always subject to error. Thus a first group of objections are set aside.

There are those, however, who hold that the earth is so heavy that it could not conceivably move. Weight, he rejoins, is purely relative, its real basis being rarefaction and condensation. The elements must be ultimately all diversified forms of some common substance, hence the usual explanation of the fall of solids towards the centre of earth applies to all bodies in the Earth's sphere. Hence this gravitational attraction has nothing to do with the alleged position of the Earth at the centre of the Universe. Magnetic attraction, however, is invoked by Marandé to explain both gravitational force and the motion of the earth round the sun, the fire at the centre of the earth being of the same substance as the Sun itself. This conception of magnetism, which perhaps came to Marandé from Gilbert,[4] is supplemented by a sort of pan-animism and a use of the principle of analogy which recalls Campanella.[5] All material objects are *animés* and exercise attraction on each other : this magnetism, he continues, is of two kinds *l'un du total, l'autre de la partie.* Hence the cohesion

---

[1] ib., p. 551.   [2] ib., p. 601.   [3] ib., pp. 641, 642.
[4] See *De Magnete* . . . Cap. 6 : De Magno magnete, telluris globae (1600).
[5] See Etienne Gilson, *Etudes de Philosophie Médiévale* : Campanella et l'Analogie.

of animal's bodies, and at the same time the semi-independence
of parts, such as nails and hair.[1]

Il n'y a rien en la nature qui ne porte en son intérieur l'idée
de ce qu'il est et la ressemblance de soi-même et qui ne s'efforce
de la mettre en évidence par un secret amour qui se chatouille soi-
même et s'excite pour éviter l'infâme reproche de la stérilité et de
l'impuissance.[2]

He does not deny outright the influence of the stars on human
destiny, nor is it incompatible with the Copernican system, but
this influence is ultimately that of the sun, whence they derive
their light, and it can only be considered along with many other
influences on human life.   The whole argument is thus a *reductio
ad absurdum* of the importance attributed to astrology.

Every body has two parts, visible and invisible, material
and spiritual, so too every element has its spiritual part.   It
is this part, called *astre* by Marandé, which exercises influence ;
there is thus an influence of the elements in man on the composite whole which is man.   Hence judicial astrology is anyhow
vain without the study of temperament.   Here we are once
more on fairly familiar ground.   The next two sections of the
book are devoted to showing the influence on men of place,
time, persons, parents, education, health and disease ; of religion
and laws, country and government, wine, wives and friends :
they are all *autant d'Astres qui répandent sur nous des influences
fort remarquables*.   Here is a passage on the force of tradition
and environment on religion :

Le Mahométan ne voit rien au delà de la créance de son père
que son Alcoran et son Prophète.   Quelque vérité qu'on lui puisse
montrer au contraire, c'est inutilement : il est engagé dès son jeune
âge, et la religion qui jette les plus profondes racines dans l'âme de
l'homme est celle qu'il a sucée avec le lait et que sa nourrice lui a
enseignée : faut donc qu'il parachève sa course.   Il ressemble à celui
qui se trouve au milieu d'une rivière, dans un bâteau, sans rames,
sans aviron, quelque signe qu'on lui fasse de venir à bord, il suit
malgré lui le courant de l'eau.   Et quelque force d'esprit dont les

[1] Marandé continues : ' L'homme seul fait le rechigné et le mal-content,
il marchande de tout et est toujours prêt de changer sa part contre le
premier venu. . . .   Mais tous ses défauts ne sont pas de notre nature,
ils procèdent du vice de notre opinion et du dérèglement de notre esprit :
contentons nous de jouer notre personnage et de considérer que nous
portons en notre sein dequoi nous satisfaire pleinement, pourvu que
notre esprit se borne aux limites que Dieu et la nature ont mis au dedans
de nous ' (p. 622).
[2] ib., p. 631.

jeunes libertins aujourd'hui se veulent armer contre Dieu et contre notre Religion, quelque mépris, dis je, qu'il en fassent, pour au dépens de leur salut, sacrifier leur âme à l'impiété, il n'y a pas un parmi eux qui n'ait peur quelquefois d'en être châtié et qui ne redoute l'avenir quand il y pense, tant il est difficile de se déffaire des loix du pays qui pour s'être rendues compagnes de nos jeunes ans, ne nous laissent jamais sans regret et sans amertume.[1]

Marandé is a sincere enough Christian, but how double-edged is his reflexion !

These influences seem to mould the whole course of our lives. What then of moral responsibility ? The author seems to imagine he has dealt with this difficulty by pointing out that these influences are neither good nor bad in themselves, but his explanations on this point are obscure. If the stars have indeed an influence, the science of astrology still remains the most uncertain of all fields of knowledge. The ' sciences ' of physiognomy and chiromancy are more dependable, indeed where simple folk, peasants and such, are concerned almost infallible. Marandé ends by recommending suspense of judgement on all the opinions expressed by him and those with whom he disagrees. The ways of God are incomprehensible.

These two chapters were published two years after the condemnation of Galileo and a year before the Papal bull against astrology. It is interesting to see the method Marandé employs on such dangerous ground—Montaigne's method in fact. But it can hardly be claimed that he was particularly advanced in his defence of Copernican theory. Already in 1630, before the publication of the *Massimi Systemi*, La Mothe le Vayer tells us that few men of learning are not won over to the new views.[2] We have seen how unwilling the prudent Mersenne was to express himself against Galileo in 1634 ; [3] and six years later Gassendi, while making clear his own convictions, ends by saying that he will not absolutely assert the earth's motion, although the opposite opinion has much need of better arguments, while the Scriptures can be explained metaphorically. Nevertheless, *hac occasione pure captivum intellectum non erubesco non quod propterea existimem articulum fidei esse.* His attitude is simply one of respect for the opinion of the Cardinals who condemned Galileo, and he defends his position with vigour against the attack of his *quondam*

---

[1] ib., p. 723.
[2] *Cinq Dialogues* (ed. Trévoux), p. 74 ; *Quatres Dialogues*, p. 356.
[3] See above, p. 174.

friend, J. B. Morin, who sought to prove him a heretic in his *Ala Telluris fracta*.[1]

To conclude then, Marandé shows the triple importance of the Essays for those of his generation.   His book is full of considerations on the vanity and incertitude of knowledge, which are valuable in two connections : first they inspire a Christian pyrrhonism, and secondly they are a weapon against the dogmatism of those who oppose scientific advance.   And finally, he preaches a human virtue which is an attainable ideal, in contrast with the presumptuous pretensions of the neo-Stoics.

[1] *Opera*, III : *Epistola II de Motu impresso* . . . (to Pierre Dupuy), p. 519.   See also Vion Dalibray's Sonnet sequence *Le Mouvement de la Terre* written before 1646.   The influence of Montaigne on Dalibray and on his friend Pailleur, who was acquainted with Pascal, would not be hard to show.   Bernier (*Abrégé de la Philosophie de Gassendi*, ed. 1684, IV, pp. 278, 279) states that those of orthodox faith who wish to maintain the earth's motion say that Galileo's condemnation was merely an injunction against Galileo and cannot apply to other forms of the theory until the contrary theory has been promulgated as an article of faith which has not been done.   Bernier's own opinion may be gathered from the *Requête des Maîtres és Arts* . . . (1671).   In 1659 Chapelain notes already that one or two of the Jesuits *s'apprivoisent à l'hypothèse du mouvement de la terre*.   He fears, however, that their mouths will be quickly stopped (*Lettres*, II, p. 67).

CHAPTER XVI

DESCARTES AND MONTAIGNE

Le grand homme n'est jamais aérolithe.

BAUDELAIRE

IN any general tableau of the seventeenth century the figure of Descartes looms so hugely that it would be necessary in any case to consider side by side certain ideas of Montaigne and of Descartes, if only to show how in some respects the success of Cartesianism in the second half of the century necessarily coincides with the discredit of the *weltanschauung* represented by Montaigne, Charron, and most of the writers dealt with in this book. In one sense, then, the purpose of this chapter is to point a contrast as well as to suggest an influence. Just as Garasse, Boucher and Silhon often share Montaigne's ideas and are even indebted to him, so it is with Descartes. It is the privilege of men of genius to appear more original than they are, and this is true even of that philosopher whose fundamental claim to our gratitude is that his ideas presented a complete break with the past. Modern intensive study of Descartes—I refer in particular to the work of M. Etienne Gilson [1]—has succeeded in showing how much the Cartesian metaphysic owes to medieval thought, and the same writer's monumental edition of the ' Discourse on Method ' shows also how much light can be shed upon the history of his mind by a study of the Essays and *La Sagesse.* What I hope to show is that the young man who went to Holland in 1616 was in many ways the disciple of Montaigne and Charron, that his *morale par provision* is taken mainly from the Essays, that his theory of animal mechanism has for its origin a dissatisfaction with the ideas of the partisans of the *intelligence des bêtes*, and finally that some obscurities of his ' enthusiasm ' of 1619 only reveal their full significance when linked up with certain features of *La Sagesse.*

[1] See above all, *La Pensée Médiévale dans la Formation Cartésienne*, 1930.

209

The numerous echoes of Montaigne which we find in the 'Discourse' have, perhaps it may be held, only a limited significance. It is a book written, as all Descartes' books were written, with a very definite end in view; carefully toned to conciliate the public, to arouse its interest and make it ask for more, so to induce, if possible, some Prince or Commonwealth to place at the philosopher's disposition the wherewithal to continue his experiments on a vaster scale. As Descartes says to Mersenne in 1630, he is searching for *un biais par le moyen duquel je puisse dire la vérité sans étonner l'imagination de personne ni choquer les opinions qui sont communément reçues.* Some of the most obvious echoes of the Essays which we find in the 'Discourse' may thus be due to an intentional adoption of themes and phrases familiar to the public for whom he was writing. That is a point on which the reader is begged to suspend his judgement.

The 'Discourse', however, is also the long-promised *histoire de votre esprit*, referred to by Balzac in a letter to Descartes, as far back as 1628—the story of his adventures *dans la moyenne et dans la plus haute région de l'air*.[1] It presents the formation of Descartes' views, and is inevitably the main document upon which we are forced to rely for our knowledge of that period where the influence of others upon Descartes' mind must be sought. We must naturally accept with caution his account of events which took place at least seventeen years before. If, however, the indications of the 'Discourse' are controlled by all the available evidence, it seems fairly clear that the 'history' of the 'Discourse' is only a 'fable' in the sense that it may serve as a lesson to others, and that (though it omits much) what it *does* tell us of Descartes' preoccupation, is materially correct.

'*Le bon sens est la chose du monde la mieux partagée.*' This, the famous opening phrase of the 'Discourse', has often been contrasted with the assumption of Montaigne (echoing Plutarch) that there is more difference between one man and another than between some men and some animals. The importance of this contrast has already been seen in dealing with Chanet, but here it is, in part, illusory. Not that the familiar ironical argument which Descartes gives for holding such a view (every one thinks they have plenty of common sense) [2] implies that he does not mean what he says. In spite of his general rejection of 'substantial forms', Descartes is in agreement with the view that reason (*bon sens*) is the 'essence' not as the Scholastics held and

---

[1] 30 March 1628. *Œuvres* : ed. Adam et Tannery, Vol. I, 570.
[2] cf. Montaigne himself, *Essais*, II, 17, p. 441.

as he says here, of *man* (that composite creature, but single substance, who comprises a body and a mind) but it is the 'essence' of *mind*, a separate substance temporarily conjoined with a part of the material universe (which is itself one substance). To conclude, however, that Descartes wishes to show that all men are equally intelligent would be false.

As Gilson has pointed out, *bons sens* (which is not the same as *esprit* or intelligence) is used by Descartes in two senses : first, the faculty of judgement, or as he sometimes says *la lumière naturelle*, that is, reason. This is indeed *naturally* equal in all men in so far as they are minds, although it is better used by some than others. Hence precisely the significance of a method.

But *bon sens* is also frequently the equivalent of *bona mens*, that is, Wisdom or Philosophy, and is hence the perfection of the *lumière naturelle* to which we may hope to attain by the use of a method. Thus the work which Descartes on the morrow of his meditation in the stove vowed to write and finish before Easter 1619, was to have been called *Studium Bonae Mentis* : *ce sont*, says Baillet who possessed the fragments, *des considérations sur le désir que nous avons de savoir, sur les sciences, sur les dispositions de l'esprit pour apprendre, sur l'ordre qu'on doit garder pour acquérir la sagesse, c'est à dire la science avec la vertu, en joignant les fonctions de la volonté avec celles de l'entendement* (*Œuvres, X,* 191). So, in the ' Discourse ', the purpose of Wisdom, in which the ' luck ' of hitting on a right method has caused Descartes to make such progress, is, he says, to raise his knowledge ' gradually to the highest point to which the modest powers of his intelligence and the short duration of his life permit him to attain '. The original title, moreover, of the manifesto of 1637 was *Le projet d'une Science Universelle qui puisse élever notre nature à son plus haut degré de perfection.* Wisdom and Science, these two terms which are synonyms for Descartes, are habitually opposed to each other by the thinkers of the Renaissance as a whole and nowhere more strongly than in Charron's *La Sagesse,* which offers a physical reason why it is impossible for the man of judgement to be a man of learning, since judgement and memory are incompatible in any high degree. Descartes, in his desire to escape from any such view, is ready to suppose, on the other hand, two types of memory—one of which, ' local memory ', is characteristic of the pedants and the ' philosophers ' (this is his usual name for the school men), whereas the other, ' intellectual memory ', is involved in many processes of the understanding.[1] We see his interest in Lull's *Ars Magna* in his correspondence with Beeckman (1619) [2] and how he insists that the true art of memory is a knowledge of causes and the order in which they follow from each other.[3] We see there also the origin of that preoccupation with the uninterrupted movement of thought which it is necessary to preserve in deductive argument, the need for ' enumeration ' which plays a great rôle in the text of the ' Rules.'

This new identification of Wisdom and Science is brought about, not only indeed through the fact that Mathematics are for Descartes the type-science, but also because we have in his conception of Wisdom a transposition onto the intellectual plane of the ethical ideal of the Renaissance, such as we have it in Charron even more than in Montaigne. As Gilson says : ' Le bonheur consiste, en effet, dans la satisfaction de tous les désirs raisonnables et dans la certitude que nos désirs non satisfaits sont impossibles à satisfaire, donc contraires à la raison. Si l'on applique cette définition au domaine de la connaissance, la raison ne pourra être satisfaite (et par conséquent l'homme ne sera heureux) que si elle peut avoir la double certitude de connaître tout ce qu'elle est capable de connaître et de l'impossibilité absolue de connaître ce qu'elle ne connaît pas.' [4] Thus in the Rules Descartes says of the contemplation of the truth that it is ' the kind of pleasure which is in this world almost the only felicity which no pain can destroy '. Thus the right exercise of reason is in itself a moral act, and Wisdom and Science or Philosophy identified. So much then for the ideas underlying the preamble to the ' Discourse ', which ends by proclaiming the author's intention to represent ' my life as in a picture '.

Ainsi mon dessein n'est pas d'enseigner la méthode que chacun doit suivre pour bien conduire sa raison, mais seulement de faire voir en quelle sorte j'ai tâché de conduire la mienne. Ceux qui se mêlent de donner des préceptes se doivent s'estimer plus habiles que ceux auxquels il les donnent : et s'ils manquent en la moindre chose, ils en sont blâmables. Mais ne proposant cet écrit que comme une histoire, ou si vous l'aimez mieux, que comme une fable en laquelle, parmi

---

[1] cf. J. Sirven, *Les Années d'Apprentissage de Descartes*, pp. 302, 303, who sees here the origin of the Cartesian Dualism. See also the important letter to Huygens on the death of his brother (*Descartes and Huygens : Correspondance*, ed. Roth, p. 182).

[2] *Œuvres*, X, 156.

[3] ib., X, 230 (*Cogitationes Privatae*). cf. Bruno's early treatize, *De Umbris Idearum.*

[4] *Discours* (ed. Gilson), pp. 225, 226.

quelques exemples qu'on peut imiter, on en trouvera peut-être aussi plusieurs autres qu'on aura raison de ne pas suivre. . . .[1]

With this we enter into the story of Descartes' youth. We may pass over his account of his schooling, except to note that he begins by describing, as it were, in a paraphrase of the *Ratio Studiorum*, the function of each discipline and the profit, which, on the authority of his masters at La Flèche, he might reasonably hope to derive from them ; and, as he writes of scholastic philosophy, a personal note of irony creeps into this repetition of the words of others.[2]

Education does not finish at school, however, or at the university ; it is completed by travel. Here the educational function of travel as stated by Descartes is obviously inspired by the Essays or Charron : travel is contemporary history, is to converse with the men of one's own age and know their lives : travel teaches the relativity of custom and educates the judgement. It is Montaigne too who may have inspired that subtle reserve that history itself, by its omission of intimate and humble details, gives a falsely noble picture of the capacities of human nature which may well lead astray those who would live according to its lessons. And insensibly Descartes enters upon a personal re-appreciation of the arts and sciences : rhetoric and poetry, mathematics, where he admits the rôle of practical application as taught him at school still came uppermost in his mind : pagan ethics, unlike mathematics in its lack of any solid basis, where the Stoics with their pretensions to insensibility had built immense palaces on the flimsiest foundation. Theology ? Theology, however, is no science. Descartes, as elsewhere, sets matters appertaining to religion resolutely aside : *pour les examiner et y réussir, il était besoin d'avoir quelque extraordinaire assistance du ciel et d'être plus qu'homme.* The real disillusionment is obviously philosophy, the basis of all other sciences, in which no single problem was beyond discussion and hence all was doubtful, so that ' I almost held all was false which was only likely '. It is important to note how different this mitigated and unwilling scepticism is from the later *voluntary* attitude of ' methodical doubt '.

[1] cf. *Essais*, III, 2, p. 29.
[2] Descartes nevertheless does not appear ungrateful to the Jesuits who taught him, and his true opinion seems to emerge in the letter (1638) to a father on his son's education, in which he says even of Scholastic philosophy that it is useful to have studied ' le cours entier en la façon qu'il s'enseigne dans l'Ecole des Jésuites, avant qu'on entreprenne d'élever son esprit au dessus de la pédanterie pour se faire savant de la bonne sorte ' (*Œuvres*, II, 378).

And so into the world ! What is the attitude of the young man who, having chosen no profession, goes like so many of his contemporaries to travel in the Netherlands, in that State which war, learning and commerce combined to render the most active in Europe ? It would not be other were he a devotee of Montaigne or of Charron. He is disabused with learning and ' resolved to seek no other knowledge than that which could be found in myself ', or in the ' great book of the world ' [1]—the acquisition of experience, which, in the school of life, must be at once put to the touch and proved true or false. This knowledge of self is, above all, an ethical knowledge ; it is not only to know the truth, but ' to understand my own actions and to walk with assurance in this life '. What is the lesson that the young philosopher learns in the brief space of two years ? That with which (one is pretty convinced) he set out : that there was almost as much diversity in the manners of men as there was among the opinions of the philosophers. Relativity of custom as well as relativity of opinion : *J'apprenais à ne rien croire trop fermement de ce qui ne m'avait été persuadé que par l'exemple et par la coutume et ainsi je me délivrais peu à peu de beaucoup d'erreurs qui peuvent offusquer notre lumière naturelle et nous rendre moins capables d'entendre raison.* [2]

A period of introspection followed, Descartes would have us believe : *je pris un jour résolution d'étudier aussi en moi-même.* Here we must intervene to offer certain obvious additions to Descartes' confidences. The period of the study of other men was that of his first residence in Holland. He was engaged as volunteer in the army of Prince Maurice of Nassau, his name was inscribed in the registers of at least one University, his enthusiasm for mathematics had not left him. Furthermore, what perhaps made him resolve one day, as he says, to ' study in myself also and employ all the vigour of my mind to choose the ways I should follow ' was the instigation of his friend, Isaac Beeckman.

The importance of this friendship, dating from 10th November 1618, has been emphasized anew by M. Cohen.[3] It is on the anniversary of their meeting on 10th November 1619 that Descartes, in a village near Ulm, has the three dreams from which he dates his great discovery : *X November 1619 cum plenus Enthusiasmo forem, et mirabilis scientiae reperirem fundamenta.* Perhaps the best explanation of the nature of the great dis-

---

[1] cf. *Essais*, I, 26, p. 203.
[2] *Discours* (ed. Gilson), p. 10.
[3] G. Cohen : *Ecrivains français en Hollande.*

covery is the unity of science and—still more—the conviction
of a personal vocation. We know that he was on the road to a
discovery of a ' new science ', concerning the treatment of all
quantitative problems, from a letter to Beeckman in March 1619.
We know also that in the autumn of that year, before the famous
' enthusiasm ', he appears to have met at Ulm, the great *foyer*
of mathematical studies in Germany, Faulhaber, who was a
Rosicrucian.[1] There are several problems of date which there
is no room to elucidate here, but there are certain aspects of
Descartes' preoccupations at this time which appear clearly
enough in his dream and which have not received enough attention. M. Leroy's book (see note) contains a comment on the
dreams written by Freud, who ignores the third. Yet the
first and second dreams, admonitory in Descartes' estimation,
are less important in his own eyes than the third, on the importance of which alone M. Maritain has insisted.[2]

In the third dream the most important point is the reading in
a *Corpus Poetarum* of a poem of Ausonius which begins : *Quod
vitae sectabor iter ?* This is the fact which is mentioned by Descartes as a *memento* in his *Cogitationes Privatae*. The other points
about the dream appear, from Baillet's account of the lost treatise,
entitled *Olympica*, to be as follows. He first found on a table a
Dictionary not knowing whence it came, and was pleased, hoping
it would be useful to him. It turned, however, into the *Corpus*
(which he had doubtless used at La Flèche) where he read the
poem mentioned. A man, however, came giving him a poem
of Ausonius which he also knew, *Est et Non*. He replied he would
find it in the book, and searched in vain, but he said he knew
a better poem than this, namely *Quod vitae sectabor iter ?* On
searching for it, however, he only found a lot of little portrait
engravings and told the man that the book must be of a different
edition. With that the dream vanished, but without waking he
began to interpret it. The Dictionary meant the body of all
the Sciences together and the *Corpus Poetarum*, even more dis-
tinctly, *la Philosophie et la Sagesse jointe ensemble*. Nor did
this astonish him for ' the poets, moved by Enthusiasm and the
Force of the Imagination, strike, as it were, fire from the tinder
of our minds, discovering certain seeds of wisdom more surely
than does the reasoning of philosophers '. Finally the poem
Quod vitae, on the uncertainty of what life to choose, represented

[1] Maxime Leroy (*Descartes, le philosophe au masque*, 1929) who has
rightly insisted on the importance of Descartes' Rosicrucian friendships,
is not convinced that Ulm is the town in question (op. cit., I, p. 66).
[2] *Le Songe de Descartes.*

the ' counsel of a wise person or perhaps of Moral Theology '.
On waking Descartes continued his attempt at interpretation,
adding that the *Corpus* signified the Revelation or Enthusiasm
with which he hoped to be favoured, while the *Est et Non* of
Pythagoras was ' the Truth and Falsity of human knowledge
and profane science '.

One may be surprised at the conviction of Descartes that
this dream was so profoundly significant, but apart from his
quite obvious interest at this time in symbolism of a non-
mathematical as well as of a mathematical nature,[1] certain
indications have perhaps not been sufficiently emphasized.

Both the poems are given by their author as from Pytho-
gorean sources.[2]   The first describes the disadvantages of every
kind of life ending with the verse : *Non nasci esse bonum aut
natum cito morte potiri.*   It is obvious from Descartes' interpretation that its importance in his mind is connected with the
question of the first verse, and his conviction that the reform
of all the sciences, the ' instauration ' of a new method, was to
be his mission.   In the ' Yes and No ' poem, which describes
how these two monosyllables form the very texture of our lives,
there are two ideas which might have remained in Descartes'
mind :—

> Hinc omnis certat dialectica turba sophorum . . . ,

the loud-mouthed disputes of the schools : or by contrast the
one specifically ' Pythagorean ' allusion of the poem :

> Hinc pauci, multi quoque talia commeditantes
> Murmure concluso rabiosa silentia rodunt . . .

some bite their lips in silence.

Descartes' interest in Pythagoras at this moment was obviously very great.   In the ' Rules ' he refers several times to
the Pythagoreans.   He notes that the first inventors of philosophy
would admit none to the study of wisdom who were ignorant of
mathematics, from which he concludes that their mathematics
were something more profitable than ours, although not perfect,
as shown by their sacrifices and insane exaltation for some
quite mean discovery.[3]   Their prodigious machines were nothing

---

[1] cf. *Œuvres*, X, 218, Sensibilia apta concipiendis Olympicis : ventus
spiritum significat (so dream of wind) motus cum tempore vitam, lumen
cognitionem, &c.

[2] Ausonius, *Idyllia*, XV, XVII.

[3] *Œuvres*, IV, 375; ref. to Pythagoras' sacrifice of oxen (Diogenes
Laertius).   Cf. also the unreasonable preference of virtue to vice, an
allusion to the Pythagorean taboos.

very extraordinary, but he suspects that writers such as Diophantus and Pappus who reveal something of the 'old mathematical philosophy' which flourished many centuries before them, are also holding something back. And Descartes ends his consideration of this topic by saying: 'these reflections led me back from study of arithmetic and geometry to General Mathematics'.[1]

It is not hard to see that all Descartes' preoccupations at this moment lead him towards Pythagoras. Not only the mathematical conception of the universe, the alphabetical notation of number ascribed to him, the arithmetical aspect of geometry and the theory of music, but also the conception of 'animal spirits' has its possible origin in Pythagoras. While, if not Pythagoras himself, Archytas,—a Pythagorean—is responsible for the first theory of the earth's movement. Indeed Copernicus admitted that it was Pythagoras who had put him on the track of his great discovery. Nor is this all by any means, for the Pythagoreans were a fraternity, with a vow of silence during a limited period. It is also a fair inference that Descartes' interest in the Rosicrucians or, as he calls them in his *Excerpta Mathematica, Cabalae Germanorum*, comes from the analogy of their doctrine.[2] They were also a brotherhood, vowed to secrecy for a hundred years after their founder's death, and aimed at a reform not of the social structure but of the sciences. Whether Descartes, in spite of his subsequent denials, knew much of them or was one of them himself must remain conjecture.[3]

To return to the dream, we must next note the title given to the treatise which related the momentous experience : *Olympica*. This has been explained as referring to 'the most exalted topics', or to the divine revelation with which he believed himself to have been favoured. This too may have, however, a Pythagorean origin, referring to the story that Pythagoras, asked by Leon, King of Phliasians to name the art in which he put most reliance, replied that he had no acquaintance with any art but was a philosopher ; and that he compared life to the Great

---

[1] *Œuvres*, X, 377.   [2] ib., X, 297.

[3] The Alexandrian Pythagoreanism, which was to have such influence on the later history of Occultism, as already on Paracelsus and other writers of the Renaissance, might offer still more important *rapprochements* with Rosicrucianism, but would carry us too far from the subject in hand. It may be pointed out, however, that the first Rosicrucian writings, and the spate of pamphlets against them, begin in 1615 (*Fama fraternitatis*).

Note also that one of the discoveries of Faulhaber was the stereometric analogy of the Pythagorean proposition.

Games where some went to compete for the prize and others went with wares to sell, but the best are spectators.[1]

As a matter of fact, Montaigne's telling of the tale is more striking in connexion with this title. In the essay on Education (I, 26), immediately after the magnificent passage on the *grand monde que les uns* (Pythagoreans again) *multiplient comme espèces sous un genre, c'est le miroir où il nous faut regarder pour nous connaître de bon biais*, he continues :

Notre vie, disait Pythagore, retire à la grande et populeuse assemblée des jeux Olympiques. Les uns s'y exerçent le corps pour en acquérir la gloire des jeux ; d'autres y portent des marchandises à vendre pour le gain. Il en est, et qui ne sont pas les pires, lesquels ne cherchent autre fruit que de regarder comment et pourquoi chaque chose se fait, et être spectateurs de la vie des autres hommes, pour en régler et juger la leur.[2]

Furthermore, the story itself is the fabled origin of the ' three lives ' as we have them in Aristotle—the Theoretic, the Practical and the Apolaustic.[3] We have seen the variation on this elaborated by Montaigne himself and the simile of the three regions of the air which is so often used in connexion with it. Nothing prevents us assuming that the two possible senses of Olympica (the games—the Olympian region of the air) were in Descartes' mind in his choice of a title.[4]

To be a spectator, θεωρεῖν, such is the theme of some of Descartes' most intimate utterances, particularly the strange opening entry of the *Cogitationes Privatae* : ' Kalends of January, 1619 : As actors warned lest they should blush, put on a mask, so I, about to ascend upon the stage of the world where I have hitherto lived a spectator, appear in disguise (larvatus).' It is during the months which follow that we see Descartes studying Flemish, Perspective and Architecture, and we gather from his letters to Beeckman that the latter attempted to recall his mind to higher problems, and is rewarded by the news that he is on the road to the discovery of an ' utterly new science ? '[5]

Further light on this dream can be shed, however, if we

[1] Cicero : *Tusc. Disp.*, V, 3 ; Diogenes Laertius, VIII, 8.
[2] *Essais*, I, 203, 204.
[3] J. Burnet : *Early Greek Philosophy*, p. 108.
[4] The other fragment in which the term is used concerns symbolism (already quoted above, p. 216, note 1) *sensibilia apta concipienda Olympicis.*
[5] Further evidence of the fact that at a certain moment Descartes appears to have thought of himself as a mere reviver or rearranger of ancient thought is provided in certain extant fragments of the *Olympica* (see *Œuvres*, X, 204).

assume what I have already shown to be probable, namely, that the young Descartes had some acquaintance with *La Sagesse*. There is a striking use made of this formula *Est et Non—Oui et Non* in that book. On opening it, the reader is confronted in all the early editions with an engraved title-page : Wisdom represented as a naked woman and chained to the pedestal beneath her feet four little figures representing : Custom, Opinion, Superstition and lastly *la Science Vertu ou Preud 'homie artificielle, acquise, pédantesque, serve des loix et coutumes, au visage enflé, glorieux, arrogant, avec les sourcils relevés, qui lit en un livre où y a écrit OUI, NON*. It is not impossible that the poem of Ausonius—the first great writer of Bordeaux—with its reference to the disputes of the schools should be also the source of Charron's symbolism.[1] At all events, Descartes' waking interpretation refers to the Truth and Falsity, not of knowledge, but of *purely human* knowledge and of *profane science*. He cannot find this poem in the book (which contains engravings) and prefers the other to it.

Descartes' interpretation becomes far more significant, however, if we suppose he had in the past read and noted another passage of *La Sagesse*.

Charron's treatment of the function of the understanding has been mentioned : (1) The search for truth, which is none the less impossible by human means, so that its employment becomes the mere opposition of one reason to another : (2) *L'autre fin moins naturelle mais plus ambitieuse est l'invention*. Creation, which seems ' image of godhead ' has given us works which have ravished the admiration of the world. And he continues thus :—

S'ils ont été avec utilité publique, ils ont déifié leurs auteurs. Ceux qui ont été en subtilité seule sans utilité, ont été en la peinture, statuaire, architecture, perspective, comme la vigne de Zeuxis, la Vénus d'Apelles, la statue de Memnon, le cheval d'airain, la colombe de bois d'Archytas, la Sphère de Sapor roi de perse et tant d'autres.[2]

These marvels present precisely the type of problem which

---

[1] The title of Abelard's treatise *Sic et Non* may have crossed Charron's mind, and in Abelard he would doubtless have seen one of the early champions of theological rationalism, one of the founders of Scholasticism. although, as a matter of fact, Abelard's view of the essentially antinomian character of the human understanding presents a certain analogy with what we find in *La Sagesse* (see above, pp. 83, 84).

[2] *De la Sagesse*, I, 16, 12. The source of this list of marvels may be Cardan, *De Subtilitate* (1561), pp. 497, 1010, 11 ; 1018, 1028–1030 ; 1034 ; 1156.

fascinated Descartes in 1619, at the moment when we see him studying Perspective, Painting and Architecture, although it is doubtless a mere coincidence that in one of the entries of the *Cogitationes Privatae* we find precisely a reference to the wooden dove of Archytas [1] preceded by a description of a statue moved by magnetism. The passage of Charron, however, concludes thus :

Mais en tout cela il n'y a pas bien de si grande admiration que l'on pense, et à proprement et loyalement parler, il n'y a point d'invention que celle que Dieu révèle : car celles que nous estimons et appelons telles, ne sont qu'observations des choses naturelles et conclusions tirées d'icelles, comme la peinture de l'optique des ombres,[2] les orloges solaires des ombres des arbres, l'imprimerie des marques et sceaux des pierres précieuses.

True invention, true discovery, then, is here represented as a gift from God.

Now I do not wish to suggest that Charron or Montaigne were writers whose ideas in general were *necessarily* prominent in Descartes' mind even at this time, but I would suggest that the whole force of his dream-experience was that it represented an epitome of elements from the most diverse sources and different ages of his life. That is clear enough with regard to the first dream of going to pray in the college chapel at La Flèche. And in the third dream the Pythagorean gambit is evident. The Dictionary which means *les Sciences Ramasseés* has its obvious connexion with that chain of reasoning, that true art of memory which had haunted his mind for more than a year. The most important event in the dream, however, was the discovery of the first poem and the rejection or disappearance of the second. The *Oui et Non* of Charron's title plate and the divine character of invention, as given in Charron, may be only reminiscences of what he had read a year or two before, but they do throw some valuable light on the poem *Est et Non* and the conviction of divine intervention in the ' discovery of the foundation of a marvellous science '.

There remains, however, the inter-relation of the idea of a choice of life, the ' spectatorship ' of Descartes and the possible allusion to the life of contemplation in the title *Olympica*. Provided we remember that the date of the 10th November 1619 is merely a beginning and that a year and a day later (by one

---

[1] *Œuvres*, X, 230, 231. Descartes' observation of the flight of birds is noted by Beeckman in January, 1619.

[2] What about the *Cogitatio* (X, 215) on the shadow garden representing trees and other figures ?

of these coincidences which astound him) he notes that he began to understand the 'foundation of the marvellous invention' (the actual method and its rules ?), and that already in the letter to Beeckman in March 1619 he is on the track of a new method of solving physical problems, we shall see that Descartes' progress was a more gradual one than perhaps he himself imagined on any of these occasions. If the entry of the *Cogitationes* which announces his appearance in the world as something more than a spectator is now considered, on the evidence we possess it can only be connected with the practical and linguistic studies announced in the letter to Beeckman, Yet surely this *larvatus prodeo* was either a false start, a mere promise to himself to adopt some other rôle than that of a mere spectator which was speedily abandoned, or else it was nothing more than the assumption of a mask in the sense that behind it the philosophic spectator lives on unchanged. To be a spectator in the Pythagorean sense is both to have a profession and to have none. Hence the subtle double meaning of that *Quod vitae sectabor iter ?* The 'counsel of a sage or even of Moral Theology', as Descartes interprets it, was to have no profession, it was to have a vocation : not merely the vocation of the speculative life as the search for truth, truth as itself the road to happiness, but a mission which might be his should he prove worthy of it, the reform of the sciences as a whole, for they were a whole and their unity seems to have been the other conviction left upon his mind by the dream. From the unity of the sciences, it follows naturally enough that their perfection must be carried out by one man, and that man, by the grace of God, perhaps Réné Descartes. This conviction is all that Descartes, most indirectly and most modestly, will vouchsafe to the public of 1637 as to his experiences of eighteen years before.

Yet the string of similes—the rebuilding of a town, the framing of a constitution, the rebuilding of a house—while they discreetly convey Descartes' certitude of his mission, are mainly directed to the end of minimizing the novelty of the task he felt imposed upon him. It is true that Descartes had no political reforms in mind. In view of the fate of Bruno and Campanella it was imperative to reassure the public on this point ; but it is also true that all his life he hoped for a reform of the *corps des sciences ou l'ordre établi dans les écoles pour les enseigner ;* not undertaken indeed by himself, a private individual, but by the qualified authorities. All his writings are directed to this end, and their different character is explained by his successive efforts to appeal to the Jesuits, the Universities, and finally such enlightened rulers as Christina of Sweden. Probably the last of all Descartes' philosophic writings, the *Recherche de la Vérité par la Lumière Naturelle*, shows him, as has recently been said, in the attitude of turning to the Gentiles and appealing over the heads of the men of learning and the theologians to the ordinary man, in a way which, despite appearances, he had not done in the ' Discourse '.

In this passage of the ' Discourse ' we have, however, not only the apparent disavowal of revolutionary intentions even in the intellectual world, but also the beginning of his explanations of ' methodical doubt '—a necessary corollary to the conviction of his mission As a *personal* experiment he was convinced that with regard to the opinions he had received on the authority of his masters or had entertained up to that time, he could not do better than ' to undertake to disbelieve them all and at the same time '—*simul et semel*—' in order that I might subsequently adopt the same or better, when I had set them out by the level of reason ".[1] This doubt, it should be repeated, is something totally different, in its voluntary character, in its intention, and in its rigour, from the mitigated scepticism of Montaigne. Descartes, however, immediately proceeds to explain the reserves with which he determined to adopt his suspension of belief.

First, he contrasts again the difficulties of social and intellectual reform and makes a renewed disavowal of the former. Here once more Descartes' considerations are inspired by Montaigne or Charron :

Ces grands corps sont trop malaisés à relever, étant ébranlés, et leurs chutes ne peuvent être que très rudes. Puis, pour leurs imperfections, . . . l'usage les a sans doute fort adoucies : et même il en a évité ou corrigé insensiblement quantité, auxquelles on ne pourrait si bien pourvoir par prudence. Enfin, elles sont quasi toujours plus supportables que ne serait leur changement . . . C'est pourquoi je ne saurais aucunement approuver ces humeurs brouillonnes et inquiètes, qui, n'étant appelées, ni par leur naissance, ni par leur fortune, au maniement des affaires, ne laissent pas d'y faire toujours, en idée quelque réformation . . .[2]

What is still more important than these resemblances are the further reserves which Descartes adds. Even in such a personal matter this ' methodical doubt ' is not everybody's duty or privilege. For almost the whole world is composed

[1] cf. last phrase, *La Sagesse*, II, 8 § 7, 3.
[2] cf. *Essais*, III, 9, pp. 236, 233 ; I, 23, pp. 151, 153.

of two kinds of intelligence. Some are too presumptuous . . . *s'ils avaient une fois pris la liberté de douter des principes qu'ils ont reçus, et de s'écarter du chemin commun, jamais ils ne pourraient tenir le sentier qu'il faut prendre pour aller plus droit* . . . The others are not too headstrong but too docile. Reasonable and modest enough to know that they are *moins capables de distinguer le vrai d'avec le faux que quelques autres par lesquels ils peuvent être instruits* [1], they are best advised to follow the opinions of others. Note what is, in effect, Descartes' transformation of the dogmatists and the peasants of Montaigne. Who then are fitted for this examination but those who have learnt the lesson of the Essays, those who have learnt the *diversity* of the customs and manners of men and of the opinions of the philosophers?

Ayant appris dès le collège, qu'on ne saurait rien imaginer d'étrange et incroyable, qu'il n'ait été dit par quelqu'un des philosophes [2]; et depuis, en voyageant, ayant remarqué que tous ceux qui ont des sentiments fort contraires aux nôtres, ne sont pas pour cela barbares ni sauvages, mais que plusieurs usent, autant ou plus que nous de raison : et ayant considéré combien un même homme, avec son même esprit, étant nourri dès son enfance entre des Français ou des Allemands, devient différent de ce qu'il serait s'il avait toujours vécu entre des Chinois ou des Cannibales . . . en sorte que c'est bien plus la coutume et l'exemple qui nous persuadent qu'aucune connaissance certaine, et que néanmoins la pluralité des voix n'est pas une preuve qui vaille rien pour les vérités un peu malaisées à découvrir, à cause qu'il est bien plus vraisemblable qu'un homme seul les ait rencontrées que tout un peuple . . .

And that one man, Descartes. If these considerations are not truly those which influenced Descartes, with what cleverness has he chosen the *biais* which was most familiar to his contemporaries in order to justify himself!

The device, however, of methodical doubt is represented by Descartes as having been postponed in his own case, until he had undertaken that *Studium Bonae Mentis* which discussed the relations of Science and Wisdom and until he had discovered ' the true method '. With regard to the four rules of the *Discours* or the twenty-one *Rules* which throw such important light on the real character of the method, it is hardly necessary to do more than draw attention to certain features. Their importance

---

[1] There is no real discrepancy with the opening sentence of the ' Discourse '. As M. Gilson points out (ed. cit. 177, 178) all are equally capable of recognizing the truth, but not of *discovering* it (' invention ' is a gift, if not a grace).

[2] cf. Cicero : *De Div.*, II, 58, 119 ; and also *Essais*, II, 12, p. 292.

above all in the condensed form in which they are given in the
' Discourse ' is due to the fact that from the multitude of logical
precepts and the numerous rules of mathematical analysis these
alone suffice, for from them, if properly understood, all those
which are of any utility can be derived.   The connexion between
Descartes' study of the memnonic treatises of Lull, Schenkel
(and perhaps Bruno) and the arrangement of causal series has
been already noted, and Descartes' own text here reminds us
of it with its reference to Lull.

We may pass therefore directly to the *morale par provision*,
necessitated by the fact that the very unity of the sciences
compels Descartes to conduct a simultaneous attack on a whole
series of problems in order to discover not only a new physics
(the trunk of the tree) but its true basis (its roots) in a new
metaphysics.   The first and the last of the maxims of the *morale
provisoire* lead us back directly, if not to Montaigne, to Charron :
conformity with custom and choice of a way of life.   While
the second (adherence to a course once adopted) seems ana-
logous with the last.   The ideas involved are familiar, and may
therefore be rapidly passed over, except to note that the similarities of *Avoir un train de vie certain* (*Sagesse*, II, 4)—considerations on choice of life and persistence in a resolution—may
possibly strengthen the supposition that reminiscences of *La
Sagesse* played their part in the dream of the poem *Quod vitae
sectabor iter ?* [1]

The third maxim, though it has still a connexion with Charron,
is more obviously stoical in inspiration.   *Tâcher toujours plutôt
à me vaincre que la fortune, et à changer mes désirs plutôt que
l'ordre du monde :*—Descartes' development of the theme, though
it again presents analogies with odd phrases of Charron, is
obviously mainly the résumé of some such book as Lipsius'
Manuductio. [2]

One important point of difference between Charron's ideas
and their presentation in the ' Discourse ' has been emphasized
by Gilson.   Charron's is a definite ethic contained in a hand-
book on Wisdom ; the chapters from which Descartes has taken
various considerations concern *la vraie preud'homie*, whereas
Descartes presents them as temporary.   Two observations must,

---

[1] For Maxim I : cf. Charron, II, 8 § 7 (and perhaps on the consultation
of the prudent ;   II, 10 § 4) ; II, 2 § 2 (contrast of the outward attitude
of dogmatists and real beliefs) ;   II, 5 § 8 (*ils se le font accroire qu'ils le
croient*, &c.) ;   II, 2 § 7 (end) opinions *commodes*.   Also Essays, III 10
(*Ménager sa volonté* and treatment of vows) and Charron, II, 2 § 7.
Maxim II, cf. Charron, II, 4 § 3 (end) : Maxim IV : ib., II, 4.

[2] See Gilson, ed. cit., 250–4.

however, be added. What difference is there between these maxims and those according to which Descartes had hitherto conducted his own life, as we have seen by examining the first part of the ' history of his mind ' ?   Nothing, I suspect, but mere fact of formulation, with the rider that they are provisional only.   Nothing perhaps but certain convictions which are here left unstated.

Further, what differences are there between this provisional ethic and Descartes' later views ?   We know that in his famous tree of Philosophy, one of the three branches springing from the trunk of the New Physics, is *la plus haute et la plus parfaite Morale qui, présupposant une entière connaissance des autres sciences, est le dernier degré de la Sagesse.*[1]   So far as knowledge of this definitive Ethic goes, we have to rely on Descartes' correspondence—above all the letters to the Princess Palatine—and certain indications of the *Traité des Passions.*   He had too much controversy already on his hands, he informs Chanut, to set out his views on such an essentially controversial matter.   It is certainly worth comparing his doctrine, as it appears in the letters to Elizabeth, with this section of the *Discours,* although as Sorbière (I think) maliciously remarks somewhere ' *on voit qu'il n'avait pas beaucoup réfléchi à ces choses-là* ', and Elizabeth herself has no difficulty in picking holes in some of his ideas.[2]   Her criticism is in effect mainly of his Stoical, idealist and libertarian bias and also the very assumption of what is almost omniscience for the practical conduct of life.   And indeed at first sight the definitive ethic differs only on a few points from the maxims of the ' Discourse ' brought forward with Seneca's *De Vita Beata* as a basis of discussion in their correspondence.

It is true, nevertheless, that in 1645 Descartes would substitute individual judgement (if enlightened by his own philosophical principles) for conformity with the opinion of our wisest fellow citizens.   A commonplace improvement indeed, only significant in so far as Descartes' whole philosophy is historically the next step after that of the Reformation and the humanism of the Renaissance towards the establishment of the freedom of the individual judgement in every sphere of life.   It is also merely putting back in the window what was perhaps cautiously omitted from the maxims of the *morale par provision,* since *le philosophe au masque,* one has every reason to believe, acted all his life on the principle of *intus ut libet, extra ut modus est.*[3]

[1] *Œuvres,* IX, 14 (*Principes : Preface*).
[2] *Œuvres,* IV ; cf. especially, 289, 404-6.
[3] cf. Descartes' own motto : *Qui bene latuit bene vixit,* and below, p. 242, Cremonini's motto.

And in so doing, he merely continues, like so many others, the Montaigne tradition, which is not that of mere conformity but of the inevitability of individual judgement : *j'ai mes loix et ma cour pour juger de moi.*

Still more commonplace appears the substitution of a constant following of right reason for constancy in a course once adopted, the second Maxim of the ' Discourse '. The third, indeed, and fourth do gain in significance by their revision. The limitation of our desires to what is within our power, hence to our thoughts, receives its full sense only with the statement of the Cartesian dualism and a new knowledge of the extent of human freedom.[1]   The review of the diverse occupations of men in order to choose the best becomes explicitly the superiority of the speculative life.   But it was *implicitly* so all along, for the conclusion which Descartes says it taught him (in 1619 or 1620 ?) was ' I could not do better than continue in that walk of life in which I was then engaged '.

The similarities with Stoicism cannot be pushed very far, however.   The eclectic mixture of Stoical and Epicurean ideas was recognized by Leibnitz, but what has perhaps been made less clear is the importance, which, despite the Cartesian dualism, he attributes to the body.   There is a *ployer la machine* in Descartes, as in Pascal, though totally different in intention.   He does not disdain something like the ' diversion ' of Montaigne. Of undeserved misfortunes he writes to Elizabeth : ' *je ne trouve à cela qu'un seul rémède, qui est d'en divertir son imagination et ses sens le plus qu'il est possible, et de n'employer que l'entendement seul à les considérer, lorsqu'on y est engagé par la prudence.'* [2] There is, none the less, a certain difference between this attitude and that of *De la Diversion*, and in the frequent discussions with Elizabeth on the interaction of bodily and mental health it is above all the action of mind on body which Descartes appears to consider.   He thus believes that his cultivation of an optimistic outlook was what cured the cough with which he was born.[3]

Yet this is too simple a method of considering the question, for the Cartesian dualism is, in fact, far less straightforward than it appears.   Just as Descartes is led to suppose two kinds of memory, he is led to distinguish two kinds of passion, and two kinds of imagination, in order to bridge the gulf which his

---

[1] This freedom is, in a certain sense, implicit in the proclamation that it is *possible* to reject *all* one's beliefs *at once.*

[2] *Œuvres*, IV, 218 (May 1645 ?).   See too, without any restriction, the letter to Pollot (ib., 278 (1641)).

[3] *Œuvres*, IV, 218.

own metaphysic has set up, and his very interest in physiology helps to readjust what might seem an inhumanly intellectualist ethic. In the correspondence with Elizabeth interaction-problems play a great part, for if the perfection of the mind is to be considered, there is also the problem of bodily health to which Descartes personally attached no little importance; witness the strange hopes he at one time cherished of prolonging human life.[1] Finally the ideal of the perfection of human nature as a whole is the inspiration of the *Traité des Passions*. It is beyond the scope of this chapter to enter into a discussion of Descartes' use of the term *passion de l'âme* and the various distinctions he establishes, but his general attitude is summed up in the letter to Chanut in which he writes of 'the passions':

En les examinant, je les ai trouvées presque toutes bonnes, et tellement utiles à cette vie, que notre âme n'aurait pas sujet de vouloir demeurer joint à son corps un seul moment, si elle ne les pouvait ressentir.[2]

It is in this aspect among others that the moral temper of Cartesianism has been compared with that of Corneille's tragedies. Descartes' attitude, however, has a further connexion with drama, and this leads us back to the theme of spectatorship. The true remedy of the passions is to cultivate the attitude of the spectator of a drama, the drama of our own emotions, as well as the drama of the universe of which we are part. Any reader of the correspondence must be struck by the constant use of the similes of the drama.[3] Controlled emotion is part of the felicity which can be enjoyed here and now. A knowledge of our immortality and our mortality teaches us to look on the events of the world as we do those of a play. Yet by its insistence on human liberty, by the fact that on the intellectual plane the accent of his philosophy is constantly laid upon what the human mind *can* know and not on what it can never know, the Cartesian philosophy is robbed of any really tragic element. The moral attitude of Descartes, although it has its roots in the humanism of Montaigne more than has sometimes been thought, differs precisely in that

[1] Note the rôle attributed by the Rosicrucians to 'perfect temperament'. In Mersenne's *Vérité des Sciences* (I, p. 596) we read: 'Il y en a d'autres qui veulent qu'un corps parfaitement tempéré soit si parfait qu'il ne puisse contracter aucune maladie, qu'il puisse subsister éternellement . . . qu'il puisse guérir les maladies . . . ce qu'on attribue aux . . . Frères de la Rose-Croix '.

[2] *Œuvres*, IV, 538.

[3] From the opening of the *Compendium Musicae* (1618) onwards such similes are common.

its moral optimism is completed by an intellectual optimism which leads us on to the ' Theodicy ' of Leibnitz, and to that *apologia* of the best of possible worlds which Voltaire exposed. A Montaigne, or a Charron in his train, may seem to ignore ' original sin ' as Descartes does, but they introduce, as it were, a compensating feature in their insistence on the limitations of human knowledge, in their fideism and what is in effect their denial of the possibility of a metaphysic.

It is doubtless to Descartes' metaphysic that we should now logically turn.   Before doing so, however, we must consider, first, the most obvious contrast of opinion which can be made between Montaigne and Descartes : their interpretation of animal behaviour.

We have seen the importance which the *intelligence des bêtes* assumed for many contemporaries of Descartes,[1] and M. Busson, in giving a long list of those who discuss this question, says he is convinced that (with two exceptions) Montaigne is everywhere *la source ou la cible*.   It is very easy to prove without the least doubt that he is also, although not named, *la cible* in the ' Discourse ' itself.   It is in a letter to the Marquis of Newcastle on this question, written in November 1646, that Descartes makes the only mention of Montaigne and Charron which can be found in his works, and repeats the reasoning of the ' Discourse '.   It may, however, be said that this is only the choice of convenient adversaries, the best-known names of those who argued the extreme opposite case—for the *reasoning* of animals.   If we examine carefully the earliest indications of his theory with Descartes' presentation of his case elsewhere,[2] we shall see that it is possible to go further.   We can say not only that Montaigne —or better Charron—is the *cible* but that he is also, in some measure, the source of Descartes' ideas.   The automaton theory would not have been evolved by Descartes except by reaction from the partisans of *l'intelligence des bêtes*—and by reaction also perhaps to the one tenet of the Pythagoreans for which he could find no credence.

In dealing with Charron it has already been indicated that *l'intelligence des bêtes* is not so flattering as it may appear.   Having

---

[1] Note that Chanet's book (above, pp. 186–193) was *written* before the *Discours*.   Descartes nowhere refers to him.   So far as La Chambre is concerned, Descartes procured and consulted his *Caractères des Passions*, but, after glancing at it, tells a friend it is ' mere words '.

[2] *Discours*, Vme Partie (ed. Gilson, pp. 55–9) : *Œuvres*, IV, 568, I, 404 ; II, 39 ; II, 121 ; V, 276–7 ; IX, 321 ; XI, 120, 202.

spoken of the most ingenious and marvellous actions of animals, Charron (there is no exact parallel in the Essays) [1] continues :

Pour rabattre tout ceci aucuns malicieusement rapportent toutes ces choses à une inclination naturelle, servile et forcée : mais outre que cela ne peut être . . . aussi ne sauraient ils dire que c'est que cette inclination et instinct naturel. *Encores ce dire se retorque contr'eux, car il est sans comparaison plus noble, honorable, et ressemblant à la divinité d'agir par nature que par art et apprentissage, être conduit et mené par la main de Dieu que par la sienne, et réglément agir [que] par liberté fortuite et téméraire.*[2]

And Charron adds that the above view accords ill with the teachability of animals. Note, furthermore, that instinct as a direct mode of God's operation upon or in his creatures presents obvious analogies with Charron's view of the divine character of true ' invention ', though he denies one and accepts the other.

Now in this connexion the earliest text of Descartes which we possess is the following entry of the *Cogitationes Privatae* :

Ex animalium quibusdam actionibus valde perfectis, suspicamur ea liberum arbitrium non habere.

We have also seen the interest which Descartes takes at this very same time in *automata*. The moving statue and the dove of Archytas have been mentioned,[3] and in the *Principia* we have again Descartes' admission that the consideration of ' *artefacts* ' have aided him much in the whole elaboration of his physics. According to Baillet, the theory was evolved by 1625 and in a letter to Mersenne in 1630 Descartes is already able to refer him to the *Monde* then in preparation.

If we bear these indications in mind, one feature of the ' Discourse ' and the letters and other passages indicated assumes the air of a personal confidence and not a mere expository device. In the majority of these passages Descartes definitely asks his readers or his correspondents to consider *automata*. Thus in the ' Discourse ' he says that his opinion will ' seem in no wise strange to those, who knowing how many diverse *automata*, or machines which move the industry of men can construct (employing very few parts, compared with the multitude of those . . . which

---

[1] See, however, *Essais*, II, 8, p. 76.　　　　[2] *Sagesse*, I, 8, 7.

[3] Curiously enough, he replies to Mersenne in 1640 that a machine which could fly like a bird is ' metaphysically ' but not ' physically possible ' (III, 130, 163). His certitude on this point (compare the many puzzles of Mersenne on which he refuses to commit himself) indicates his close consideration of the matter, doubtless in 1619, as Beeckman's notes show.

compose the body of any animal), will look upon this body as a machine which, being made by God, is incomparably better organized '. Given a machine of such a type, says Descartes, there is no means of distinguishing it from an animal. Yet there will be means of distinguishing such a machine from a man.

Descartes sees clearly enough that the crux of the problem, which has to be judged from the point of view of behaviour, is the question of speech, and perhaps, in a lesser degree, adaptation. He replies directly to the objections of Montaigne and Charron [1] who confuse the emotional cries of animals with the rudimentary symbolism evolved even by deaf-mutes. We can further see how this distinction was clear to him from the time of his early interest in symbolism. He takes up the familiar saying of Montaigne that men are so unlike in capacity that there are some beasts nearer to men than some men to others,[2] and points out the inequality of animals of the same species, and remarks that the stupidest child speaks better than the cleverest animal. Finally he denies, as Montaigne had playfully suggested, that animals speak but we don't understand them. The objection here, as on another point, is clearer in the letter to the Marquis of Newcastle. Dogs certainly communicate their feelings to their masters but not their thoughts, and on the ' industry of animals ', he adds : ' *Je sais bien que les bêtes, font beaucoup de choses mieux que nous, mais je ne m'en étonne pas : car cela même sert à prouver qu'elles agissent naturellement et par ressorts, ainsi qu'une horloge, laquelle montre bien mieux l'heure que notre jugement ne saurait le faire.*' This indication is better explained by the letter of March 1638 [to Pollot], where again the supposition of a man brought up among *automata* is introduced, for here Descartes makes it clear that the very perfection of animals in certain specific acts would prove to such a man that animals were the machines of a greater Artificer than any he knew. The same supposition appears in a letter to Mersenne and one to More.

It is in this letter to Henry More that the position of Descartes is made most clear. He here begins by admitting that,

---

[1] For full list of parallel passages, showing where Descartes replies to the Essays, see *Discours*, ed. Gilson, 420–9.

[2] See in Letters to Newcastle (IV, 568) : ' Car bien que Montaigne et Charron aient dit qu'il y a plus de différence d'homme à homme que d'homme à bête, il ne s'est toutefois jamais trouvé aucune bête si parfaite qu'elle ait usé de quelque signe pour faire entendre à d'autres animaux quelque chose qui n'eût point de rapport à ses passions ', &c.

though it is impossible to prove that animals 'think', he does not believe it is possible to demonstrate that they do not think, since we have only their behaviour by which to judge. Yet there is no reason *for* except similarity of visible structure, from which our natural inference of similar mental processes is derived. This unreasoned inference, however, arises in childhood and should not be given undue weight, since far stronger contrary evidence can be produced.[1] 'This argument also has its place that it is not so probable that worms, fleas and caterpillars should have an immortal soul as that they function after the manner of machines'. It should be noted what a minor place is held by this argument, to which we must refer later. Secondly, it is very likely, since art can imitate nature and since men can make *automata* which move without consciousness, that nature also should produce her own *automata*. So that truly we ought to think it more strange that a soul is found conjoined with each human body. But *above all*, although there are differences of aptitude and 'perfection' among animals, as among men, and although all (*sic* !) can easily signify their emotions and appetites by voice or sign, there is no evidence of non-emotional speech. Finally Descartes reminds More that he does not deny either life or sense to animals (as he is commonly represented to do), so that his opinion *non tam crudelis est erga belluas quam pia erga homines, Pythagoreorum superstitione non addictos.*[2]

The piety of Descartes in this matter seemed ill-advised to many contemporaries, although he presents his views in the 'Discourse' and elsewhere not as caused by a consideration of the greater likelihood which the immortality of the soul obtains by their acceptance, but as a profitable *result* which follows from it. How little real weight he wisely attached to it is surely indicated by the fact that it is not urged in the *Méditations* where he is most anxious to persuade that doctrine of immortality—and indeed we shall see that he does not think that immortality can be proved. The theory of animal mechanism, however, when thus examined in detail, does show how reasonable in the main—and, in the light of modern mechanistic biology, how profitable, in spite of its paradoxical form—that theory was.[3] The theory, however, seemed dangerous to some contem-

---

[1] Compare the argument in *Méditations*, VI, on the veracity of sense-perception.

[2] *Œuvres*, V, 276–8.

[3] If to-day biology cannot dispense with the notion of intention whether it considers behaviour or structure, it must be remembered that evolutionary theory is responsible. Descartes' refusal to entertain any such notion is exactly paralleled by his antifinalism in metaphysics.

poraries as much because it seemed to them to make things easy for the atheists (*viam sterni Atheis*) as because it conflicted with the Aristotelian ' substantial forms '. Descartes' reply to one of these critics, (3rd October 1637), provides an intriguing passage where he appears to transform Charron's objection against the ' instinct ' theory (quoted above) into an argument for his own view.

' I cannot understand (he says) how after positing so small a difference between the actions of men and animals, they can persuade themselves that there is so great a difference between the nature of " rational " and " sensitive " souls. For wherein do they imagine sense to be distinguished from reason ? Because, forsooth, sense-knowledge is alleged to be simple and apprehensive, and hence not liable to error : but rational knowledge to be rather more complex, and to be conducted by the ambiguities of syllogisms. And this does not seem in any way to argue a greater perfection : particularly since these same men say that the knowledge of God and the Angels is also simple and intuitive, or merely apprehensive, and not fettered by any of the wrappings of discursive thought : so that, on their own showing, the sense of brutes more nearly resembles, if one may dare to say so, the knowledge of God and the Angels than human reasoning.' [1]

It may appear that too much space has been devoted to this question, but it must surely be evident that this theory (dispensing with ' substantial forms ' where they appeared most inevitable), together with the method and the discovery of a single attribute of matter, namely extension,[2] in terms of which all physical phenomena can be explained, are the first and the essential steps in the elaboration of Descartes' whole philosophy. And if this be admitted, may we not add the suggestion, which seemed too bold to put forward at an earlier stage, that in the notion of the divine character of ' true invention ', we have the germ of that doctrine of innate ideas, which, developed more logically by Malebranche than by his master, ends in Occasionalism.

It is unnecessary to linger over the reaction of Descartes to Scepticism which leads to the discovery of an irrefutable point of departure in the *Cogito*, although it should be remembered that his own reason for not discussing at length the sceptical

[1] *Œuvres*, I, 416.
[2] Motion being treated very unsatisfactory as a ' mode ' of extension.

critique of knowledge in the ' Discourse ' was a wish to avoid all appearance of encouraging ' dangerous thoughts '. Our examination of the young Descartes of 1616–19 and of the probable genesis of the *bête machine* must inevitably suggest more precise reasons than hitherto adduced for supposing Montaigne to have been ultimately responsible, either through Charron or directly, for providing the fecundating doctrine against which Descartes reacted, as in the explanation of animal behaviour.

It is important, however, to be clear as to Descartes' attitude towards fideism. He was not content with the perfunctory division of theology from the sphere of philosophy and the sciences. He rightly pointed out that there is a neutral ground, that two problems, the existence of God and the immortality of the soul, are claimed both by theology and philosophy. His position is, in this respect, strictly orthodox. Nevertheless, M. Busson has recently pointed out that it is possible to speak of Descartes' fideism—and even of Descartes' fideist influence. Not so much because his own implicit claim and the explicit claim of his followers was that, *only* on their principles could these doctrines be proved. But because, with respect to immortality his very honesty shows this founder of a later theological rationalism as singularly modest in his claims. It is only necessary to point out that the first edition of the *Méditations* claimed to prove the doctrine of immortality, but that this claim was subsequently withdrawn. All he professes to do is to show that the mind or soul is simple and the body composite, that ' the death of the soul cannot be inferred from the corruption of the body ' and hence that men may ' hope for a second life after death '.[1]

Descartes' reasoning in this passage is only intelligible in connexion with the whole of his ' physics ', as he himself is careful to point out. From his law of the conservation of matter it follows, in a sense, that the substance, Matter, is naturally as incorruptible as the substance, Mind ; both continue to exist as long as God grants them his ' concourse '. But matter differs from mind in this, among other respects, that it is composed of parts, that it is diversified by various changing configurations, whereas mind remains identical with itself. Furthermore, any body, human or otherwise, is only itself part of the substance, matter. In one particular, therefore, Descartes' view is peculiar to himself, in that he invokes the wrongly formulated law of conservation of matter (instead of conservation of energy). In so far as the argument is founded on the alleged simplicity of the

[1] See the *Abrégé des Six Méditations.*

mind or soul and the composite nature of the body, it is superficially in accordance with the whole scholastic tradition.   In, a
third respect, which explains his unwillingness to claim to *prove*
immortality, it is again an innovation.   He refuses to say that
mind is *necessarily* immortal or bodies necessarily mortal, because
he refuses to limit the omnipotence of God.   His position here
is the result of his whole attitude to the question of ' eternal
verities ', and offers us a striking exception to his avoidance of
all theological questions.

Already when many of his views, except perhaps some of
his leading ideas on physics, were hardly developed, Descartes
has a most decided opinion on what appears a purely theological
matter, an opinion he stuck to all his life and to which he evidently attached considerable importance.[1]   He maintains that
there is no distinction between God's understanding and his will,
as the scholastics held.   For them part of the content of God's
understanding were the ' eternal verities ', some of which at least
are known to us, such as the principle of contradiction.   Descartes refused to recognize, as the Scholastics did, any of these
' eternal verities ', the existence of a Good, for example, as sub-
sisting in the understanding of God and independent of his will.
What is the explanation of his attitude ?

For the Thomists the will of God, being distinct from his
understanding, merely carries out what his omniscient intelligence has seen and understood from all eternity.   His will is
limited by his intelligence, and has always some end in view.
These ends are the reasons why the world is just as it is.   God
was free not to create the world—supposing he had not wished
to do so—but he had to create it in the way most resembling his
own perfection, and the good which he put into it is the explanation why it is ordered just so and so.   Thus it is impossible to
understand the world excepting by trying to find out what ends
God had in view.   The consideration of ends is no less necessary
to the physicist than to the metaphysician, for the ultimate cause
of any determinate effect is a final cause, and everything which
exists is fundamentally explained by one consideration—the best
possible order of the world.   Thus for the Scholastics the human
eye is placed below the eyebrows in order that they may shield
it ; in the top of the head in order to see farther : yet not absolutely on the top, like a beetle's, for then it would lack the pro-
tection of the eyebrows (cf. Coimbran Commentary on the *De
Anima*).   *Concipimus Deum*, writes Descartes with indignation,

[1] See E. Gilson, *La Liberté et la Théologie chez Descartes*, pp. 85–8,
92–5, 103–8).

tamquam magnum aliquem hominem, qui hoc et hoc sibi proponit, et ex his et his mediis tendit, quod certe Deo maxime indignum. Not only unworthy, but an effective bar to the founding of true physics, which was Descartes' real object even in writing the *Méditations*.[1]

For Descartes it is not true that God wills what is good, but that what he wills is by that very fact good. God, just as an absolute King is the efficient cause of the government of his state, is the efficient cause of the world, and physics is concerned with efficient causes and not with final ones.

In the *Méditations* and the *Principia*[2] Descartes took an intermediate course, which without insisting on the identity of God's will and his understanding or denying the existence of these ' eternal verities ', no less effectively dealt with anthropomorphism, and with finalism. These ' eternal verities ' or necessary truths *may* exist but we know nothing about them, and those truths to which we give the name are the simple ordinances of God, which can be changed to-morrow, if he so decrees. We can grasp these truths, such as the principle of contradiction, or the truth that the sum of the angles of a triangle is equal to two right angles—whereas we can only know that God exists without actually knowing or understanding him. We therefore know these truths to be of the order of finite things, whereas God is infinite. Suppose these truths, which seem necessary to the human mind, are not the ' creatures ' of God, and he their efficient cause, as of all else in the universe, they must be God himself. We should then necessarily understand God himself and have pretensions to comprehend his infinite nature, which is absurd, since our minds are finite.

Thus Descartes' invasion of the realm of theology is a negative one. It is made for the purpose of denying that we can profitably inquire into the ends which the Divine intelligence has in view. In the form it assumes in the *Principia* it is parallel with the fideist tendency which denies that we know anything of God except that He exists. It provides a remarkable example, particularly coming from Descartes, of the way in which this trend was used in the interests, not only of lay morality or of tolerance, but of rational speculation. It shows a far more subtle and profound attack on anthropocentrism than those which were inspired by Montaigne's work, and reminds us of an aspect of the great philosopher's thought implicit throughout his system. To judge how effective it was compared with theirs

---

[1] See Introduction, p. xx.   [2] *Principia*, I, 19, 26, 27.

would involve a contrast between the 'eternal verities' and 'pre-established harmony' of Leibnitz and the anti-finalism of Spinoza, with a disquisition on the finalism of eighteenth-century apologists, which is far beyond the scope of this chapter.

It is certain, at all events, that Descartes is not only the stepping-stone to Newton, and the ancestor of La Mettrie and ultimately of the modern Behaviourists, he is also the defender of the faith who puts new heart into the inwardly quailing ranks of the apologists. M. Gilson has shown what inspiration he himself drew from the Augustinian idealism of his friends of the Oratory, Gibieuf and Silhon, inspiration repaid them with interest.[1] Despite the Papal condemnation of 1674, not only the Jansenist, hence Augustinian, Arnauld, but Bossuet, Fénelon and a host of lesser writers hasten to borrow the Cartesian arms, and by the end of the century 'rational theology' is à la mode.[2] This development coincides with that partial eclipse of Montaigne which the final pages of this book describe.

Yet if Descartes brought gifts of doubtful value to the cause of religious orthodoxy and thinned the ranks of those who believed in a Christian—or to be safe, let us say, a pious—scepticism, his own temper on religious matters singularly resembles that of many of the 'latitudinarians' on whom the influence of the Montaigne was paramount. The Descartes of M. Leroy, the friend of Rosicrucians and Deists, the man who never made the pilgrimage to Loretto, and who was determined not to be the prisoner of the great machine of the Counter-reformation— that is the real Descartes, rather than the essentially Catholic philosopher of the Baillet legend, endorsed by M. Espinas or M. Chevalier. M. Leroy's one mistake is to imagine that Descartes is unique among latitudinarians. There were others whose best friends were Protestants, Deists and *Athées couverts* : others who, like him, saw no reason why most of Lord Herbert's ideas on religion could not be received by the Church, others, who while finding the criticism of hell-fire doctrine, such as we have seen in *Les Quatrains du Déiste*, merely frivolous, would endorse that noble letter to Huygens on the death of his brother :

je ne puis concevoir autre chose de ceux qui meurent, sinon qu'ils passent à une vie plus douce et plus tranquille que la nôtre, et que nous les irons retrouver quelque jour, même avec souvenance du

---

[1] L'Innéisme Cartésien (in *La Pensée Médiévale dans la Formation Cartésienne*) and above, p. XX.
[2] Above all in Protestant circles, cf. Spink, *Rousseau et Génève*.

passé, car je reconnais en nous une mémoire intellectuelle, qui est assurément indépendante du corps.[1]

A colossus, with one foot in the modern and one in the medieval world—it is thus that modern scholarship and the historians of philosophy represent Descartes. I have sought to make clear what he owed to Montaigne, who died only four years before he was born, and Charron, Montaigne's imitator, who died when he was six. If we may trust at all the veiled autobiography of the ' Discourse ', the young Descartes who went to Holland in 1616 knew these writers well and found the lesson of the diversity of men as true as their other lesson of the diversity of philosophical opinions. It is pretty clear that the *conformisme* of the *morale provisoire* comes from the Essays. It is certain that the mechanistic interpretation of animal behaviour is directed against Montaigne and Charron and it is extremely likely that it was originally conceived through a consideration of their view together with a study of mechanical ' toys '. Finally, when we notice that certain obscure features of the dream of Descartes on the eve of St. Martin 1619 become quite plain in meaning and in origin, if we may link them with two passages of *La Sagesse*, it may be claimed that we have shown that the long-suspected influence of the old sceptic on Beeckman's young friend from Poitou is greater than has been hitherto supposed.

[1] *Correspondence of Descartes and Huygens*, p. 182. Note the numerous changes introduced by the pious Clerselier into the whole passage.

CHAPTER XVII

GASSENDI AND HIS FRIENDS

IN 1624, the year which saw the appearance of the *Jugement des Actions Humaines*, Descartes' great rival in the eyes of his contemporaries, Pierre Gassendi [1592–1655] published his first work, his attack on the Aristotelians,[1] almost simultaneously with the famous pronouncement of the Parlement of Paris, made at the University's request, that nothing contrary to Aristotle should be taught in physics.

There was no question of awaking Gassendi from his dogmatic slumbers : he tells us he never could abide Aristotle from his youth up. It was, however, above all ' my Charron ' (he prints the name in heavy type) whose book encouraged him to give expression to his criticisms of the Stagyrite.[2] Gassendi's earliest correspondence also shows his admiration for Charron. In 1621 Henry Faur, a grandson of the famous Faur de Pibrac, sends to Aix a copy of the *Discours Chrétiens, quia scio ejus ibi authoris genium et ingenium placere*. In a reply Gassendi, after declaring himself a disciple of Sextus and the Sceptics, says he has not yet really had time to deliver judgement on the substance of the *Discours*, and continues as follows : ' Yet I have devoured the little work eagerly enough, nor indeed did you err in guessing that this author's genius and disposition please me. I will freely confess to you what I feel, namely, that, though all of him pleases me, nothing indeed charms me so much as that Wisdom itself, which he says in his own preface puts the crown upon his studies. Fitly indeed you counsel me to take this author as companion in my solitude, for there is a philosophy which is content with few judges, and which of set purpose shuns

---

[1] *Exercitationes Paradoxicae adversus Aristoteleos.*

[2] Verum mihi animos adjecit, timoremque omnem depulit et *Vivis* et **MEI CHARRONII** lectio, ex qua visus sum non injuria suspicari Sectam illam non esse penitus probandam, quod probaretur quam plurimis (ib., Preface). To these names he adds those of Ramus and Pico della Mirandola ; also later Francesco Patrizzi.

the multitude. Who in sooth is a saner judge than Charron ? Above all, if those are set by him from whose works he himself derived profit : Montaigne, Lipsius, Seneca, Plutarch, and Tully. These, truly, and few others would I add to bear him company : few, I say, for such authors seem to me rare indeed in so vast a sea (*admodum rari in tam vasto gurgite*). For whom I would sometimes substitute Lucretius, Horace, Juvenal, sometimes Lucian or Erasmus . . .'

A month later Gassendi is on the point of finishing his work on Aristotle, ' the man with the wax nose ', as he disrespectfully called him, ' for he can be interpreted as you will '.[1] Gassendi's attack is rather against the Scholastic interpretation than a criticism of the Latin Averrhoists of the Paduan school.

Such are the only places in which the Canon of Digne mentions Montaigne and his disciple, the Canon of Condom, nor are allusions to them to be found elsewhere in his work. The indirect influence is clear enough, however, in the *Exercitationes adversus Aristoteleos*.[2] In reaction from the Scholastic dogmatism Gassendi indeed passed through the Sceptical stage before he attempted constructive philosophy by his revival of the Epicurean atomism and the Epicurean utilitarianism. He remains, however, above all, a critic, the critic of Aristotle, of Fludd, of Descartes, of Lord Herbert, one whose cautious *videtur* was a by-word of the age.[3]

He makes the confession of his own development in the Preface of 1624. No ideal ever pleased him so much as the suspense of judgement of the Pyrrhonians and Academics ; for, when he came to understand how far human ingenuity was from ever grasping the inner causes of natural phenomena, he saw the levity and arrogance of the Schoolmen, whose manner is at once an illustration of the presumption and uncertainty of human science. For the Aristotelians trespass constantly the bounds of philosophy in treating of theological questions. Their metaphysics include speculations on the Trinity and the Incarnation, their ethics discussions of supernatural felicity, their physics debates on transubstantiation, the creation of the world and the resurrection.[4] But within the bounds of philosophy it is un-

---

[1] *Opera* (1658), VI, p. 391, p. 1, 2.

[2] For further attacks on Aristotle, see Jean de Launay, *De Varia Aristotelis Fortuna*, 1656, and the *Requête des Maîtres ès Arts, Professeurs et Régents de l'Université de Paris présentée à la Cour Souveraine du Parnasse* 1671 (by Sorbière and Bernier).

[3] Bernier : *Abrégé de la Philosophie de Gassendi*, 1678, I.

[4] *Exercitationes*, I, I, § 9.

worthy of a philosopher to subject himself to any purely human authority such as that of Aristotle. The tone of all discussions should be doubting and probing.

Gassendi then occupies himself with a critique of Aristotle himself. How much in him is contrary to faith, how uncertain is the canon of his writings, how many matters lack treatment, how much repetition, contradiction and downright falsehood there is in them ! [1]   The most serious ground of attack is Aristotle's dialectic ; his ideal of science by demonstration either *a priori* or *a posteriori* is useless and impossible. All deductions are based on previous induction ; all general notions are formed from particular instances given in experience and formed by abstraction.[2]   But no induction which does not rest on complete enumeration can be the ground of a truly universal proposition. Concepts are purely mental ; the ten categories are not the only possible categories of thought. As for the so-called ' eternal verities ' or necessary truths, where shall we find them ? [3]

The final chapter is entitled : *Quod nulla sit Scientia et maxime Aristotelea.* Knowledge by faith of the articles of faith is excepted. There is only a knowledge of objects as they appear to the individual. There is no absolute standpoint anywhere ; for, first, how can sensible things appear the same to various animals ? Would you say that the temperament of this or that animal is vitiated, not natural ? Absurd excuse ! They are each natural after their own nature and far more so than men, who have indeed vitiated their natural temperament by misuse of reason. Secondly, human customs and usages show there is no absolute standpoint. He refuses to give instances from religion, but he gives others as to marriage, beauty, &c. Hence the ' essence ' of natural objects is unknown, as Solomon confesses, and after him almost all the ancient philosophers, to whom some moderns might be added. Nothing is certain in metaphysics except by faith, and even mathematics do not conform to Aristotle's ideal, for they are merely a science not of existence but of relations, and in which our conclusions are contained implicitly in the premises from which we start.[4]

We have spoken of Gassendi's caution ; we must not forget that the publication of the book just analysed was also an act of courage. Indeed only the first of the six promised *Exercitationes* were ever published, and we know from a letter of the author, written in 1630, that ' the prefatory book having appeared

[1] *Exercitationes*, I, IV–VIII.   [2] ib., II, II, § 4.
[3] ib., II, IV, § 4, p. 778.
[4] ib., II, VI, § 4 ; ib., § 6 ; ib., § 8.

without the customary approbation [of ecclesiastical superiors] almost provoked a tragedy. I leave you to imagine the treatment which might be expected for the rest.'

Already in the negative framework of the *Exercitatio* is sketched the ideal of a science of appearances, and the philosopher whose teaching Gassendi chose to revive and defend was naturally the most empirical of the ancients, Epicurus.[1] In his copious exchange of letters with the handsome Comte d'Alais, Governor of Provence, he rebukes his noble correspondent for exaggerating the weakness of the human intellect whose science is rather ignorance : *Ea nempe est, ut nihil nosse praeter rerum corticem liceat : et ne minimae quidem rei intima natura introspici.*[2] This sums up his epistemological position.

Philosophy, as Gassendi saw it, was, according to Bernier, *une certaine recherche ou poursuite de la Vérité, et tout ensemble de l'Honnêteté* ; while ' wise ' and ' wisdom ' were terms we should only apply to God. We see then that if henceforth *l'humanité va méditer en vue de la vérité, non plus à partir de la vérité,* as M. Brunschvicg has said of philosophical ' revolution ' of the seventeenth century, Gassendi as well as Descartes has a part in that new conception of philosophical speculation, while both agree also that the pursuit of the good and of the true are inseparable.

Perhaps Gassendi's greatest influence on his age was his revival of a utilitarian hedonism, founded on these four canons : any pleasure which does not involve some unpleasure *(molestia)* is to be embraced ; any unpleasure without pleasure is to be shunned ; any pleasure which is incompatible with a greater pleasure is to be shunned ; any pain which renders it possible to avoid a greater pain is also to be accepted. Quoting this, Gassendi says in the course of the above correspondence :

Fecunditas magna horum Canonum ; nam professioni etiam Christianae quam maxime accommodantur. Verum et res est per se nota, meditationeque sola indiget, et cum universa moralis Philosophia hinc pendeat, non est quod multis iam dicatur.[3]

Gassendi's meditations on this ' self-evident ' foundation are, however, largely of a question-begging nature.[4] What is important is his pretension to found a Christian Epicureanism, his

---

[1] A number of friends, chiefly among them Luillier (protector of Théophile), appear to have encouraged him to consider the reconciliation of atomism with the doctrine of Divine Providence. A rehabilitation of Epicurus had been already undertaken in the sixteenth century by Vicomercato.

[2] *Opera*, VI, pp. 344, 154.   [3] *Opera*, VI, p. 153.

[4] For a good critical account, see G. S. Brett, *Gassendi*, 1908.

insistence on the fact that it was pleasure as a *mental state*, not the objects which gave rise to it, which had to be considered, and his attempt to establish a single criterion of value. Gassendi's influence by this part of his teaching—the ' art of spending one's life happily '—was undoubtedly great and the indirect influence through Bernier's *Abrégé* must also have been considerable.

I have shown Gassendi's original contact with the Essays and with Charron, and how much both the modesty of his claims for philosophy and the basis of his ethics have in common with those of Montaigne. The influence is not the same, but it is in the same direction.. His intimate friends, Naudé, Patin, Sorbière, have the same great admiration for Montaigne and Charron (as also for Epicurus), and their writings contain constant references to these authors. Adding to them some of those who also met at the house of the Royal Librarians, the brothers Dupuy, such as La Mothe le Vayer, Luillier (both intimate with Gassendi) Chapelain, the Abbé de Marolles, Perrot d'Ablancourt, and one or two others of this circle of friends, we get an impression of a common philosophy of life, in which the influence of the Essays has counted for much. They are sincere Christians (in spite of some mutual accusations), but most of them are obviously in secret reaction, consciously or unconsciously, against some feature or other of seventeenth-century orthodoxy—*guéris du loupgarou*, as Gui Patin would say, who tells us that his own master, Moreau, and Naudé, in their hatred of religious controversy, took from the Paduan, Cremonini, their motto : *intus ut libet, foris ut moris est*. Such an adjustment is hardly sufficient for a man of sincerity, and their tendency to fideism is largely due to their attempt to arrive at some harmony of their religious convictions with their other beliefs.[1] Let us turn first to Gabriel Naudé (1600–53).

Terrible puritain du péripatétisme, says his friend Patin. Naudé's own account of his intellectual development is different.

J'ai passé par la Philosophie Scholastique sans devenir Eristique, et par celle des plus vieux et modernes sans me particulariser . . .

---

[1] Of Gassendi's piety there is no doubt. See even what Patin, who, though a *cœur d'or* was a *mauvaise langue*, has to say of him. He is very angry because Gassendi, an invalid, has taxed his strength in Lent (éd. *Réveillé Parise*, II, 153). Patin writes after his death : ' Pour Monsieur Gassendi, il était homme sage, savant et bon, tempéré et habile homme, en un mot un vrai Epicurien mitigé. Comme je lui dis en sa dernière maladie qu'il n'en echapperait point et qu'il donnât ordre à ses affaires, il leva gaîment la tête, et me dit à l'oreille ce beau vers : *Omnia praecepi, atque animo mecum ante peregi*.'

Sénèque m'a plus servi que Aristote ; Plutarque que Platon ; Juvenal et Horace plus qu'Homère et Virgile ; Montaigne et Charron que tous les précédents . . .

In the *Avis pour dresser une Bibliothèque* (1627) he advises his readers to set Montaigne, Charron and Bacon besides Seneca and Plutarch—not, let it be noticed, among those critics of the sciences whose usefulness he acknowledges : Sextus, Sanchez and Agrippa. He would put the two of them, Montaigne and Charron, among the seven wise men of France.[1] In the *Naudiana* we read :

La Loi de Nature est la vraie règle d'un honnête homme, pourvu qu'il pratique ce premier point : *quod tibi fieri non vis, alteri non feceris.* Il y a quelques livres qui conduisent un homme en cette . vie : savoir *Epistolae Senecae,* la Sagesse de Charron, *Vita Pomponii Attici,* Essais de Montaigne, les Dialogues Sceptiques de la Motte le Vayer, *Epistolae Plinii,* Horace, Juvenal, *Officia Ciceronis, Marcus Antonius Imperator et Philosophus.*[2]

He preferred, however, *La Sagesse* to the Essays. Charron and Bodin (*La République*) are, to his mind, the best books in the world,[3] and comparing Montaigne with his ape, Charron, he says in 1633 :

Pour Michel de Montaigne, comme ses Essais sont remplis d'une plus grande abondance de sentences et qu'à la façon de Sénèque il frappe plus souvent, il est aussi beaucoup au dessous en ce qui est de l'ordre et de la pureté. Au regard de Pierre Charron, je l'estime en cela plus sage que Socrate, que le premier avec une méthode tout à fait admirable et avec une grande doctrine et un grand jugement, il réduit en art les préceptes de la sagesse même. Il est vrai que son livre nous donne à la fois Aristote, Sénèque et Plutarque et qu'il contient en soi quelqu'chose de divin qu'avant lui n'ont eu tous les anciens et tous les modernes.[4]

Naudé, like all his century, prizes method ; he prizes also compendious instruction. Such is the basis of his preference, while his constant references to both Montaigne and Charron show how sincere his admiration was.[5]

What were the interests of the man ? Bibliography and the

[1] *Ie Mascurat,* 1649, p. 553.   [2] *Naudiana* (ed. 1700), p. 54.
[3] ib., p. 289 : Patin, *Lettres,* II, 479.
[4] *Bibliothèque Politique* (trad. fr. 1642), p. 16.
[5] *Apologie pour les Grands Hommes* (Montaigne, pp. 6, 7, 46, 244, 312). *Considérations sur les Coups d'Etat* (ed. 1668) (pp. 32, 36, 129, 320 on Montaigne ; 15, 18, 36, 54, 120, 131, 191, 234 (329) on Charron). *Mascurat* (pp. 180, 181, 287, 288, 446, 447, 553, 630 on Montaigne ; pp. 118, 287, 288, 289, 553 on Charron).

exposure of vulgar errors : almost all he wrote may be ranged under these two heads. Take his third publication the *Apologie pour les Grands Hommes Accusés de Magie* (1625). *Multos absolvemus, si coeperimus ante judicare quam irasci*, that is his epigraph. He has read many of Demonologists and in particular Lancre and Delrio.[1] Most of them lack the critical faculty. He has also been reading Garasse ; he has noted his invectives against Virgil and Homer and has come to the conclusion that all great men are accused of relations with the devil. Is this likely to be true ? His book is an examination of the question.

Naudé is here very cautious ; he does not deny the existence of witchcraft,[2] for example, or of demons. His conclusion is merely that the Demonologists, for their own honour and the elucidation of the truth, should examine their evidence with care. It is a different matter in his *Mascurat*, written twenty-four years later. In the earlier book what interests us rather is the attitude of scientific prudence with which the author begins. Its method is simply the rationalization of those legends which cannot be shown to be completely baseless. Empedocles was the victim of scientific curiosity, like Pliny, in wishing to observe the eruption of an earthquake. Is it likely that a man like Aristotle, who did not believe in any supernatural creatures, should have had any relations with them ? The ' voice ' of Socrates was, as Naudé, a thorough intellectualist, puts it :

la bonne règle de sa vie, la sage conduite de ses actions, l'expérience qu'il avait des choses, et le résultat de toutes ses vertus, qui formèrent en lui cette prudence laquelle peut être à bon droit nommé le lustre et l'assaisonnement de toutes ses actions . . . en un mot, l'art de la vie, comme la Médecine est l'art de la santé.[3]

Thus Naudé has summed up, in a word, his conception of Ethics, Montaigne's conception, the conception of all these humanists.

He holds his own to be the age of progress,

plus propre à polir et aiguiser le jugement que n'ont été tous les autres ensemble, à cause des changements notables qu'il nous a fait voir, par la découverte d'un nouveau monde, les troubles survenus en la Religion, l'instauration des lettres, la décadence des sectes et vieilles opinions et l'invention de tant d'ouvrages et d'artifices.

Now indeed is the time to rouse men's minds, to throw off an infinity of false and absurd opinions. There are three fallacious principles chiefly responsible for vulgar errors : that general

---

[1] On these authors see above, pp. 23, 41, 42.
[2] *Apologie*, pp. 36, 37.   [3] *Apologie*, p. 312.

consent is a proof of truth ; that to quote authorities constitutes demonstration ; and thirdly, *polymathie*, a new fad which Naudé defines as *parler à chaque sujet de toutes choses et à chaque chose de tous sujets*.[1] Some years later, however, he is inclined to look back with regret at the glories of the Renaissance. Learning, he notes, always involves a decline of orthodox religion.[2] There are too many novelties in the sciences. Naudé was at bottom conservative by temperament ; for example, he thinks that Aristotelianism is doomed, not by its intrinsic defects so much as because its day is over and the circle has turned.[3] The fideism of this rationalist-by-temperament takes this odd form :

> . . . Dieu ne permet jamais que l'on puisse tellement faire glisser un mensonge en chose d'importance qu'il n'y reste assez de lumière pour découvrir la fausseté qui est cachée au dessous, si on y regarde de près.

Hence perhaps the assurance with which he tilted against vulgar errors. The words which he gives his spokesmen in the *Mascurat* were true of him all his life :

> A te dire vrai, Saint Ange, l'une des plus grandes satisfactions que j'aie au monde, est à découvrir, soit par ma lecture, soit par un peu de jugement que Dieu m'a donné, la fausseté et l'absurdité de toutes ces opinions populaires.[4]
>
> Qui pourrait établir dans le monde l'incrédulité jusqu'à un certain point, en chasserait bien de la folie, *nervus enim sapientiae non temere credere*.[5]

His years in Italy, ' where some have too little faith, the others too much ', strengthened him, no doubt, in this opinion.[6]

The *Mascurat* contains downright words of sense on the chief of these vulgar errors. He does not believe in demoniac possessions.[7] He denies that the witches' ' coven ' has any

---

[1] ib., pp. 606, 629 ; cf. *Avis pour dresser une Bibliothèque* (1627), p. 74.

[2] *Considérations sur les Coups d'Etat* (ed. 1668), p. 220. On the question of progress or decline in the seventeenth century (part of the history of the quarrel of the Ancients and the Moderns) consult : Sieur de Rampalle *Discours Académique . . . Que le Monde ne va point de mal en pis.*, 1639. A.C. : *Discours sur les Sentiments Communs d'Aujourd'hui*, 1653. Le Père Zacharie de Lisieux : *Genius Saeculi*, 1656. The authors are convinced, respectively, of variation, no direction ; of real progress ; of real regress. Note that in Fontenelle's *Dialogue des Morts* Socrates blames Montaigne for holding that everything was superior in antiquity.

[3] *Apologie*, p. 331.

[4] *Mascurat*, p. 93. (Saint Ange and Mascurat are the characters of the dialogue.)

[5] ib., p. 143.   [6] *Naudiana*, p. 90.   [7] *Mascurat*, p. 310.

reality.   One does not believe a lunatic who confesses to seeing visions or a monomaniac who thinks himself God the Father, a hare or a waterjug.

Quand une belle et grosse fille . . . se plaint d'avoir quelque homme noir qui la suit, de voir des Diables, d'entendre du bruit à la maison, d'être entourée de fantômes, on dit en se moquant d'elle que son pucelage l'étouffe ; si l'on parle que des esprits, ou follets ou sérieux, reviennent dans une maison, on répond communément que la Maîtresse ou la servante sont amoureuses : et pourquoi donc brûler une pauvre femme qui par maladie, par sottise, par force ou autrement, confessera d'avoir été portée en moins de rien sur un Bouc, sur une fourche ou sur un balai à ces assemblées, tantôt éloignées de cent lieues, tantôt proche de leurs villages, où elles auront fait mille extravagances puériles, ridicules, impossibles, et qui mériteraient mieux qu'on les fit panser ou enfermer aux Petites Maisons, que non pas exterminer, comme l'on fait, par le feu et la corde ?

For Naudé, as for Montaigne, actual presence at the ' coven ' is the main point.   He treats the matter historically, and shows that the early Church did not believe in witches, or, even when they did, denied that their cult should be treated as anything but illusion, since it involved the divinity of gods other than the Christian God, and would thus bring back paganism.   In 1491 the Parlement of Paris still generally acquitted on this charge.   He quotes how Lestoile, commenting on a burning even in 1587, *trouva cette punition bien étrange, parce que cette vermine y était toujours demeurée libre et sans être recherchée.*   The witch-mania, he concludes, has come since that date, although rehabilitations are not unknown.[1]   Naudé is against the extraction of evidence by torture in any legal case, and quotes a notable test carried out by a certain Cardinal.[2]   The philosopher's stone is nonsense, as also magic and alchemy, divination and astrology.[3]

Naudé insists yet again in the *Mascurat* on the duty of individual judgement.   The credulity of men of learning like Mersenne and Peiresc is appalling, but credulity in ethics and in politics is far more dangerous than in physics.   What then are Naudé's own leading ideas on Ethics ?   The following passage

[1] ib., pp. 314–22.   For the average educated opinion of Possession, &c., see Nicolas de Campion, *Entretiens sur divers sujets* . . . 1704. Entretien III.   These conversations are founded on actual conversations among the members of the Campion family in the 1640's.   Apiste (M. de Trancé), admirer of Charron and great traveller, is the only sceptic on this matter.

[2] ib., p. 327. .   [3] ib., pp. 468, 469, 684.

shows the relation both with enlightenment and with the ideology
of emotional fideism and its sceptical basis. He is defining the
force of mind he desires in his ideal minister of state :

> . . . certaine trempe et disposition d'esprit toujours égale en soi,
> ferme et stable, héroïque, capable de tout voir et tout faire sans se
> troubler, se perdre, s'étonner : laquelle vertu se peut facilement
> acquérer en faisant de continuelles réflexions sur la condition de
> notre nature faible, débile et sujette à toute sorte de maladies et
> infirmités, sur la vanité des pompes et des honneurs de ce monde :
> sur la faiblesse et l'imbécillité de notre esprit : sur les changements
> et révolutions des affaires : les diverses faces et métaschématismes du
> Ciel et de la terre ; sur la diversité des opinions, des sectes, des reli-
> gions, sur le peu de durée de toutes choses : bref sur les grands
> avantages qu'il y a de fuir le vice et suivre la vertu.[1]

Naudé is outspoken against an excess of religious scruples and
observances :

> Il ne faut point tant de mystères et de cérémonies pour être homme
> de bien . . . Etre homme de bien c'est vivre selon les loix de Dieu
> et de la Nature, noblement, philosophiquement, avec une intégrité
> sans fard, une vertu sans art, une religion sans crainte, sans scrupule,
> et une ferme résolution de bien faire sans autre respect et considération
> que de ce qu'il faut ainsi vivre pour vivre en homme de bien et
> d'honneur.[2]

Virtue then is to be followed, ultimately, for its own sake, but
Naudé is fond of insisting that, where the demands of morality
and expediency coincide, the higher motive should not be invoked. So far as political philosophy is concerned, the great
problem is, however, how far the good may be sacrificed to the
useful.

The relations of ethics and *real-politik* form the subject
matter of the *Considérations sur les Coups d'Etat*, written in
1639 for Naudé's patron, Cardinal Bagni, and in reply perhaps
to Silhon's *Ministre d'Etat* and Balzac's *Prince*.

The prince must not be the prisoner of the law. Obviously
certain things must be allowed him which are not permitted
to the individual : this is the foundation of Naudé's attitude
(cf. *Essais*, III, 1). He takes his rules for permitting the action
of the sovereign against law or morality from Charron : the
end must be defensive, the crisis must be grave, the action itself
understood to establish no precedent. It must be done without

---

[1] *Considérations sur les Coups d'Etat* (ed. 1668), p. 307.
[2] ib., pp. 320, 321.

vindictiveness and with a sincere regret.[1] Naudé declares that there is much to be said for Machiavelli, but there is one favourite maxim of politicians—the danger of generosity—to which he will never subscribe.

L'ajoute qui voudra à ses écrits, pour moi je ne la mettrai jamais aux miens, n'estimant pas raisonnable de préscrire des fins et des limites à la clémence et à l'humanité : qu'elle étende ses bornes si loin qu'elle voudra, elles me sembleront toujours trop courtes et reserrées . . .[2]

No doubt the right thing cannot always be done in the right way. Charles V and Cardinal Cajetano might have dealt in a variety of ways with Luther, but the one unwise measure would have been assassination. Don't make martyrs, *it doesn't pay* ; Henri II only encouraged heresy in France by doing so. Much of Naudé's attention is taken up with the political aspects of religion. From this point of view the truth or falsity of any particular cult seems to him totally irrelevant. He notes the claims of those in search of authority to have divine revelations or mystical experiences or portents in their favour. Providence and punishment after death are, no doubt, necessary principles of society, and the people are always full of superstition—Naudé here shows the true Renaissance scorn—but they are the strongest force in the State. Knowledge of their character helps to know how secretly to lead them by the nose, as they must be led, but there are only two real ways : the fear of God or the rigour of the law.

In the *Mascurat*, Naudé holds that books against morals should be suppressed rather than those against faith. The heretic is a danger to himself, the vicious man to society, and he is not certain that heretics should be punished at all—they are merely mistaken. With the wicked it is otherwise. Ethics are then more important and more certain than dogma : he makes the sensible remark about the question whether the great Pagans were ' saved ', that, if they were, Christians must hold this to be due to their actions and not to their beliefs.[3]

---

[1] *Considérations sur les Coups d'Etat* (ed. 1668), p. 120. Most of the ideas of the *Considérations* are derived from *La Sagesse*, Book III, and ultimately from Bodin and Montaigne. According to Naudé himself, only ten copies were printed. This may, however, be doubted. Brunet put the number at 100.   [2] ib., p. 129.

[3] *Mascurat*, p. 346 et seq. Naudé attaches a good deal of importance to the Science of Character (*Mascurat*, p. 665 et seq.). He admires Barclay's *Icon Animarum* enormously, but he has certain reserves to make and he does not imagine that this type-psychology can be more than a rough guide in dealing with individuals. See further and on Education the paragraph on Naudé's *Syntagma de Studio Liberali* below, pp. 311, 312.

Patin was perhaps right when he said that his friend Naudé :

avait une grande pente naturelle à ne prendre aucun parti de religion, ayant l'esprit tout plein de considérations, réflexions et observations politiques sur la vie des princes et du gouvernement du monde et sur la moinerie aujourd'hui dans l'Europe de sorte qu'il était bien plutôt politique que c[royant ?].

But was he also right when he went on to ascribe to Naudé the opinions of his master at the College de Navarre, Claude Belurgey to whom the *Quatrains du Déiste* have been attributed ? [1] Belurgey laughed at the Bible, especially Genesis and the prophets, and admitted neither miracles, visions nor revelation, hell, heaven or purgatory. Even so, how did he differ from Patin himself [1602–72] who certainly was a Christian, though perhaps hardly orthodox, *vieux Chrétien, ennemi juré des fourberies de Rome* ?

En notre religion Chrétienne je crois, comme nous devons croire, beaucoup de choses que nous ne voyons point *quaeque sub sensus non cadunt* mais c'est par le moyen de la foi, qui nous y oblige, *et quae est rerum non apparentum* : mais en fait de médecine je ne crois que ce que je vois . . .
Je crois tout ce qui est dans le Nouveau Testament, comme article de foi, mais je ne donnerai pas telle autorité à toute la légende des moines . . . *Credo* in unum Deum, *Christum crucifixum, etc, de minimis non curat praetor.*[2]

Again he imagines what kind of a sermon he would make if he had to :

. . . Je ferai le sermon bien court ; autrement je ferais comme les autres, je dirais bien des fadaises, bien des extravagances, aux quelles je ne croirais non plus qu'eux.

Patin seems to resent the ascription of every unpleasant feature in man to original sin. He thinks the celibacy of the monks, whom he hates, neither natural nor expedient. Witchcraft is nonsense, as the Parlement of Paris now recognizes,[3] demoniac possessions are *des maux de matrices.* Purgatory is a fine Papal fable for robbing rich and poor.
But Patin hates apostasy. Sorbière can do nothing that

---

[1] See above, pp. 151–153.
[2] *Lettres* (ed. Réveillé—Parize), I, p, 9, and p. 90. But to put occult qualities everywhere is *trop relever inscientiam veterum academicorum* (I, 447).
[3] *Lettres* (ed. cit.), III, p. 210 : cf. ed. Triaire, p. 344, on the *Démonomanie.*

pleases him since his conversion to Catholicism.[1] He hopes to meet the great men of the ancient as well as of the modern world in paradise. He certainly believes in the efficacy of prayer, as many passages show. He is scandalized above all by the prosperity of the wicked. His reflexions on Browne's *Religio Medici*, which he admired, are significant. He finds himself wishing there was the same liberty of expression in France ; *la subtilité de l'esprit humain se pourrait découvrir par cette voie* : but his final conclusion is that Browne

cherche maître en fait de religion, comme beaucoup d'autres, et peut être qu'enfin il n'en trouvera aucun. . . . Il est encore en vie, il peut aussi bien empirer qu'amender.

In his library, where Erasmus and Joseph Scaliger flank a crucifixion over the mantel, St. François de Sales, Jean Pierre Camus and Justus Lipsius hang by the side of François Rabelais. For Camus he has a special respect, due to his attacks on the abuses of the regulars, and he had also some personal intimacy with him.

What are the other portraits of his favourite authors and friends ? Apart from the doctors, there are Gassendi, Saumaise, Heinsius, Grotius, Naudé, Muret, Buchanan, J.-A. de Thou, Campanella, Paolo Sarpi, Casaubon, L'Hôpital, Charron and Montaigne.[2]

A list of his favourite authors gives us Rabelais, the Satire Ménippée, Bodin's Republic, Lipsius' Politics, Montaigne's Essays, Charron's *Sagesse*, and—*pour rire*—Garasse, his *Doctrine Curieuse* and *Recherches des Recherches*.

Voilà des livres qui sont capables de prendre le monde par le nez : j'en excepte les deux derniers qui sont bons à autre chose. Ne les négligez point, en faites une petite bibliothèque laquelle soit *a reductis et extra insidias monachorum*.[3]

Among these, Charron (*ah ! le beau livre*) and Montaigne may be considered his favourites, along with Erasmus' *Colloquia* which he re-read every year. He even forgave Montaigne his aspersions on the medical profession [4] *c'est tout dire*—and the references to the Essays in Patin's letters are frequent. As with Lestoile (Chap. I) so with this other good burgess of Paris, it is the ' Ecclesiastes touch ' which is most intimately connected in both their minds with the Essays.

[1] Equally hatred for converted Catholics (III, pp. 143, 144) and ed. Triaire, I, p. 594.
[2] ed. Réveillé Parize, II, p. 283.
[3] ib., I. p. 267.   [4] ib. (ed. Triaire), I, p. 465.

Je conclus que l'homme est un chétif animal bien bizarre, sujet à ses opinions, capricieux et fantasque, qui tend à ses fins et qui toute sa vie n'aboutit guère à son profit, particulièrement en pensées vagues mais quelquefois bien extravagantes.

Patin always concludes thus as to this *bizarre et fantasque animal qu'on appelle homme.* Death lifts the mask.

et fait connaître que la vanité de la vie n'est qu'une comédie assez chétive, qu'un farce assez courte, qu'une ombre ou le songe même d'une ombre.[1]

The influence of the Essays on Patin remains much less clear than the influence on Naudé. Before turning to Samuel Sorbière, a real disciple of Gassendi, not a mere friend like the last two, we may mention two other Epicureans who belong vaguely to the *ambiance* of Gassendi.

Charles Cotin [1604–82] poet, priest and academician, the victim of Boileau and Molière, serves to remind us of the spirit of piety in which Gassendi's rehabilitation of Epicurus was undertaken. For his *Théoclée* (1646), while setting out to condemn the Epicurean denial of Providence, ends by proving that here, as in his Hedonism, the master of Lucretius has been gravely misrepresented. In J. Fr. Sarasin [1614–54] we have another admirer of Gassendi, another poet. Sarasin boasts himself an Epicurean in the preface to his *Œuvres* (1656), as in the delightful *S'il faut qu'un jeune homme soit amoureux,* and his *Discours de Morale* [2] is written in defence of Epicurus and of a Hedonist utilitarianism in general. All suffering, he points out, is only accepted to avoid worse suffering, and it is self-evident that no one despises pleasure as such. Sarasin (unlike Cotin) again and again reminds us of the Essays—but Sarasin also shows how Montaigne's influence sometimes becomes merged in that of Gassendi so far as a Hedonist ethic is concerned. The attitude of Sarasin to Montaigne and Charron is presented to us in a most interesting light, when attacking a certain superficial irreligion to be found in those who make it their business ' to employ the utmost resources of their intelligence to debauch the

---

[1] Patin's heart—what a subject! He seems mean and cruel only through cowardice. Hence his horror of thieves. St. Cyran was for their most severe punishment : this comforts him. He insists on taking a young man to witness an execution at the Place de Grève for his good, but to attend a prisoner at the Châtelet so upsets him he swears never to enter a prison again. His wife's one fault is her cruelty to servants, and he cannot forgive Richelieu for oppression, for bringing war and grinding taxation on the poor.

[2] J. Fr. Sarasin : *Œuvres* (ed. Festugière), II, pp. 37–74.

conscience of women out of pure natural perversity '. These are they, he continues, who *sans avoir aucune raison de douter, comme ont les savants libertins*, mock openly at religion and cause scandal in churches, retail a few indecent tales about monks, and ' with five or six passages of Charron and Montaigne which the most intelligent among them preach to the others ', profess to confute all theology, and challenge ' the combined wisdom of all the priests and monks of Paris '. The distinction is once more clear between the real character of Montaigne and Charron (ambiguous as it may be) and the uses to which they can be put.[1]

Samuel Sorbière [1610–70] may be no eagle, but he was a man of great intelligence, open to all the new ideas of the age,[2] particularly interested in philosophy. He acted as a go-between for Descartes and Gassendi, and translated Hobbes. François Bernier said he knew no one except himself who was a better Gassendist than Sorbière. In 1652 he had already prepared but never published an adaptation in French of Gassendi's *Syntagma* (of the life and philosophy of Epicurus), and in his letters he has left a brief but excellent defence of atomism. It is, in effect, he says a scientific hypothesis which seems to work. *Charron et Montaigne était pour ainsi dire ses héros*, writes Graverol in his Memoir.[3] He was indignant at the attack of Chanet on these two authors—*quales viros*—and meditated a reply.[4] Of his favourite books he says :

> Je loge Monsieur de Balzac dans mon étude immédiatement après Charron et Montaigne, les deux seuls Auteurs français que j'égale aux Anciens, et que je préfere à tous nos Modernes en ce qui est de la profonde Doctrine. Monsieur de la Mothe le Vayer les suit de fort près, et ces quatre Messieurs sont presque toute ma Bibliothèque française.[5]

Balzac, however, is merely a fine stylist :

> je trouve mieux mon compte dans celui qui sait ce qu'il dit, qui voit toujours où il veut aller. C'est pourquoi je m'attache plus à Plutarque qu'à Sénèque, à Charron qu'a Montaigne : à Du Perron, d'Ossat et Coëffeteau qu'à Balzac et ces autres Modernes, quoique je les estime tous infiniment les uns et les autres. Mais les genres sont différents, et il n'est question que de ne mettre pas ce dernier hors de son prix.[6]

He prefers, as Gassendi, Naudé, and Patin do, Charron to Mon-

---

[1] J. Fr. Sarasin : *Œuvres* (ed. Festugière), II, p. 181.
[2] Contrast with Naudé who did not understand Descartes, or Patin who did not understand Copernicus or Harvey.
[3] *Sorberiana*, 1695.
[4] See above, p. 186 et seq.
[5] *Sorberiana*, p. 32 et seq.
[6] ib., p. 41.

taigne, but it is chiefly that part of *La Sagesse* which came from
the Essays which has influenced him ; so much is clear. He
has not the same interest as Naudé in political matters for which
Charron went to Bodin, or for the Latin Stoicism, which appeals to
Patin. Wisdom, is for Sorbière as for Montaigne, smiling because
sceptical :

> Il n'y a rien de plus sérieux que l'étude du bon sens, et il n'y a
> rien pourtant de plus enjoué que la sagesse.[1]

In the prefatory letter to his translation of Sextus, Sorbière
enumerates the lessons of Scepticism according to Marcus Aurelius
—modesty and civility, a firm resolution to live according to
nature, and a tolerance, even of ignorance itself, without thrust-
ing one's enlightenment on those who follow vulgar opinions.
Scepticism is not merely to be taken as a purge of prejudices
once in a man's life. Of Descartes, whose dogmatism he disliked,[2]
he writes well :

> Il ne suffit pas, comme vous le savez, Monsieur, pour mériter le
> modeste nom de Sceptique ou d'Académicien, qu'on ait douté une
> seule fois en sa vie, ne qu'on ait supposé cet horrible fracas d'opinions
> dont on a prétendu de s'être délivré par une purgation universelle
> et par un bouleversement entier de toutes nos idées qui est tout-à-
> fait impossible, ou duquel il serait très malaisé au raisonnement
> humain de se relever. Il n'en faut pas tant faire pour s'acquitter à
> la Sceptique ; *mais il faut le faire plus sérieusement et plus constam-
> ment.* L'époque doit être prise en moindre dose : et l'on s'en sert
> pour la santé de l'esprit comme un rémède doux et bénin qui nous
> délivre des opinions mal digérées, et non pas comme d'un poison qui
> arrache jusqu'au premiers principes de nos raisonnements.[3]

Sorbière, however, in his letters dealing with the controversy
between Gassendi and Descartes (which he rightly represents as
partly a difference of fideist *versus* rationalist) has given all the
ordinary proofs of Theism and of Immortality, including the
Cartesian variation of the Ontological proof His conversion to
Catholicism (in which his motives may not unjustly be questioned) imposed certain demonstrations of zeal on his part.
Even if his presentation of such arguments are not to be taken

---

[1] *Lettres et Discours* (1660), p. 356.
[2] Above all he found Descartes' originality exaggerated. ' Je le vois
tout Platonicien dans sa Métaphysique et assez Scholastique en la substance de ses réponses [aux Objections] de même qu'en sa Latinité.
Sorbière called the *Traité des Passions, le roman des passions* (*Lettres et
Discours*, No. 63).
[3] *Lettres et Discours*, p. 690.

at their face-value, it is not in Sorbière's religion that one may look for the results of his scepticism.　The most important result is one in which the Essays cannot have had any direct part, but which came to Sorbière probably from his study of Sextus : a realization of the conventional nature of speech, the double use of language, *scientific or emotive*, and of the dangers of symbolism.　Hence some acute reflexions on literature or literary criticism.[1]

Truth is a notion which applies to propositions and their meaning.　It is a quality of the proposition not of the object. We should not omit to reflect that :

raisonnant sur les autres choses, nous avons employé tout de même les paroles et l'écriture par un abrégé qui produit cette merveilleuse agilité des pensées et du raisonnement.　Et c'est là que nous sommes sujets à prendre le change, si nous ne rapportons ces images artificielles, les paroles et l'écriture, aux idées naturelles des sensations qu'elles signifient.[2]

Sorbière quotes Hippocrates with approval : *absurdum est existimare ideas crescere ex nominibus et impossibile est. Nomina enim sunt ab hominibus sanctita, ideas vero nequaquam, sed sunt veluti quaedam naturae germina.*　These last words imply some doctrine of innate ideas.　It is not clear that Sorbière himself altogether rejected such a view.　*La Nature produit les idées, et nous faisons les mots, qui ne sont chose que certaines répresentations des idées.*　Nature, that is to say sense-experience, is the source of all knowledge, nay even of faith itself—*fides ex auditu.* When in doubt as to a question of meaning, reference must thus be made to sense-experience.

As to the double use of language, Sorbière says poets and orators arrange the words they use *comme si c'était le son des cloches ou des figures tracées par le hazard.*　This is obviously not a very satisfactory formulation of the emotive use of language, but this author seems to have got hold of the distinction well enough, to judge from some of his other observations :

La Poésie (he says) me paraît au regard de la Prose *une certaine danse des paroles*, inventée pour le plaisir de l'oreille, plutôt que pour la décision des matières de raisonnement : [3]

Lucretius, Lucan, Pibrac and Theognis are historians or philosophers not poets.　Sorbière seems to be one of the few Frenchmen of the seventeenth century who realized the fundamental fallacy

---

[1] *Lettres et Discours*, p. 694 et seq.　　　[2] ib., p. 332 **et** seq.
[3] *Lettres et Discours*, No. 57.

of all the critical writing about *le vrai et le vraisêmblable*. He declares that :

Le sujet d'un poème [epic or tragedy] sont les moeurs des hommes, et non par les causes naturelles : les moeurs réprésentées *et non pas les moeurs que l'on raconte historiquement, les moeurs feintes (comme porte le nom de Poésie) et non pas les moeurs trouvées dans les hommes.*[1]

As for Sorbière's views on Ethics, he has defended the hedonism of Epicurus (as interpreted by Gassendi) in a letter to Conrart. He shows elsewhere his tendencies in a *Discours de l'Amitié*. Friendship does not arise from utilitarian motives, but its durability depends largely on them. His naturalism is best seen, however, in a *Discours Sceptique*, exchanged with Michel de Marolles, and printed in the latter's works.[2] Has limited monarchy increased human malice, asks this student of Hobbes ?

Je soupçonnais depuis fort longtemps que les hommes ne valaient guère : mais je ne considérais que ceux parmi lesquels nous vivons ramassés dans les Villes et réunis en les Sociétés. Il me semblait qu'il n'en était pas tout à fait de même de ceux dont on nous fait des Relations, qui vivent en l'état de Nature, ou en un état qui en approche plus que le nôtre.

Don't despise such men as barbarians. Don't even despise animals ; do we know more of Nature than they do, except in so far as we know we don't ? Is commerce, for example, one of the most obvious results of man's social life, really an advantage ?

Sorbière inclines to the view that the misfortune of the European state is that it has neither the simple organization we find in the West (Canada and Brazil) nor the absolute Government found in the East (India and China). There is more real liberty in the East than with us, and less war. Marolles disagrees in his reply but maintains that the real trouble in Europe is the unequal treatment of the poor man and the man of influence before the law.

More important in connexion with Montaigne is Sorbière's admiration for Cicero's *De Officiis*.

Je mets son traité *De officiis* à la tête de toute sorte de livre, sans en excepter aucun que la Sainte Ecriture. . . . L'excellent livre qui c'est pour former l'homme de bien et l'honnête homme.

The reader has had his attention drawn to the use Montaigne makes of this treatise, and to Cicero's emphasis on the impor-

[1] loc. cit.
[2] Michel de Marolles : *Suite des Mémoires* (1656), p. 80 et seq.

tance, for the good life, of adaptation to circumstance. To the influence of this book on the idea of *honnêteté* and to Sorbière's attempted definitions of the *homme de bien* and *l'honnête homme*, we will return later.

Sorbière was himself a traveller [1] and he attributes importance both to travel itself and still more to the reading of books of travel as a means of broadening the mind and curing prejudices. We have seen the importance which must be attached to this train of thought, and will see it still more clearly. Gassendi's other chief disciple, François Bernier [1625–88], is best known for his travels in the East. The long letter to Chapelain written in 1667, and ' sent from Chiras in Persia . . . concerning the Superstitions, strange fashions, and Doctrine of the Native Indians or Gentiles of Indostan ' is written, as he announces elsewhere, to show ' that there is nothing which opinion, pre-possession, custom, hope and the point of honour, &c., may not make men do or suffer '. Bernier has a keen eye for less general lessons to be learnt from Oriental customs and opinion down to the very practice of their medicine. On the whole, however, Bernier—one of whose duties in India was to instruct his master, Aga Danechmend Khan, in the philosophy of Descartes and Gassendi, (which they discussed together nearly every day)— is too widely read and too solidly grounded in philosophy for much trace of any influence of Montaigne to be visible in his work. The letter to Chapelle [2] ' On Atoms and the Mind of Man ' [3] and the *Abrégé de la Philosophie de Gassendi* (1678), written for Mme. de la Sablière, have considerable interest for the question of what the eclectic philosophy of Gassendi represented in the

---

[1] His account of his journey to England raised a storm of protest in this country and was the subject of a diplomatic protest (see art. of M. Morize in *R.H.L.*, 1907).

[2] Claude Emmanuel Luillier [1626–86], the son of François Luillier, is destined constantly to cross our path. His Gassendism is well known, as is his friendship with Molière, La Fontaine, Boileau and Racine. The *Voyage*, written with Bachaumont, and the many charming poems and letters do not reveal anything of interest in connexion with Montaigne.

[3] This letter, apart from providing a good analysis of how men become *esprits forts* or free-thinkers, is chiefly remarkable for a realization that the materialist problem, or the problem of dualism, does not arise at the level of human reasoning, but at the level of sense. Note further in this connexion that Bernier shares Bayle's view of the Cartesian theory that animals were machines as dangerous to religion : ' C'est vouloir fonder cette différence, c'est à dire la Spiritualité de l'âme humaine, sur l'insensi-bilité des Brutes, ou ce qui est le même, c'est vouloir fonder un article de Foi sur un principe qu'ils ne prouvent par aucune raison et qui paraît évidemment faux '.

minds of contemporaries, but apart from the rebuttal of the charge that atomism involves materialism, lie outside the scope of our study.

It seems convenient, however, to examine here the influence of Montaigne on at least one earlier traveller in the East. So far as America is concerned, M. Chinard has shown that most of the French missionaries and travellers of the first half of the seventeenth century owe nothing directly to the Essays, although certain disciples of Montaigne, notably La Mothe le Vayer and also Cyrano de Bergerac, owe much to the travel-book.[1] The reflexions to which the books of travels might give rise in the way of a critical attitude to Western Civilization, may be seen with remarkable clearness in a writer who merits a place in the present study : Michel Baudier. In his *Histoire de la Religion des Turcs* (1625), he devotes a chapter to the almsgiving of the Turks, with its clear benefits to the community by the founding of hospitals, and to the poor and beggars, while scoffing at the intention of ' saving ' the dead. Baudier insists on the monstrous inequality of riches in the West and recalls Montaigne's story of the savages at the Louvre who were astonished at the contrast of pomp and poverty (p. 122). He deals at length with the charitable actions of Mohammedans towards animals, he notes that there are fewer fathers who refuse to provide for their children except by their wills (again echo of Montaigne). He says the Turk does not marry for money, and describes their divorce. There is no professional legal pleading and justice is given with speed (p. 173). Elsewhere in his *Histoire du Sérail* (p. 111), the contrast with France is pointed out. An extraordinarily prevalent heresy among the Turks is that any man may be saved in his own religion.[2] He thinks that God has permitted their sway so long solely on account of their good works. A chapter on Turkish Law is calculated to encourage belief in the ethical basis of the Law of Nature common to all men. Finally, Baudier in his *Histoire de la Cour de Chine* (1631) says if the use of drugs and remedies brought from the East is approved, one may hope that the observation of Oriental customs and usages may *cure* our social ills. This book explains the points of contact between Christianity and Buddhism (which is doubtless, he thinks, a perverted form of it, Buddha's mother being identified with the Virgin).

It was not only the ' voyage ' to the Far East or Far West, which played an important part in the broadening of men's

[1] See G. Chinard : *L'Amérique et le Rêve Exotique*, 1913.
[2] cf. Bernier : *Letter to M. Chapelain* (English translation 1676), p. 149.

minds—often unconsciously both on the part of the author or the reader—there was also the imaginary voyage, intentionally used as a vehicle of criticism.   The first of these in France (apart from certain episodes in Rabelais) is a rare book published in 1616, *Le Royaume d'Antangil*.[1]   Curiously enough, this book bears no trace of Montaigne's influence.   The second of these imaginary voyages is probably Cyrano de Bergerac's *Voyage dans la Lune* (1650) and his *Etats du Soleil* (1656).   According to Nicéron, Cyrano [1619–55] had been the pupil of Gassendi, who was undoubtedly, with La Mothe le Vayer and Campanella, his favourite among modern philosophers.   Cyrano is not only a sceptic, but an anti-Christian sceptic.   How daring his satire was has only been revealed in recent years by the publication of the original manuscripts by M. Lachèvre.[2]

Cyrano is the sworn enemy of dogmatism : note the way in which he ridicules the Spaniard who has fled his country in order to dogmatize in his own way.   He particularly loves to show the absurdity of various forms of anthropocentrism—

l'orgueil insupportable des humains qui se persuadent que la Nature n'a été faite que pour eux, comme si c'était vraisemblable que le Soleil . . . n'eût été allumé que pour mûrir ses nèfles et pommer ses choux.

It is commonly said that man's upright position is a sign of his superior nature.   The inhabitants of the Moon find an equally good reason for thinking that their position on all-fours ' proves ' the nobility of their species and its value in God's sight.   The same people conclude from Cyrano's lack of feathers and wings that he cannot be the favoured child of God as they are.   Cyrano notes the effect of atmosphere on the mind when he pretends that on the sun no criminal case may be tried in stormy weather.[3]

Within a few pages one may find a long passage on influence of the imagination.   This should be read with the episode of the witch trial in the *Etats du Soleil* and also the 13th letter of the *Œuvres Diverses* (1654), in which Cyrano attacks the belief in sorcery.   If this letter is compared with Montaigne's *Des*

---

[1] Recently republished by F. Lachèvre (1933).   The author is unknown. Some of the topography is borrowed from contemporary accounts of Madagascar.

[2] Frederic Lachèvre : *Le Libertinage da XVII siècle : Cyrano de Bergerac*, 2 vols.

[3] *Cyrano de Bergerac : Histoire Comique de la Lune, &c.* (ed. Garnier), pp. 103, 133, 134, 143, 144, 287.   Note further passages on Angels (p. 162) : and on Death.

Boiteux (III, 11), it is obvious that Cyrano had just re-read that essay before he sat down to compose his letter.

Je ne défférè à l'autorité de personne, si elle n'est accompagnée de raison, ou si elle ne vient de Dieu, qui tout seul doit être cru de ce qu'il dit à cause qu'il le dit . . .[1]

The cases one hears of, always happened three or four hundred miles from the abode of your informer.

La Foi d'une personne seule doit être suspecte en chose si miracu-leuse . . . C'était une pauvre vieille : elle était pauvre : la néces-sité l'a pu contraindre à mentir pour de l'argent : elle était vieille : l'age affaiblit la raison : l'age rend babillard, &c., &c. . . . Car enfin il est plus facile qu'une de ces choses soit arrivée qu'on voit tous les jours arriver qu'une aventure surnaturelle sans raison et sans exemple . . . Si cependant il ne dit mot, chacun crie qu'il est convaincu de sa conscience, et aussitot on le jette au feu.[2]

And Cyrano's explanation of the illusion of the *transport* to the ' coven ' suggests the possibility of the use of drugs, which he imagines to be applied externally.

Cyrano is to-day recognized as the boldest of the free-thinkers of the period, and the famous scene in his *Agrippine* (II, 4), where Sejanus laughs to scorn the existence of the gods, has been taken as the work of one of the rare authentic atheists of the seventeenth century. The sources of his ideas are varied and, while they certainly include the Essays, the debt would be hard to estimate. Similarly Cyrano's personal connexion with Gassendi remains doubtful.

The enthusiasm of Gassendi's friends, Naudé, Patin and Sorbière, for the Essays and even more for *La Sagesse* has been seen, and their probable influence on Cyrano. The utilitarian influence of Gassendi exercises itself on Sorbière, Sarasin and Cotin, as also on Bernier and Naudé. Even Patin shows traces of it, which may not be directly due to Gassendi. All these writers except Cotin and perhaps Sarasin, show various nuances of the humanistic scepticism with which we have become familiar. It is time to turn to the great sceptic of the century, La Mothe le Vayer, who more than any of his contemporaries, perhaps, profited by some perusal of *relations de voyage* which had played their part in the evolution of Montaigne's relativism.

[1] ed. Lachèvre, II, p. 211. cf. *Essais*, III, 11, pp. 332, 333.
[2] *Essais*, ib. and on conscience perhaps, III, 9, p. 239.

CHAPTER XVIII

LA MOTHE LE VAYER: LA DIVINE SCEPTIQUE

*L'on peut dérober à la façon des abeilles sans faire tort à personne :
mais le vol de la fourmi qui enlève le grain entier ne doit jamais être imité.*
LA MOTHE LE VAYER.

OF the writers examined in last chapter, all (but Cotin)
have avowed their admiration for François La Mothe
le Vayer [1583–1672]; and Gassendi, Naudé, Patin and
Sorbière were his intimate friends. It was to him that Marie
de Gournay left her library. It is a letter from François Luillier
to Peiresc which supplies the real date of La Mothe's first published work (1630), informs us of Gassendi's admiration for the
book, but shows that both he and Luillier had yet to make the
author's acquaintance.[1] He was a friend of Mersenne, to whom
he addressed one of his many little works. He was an early
member of the Academy along with Silhon, and it was Bernier
who closed his eyes. Molière was the intimate friend of his son,
on whose premature death he wrote a sonnet to the father. The
brief list of the great dramatist's few books, drawn up after
his death, begins with the two folio volumes of La Mothe's works.

La Mothe was already forty-seven years old when he caused
to be printed in Germany under the assumed name of Orasius
Tubero, his *Cinq Dialogues faits à l'Imitation des Anciens* (1630),
almost immediately followed by another collection of four dialogues. These two books are the boldest he ever produced. All
he wrote later, and he wrote much, only supplements, attenuates,
or reaffirms the philosophy of these nine dialogues.

In La Mothe we find a fideist in religion,[2] a sceptic in all

[1] Luillier, whose son Chapelle was later taught by La Mothe, was on
close terms with Des Barreaux and Théophile, as also with Gassendi.

[2] Note that La Mothe's sincerity cannot be questioned, at any rate,
during the latter part of his life. His own son was a priest; he refers
to certain ' homilies ' composed for his own use (II, 185), and he goes
out of his way to declare that things human cannot be understood without things divine (II, p. 237). Huet, bishop of Avranches, thought La
Mothe the most suitable person to refute the *De Tribus Impostoribus*.

branches of philosophy and science, fascinated by diversity, a devourer of books of travel, a man of universal erudition which he delighted to use against all forms of dogmatism, a friend of tolerance and humanitarianism. La Mothe's ideal is that of the Essays : *la satisfaction que donne un esprit bien fait.*

Il faut se contenter de la jouissance de soi-même, la plus charmante de toutes, si l'on en sait bien user . . .

and he rediscovers something of the accent as well as the words of the Essays in his most heart-felt utterances :

Si celui qui lira ce qui je viens d'écrire se souvient qu'il est homme comme moi, il se devra contenter du vraisemblable comme je fais et ne rien désirer au delà . . . Non content de cette déclaration, je réitère ici ma profession d'ignorance, dont la Sceptique m'a fait faire le premier vœu, et me jettant doucement entre ses bras, comme entre ceux de ma mère nourrice, je m'y promets le repos qu'elle donne à tous ses Sectateurs, et de trouver dans son giron le plus doux chevet que puisse choisir pour se reposer une tête amie de la tranquillité.

Self-knowledge and examination more than any other topics, except *vanitas vanitatum*, bring with them echoes of Montaigne. La Mothe is an independent disciple who is at pains to avoid direct reminiscence, but he is a disciple and among the ablest and the most influential of the many who followed Montaigne's general way of thinking in the first half of the seventeenth century.

The quotation above, bearing so clearly the mark of the Essays upon it, concludes what is probably the earliest composition of La Mothe.[1] Scepticism and the Gospel have at least in common, he tells us, their condemnation of intellectual presumption, a presumption which is implicit in our judgement : this or that person lacks common sense. ' To lack common sense ' is a phrase which rarely means more than ' to have an opinion we do not share ', though it ought to mean the general consensus of humanity. Even then such a general consent has no logical value, nor is it easy to find general consent on any matter of importance. Has the ordinary man who uses the expression, attempted to arrive at ' common sense ' by any enumeration of opinions ? Ethics are as doubtful as any other branch of knowledge apart from religion. Men talk of the necessity of choosing a certain end in life. Has life any end or

[1] *Œuvres,* (1663), II, *Opuscule ou Petit Traité Sceptique sur cette commune façon de parler : N'avoir le sens commun.*

can it have ? And if it has, fortune would make such choice most often useless.

We find an echo of this early essay in the first of the Tubero dialogues, La Mothe's boldest work. *De la Philosophie Sceptique*, takes place between Eudoxus and Ephestion. The former, an Aristotelian, demands the recognition of self-evident truths, admitted by all. Ephestion replies with one of his vast stock of apposite proverbs : *la và male quando si chiama gente a soccorso*. You can't talk about the general consent of mankind when half the surface of the globe remains uncharted. After defending the sceptical position from the alleged impossibility of a regress of doubt, Ephestion expounds the ten methods or ' means ' of Sextus. The tenth is his favourite : the diversity of custom and opinion. In this way some common notions are criticized : filial and parental affection : the connexion between health and longevity, and the advantages of reason : but the Aristotelian is unconvinced.

The second dialogue (*Banquet Sceptique*) may be considered as a pendant, for here the characters discuss in the same style different foods, manners of eating, cannibalism, sexual life and its various perversions ; while the third, on private life, presents Hesychius (La Mothe himself) who tries to persuade Philoponus that the contemplative life is best. The latter cannot understand this point of view because he doesn't know how to be alone with himself. Hesychius admits he was once a slave to ambition, but philosophy and, finally, travel cured him. The fourth dialogue is more directly satirical : *Sur les rares et éminents qualités des Anes de ce Temps*. It is primarily a criticism of those who believe in progress : Philonius, the lover of asses, is questioned by Paleologue.[1] The former maintains that the world changes for better. Above all, the asses are more perfect in all the offices of life *que de père en fils nous les voyons soigneusement conserver dans leurs familles*. The conception of beauty is examined at length, and the beauty of the ass is described in an admirable parody of the usual enthusiastic descriptions of man. Must not each animal imagine God after its own image ?

The fifth of these dialogues (*De la Divinité*) sets out to show that faith is the sole basis of religion. Theology is not a science, its principles are given by faith which is a matter of the will. The five Thomist proofs of God and four others are examined and shown to be logically imperfect. The ordinary anthropomorphic conception of God is a mere political convenience (as

[1] For this question which underlies the quarrel of the Ancients and the Moderns see above, p. 245, note (2).

the Mandarins of China hold). As to the action of God in the world, it may be asked why people should continue to pray, if their prayers are not heard ; for of the frequent prosperity of the wicked there can be no doubt. The irreligious hold that there are as many religions as there are hypothetical accounts which can be given of the universe. Thus, too, an Ethics founded on new principles explaining equally well the duties of life, could give rise to a new religion, just as Copernicus has revolutionized astronomy by his hypothesis,

puisque finalement une religion, connue de la sorte, n'est autre chose qu'un système particulier qui rend raison des phénomènes moraux et de toutes les apparences de notre douteuse Ethique.[1]

This modern conception of science is worth noting.

Each religion is held by its adherents to be true to the exclusion of all others, but Themistius held that variety of worship was agreeable to God, and toleration is more common in the East than is generally supposed. Not all religions believe in immortality ; some set store by much ceremony, others will have none. Some employ inquisition and torture, but Tertullian and Justin Martyr were against all force. Are natural law and religious ethics compatible ? Can one have an excessive piety ? Is Atheism worse than superstition ? Bacon did not think so. It has not necessarily any evil social results.[2] Every kind of natural object and animal has been deified somewhere or at some time, and indeed *la théanthropie sert de fondement à tout le Christianisme*. Faith, then, is the sole basis of religion.

The first of the second set of dialogues shows the conversion of an Aristotelian, Telamon (Mersenne ?), to scepticism. He claims that, since God can only be known through his works, natural philosophy is of prime importance for the knowledge and love of God. Orasius (La Mothe himself) replies that even if natural philosophy is as important as alleged, it is hardly fitted for its task. How does one define Nature ? Is the causal law that nothing is in the effect which is not in the notion of the cause, really valid ?

Je ne m'arrêterai point non plus sur ce que tous les hommes conviennent quasi avec les Stoiciens à se persuader que ce monde n'est fait que pour eux, et que particulièrement ils sont maîtres de la vie de tous les autres animaux, comme les chats, peut-être, se persuadent que Dieu n'a créé les rats et les souris que pour les engraisser.

---

[1] La Mothe : *Deux Dialogues* (ed. Chefs d'Œuvres Méconnus), p. 117.
[2] cf. Bayle's *Pensées sur la Comète*.

Pythagoras and Epicurus held that we had no jurisdiction over them, Holy Scripture enjoins our care for beasts, and the Turks admit sheep into Paradise according to a text of the Koran.

Passing over the ubiquitous question of immortality, we have Telamon's statement on ethics. All philosophers really agree as to the good which is the end of life : the love of God, the practice of virtue, the life according to reason are all identifiable. The passions are neither good nor bad in themselves. Orasius replies : I speak only as a philosopher, of course, but we sceptics fall back on customs and adapt ourselves to them, for there are no other principles. The differences of opinion as to the ' sovereign good ' are not merely verbal. Further, Aristotle confounds man's end with his happiness. Apply this to animals : it *may* be true that it is their function or end to exist for the service of man. It is hardly evident, though, that it is their greatest happiness. Again, is power or lack of responsibility more valuable to a man ? Happiness hardly seems to depend on knowing oneself happy, for we do not know our happiness as *present* happiness.

As to actions, circumstances make them good or bad, and this fact is enough to show that there are no actions which are naturally (that is intrinsically) good or bad. As to passions, it is hard to accept Aristotle's view that they are indifferent. How can something admittedly vicious in a greater degree, be indifferent in a lesser degree ? Is virtue innate in any sense, so that the science of ethics can be, as Bacon said, the Georgics of the Soul ? If so, it is hard to see how responsibility for crime can be maintained, where the propensity to it can be shown to be hereditary. On the other hand, if intention is what makes actions moral or immoral, if the principle *nemo fit sponte nocens* is also true, how do you account for the commission of crimes or evil actions of any kind ? Degrees of blame gave rise even among the ancients to the interminable disputes of casuists ' who caused no less turmoil than our modern ones '. If evil is something positive, how can you reconcile this with the goodness of God ? And so far as specific vices are concerned, if a wish to resemble his Creator is natural to man, how can any excess of ambition be possible ? Whatever seems most criminal to-day in sexual matters must be admitted to have been innocent under the simple law of nature. Life would be impossible without anger,

ceux là étant bien dignes de compassion ou de risée, lesquels empêchant seulement que sa pointe n'agisse au dehors, la font replier contre eux mêmes, et ne voulant permettre à ce feu de prendre l'air et s'éventer, comme si c'était chose honteuse.[1]

As for idleness, it has much in common with the admirable suspense of the Sceptics. Under this spate of objections, Telamon gives in and admits his conversion to scepticism.

In the next dialogue (*De l'opiniâtreté*) [2] there is some more interesting criticism of ethics. A defence of the parricide of aged parents is possible, and if from the population point of view some infants have to be killed, as is done in many parts of the world, would not abortion be far less cruel ? Prejudice has nowhere so strong a hold as in ethics, and yet if one accepted what is supposed to be perhaps the one evident principle of conduct : do not do unto others what you would not have them do unto you, all punishment must be abandoned, for who would not rather be forgiven than punished ? Lastly, this dialogue contains a discussion as to whether the discovery of America was really a good thing for mankind. What cruelty and suffering has not been caused there ? As far as life goes, the inhabitants have been forced to abandon their innocence, exchange the pure Law of Nature for our corrupt laws, and we have imitated in nothing the example which they set us of what almost seemed a golden age. As for religion,

tant s'en faut qu'on ait avancé quelque chose pour le royaume du Ciel, comme l'on parle, que les Indiens qui se pouvaient sauver, au dire des plus équitables théologiens, dans l'innocence de la loi naturelle selon laquelle ils vivaient pour la plupart, recevant la lumière de l'Evangile chrétien de si mauvaises mains, l'éteignent aussitôt qu'ils en ont la liberté et tombent ainsi dans les malédictions de l'apostasie.

The fourth of these dialogues (*Du Mariage*) contains a debate on women which is rather banal, but the third, dealing with Political Science, is full of interest. Does such a science exist ? Is man a political animal ? It is clear at least that social organization has robbed us of our natural liberty :

les belles polices . . . ont causé les guerres, les tyrannies, les pestes les famines et généralement tous les maux que nous souffrons.[3]

There is such a thing as political routine but no general principles, for indeed the opportunism necessary for dealing with a diversity

---

[1] ib., p. 162 (cf. *Essais*, II, 31, p. 521).

[2] The *Crates* of this dialogue has been identified with Vaugelas. This is inadmissible as Crates, who appears elsewhere in La Mothe's dialogues, was a priest (see below, p. 275).

[3] Quatre Dialogues (ed. Trévoux), p. 257.

of circumstances makes all such almost useless. Spain is an
example of a nation which has become a byword for political
wisdom. And yet the Spaniards threw away their chances of
universal domination, chiefly through cruelty and intolerance.
They would still possess the Netherlands, if they had shown a
grain of moderation, and their expulsion of the Moriscoes has
damaged their prosperity at home.

La Mothe goes on to a comparative study of kings and types
of kingship. He examines, as Montaigne does, their alleged
divinity and their religious functions, accompanied sometimes by
various forms of subjection, all this with a wealth of example
which recalls to the modern reader Frazer's ' Golden Bough '.
Ought they to be above the law, elected or hereditary ? Should
women or bastards have a right to succeed ? Finally, is the
Earth itself, a mere point in comparison with the Universe,
worth all the heat of political life ?

C'est donc pour ce point que les Rois de France et d'Espagne
commettent tous les peuples Chrétiens les uns contre les autres,
réduits qu'ils sont à prendre l'un ou l'autre parti.[1]

The sage will live in retirement as far as possible.

The sage, Orasius Tubero, was not destined to live in absolute
retirement. He was to live twenty years at Court, and compose
a number of works, political and religious, at the bidding of the
great Cardinal Richelieu. La Mothe gradually restated under
his own name most of what he had first prudently declared
under his pseudonym. First come two little treatises against
the Spaniards.[2] What is here of importance is the attack on
the character of the Spanish zeal for religion. They make it a
specious excuse for all their projects.

Il n'y donc pas beaucoup de quoi les Espagnols se puissent vanter
d'avoir tant exterminé de créatures humaines sous un faux prétexte
de religion.

A forced religion is of no value, and the fanaticism shown in
stamping out all heresy in Spain has simply given them a vast
quantity of secret Jews and Mahometans in Spain, while to
former Spanish interference in France the success of Protestantism
is directly due. La Mothe repeats, almost word for word, his
accusation that the Spaniards have made innocent pagans into

---

[1] *Quatre Dialogues* (ed. Trévoux), p. 351.
[2] *De la Contrariété des Humeurs qui se trouvent entre certaines Nations :
En quoi la Pieté des Français diffère de celles des Espagnols* (1636).

apostates—damned them, not saved them, in fact. In a third work, published two years later,[1] he again exposes the assumed piety of the Spaniards in their conquest of Mexico and Peru. The angle from which the question of the ' savages ' is here viewed, leads us on to a work which was written against St. Cyran and the Jansenists by the orders of Richelieu : *De la Vertu des Payens* (1642).

The importance attached to this matter and its connexion with the problem of the Law of Nature and the separation of Ethics and Religion has been already seen. Its treatment here presents little new interest. Three cases are distinguished : from Adam to Abraham (the age of the Law of Nature) ; from Abraham to Christ (the age of the written or Mosaic Law) ; from Christ to the end of the world (the age of grace). The first case still applies wherever there has been no chance of becoming acquainted with Christianity. The position of the Gentiles during the period of the Mosaic Law is doubtful, but the best theological opinion is that many are saved. He is personally inclined to think that none of the pagans have a better chance of salvation than those who were supposed atheists (with the exception of Diagoras, Euhemerus and Theodorus of Cyrene), just because they denied the false gods of the heathen.

The second part of the book is devoted to an examination of the lives of the great men of Antiquity, among them Sextus, Julian the Apostate, and Confucius. La Mothe finishes by insisting that virtue must be recognized even when salvation is out of the question. Elsewhere he declares that all laws are interpretations of the law of Nature *gravée dans nos coeurs et qui nous est insinuée avec ce rayon de lumière raisonnable dont le ciel nous gratifie en naissant.* When such interpretations are unreasonable, they must be rejected. Yet, since he holds like Montaigne that the laws must be obeyed because they are laws not because just, since he sets aside, like Montaigne, the claim of the philosophers of antiquity to disregard social laws in the name of a higher morality, it is difficult to see what form this rejection can take.[2]

The *Petit Traité de l'Immortalité de l'Ame* (1637) does not require more than a mention. It naturally takes up a fideist, though not an extreme fideist point of view : immortality cannot be demonstrated, but probable proofs can be given.

There is yet another section of La Mothe le Vayer's work which does not demand much attention : his *Discours de l'In-*

---

[1] *Discours de l'Histoire* (1638).
[2] *Petits Traités en forme de lettres.* No. 38.

struction de M. le Dauphin (1640) written at Richelieu's request, who intended that the author should be the tutor of the future Louis XIV. The great Cardinal died too soon, and his successor, Mazarin, refused to choose between Gassendi, La Mothe, Arnauld d'Andilly and Rigault, and since the Queen-mother insisted on a priest, Hardouin de Péréfixe was finally selected. La Mothe, however, became tutor to the King's brother, duc d'Anjou, and from 1652 to 1656 he was also in fact the chief instructor of Louis himself. In connexion with these duties he prepared a series of manuals : *La Géographie du Prince, La Morale du Prince,* &c. In these he not unnaturally displays a certain timidity in putting forward his personal views. He suggests, for example, that peace is generally the best policy on grounds of utility and self-interest, that it is probably a bad thing to employ force in converting the Protestants, but all this with such circumlocution and caution, that one may doubt whether the influence of the ' Plutarch of France ' would ever under more favourable circumstances have left its mark on the mind of Louis deeply enough to modify the policy of aggrandizement and intolerance which he was later to adopt.[1]

It is rather in the continuous stream of *Opuscules* and *Petits Traités* which, from 1643 onwards, came from La Mothe's pen that we must look for his advocacy of *la divine Sceptique.* Scepticism has disappeared in modern times as a philosophical doctrine, because it has been incorporated in the critical attitude of a scientific probabilism. Some of these little works of La Mothe illustrate this change at work ; he distinguishes the cases included under some loose general statement, he weighs the pros and cons. Take a chapter on dreams and their meaning. The problem must be simplified by first setting aside visions or dreams from God. Though Aristotle denies their existence they are easily recognized, how we are not told, but since they are put in a class apart, a free discussion becomes possible, which is, of course, what La Mothe wants. Three cases must next be distinguished : dreams which are (1) the result of temperament and character, (2) caused by the thought of actions we wish to undertake or to avoid, (3) purely fortuitous. Their interpretation is always doubtful. And yet the Canadians believe all dreams to be literally true. So too the Islanders.

En verité, il y a des hommes, partout merveilleusement enclins à se tromper eux-mêmes : et c'est une chose étrange que ceux du

[1] For a full account of La Mothe le Vayer's life, see R. Kerviller, *Etude sur la vie . . . 1879.*

vieil et du Nouveau Monde s'accordent si bien en cela, notamment au fait des Songes.[1]

In other chapters, however, La Mothe indulges in the sterile procedure of paradox and counterparadox. For example, he will argue first that theft is not an offence against the Law of Nature, since private property is not a positive right under that law. Did not God command the Israelites to despoil the Egyptians ? As for punishment, he exclaims :

Mais quoi ! le gibet est plus pour les malheureux que pour les coupables !

Turn the page, however, and you will find a little essay against theft. The passage of the Bible is easily explained (La Mothe delights in these difficult cases from the Scriptures and he does not always explain them). Theft has everywhere been disapproved, and though the Chinese do not punish it with death, the Americans impale thieves and most people agree, and he with them, that you cannot be too severe in this matter.[2]

Following on what La Mothe says of theft, it should be noticed that he abominates any form of execution with torture, he condemns the practice of the Inquisition in punishing children for the faults of their fathers, though, for example's sake, punishment should always be public. His humanitarian tendencies appear most clearly in his protests against cruelty to animals. This matter is referred to already in the Dialogues of Orasius Tubero, and a later passage on the subject is worth quoting in full : Christians ought to be ashamed of their attitude to the brutes when they see how animals are treated in the East.

Je vous avoue que je leur vois faire souvent des traitements qui me ferait souhaiter qu'il y eût quelque peine établie contre de certains bourreaux qui ont cent fois plus de brutalité qu'elles. Il me semble même que ce point devrait être touché par ceux qui se mêlent d'instruire aux bonnes mœurs, et qu'on devrait apprendre à un peuple farouche et cruel que Dieu plein de miséricorde veut que nous en usions envers les animaux afin de nous la rendre plus familière par accoutumance.[3]

Those we call ' wicked ' are made so by the treatment given them by men. La Mothe ends with his usual moral : all the evil in the world is to be imputed to the vanity and presumption of man, who thinks all things were made for his convenience. In De l'Ingratitude he says that gratitude lies in intention not in

---

[1] Œuvres (1663), II, p. 16 et seq.
[2] ib., II, p. 533 et seq. (cf. Mémorial, No. 29).
[3] Petits Traités en forme de lettres, p. 613.

return made, and that in the East it is considered a duty to be kind to animals just because they cannot make any real return.[1] How important this subject is, may be understood when it is remembered how the *Entretien avec M. de Saci* begins by speaking of the results at Port Royal of the Cartesian theory that animals were machines and how *on n'avait guère de solitaire qui ne parlat d'automate* ; not only that, but convinced that animals felt nothing, practised vivisection without any attempt to lessen the sufferings of the objects of their experiments.[2]   There is also the well-authenticated story of Malebranche kicking a dog. That is to say a scientific theory ill-understood was about to reinforce Catholic prejudice, which with its absolute anthropocentrism already helped to excuse natural brutality and negligence.

In the *Mémorial de Quelques Conférences avec des Personnes Studieuses* (1669), La Mothe notes a conversation in which the company were strongly of opinion that one of the most necessary things in the education of a prince was to prevent a delight in cruelty even to animals.   As so often he supports this view by quoting, not the Essays—the well-known *C'est passetemps aux mères de voir un enfant tordre le col à un poulet*, &c.—but a classical authority, Varro.   It is sometimes hard not to have the impression that La Mothe wishes to avoid the constant mention of an author whose ideas he so often expressed.

La Mothe attacks also some rather unimportant prejudices which loomed large in his day : for instance, the burial rites of various nations (cf. Charron and Sorel above, p. 108).   Has the matter any real importance, he asks.   The Church says yes, so one must agree with her.   And since Christianity allows the use of reason more than the Mahometans do, less than the pagans, he would have us admit that there are certain unworthy superstitions, which reason is competent to deal with :

Quelle bonté de mettre le Paradis à prix d'argent ? de préférer l'encens ou le culte à la probité ? et d'attribuer des sentiments à Dieu que nous aurions honte d'imputer à un homme raisonnable ? [3]

Elsewhere he protests both against prejudice against foreigners and against the idea that patriotism is only a useful political expedient.   There are countries of choice as well as countries of birth, and he ends with a passage which recalls Charron (and Michel Baudier) :

---

[1] *Œuvres*, II, Opuscules IVme Partie (cf. Baudier, p. 257).
[2] cf. Pascal (ed. Grands Ecrivains), I, pp. 26–8.
[3] *Œuvres*, II, p. 498.

Et je ne doute point que vous ne reconnaissez combien ce serait une chose ridicule qu'il fût permis de faire cas, et d'avoir soit des chiens, soit des chevaux qui viennent des pays fort éloignés, lorsque nous les trouvons excellents, et qu'il ne fut pas loisible de se prévaloir des hommes du dehors qu'une vertu extraordinaire peut nous rendre recommandables.[1]

The only part of Ethics in which La Mothe is not completely sceptical is introspection and self-examination. This is difficult, and half the battle is to recognize one's defects :

. . . le plus déréglé des hommes changerait indubitablement de mœurs et aurait horreur de sa turpitude, s'il se donnait le loisir de l'envisager comme il faut.[2]

The true principle of ethics is conscience, and one of its most important precepts is consistency of life. La Mothe develops these notions in *De l'Examen de Conscience des Pythagoriciens* in language obviously inspired by the Essays. It is difficult to be *one* person. The author justifies the versatility of Alcibiades as a wise prudence. Philosophers have unwisely held that true wisdom is always to will or not to will the same thing, but our desires change like water and the mind must be constantly in acquisition of knowledge, intellectual and moral, if only to make up for what is lost by memory or revision of judgement. And it is just because they know how to revise their judgements that the truly wise and virtuous are *simples et traitables*.

It is in La Mothe's *Prose Chagrine* (1661), one of his most readable works, that he makes his own self-examination and confesses himself in public.[3] This book is thus in a very special sense in the tradition of the Essays, for the underlying idea is the value of analysis and of the expression of one's temporary mood to restore moral health and balance. It is also the most loosely constructed and the most personal of his works.

The times are out of joint, for we hardly know Life before it is done. The young have the Arts and Sciences indifferently thrust upon them without any attention being paid to their natural temperament. Hence so many ' lettered fools '. Is ignorance the alternative ? Why accuse those of ignorance to whom nature has given a gift of common sense ? [4] The more

[1] cf. Charron : *Petit Traité de Sagesse :* and Baudier above, p. 257.
[2] *Œuvres*, II, p. 618 (cf. *Essais*, III, 5, p. 82).
[3] This title has its parallels in the *Epîtres Chagrines* of St. Evremond and Madame Deshoulières. On the *Prose Chagrine* and *Le Misanthrope*, see below, p. 391, note 2.
[4] Contrast with p. 261, above.

learned one is, the more conscious of ignorance. Philosophy (moral philosophy) is perhaps the one exception to all these useless disciplines, yet what absurdities and disagreements are to be found here ! The casuists have so confused people's minds that good and evil are hardly recognizable. For himself—and it is rather his own life he would examine—he is a philosopher by inclination and yet a courtier by accident. Perhaps his disgust is due to the social evils he sees : superstition, venality, and dissension in religion ; venality in the law courts, unlike the free justice of China, Persia and Turkey ; extortion and waste in public finance. Perhaps in another mood he would not be so bitter, but, says La Mothe, one should speak out one's mind and one's mind should change. These two things are connected.

De n'en avoir qu'une sorte (de sentiment) c'est dans ma philosophie aussi bien que dans la Politique de Cicéron un vice plutôt qu'une vertu,

Invariability is in Ethics—where his three masters are Cicero, Seneca, and Plutarch—a fallacy comparable to the theological heresy of the Monotheists.[1]

La Mothe goes on to a short re-statement of his sceptical philosophy. He recalls his recent annoyance with a cocksure person who would not yield to any argument on any point, and whose last resort was always to declare that the argument which put his back to the wall was contrary to faith. This man also maintained that scepticism was incompatible with Christianity. The precise opposite is true, for all philosophical sects are contrary to Christianity except the Sceptics. They only hold that sense-experience is fallible, not that it is always fallacious, so that scepticism does not imply a rejection of all miracles as evidence for Christianity, although their importance is frequently exaggerated, and many must be rejected, even those attributed to the Christ-child. It is even true that Theism can be established by human reason, but it is preferable to make all that concerns religion a matter of faith, since (it is implied) argument will not do more than establish the existence of a God and of his Providence. The perfection of learning (*science*) is not the attainment of ultimate truths : it is, as the Caliph Gali was wont to say, *douceur de moeurs*.[2] To acquire this, knowledge of how customs, odd to our way of thinking, seem natural to other nations is especially valuable.

To return to himself, when depression descends—and though old, his is not due to old age—that is the time to examine one's

[1] *Œuvres*, II, pp. 1119, 1120.   [2] ib., p. 1136.

life and repent of one's vices. Instead, we generally attack those of other people when in this mood.[1] Anger and cruelty are the vices La Mothe particularly hates, hence a return once more to the subject of cruelty to animals.[2] He cannot approve, however, the common discourses on the general extirpation of the passions, and cannot forget all Aristotle has said in their favour. What would life be without them but a perpetual contemplation of our own misery : *peu s'en faut que je ne mette notre essentielle félicité dans le ressentiment de ce qu'elles ont de plus impétueux.* But they are chaotic and attachment to them spells a chaotic life.

His own life has been useless to society and idle even on the most indulgent interpretation. Studious retirement is not to be despised, but such an existence too often seems to have a fictitious consistency which is just its uniform indolence. And his writings ? Others must judge whether they have had their justification. As for the self-satisfaction of the virtuous, justly suspicious to many minds, he has no experience of it, but perhaps his life is cause. Here La Mothe feels his *chagrin* is beginning to dissolve (Pascal would have found him as lacking in a real sense of sin as Montaigne). We weep and laugh by turns; he feels he exaggerates the evils of existence, and would rather look at the brighter side. Heraclitus and Democritus belong together ; one must temper the attitude of one with that of the other.

Je veux imiter les railleries de ce dernier, en me moquant de lui-même d'avoir placé la vérité, dont il était grand amateur, au fonds d'un puits, au lieu de dire qu'elle n'est trouvable qu'au Ciel, où il la faut seulement chercher, ne se rencontrant point ailleurs.[3]

So too Montaigne, it will be remembered. This comparison is indeed the symbol of fideism as opposed to a radical scepticism.

[1] If we may believe Tallemant, this was La Mothe's own failing.

[2] ib., p. 1149. 'Soyons pleine d'indulgence et de douceur, même envers les bêtes afin de n'en manquer jamais à l'égard de nos semblables. . . . Considérez ces brutaux et dénaturés qui commettent tous les jours devant nos yeux de si énormes barbaries, tantôt contre des chevaux, tantôt contre des chiens : ils n'useront pas de plus grande indulgence envers les hommes, autant de fois qu'ils croiront que leur férocité pourra demeurer impunie . . .' After quoting a text of Cicero, La Mothe continues : 'Ha ! qu'on entretient tous les jours le peuple de discours qui ne valent pas ceux-ci, et dont il ne tirera jamais le profit qu'il pourrait faire d'une doctrine si pleine d'humanité. Je remarquerai encore à notre confusion qu'autrefois les Athéniens punirent très sévèrement un de leurs bourgeois pour avoir eu la cruauté d'ôter la peau à un mouton vivant. Nous voyons tous les jours faire pis devant nos yeux à une infinité d'animaux sans que personne s'y oppose.'

[3] ib., p. 1161 (cf. *Essais*, III, 8, p. 192).

In all this, says La Mothe, I hope I offend none ; I only follow my *humeur bigarre*.

Elle me fait souvent passer brusquement d'un sujet à un autre selon que mes caprices sont violents : et je me suis vu réduit au style concis et coupé, qui lui plaît comme lui étant naturel, encore que je n'ignorasse pas que c'était s'éloigner étrangement de celui qui est le plus en vogue aujourd'hui.[1]

Such is his humour. His design has been to show how one might deal with depression, by his own example, and we leave him determined to take leave of all other thoughts *pour prendre celles qui portent sinon à la joie, du moins à un rire Abdéritain qui en est fort voisin.*

In 1670, two years before his death, La Mothe sums up his philosophy for the last time in a slender volume : *Les Soliloques Sceptiques.* The most important maxim of science is that there are not only things unknowable but things not worth knowing. Desire of knowledge is natural to man. This is his distinctive mark, and not his reason (compare with Marandé, contrast with Chanet and with the Cartesians.) But ' science ' is not in our power nor ' natural ' to us.

L'homme n'est pas capable de savoir la raison d'autre chose que de ce qu'il exécute à sa mode, ni comprendre d'autres sciences que celles dont il fait soi-même les principes.[2]

To reason about religious matters is to discover that logic and religion don't agree. Once admit reasoning, individualism must creep in, and each man chooses among the articles of religion those he prefers.

Is Scepticism not pernicious outside religion ? No, for the great danger is that one should imagine it necessary to believe the expert. Once having come to a conclusion, most people are too obstinate to be re-persuaded. Yet so far as the vulgar are concerned, it is vain and even undesirable to try and establish the superiority of doubt. It would only afford them an excuse

---

[1] *Œuvres*, p. 1161. Compare Montaigne on his own style, p. 123 above. There is no room here to deal with La Mothe's attack on the tendencies of the stylists grouped round the Academy (of which he was member) nor his attack on Vaugelas. He backed up Mademoiselle de Gournay in his *Eloquence Françoise* (1638), attacking especially the prudery of the purists, their notion that a thing well said in one way is always badly said in another, their dislike of archaisms, of neologisms, of metaphor, and their fallacy that hiatus is always ugly. He lays stress, however, on the importance of the building up of periods.

[2] i.e. Mathematics (*Soliloques*, II).

for sticking to their own prejudices. It is better to pay an external homage of conformity to conventional ideas. In this admission we lay our fingers on the crucial difference between the liberals of the seventeenth and those of the eighteenth century.

Even on ethical questions, as on all others, there seems to be no agreement of opinion. La Mothe adapts Montaigne's famous observation on the strangeness of a morality which changes as one crosses a mountain,[1] and he adds later with that shade of regret which reveals the double rôle of *la divine Sceptique* :

> Cette grande discordance des Nations fait voir entre autres choses, qu'il n'y a point, à le bien prendre, de communes notions parmi les hommes. . . . Certes, c'est une chose pitoyable de voir d'un œil exempt de prévention, comme chacun prend les choses à sa mode et comme il n'y a presque personne qui n'aime mieux reprendre Dieu et la Nature que de reconnaître ingénuement l'ignorance où il est.

It is hardly necessary to point out how closely the substance of La Mothe's philosophy is that of the Essays. The analysis of his views may seem tedious, for the apparent lack of any intellectual development between his earlier and his later works gives an impression of the philosophical barrenness to which a consistent Christian Scepticism of this kind seems to be condemned. This judgement would, however, not be quite fair to La Mothe nor to the many friends who shared his views. They did a great service by their opposition to dogmatism, and their encouragement of the critical spirit. They felt themselves all the more intellectually free, since religion was best kept entirely separate from all rational speculation. And not even in La Mothe's case did scepticism totally shake a belief in a humanist ethic of some kind. No matter how often he shows that notions of morality differ from land to land, even if the conception of the Law of Nature is criticized by him, a belief in some intrinsic principle in man which permits him to know good from evil does remain.

Another error must be banished. La Mothe was not the lonely champion of his way of thinking, nor was he merely supported by the few friends whose views were examined in the last chapter. Attention must be drawn to two books of his : the *Mémorial de Quelques Conférences avec des Personnes Studieuses* (1669) and the *Hexaméron Rustique* (1670). Here we meet under various pseudonyms all La Mothe's chief friends and acquaint-

---

[1] *Essais*, II, 12, p. 338 (Quelle vérité que ces Montagnes bornent, &c.). cf. Pascal : *Pensées* (ed. Brunschvicg), No. 294.

ances.   Nor is this all, for if one looks at the Dialogues of Tubero
after reading the *Mémorial*, it will be realized that here the
characters are often the same people, the author's friends.   The
Mémorial is a record of conversations held over a number of
years, at the house of the Du Puy brothers, the Royal Librarians.
Le Cabinet de Messieurs Du Puy was indeed a learned *cénacle*
frequented by many of those who like La Mothe himself, were
also of the Academy.   Two subjects constantly recur, the problem of faith and reason, and an interest in books of travel.   It
is worth while touching on the ideas of some of this set on religion
and ethics.

CHAPTER XIX

LE CABINET DE MESSIEURS DU PUY

MICHEL DE MAROLLES, abbé de Villeloin, and indefatigable translator, was one of the most intimate friends
of Mademoiselle de Gournay. We have also seen his
exchange of *essais sceptiques* with Sorbière, and mentioned the
presence of the Essays of Montaigne in his father's modest
library. He appears as *Marulle* [1] in the *Heptaméron Rustique*
of La Mothe, but it is from his own works that we may judge
the outlook of a broad-minded Christian of the seventeenth
century. He inveighs against images, relics and other forms of
superstition. He is very sceptical about sorcery.[2] He considers that the reunion of the Churches *ne dépend que d'une bonne
reformation de notre côté*.[3] Having remarked that difference of
character is the result of temperament, a friend of his, the Comte
de Barraut, asked him whether this was not an opinion dangerous
to the doctrine of the Immortality of the Soul:

Mais on lui répondit que quand l'âme de l'homme ne serait pas
immortelle par sa nature, comme celle des bêtes, qu'elle le serait par
grâce, et qu'il suffit de dire que c'est un point de foi : car d'en
raisonner par les maximes et les principes de la Philosophie, soit
d'Aristote, soit de Platon, comme a fait encore depuis peu de jours
un de nos Amis, il est impossible de le démontrer.[4]

He agrees elsewhere with Sorbière (and Silhon) that if it were
not for his immortality man would be worse off than the beasts.[5]
Marolles' comments on his translation of Lucretius are also

---

[1] The nickname of Marulle was obviously chosen by allusion to what
La Mothe considered his friend's most important work, his translation
of Lucretius (1650). Michael Marullus (died 1500) was the brilliant
humanist emendator of Lucretius. Marolles says of his translation that
it has had the largest and quickest sale of all his books, contrary to his
expectation.

[2] *Mémoires* (1656), I, pp. 132, 146–49, 170, 171, 276–8.

[3] ib., I, p. 241.   [4] ib., p. 249.

[5] ib., II, p. 94.

worth noting.   He sticks up for pagan religion as socially useful.
The origin and nature of the soul is unknown except by revelation, but the existence of God is *almost* demonstrable by reason.[1]
Of the maxim *de nihilo nihil* he says that all physicists have
accepted it as true, *mais cela n'empêche pas que par la foi nous
ne soyons persuadés que de rien Dieu a fait toutes choses par sa
parole*.   He declares himself however outright in favour of
Copernicus and Galileo.   Finally, a paragraph on Ethics may
be fittingly quoted.

Vous ne sauriez être plus Sceptique (he writes to Sorbière) que
je le suis dans la plupart des choses.   Mais dans les questions de la
Morale qui peuvent être de notre portée, je prends volontiers le parti
de ce qui me semble le plus honnête et le plus juste sur les coutumes
reçues de nos Pères, et sur les fondements de la doctrine : car je tiens
qu'il ne faut rien changer et que nous sommes redevables à notre
divin Legislateur, de la plus excellente Morale et de la plus noble
Politique qui se puisse imaginer.[2]

Marolles has been mentioned as a type of the seventeenth-
century humanist Christian, but it is hardly possible to speak of
him as being influenced by Montaigne.   The other indefatigable
translator of the time, Perrot d'Ablancourt [1606–64], whose
father's *Gigantomachie* has been mentioned, and who visited the
Du Puys almost every day, does sometimes echo the Essays.
Tallemant says :

D'Ablancourt est un esprit comme Montaigne mais plus réglé :
il s'est amusé par paresse aux traductions . . . Après avoir bien
lu les Pères, il dit que pour trouver du sens commun il faut aller an
dessus de Jésus Christ.[3]

and it is not for nothing that a contemporary memoir of his
life declares :

Son génie approchait fort du génie de Montaigne ; et s'il eût
voulu travailler de lui-même, il ne lui manquait rien de tant ce qu'il
faut pour cela.[4]

His preface to the *Honnête Femme* of Du Bosc bears out this
judgement, but it is enough for our present purpose to draw
attention to his fideism as expressed in his *Discours à M. Patru*.
Finalist arguments such as the desire to believe in immortality

---

[1] *Les Six Livres de Lucrèce* (1659), p. 427.
[2] *Mémoires*, II, p. 136.   On *Honnêteté*, see below, p. 317.
[3] Tallemant des Réaux : *Historiettes*, V, p. 24.
[4] *Recueil de Diverses Harangues*, 4ᵐᵉ partie. Bruxelles, 1682, p. 233.

as taking thought for posterity, or knowledge of the future are good enough to help a man already illuminated by faith, but useless for any other purpose. I may hold as a physicist that resurrection is impossible, if I believe that God can do things impossible in the ordinary course of nature. ' It is not necessary to be stupid to be a good Catholic, and we are not forbidden to raise our eyes to heaven, to contemplate the beauty of the world, nor to investigate the limits which God has given to Nature ', *so long as* a sphere of things beyond reason is recognized. Rationalism in religion, were it possible, would take away the merit of faith :

Tu crois l'immortalité de l'âme, à cause que ta raison te le fait voir ainsi ; et moi, contre mon sens, je crois que nos âmes sont immortelles, parce que notre Religion me commande de croire de la sorte . . . et croyant de cette façon l'immortalité de l'âme, tu te peux bien vanter d'être savant, mais non pas d'être Chrétien.

Exactly in the same way as intention alone can make an action good, so understanding is nothing without belief.

Tel pense croire l'évangile, qui ne croit que sa raison, et bien souvent ce n'est pas en Dieu, mais en nous-mêmes que nous nous fions.

Finally, if it were not true that men know nothing with certainty, there might be some excuse for this rationalism, but nothing is so necessary in order to counteract human presumption, as to realize the ' imbecility ' of man.[1]

Before passing on to Chapelain and Balzac, another friend of the Du Puys, clearly a student of the Essays, is worth our attention. Philippe Fortin de La Hoguette [1585–c. 1670] after a military career, became tutor to the sons of the Duc de Longueville, and composed three works, one of which enjoyed considerable success up to the very end of the century, his *Testament ou Conseils Fidèles d'un Bon Père à ses Enfants* (1648). He also knew Gassendi, La Mothe, and the astronomer Diodati, and in 1623 he came to England in order to meet Francis Bacon, *mon grand chancelier*, for whom he had the greatest admiration and whose portrait he obtained for the Du Puy brothers.[2] La Hoguette's letters to Pierre Du Puy and Louis le Pelletier already indicate the influence of the Essays on this attractive personality.

---

[1] *Recueil de Diverses Harangues*, pp. 749 et seq. Notice D'Ablancourt's preface to his translation of Lucian recommends Lucian specially as one who exposes better than any one else the vanity and ignorance of philosophers and the feebleness of man.

[2] La Hoguette : *Correspondance* (ed. Larroque), Lettre du 26 Sept. 1623 from London.

When ill, he writes :

Notre bonne mère Nature est celle qui me doit guérir pourvu
que je sois assez sage pour ne la surcharger point d'aucuns excès.
Le soleil remonte, les jours croissent, et mon espérance comme les
jours, qui me fera prendre patience jusqu'à la St. Jean et au delà,
s'il est besoin. Aussi bien est-ce un mauvais emplâtre à tous maux
que l'impatience . . . Peut-être suis-je comme le curé de Montaigne
qui argumentait de l'ire de Dieu contre le genre humain parce que
sa vigne avait été gêlée.[1]

Three weeks later he is still harping on the misery of man and
the happiness of the animals. But once unburdened, he feels
better and he likes to note his changes of mood :

Je partis de Paris avec une âme de pagnotte et en résolution de
me cloîtrer chez moi. Cette fantaisie me passe, et l'envie de retourner
dans le grand monde lui succède. Je ne sais si ce nouveau désir est
produit en moi par un excès de santé . . . ou si c'est un effet de
l'intempérie de mon cerveau, tant y a que s'il se fait quelque chose
par deçà par mer ou par terre, je suis encor soldat.

A month later he changes his mind again and reflects :

que cette bonne dame [Nature] est heureuse de servir à deux effets
si contraires et de conserver encor son nom.[2]

La Hoguette's books contain a fair number of references to
Montaigne and his ideas are often evidently inspired by the
Essays. He is not, however, a sceptic or a fideist of the type
of La Mothe, or D'Ablancourt, or even Marolles. He differs
from them in the strength of his conviction that ethics can be
founded on natural law, that man is naturally good, but agrees
that the supernatural must be kept in its proper place.

The preface of La Hoguette's *Testament* contains a defence
of neologisms. They are valuable because expression is the
ultimate aim of all writing. Further on, he writes :

Soit que tu parles ou que tu écrives, ne recherche nulle autre
diction que celle qui sera la plus propre et la plus significative pour
exprimer les notions de ton âme. La diversité des visages ne procède
que de la diversité des esprits, ni celle du style que de celle du tempérament et des moeurs.[3]

Such considerations, not in favour in the French seventeenth
century, have been seen to be characteristic of the disciples of
the Essays from Marie de Gournay onwards.

The book begins with the duty of man to God. The sacrifice

---

[1] La Hoguette : *Correspondance*, p. 75. *Essais*, I, 26, p. 202.
[2] ib., p. 208.   [3] *Testament* (ed. 1655), p. 102.

of reason is part of this duty so far as religion is concerned, elsewhere reason is the one criterion. Touching on the free-thinkers,
La Hoguette notes that there are two kinds of believers, and it
is the ' middle class ' of minds who have the presumption of
wishing to cast religion out of their lives.[1] Two years later in
his *Catéchisme Royal* he says that it is only the open profession
of Atheism or public attacks on the Christian religion, as being
that of the State, which are offences before the law. Frédéric
Lachèvre has shown that French practice in the seventeenth
century generally acted on these lines. La Hoguette continues :

> La Foi véritablement est un don de Dieu, il ne l'a pas qui veut :
> mais la discrétion de ne pas condamner les mystères est en la puis-
> sance de l'homme.[2]

And, in the same place, he continues, dealing with the proper
manner of conceiving the Deity :

> Donnons-lui ce qu'elle désire de nous, à savoir une soumission
> simple, ignorante et sans aucun raisonnement . . . Il serait à
> souhaiter qu'on en parlât plus sobrement et qu'on eût cette discrétion
> de ne point assujettir aux mesures des hommes l'immensité de Dieu ;
> de laquelle on a pris l'autorité de décider aussi hardiment et de ses
> attributs incompréhensibles, comme s'il n'était question que de pro-
> noncer sur des passions humaines. La fleur de la plus belle saison des
> esprits se passe en cette vaine altercation : et de la vanité qu'on prend de
> juger de la Nature Divine, il se forme une certaine présomption qui
> rend la personne qui en est atteinte incapable de toute autre société.[3]

We only know *that* God exists not *what* He is. An adequate
notion of Him can only be got by abstract thought and by negation ; above all, mental imagery must be banished.[4] God's
power is palpably evident in the world, however, and Christianity
is in its essence conformable to natural reason.[5]

[1] ib., pp. 48–50 (cf. p. 254 the further use of comparison with the
three regions of the air).

[2] *Catéchisme Royal*, 1650, p. 16.

[3] ib., p. 17. In this little work note also echoes of Montaigne on pp. 1,
2, 27, 28).

[4] *Eléments de la Politique*, Chap. I.

[5] *Testament*, pp. 108, 109. A not very convincing section on Immortality, interesting for the utilization of personal experience, was added
to the *Testament* in 1655. One other addition to this edition may be
noted. The first edition contained a chapter on superstition, which La
Hoguette begins by repeating Bacon's condemnation of superstition as
worse than atheism. Later he adds a special section on hypocrisy and
des faux Directeurs des affaires, de la santé, de la conscience. (This is one
year before the Provincial Letters, and nine before the first Tartuffe.)
He expresses himself pretty strongly elsewhere on this subject (p. 73).

As to the nature of man, La Hoguette is among those who protest, like Marandé, against the notion that man is by definition the 'rational animal'.

Il le peut devenir mais qu'il le puisse être sans étude et sans en faire les actions, c'est ce que je ne comprends point. La raison est plutôt une qualité propre de l'homme qu'essentielle à lui seul. Appelons comme nous voulons l'intelligence de l'éléphant, du cheval et du chien, elle ne se fait point sans réflexion non plus que la nôtre, qui est une espèce de raisonnement.[1]

Man ought rather to be called the *animal enquérant*. It is neither his reason nor his sociability which make him different from other animals.

La Hoguette asserts the essential freedom of man. So it was in Eden, so it may be seen even in children, who possess a natural wish for independence.[2] The will tends naturally to good, contrary tendencies are to be counted due to passions, ignorance, inexperience, or original sin (inherited). But man's original goodness is not lost. Though he may do evil, he almost always knows it to be evil. The keyword of La Hoguette's remarks on ethics is his notion of *pudeur originelle* which he opposes to original sin. Still more striking is the psychological justification of right conduct.

Ainsi, mon fils, puis qu'il ne peut jamais y avoir un parfait accord entre notre pensée et notre libre consentement (qui est notre parole intérieure) que dans le dessein d'une action qui soit bonne, rends toi capable de cette harmonie, et intérieurement véritable.[3]

Characteristic, too, of his moral optimism and the harmony-not-conflict view of ethics is La Hoguette's identification of virtue and innocence in the *Catéchisme Royal* :

Qu'appelez vous vertu ?—Je n'oserais vous la dépeindre des couleurs de l'Ecole de peur qu'en vous la faisant voir triste, sévère et renfrognée, elle ne vous fût plutôt un sujet d'aversion que d'amour. Je la conçois sous un visage plus doux, et qui est (ce me semble) son vrai portrait, à savoir que la vertu est une constante et gaie application de toutes nos actions au bien : constante, parce qu'il ne faut jamais qu'elle varie : et gaie parce que toute action libre l'est. En un mot, la vertu et l'innocence ne sont qu'une même chose ; et puisque la saison de notre vie la plus innocente est la plus enjouée, il faut que notre vertu lui ressemble, ou pour le moins que la gaîté

[1] *Testament*, p. 135.
[2] ib., p. 64. ' L'opiniâtreté de l'enfant n'est autre chose qu'un brut et informe raisonnement de l'ame encore imparfaite qui veut jouir de ses droits avec le temps.'
[3] ib., pp. 69, 70.

soit un assaisonnement de ce qu'il y a de plus austère en la pratique des vertus : et un témoignage de ce que je dis, c'est que celui de tous les hommes qui a été jugé par l'Oracle avoir été le plus sage et le meilleur, a été le plus enjoué.[1]

La Hoguette insists in a number of ways on the analogies and interaction of body and mind. The soul is best known through the body. Instruction in self-knowledge should begin with some study of anatomy. The other study which should be begun early with children is geography, particularly in connexion with the influence of climate on racial characteristics. On asceticism [2] he directly echoes the Essays :

Quelqu'un a dit que c'est une espèce de trahison de mal traiter le corps et de rendre ses fonctions stupides et esclaves pour épargner à l'ame la sollicitude de les conduire selon raison.[3]

It would be misleading, however, to suggest that La Hoguette's views on ethics are not thoroughly orthodox. Asceticism has its place in the priestly life, which he expects one of his children to adopt, though ' civil devotion ' pleases him more. He insists on the importance of charity, and his remarks about love are very puritanical. His opinions on music, dancing, novel-reading and many other practical questions are interesting but need not detain us, nor most of his remarks on education. Except to note that he adopts Montaigne's protest against the way in which parents hold more aloof from children as they grow up. The book originally ended with a meditation on death, to which a discourse on immortality was later appended.

La Hoguette's third work is entitled *Les Eléments de la Politique selon les Principes de la Nature* (1663). The introduction gives an attractive account of his life where the author declares that, after long research on political science,

j'ai trouvé qu'il n'y avait point de meilleure ni de plus saine que celle qui était le plus conforme à la Loi de nature non corrompue : et que cette loi non corrompue, celle de Dieu et de la droite raison, n'étaient qu'une même loi.

Unlike Montaigne and Charron he does not seem to believe that there is much difficulty in detecting this law. The soul is neither good nor bad except in a transferred sense. It requires no

---

[1] op. cit., pp. 2, 3.
[2] La Hoguette is very much opposed to allowing people to make vows at the age of fifteen. He wants the age raised. A measure of the kind was eventually put in force under Louis XIV.
[3] *Testament*, p. 191.

' purging ' in itself. Its actions only are good or bad according
to their naturalness or appropriateness.

Chapters on imaginary prehistory, giving a democratic character to primitive societies, the derivation of all social laws from
such principles as gratitude, self interest, &c., reducible to ' do
as you would be done by ' and the recognition and worship of
God, are features of this book. The law of Moses was simply
the law of nature written down in order to impress the Jews.[1]
Human law preceded divine law, in the sense that ' do as you
would be done by ' (and the laws derived from this rational
foundation) are sufficient for social life, without any knowledge
of God—as may be seen in the case of social animals. Thus
religion indeed is the only respect in which beasts greatly differ
from man, but no religion can be good whose precepts are not
conformable to natural, civil and international law (loi des gens).[2]
The book contains also a remarkable downright condemnation
of all war from this soldier, who said it was better to be a butcher
than a soldier.[3]

La Hoguette ends again with an echo of the Essays. The
ugliness of vice and its results are enough to keep men in the
right path.

Toutes les austérités qui prennent le change, en punissant le ser-
viteur pour les fautes du maître, contristent plutôt l'âme en affligeant
le corps qui est son associé, qu'ils ne la rendent meilleure. Nous
autres qui sommes un peu plus matériels, laissons l'usage de ce ragoût
et de cet entremets de dévotion à ceux qui l'aiment, sans en condamner la pratique, et voyons s'il n'y a point de voie moins épineuse
et plus conforme à notre nature que celle là . . . Enfin on peut par
son moyen aller au Ciel par le Paradis terrestre, tâchons donc de
l'acquérir si nous voulons y aller et posseder nos âmes en paix.[4]

---

[1] Eléments, p. 170.   [2] ib., chap. 12, pp. 225, 255, 256, 271.
[3] Correspondance, p. 57 ; Eléments, pp. 457 et seq., note especially
p. 461 on the dangers of winning a war. It may be worth quoting in
this connexion the remarkable verses of a Protestant, the Bordelais poet,
La Vergne (Essias de Poésie, 1643) :

> O Dieu ! changez l'horrible face
> De cet élément de malheurs,
> Tarissez la source des pleurs,
> Avec celle d'une disgrâce.
> Réunissez par des accords
> Les sentiments de tous les corps,
> Etouffant ceux d'une victoire
> Qui fait le crime des guerriers :
> Et qu'on ne cherche plus de gloire
> Dans l'amertume des lauriers.

[4] ib., p. 471 et seq.

It is illuminating to see how many elements of the naturalistic rationalism of this author come from the Essays. This gives us some indication of the wideness of Montaigne's influence ; while the limited fideism of La Hoguette, apparent at least in his earlier works, helps to show how prevalent this tendency was to have effect on a temperament of this kind. He reflects Montaigne's moral optimism more than his intellectual pessimism.

A different kind of influence may be seen in the little book written by George Pellisson, brother of the Historian of the Academy : *Mélanges de Divers Problèmes* (1647). This contains much acute psychological analysis. The whole method is interesting. As an explanation of any fact it is not enough to give one reason, for any fact has generally a number of contributing causes. So particularly with regard to human actions and emotions :

je puis dire que toutes les passions ensemble y paraissent toujours, et y jouent leur rôle encore que ce ne soit pas toujours d'une semblable façon . . . et comme l'on dit qu'aucun Elément ne nous paraît jamais en sa pûreté, je pense aussi que tout de même aucune de nos passions ordinaires—qui sont comme les principes et les éléments de nos moeurs—ne paraît jamais en sa pûreté et sans aucun mélange des autres.

Why do we desire fame ? As a ' second life ', no doubt ; but we also desire it in order to think well of ourselves, as a means of making ourselves loved. Again, we wish to be loved, no doubt, just for the sake of being loved, but also for incidental advantages. So vengeance is desired partly to restore our opinion of ourselves, partly for the sake of the opinion of others and our power over them, partly by a wish to make sure we shan't be injured again.[1] When direct signs of Pellisson's interest in certain ideas of Montaigne's are seen, it seems fair to suppose that it was the Essays which taught him this method of psychological analysis.

The third problem—why rage should be often calmed by opposition rather than supplication—is simply a development, and a subtle development, of the first of all Montaigne's Essays. The 22nd problem discusses Montaigne's opinion that matters to do with sex ought to be openly discussed.[2] Such examples could be multiplied. It is enough here to draw attention to certain of his views. It astonishes some people that wicked men

---

[1] *Mélange de Divers Problèmes*, Preface (cf. above, p. xxxiii).
[2] Montaigne is quoted here. Pellisson disagrees with him and makes a good case.

make good friends : but nothing and no one is wholly good or bad, and all of qualities have their compensating disadvantages,[1] It is a received maxim that the mean is best and extremes to be avoided : but it is just as often the other way round. The middle region of the air is always troubled.

Il faut ou ne raisonner point du tout, mais suivre le simple sens commun comme les Paysans, ou bien raisonner exactement et profondément et se rendre véritablement savant ; pour ce que raisonner à demi et être à demi savant, c'est le moyen de s'embrouiller en mille doutes inconnus aux autres.[2]

Further on Pellisson says of the usual condemnation of the vulgar :

En cela il y a de l'aigreur, car il ne faut pas considérer les seuls défauts du peuple, mais aussi considérer ce qu'il a de bon, et pour lors nous trouverons qu'en beaucoup de choses il a les premières connaissances du sens commun très vives et très nettes, encore qu'il n'en sache pas discourir exactement et d'une façon subtile.

The opposition of common sense and reason is harped upon. Pellisson thinks there is a tendency to expect either too much or too little of reason, as also of human goodness. People do not realize that it is almost impossible to be wholly bad, and this is just where Machiavelli's maxims fail.[3] In various connexions Pellisson notes the importance of spontaneity, of doing things unconsciously. He must be set down as an anti-intellectualist, and he also reflects the usual fideist tendencies as to the conception of God.[4]

[1] *Mélange* . . . pp. 32, 33.   [2] ib., pp. 68–71.
[3] ib., pp. 296, 297 (and Prob. 42).
[4] '. . . Il est si aisé de dire en quoi les choses ne consistent pas, que de cette sorte nous sommes savants de la Nature de Dieu même, puis qu' ignorant ce qu'il est, nous le connaissons néanmoins par négation et sa vons qu'il n'est rien de materiel . . . de sorte que sans pouvoir décrire sa grandeur, nous pouvons néanmoins facilement blâmer et reprendre ceux qui en parleraient trop bassement.'

CHAPTER XX

THE ACADEMY: CHAPELAIN AND BALZAC

JEAN CHAPELAIN, poor poet, good critic and worthy man, forms, like La Mothe, an important link between the *cénacle* of the Du Puys and the Academy. The manuscript of his philosophical dialogues has been apparently lost,[1] but there is still enough in his voluminous correspondence to show how much his general ideas are those of the Essays. It would not be possible to take at face-value the praise of their author in which Chapelain indulges in one of his letters to Mademoiselle de Gournay, for whom we know he had no great regard,[2] were it not borne out by the many passages where he follows in Montaigne's footsteps, while we have already mentioned his connexion with an impression of the Essays which the Elzevirs were to have brought out (above, p. 54).

George Collas has collected, in his book on Chapelain,[3] the most important of Chapelain's declarations. In a letter to Balzac, he writes:

Lorsque je pense avoir établi un fondement assuré pour bien juger des choses et raisonner raisonnablement, je trouve que je n'ai rien fait encore. Car comme il est vrai que la droite raison est le seul juge naturel de toutes choses, il est aussi véritable qu'elle n'est guère connue et qu'il n'y a point d'homme qui se puisse assurer de l'avoir. Il n'y a que peu de principes dont on convienne universellement dans toutes les familles de philosophes. Il n'y a point de loix qui ne soient détruites ou affaiblies par d'autres. Les coutumes locales dérogent le plus souvent au droit général. Chaque nation s'est fait des maximes de conduite différentes de celles des autres. Enfin il s'est rencontré des novateurs dans les derniers temps, qui ont contesté à Euclide sa méthode et son système à Ptolémée, qui est tout dire pour faire voir l'incertitude du raisonnement le plus certain.

[1] *Correspondance* (ed. Tamizey de Larroque), II, p. 270.
[2] ib., I, pp. 18, 19.
[3] *J. Chapelain*, 1912, pp. 60 et seq.

287

Hence his hatred of dogmatism and his adherence to the Sceptics :

De toutes les sectes . . . je n'en crois point de plus téméraire que les Dogmatistes ni plus sages que les Sceptiques et que dans tant de sujets de douter je ne trouverais rien de plus juste que le doute et l'irrésolution . . . Ne serait-ce point une des vanités de cet orgueil-leux animal qui s'appelle l'homme, de s'imaginer qu'il est favori de Nature et qu'elle a soumis toutes ses richesses non seulement à sa vue mais encore à son jugement. Je voudrais que l'homme crut que Dieu a mis des bornes à l'action et à la jurisdiction de toutes les choses créés, et que dans ces bornes chacun agit parfaitement. Mais en l'homme la raison la mieux constituée s'abuse et tombe en erreur : elle ne voit rien de bien clair, et toute son opération ne consiste, à bien parler, qu'en soupçons et en conjectures. D'où l'on pourrait tirer que nous ne sommes pas si raisonnables que nous pensons, que nous sommes renfermés dans d'étroites limites aussi bien que les autres Créatures, que, hors certains principes qui regardent le bien vivre, selon nous toutes autres lumières sont trompeuses à notre esprit, et que la raison générale n'étant que dans le Créateur, s'il y a des Créatures qui la possèdent quelquefois, c'est par grâce et non par nature. . . . Toutes choses sont dans l'ordre : il n'y a que l'homme qui en sort et qui ne se cherche où il n'est pas par une fatale pré-somption . . . Il a sans doute plus de participation de la Raison souveraine que tout ce que nous voyons de créé et il est le favori de la Nature en un certain sens, pour ce qu'elle lui a fait plus de faveur qu'à ses autres productions. Mais elle ne l'a pas associé à son Empire, et quoi qu'il soit un aigle au respect des autres animaux, il n'est qu'un aveugle auprès d'elle, et pour son supplice il a obtenu d'elle cette ambition qui le fait se méconnaître et qui en le jettant hors de ses bornes, lui fait faire bien plus imparfaitement ses actions propres que ne font ceux à qui elle a été plus avare de ses grâces qu'à lui. Elle l'a revêtu de ses dons avantageusement mais en récompense elle lui a laissé une mauvaise liberté de se feindre des chimères et de ne se contenter pas de ses trésors, d'entrer dans la maison d'autrui et de laisser perdre la sienne, de chercher la cause des effets qui passe sa capacité, et de négliger celles dont la connaissance est née avec lui, dont le profit lui sera indubitable. Je conclus après un si mauvais sermon que l'homme, qui se pique de raisonnable par excellence, ou ne connaît point certainement la raison ou ne la connaît qu'en bien peu de choses et seulement en celles qui regardent le bien vivre selon la Nature.

In spite of Chapelain's leisurely style of expression the above passage sums up so well his position that I have not hesitated to reproduce it at length. The substance of Montaigne's doc-trine is there, even some of the phraseology, though this may be seen more clearly elsewhere.[1] Once more we have ethics

[1] e.g. *Correspondance*, I, p. 606.

excepted from a cautious scepticism, comparable to that of his great friend, Gassendi, the one contemporary philosopher whom he admired. Chapelain liked to consider himself a Stoic, but his stoicism mostly seems to provide the matter of much mild pleasantry between himself and Balzac.[1] It is simply the cultivation of what he calls *sa chrétienne ataraxie*, for Chapelain was certainly a man of piety. His extreme anxiety for the conversion of his friend Conrart seems proof of his Catholicism, and he was sympathetic towards the Jansenists, though chiefly for non-religious reasons.[2]

Chapelain was certainly more or less of a fideist. He hardly ever speaks directly of religion, except in connexion with matters which obviously in his mind are not essentially the affair of the theologians or ' scholastics ' as he generally calls them. One sees constantly, in reading his *Correspondance*, how the sciences were hemmed in on every side by some barrier of dogma, and Chapelain is conscious of it. He doubts whether the Jesuits are really going to accept Galileo. He sympathizes with Vossius in the attacks levelled at his *De Vera Aetate Mundi* and hopes to see the question of chronology, to which Martini's *Histoire de la Chine* (1658) had recently given prominence, thoroughly aired. His fideism seems indicated too by the reproach levelled at Bentivoglio's History of Flanders : he has mixed religion and history. This is to be condemned, but not the mixture of history and ethics.[3] Chapelain's observations on history seem frequently inspired by the Essays.[4] Finally, he makes himself the advocate of religious tolerance in a letter to a German correspondent. He hopes the Elector of Brunswick will set up a University where full freedom of conscience and open profession of any cult is admissible.[5] As to political theory he adopts some kind of contract theory, limiting monarchical authority.[6] His interest in foreign travel is constantly reflected in the letters to Thevenot, D'Ablancourt and Bernier, though the complete absence of

[1] e.g. ib., I, p. 600, 697.

[2] The matter of the controversy appears to him unimportant (II, p. 136).

[3] ib., I, pp. 15, 16.

[4] cf. ib., I, p. 36 (*Essais*, II, 1, p. 12) ; p . 274 (II, 1, pp. 8, 9 and especially 10) ; pp. 326, 337 (II, 10, pp. 118, 119) ; see also on Montaigne, I, pp. 352, 353 ; II, p. 413.

[5] ib., II, p. 596. Here and elsewhere (II, 199, 200, 206, 809) Chapelain discusses Bodin's *Colloquium*, which he seems to take to be the same as the famous *De Tribus Impostoribus*.

[6] ib., II, p. 249 (1662). It is not till one reaches Bossuet that absolute monarchy finds a convinced exponent. Note the attack on Claude Joly, however.

any notion of progress comes out amusingly in a letter to the latter.[1]

What of the ideas of the rest of the Academy ? In the majority of cases the first members of the new body do not seem to have had any general ideas at all. It is useless to inquire whether Maynard, Malleville, Boisrobert, or Godeau admired Montaigne, although we have seen his influence on Racan. Did Saint Amant allude to him (or to Charron) when he wrote the following epigram ?

SUR UN FAMEUX ECRIVAIN

Cet auteur que je viens de lire,
Dit bien les choses qu'il veut dire
  Mais pour rebattre son crédit,
On dit qu'il devait s'interdire
De dire les choses qu'il dit.

Guillaume Colletet, another of the poets of the Academy, the friend of Marie de Gournay, certainly held Montaigne in honour. Of the prose writers Gombauld contains nothing of interest, nor Gomberville ; Conrart is very guarded in his only allusion to our author.[2] With Silhon, La Chambre (and Cotin) we have dealt and with La Mothe and Marolles. Faret and Bardin who both owe something to the Essays will find their place later. Vaugelas is a mere grammarian.

Grammar indeed, and style seen from the point of view of the grammarian were the chief interests of the first Academicians, and their first duty was to produce a grammar and a dictionary of the language. We may notice at least that Montaigne was still numbered by them among the best writers of the language, along with Amyot, Du Vair, Charron, Du Plessis Mornay, the Satire Menippée and other classics of the preceding century. The influence of the evolution of style on Montaigne's fortunes may be reserved, however, until another member of the august assembly has been considered : Jean Louis Guez de Balzac [1597 ?–1654]—with Corneille the most important figure in French literature between 1624 and 1656.

---

[1] cf. *Correspondance*, II, p. 166. Perhaps no European after Bernier (at least, of his intellectual interests) will ever visit India. Note the interest in the social position of Indian women, and the query whether they have any influence on the development of literary style.

[2] Conrart : *Correspondance* (ed. Kerviler), p. 300. After recalling that Charron is the tailor who wished to re-dress Montaigne *ce philosophe naturel (et non pas toutefois cynique)* he goes on to say they are both dangerous authors for those who have not yet ' found a master '.

Balzac began his career as the pupil of François Garasse at Poitiers, studied at Leyden with Théophile, and posed as the defender of Dutch liberty of conscience in an anonymous *Discours Politique sur l'Etat des Provinces Unies*, which he afterwards disclaimed. Even in later life, however, we see him pleading for the liberty of the Press.[1] He disclaimed also his intimacy with Théophile, when the latter was attacked and put on trial. He never tired from this time on to affirm his orthodoxy in religion, and he was, no doubt, sincere. The manner, however, in which he denounced his former friend, (while indeed attacking Garasse at the same time) reveals the less amiable features of Balzac's character. He was always out to be on the popular side in any difference of opinion. Thus, although a very large number of passages in Balzac's work testify to the influence of Montaigne, his direct references to an author, whose disciples did not always escape the accusation of impiety, are not characterized by any very generous approval. There can be little doubt, however, that we must count Balzac himself as a disciple of Montaigne, and the editors of the recent critical edition of Balzac's letters [2] point out that even the antipathy of Balzac (and Chapelain ?) for Mademoiselle de Gournay seems founded on his common admiration for an author whom he did not admire for the same reasons nor to the same degree.

There was no difference, however, so far as fideism is concerned. In 1623 Balzac presents himself to Sebastien Bouthillier, Bishop of Aire, and friend of Richelieu and St. Cyran, as a man

qui ne veut rien croire de plus véritable que ce qu'il a appris de sa mère et de sa nourrice.

Not only is his attitude to consider religion above all as a heritage, and piety a duty by respect for tradition, but he definitely distrusts reason in religion and elsewhere. In the same letter he writes that ' *il est certain que la raison des hommes ne s'étend pas si loin que la vérité des choses* '. In *Le Prince* (1631) the liberalism of this conservative is seen in what he has to say about superstition and hypocrisy, most of it too familiar to bear quotation. On hypocrisy he only rises to real eloquence when he is attacking the Spaniards. He condemns in the grand style their treatment of the Indians in America under the pretext of converting them. In *Le Prince* Balzac condemns also credulity as to demoniac possessions and the morale *relâchée*

[1] Balzac : *Œuvres* (1665), II, Lettres latines, p. 84.
[2] *Les Premières Lettres*, ed. H. Bibas and R.-T. Butler, I, p. 271.

of a ' new theology ', while a later chapter on the relations of individual morality and political honesty adopts an attitude of compromise, reminding one of the Essays (III, 1). Loyalty to obligations is the foundation of the *jus gentium*—a favourite conception which he appears to identify sometimes with the law of nature (*jus naturale*) and with reason itself. In this connexion his attitude to reason again finds a characteristic utterance. The wisest of the pagans believed that though

la raison eût son étendue plus libre et moins indéterminée en la Politique qu'en la Morale, ils n'ont pas cru pourtant que cet espace dût être infini, et que tout ce qui est mauvais et défendu dans les Familles fût bon et légitime dans l'Etat. Ils ont dit que les Dieux eussent bien plus obligé les hommes de ne leur point donner cette Raison, que de la leur avoir donnée pour incommoder le Monde et pour se tourmenter eux-mêmes ; que ce rayon de Divinité, ce vite mouvement de la pensée, cette pointe qui perce et pénètre tout, leur était un présent funeste et une libéralité ruineuse, s'ils ne s'en servaient qu'au dommage et à la perte d'autrui, et si ce qu'ils ont de commun avec les Dieux les rendaient plus farouches et plus misérables que les bêtes.[1]

Balzac himself accepts more or less this view that the ' divine ray ' is of little advantage to man, as may be seen very clearly in his comments on the long passage of Chapelain which has been quoted.[2] Of their common philosophy, he writes :

Nous en professons une, comme vous dites excellemment, qui a été découverte pour la ruine de toutes les autres. Suivons ses maximes et celles de l'Evangile et nous aurons compassion de toutes les Sectes et de tous les Sectaires.

Again Balzac takes up Montaigne's refrains :

Je sais il y a longtemps que l'homme est un animal composé de pièces toutes contraires, que tel est raisonnable aujourd'hui qui n'est pas assuré de l'être demain . . . et à ce que je vois il y a autant de différence entre lui et lui-même qu'il y en a entre lui et un autre.[3]

In the *Socrate Chrétien* (written about 1640–1) the preface shows the fideist intention of the whole book. Later during the fifth conversation two Spanish friars arrive with a new theological *summa*. Socrates, the hero, does not approve of their rationalist treatment of religious matters. Discussions of God's essence, attributes and intentions in the jargon of Aristotle are absurd. The early Church had a proper distrust of philosophy.

---

[1] *Le Prince*, chap. 25.   [2] *Œuvres*, II, pp. 853, 854.
[3] *Lettres*, XX, 20.

He thinks of St. Thomas as merely sent into the world to convert the Peripatetics—*nation présomptueuse et mutine qui défère si
peu à l'autorité qu'il se fonde toujours en raison.* The sacrifice
of reason is not only agreeable to God, but

> Plus nous sommes vides de nous-mêmes, plus nous avons de
> disposition à être remplis de Dieu. D'ordinaire, il observe ce silence
> de notre raison pour s'entretenir, sans être interrompu par le babil
> et par les questions de cette Importune.[1]

The sketch of Balzac's fideism and his mitigated scepticism
may be completed by his reply to certain criticisms of his orthodoxy in *Le Socrate Chrétien.* Balzac had spoken of the soul
as *une partie de Dieu, un rayon de la Divinité, la partie divine
qui est en l'homme* ; he makes his apology and pleads that his
language was metaphorical.[2] Again he had said that ' I know
not what more ancient than the world has built the world '.
On behalf of Socrates he submits that

> C'est un aveu d'ignorance par lequel il confesse que Dieu est une
> chose inconnue à l'homme, et qui ne se peut ni bien définir ni bien
> nommer.

The first of these two points has some interest. The notion of
the soul or reason (an identification favoured by such nomen-
clature as the ' rational soul ') as part of the Divine nature has
been seen elsewhere (somewhat paradoxically) in conjunction
with scepticism and fideism, but it seems to lie most often implicit
in the minds of those whose ethical ideas are summed up in the
notion of the Law of Nature. It was, of course, a favourite
notion of the Stoics, and it will be recollected that, in the *Entretien
avec M. de Saci,* Pascal names it as one of the errors characteristic
of Epictetus. Balzac is dominated by a kindred conception, the
jus gentium—of more legal reality, but in whose meaning (I
repeat) he seems inclined to merge that of natural law.

It is a commonplace to say that Balzac is not a thinker—
though he is a juggler with words and commonplaces. The

---

[1] *Œuvres* (1665), I, p. 231. cf. *Lettres Latines*, p. 96, 'neque sine
aliquo horrore vides funambulos ullos in rebus Theologicis, imo Icaros
et Phaethontas. . . . Ego qui imbecillitatem humanam qui propriam
infirmitatem optime novi, non modo non volare sed nec navigare quidem
velim . . . Ita impii simul et superstitiosi sunt miseri mortales, atque
ex contrariis partibus constat animal illud quod hominem vocamus'.
also the poem, *Cede Deo.*, II, p. 30.

[2] *Œuvres*, I, p. 600 et seq. I note this error specially condemned in
R. Fornier's *Discours Académiques de l'Origine de l'Ame*, 1619, p. 15.
It is one followed, says the author, by some Catholics (cf. p. 188 above).

inventory of his general ideas is short and they are none of them original.   His notion of the limitations of reason and its relation to faith are simply those more or less of the other authors in this and the preceding chapter—Montaigne's ideas and those of the Paduan school.   He is, however, more orthodox, less bold, and perhaps more genuinely religious than some of them.   There are innumerable occasions on which he echoes the Essays in one way or another, but these reminiscences are not significant enough to warrant more detailed treatment.

Balzac, however, has written one of the chief mid-seventeenth-century criticisms of our author.   This, the temper of his direct allusions to Montaigne elsewhere, and those of some of his contemporaries will find their place at the head of the next chapter.

In our study of Marandé and of the *Gassendistes*, of La Mothe and his many friends, we have shown how a number of ' intellectuals ', as we should say to-day, manage to reconcile their religious convictions with the rest of their knowledge by the adoption of a Christian scepticism.   They are liberal Churchmen (with the exception of Cyrano), and in reaction against many features of the religious life of their day.   Their attitude in this matter and their debt to Montaigne constitute what they all have in common.   Only some of them reflect Montaigne's ethical views, all of them, however, are forced to insist on the distinction between religion and ethics, not only by their fideism, but also by their condemnation of the inevitable concomitants of a period of religious revival, superstition and hypocrisy.   It is obvious that if most of them were consistent, which few men are, they would eventually sever their connexion with the Catholic Church. Does Montaigne's philosophy necessarily involve that ?   The answer already given is no.   It will be time to re-examine that answer when Pascal is dealt with.

CHAPTER XXI

THE EVOLUTION OF TASTE

SINCE taking leave of Camus, we have been mostly occupied with the influence of the Essays, not with critical appreciation of the Essays. Camus' letter to Achante was published in 1613, the *Dissertations Critiques* containing Balzac's opinion of Montaigne, though written in the forties, were not published until 1657, three years after his death. The gap in years between these two criticisms is considerable. Can we fill the gap, except in so far as we have shown the admiration of so many writers for our author ?

Corneille quotes Montaigne in his defence, when, at the height of *la Querelle du Cid*, he pleads for a generous interpretation of the ' laws ' of the drama.[1] Tristan voices his admiration in defending his own autobiography *Le Page Disgracié*.[2] By the middle of the century we can point to traces of a Montaigne legend ; [3] we have people saying ' So-and-so is a second Montaigne ', or ' just like Montaigne ', or with Madame de La Fayette ' how nice to have him for a neighbour '.[4] That is a tribute to the success of his self-portrait, but is hardly significant except

[1] See *La Suivante* (1637), Epitre. *Heraclius* (1647), Au lecteur. Note also the extract of *Essais*, I, 23 at the head of Cinna.

[2] ' Que dira-t-on de ma témérité d'avoir osé moi-même écrire ma vie avec un style qui a si peu de grâce et de vigueur, vu qu'on a bien osé blâmer un des plus excellents Esprits de ce siècle, à cause qu'il se met quelque fois en jeu dans les nobles et vigoureux essais de sa plume. Il est vrai que ce merveilleux Génie parle quelquefois à son avantage en se dépeignant lui-meme : et je puis dire qui n'ayant aucune matière de me louer en cet ouvrage, je ne prétends que de m'y plaindre '. (Bib. Elzevirienne, p. 10.)

[3] *Tallemant*, VII, p. 466. ' Montaigne étant un jour malade, on le pressa tant qu'il souffrit qu'on fit venir un médecin. Il demanda à ce monsieur comment il se nommait : " Les Savants, dit l'homme, me nomment Aegidius et les ignorants m'appellent Gilles ".' *Menagiana* (ed. 1715) : ' Montaigne en son livre de dépense mettait : *item* pour mon humeur paresseuse, mille livres.'

[4] D'Ablancourt (see above, p. 278) ; one of the Bautrus (*Menagiana*, I, pp. 268, 269) : Madame de la Fayette (*Segraisiana*, 1731, p. 143).

in so far as it points to the position of the Essays as a classic, a position which it held from the beginning of the century. There are signs, however, that the attitude to the Essays as literature was slightly changing. Style was the preoccupation of the age, and construction—a kind of style and a type of construction which the Essays lacked. More people were inclined to make seriously the ironic comment which La Luzerne, puts in the mouth of an ' ignorant critic '.

> Montaigne est trop volage
> Trop de sujets divers y tiennent même page.

All this is reflected in Balzac's two *Dissertations Critiques* which have, as their point of departure, a discussion between a certain Gandillaud, magistrate at Angoulême, Balzac and others (*Dissertations Critiques*, XIX).

He begins by some adverse comments on the style of Seneca —the usual ones, which Montaigne himself made. These he applies implicitly to the style of the Essays. There is nothing new in this, for if Camus is right, such was the criticism of Beza half a century before.[1] The flowing sentence and period had, however, in the meanwhile, banished the short pithy phrase, largely thanks to Balzac himself, who sought for a long rolling sound even at the cost of tedious redundancy.[2] In his next Dissertation (*Qu'au temps de Montaigne notre langue était encore rude*) Balzac makes a more generous estimate of Montaigne's style ' in spite of his age and his province '.

Il faut avouer avec cela que son âme était éloquente : qu'elle se faisait entendre par des expressions courageuses ; que dans son style il y a des grâces et des beautés au dessus de la portée de son siècle.

It is rather construction than style which Balzac insists on : *Montaigne sait bien ce qu'il dit : mais je pense aussi qu'il ne sait pas toujours ce qu'il va dire.* And yet like every one else who has written on our author, he owns he falls under the charm of Montaigne's digressions ; *quand il quitte le bon, d'ordinaire il rencontre le meilleur.*

The next remark is illuminating :

Il faut avouer qu'en certains endroits il porte bien haut la Raison humaine. Il l'élève jusqu'où elle peut aller, soit dans la Politique, soit dans la Morale.

Montaigne, is indeed, as we know, a rationalist of sorts in ethics and in politics,—a rationalism tempered with conservatism it

---

[1] See above, p. 119, note 1.
[2] On evolution of Balzac's style see Chapelain, *Correspondance*, II, 836.

is true—but Montaigne is surely far more remarkable for his mistrust of reasoning. Balzac's statement here corroborates what we have said of his own fideist tendencies.

To return to a purely literary question, Balzac tells us (it should be noticed), that Montaigne is not a good critic of literature. Was this because of his praise of the Pléiade and Du Bartas ? Rather I think it was Montaigne's remarks on Latin authors—that he put Lucretius beside Virgil, Plautus before Terence, Seneca before Cicero, for Balzac speaks elsewhere of Montaigne's latinity in this very connexion. He refuses to quote him as a critical authority :

Je ne parle point d'un autre homme de mon voisinage, Père d'alliance de Mlle. de Gournay, estimé de Fra Paolo, et allegué par le Chancelier Bacon. Quoique le pays latin ne lui fut pas inconnu, il était néanmoins étranger et hôte en ce pays là. Par conséquent, il devait y aller plus retenu et se donner moins de liberté qu'il ne s'en donnait. Il ne devait pas faire le Magistrat où il n'avait pas droit de bourgeoisie. Pour décider des vers Latins comme il prétendait de le pouvoir faire il n'entendait pas assez ni le Latin ni les vers. Aussi en pareilles occasions, combien d'équivoques et de méprises de son jugement. Je ne vois presque autre chose dans les Essais.[1]

All this because Balzac doesn't agree with a man who knew Latin before he spoke French, while the one instance quoted of Montaigne's lack of taste is his number of quotations from the Pseudo-Gallus (ten as a matter of fact in the three Books).

Otherwise Balzac is all for Montaigne's ' liberty '. · He defends his confidences and finds their detail agreeable.[2] He would always like to know those he admires through and through, *dans la pûreté de leur naturel*, and hence thoroughly approves the manner of the Essays. Why did he not give particulars of his term of office at Bordeaux ? A friend has suggested pride. That he does not believe, but the same man also asserts that Montaigne was not a success as Mayor of Bordeaux. Nay more, it is a pity that Montaigne did not confide to the readers of his book more of his experiences as a member of the *Parlement*. The one confidence which the company agree in regretting is that Montaigne boasted of having had a page. First he ought

---

[1] *Œuvres* (1665), I, p. 597. As to Paolo Sarpi's praise of our author see his life (*Vita del Padre Paolo*, Leiden, 1646, p. 253). Sarpi struck by the perfect friendship of his friend Trevisano with Barbarigo ' ordino a Maestro Fulgentio di tradurgli nell'Italiano dalla lingua francese il saggio di Michiel di Montagna dell'amicitia,' &c.

[2] Balzac would hardly do otherwise; it was said of him : ' How can you expect him to be *well* ? He always speaks of himself, and never without hat in hand ! ' (cf. *Lettres de Costar*, p. 128 and elsewhere).

not have had one, secondly he ought not to have confessed in the Essays that he had had one.

This seems the one utterly unfounded accusation of Balzac's article. Why should not Montaigne have had a *page gentil-homme Italien qu'il nourrissait soigneusement*? Why shouldn't he have mentioned his untimely death? [1] It is as unfounded as the complaint of Baudius that Montaigne wished to create the impression that he had a vast household by telling us he could only remember his servants by their provinces (*nations*).[2] The same man who cast doubts on the efficiency of Montaigne as Mayor of Bordeaux also asserted that he had the affectation of sometimes dressing entirely in white, green or other colours. Balzac takes up this remark in one of his letters to Chapelain. We have to set against Montaigne's own declaration that, as his father before him, he always wore black or white.

Balzac then, in short, admires Montaigne, even, with certain reservations, his style, his digressions and his confidences, except where they seem to him a trifle vain. The *moi* is not yet entirely *haïssable*. As for Montaigne's thought, the sceptic is still some-times too much of a rationalist for Balzac, who as we have seen, owes him so much. Yet Balzac is very sensitive to the tendencies of his day, and we note in these two dissertations the underlying truth that Montaigne is a trifle old-fashioned. He was also a ' dangerous author ' in many people's eyes. Balzac reflects this too, in some rather ungenerous allusions elsewhere. His defini-tion of *les demi-sages et les demi-savants* is those ' who have read Montaigne and Charron and have heard tell of Cardan and Pomponazzi '.[3] He considers La Mothe le Vayer, against whom he had some deep-rooted personal grievance :

comme une des grandes lumières, un des grands ornements de l'Académie française, comme restaurateur de la philosophie sceptique, comme le successeur de Montaigne et de Charron, voire même, s'il lui plaît, de Cardan et de Vanini, la mémoire duquel est en bénédiction à Toulouse.[4]

Such implicitly adverse comments—the last is said half in jest —are of more importance as showing the tendencies with which Montaigne was increasingly identified, rather than as reflecting the considered opinion of Balzac on the man himself.

Ménage too seems to share Balzac's view of Montaigne as a stylist and as a ' dangerous author '. He says pertinently :

---

[1] *Essais*, I, 5, p. 48.   [2] See above, p. 23.   [3] *Œuvres*, I, p. 398.
[4] *Lettres Inédites* (ed. de Larroque), p. 800, allusion to the burning of Vanini at Toulouse.

Comme de Bertaut, on peut dire de Montaigne (le meilleur auteur de son temps) que venant au monde plus tard il aura mieux écrit. Il aimait les Relations de Voyage. Il aurait bien profité de celles qui sont faites depuis.[1]

A letter of Roland Desmarets [2] shows a real appreciation of the qualities of the Essays but adds nothing new. Montaigne above all forms the judgement, hence his place among the classics. Indeed his study was to model himself on the philosophers of antiquity, to know and introspect himself (in se descendere), to study his own life that he might leave at last an adequate picture of himself to his friends. Apart from this wish he rejected all claims to literary fame. Would that this enthusiast for freedom and independence had not so indulged his natural bent and neglected the promptings of ambition, for he could have left us the most finished philosophical treatises, which would leave no place for carping criticisms, as (forsooth!) his lack of system and his digressions. Above all, Desmarets admires his subtle analysis of his daily thoughts, his happy neologisms and admirable metaphors. Here we have an estimate by one who does not have the same fashionable preoccupation with style as Balzac or Ménage.[3]

The best mid-century review of Montaigne's position, perhaps is to be found in the Bibliothèque Française of Charles Sorel [1599–1674]. This was only published in 1664, two years after the first edition of the Logique de Port Royal. Now the second edition of the latter book (1666) introduces a new attack on Montaigne which is the reflexion of Pascal's views and their first expression in print, and thus marks the beginning of a

[1] Menagiana (ed. cit.), III, pp. 102, 103.
[2] R. Maresii Epistolarum Libri, p. 79, see above, p. 55.
[3] The same may be said of an anonymous author who writes defending Montaigne from the charge of vanity or presumption :
Je trouve que le livre des Essais de Montaigne est une vraie école de vérité et de vertu, où tout ce que la Philosophie a de beau et d'utile est montré d'une manière si humble qu'il semble que la principale intention de cet auteur en écrivant ait été de publier qu'il ne savait rien. Je ne crois pas qu'on puisse voir ce caractère de modestie et d'humilité gravé dans aucun livre plus profondément qu'en celui-ci : de même que cet auteur a intitulé son Livre les Essais, aussi a il bien pris garde d'exprimer toujours ses pensées en la forme des apprentifs. . . . Pourtant cet apprentif est un habile maître et tous ses Essais sont autant de Chefs d'Œuvres, car on ne peut, à mon avis, écrire plus fortement et mieux qu'il a fait touchant la mort, la pauvreté, l'ambition, la vengeance, la fausse dévotion, l'amitié et généralement sur tous les sujets de nos désirs et de nos craintes dans tous les états et conditions de cette vie. (Jugement de M.D.L. in G. Béranger : Réponse à plusieurs injures . . . contre Michel . . . de Montaigne . . . 1667, p. 74. See later, pp. 411–413).

new chapter in the history of the Essays. Sorel and his views belong to the first half of the century.

The fifth chapter of the *Bibliothèque* treats of books on ethics ' with a special judgement of the works of Montaigne and Charron '.

Nous dresserons maintenant une manière de dissertation pour rechercher si on doit conserver à cet auteur toute l'estime que beaucoup de Gens font de lui.

This beginning underlines the curious position of the Essays— a classic, that is a book on whose value there is a general consensus of opinion, in spite of smaller variations, and yet not quite a classic, for its readers seem to be inevitably partisans—or censors. The discussion is important, says Sorel,

puisque cet ouvrage a tant de cours et qu'on rencontre souvent l'occasion d'en parler, et que même on peut être en balance si on en doit faire la lecture.

License of language ; questionable attitude towards religion ; ignorance of ethical theory (except for Seneca and Plutarch) ; ignorance of philosophy in general and even of the humanities ; and finally the accusation that the Essays would totally disappear, if the subtraction of quotations and personal confidences were made : these, says Sorel, are the usual criticisms of those who dislike the Essays. Special attacks on Montaigne's and Charron's theory that the animals reason have been made by Silhon and Chanet. He will not defend the opinion of Montaigne and his disciple on this question, which he thinks was made without due consideration of the issues involved.

Among Montaigne's defenders, Sorel sets Marie de Gournay aside as too passionate an admirer. He quotes (without acknowledgement) Camus pleading for Montaigne's free speech and his undoubted submission and loyalty to the Church. He quotes Pasquier on the titles of the Essays and suggests that Montaigne's intention is to hide his attacks on doctors and other people or ways of thinking under cover of a false title. As for Chanet's argument that the lack of orderly construction proves Montaigne's lack of judgement, Sorel roundly declares this will never hold water. Montaigne's numerous Latin quotations are to be excused since there was not much French worthy of quotation in his day, and against his rare Gasconisms (retailed by Pasquier) one must set such admirable neologisms as, for example, the word *enjoué*. Montaigne's wide reading is too obvious for accusations of ignorance to be tenable, nor does he believe that Scaliger ever called him *un hardi ignorant*. Of his confidences, Sorel says acutely :

il ne prétend pas que ce qu'il dit de lui-même soit pris pour autre chose que pour ce que c'est, ayant assez reconnu toutes les faiblesses humaines et les siennes propres.

His knowledge of human psychology ought to make him, according to another writer quoted in this article, *le manuel ordinaire des gens de la Cour et du Monde*.[1]

On ' mere trifles ' Sorel has a caustic page directed against Balzac. Why shouldn't Montaigne have a page ? It was the custom in his day. Why crack jokes about his having been a lawyer, or accuse him of not being a success as Mayor of Bordeaux ? Perhaps he was a bad mayor, but

Quand il est question du prix des Ouvrages de quelque auteur, il n'est pas besoin de s'attacher à des accidents particuliers touchant la personne et la condition.

Read him, says Sorel, and you will find him all the more readable for his discursiveness. He may be taken and left where you will. But some people hold that far from being the best of all books for those whose reading is limited, it would be better were he forbidden entirely to those who read nothing else. Above all, he is capable of offending feminine taste. He is not an author for the ignorant, the novice or those of mediocre intelligence.

As so often the substance of Montaigne's thought comes in for more close consideration when Sorel passes on to Charron, and the dangers of reading these two writers are further discussed. *La Sagesse* is a book about which opinions differ even more than about the Essays. Charron's enemies say that his views may be excusable in a trooper but not in a theologian. They point to his emphasis on the human means by which religion is received and with what abuses it is bound up, and to his declared opinion that Immortality is undemonstrable. He is thus bound to have an unfortunate effect in arousing religious doubt. Sorel pleads his good intentions, as shown both by his life and his frank statement of difficulties. He does not approve of the attacks of Scipion Dupleix—a personal enemy he feels—and of Garasse.

La Sagesse is sound and useful on Ethics and ' wisdom ', but its tendency is to make man out to be the most abject and miserable of creatures, which is good indeed for his pride but not enough without also showing his capabilities, and how he may escape from his misery (compare *Entretien avec M. de Saci*, and contrast with Balzac).

Some people think Charron's opinions are, on the whole,

---

[1] See above, p. 116, note 3 (*bréviaire des honnêtes gens*).

sound, but Sorel is inclined to doubt whether these persons are conspicuous for their virtue or piety :

il suffit de savoir que parce qu'il ne s'en trouve guère de leur trempe, chacun n'est pas propre à la lecture de tels livres.

He rejects, however, the extremists on both sides, for there is much that is admirable in Montaigne and Charron, and those who condemn them out of hand appear to wish to rob France of two of the best authors who have added lustre to her name.

Sorel's review of the position of Montaigne and Charron is none the worse for its plain wish to hold the middle opinion, for it informs us all the better of the increasing tendency to mistrust Montaigne's ideas and to underestimate his literary qualities. That Montaigne's language was becoming out of date, we have known ever since dealing with Marie de Gournay, and also (as Sorel notes) that there were those who proposed as a remedy to ' bring him up to date '. (Marie de Gournay, the reader may be reminded, should be absolved from most of the burden of this charge).[1] Sorel rightly objects and denies that the language has changed so much as to warrant such a proceeding. He objects also to those who suggest a systematic arrangement of the Essays (*ranger Montaigne par matières*).

So far as I am aware, such an arrangement of the Essays was merely a suggestion when Sorel wrote and has remained so until 1783, although anthologies of the Essays were soon to begin : but already some one had tried his hand at modernization of our author. Sorel names him—Plassac-Méré, brother of the better-known chevalier de Méré. For an introduction to Plassac-Méré let us return to Balzac's *Entretien* on Montaigne. He appears there as ' *admirateur de Montaigne* ', setting him above Cicero. He was a friend and neighbour of Balzac, and of La Thibaudière (a habitué of the Hôtel de Rambouillet), as also of Mitton. The relations of his brother, the *chevalier*, with Mitton and with Pascal are well known. His letters, published in 1648, show many traces of his reading of the Essays, and contain a warm appreciation of the book.[2] Plassac's project of modernization is all the more important because of his enthusiasm for Montaigne, and because in him and his brother we begin to see how the Essays were considered in a slightly different *milieu* from those studied so far. If Montaigne is the ' breviary of a gentleman ', the manual of the *gens du monde*, these authors will show us more clearly how they read him.

Writing to a doctor friend, Plassac declares that antiquity never produced a better wit, a clearer intelligence nor a broader

[1] See above, p. 63.   [2] On Plassac-Méré, see below, pp. 321–326.

one than Montaigne's ; not as to scientific knowledge, of which he is not fit to judge ;

je m'arrête seulement aux choses exquises qui sont honnêtes et nécessaires à l'usage [de la vie].

His knowledge is unclouded by the prejudice of custom ; like Socrates, he possesses the universal spirit, but few understand him well, for he requires intelligent reading. Comparison with Charron, a bad copy of an excellent original, is merely absurd. Of the dangers of Montaigne's philosophy, Plassac says :

Ses ennemis lui reprochent d'avoir gâte quantité de personnes : mais ce malheur vient de leur faiblesse ; et vous savez qu'Aristote a rempli toute la terre de pédants. Ce sont les singes qui se tuent eux-mêmes en maniant les armes des hommes et qui, au lieu de de s'instruire, se corrompent.[1]

He thinks the Essays would have been incomparable, if only their author had taken more pains to please, if he had pruned, cut out trivialities, and not neglected order and style. In ' elocution ' he has the faults of his age and his province, no doubt, but he would have overcome these if he had not despised the art of eloquence. Plassac repeats these criticisms in another letter to ' Monsieur de Mitton, Conseiller du Roi et Trésorier Provincial de l'Extraordinaire des guerres en Picardie '. This letter begins with the following tribute :

Monsieur, Je vous ai souvent parlé des obligations que j'avais à l'excellent Montaigne. Je n'oserais pas dire qu'il m'ait conduit dans le monde, de crainte de lui faire du tort ; mais si je n'ai pu faire mon profit des biens qu'il m'a présentés, au moins j'avoue qu'il a toujours été le Consolateur de ma vie.[2]

He adds that perhaps Montaigne's admiration of Seneca has contributed to make his style brusque and uncultivated, he has therefore made an attempt at modernizing an essay he has been reading by way of encouragement to Mitton, who, he has heard, had some such intention of improving the Essays by removing those faults of his style which were due to his century.

Sans doute vous êtes capable de l'éclaircir et de l'ajuster sans l'affaiblir ni l'étendre. Vous en pouvez retrancher de petites comparaisons et des superfluités qui ne font rien à son sens et vous conduire dans les choses essentielles avec autant de scrupule que vous feriez aux mystères d'une Religion.[3]

---

[1] *Lettres de M. de Plassac*, 1648, p. 352 et seq.

[2] Elsewhere he recommends to a friend the four French authors he considers worthy of study : first, his friend Balzac, then Montaigne, d'Urfé and Corneille (ib., p. 464). Note that d'Urfé is singled out as teaching ' la delicatesse et la parfaite honnêteté '.

[3] ib., Lettre 90.

It seems not out of place to give some idea by quotation of this singular enterprise which Plassac invited his friend to emulate.

LIVRE I
CHAPÎTRE LI
DE LA VANITÉ DES PAROLES

MONTAIGNE

Un Rhétoricien du temps passé disoit que son mestier estoit, de choses petites les faire paroistre et trouver grandes. C'est un cordonnier qui scait faire de grands souliers à un petit pied. On luy eut faict donner le fouet à Sparte de faire profession d'un art piperesse et mensongère. Et croy que Archidamus, qui en estoit Roy, n'ouit pas sans estonnement la responce de Thucydide, auquel il s'enqueroit qui estoit plus fort à la luicte, ou Pericles ou luy : Cela, fit il, seroit malaisé à vérifier : car quand je l'ay porté par terre en luictant, il persuade à ceux qui l'ont veu qu'il n'est pas tombé, et le gaigne.

Ceux qui masquent et fardent les femmes font moins de mal : car c'est chose de peu de perte de ne pas les voir dans leur naturel : là où ceux cy font estat de tromper non pas nos yeux, mais nostre jugement et d'abastardir et corrompre l'essence des choses. Les republiques qui se sont maintenues en un estat reglé et bien policé, comme la Crétense ou Lacédémonienne, elles n'ont pas faict grand compte d'orateurs.

PLASSAC

Cet Orateur du temps passé, qui die que son Mestier estoit de faire paroistre les choses grandes petites et les petites grandes n'eust esté bien recu en Lacédémone, où la peuple déclarait la guerre au mensonge et à toute sorte de piperie. Je m'asseure que leur Prince fut fort surpris de la réponse de Thucydide, quand il lui demanda lequel estoit le plus fort à la lutte de Periclès ou de luy : C'est, dit-il, une question difficile à resoudre. Car quand nous luttons tous deux, il me semble bien que je le mets bas et le renverse sans beaucoup de peine ; mais nous ne sommes pas relevez, qu'il regarde l'Assemblée avec un visage riant et ne cesse point de parler qu'il n'ait fait croire à tout le Monde qu'il m'a vaincu et souvent il me le persuade à moi-même. Ceux qui fournissent de fard aux Dames sont moins à blâmer : il nous importe peu de les voir en leur naturel et mesme si l'artifice les embellit, nous y gaignons. Mais ces Messieurs qui déguisent toutes choses veulent tromper nostre jugement et cette tromperie est bien plus à craindre que celle de nos yeux. Les plus sages Républiques et les mieux policées comme celle de Crete et de Lacédémone n'ont jamais fait grand conte des Orateurs

Even if such a modernization of the Essays had been necessary, the above is hardly a very happy attempt. It is sometimes supposed that Montaigne was already becoming partly unintelligible to those who were not well read in the literature of the previous century. Some remarks of Mademoiselle de Gournay might encourage this error, which has little justification. Plassac wants a new Montaigne primarily for the sake of style. So far as intelligibility goes we have a useful document in the shape of a Mazarinade, published during the Fronde, in 1652.[1]

This pamphlet is entirely composed of extracts from a number of different Essays (I, 37 23 ; II, 37, 32). A comparison of the text as given in these extracts with the original shows practically no changes except in spelling.[2] It is obvious that a political pamphlet is designed to be understood and appreciated by the largest possible public. The fact that there is some revision of the text, necessitated by the uses to which it was being put, and yet so few modernizations, is a most convincing proof that it was merely literary fashion, not the natural evolution of the language as it was then spoken and written, which appeared to render the Essays archaic.

It would sum up the general estimate of the Essays in the middle of the century to say that the literary ideals of the age were tending not so much to make men ignore the great qualities of Montaigne's style, for of that there is recognition everywhere, but rather to set against them in the balance those qualities which he lacked and by which men of letters set more and more store. As to Montaigne's thought, it would be a fair conclusion that, although its leading ideas dominated the minds or were congenial to the temper of so many men of the day, the repeated warnings of theologians and others that the book was dangerous had not been without their effect. Even Damien Mitton [c. 1618–1690], to whom Plassac suggested a re-writing of the Essays and who was clearly a *Montaignisant*, as will be seen, is reported to have expressed his doubts :

Sur le sujet de Montaigne, qui est si tendu, il dit qu'il n'en fallait pas faire son ordinaire mais en user sobrement, comme on boit les

---

[1] *Ovide parlant à Tieste*, 1652, 4°. I Que la Coutume doit être observée sans que l'on y puisse mettre empêchement. II Que les Loix reçues ne se doivent aucunement changer. III Que l'Epée rouillée de la Justice peut perdre le Mazarin par ses nouvelles Loix. IV. Que les loix permettent d'appeler mains ennemies pour éviter une continuelle guerre, &c., &c.

[2] I note the suppression of an asseverative ' *si* ' : *prendrois* for *prendroye* : *infonde* for *infond* (*Essais*, I, p. 299) ; *extrennes annuelles* for *estrennes* : *un poul* for *un pouil*.

vins de liqueur, qui sont trop fumeux et qui feraient mal à la tête.[1]

Lastly there is perhaps an increasing inclination, which will be seen more clearly as we proceed, to criticize Montaigne for speaking too much of himself. It is not new, for we have seen how early it began, but owing to the ties which bound literature and the life of upper-class society closer and closer as the century went on, this inclination becomes certainly stronger. Apart from the *précieux* and *précieuse* the most important product of this social life was the conception of *honnêteté*. Montaigne's influence on this conception must now be examined.

[1] *Portefeuille de M. de la Faille*, p. 9 et seq. Bon mots de feu M. [note: C'est M. Miton.] Note also his reply to the gentleman who boasted he knew 'all Montaigne by heart' 'I have the book' (loc. cit.). On Mitton, see below, pp. 359–362.

CHAPTER XXII

L'HONNÊTETÉ

IT is not easy to give a satisfactory definition of *honnêteté* as understood in the seventeenth century. It is certainly far more than deportment : on the other hand, the use of *honnête homme* simply to mean ' a good man ', though not infrequent, certainly fails to bring out the full connotation of the term. The author of an exhaustive tome on the subject, M. Magendie,[1] seems inclined to treat *honnêteté* as the part of ethics, whose sphere is limited not only to a certain social class but. also to the life of social intercourse. He distinguishes, however, the *bourgeois* conception, where *honnêteté* is recognized as limited in this way as a supplementary morality, and the aristocratic conception where it is raised to the dignity of a complete rule of life. The second of these is more or less the same as the English notion of the ' gentleman '. M. Magendie's conclusion is that in the first half of the seventeenth century the French treatises on *honnêteté*—inspired chiefly by Italian and Spanish manuals of civility such as Guazzo's *Civil Conversazion*, Guevara's *Clock of Princes* and that more ambitious masterpiece, Castiglioni's *Cortegiano*—were written by *bourgeois* writers chiefly as guides to Court life. They aim at providing the *art de parvenir*. It is only about 1660, with St. Evremond and Méré, that the second, the aristocratic conception, largely inspired by Montaigne, comes to the fore. It is with the first period that the present chapter is concerned.

Guazzo, Guevara and Castiglione were read and pondered by Montaigne himself, and according to Magendie, much that derives ultimately from them in the writings of Faret, Bardin and others seems to have come through the Essays. Montaigne's independence, both by social position and by character, gives what he derived from his predecessors its own special stamp,

---

[1] *La Politesse Mondaine et les théories de l'honnêteté en France au XVIIme Siecle, de* 1660 a 1660. Alcan (2 *vols.*).

which is lacking to the narrow utilitarian spirit of the early French theorists.   M. Magendie sums up their debt to the Essays in these terms :

Ils semblent avoir surtout mis à profit en la détachant, pour ainsi dire, de l'ensemble de l'œuvre, la pédagogie de Montaigne, qui vise à former un homme de monde plutôt qu'un pédant alourdi de doctrine.[1]

The border line between the literature of civility and education is obviously very vague and there are many reasons for taking them together.   French pedagogic writings are rare, however, in the period under review : a collection of such made by Grotius, who was for long resident in France, contains one contribution by a Frenchman (Naudé) out of a total of twenty-five.   The influence of Montaigne may be discovered, nevertheless, not only in Marie de Gournay's *De l'Education des Enfants de France* and her *Abrége de l'Instruction du Prince* but in one or two other efforts of the same kind.

In *La Nourriture de la Noblesse* (1604) by a certain Pelletier, reminiscences of our author are very frequent.   The author insists in a chapter on vice upon

je ne sais quel congratulation de bien-faire qui la réjouit [la jeunesse] en soi-même.

It is *à propos* of religion (into whose mysteries the young should not too deeply inquire) that the author inculcates the lesson that one must learn to hear criticism of the Church without annoyance and have a constant respect for the truth even if disagreeable.[2]   Education of the judgement more than the memory was a popular text of the day, but Pelletier shows that it is from the Essays particularly that he has learnt this lesson.   (*C'est plutôt un habile homme qu'on en veut faire qu'un savant homme.*)   History as moral instruction is to be given a prominent place in the studies recommended.   Above all, Pelletier shows the same appreciation as Montaigne, of the fact that nothing worth doing in education can be done by constraint :

La vertu même désire qu'on aille joyeusement au devant d'elle. Il faut rire aux Muses, celui qui en veut gagner les grâces.   Car il n'y a rien de si aisé qui ne semble extrêmement difficile si on le fait par contrainte.[3]

The knowledge of *belles lettres* is highly esteemed by Pelletier as the sovereign remedy for vicious inclinations (in which the

[1] op. cit., p. 335 et seq.   [2] cf. *Essais*, I, 26, p. 198.
[3] op. cit., p. 27a.

average page finds only too much encouragement), but he does not underestimate the importance of everyday experience in favour of book-learning, as this echo of the Essays shows :

Tous lieux seront sa classe, et toutes heures le temps de sa leçon. Aussi bien l'instruira la sottise d'un valet que le grave discours d'un maître aux arts. Il ne doit pas toujours être bandé à même chose : son âme sera donc à divers étages, qui se sache tendre et démonter. Il devisera avec son voisin de son batiment, de sa chasse, de sa querelle, du mariage de ses filles, s'approvoisant avec plaisir au moindre charpentier ; tantôt il entretiendra un jardinier. Un Amphitheâtre, un château ruiné, le lieu où s'est autrefois donnée une bataille seront d'autant de pièces de son instruction.

Again he writes from the same inspiration :

Le maître ne doit pas toujours parler : il faut qu'il écoute l'écolier à son tour ne lui demandant pas seulement compte des mots de sa leçon mais de son sens et de sa substance, &c.

The boy must not be overworked.

Il faut que le corps exhale je ne sais quoi de doux et de gracieux à l'âme, sans le laisser sécher de tristesse et de mélancolie.

He should have as much liberty as possible. As to all admonitions Pelletier adopts Montaigne's sound principle that they should be given always in private, and that the pupil must be watched without his being conscious of it.

It is worth noticing that the quotations above are mostly taken from the sixth chapter of this little book (*De l'Obéissance*), although there are traces elsewhere of the Essays. The question of travelling is treated in detail, but clearly on lines suggested by Montaigne (I, 26), who has also inspired the last chapter on death. Seneca and Plutarch are also largely drawn upon as the author acknowledges. The spirit of Montaigne's famous essay as well as much of its actual advice seems to have passed into the *Nourriture de la Noblesse*. One would like to have been Pelletier's pupil. It is indeed irony if he is the same tutor whose cause was pleaded at Grenoble in 1606 by Claude Expilly, and who was forced to sue for his salary.[1]

Of other treatises on education published in the first decade of the century *L'Academie des Vertueux* (1600) by Du Souhait, and *Le Dauphin*, a poem by Jacque de la Fon, have no interest for us. Nor does *L'Institution du Prince* (1609) of Jean Héroard,

---

[1] We may take it that he won his case, or doubtless Expilly's eloquent summing up would not have been published among his most notable harangues (Claude Expilly : *Plaidoyers*, 1608, No. 18).

tutor of the said Dauphin, the future Louis XIII, bear any trace
of Montaigne's influence.   It is at this point, however, that it
seems fitting to mention an *Institution du Prince* by that eccentric
epicurean, Nicolas Vauquelin des Yveteaux (1567–1649), who
was for a time charged with the education of the Dauphin and
previously with that of the Dauphin's half-brother, the Duc de
Vendôme.   He wrote a poem on this subject in 1604 in which
he recommends *leçons de choses*, a school out of school, as Montaigne did.[1]   The influence of the Essays is quite apparent in
the interesting memoir which Des Yveteaux drew up at the end
of his life for the next Dauphin, the future *Roi Soleil*.   This
document, made at the Queen-Mother's request, contains some
historical information in the shape of criticisms of tendencies
into which Louis XIII had been allowed to fall (his superstition,
his excessive taste for the chase, for mechanical hobbies, &c.).
Des Yveteaux is a man of ideas and it is therefore worth noting
that he gives a proper prominence to Montaigne's most important recommendations: pleasure and profit must be mixed ;
' there is no place, time nor conversation which does not give
opportunity for teaching or administering praise or blame ' ;
the tutor should get his pupil to express his opinion on what he
has read, even pretending to ask him questions for his own information.[2]   Every lesson should begin with some amusing story
*car il faut mettre en riant l'instrument dont on veut jouer, premier
que de la toucher sérieusement*.   Most of this document is concerned with practical details as to studies, régime and so on.
Certain books are recommended :   among them Plutarch and a
number of other lives ;   Commines, Seneca's *De Beneficiis* ;   Aristotle's Ethics, Politics and the second book of Rhetoric ;   Botero,
the refuter of Macchiavelli and

les essais de Monsieur de Montaigne pour le pureté de la langue avec
la bonté du livre.[3]

With Des Yveteaux's *memorandum* we may mention another
treatise on education which was little more than a private document, no doubt.   It is contained in a volume printed for private
circulation by Charles de Gamaches, the second husband of
Montaigne's daughter :   *Le Sensé Raisonnant sur les passages de
l'Ecriture Sainte contre les prétendus Réformés* (1623).   This
book, written at Montaigne, whose nineteen chapters are each
separately dedicated to various relations and friends, begins with

---

[1] Vauquelin des Yveteaux : *Œuvres* (1921), Institution du Prince,
verse 161.

[2] ib., pp. 161, 162, 164.   [3] ib., p. 164.

a letter of Gamaches to his son, *contenant l'institution d'un Enfant de Qualité. Avec quelques instructions nécessaires à un Cavalier et entr'autres un avertissement à harder chevaux avantageusement.* The mixture of piety and very material common sense is sometimes irresistably comic, but Gamaches takes all his leading ideas from his father-in-law. The tutor is to ask the boy questions in order to form his judgement and make every occasion the subject of a ' lesson '—*C'est le moyen d'avoir la tête bien faite plus que remplie et d'être habile homme plus que savant.* There is here and there a touch of Montaigne's moral optimism, and we may note that the book as a whole shows that the hospitable and tolerant traditions of the château de Montaigne have not been lost.

The *Syntagma de Studio Liberali* (1633) of Gabriel Naudé, much the ablest of the works on education here under review, shows even more than Des Yveteaux the influence of Montaigne. The *Syntagma* begins by criticizing the tendency of this class of book to enter into needless and otiose details without defining general methods, the end of each study, and providing a good bibliography of the subject. The chief defect of the contemporary education is found, as usual, to be the abuse of memory. Even under the most favourable circumstances this gives a bookish culture which has learnt nothing not only not from life, but not even from the lives of men of other ages.[1] The fault lies with the pedant, who is the ' Pandora's Box ' of all educational abuses, attacked and ridiculed by the ancients, and pilloried by them on the comic stage.

Sed non defuere etiam ex recentioribus viri certè graves, inter quos nostrates duos Michaelem de Montaigne et Petram Charondam honoris causa nominabo, qui vitium hoc, tamquam ingeniorum pestem et bonæ mentis prorsus inimicum, cane pejus et angue, vitandum esse monuerant.[2]

Naudé is inclined to pay far more regard than Montaigne to the importance of temperament in education ; indeed it is one of the chief burdens of the *Syntagma*.[3] Montaigne, it will be remembered, thought all early conjectures as to character a little premature. It is, however, this consideration which makes Naudé insist, again in contrast with the Essays, that education ought to begin at home where individual inclinations can be

[1] History is ' Magistram et ducem bene beateque vivendi '.
[2] op. cit., p. 21.
[3] see op. cit. *passim* and also in Naudé's other works *Biblioth. Polit.*, pp. 136, 137 ; *Mascurat*, p. 665, et seq. *Considérations*, p. 324.

studied in a way they can never be at school.   Montaigne, however, presupposed a private education, and appears to have disapproved of schools altogether, so far as a young nobleman was
concerned.   Similarly, Montaigne approved of the custom of
sending young men of good family away from home as pages
(which appears to be generally condemned in the seventeenth
century) only on the understanding that the page had a tutor
in charge of him and his fellow-pages.   Naudé does not indeed
approve entirely of education at home, on account of the possibility of meeting all kinds of people, many unsuitable for the
child, but he does appreciate the benefits of intercourse with
grown-ups, liberty of speech with merchants and artisans in order
that the boy may learn from everybody.   The system in force
amounts to shutting them up together in complete subjection
and then letting them out into the world quite unprepared.[1]   The
tutor, who ought to have had himself a similar education to his
pupil ' should instruct him in a familiar manner either in the
schoolroom or walking in a garden, or, if it so chances, upon
a journey : [2] let him set before himself everywhere this triple
purpose, that being educated in virtue and elegance of manners at the same time as knowledge, the young men committed
to his teaching shall become not less honest than lettered and
polite '.

Like Montaigne, Naudé warns against severe punishment
which makes either for timidity and stupidity or for rebellious-
ness.   Hence the tutor must not be morose or fussy but easy-
going and indulgent, coming to his pupil's help in everything
profitable that meets his taste, be it horses, hounds, books or
clothes ; and this without condescension.   In this way he will
gain his pupil's affection which is the only real source of an
authority which fear cannot give.[3]

One more work which is almost wholly derived from Montaigne's *Institution des Enfants* requires some mention, and leads
us back to the question of *honnêteté*.   We read in the *Sorberiana* :

Il y avait à Paris environ ce temps ci (1640) un certain Grenailles,
Sieur de Chatonnières, Limousin, jeune homme de 26 ans, qui décocha
tout à coup une prodigieuse quantité de livres.

L'Honnête Garçon (1642) by this author is built up of quotations
from Montaigne, a fact which Grenailles does not attempt to
hide.   On the contrary, he lavishes praise on Montaigne at
every turn.   He recalls that Du Perron said the Essays were
the *Bréviaire des Honnêtes Gens*, calls Montaigne *le Plutarque*

---

[1] *Syntagma*, p. 45.   [2] cf. *Essais*, I, 26, p. 200.   [3] ib., p. 48.

Chrétien, and remarks on his popularity among the nobility of France. Elsewhere he writes sententiously of his agreement with Montaigne :

Or je suis d'autant plus volontiers de son avis qu'outre que nous sommes tous deux de même climat, je crois parler comme Sénèque et Plutarque, lorsque je parle comme Monsieur de Montaigne. Cet auteur ne semble être que leur interprète and il s'est tellement plu à leur doctrine qu'il se l'est incorporée, ainsi qu'il parle lui-même.

Grenailles is simply a literary hack out to make his way in the world. His book with its undigested but rearranged chunks of Montaigne is only of importance as showing that it was still ' good business ' to trade on the reputation of our author.[1]

These few works on education show, at least, the assimilation of the general trend of Montaigne's *Institution*. To them must be added *La Logique de Port Royal*, to which we must refer later.

The chief reason why the writers on *honnêteté* afford an interesting field for the student of the Essays is because round this notion there forms itself a kind of *sous-morale*, which, without making explicit claims, comes to be considered a complete code of conduct. In the elaboration of this code many criterions used are, one would say, more aesthetic than moral. It is from this point of view that the writings of Méré and St. Evremond are especially important. The earlier writers, referred to Magendie as *bourgeois*, certainly borrow from Montaigne, but all they take in general are isolated ideas without adopting anything of the outlook of the Essays. For this reason it is not necessary to spend much time examining their books.[2]

Nicholas Pasquier, son of the more famous Etienne and author of *Le Gentilhomme* (1611), is obviously acquainted with the work of his father's friend, and it has left a few traces in his book, which is chiefly drawn from the *Cortegiano*.[3] Much his most

[1] Grenailles thinks every one should discuss Theology, and praises St. Thomas. Silence on such subjects favours the atheists (ib., pp. 162, 265).

[2] The age swarms with popular books on ethical subjects. Most of those which date from the beginning of the century show no traces of Montaigne's influence, though this is just the period in which one might expect to find it. See, for example, such books as the *Epîtres Morales* of D'Urfé (1603) and Nervèze (1603) : Guillaume Chevalier, *De la Vaillance* (1603) ; Christophe de Bonours, *Discours de la Vraie Noblesse* (1616). *Le Cabinet du Vrai Trésor* (1606) shows some echoes of the Essays (pp. 27, 95, 116). *Entregent* and *bienséance* are keywords which have more and more attention devoted to them. Already Scipion Dupleix's solid *Ethique* (1617) has a special section at the end devoted to these topics.

[3] e.g. pp. 18, 19 (on Latin, the teaching of), p. 72 and perhaps pp. 123, 124 (compare Magendie : op. cit., p. 346). For Pasquier's ideas on education see *Lettres*, 1, 5. Note also his exchange of letters with

significant remark, however, is that vice *n'est qu'une inégalité et discorde de mœurs qui se répugnent à elles-mêmes*.   Here we have the idea of appropriateness which becomes more prominent as the century proceeds.

The popular *Traité de la Cour ou Instruction des Courtisans* (1616) [1] of Eustache de Refuge, although it is not certain that it owes anything to Montaigne, illustrates certain points about this literature which require emphasis.   It is a general manual of conduct, the first half of which is devoted to psychology in general, and reads in places remarkably like a résumé of *La Sagesse*.   The passions are dealt with in some detail—note their control and moderation by various methods, among them *divertissement* (compare Charron).   Temperament is given great prominence,[2] while the second part of the book contains much practical advice as to the courtier's life.   Thus the scope of these treatises on civility is often wide, if superficial, and, just because they are written in a utilitarian *arriviste* spirit, they stress certain features in which we are interested such as temperament, diversity of character and adaptability—for one condition of a courtier's success is suiting himself to others.   Ease and grace must mark all the courtier's activities; here again it is seen what ground is being prepared for the influence of Montaigne's artistic conception of right conduct.

The main crop of these writings begins, however, with *Faret's Honnête Homme ou L'Art de plaire à la Cour* (1630),[3] its popularity calling forth a host of imitators or emulators.   In spite of its debt to Castiglione and to Montaigne, who are both inspired by a more liberal conception of what ' being a gentleman ' means, the second title of this book is a more accurate guide to its spirit. It is enough to mention the nature of the various passages of this book inspired by the Essays.[4]   Protesting against the prevalent idea that letters are not necessary to a gentleman, Faret argues that learning is only truly used for the worthiest ends, when, at the hands of those whom fortune has put in a high

Montaigne's nephew, Seigneur de St. Genêt (I, 11, III, 11, &c.) remarks on reform of justice (I, 6) and reunion of Protestants with the Church of Rome (V, 7).   ' Les differends qui naissent de ces disputes ne doivent empêcher les hommes de vivre en société, et *sous un même curé et en un même temple de faire le salut de leurs âmes* ' (cf. above, p. 148 note, 1).

[1] Republished 1617, 1618, 1619, 1622, 1636.   The author, *maître des requêtes* at the *Parlement de Paris*, died in 1617.

[2] op. cit., pp. 17–27, 40, 41, 120.

[3] *Edition critique*, M. Magendie, 1925.

[4] Nicholas Faret (*c.* 1600–46) was a member of the Academy.   His *Vertus Nécessaires à un Prince* (1623) owe nothing to the Essays.

position, it can be used ' to govern peoples, to lead armies, to cultivate the friendship of a prince, or a foreign nation, to make treaties between kings ' rather than to languish among the school-rooms of the University, among the pleas and intrigues of the Courts and the disputes of doctors.[1] Books are both profitable and add pleasure to life, but the great book of the world is more so than all Aristotle. Yet the *honnête homme* should be acquainted with various sciences, above all ethics, ' politics ', and history, which is the source of worldly wisdom.[2] Real wisdom, however, comes not so much from learning or even experience : ' its seat is in the understanding, not in the memory '. Experience does not teach much without a power of judging of difference of circumstances.[3]

Faret, however, also notes that *le prix d'une âme ne consiste pas à s'élever haut mais à marcher réglément et également* ; [4] and under the heading *De la Complaisance*, he writes :

> Cette souplesse est l'un des souverains préceptes de notre art. Quiconque sait complaire, peut hardiment espérer de plaire : Et en vérité l'une des plus infaillibles marques d'une âme bien née, c'est d'être ainsi universelle et susceptible de plusieurs formes, pourvu que ce soit par raison et non par légèreté ni par faiblesse. Il y a du rustre et du stupide d'être tellement pris à ses complexions qu'on ne-puisse jamais en relâcher un seul point. Un esprit bien fait s'ajuste à tout ce qu'il rencontre et, comme on disait d'Alcibiade, il est si accommodant et fait toutes choses d'une certaine sorte qu'il semble qu'il ait une particulière inclination à chacune de celles qu'on lui voit faire.[5]

Hence in conversation the *honnête homme* should always express his opinion in the form of a doubt.[6] This last passage of Faret is much the most important debt to Montaigne so far as the fruitfulness of the idea goes. In *L'Honnête Homme*, however, it remains undeveloped and lost among much good though super-ficial advice, and his conception of *l'honnête homme* requires no separate discussion.[7]

Another member of the future Academy, Pierre Bardin, had

---

[1] op. cit. (ed. cit.), pp. 24, 25 (which give necessary references to the Essays).
[2] ib., pp. 26, 27.　　　　　　　　　[3] ib., pp. 29, 30.
[4] ib., p. 57.　　　　[5] ib., p. 70.　　　　[6] cf. ib., p. 79.
[7] Note Faret on religion, p. 32. It is the foundation of all virtues, but a special warning is given against the discussion of matters concerning God. (Note also in *L'Homme Content* (1629), by Le Page, criticism of the presumption of theologians *and* philosophers, the first speaking rashly of God, the second rashly of nature.)

the intention of publishing a book under the same title as that of Faret. Being anticipated, his work appears two years later under the title of *Le Lycée*.[1] Not only is the scope of his book far wider than that of Faret, but moral preoccupations dominate it : *J'avoue*, he says, *que les intentions d'un honnête homme vont bien au delà des desseins d'un courtisan*. Although *Le Lycée* does not show direct signs of much borrowing from the Essays, his first book, *Essai sur l'Ecclésiaste* (1626), a paraphrase of Ecclesiastes (later republished in a more complete form under the title of *Pensées Morales sur Ecclésiaste*), contains a letter, by way of preface, in which the inspiration of Montaigne is clearly apparent.[2] The author has chosen to paraphrase Ecclesiastes, as showing how much better ethics were taught in the Bible than elsewhere. An interesting sceptical development on the vanity of science should be noticed. There is no appeal from individual judgement, but what cannot be proved false cannot either be proved true. The notion that some opinions are ' natural' does not help matters :

Car c'est une folie de dire que cette opinion est plus selon l'ordre de la Nature que celle là, puisque c'est l'entendement humain qui suppose un tel ordre et non pas la Nature.[3]

Le Lycée begins by giving Socrates as the model of the *honnête homme*. Bardin formulates the connexion of Stoical physics and ethics well when he says : Virtue for them was natural to men, and if they came to depart from it, this could only happen by allowing some external cause to act upon them. He himself accepts this view only to the extent that virtue can be taught, and it is a capability not a possession. *Honnêteté* is identified with the Stoical formula of the ' life according to Nature ', founded on universal consent. Hence *honnêteté* is recognized wherever found. It is recognized, at all events, in the historical actions of famous men which are admired by all. The quality of any act depends on its appropriateness, on time, place and circumstances, even according to religious doctrine.

The knowledge necessary to the *honnête homme* is ranged under knowledge of God, of self, of others, and of prudence in general. The causal proof of God's existence is given, Bardin

---

[1] *Où en plusieurs promenades il est traité des Connaissances, des Actions et des Plaisirs de l'Honnête Homme.*

[2] See passages beginning : ' J'ai remarqué que comme un nain porte la forme entière de l'homme . . . ' : ' L'éloquence des premiers siècles était mâle . . . ' and end.

[3] ib. (2nd ed.), I, p. 51.   cf. ib., I, pp. 230, 231.

recommends conformity with the established cult, reminding his readers of Socrates' dying wish (a cock to Aesculapius). Knowledge of self involves an examination of the place of man in nature, a study of one's particular aptitudes and capabilities, and a scrutiny of one's conscience. Knowledge of other people is necessary not only in order to know how to live with them, but because *les choses n'ont point d'action sur elles mêmes : et il afut un miroir à nos yeux, autrement il ne se verront jamais.*[1] The real characters of others are hard to know ; external signs require much study and are more trustworthy than elsewhere with regard to private conduct and habit.

Of the sciences moral philosophy and history are the most important. The education of the *honnête homme* must be quite general, but he may also add to it, later, technical knowledge of his own profession. Travel is recommended to the young man for the profit to be derived from observation of men, customs and political institutions.[2] Prudence is the strategy of success, the science of expediency : it is a quality which depends largely on temperament, which therefore receives ample attention. The difference of the good (dependent on motives) and the useful (results) is discussed. In the second volume of *Le Lycée* (1634), Bardin, however, defines good as what is natural to anything and desired by it, and comparing the active and contemplative life, he is led to claim, to the advantage of the former, that the degree of excellency of any act depends on its effects.

Bardin's book is interesting for his insistence that the *honnête homme* is more than a courtier and for his identification of *honnêteté* and ' follow nature '. His interpretation of this formula is extremely vague however, and in spite of the place he allots to the study of individual character and to appropriateness it is not possible to estimate with any certainty his debt to Montaigne as more than the adoption of a few isolated ideas.

L'Honnête Femme (1632) by the Père du Bosc is chiefly an exercise in style.[3] The second edition (1633) contains an introduction written by Perrot d'Ablancourt, who gives the book the supplementary title of *L'Introduction de l'Introduction à la Vie Dévote.* D'Ablancourt here, as elsewhere,[4] reminds one constantly of Montaigne, but apart from saying that virtue must be made attractive, that precepts are dangers, since a single circumstance changes a whole situation, and apart from a very Montaignesque passage on the excessive use of examples to illustrate general

[1] *Lycée*, I, p. 137.   [2] ib., I, p. 414.
[3] Note pp. 33, 179, 185, 186, possible reminiscences of the Essays.
[4] See above, pp. 278, 279.

principles, this preface contains nothing of interest. Grenailles'
Le Bon Esprit (1641) is almost entirely concerned with the
humours, so too *Les Entretiens du Cours* (1654) by Marmet de
Valcroissant. Grenailles' *La Mode* (1642) and *La Contre Mode*
(1642) of his friend Fitelieu both set out to be thoroughly orthodox
—with a smattering of scholastic jargon—on religious matters.
We must note Grenailles' censure of pyrrhonism, an uncompli-
mentary reference to Montaigne in Fitelieu,[1] and both authors'
anxiety to defend the idea of eternal punishment. *Le Gentilhomme Chrétien* of Yves de Paris is excellent but has naturally
no point of contact with the Essays. *La Conduite du Courtisan*
(1646) by F. de Soucy and *Le Courtisan Désabusé* (1658) by
Bourdonné are both insignificant.

Le *Traité de la Fortune des Gens de Qualité* (1661) by F. de
Caillière is written not to show how to become an *honnête homme*,
but how, being one, to succeed in society or at court. For such
a man, study of his own character and capabilities and of the
qualities of those he wishes to serve are the most necessary
training. Temperament is already of great importance in becoming an *honnête homme*. Versatility is to be prized :

Il n'y a que les esprits universels agréables à tout le monde, parce
qu'ils ont l'avantage de se transformer sans peine comme des Pro-
thées . . . de sorte qu'ils semblent nés pour toutes les professions
de la vie civile.[2]

Far more valuable than these writings is the discussion of
the terms *honnêteté* and *honnête homme* by a *Montaignisant* already
mentioned, Samuel Sorbière. His interesting definitions will
enable us to bring this chapter to a close. In one of his letters
Sorbière describes what he understands by the four terms :
homme de bien, homme dévot, honnête homme, and *galant homme*.[3]

The terms are not mutually exclusive but to some extent
cumulative. The first is the good but plain man, not given to
the discussion of the principles of society but obeying what
his superiors in station tell him. The second is the religious
man, conscious of the vanity of human knowledge, for whom
the moral virtues are not enough. His own virtues he hides as
far as he can, content so far as the world goes to set a good

---

[1] cf. op. cit., p. 60. Fitelieu expresses his scorn ' pour ces petits
savants qui pour avoir appris par cœur quelque piece de Montaigne,
s'ingèrent à tous moments dans les bonnes compagnies,' &c. (cf. Sarasin
above, p. 251).

[2] op. cit., p. 210. (Note p. 20 defence of the Epicureans.)

[3] *Relations, Lettres et Discours,* 1660, p. 320 et seq. (Sorbière adds a
description of the *faux homme de bien, faux dévot*, etc.)

example. Knowing he cannot please every one he is apt to consider the faithful alone as his neighbours and these only in accordance with their merit. 'This makes him appear a little hard and presumptuous, although tenderness of heart and humility are the foundation of all Christian virtues.'

The description of the *honnête homme* is worth quoting at length. He is

bien plus éclairé que l'homme de bien, et il ne suit pas les seules lumières qui conduisent l'homme dévot. Il se laisse guider aussi aux clartés naturelles du bon sens et de l'équité vers lesquelles il fait autant de réflexion que sur celles que la piété lui donne. C'est pourquoi sa vie est plus en dehors ; sa science est plus étendue et ses actions, de même que ses paroles, sont plus accommodées à quelque bienséance et à quelques civilités, par lesquelles il tâche de se rendre utile et agréable à tout le monde. Ses pensées sont plus vastes que celles de l'homme de bien et elles lui font entreprendre plus de choses qu'il ne ferait, s'il renfermait son activité dans une moindre sphère. Sa vertu est plus détachée de la matière : et ses maximes d'honneur lui font trouver de quoi enchérir sur la pratique ordinaire de ses concitoyens. Il veut faire plus que les Loix ne commandent, et il ne s'estimerait pas digne du titre qu'on lui donne, s'il ne faisait que ce que doivent faire les autres hommes. Il est soigneux de tenir ce qu'il a promis, et jamais il ne cherche de prétexte pour s'empêcher de faire du bien à ceux qui ont besoin de lui. Il ne se met pas tant en peine de ce qui ne regarde que leur divertissement ; et de ce côté là il vit avec quelque négligence. Car de même que notre homme de bien n'a pas voulu aller au delà des Loix, et que notre dévot a cru qu'il n'était pas obligé de pratiquer les Vertus Morales indifféramment envers tous ceux qui le reçoivent pour peu qu'ils valent ; cettui-ci n'estime pas qu'il doive passer les bornes de l'honnêteté pour donner du plaisir aux personnes voluptueuses. C'est pourquoi il leur paraît quelquefois un peu difficile : quoiqu'il n'y ait rien de meilleur ni de plus accommodant que lui.

The *galant homme* lives more in the world of society and at court, gives more time to fashion and amusements, studies to please every one, particularly the ladies. He is a little lacking in sense of proportion, but he carries it off with his *bel air*. With time and years he may become *honnête homme, homme dévot, homme de bien* ; but the contrary is not true. Experience will not give them what they lack to earn the qualification of *galant homme*.

Sorbière has here attempted not an arbitrary definition of what he thinks *l'homme de bien, l'honnête homme*, &c., should be, but he has tried to convey the connotation of these terms by a description of the character which seems in keeping with each.   Thus *l'honnête homme* has primarily an ethical meaning, not merely a social one ; [1] his code of conduct is superior to the conventional one of the *homme de bien* and wider than the purely religious one of the *homme dévot* (though religion is vaguely implied to have its proper place in his life).   *L'honnête homme*, according to Sorbière is, to some extent, a rationalizing philanthropist as well as a ' man of the world '.   He studies to help and to please. To please is not his one aim, however, and especially in matters of sex his morality sets bounds to his complaisance.   *Le galant homme* differs from him only in this and because his life is predominately that of the fashionable world and the court.   *Le galant homme* is, above all, *natural* ; *l'honnête homme* is amiable.

In an exchange of views with Marolles, Sorbière quotes Montaigne :

Un honnête homme doit savoir faire toutes choses sans en excepter les mauvaises ; mais il ne se doit plaire qu'aux bonnes, dit Michel de Montaigne, après avoir demandé à un Ambassadeur de Roi en Suisse combien de fois il s'y était énivré pour le service de sa Majesté.

This conduct Marolles in reply calls *une pure galanterie*, and insists that the *honnête homme* should accommodate himself to circumstances but not to the extent of doing anything against his conscience.   The *honnête homme*, Marolles continues, is indeed ' the Sage ', but *cet honnête homme, qui se produit diversement dans toutes les conditions, ne peut jamais être séparé de l'homme de bien*, nor can he be *honnête homme* without piety.   Thus Marolles and Sorbière agree in the sense they give to these terms.

To see the import of these distinctions and the full influence of Montaigne on *l'honnêteté*, it is necessary to turn to the Méré brothers, St. Evremond and other representatives of *le monde—le monde* which plays an increasingly important rôle in the history of literature and thought as the century moves on.   We cannot approach them simply from this angle of *honnêteté*, for Montaigne's influence upon them is far too general to fit in with such an arrangement, except perhaps in the case of the chevalier de Méré. They are to be treated primarily as disciples of Montaigne. Such treatment will show incidentally how the Essays have affected their conception of *l'honnête homme*.

---

[1] Note that in the passage quoted *honnêteté* means simply morality. The *Recueil Général Des Questions traitées és Conférences du Bureau d'Adresse*, I, p. 365, says that *l'honnête homme* possesses ' *le bien honnête qui est la Vertu* ', but to be *homme d'honneur* this virtue must be recognized by others :   a good distinction.

CHAPTER XXIII

THE MÉRÉ BROTHERS

On dit bien vrai qu'un honnête homme, c'est un homme meslé.
MONTAIGNE

*H*ONNÊTETÉ is the password which gives an entry into *le monde*, into French society from the time of Louis XIV to the Revolution. In this and in the next chapter some of those who helped to form and to formulate its meaning are dealt with. The influence of Montaigne upon them will be seen, and how the term *honnêteté* is, like Montaigne's ideal, something which transforms purely ethical considerations and transcends them in an art of life, of which one of the most important parts is that of living with one's fellow-creatures. It is through this conception that the hedonist humanism and the tolerance of the best Renaissance thought is eventually diffused and propagated to form the soil on which the *philosophes* were to work.

Those whom we deal with here were rationalistic only in their ethics, they were fideist, more or less, in religion and found no contradiction between a naturalistic conception of life and the tenets of revealed religion. That was due largely to their lack of logic and to their insufficient understanding of what Christian ethics imply. It was Pascal, a fideist, the last great fideist of the century, who exposed the contradiction, and who used and rewelded the weapon of the *Apology* in the service of religion. At the same time and later, partly influenced by the *Pensées*, no doubt, come a series of attacks on the Essays, and by the end of the century, we shall see how far Montaigne's popularity had declined.

The letters (already mentioned) of Josias de Gombauld, Seigneur de Plassac-Méré,[1] elder brother of the chevalier de Méré, friend of Maynard, and Balzac, claim to contain ' an ingenious ethick ', drawn not from Aristotle, Cicero or Plutarch, but from

[1] See above, p. 302.

the observation of life ' in the best circles '. Balzac writes to him in 1639 :

> Mais où prenez vous tout ce que vous écrivez, vous, Monsieur, qui faites peu de voyages en pays latin, et qui allez rarement en Grèce ? Sans doute . . . dans l'Idée universelle des choses.

A few years later Balzac blames his friend for having gone to the unnecessary expense of a ' coach ' to read Cicero with him.[1] He owes so much to the Essays, probably just because of his lack of a classical education, and the foundations of his ' ingenious ethick ' are to be sought as much there as in his experience.

For him it is true that

> Le véritable secret ˉde la Sagesse est de vivre et que c'est la diversité des actions qui étend la vie et la fait sentir davantage.[2]

He declares his ' naturalism ' in no uncertain terms :

> A parler tout de bon, je ne connais point d'autre secret que de se contenter. La plus fine morale, si je ne m'abuse, ne tend que là. Et de fait, que veulent dire, je vous prie, ces Sages qui parlent toujours du mépris de la gloire, et qui font consister le souverain bien de l'homme dans la satisfaction de lui même ? N'est ce pas nous dire en termes exprès qu'il ne faut point dépendre des opinions d'autrui et qu'on doit se satisfaire des choses qu'on aime. En bon principe de Nature nos appétits sont toujours innocents et nos dégoûts toujours criminels. Il faut laisser pour les dupes la piperie du monde qui nous incommode et qui traverse la douceur de la vie. J'entends des choses qui ne choquent point la foi. Du reste, si nous sommes bien avisés, toute notre complaisance ne sera que pour nous.[3]

Tolerance is another lesson Plassac has learnt :

> Nous serions dans une grande erreur, la Religion à part toutefois, de croire qu'il n'y ait rien d'excellent que les choses que nous pratiquons. Les opinions qui nous sont contraires ne laissent pas de rendre heureux ceux qui les suivent. Il faut avoir l'esprit extrêmement borné pour se figurer qu'il n'y a rien de bon ni d'honnête hors de nous.[4]

Indeed tolerance is so much the mark of an *honnête homme* that the false *honnête homme*, so he tells his friend La Thibaudière,[5]

---

[1] *Œuvres* (1664), Lettres, XIV, 34. See also VIII, 44, IX, 46 and XIV, 35, where the ' coach ' is mentioned. For Plassac's letters to Balzac, see op. cit., Nos. 3, 43, 44, 71, 72.
[2] *Lettres de M. de Plassac* (1648), p. 235.
[3] ib., p. 264.   [4] ib., Lettre 20.
[5] M. de la Thibaudière was the uncle of the Gandillaud for whom Balzac recorded the conversation on the Essays in his *Dissertations Critiques* (v. ante), and Gandillaud was told to show the dissertation to

is characterized as the man who cannot abide anything but his own way of thinking. He, like Socrates, prefers the people to such dogmatists, for their good sense is less corrupted. Dogmatism about new opinions is especially foolish : ' if Descartes refutes Aristotle, another will come who will do the same to him '.[1] A man of sense will not bother his head about things which make him neither happier nor better, but will live as he pleases within the limits of law and custom without declaring war on them.

He describes those who shock good manners by their pedantic austerity as imitators of Diogenes. They seem to imagine it only necessary to be forbidding and peculiar in order to be like him :

Sans mentir ils sont bien loin de leur compte : ce philosophe agissait des propres mouvements de la Nature, portant dans le cœur ses vrais caractères. Il disait ce qu'il pensait et pensait grandement, ayant le cerveau très épuré par l'étude et par la méditation. Ceux ci sont de mauvais Comédiens qui représentent mal les actions de l'autre et qui voudraient tromper le monde . . .

They are always sensitive about their lack of conformity and not without inner conflict. Some of his own friends indeed make short shift with common usages *mais pour embellir leur vie et la passer avec plus de douceur et d'innocence.* To be natural is not only the secret of happiness, but of the gracefulness which is an essential qualification of the *honnête homme,* for it is only thus that the art of pleasing can be acquired. It is this art which Plassac calls *la véritable galanterie,* which ' polishes manners, puts charm into the most everyday conversations, distinguishes the real *honnête homme* from the sham, the civilized man from the boor, the court from the country '.[2] Some people fail in this ideal because they try and model themselves on some hero of a novel :

Et comme ils veulent imiter la vie de quelque Héros, qui n'est qu'une vie d'imagination, la leur est toute en chimères, et ne paraît qu'une fable. Il me semble qu'un honnête homme est réel et humain, et que celui qui ne l'est pas est faux et brutal.[3]

his uncle, who was not apparently an ardent admirer of Montaigne. On La Thibaudière, see Balzac, *Œuvres,* I, pp. 247, 572, 661, 703, 705, 721, 724 ; II, *Lettres,* XII, 31–3 ; XVI, 30 ; XXI, 9. Plassac : Lettres 9, 87, 88, 89. P. Costar : *Lettres* (1658), I, p. 237.
    [1] cf. *Essais,* II, 12, p. 325. (cf. Lettre 91 some one accused of being *Moine de Descartes*).
    [2] ib., Preface.   [3] ib., p. 333.

Note the implication that, above all, the *honnête homme* is humane and tolerant. The real translation of that expression as the 'civilized man' begins to make itself clear in the letters of Plassac.

It needs the advantages of birth, education and natural qualities to make an *honnête homme*, however, and not least of these are natural qualities. Discussing a miserly abbé, he writes to the Marquis de Jonzac :

> N'en déplaise à la Philosophie, nous naissons vertueux ou vicieux : et je conclus par là que l'abbé sera toujours avare, que vous aurez toujours de dignes sentiments, et que Monsieur X sera toujours un brutal.[1]

Peace of mind, Plassac says in speaking of a general—probably La Meilleraie in whose household he had lived—peace of mind is the perfection of wisdom ; and, one may add, it is this peace which is at the bottom of the 'grace' or the *bel air* of the *honnête homme*. Yet it comes in different ways ; it is dependent on acting in accordance with one's nature, which is capable of little alteration. Reflecting on the character of his late patron, he writes :

> Toutefois avec la clarté de son jugement, qui lui devait bien faire connaître que le repos est le vrai partage du Sage, je vous puis assurer qu'il n'en a point et qu'il n'en recevra jamais que dans la vie pénible, pleine d'inquiétude et de péril . . . Faisant réflexion là dessus . . . je suis en doute si la philosophie qui établit le repos pour souverain bien ne nous abuse point et que l'âme, à qui la gloire a été donnée pour dernière félicité, ne peut pas dès ce monde anticiper quelque partie de cette gloire. Les choses d'ici-bas n'étant jamais pures, on peut conclure par là que faire et non-faire est indifférent : et qu'un naturel qui est porté au travail, à qui le repos est peine, peut trouver dans l'agitation une profonde félicité. Si l'erreur se fait voir par les inconvénients qui suivent nos actions, qui sont celles, je vous prie, qui en sont exemptes : et quel plaisir peut être plus grand à l'homme que de faire ce qu'il aime ? Ceci est toujours le refrain de ma morale ; et plus je considère le petit nombre de nos jours, et ce qu'un chacun doit à des inclinations, et plus je me la reconfirme. En effet nos joies et nos déplaisirs viennent de notre opinion et non pas de celle d'autrui.[2]

The disciple of Montaigne can be read between the lines of such a passage. To see this still more clearly one has only to turn to Plassac's reflexions on his sufferings when ill :

[1] cf., *Essais*, II, Lettre 84.
[2] ib., p. 475, 6, cf. *Essais*, II, 12, p. 323.

Je n'essaie point de me rendre insensible aux accidents, ainsi que les Sages conseillent. Car j'ai trouvé par expérience, que le meilleur rémède était de souffrir. Si je faisois d'autre sorte je pâtirais trop en agissant. Plus je cherche des moyens pour me consoler, plus je raffine mon mal, et je n'ai pas guéri une blessure qu'aussitôt j'en découvre une autre. J'aime bien mieux recevoir tout d'un coup les atteintes de la Fortune que de tenir quelque temps dans un mauvais fort, où il faudrait à la fin que je me rendisse. Je n'ai su faire encore mon profit de ces Romans de Philosophie. Ce sont de vaines idées de choses qui ne furent jamais : au moins qui ne peuvent, selon moi, soulager un esprit affligé. La vertu ne me vaut pas l'endurcissement. Et d'ailleurs il me semble qu'on doit suivre son naturel, et qu'il n'est rien de plus miserable qu'une joie forcée. En faisant comme je fais, les premiers moments de joie qui viennent sont toujours suivis d'une entière guerison.[1]

Other pages of these letters serve to show still further how much Plassac has formed himself on Montaigne. His philosophy of life is somewhat lacking in the *generosity* which combines with wide-eyed disillusionment to make up the charm of the great Gascon. He may echo faithfully some remarks from the Essays on the disadvantages of marriage, or how readily he would travel, if need be, to find congenial company and intelligent conversation : [2] the atmosphere is very different ; at bottom, if I am not mistaken, because Plassac, though he has assimilated the precepts of Montaigne's ethics, lacks the aesthetic spirit which informs them. Or perhaps more truly there is an emptiness at the centre of his life which comes from a certain selfish hedonism, an emptiness which yawns when he writes :

Tous les matins il me prend envie de ne me point lever du lit— Quoi, dis-je, quelle affaire ai-je dans le monde qui mérite du soin ? [3]

So far as Plassac's religion is concerned, his respectful expressions will have been noted, he boasts in a love letter [4] of going to Mass every day, but we may put him down as perhaps hardly conscious how far his leading ideas on conduct were ultimately at variance with the teaching of the Church. The one letter which turns on any such subject is, however, a very sharp reply to a priest who appears to have attacked him in his pulpit for supposed irreligion. ' I believe (he says) everything which the Church commands me to believe ; and if you are not content with my written assurance, I am ready to tell you so in

[1] ib., Lettre 54 (cf. perhaps *Essais*, III, 13, p. 418, &c.).
[2] ib., Lettre 17, 65.   [3] ib., pp. 195, 196.
[4] The business-like love letters of Plassac are often amusing but do not interest us here.

confession.' The letter is remarkable if, as I fancy, it contains an early reference to the *Cabale des Dévots*.[1]

Plassac's letters appear to have been mostly written between the years 1638–48, which he spent chiefly in retreat at Beaussais, a country-house near Poitiers where he died in 1661. His younger brother, the Chevalier de Méré,[2] after seeing some military service and a society life which brought him into contact with most of the celebrities of his day, retired in 1662 or 1663—a bachelor too—to the same property, which he had inherited and where he wrote most of his little books and many of his letters.[3] The resemblance between these two brothers goes still further. The background of their ideas is very much alike.

M. Bridieu a oui que M. Voiture rêvait deux heures le jour ce qu'il devait dire la journée. · Le chevalier de Méré fait la même chose ; il rêve deux heures le jour et écrit toutes ses pensées, relit ses mémoires et est un mois à faire une lettre : il travaille sur le fonds de Montaigne.

So we read in a contemporary scrap-book.[4] The observation gives the key to both the difference and the resemblance of the brothers. They both work on the ' matter ' of the Essays, but the *chevalier* has some of the capacity for taking pains which is said to constitute genius. He made himself by hard work an author of many subtle and witty pages. Sorbière says of his *Conversations :*

Il me semble, que je me promène dans ce livre comme dans un jardin, où je découvre à chaque pas de belles allées et, au bout, des jets d'eau, des statues et des perspectives.[5]

Méré is not a genius, but he possessed more vanity than most, resulting in a tendency to didacticism. He considered himself as a professor of *honnêteté*, for round that conception all his writings turn. He considered himself an authority on other matters as well. One of his books tells us of a journey to Poitiers (or

---

[1] ib., p. 282 ; cf. Raoul Allier : *La Cabale des Dévots*.

[2] Antoine de Gombauld (1604–84), knight (or *supposed* knight) of St. John or ' of Malta ', hence known as the *Chevalier* de Méré, has been often confused with Georges Brossin, marquis de Méré.

[3] *Les Conversations du Chevalier de Méré et du Maréchal de Clérambaut* (1668) ; *Discours de la Justesse* (1671) ; *Des Agréments, De l'Esprit, De la Conversation* (1677) ; *Lettres* (1682) ; *Œuvres Posthumes* (1701). Consult : E Chamaillard, *Le Chevalier de Méré* (1921) ; *Revue de l'Histoire Litt. de la France*, 1913, Ch. H. Boudhors : *De Méré et Pascal* ; ib., 1922–4 id., *Le Cahier du Chevalier de Méré* ; M. Magendie, *La Politesss Mondaine* ; and, above all, *Œuvres Complètes* (ed. Boudhors).

[4] E. Griselle : *Revue de Fribourg*, 1907–8.

[5] *Sorberiana*, p. 169.

in Poitou) made in 1652 by the Duc de Roannez (then Governor of the Province), Mitton, Méré himself and a mathematician, who is undoubtedly Pascal.[1] It was certainly Mitton and Méré who opened Pascal's eyes to all that he called later *esprit de finesse*, and to them he owed almost certainly his first introduction to the Essays. Méré, however, characteristically made pretensions to know more about mathematics than the mathematician, and, though his thesis was an absurd one, stuck to his guns and published his letter to Pascal on the subject more than twenty years after the latter's death.[2] So much for the character of the man. His untiring analysis of moral and social qualities and his search after perfection—*rien n'empêche tant de trouver la perfection que de croire qu'on l'a trouvée*—gives a certain attractiveness to him for all his faults, and the interest of his ideas for our study is considerable.

Let us piece together from Méré's books and letters his conception of *honnêteté*, and supplement some of the definitions and distinctions which he loves.

The perfect *honnête homme* is probably never to be found. He is an ideal, but happiness depends on the approach to this ideal, *car il est impossible d'avoir cette honnêteté sans la connaître ni la connaître sans l'aimer éperduement, et c'est ce qui fait qu'on est heureux de la posséder.*[3] But although *honnêteté* includes everything, it is no science ' of living and dying well ' *car si l'on ne mourrait point on ne laisserait pas d'être honnête homme, même on y pourrait faire un plus grand progrès.*[4] Nor is it *bien dire et bien faire* ; the sign of *honnêteté* is *savoir plaire* :—Not out of pure benevolence, for

Quand on est de bonne compagnie à l'égard des honnêtes gens, on l'est aussi pour soi-même, et de là dépend le plus grand bonheur de la vie.[5]

One must please ' those who recognize real merit '. It is in this circle that Méré constantly argues.

Honnêteté has to be learnt, and is rarely self-taught, but it is never too late to acquire it by adding to the good heart which entitles a man to the name of *homme de bien* the further essential qualities of *bon air, l'esprit agréable* and *l'adresse*.[6] The ethical

---

[1] Méré : *De l'Esprit* (1677), p. 99 et seq. (cf. R.H.L., 1913, art. of Ch. Boudhors). See Marquis de Roux, *Pascal en Poitou*, for date.

[2] *Lettres* (ed. 1682), No. 19. cf. *Le Cahier du Chev. de Méré* (R.H.L., 1923), p. 56, an accusation that Pascal had ' stolen from the *chevalier* ' and p. 69 ' M. Pascal, M. Mitton, M. du Bois, M. de Roannez et beaucoup d'autres n'auraient jamais rien su sans moi.'

[3] *Lettres*, No. 147.   [4] *Conversations*, pp. 144, 234.
[5] ib., p. 158.   [6] *Lettre* 89, 121.

side of *honnêteté* cannot be disregarded when we are told that it depends above all on ' setting head and heart in good order ' ; yet, since above all it makes people lovable, it reveals itself an art.   True gallantry appears to be the same as perfect *honnêteté* : its end is to please.[1]   There is a distinction between them though, summed up in the comparison of Alcibiades and Epaminondas.[2] Alcibiades adds physical attractiveness, tact and adaptability to the gifts of the Theban.   The *galant homme* makes everything becoming to himself and possesses ' urbanity '—*je ne sais quoi de railleur et de flatteur tout ensemble.*[3]   There is indeed a false gallantry which is only exterior : in the ' old court ', under Louis XIII, physical qualities were considered sufficient.   Its most brilliant members found the expression of their qualities in action, but *on est souvent acteur de rien, comme riseur de rien.*[4] The court itself contains few persons of real merit, it is a model only for language and fashion.   So that, although without a knowledge of its manners, one cannot please those who are of it, nothing is more ridiculous than the mere courtier who is like a fish out of water elsewhere.

Tous ces courtisans sont comme autant d'enfants de tribut, qui ne se souviennent ni de leurs parents ni du lieu de leur naissance.   Ces sortes de gens charmés de la Cour ne pensent qu'à satisfaire à leur ambition.   Et s'il arrive qu'on les éloigne et qu'ils soient contraints de retourner chez eux, l'abord de leurs maisons leur fait plus de dépit qu'Ulysse n'eut de plaisir à revoir la sienne.[5]

Méré himself professes to prefer ' the world of natural objects ' to the ' artificial world ', which pleases exclusively at Court. He is constantly trying to explain his country-pleasures to Mitton, the true Parisian, the barber-surgeon's son.   Though his love of Nature may be taken with some reserve, it is well to see the importance he gives to ' nature ' in the sense of individual character, for it is the basis of the art of pleasing which is *honnêteté*. Felicity ' depends much more on temperament than on those things which we think impart it ' :

Rien ne saurait plaire qui ne soit naturel ou du moins qui ne la paraisse et . . . il est presque impossible de bien jouer le personnage d'un autre.[6]

La bonne conduite consiste encore bien fort à suivre les voies qui nous sont les plus propres.   Il faut pour cela s'examiner de tous côtés,

---

[1] *Des Agréments*, p. 123.   [2] *Œuvres Posthumes*, V, p. 195.
[3] *Lettres*, No. 68.   [4] *Conversations*, p. 128.
[5] *Lettres*, No. 143 (cf. *Essais*, III, 9, p. 271).   *Œuvres Posthumes*, pp. 221, 240.
[6] *Lettres*, No. 116.

et se ressouvenir que ce ne sont pas les choses de même nature qui peuvent rendre toute sorte de gens heureux. Quelques personnes de ma connaissance passent leur vie a jouer des rôles qui leur déplaisent, et c'est une simplicité bien grande, à moins que de ne pouvoir faire autrement.[1]

Tout le monde a besoin d'un livre à part . . . même pour coiffer les brunes et les blondes.[2]

Effort spoils pleasure so much that he knows a man who dislikes trumpets simply because of the palpable efforts made by those who blow them. If one is offered some part to play which cannot be done ' agreeably ' (that is both from the point of view of oneself and others) the *honnête homme* should refuse it. It is this knowledge of what suits one, the possession of this special sense of values, which makes an *habile homme*.

However, since a fittingness in all things is the mark of *honnêteté*, it is not only a question of studying one's aptitudes but also of adapting oneself to circumstances. Méré expressly rejects the foolish idea that whatever is ' natural ' is *ipso facto* pleasing.[3] He himself clarified his intelligence, but that was not going against his temperament, which should be followed in physical movements, manners and action. He believes, though, that ' one should correct in a day one's faults when one is advised of them : *Le cœur s'accommode aisément à ce que la nature lui conseille*,[4] especially if one possesses intelligence.

Just as the *honnête homme* should not live in constraint, or if he must, will hide any effort that he may have to make, so he must be tolerant and indulgent with others, and, bearing everything lightly, *ne se ƒîquer de rien*. It is here that one may profitably be a ' gool actor ', not taking anything too much to heart.[5] In a way, this should be easy, for *qua honnête homme* he is of no profession.

Un honnête homme n'a rien de particulier qu'à bien vivre et à se communiquer de bonne grâce par les discours et par les actions.[6]

On artistic matters, for example, he *speaks* as an amateur, but he does not *practise* (when he writes or paints or acts) as an amateur.

Plus on a de discernemen exquis, plus on se fait d'honneur d'être indulgent.[6]

It is almost unnecessary to say that the *honnête homme* is not dogmatic, for how could be hope to please in such a manner.

[1] *Œuvres Posthumes* (end).
[2] *Cahier* (R.H.L., 1924, 9, 490) (cf. *Essais*, III, 13, p. 444).
[3] *Lettres*, No. 36.   [4] *Cahier*, pp. 81, 82.
[5] *Œuvres Posthumes*, V, p. 204.   [6] *Conversations*, p. 222.

Méré's dislike of the ' pedants ' is strongly expressed in the fifth talk of his first published book, *Les Conversations du Chevalier de Méré et du Maréchal de Clérambaut*. Clérambaut hoped to be appointed governor to the Dauphin and Méré himself hoped to be tutor. Alas for their plans ! the marshal died too soon.

Ordinary education has little to do with *honnêteté*, but it is towards this ideal that the prince's education should be directed. He will learn Latin in spite of the time it takes and other difficulties, but there are to be few lessons, amusingly diversified to keep the pupil always in a good temper.

Le Maréchal : Je crois que le meilleur moyen pour se rendre habile et savant n'est pas d'étudier beaucoup mais de s'entretenir souvent de ces choses qui ouvrent l'esprit.[1]

The second Conversation asks the pertinent question why the knowledge of the Greeks, those masters of all the arts, does not profit us more. Méré attributes this largely to Aristotle, whom he contrasts unfavourably with his predecessors.

Ceux là faisaient leur félicité de connaître, et disaient qu'ils ne savaient presque rien. C'était d'honnêtes gens et de bonne foi, qui traitaient douteusement des choses douteuses.

Aristotle sought, on the other hand, to make a reputation and knew well that all but a few clear-sighted people prefer a philosopher who lays down the law. Whatever the actual value of his work, says Méré, ' I would that so great a man *eût un peu plus naturalisé l'art et les règles* '.[2] Aristotle is clear and admirable on many matters, but what is most obscure in him is most esteemed, and through him men have come to value obscurity as the synonym of profundity, and this has become one of the chief reasons why education has so little result. The mathematical sciences are greatly superior to all others, but they tend to make a man too speculative. Méré attributes great importance, none the less, to *l'esprit géométrique*, the deductive abstract method. He is inclined to set less store by history than the Marshal, because past experience is no sure guide to the future.

As with the *honnête homme* so with the child, it is *savoir-faire* he must be taught ; but he must not display it on all occasions, he must not hope to excel in every way. Most of all :

Il faudrait principalement faire considérer au jeune Prince que les rois et empereurs qui ont été honnêtes gens, outre la gloire qui leur en reste, ont passé encore une vie heureuse et agréable.[3]

[1] *Conversations*, I.   [2] cf. *Essais*, III, 5, p. 120.   [3] ib., p. 104.

That too was the lesson of the Greeks : the art of living (above all they knew how to love). Méré is one of the few Frenchmen of his age who preferred the Greeks to the Romans. It is not merely that Socrates, not yet enough esteemed, is more his hero than even Caesar. To the Romans, besides their pride, he ascribes :

Une injustice manifeste et une avarice insatiable de Bourgeois arrogants, qui par quelque adresse à faire la guerre, et par la discipline de leurs armées, pillaient et ravageaient toutes les nations de la terre [1]

—whom they insulted at the same time by dubbing them ' barbarians '. Méré in a letter to the Duc de Mazarin, after touching on the brutality of Augustus to Cleopatra, and the ingratitude of Pompey and Brutus to Caesar as traits characteristic of the Romans, goes on to say of even Scipio Aemilianus that

s'il n'eût pas été si formaliste et si grand observateur des coutumes de son Pays, ce qui marque un esprit de peu d'étendue, je le mettrais au nombre des plus excellents hommes.[2]

As for Cato of Utica, he always acted on ' false principles ', he believed in the letter of the law only

sur quoi je prends garde que les gens simples qui se laissent conduire à leur instinct naturel sont moins sujets à se tromper que la plupart de ces grands personnages qui pensent tout savoir.

Méré mocks the fanatical patriotism of the Romans in the story of the Greek who tried to dissuade Cato from his suicide : What do you mean by the ' air of your country ' ? It has been round the world since you were born. And even Tiber water and fields and houses, too, have all changed. And if they had been the same, have you an obligation to inanimate things ? These were the heroes of the Romans, says Méré, and yet Balzac persuades people they were demigods ! [3]

This hellenism and this cosmopolitanism are essential traits in Méré's character. By these tastes he looks back to the Renaissance and on to the eighteenth century :

Il me semble que je suis citoyen du monde, à peu près comme l'est Socrate, et je ne laisse pourtant pas de tourner de temps en temps les yeux vers mon village.

In the third Conversation, it is recommended that the prince should be hardened and taught to be able to lead a frugal life.[4]

---

[1] Œuvres Posthumes, p. 64.
[2] Lettres, No. 36, cf. Essais, II, 36, pp. 571, 572.
[3] ib., cf. on the same subject a letter (56) to Balzac.
[4] cf. Essais, I, 26, pp. 197, 198.

He will thus realize that magnificence and luxury do not make one the more an *honnête homme*.[1] As one trains the body by physical exercises, so the mind, which is naturally supple, must be formed, but once formed only a little further advice is necessary. It is a question of intelligence not of memory. This is where education by bringing out natural aptitudes can be of great importance. One of the main results of intelligence is insight into the character of others—their real qualities of mind and their limitations. Hence it is particularly desirable that the prince should be a good deal in the company of grown-ups.[2]

Part of *honnêteté* is the art of pleasing—an art which like all others must be hidden—it depends on having good taste. With taste for guide the pupil will know

ce qu'on doit souhaiter acquérir, et les moyens pour y pouvoir exceller : s'il avait par avance le sentiment juste du bien et du mal, il mettra de lui même à profit tout ce qui se passe autour de lui.[3]

Avoir le goût bon—taste does not appear in this passage to be used in the ethical sense which it is given elsewhere, though the transition is clear when Méré writes some pages later that ' the first emotions of the heart give an inclination to good or evil which lasts a lifetime '. Taste and intelligence (*esprit*) are the two kinds of mental qualities, the two *justesses*, intuitive and intellectual respectively. But we may ask : Is taste objective ? Can one dispute about taste or say when it is good ? Yes, says Méré and gives us one of his shadowy but instructive definitions :

Le goût bon se fonde toujours sur des raisons très solides : mais le plus souvent sans raisonner. Il consiste à sentir à quel point de bonté sont les choses qui doivent plaire, et à préférer les excellents aux médiocres. Mais d'où vient que c'est avoir le goût bon que d'aimer les bonnes choses : c'est qu'une bonne chose contribue à notre bonheur et que plus elle excelle plus elle y contribue. Il ne faut pas chercher plus avant, car ce serait demander pourquoi nous voulons être heureux.[4]

He will allow us to add, however, that the test of true or false pleasure is durability or consequences.

Intelligence (*esprit*) is seeing things as they are, or more especially the relations between one fact or set of facts and another. It is a matter of common sense and discursive reasoning, and its results are evident once stated. The other *justesse* (taste) is concerned with *les mesures jusqu'où on peut aller*, with a mean between excess and defect. *Justesse* of taste is exercised

---

[1] *Les Conversations*, p. 115.
[2] ib., p. 140.   [3] ib., p. 168.
[4] *De la Conversation*, pp. 100, 101.

always on particular cases, and in unique circumstances, and hence has no rules.[1] One is of ' heart ', the other of the head, but they are often mixed, yet, as often as not, do not belong in an equal degree to the same individual. The analogy with Pascals' *esprit géométrique* and *esprit de finesse* is obviously fairly close.

Méré's conception of these two qualities is developed in *Des Agréments*, and *De l'Esprit*.

An *agrément* is anything that pleases. The secret of this ' charm ', when of manner, consists generally in almost imperceptible spontaneous detail. The more unanalysable, the more fascinating they are. Of these accomplishments some make their possessors loved, others, less estimable, only make one admired ' because one succeeds in one's rôle '. Spontaneity being essential to the air with which one must carry one's accomplishment, personal inclinations must carry great weight especially in all indifferent matters. Few are as supple as Alcibiades. As for such characteristics as make one unjust, envious or malicious they must be got rid of ' because they are unbecoming '.[2]

Le bon air is much the same as *agrément* in a higher degree (Compare *galant homme* and *honnête homme*). Its charm is more evident in its causes, it includes the self-confidence of those who have been accustomed to command from childhood up. Since its causes are more obvious, it is less subject to change. Both, however, depend more than anything else on becomingness (*bienséance*), a knowledge of which comes from both the heart and the head, but not from mere good fortune. It is a very moot point, however, if one should attempt to please as many people as possible or only one's especial friends.

After a somewhat otiose discussion on *bienséance*, we come to one of the most important passages in Méré's works. He writes two pages on the importance given by Christ himself to what was done fittingly—the anointing of his feet for example ;[3] and continues—*aussi le plus grand défaut des mauvaises choses c'est qu'elles sont désagréables :*

> Enfin qui me demanderait une marque infaillible pour connaître le bien et le mal, je n'en pourrais donner ni chercher une plus forte ni moins trompeuse, que la décence et l'indécence : *car ce qui sied bien est bon, et ce qui sied mal est mauvais ; de sorte que tout ce qu'on fait approche de l'un ou de l'autre, plus on y voit de vertu ou de vice.*[4]

---

[1] *Les Conversations*, p. 40, &c. *De la Justesse.*
[2] *Des Agréments*, p. 35. [3] ib., p. 67.
[4] ib., pp. 70–3.

Here we have in black and white an identification of aesthetic and ethical value which we saw to be implicit in the approach of the later Essays to all problems of conduct. Méré arrives at it from this basis that an *honnête homme* is not only a good man but a lovable one, and the question arises ' lovable by whom ? ', ' pleasing to whom ? ' He answers with the usual circular argument : to those who judge sanely.[1] In an attempt to avoid this dilemma, he insists that the absence of qualities ' which shock ' is even more important than the presence of good qualities. The personality must be a whole, at all costs, and Méré makes a striking comparison with the proportions, nay even the symmetry, of Architecture.[2]

Though in the matter of *agréments*, the intent to please is always displeasing, and though ' in such cases the conflict of passions is unbecoming ', it is not so in those matters where honour is the motive (love and war). Here the more conflict there is, the more *merit*,[3] always on condition that *la bienséance* is preserved. It is not easy to systematize Méré's over-subtle distinctions. A new confusion is introduced after this apparent exclusion of ' honour ' from what concerns polite manners, when he says that *agréments*, previously defined in terms of their *effect*—that they please—are said to be valuable in proportion to the value of their *cause*. The rest of this discourse, however, makes it clear that the sphere of *les agréments*, and even of *honnêteté* in general, is social intercourse between men and women. It is the second *commerce* of the Essays,[4] its sphere the *salon* of Madame de Rambouillet. The lovableness which is part of *honnêteté* is the art of touching the heart especially of members of the other sex not to the extent of love with a capital L but to the extent of ' inclination ', as the phraseology went, or as he himself says *à cette sorte de galanterie qui ne paraît qu'à se communiquer agréablement*.[5] Méré is no enemy of ' the passions '.

Elles sont ordinairement si bonnes, que tant s'en faut qu'on les doive retrancher, on fait bien d'en augmenter le nombre, et d'être touché de tout ce qui plaît aux personnes raisonnables. Car si peu qu'on leur revienne d'ailleurs, c'est un moyen sûr d'en être aimé.[6]

Without them life would be boring for every one, they appear in all one says or does. Those that are bad, sadness (a mixture of anger and depression), envy, avarice, emulation, must be suppressed, but it is not enough to suppress outward signs, it

---

[1] *Des Agréments*, p. 76. [2] ib., pp. 91, 96.
[3] ib., p. 123. [4] *Essais*, III, 3, p. 53 et seq.
[5] ib., p. 145. [6] ib., p. 136.

is necessary to render the heart *comme l'ont ceux qui sont les mieux nés*.[1] So much for the 'heart', so much for taste.

The intellectual quality, *esprit*, is, says Méré, almost the same thing as 'to judge rightly of all things'. It is not the same as prudence, for imprudence is generally due to lack of making any reflexion or judgement at all. Who would deny intelligence (*esprit*) to Socrates or to Caesar (who had no time for deep reflexion), and yet both met their death by lack of prudence. Prudence, dependent on temperament, makes us look differently on the same thing at different times. If one possesses intelligence, however, the imprudent temperament is easily corrected. Nor is intelligence the same as imagination, which often imitates it: the intelligent man can recognize intelligence in others, while the brave or the beautiful are not necessarily judges of courage or beauty. Indulgence is another characteristic of intelligence. Intelligence can be acquired most of all by hard thought, but the right kind of company, natural aptitude, and good masters may all help:

A mon sens, la plus grande preuve qu'on a de l'Esprit et qu'on l'a bien fait, c'est de bien vivre et de se conduire toujours comme on doit. Cela consiste à prendre en toutes les rencontres le parti le plus honnête et celui qui paraît le plus conforme à l'état de vie où l'on se trouve.

One recalls Montaigne's *notre grand et glorieux chef-œuvre est de vivre à propos* ; but since the answer to such questions of conduct, which are particular cases, dependent on unique circumstances and on the judgement of the individual, is clearly supplied by the *justesse* of taste, it is hard to see what is the distinction Méré really draws between *esprit* and taste.

Méré sees also some distinction between intelligence and reason. Reason is a faculty of the soul common to intelligence and sensory experience (*sentiment*). Intelligence then is something more abstract and more purely intellectual than reason. Yet *esprit* is evidently not the *esprit géométrique* of Pascal, for it is in this little treatise that Méré tells the story of the journey to Poitiers made with Pascal. 'The young mathematician' found himself initiated for the first time here into the secret of 'intelligence' or *esprit de finesse*. Nothing solid emerges from *De l'esprit* in spite of Méré's many distinctions, and his sometimes acute observations. It is in his dominating notion of 'taste' that his originality and interest lie.

Of religion he speaks but rarely. In the *Cahier* we read:

[1] ib., p. 150.

Il faut être bien fou pour n'avoir pas de religion, et il faut être bien fou pour en avoir. St. Paul même l'a dit. One of the *Œuvres Posthumes* ends with the good advice to put one's hope in God —' sure means of being happy in this world and the next '. Though *honnêteté* and piety go well together, the former is in no way dependent on the latter :

Quand un [honnête] homme ne saurait pas tous les préceptes divins il y en a bien peu qu'il n'observât de lui-même.[1]

It is worth glancing at some of Méré's *dicta* on literature, not the pedantic examination of Voiture undertaken for Madame de Sablé,[2] but the passing comments, which give the most favourable idea of where the *chevalier's* best gifts lay. He notes the double use of language :

On ne parle pas seulement pour faire entendre ses pensées, on parle aussi pour exprimer ses sentiments, et ce sont deux choses bien différentes.[3]

Two things, moreover, which it is generally necessary to combine. In order to touch others, it is necessary oneself to be touched, at least as much as actors are on the stage.[4] He notes that there is a problem of communication : it is not always easy to say what one wants.[5] The real eloquence is of thought, but ' invention ', which is dependent on inspiration, is not necessary even to the highest eloquence.[6]

Literary talent is a question of personality, doing what suits one. A ' formed style ' is a personal style :[7] when he wished to write like Plutarch *à la barbe carrée*, it was not a success. To a friend who asks him : shall I imitate Balzac or Voiture, he replies : follow rather your bent and your own taste and *observe* all you can in both the natural and the social world. *Il me semble que c'est le moyen de se faire en chaque chose une idée de la perfection.*[8] Observation touches the *chevalier*, and he objects that, the love-letters of Voiture, for example, are false because a strong emotion is not so analytically expressed.[9]

---

[1] *Œuvres Posthumes*, pp. 91, 92. This passage is preceded on p. 86 by yet another statement of a certain utilitarianism. See also *Lettres*, No. 187 (a mere joke ?).

[2] See *Lettres*, No. 58. [3] *Les Conversations*, p. 224.
[4] ib., p. 226. [5] ib., p. 51.
[6] *Lettres*, No. 147.
[7] ib., No. 105. [8] ib., No. 116.
[9] *Les Conversations*, p. 173. (Of course Voiture often *intended* to be unreal.)

Finally on the necessity of the individual judgement in criticism he writes to Costar : [1]

. . . Quelques grands critiques que vous puissiez consulter vous ne sauriez vous passer de votre sentiment particulier pour juger des bons auteurs . . . Il me semble d'ailleurs que les jugements qui sentent le panégyrique ou la satire sont toujours faux et que pour connaître le vrai mérite des écrits on fait mieux en les lisant d'examiner ce qui se passe en soi-même sans prévention que d'en croire les flatteurs ni les envieux ni la foule des ignorants.

As for the rules :

Je prends bien garde que ceux qui s'attachent fort aux règles n'ont que bien peu de goût, et c'est pourtant le bon goût qui doit faire les bonnes règles pour tout ce qui regarde la bienséance.

In this letter the *chevalier* recalls the fact that Montaigne (*qui avait plus d'esprit que Scaliger et je crois encore qu'il était plus savant*) put Ronsard at the head of all French poets. Any man, however great, is subject to error, he implies.

If there were only the many echoes, direct and indirect, of the Essays to judge by, it would still be clear how much Méré owed to our author.[2] On occasions he even seems to imitate his style of composition, as in the development of an argument by examples of cases *for* and *against* in *De l'Esprit* ; what is almost a pastiche opens *De l'Eloquence et de l'Entretien*.[3] When, in addition to such evidence, it is possible to point to Méré's admiration and *the nature of* his admiration for Montaigne, it may be claimed that the *chevalier* was above all formed by the Essays, whose naturalism, whose moral aestheticism, whose fund of psychological observation nourished all that is most original in him.

To Mitton he writes :

---

[1] *Lettres*, No. 22. Pierre Costar (1603–60)—*le pédant le plus galant et le galant le plus pédant du monde*—' disait avec Montaigne : L'histoire, c'est plus mon gibier ou la poésie que j'aime d'une particulière inclination.' (*Vie de Costar*, Tallemant, IX, p. 127 : cf. p. 76.) For Costar and Montaigne, see *Les Entretiens de Voiture et Costar*, 1655, 147, 148, pp. (472), 487, 541, 556.

[2] Apart from passages quoted, see *Des Agréments*, pp. 62, 63. *De l'Esprit*, p. 22. *Œuvres Posthumes*, pp. 75, 155, 247, 248, 277. *Lettres*, No. 9, pp. 69, 70 ; No. 27, No. 79. *Cahier*, R.H.L., 1925, p. 596.

[3] *Œuvres Posthumes*, pp. 95, 96. See also perhaps *Lettres*, No. 91. Théophile and Balzac, to whom we may perhaps add Voiture, were Méré's other masters. It has been seen what Balzac and above all Théophile owed themselves to the Essays. (cf. *Bib. nat.*, n.a.f. 433, f. 298A remark of Boisdauphin, brother of Madame de Sablé.)

Vous savez dire des choses et vous devez être persuadé qu'il n'y a rien de si rare. Vous souvenez vous que Madame la Marquise de Sablé nous dit qu'elle n'en trouvait que dans Montaigne et dans Voiture et qu'elle n'estimait que cela. Je m'assure qui si vous l'eussiez souvent vue ou qu'elle eût eu de vos écrits, elle vous eût ajouté à ces deux excellents génies.[1]

Again in the *Cahier*, he says of the *Provinciales* :

Les géomètres ne manquent pas de méthode, mais souvent elle n'est pas agréable. Ce ne sont pas des *livres de choses*, comme les Essais de Montaigne : ce sont des rhapsodies.[2]

What are these 'things' common to Montaigne and Voiture ? Things 'that please' ? Things which show *l'esprit juste* ?— Madame de Sablé always said of Voiture qu'il *parlait, écrivait juste*, and even that he laughed so appropriately that one could tell what had been said.[3] Can we go further than this ? Yes, for the *chevalier* seems to identify these things with what he calls *l'esprit metaphysique*.[4] The adjective ' metaphysical ' means, as it meant still in the eighteenth century when Marivaux's comedies were called metaphysical, what we should call ' psychological '. It is the accurate and subtle psychological observation of the Essays which Méré and Madame de Sablé call *choses*. Yet another nuance is also perhaps intended. What is called in England ' metaphysical poetry ' is the poetry of conceits. The conceit differs from the *pointe* in that it is not merely a juggling with words but a juggling with ideas, which results in a novel and striking utterance. *L'imagination contrefait l'esprit*, says the *chevalier*. When the conceit is not only striking but true, when it is *psychologically* true, we have *esprit*, not imagination, and this, in prose, is the maxim, Madame de Sablé's favourite *genre*.[5] I would suggest that it is of the ' conceit ' as seen in Voiture that Méré is thinking when he says :

Il est difficile de trouver de bonnes choses en Montaigne. On croit avoir trouvé quelquechose, qu'on n'a rien trouvé.

Or more emphatically of the *obiter dicta* of the philosophers in Diogenes Laertes :

---

[1] *Lettres*, No. 174.   [2] *Cahier*, p. 68.   [3] *Lettres*, No. 58.
[4] *Cahier*, p. 65 . . . ' Je dis à Pascal que je ne connaissais que Montaigne et Voiture qui dissent ces choses là.'
[5] There remains, however, a distinction, which Méré himself notes, between *choses* and maxims. These 'things' arise directly from the subject of conversation, they are not couched in general terms, they *suggest* a general application which the maxim *declares* (R.H.L. 1923, art. cit.).

Montaigne eût trouvé bon tous les bons mots de ces philosophes :
il n'en a jamais dit un bon.[1]

Ungrateful man! It was to Montaigne that he, like his
brother, owed the whole orientation of his mind. Yet Plassac
wanted to bring the Essays up to date, and Méré, although he
found him full of *choses*, seems equally dissatisfied with their
expression. Poor Méré! he could hardly dream that, if posterity
has remembered his name, it is, because by perhaps introducing
the Essays to a mere mathematician, he prepared young Pascal
to become the author of the *Pensées*!

[1] *Cahier*, p. 15, 21.

CHAPTER XXIV

LA ROCHEFOUCAULD AND ST. EVREMOND

WHETHER the influence of Montaigne is visible in Voiture or not,[1] we have not yet by any means exhausted the evidence of his popularity during the Regency, the great period of the *salons* and of the *Précieuses*. There is no room to do more than mention some of its signs in the productions of the industrious Scudéry—Madeleine, of course, not her brother—who set herself the task of elaborating an agreeably romantic picture of the fashionable society of her own day. She was not without some tincture of philosophy and the *Conversations* (1680) which she extracted from *Cyrus*, *Clélie* and the rest (once their hey-day was over) and which were widely read, show again and again signs of Montaigne's influence. One of these conversations, reprinted from *Mathilde d'Aiguilar* (1667) gives us an imaginary discussion of Montaigne's merits by a group of sixteenth century Spanish characters.[2] In *Clélie* (1656) we find a discussion of the ' intelligence of beasts ', where Hésiode and Climène show a perfect understanding of the philosophical implications of the question. Animals know *ce qui leur est propre . . . sans nulle variété dans leur espèce.* While men's happiness is varied with their temperaments, so that

. . . ce qui fait le bonheur de l'un fait le malheur de l'autre, et qu'ils voient les choses si différemment qu'ils ne conviennent ni des Dieux qu'ils adorent ni des loix qu'ils suivent, ni des vices ni des vertus, ni même de leurs propres plaisirs . . . Chaque espèce d'animaux a une raison immuable qui la gouverne, s'il est permis de parler ainsi . . . car parmi nous chacun se fait une raison à sa mode . . .[3]

If human reason is something more noble, it is also the cause of all our ills—of property, of laws and of those wars which are

---

[1] See, however, Voiture : *Œuvres* (ed. Roux. 1856), p. 568, Epitre à M. le Prince : Tout cet appareil de Mourants, &c. (and *Essais*, I, 20, p. 120).

[2] *Conversations sur de divers sujets*, 1680, 2 vols., pp. 787 et seq.

[3] *Clélie*, ed. 1660, Vol. IX, pp. 959–70.

their result. Finally, in a direct transposition of the Essays, Belinthe brings the conversation back to Climène's dog. 'Who would bother to play with a dog?' *Je vous ai déjà dit reprit Climène que l'amour des bêtes est une marque de l'humanité et qu'il y a de la cruauté de leur faire du mal.* This conversation is the prototype (in some sort) of certain poems of La Fontaine and Madame Deshoulières.

Nor must we forget (seeing Mademoiselle de Scudéry through eyes of Boileau and Molière) to insist on the character of her feminism. It is she, the alleged inspirer of Philaminte, who writes :

> Je veux donc qu'on puisse dire d'une personne de mon sexe qu'elle sait cent choses dont elle ne se vante pas, qu'elle a l'esprit fort éclairé, qu'elle connaît finement les beaux ouvrages, qu'elle parle bien, qu'elle écrit juste et qu'elle sait le monde, mais je ne veux pas qu'on puisse dire d'elle : c'est une femme savante.

And if she does not go on to say as Montaigne does that poetry is the only fitting intellectual pursuit for women, she appears his disciple, when she writes of the way to make sensible and virtuous women, and she reminds us of Mademoiselle de Gournay when she says bitterly of the lot of her sex :

> En quelle condition pouvons-nous trouver la liberté ? Quand nous naissons nous ne sommes pas seulement esclaves de nos parents, nous le sommes de la coutume et de la bienséance. Nous n'avons pas même la liberté de choisir nos maîtres, puisqu'on nous marie bien souvent contre notre inclination. De sorte que de la manière dont le monde est établi, nous naissons avec des passions qu'il nous faut toutes enchaîner, car il ne nous est pas permis de rien aimer ni de rien haïr. L'ambition nous est inutile et l'obéissance seule est notre partage.[1]

From Mademoiselle de Scudéry we must pass on to the Marquise de Sablé (1599–1678) who has been already mentioned, and to the group of writers who frequented her drawing-room. She herself reflects the influence of the Essays now and again, not so much in the Maxims published soon after her death, as in her letters and papers contained in the Portefeuille Vallant and elsewhere.[2] The Maxims of the abbé d'Ailly, another *habitué* of her *salon*, and those of A. Rousseau show no signs of the reading of the Essays. Of the crop of maxim-writers who follow La Rouchefoucauld only one seems to display this

---

[1] C. Aragonnès : *Mademoiselle de Scudéry*, p. 101.
[2] See *Maximes de Madame de Sablé*, 1678, on necessity and benefits of doubt, XV, LVIII. See echoes of Montaigne in writings printed by N. Ivanoff (*La Marquise de Sablé et son Salon*, 1927) : On friendship, p. 146 ; on education, pp. 150–3 and on family affection, p. 49.

influence. The collection I have in mind [1] has indeed been attributed to Méré, but the authorship is doubtful. It certainly is reminiscent often enough of his views and is much the most original of these books after the masterpiece of La Rochefoucauld [1613–80] to whom we must now turn.

One knows how Madame de St. Maur summed up the general opinion of her contemporaries, when she said that the Duke *fait à l'homme une âme trop laide.* The preface to the first edition [2] (1664) which defends the author invokes not only the backing of the Church fathers for the corruption of man, but also that of Montaigne.

Montaigne que j'ai quelque scrupule de vous citer après les Pères de l'Eglise, dit assez heureusement sur ce même sujet : 'que son âme a deux visages différents'. Si j'osais enchérir sur une métaphore si hardie, je dirais que l'âme de l'homme corrompu est faite comme ces médailles qui réprésentent la figure d'un saint et celle d'un démon dans une seule face et par les mêmes traits . . .
> Guarda, garzon superbo
> Che, nel dishumarti,
>   Non divenghi una fiera anzi ch'un dio . . .
Je vous avoue que je n'ai rien lu de notre temps qui m'ait donné plus de mépris pour l'homme et plus de honte de ma propre vanité

Another friend of Madame de Sablé writes to her :

Quiconque saura bien cet écrit n'a plus besoin de lire Sénèque, ni Epictète, ni Montaigne, ni Charron, ni tout ce qu'on a ramassé depuis peu, de la morale des sceptiques et des épicuriens. On apprend véritablement à se connaître dans ces livres, mais c'est pour en devenir plus superbe et plus amateur de soi-même.

What influence did the Essays have on La Rochefoucauld ? A dozen or so of the maxims are certainly derived from Montaigne,[3] and many others present close agreement of thought,

---

[1] *Maximes, Sentences et Réflexions Morales,* 1687. Note No. 334 : ' Peu de gens sont exempts de dire des fadaises, mais le malheur est qu'on les veut dire agréablement.' (*Essais,* III, 1, p. 6) and 116, 124. Also maxims of interest No. 505, 507, 531.

[2] By Henri de la Chapelle Bessé. See Grubbs, R.H.L., 1933.

[3] The debt is clearest for the family of reflexions on death : No. 21 (the constancy which is a fear to look on death) and *Essais,* III, 4, p. 65 (cf. 23 and 26) ; and especially 504, the last and one of the longest with *Essais,* III, 4, pp. 65, 66. On old age, 112 with *Essais,* III, 2, p. 43. On fortune, 323 and 470 with *Essais,* I, 47, p. 365 ; III, 8, p. 200. On the folly of wisdom, 592 and *Essais,* II, 12, p. 219 ; 92, 528, 588 (the mad Athenian) and *Essais,* II, 12, p. 224 (?). On stubbornness and stupidity, 265 and *Essais,* III, 8, p. 206 ; III, 13, p. 394. See also 182 (mixture of vices and virtues), 48 (félicité dans le goût), 549 and 571 ; and on diversion perhaps *Lettres* (*Grands Ecrivains*), p. 192.

but unless some attempt is made to interpret the book as a whole these reminiscences are not in themselves of importance. Granted that the Essays helped to make him the keen observer of human psychology which he was, did Montaigne with his refrain of ' vanity, all is vanity ' really have any great part in tinging the gloomy spectacles through which La Rochefoucauld saw the world, or was that not the result of his own thwarted ambitions, of that curious hesitation, analysed by Retz ?

In the two quotations above, the Maxims are given an almost religious intention, the book is treated as a ' critique of *self-satisfaction* '. Does this critique imply that there is no goodness in man, that there is nothing he can do for himself but wait for ' redemption ' by the grace of God ? There is among the letters of the *chevalier* de Méré a record of a conversation with La Rochefoucauld.[1] The duke complains that because he has shown in their true light the defects of heart and head from which most people suffer, every one thinks he has himself all these defects criticized, and make him a monster of corruption. Yes, you have had the same fortune as Epicurus, says Méré, whose life even has been attacked because he made the self-evident observation that happiness depends on pleasure and unhappiness on pain. La Rochefoucauld's reply is interesting : the terms virtue and vice in their conventional sense, according to which most pleasant things are wicked, most unpleasant things virtuous, do, of course, make the Epicurean criterion sound absurd, but, at any rate, even in the conventional sense well-regulated vice is better than ill-understood virtue.

Aussi n'usé-je de ces mots, me dit-il, que pour m'accommoder au langage de certaines gens qui donnent souvent le nom de vice à la vertu, et celui de vertu au vice.

Let us attempt to interpret La Rochefoucauld in the light of this crucial remark.[2] Let us take it that when he proves *la fausseté des vertus*, he means the conventional idea of virtue.

---

[1] *Lettres*, No. 20.

[2] H. A. Grubbs in the article quoted (R.H.L., 1933) reproduces a letter of La Rochefoucauld's to the Pére Esprit, brother of Jacques Esprit, his friend and—some have supposed—collaborator. Here the Christian, nay even Jansenist, interpretation of the book is to the fore : the virtue of all who are not touched by grace is not real virtue, for an element of vice enters into the magnanimity of Alexander and the clemency of Augustus. An element of apology—apology to a priest—enters into this, and the letter coincides almost to a word with the assertion that men prefer to label certain acts Virtuous ' rather than anatomise the secrets of the heart '.

Les faux honnêtes gens sont ceux qui déguisent leurs défauts aux autres et à eux-mêmes : les vrais honnêtes gens sont ceux qui les connaissent parfaitement et les confessent.[1]

Hence introspection is the first of all duties for La Rochefoucauld as for Montaigne, and they agree further as to the extreme difficulty of self-knowledge. *Il est plus aisé de connaître l'homme en général que de connaître un homme en particulier* : but even this general knowledge is difficult enough : man is *le sujet du monde le plus changeant* [2] for both of them, his good and bad qualities inextricably mixed.[3] For La Rochefoucauld *l'amour propre* is perhaps the greatest single impediment to self-knowledge, yet it is not fair, however, to say, as Gide does, that

le jour où La Rochefoucauld s'avisa de ramener et réduire aux incitations de l'amour propre les mouvements de son coeur, je doute s'il fit tant preuve d'une perspicacité singulière, ou plutôt s'il n'arrêta pas l'effort d'une plus pertinente investigation.[4]

Such indeed is the burden and refrain of the greater number of the maxims perhaps, but the book cannot be reduced to a series of variations on this theme. The author himself seems to have been conscious that the Maxims were originally over-weighted in this direction, for the majority of the maxims suppressed deal with *l'amour propre*, and among them the most important of all.[5] Even the *ambivalence des sentiments*, so dear to Gide himself, finds its place in the maxims : each passion engenders its opposite (No. 11), each humour has its agreeable and disagreeable side like most buildings (292), ' the imagination cannot invent so many diverse contradictions as there are natur-

---

[1] No. 202.

[2] No. 65, 135. *De l'Amour et de la Vie* : ' Nous nous accoutumons à tout ce qui est à nous, les mêmes biens ne conservent pas leur même prix et ils ne touchent pas également notre goût ; nous changeons imperceptiblement sans remarquer notre changement : ce que nous avons obtenu devient une partie de nous-mêmes '.

[3] No. 182 : ' Les vices entrent dans la composition des vertus, comme les poisons entrent dans la composition des remèdes. La prudence les assemble et les tempère, et s'en sert utilement contre les maux de la vie ' (cf. *Essais*, III, 1, p. 7).

[4] *Morceaux Choisis*, p. 102 (N.R.F. juillet 1910). It has been asserted that the inspiration of this side of the Maxims comes from *The Mystery of Self-Deceiving*, by Daniel Dykes (translated into French 1634). It is possible that La Rochefoucauld had read this book, but M. Jovy has not done more than make some vague *rapprochements* (*Deux Inspirateurs peu connus de La Rochefoucauld* . . . 1910).

[5] No. 563.

ally in the heart of every man ' (478), *on se console souvent d'être malheureux en effet par un certain plaisir à le paraître.*

If *amour propre* is always present among the motives of any ' virtuous ' action, and accompanies even humility (' Humility is the proof of Christian virtues ' : but there is no such humility [1]), there are other lines of criticism which play almost as large a part in the maxims. Responsibility is generally exaggerated by the insufficient weight given to circumstances, to ' fortune '.[2] Even more important than fortune (that is external circumstances) are the inner circumstances equally uncontrollable, whether they are fixed and unalterable, temperament and character, or changing and equally uncontrollable, the passions.[3] This criticism is not made from any one point of view. It is temperament or other ethically irrelevant facts which make the courage of men and the chastity of women (220) : elsewhere La Rochefoucauld distinguishes between qualities such as goodness or courage, which should depend on nature, that is temperament, and those, such as prudence which are acquired and are dependent on reason (365). A further wavering between some kind of utilitarianism (results, success) and some kind of harmony of personality as the characteristics of real virtue may be seen, where La Rochefoucauld asserts that the real and rare courage is that which fulfils its purpose and wins the day, not that which saves the single combatant's ' honour ' ;[4] and where he says *il ne peut avoir de règle dans l'esprit ni dans le cœur des femmes sans que le tempérament soit d'accord.*[5] What is wisdom itself but ' folly proportioned to one's age and fortune '. Not conflict but harmony is needed : *Le sage trouve mieux son compte à ne point s'engager que de vaincre* (549).

The ideal of some balance of the individual personality does seem to raise its head in the negative wastes of the Maxims. For the more positive utterances of La Rochefoucauld it is

[1] No. 358 and 254, summed up in the variant : ' C'est l'orgueil qui joue tous les personnages que l'on prend pour l'humilité.' Would such a Christian as Pascal have approved La Rochefoucauld on repentance any more than he approved Montaigne (' On doit se consoler de ses fautes, quand on a la force de les avouer ', 651). The ' Jansenism ' of La Rochefoucauld appears to me a fable.

[2] ' Comment peut on répondre si hardiment de soi-même, puis qu'il faut auparavant répondre de sa fortune ' (574). See also 435, 344, 345, 380, and 470, 323.

[3] This is the distinction made, for example, in 252 : ' Il est aussi ordinaire de voir changer les *goûts* qu'il est extraordinaire de voir changer les *inclinations*.'

[4] cf. No. 219 with a letter to J. Esprit (ed. Garnier, p. 108).

[5] cf. Montaigne on Chastity.

necessary to turn to the Reflexions, first published in the eighteenth century. Here we have something really constructive about the art of living.

Il y a un air qui convient à la figure et aux talents de chaque personne . . . Il faut essayer de connaître ce qui nous est naturel, n'en point sortir, et le perfectionner autant qu'il nous est possible.[1]

Little children have delightful manners, but they spoil them as they grow up by imitating others, and there is always something false in imitation.[2] *Chacun veut être un autre et n'être plus ce qu'il est.* So La Rochefoucauld reflects in *De l'Air et des Manières.* But just because this air, these manners are part of *honnêteté* and *honnêteté* is in process of becoming a conception which includes the whole of life, these reflexions have a moral significance too. From imitation of manner he passes in *Des Exemples* to criticize imitation as a guide to moral choice, the jurisprudence formed by the actions of famous men.

Where qualities are acquired, these also must be in proportion to and combine with our natural ones. But La Rochefoucauld goes further, he rejects the prudent counsel of Montaigne (and Méré) not to mix or mingle the man and his office, he is dominated by the conception of the artistic wholeness of the individual ; the position of marshal or of lieutenant-general have a certain dignity appropriate to them and it is necessary to combine them and mix them with one's natural air so that they appear inseparable.

Ce qui fait qu'on déplaît souvent, c'est que personne ne sait accorder son air et ses manières avec sa figure, *ni ses tons et ses paroles avec ses pensées et ses sentiments,* on trouble l'harmonie par quelquechose de faux et d'étranger : on s'oublie soi-même et on s'en éloigne insensiblement : tout le monde presque tombe dans ce défaut ; personne n'a l'oreille assez juste pour entendre parfaitement cette sorte de cadence.

Appropriateness has its beauty even when involuntary : as of Turenne's death he asks :

La fortune ne s'est-elle pas servie des circonstances de la mort de César pour la rendre plus convenable à soi ? [3]

The musical metaphor comes in again in *De la Société,* where La Rochefoucauld shows, more than anywhere else perhaps, his

---

[1] III, *De l'Air et des Manières* (ed. Grands Ecrivains).
[2] One cannot but think of the Essays : ' il n'est rien si gentil que les petits enfants en France ' (cf. I, 26, p. 211).
[3] *Réflexions Diverses,* No. 14 (cf. *Essais,* II, 11, p. 128).

indulgence, his delicacy and his observation. There is room for
infinite variety of minds in social intercourse,

on peut prendre des routes diverses, n'avoir pas les mêmes vues ni
les mêmes talents, pourvu qu'on s'aide au plaisir de la société et qu'on
y observe les différentes voix que les divers instruments doivent
observer dans la musique.

All La Rochefoucauld finds itself summed up, though, in the
reflexion *Du Faux* with which we may conclude :

Ce qui fait cette fausseté si universelle, c'est que nos qualités sont
incertaines et confuses, et que nos vues le sont aussi. On ne voit point
les choses précisément comme elles sont : on les estime plus ou moins
qu'elles ne valent, et on ne les fait point rapporter à nous en la manière
qui leur convient, et qui convient à notre état at à nos qualités. Ce
mécompte met un nombre infini de faussetés dans le goût et dans
l'esprit ; notre amour propre est flatté de tout ce qui se présente à
nous sous les apparences du bien : mais comme il y a plusieurs sortes
de bien qui touchent notre vanité ou notre tempérament, on les suit
souvent par coutume, ou par commodité : on les suit parce les autres les
suivent, sans considérer qu'un même sentiment ne doit pas être également embrassé par toute sorte de personne, et qu'on s'y doit attacher
plus ou moins fortement *selon qu'il convient plus ou moins à ceux qui
le suivent* . . . Il faut discerner ce qui est bon en général et ce qui
nous est propre, et suivre alors avec raison la pente naturelle qui nous
porte vers les choses qui nous plaisent. Si les hommes ne voulaient
exceller que par leurs propres talents, et en suivant leurs devoirs, il n'y
aurait rien de faux dans leur goût et dans leur conduite . . . il y aurait
de la proportion dans leurs vues et dans leurs sentiments, leur goût
serait vrai, il viendrait d'eux et non pas des autres, et ils le suivraient
par choix et non pas par coutume ou par hasard . . . Un magistrat
est faux quand il se pique d'être brave, bien qu'il puisse être hardi dans
de certaines rencontres : il doit paraître ferme et assuré dans une sédition
qu'il a droit d'apaiser sans craindre d'être faux, et il serait faux et
ridicule de se battre en duel.[1]

The man who writes these lines sees humanity under the same
light as the author of the Essays, and his leading idea on value
is the distinction between good in general, (if such a thing exist)
and good for the individual, as was Montaigne's also.

To treat La Rochefoucauld as a ' Jansenist ' is simply to
confuse that masterpiece, the Maxims, with that tiresome copy,
La Fausseté des Vertus Humaines (1678) by Jacques Esprit,
which will find its place among later attacks on Montaigne.

Even more than the maxim the literary portrait fascinated

[1] ib., No. 13, p. 312 et seq.

the *salons* round the year 1660.[1]   Here is a *genre* which might
be expected to revive interest in the great self-portraitist.   The
vogue of the portrait arose through the key-portraits in Mademoiselle de Scudéry's novels, *Clélie* and *Le Grand Cyrus*, but
more illustrious ancestors, Plutarch and Montaigne, are claimed
by the preface of the *Galerie des Peintures* (1663).   La Rochefoucauld's own self-portrait shows traces of the Essays,[2] but one
would hardly expect the real complexity of human psychology,
as seen by Montaigne, to emerge in the superficially clever description which makes up most of the *Galerie des Peintures*.   Even
a masterpiece such as Bussy-Rabutin's portrait of Turenne,
written though it was by a keen admirer of the Essays, would
have been written just the same had the Essays never existed.[3]
We possess, however, a ' portrait,' of Montaigne, published in 1661,
and composed out of various passages of the Essays.[4]   The
intrinsic interest of this pastiche is small.   Montaigne is allowed
to speak for himself, except in two places which may be quoted
since, less directly derived from the Essays, they throw some light
on the author's conception of Montaigne's character :

Pour ce qui est de l'opinion d'autrui, bien que j'aie quelque peine
d'avouer ici la vérité, je veux néanmoins demeurer d'accord que je ne
connais personne digne d'une parfaite estime : possible est-ce parce que
je vois peu de personnes de condition qui ne soit d'épée, profession qui
ne se propose que la vaillance . . .
La philosophie où je m'attache le plus est celle qui apprend à
s'humilier.

The interest of this rather unattractive portrait of Montaigne
lies in the fact that there is in the Bibliothèque Nationale a
copy of it, detached from the volume in which it appeared and
bound separately, which bears a manuscript title :

Portrait/d'un Inconnu/(l'Illustre Montaigne)/suposé fait par lui-même.
/Imprimé en 1661.

---

[1] On La Bruyère, see below, p. 421.

[2] See La Rochefoucauld (ed. Grands Ecrivains) for *rapprochements*.

[3] Bussy Rabutin [1618–93], *Mémoires* (1693), p. 344, &c.   Bussy, like
Patin, adorned his library at the château de Bussy with the portraits
of his favourite authors : those remaining in 1805 were three : Pibrac
in whose quatrains, according to the inscription, ' toute la morale chrétienne
et civile est renfermée ' : Rabelais, author of ' cette folle et fine satire
contre son siècle, qui eut un cours merveilleux, et qui en aura toujours ' :
and lastly ' Michel de Montaigne, gentil'homme gascon, qui, dans un livre
intitulé ses Essais, a mis tout le bon sens du monde ' (A. L. Millin, *Voyage
dans le Midi*, 1807).

[4] *Recueil de pièces en prose* . . . Paris, Charles de Geret (?) 1661,
IV, pp. 326–36.

Des anecdotes m.s. de Lancelot de l'académie des belles lettres, le disent de la *fameuse Ninon*, admiratrice de Montaigne, ou de Saintévremond, qui *le fit* à Ninon sa bonne amie : [1]

M. Magne also attributes it to Ninon.[2]

That Ninon [1623–1705] must be classed among the disciples of Montaigne, is common knowledge. Tallemant says of her education as a free-thinker by Charleval, d'Elbène and Miossens :

Ils lui ont fait prendre un certain air de dire et de trancher les choses en philosophe : elle ne lit que Montaigne et décide de tout à sa fantaisie.[3]

Unfortunately none of Ninon's published letters, with one possible exception,[4] not even those delightful exchanges with her old friend, St. Evremond, nor her satire, *La Coquette Vengée*, offer any traces of the influence of Montaigne. The interest of this *Portrait d'un Inconnu*, if it is really hers, is all the greater, as it corroborates the accounts of her admiration for the Essays, and shows a close acquaintance with them. M. Magne quotes her, however, as affirming the complete independence of religion and ethics :

On est à plaindre quand a besoin de la religion pour se conduire dans le monde, car c'est une marque évidente que l'on a l'esprit bien borné ou le cœur bien corrompu.[5]

Her attitude towards religion was one of independence if not of hostility—a mutual hostility, given the ideas of the Church on sex and on women in general—but, if, as M. Magne has shown, she was reconciled to Catholicism at the end of her life, the importance once attributed to her *milieu* at the close of the century as a centre of free thought, when fashionable piety was at its height under the auspices of the King and Madame de Maintenon, has obviously been exaggerated. If she left a thousand francs to buy books to a little boy of twelve, called Arouet, the son of her lawyer, it is obvious enough that she had no inkling of the future, and she might never have made the legacy had she known. It is Ninon's life, which is important. Had you asked any of the men named in the last two chapters whether she was *une honnête femme* in the sense they gave to the word

---

[1] Bib. Nat. Res. Ln²⁷ 32296.

[2] E. Magne : *Ninon de Lanclos*, 1925, p. 343.

[3] Tallemant : *Historiettes* (ed. Monmerqué), VI, p. 6.

[4] E. Colombey : *Correspondence Authentique de Ninon de l'Enclos*, 1885, p. 141. See Note of editor which does not seem convincing.

[5] Magne : op. cit., p. 105.

honnêteté, their answer in spite of her way of life and her scepticism, would have been a definite yes.[1]

St. Evremond [1613–1703] himself will complete our picture of the influence of the Essays on *le monde et la cour*. Though he lives on into the eighteenth century, an exile in England, his active life comes to an end, like so much else, as a result of the downfall of Fouquet in 1661. St. Evremond belongs to the Regency of Anne of Austria and the period of the Fronde, but by his literary activity, much of which bears the mark of the Essays, he almost bridges the period of fifty-four years when Montaigne's book no longer appeared in the press, and when other signs show us that his popularity was on the wane. St. Evremond has another claim on our attention. In him we see combined the influence of those two humanists, Montaigne and Gassendi.[2] He is fittingly treated here before Pascal, a younger man who so long predeceased him, and fittingly contrasted with him, the real disciple of Montaigne set over against one who reacted as much against the Essays as he was drawn to them, and whose genius transformed what he borrowed and put it to his own uses.

Speaking of his favourite French authors, St. Evremond writes as follows to the Maréchal de Créqui :

Les Essais de Montaigne, les Poésies de Malherbe, les Tragédies de Corneille et les Œuvres de Voiture se sont établis comme un droit de me plaire toute ma vie.[3]

---

[1] Note that, according to Tallemant (VI, p. 3), Ninon had a son by the *chevalier* de Méré. Magne thinks Tallemant as a neighbour is probably well informed. Note a letter of Méré to Ninon, and see his *Cahier*, p. 69.

[2] Notice St. Evremond on his relations with Gassendi (I, pp. 164, 165). He had just realized that all the admittedly great philosophers of the past disagree : ' Au milieu de ces méditations, qui me désabusaient insensiblement, j'eus la curiosité de voir Gassendi, le plus éclairé des philosophes, et le moins présomptueux. Après de longs entretiens, où il me fit voir tout ce que peut inspirer la Raison, il se plaignit que la nature eût donné tant d'étendue à la curiosité, et des bornes si étroites à la connaissance . . .' &c. St. Evremond concluded the uselessness of philosophy. He was also influenced by Bernier.

[3] *Œuvres* (ed. Desmaizeaux, Amsterdam, 1739), III, p. 103. See also : *Lettre au Comte d'Olonne* (III, 159, 160) : ' Montaigne vous fera mieux connaître l'homme qu'aucun autre, mais c'est l'homme avec toutes les faiblesses : connaissance utile dans la bonne fortune, pour la modération, triste et affligeante dans la mauvaise.' *L'Amitié sans Amitié* (III, 137) ; *Jugement sur César et Alexandre* (II, 120) ; *Sur Epicure* (IV, 395, 396) : *Jugement sur Sénèque, Plutarque, et Pétrone* (II, 152, 153, 159 : the comparison of Seneca and Plutarch is chiefly derived from Essays, see II, 10, pp. 112–15 ; II, 32 (end)).

Montaigne, he adds, has not the same appeal to all ages as these other authors, but this is indeed due in some sort to his profundity :

> Comme il nous explique particulièrement l'Homme, les jeunes et les vieux aiment à se trouver en lui par la ressemblance des sentiments. L'espace qui éloigne ces deux âges, nous éloigne de la nature pour nous donner aux professions ; et alors nous trouvons dans Montaigne moins de choses qui nous conviennent . . . Montaigne revient à nous quand la nature nous y ramène, et qu'un âge avancé, où l'on sent véritablement ce qu'on est, rappelle le Prince, comme ses sujets, de l'attachement au personnage à un intérêt plus proche et plus sensible de la personne.

St. Evremond goes on to defend Montaigne's self-portrait and to show indirectly the pleasure, not to say profit, which can be derived from it.

> Je n'écris point ceci par un esprit de vanité qui porte les hommes à donner au Public leurs fantaisies. Je me sens en ce que je dis, et me connais mieux par l'expression du sentiment que je forme de moi-même, que je ne ferais par des pensées secrètes et des réflexions intérieures. L'idée qu'on a de soi par la simple attention à se considérer au dedans, est toujours un peu confuse : l'image qui s'en exprime dehors est beaucoup plus nette, et fait juger de nous plus sainement quand elle repasse à l'examen de l'esprit après s'être présentée à nos yeux.

Besides, such self-expression is the surest way of undeceiving ourselves of our own vanity. St. Evremond then understands perfectly what is truly the centre of the Essays, but he does not recognize any more than many other writers we have dealt with, that to *be* known for what one is, is also one of the conditions of personality.

This letter to the Maréchal de Créqui is as good an example as one can find of the influence of Montaigne. St. Evremond is old now. Like Montaigne,

> aujourd'hui mon esprit se ramène au corps, et s'y unit davantage. A la vérité ce n'est point par le plaisir d'une douce liaison : c'est par la nécessité du secours et de l'appui mutuel qu'ils cherchent à se donner l'un à l'autre.

Alas ! if he is wiser, and if he ' has lost all feelings of vice ', it is simply due to the infirmity of age, let there be no confusion on the point. ' Constancy ', he says, with Montaigne, *n'est qu'une longue attention à nos maux* : he makes no pretence to it when he suffers but leaves all to nature.[1]

---

[1] Compare I, 98, Lettre au Maréchal de Grammont (1664) : ' Je n'aime pas ses résistances inutiles qui, au lieu de nous garantir du mal retardent l'habitude que nous avons à faire avec lui.'

Still more characteristic of the Essays are the reflexions on ' virtue ', which St. Evremond contrasts with wisdom. Virtue is a state of conflict :

celui de la sagesse est doux et tranquille. La sagesse règne en paix sur nos mouvements, et n'a qu'à bien gouverner des sujets : au lieu que la vertu avait à combattre des ennemis.

As for himself he confesses that, strangely enough, he has never felt the conflict of reason and passion. But he pleads that he has certainly nothing to boast of in the fact, he ought rather to be sorry not to have recognized some pleasure as vicious. Accepting this apology as sincere, it is still undoubtedly St. Evremond's utilitarianism, which has saved him from such conflict. If the goodness of an action depends on its results, entirely or even *mostly*, as he would have said, then the demands of duty and expediency can rarely clash.

It would be a mistake to make such a disciple of Montaigne into a systematic philosopher, however. Who more conscious than St. Evremond of the ' contrarieties ' of man not merely of *la différence des humeurs et des génies* but of the changes in one man's own life.

J'avoue que je me contredis quelquefois. Je loue la constance à une demoiselle dont je crois être aimé : je conseille l'infidélité à celle qui aime un autre amant. Je ne suis pas de même humeur, de même sentiment, à trente ans qu'à soixante ; à soixante qu'à quatre vingt. Aucune contradiction.

People differ so much in their accounts of Epicurus because they wish to make him a statue, not a man. He knew there was a time for abstinence, a time for indulgence, a time for the pleasures of the body and for those of the mind.[1]

It is significant to find St. Evremond writing :

Notre jugement doit toujours être le même. Il nous est permis de vivre et non pas de juger selon notre humeur.

Despite this conviction, no man ever applied his observation of the essential changeableness of men more faithfully even to religion than St. Evremond. Men turn to God, as often as not, for the sake of change. *Le doute a ses heures dans le couvent : la persuasion a les siennes*, and most lives show a constant ebb and flow from Nature to religion and back again. Hence precisely St. Evremond's fideism :

[1] Compare III, p. 393.

A moins que la foi n'assujetisse notre raison, nous passons la vie à croire, et à ne croire point : à nous vouloir persuader et à ne pouvoir nous convaincre.

In the early *L'homme qui veut connaître toutes choses* (1647) St. Evremond reproduces the usual fideist attitude : lack of knowledge about not only the supernatural but even about the human soul. Its immortality is an opinion which has never been proved or disproved. Nor, he remarks elsewhere, do Descartes' Meditations seem persuasive.[1] Later in his *Réflexions sur la Religion*, St. Evremond takes a more original line. From the point of view of happiness here and now (the point of view he always prefers), it is a pity religion has not either more or less power over men.

Nous disons par docilité que *nous croyons* ce qu'on dit avec autorité qu'il faut croire : mais sans une grâce particulière, nous sommes plus inquiétés que persuadés d'une chose . . . qui ne fournit aucune sorte de démonstration à notre esprit.

The real Christian life involves a reversal not only of what seems intellectually sense, but what seems morally sense.

Le vrai dévot rompt avec la Nature, si l'on peut ainsi dire, pour se faire des plaisirs de l'abstinence des plaisirs.

The hedonist basis, however, according to St. Evremond still remains, as one sees. Philosophy only teaches us to put up with ills, religion to enjoy them. All who are not fortunate enough to possess the miraculous gift of faith are, whatever their other advantages, made wretched by uncertainty.

And yet the world laughs as much at those who forsake the world for God, as it abuses those who forsake God for the world. Both courses involve a downrightness which the ordinary man does not understand ; he does not appreciate these heights. He, St. Evremond, though an ordinary man, does admire any one who is full of conviction, but he sees that, with most Christians,

l'envie de croire tient lieu de créance : la volonté leur fait une espèce de foi par les désirs que l'entendement leur refuse par ses lumières.[2]

---

[1] *Œuvres*, III, p. 183. St. Evremond disliked Descartes thoroughly. In his old age, he writes : ' Je ne vis plus que par réflexion sur la vie, ce qui n'est pas proprement vivre ; et sans la philosophie de M. Descartes qui dit : je pense, donc je suis, je ne croirais pas proprement être. Voilà tout l'avantage que j'ai retiré de la lecture des principes de ce grand homme qu'on estime tant en France, mais qui, ma foi, était un peu bien fou.'

[2] *Œuvres*, IV, p. 301. *Entretien de Deux Dames avec une Religieuse : Sur le quiétisme* (IV, 294–302).

St. Evremond goes on to note acutely enough that there are many persons of piety who love God without entirely believing in his existence. Emotion is there, but not intellectual conviction. To understand his attitude to religion it is necessary to bear in mind constantly thi͡ distinction. He is always insisting, but not over-insisting, on the close connexion of the psychology of love for a human and for a divine person, and he will not let us forget that fundamentally the same emotion is involved especially in the case of women.[1]

Yet this psychological analysis of devotion interests us less than the intellectual side of religion and St. Evremond's attitude towards it. There his views are summed up in the last paragraph of these *Réflexions* :

Dieu seul nous peut donner une loi sûre, ferme et véritable. Ce que nous pouvons faire de nous est de captiver l'entendement malgré la répugnance des lumières naturelles, et de nous porter avec soumission à exécuter ce qu'on nous préscrit. L'humanité mêle aisément ses erreurs en ce qui regarde la créance : elle se mécompte peu dans la pratique des vertus.[2]

On all that concerns justice and charity, Nature and Reason seem to him to be in constant agreement. Rationalism in ethics, fideism of sorts in religion, as usual.

Such a summary account does not do justice to St. Evremond, however. If his ironical comment on theology is : *On brûle un homme assez malheureux pour ne pas croire en Dieu, et cependant on demande publiquement s'il y en a un*, he is equally ironical—too ironical, thinks Busson—in that little masterpiece, the *Conversation du Maréchal d'Hocquincourt avec le Père Canaye*,[3] when he makes the Jesuit go into ecstasies over the marshal's fideism : *Point de raison, c'est la vraie religion cela*. His attitude towards the Jansenists and the Molinists, as we see it in his conversation with D'Aubigny, holds a middle course, but the most important remark in it is his dictum on Jansenism : *rien n'est durable qui ne s'accommode à la nature*. If human reason can be and ought to be overruled by revelation, the more fundamental human impulses cannot and ought not to be disregarded.

---

[1] See : *Que la Dévotion est le Dernier de Nos amours* : *Discours de la Religion à la Duchesse Mazarin.*

[2] ib., IV, p. 302. Elsewhere : ' C'est dans le cœur que se forme la première disposition à recevoir les vérités Chrétiennes.' cf. Pascal.

[3] *Œuvres*, II, p. 183 et seq. Busson points out that the Père Canaye as a Jesuit is unlikely to have held so extreme a fideist view ; yet note the remark of Amiraut (Introd., p. xxiii).

This is the key to the relation between St. Evremond's Catholicism and his hedonist ethics.

Though he was a Catholic, St. Evremond was a liberal one, not only a constant defender of toleration—*Les temples sont du droit des souverains . . mais notre cœur est un secret, où il nous est permis d'adorer leur maître*—not only one who hoped for a reunion of the Churches, but who had given some thought to essential conditions of such reunion, who had studied objectively the actual characteristics of religious practice and life among Protestants and Catholics, not merely their theoretical professions of faith.

Ce que nous appelons aujourd'hui LES RELIGIONS, n'est à le bien prendre, que *Différence dans la Religion*, et non pas Religion différente. Je me réjouis de croire plus sainement qu'un Huguenot : cependant, au lieu de le haïr pour la différence d'opinion, il m'est cher de ce qu'il convient de mon principe. Le moyen de convenir de tout, c'est de se communiquer toujours par quelquechose. Vous n'inspirerez jamais l'amour de la réunion, si vous n'ôtez la haine de la division auparavant. On peut se rechercher comme sociables, mais on ne revient point à ses ennemis. La Feinte, l'Hypocrisie dans la religion sont les seules choses qui doivent être odieuses : car qui croit de bonne foi, quand il croirait mal, se rend digne d'être plaint, au lieu de mériter qu'on le persécute.[1]

The tyranny of Christians in forcing people to say they believe compares unfavourably with the greatest period of political tyranny in the Ancient World.

The Catholic ideal is characterized by its emphasis on the love of God, and hence the *pleasure* of doing good works. Its danger is that this love should become too much a merely human passion, and also that we should please God simply in what pleases ourselves. The Protestant religion is overcast by the shadow of predestination.

Elle ne cherche pas à plaire, elle se contente d'obéir : et dans un Culte exact et commun, elle fait Dieu l'objet de sa régularité plutôt que de son amour.

The letter to the Maréchal de Créqui provides many other interesting but debatable remarks on the contrast of Catholic and Protestant religious life. St. Evremond's real interest, though, is seen to lie on the ethical side of religion, and it is from this point of view that he hopes to see the differences among Christians healed : *faisons tant que de bien agir ensemble, et nous ne croirions pas longtemps séparés.* Thus, by way of conclusion,

[1] ib., III, pp. 234, 235.

St. Evremond contrasts the real character, the original genius of Christianity with its present state. From superstitions have come disputes on doctrine instead of agreement in good works.

De la diversité des opinions on a vu naître celle des partis, et l'attachement des partis a produit les Persécutions et les guerres. Des millions d'hommes ont péri à contester de quelle manière on prenait au Sacrement ce qu'on demeurait d'accord d'y prendre. C'est un mal qui dure encore et qui durera toujours, jusqu'à ce que la religion repasse de la curiosité de nos esprits à la tendresse de nos cœurs : et que rebutée de la folle présomption de nos lumières, elle aille retrouver les doux mouvements de notre amour.[1]

We may pass over St. Evremond's various writings against superstition and intolerance,[2] for lack of time and space, and we have seen already, to some extent, how he conceives of the morality which would heal the divisions created by vain, metaphysical dispute.

It only remains to add that it is easy, moreover, to exaggerate the rôle of ethics in St. Evremond's estimation. Its use as a science (he says indeed) is ' to form methodically a sound conscience ', but then *les vrais honnêtes gens n'ont que faire de ses leçons : ils connaissent le bien par la seule justesse de leur goût, et s'y portent de leur propre mouvement.* Again, given some ordinary sound feelings of charity and justice,[3]

un cœur aime innocemment les objets que Dieu a rendus agréables : et ce qu'il y a d'innocent en nos âmes est ce qu'il y a de plus doux et de plus tendre.

Naturally, adaptability and diversion are two of his favourite themes. In the reply of a *honnête et habile courtisan* to the self-seeker and the rigorist he rejects at once a base self-interestedness

---

[1] *Œuvres*, III, p. 149. Compare his *Réponse au jugement de l'abbé Renaudot sur le Dictionnaire de Bayle* (V, p. 265) and his Portrait of himself (1696).

De justice et de charité	Mettant en Dieu sa confiance,
Beaucoup plus que de pénitence,	Espérant tout de sa bonté,
Il composa sa piété,	Il trouve son repos et sa félicité.

[2] See not only such things as the satirical story : *Le Prophète Irlandais* [*Œuvres*, II, 379] and the poem *Sur la Vanité des Disputes de Religion* (III, 150) but also in the *Réflexions sur les divers génies du peuple romain*, St. Evremond's hatred of ' admiration founded on legend or established by the error of faulty judgement '. (For reminiscences of the Essays in these Reflexions see *Œuvres*, II, pp. 30, 60, 61.)

[3] A charitable justice, though : ' toute seule, sans aucun mélange de bon naturel, de douceur, d'humanité, elle est plus sauvage que n'étaient les hommes qu'elle a assemblés : et on peut dire qu'elle bannit tout l'agrément de la société qu'elle a établie '.

which defeats its own ends, and a virtue which is too rigid to be *useful*, and comments, like Montaigne, on the character of Cato, a great and virtuous man, who because he would not adapt himself to times and circumstances, did more harm than good.[1] Here too he insists that reason, which may teach a moderation of desires and an acceptance of fortune, is not enough to command admiration to-day. Something more is wanted—something more which constitutes *honnêteté*, in fact,—tolerance and taste.[2]

On diversion the following passage may be worth quoting :

Pour vivre heureux il faut faire peu de réflexions sur la vie, mais sortir souvent hors de soi, et, parmi les plaisirs que fournissent les choses étrangères, se dérober la connaissance de ses propres maux. Les divertissements ont tiré leur nom de la diversion qu'ils font faire des objets fâcheux et tristes, sur les choses plaisantes et agréables : ce qui montre assez qu'il est difficile de venir à bout de la dureté de notre condition, par aucune force d'esprit : mais que, par adresse, on peut ingénieusement s'en détourner.[3]

And again, advising the Comte d'Olonne what books to read :

Attachez vous à ceux qui font leur effet sur votre humeur par leur agrément plutôt qu'à ceux qui prétendent fortifier votre esprit par leurs raisons. Les derniers combattent le mal ; les premiers le font oublier, et à une douleur oubliée, il n'est pas difficile de faire succéder le sentiment de la joie.

So, with Montaigne, he disapproves of those who ' trouble the joy of their prime by the meditation of a carefully arranged death '. A little pain generally upsets all their fine resolutions. He recalls Montaigne's own experience :

Montaigne, étant jeune encore, a cru qu'il fallait penser éternellement à la mort, pour s'y preparer : approchant de la vieillesse, *il chante*, dit il, *la palinodie*, voulant qu'on se laisse conduire doucement à la nature, qui nous apprendra assez à mourir.[4]

Space forbids us to follow up many parallels between St. Evremond and Montaigne, and this summary treatment may be excused, since he is an author better known than most of those dealt with in this study. We have seen what is essential to his humanism and its resemblance with that of Montaigne, who, like

[1] ib., III, p. 69 et seq. Note how St. Evremond treats friendship from the utilitarian viewpoint in the letter which the Duchesse Mazarin maliciously called : *L'Amitié sans Amitié (Œuvres*, IV, p. 123).

[2] For a careful examination of St. Evremond from the point of view of *honnêteté*, see M. Magendie, op. cit.

[3] ib., I, p. 144 (*Des Plaisirs*).

[4] ib., IV, p. 395.

him, found his smiling philosophy in no way incompatible with his religion.

In the Méré brothers, La Rochefoucauld and St. Evremond, all students of *individual* psychology, we have seen the form which Montaigne's influence took in aristocratic society, and how, through the conception of *honnêteté*, a new ideal, with more or less of a utilitarian or hedonist foundation, but not purely ethical, makes for itself a place alongside, or in the case of St. Evremond reinterpreting, Christian Ethics. Thus *honnêteté* helps to establish the independence of religion and ethics.

CHAPTER XXV

PASCAL AND MONTAIGNE

Ainsi notre religion est folle en regardant à la cause effective, et sage en regardant à la sagesse qui y prépare.

PASCAL

WE have mentioned Méré's account of Pascal's journey to Poitiers with the Duc de Roannez and Mitton, a journey which marks the introduction of Pascal to what he was to call (with Méré) the *esprit de finesse*, and also (as I believe) his introduction to Montaigne. Méré we now know, what of Damien Mitton [*c.* 1618–90] ? If M. Brunschwicg is correct in seeing in Pascal the unnamed friend who tells Méré that he puts Mitton before Plato and Descartes, he is obviously worth some attention.[1] We have met him already in these pages as a correspondent of both the Mérés, besought by Plassac to undertake a modernization of the Essays, as being at once a devotee of Montaigne and something of a theorist on style. According to Méré, he is one of those who, like Montaigne, know how to say ' things '. A letter of his to the *chevalier* de Méré is nothing more or less than an essay in which Montaigne's manner of composition is closely imitated. The subject-matter is rather small-beer, the different emphasis of sense given by referring, for example, to Charles the Fifth as ' the Great Emperor ' or as simple ' Charles '.[2] His only other composition, so far as I am aware, are certain *Pensées sur l'Honnêteté*, falsely attributed to St. Evremond, and included in a volume of the latter's *Œuvres Mêlées* in 1666.[3]

There is a universal desire for happiness, impossible to

[1] *Pensées* (ed. Brunschwicg), p. 118. Méré : *Lettres* No. 112. On Damien Mitton, see the recent study of H. A. Grubbs.

[2] Méré : ib., No. 175. H. A. Grubbs has mentioned, since these lines were written, that Th. Corneille consulted Mitton when re-editing Vaugelas (op. cit., p. 40).

[3] ib., No. 174 : *Œuvres Mêlées* (ed. 1680), Tome 6, pp. 1–44. H. A. Grubbs has reproduced these *Pensées* in their entirety.

achieve with certainty unless other people are made happy too :

Car si l'on prétend songer seulement à soi, on trouve des oppositions continuelles, et quand nous ne voulons être heureux qu'à condition que les autres le soient en même temps, tous les obstacles sont levés et tout le monde nous prête la main.   C'est ce ménagement de bonheur pour nous et pour les autres que l'on doit appeler l'Honnêteté, qui n'est à la bien prendre que l'Amour-Propre bien réglé.

Mitton's definition of *honnêteté*—to which he gives an ethical sense—is, then, the conciliation of social and individual good. It is the duty of kings to re-establish reason, justice and honesty (*honnêteté*) by favouring *les honnêtes gens* and rendering the wicked unhappy.   Mitton is an optimist, but it is to his credit that he wishes to see snobbery abolished (though he believes class-distinctions to be necessary).   Such words as *hobereau gentillâtre, bourgeois, provincial, campagnard* should be done away with, ' they only keep alive hatred between men '.   Cheat and traitor form the only legitimate kind of abuse, and scorn for the poor and needy is mean.

Mitton has in him perhaps something rare in the seventeenth century :   the impulses of a social reformer.   His utilitarianism and his respect for Christianity both appear in his reflexion that

la religion et la piété rendent heureux, et c'est la base la plus solide et la plus sûre de l'honnêteté.

Yet *honnêteté* is not simply morality, Mitton, in his turn, repeats, unless we include in the conception the necessity of pleasing others.   At the Court men only study to please in order to succeed, in the provinces they work and do not study to please at all—both wrongly.   Success at Court—and Mr. Grubbs has shown how the respect of Mitton for the Court is connected with his bourgeois extraction—is generally learnt by experience ; it ought to be learnt by its causes.   *Il faudrait pour cela connaître la nature des choses qui doivent plaire, et connaître le cœur des hommes.*   The characteristic form of this art of pleasing, chosen as an example by Mitton and all these writers on manners, is the art of conversation.   Its fundamental principle is adaptation to one's company ; its chief school the society of women. When we realize this, we can see how Pascal, in naming Montaigne ' *l'incomparable auteur de L'Art de Conférer* ', refers not only to what he himself chiefly (or even mainly) prizes in the Essays. He speaks for Mitton, Méré, St. Evremond and a host of others. The passage of Mitton quoted on *l'honnêteté* has however a far greater importance in connexion with Pascal's note :

le moi est haïssable : vous, Miton, le couvrez, vous ne l'ôtez pas pour cela ; vous êtes donc toujours haïssable.[1]

Pascal makes his friend object :

Point, car en agissant, comme nous faisons, obligeamment pour tout le monde on n'a plus sujet de nous haïr.

I hate this *moi*, replies Pascal, not only because of the conflict of interests, which can be avoided, but because each *moi* injustly makes itself the centre of everything—*car chaque moi est ennemi et voudroit être le tyran de tous les autres.* Indeed, Mitton's definition of *l'honnêteté* explains the rejoinder which we find in the *Pensées.* My supposition, he says in effect, is that if people realize that their own intelligent self-interest is bound up with the interest of others—that they cannot be happy *qu'à condition que les autres le soient en même temps*—then the ' I ' is no longer hateful. For Pascal the *injustice* of egoism, be it never so enlightened, will still subsist. The centre of his thought is total self-renunciation for the sake (paradoxically) of personal salvation not for the sake of social service, and Mitton's answer is, of course, unacceptable to him, but we see at least that Mitton's ' disguising the *moi* ' was something more than a maxim of polite society—don't speak of yourself—such as most of Pascal's commentators have supposed on the authority of a passage of the *Logique de Port Royal.*

This fundamental difference of view, which represents (on the part of Pascal) the memory of an argument or a repeated exchange of views, finds its analogy just a century later in the quarrel of Rousseau and Diderot—its crucial subject the article *Économie Politique.*[2] There again we have the pessimism of the more religious mind, that of Rousseau, and the (relative) optimism of the humanist, Diderot, contrasted upon precisely this same question of the conciliation of the good of the one and the good of the many. Rousseau, like Pascal, hates *le moi qui voudrait être le tyran de toutes les autres,* but at the same time the idea of personal liberty dominates his work, as the thought of personal salvation dominates Pascal's book. Mitton, like Diderot, appears to believe in the conception of natural law,[3] which Rousseau and Pascal (in

[1] *Pensées* (ed. Brunschwicg), No. 455.
[2] See R. Hubert, *Rousseau et l'Encyclopédie.*
[3] When Pascal says elsewhere : ' Miton voit bien que la nature est corrompue, et que les hommes sont contraires à l'honnêteté : mais il ne sait pas pourquoi ils ne peuvent voler plus haut ' ; he alludes, not to Mitton's admission of original sin (the last member of the sentence excludes such an interpretation), but to the familiar humanist notion of nature perverted by custom, or, as Charron would put it, the perversion of natural law.

this both like Hobbes) reject.   The mystical geometry of the *Contrat Social*, as an attempt to solve the problem, is truly a religious, a supernatural, solution involving implicitly an intervention of Grace just as Pascal's Christian *apologia* involves it explicitly.

The full significance of this comparison of *Le moi est haïssable* with Mitton's *Pensées sur l'Honnêteté* will only be seen after we have studied the relation of Pascal to the Essays.   Our treatment of Pascal must, however, be brief.   A detailed consideration of what the *Pensées* alone owe to Montaigne would require a book in itself ; an author so well known does not need to be quoted for illustration of his views at every turn, and it will be seen that the whole course of this study has prepared us for the present task.

Pascal's first or, at any rate, first serious reading of the Essays was, no doubt, a result of the journey to Poitiers with Roannez, Méré and Mitton in 1652.   The first account, however, of the impression Montaigne made on him is contained in Fontaine's record of the Conversation of M. de Saci and Pascal on Montaigne and Epictetus,[1]—his two favourite authors—which must have taken place in the month of January 1655.   Pascal, it will be remembered, gives a general account of the philosophy of these two authors, of whose writings M. de Saci appears to be ignorant. Montaigne sets out to see what rationalistic non-religious ethics he can discover, and thus considering man apart from all revealed doctrine, he finds him enveloped everywhere in doubt, and the *one* purpose of *all* the Essays is to establish the universality of this doubt and the contradictory nature of all received maxims. (Notice how Pascal lends a singleness of purpose, more characteristic of himself, to the volatile Montaigne).   Montaigne thus finds himself in a position to ruin, in the interests of the Church, all the arguments and the dogmatism of both heretics and atheists.[2]

---

[1] Notice that Méré (loc. cit) speaks of Pascal's admiration for Du Vair. It is likely that Du Vair's translation of the ' Manual ' and the adaptation of it which he composed under the title of *De la Philosophie Morale des Stoiques*, formed Pascal's introduction to Epictetus, the letter of consolation to his sister on the death of Etienne Pascal (17 Oct., 1651) not only derives from Du Vair, but if Marquis de Roux's date (1652) for the Poitiers journey is accepted, it is the last work containing moral reflexions which we have between that time and the record of the Conversation with M. de Saci (provided the attribution to Pascal of the *Discours sur les Passions de l'Amour* is rejected).

.[2] Pascal evidently believes in the good faith of Montaigne, but he seems to consider that it is *incidently* in his conviction of universal doubt, already acquired, that Montaigne discovers a method of defeating the arguments of the heretics and atheists.   Is this not perhaps something in the nature of a personal confidence as to Pascal's own train of thought during the *période mondaine* ?

He shows the uncertainty of all the sciences, including mathematics, and that reason without faith is so little reasonable that it is probable that the animals are as much so, or more so, than man.[1]

Saci replies : What is all this subtle argumentation worth ? As St. Augustine would say : since this man speaks, setting faith aside, so we may safely set all he says aside. And he adds : I know that St. Augustine himself escaped from his Manichaean errors by the door of Academic doubt, but he passed beyond that stage of development. Such considerations appear to me dangerous and ultimately unsatisfying.

Pascal's answer gives us the key to what drew him to Montaigne. He cannot see *without pleasure* this vengeance of reason on reason, and he would have loved Montaigne with all his heart, if, being a disciple of the Church by faith, he had founded Christian ethics on this salutary foundation, the humiliation of man. Pascal sees the idea of conformity with custom as the basis of Montaigne's morality. A conformity with laws and customs, —with what is considered virtuous—not because they have any intrinsic merit, but because the results of disregarding them are generally painful or unpleasant.

For Pascal, hedonism is the great reproach against Montaigne. In other words, he agrees with Montaigne's intellectual position, with what is purely critical and negative in the Essays, he disagrees with what is positive.[2] Pascal agrees with Montaigne intellectually as a fideist who recognizes another fideist. The fact that he does agree so far shows his conviction of Montaigne's sincerity. Yet if, as he rightly insinuates, Montaigne sets out to search for a humanist ethic, Pascal ought hardly to be surprised that Montaigne did not find a religious one. He *is* surprised, though, and a large part of the *Pensées* are precisely intended to be some such search as Montaigne's with just such an ending. So for Pascal, the hedonism of Montaigne is no ethic at all. Owing perhaps to the exaggerated place which conformity assumes in his interpretation of the Essays, it is simply an attitude of despair, of the despair which must follow universal doubt, if faith does not supervene, and if the primitive state of man

[1] Note that Pascal adds to Montaigne's sceptical arguments Descartes' hypothesis of a *deus deceptor*.

[2] ' Montaigne est incomparable pour confondre l'orgueil de ceux qui, hors la foi, se piquent d'une véritable justice ; pour désabuser ceux qui s'attachent à leurs opinions, &c. Et Montaigne est absolument pernicieux à ceux qui ont quelque pente à l'impiété et aux vices, (*Pensées*, &c., ed. cit., p. 162).

before the Fall is not known. Montaigne forgets the Garden of Eden ; Epictetus is ignorant of original sin. They see two sides of man only to be understood through the Scriptures.

Montaigne, like Mitton, is the upholder of intelligent self-interest. It has been seen how Pascal disapproved of Mitton's mitigated *moi*, and for the *moi* in excelsis, the self-portrait of Montaigne, he can only find ridicule adequate to express his indignation : *le sot projet qu'il a de se peindre.* Self-knowledge is not an exploration whose results are obscure for Pascal ; it is either superficial and false (as with Epictetus) or true, when it arrives at a recognition of the monstrous inanity of man, a gulf to be filled only by the grace of God and the love of God which it inspires. Such seems the essence of Pascal's view, but he is fair enough to observe acutely elsewhere :

Il faut se connaître soi-même : quand cela ne servirait pas à trouver le vrai, cela au moins sert à regler sa vie, et il n'y a rien de plus juste (No. 66).

Pascal is less sympathetic to Montaigne in the *Pensées* than in the *Entretien avec M. de Saci*.[1] His other faults are faithfully detailed. The list begins with his ' lascivious words '. Pascal, whose squeamishness appears clearly in his sister's account of his life, rejects Mademoiselle de Gournay's sensible remark that outspoken language is not lascivious, but that veiled allusions are. Pascal next finds our sceptic credulous : has he not spoken of eyeless men, and squaring the circle ? It hardly seems to occur to his over-serious mind that Montaigne was capable of some very subtle jokes ! He cannot accept Montaigne's views on suicide. Yet Montaigne has only named the most excusable reasons for taking this extreme course, he never says he approves of suicide.[2] The fundamental reproach is, however, revealed as follows :

on ne peut excuser ses sentiments tous paiens sur la mort ; car il faut renoncer à toute piété, si on ne veut au moins mourir chrétiennement ; or il ne pense qu'à mourir lâchement et mollement par tout son livre,

and in more general terms still : *il inspire une nonchalance du salut sans crainte et sans repentir.* Let us accept Pascal's general statement as true. We shall see later that if he had here adopted the method of the *Provinciales* [3] and quoted texts, he would have

[1] See *Pensées* (ed. Brunschwicg), No. 66.

[2] See above, p. 35.

[3] Note that not the faintest echo of the Essays can be found in the *Provinciales.*

found that those apparently illustrating his assertions are capable of defence. It will be seen, too, how much influence Pascal's remarks had on later critics ; it is therefore necessary to notice his other comments on Montaigne before attacking the general question of the relationship of the Essays to the *Pensées*.

Montaigne jumps from subject to subject—*il cherchait le bon air*.[1] Montaigne shows up the fallacy of the dilemma : either the soul goes to a better place or ceases to be. It may go to a worse.[2] And on miracles :

Montaigne en parle comme il faut dans les deux endroits. On voit en l'un combien il est prudent, et néanmoins il croit, en l'autre, et se moque des incrédules.

Montaigne contre les miracles.
Montaigne pour les miracles.[3]

Finally, there is Pascal's tribute to Montaigne's style—which sticks in the mind, like the thoughts of Epictetus and Salamon de Tultie (Pascal himself) ; [4] and his tribute to Montaigne (to which we have already referred) as ' the incomparable author of the Art of Conversation ', who shows how one must endeavour to understand not what a man says but what he means ; [5] and to the truth of Montaigne's psychology

Ce n'est pas dans Montaigne mais dans moi que je trouve tout ce que j'y vois.[6]

That remark is also, of course, the justification of Pascal's originality as it was the justification of Montaigne when he wrote *ce n'est non plus selon Platon que selon moi.*

Pascal had no need of the Essays to become a fideist. We know from Madame Périers' account of his life that Etienne Pascal founded the religious instruction of his son upon the principle that *tout ce qui est objet de la foi ne le saurait être de la raison, et beaucoup moins y être soumis.* It was to this sheet-anchor that both Blaise and his sister attributed his preservation from the *libertinage* which might be expected of a young scientist.

---

[1] loc. cit., No. 62 (cf. perhaps Malebranche, p. 415).

[2] ib., No. 220 (cf. below, p. 410).

[3] ib., No. 813, 4 (cf. below, p. 413). The Essays in question are III, 11 and I, 27.

[4] ib., No. 18 (cf. Méré's *choses* ?).

[5] ib., p. 192 (*De l'Esprit Géométrique*). For this distinction between *what seems to be said* and the *mental operations* of the speaker, between ' statement ' and ' expression ', see I. A. Richards, *Practical Criticism*, 1929, pp. 6–8.

[6] ib., No. 64.

Again, Jansen and St. Cyran, the founders of the Jansenist movement, were in reaction against the rationalism of the neo-scholastics, and it is not surprising to find Pascal, at the time of his first ' conversion ' in 1647, pursuing with an inveterate hatred the poor friar, Forton de St. Ange, who claimed to ' prove ' the doctrine of the Trinity,[1] nor to hear him express in his *Fragment d'un Traité du Vide*, his pity for the blindness of those who invoke authority in physics, and his horror for the malice of these others who use only reason in theology. He has still at this time high hopes for empirical science, he continues his own researches ; nature's secrets, he says, are being gradually discovered by experimental methods. He has only indignation for those who suppose that antiquity, the youth of the world, is wiser in knowledge of the world than we moderns are : *N'est il pas là traiter indignement la raison de l'homme et la mettre en parallèle avec l'instinct des animaux*, instinct whose main characteristic is invariability.[2]

Pascal, then, was conscious of the dangers of rationalism in religion before he made a study of the Essays. Compare, however, with the passages we have quoted, his attitude in *De l'Esprit Géométrique*, written some ten years later, and in which the influence of Montaigne is very marked. The condition of any science worthy of the name is an ability to give definitions (nominal definitions) of all terms, and proofs of all propositions, but

en poussant les recherches de plus en plus, on arrive nécessairement à des mots primitifs qu'on peut plus définir et à des principes si clairs qu'on n'en trouve plus qui le soient davantage pour servir à leur preuve. D'où il paraît que les hommes sont dans une impuissance naturelle et immuable de traiter quelque science que ce soit dans un ordre absolument accompli.[3]

Pascal's demand is impossible for mankind even in geometry, as he recognizes himself. He is moving over to a certain intellectual pyrrhonism which is absent from his earlier writings, while in the *Pensées* we find the intellectual position of Montaigne fully adopted. This is not where the originality of Pascal lies. This study of the fortunes of the Essays has shown not only how widespread fideism was in the first half of the seventeenth century but also how prevalent its emotional side, the ' critique

[1] See E. Jovy, *Pascal et St. Ange*, 1927.
[2] *Pensées et Opuscules* (ed. Brunschwicg), pp. 76, 78, 79.
[3] For the excessive nature of Pascal's demands, and critique of realism in general see a work already quoted in the connexion (p. 449) : L. Rougier, *Les Paralogismes du Rationalisme*, passim and p. 132.

of satisfaction ', the realization of the vanity of life, of all natural desires.

Yet Pascal develops all that side of the Essays with his own genius, not only because of the undoubted attraction which Montaigne had for him, but also because to do so gave him a hold on such men as Méré, Mitton and all those others whose humanism was grounded on the Essays and who admired the book. There is the religious side of Montaigne and the pagan, humanist side ; they are mixed, though possibly at bottom incompatible. Those whom Pascal wishes to convert stress the humanism of Montaigne, but the fideism with which the book has also imbued them makes clear the angle from which they should be attacked.

It is not necessary to accept as accurate the assertion of a contemporary, Bridieu, who was not only of Pascal's *milieu* but himself a Poitevin, that

M. Pascal a fait ses fragments contre huit esprits forts du Poitou qui ne croyaient pas en Dieu. Il veut les convaincre par raisons morales et naturelles.

We may suspect that, in the mind of Bridieu, Plassac and the chevalier de Méré, his brother are among them. But what little we know of the genesis of the *Pensées* also points to a similarly-minded public whom the book was intended to convert, while the internal evidence is very strong. Yet before examining that evidence, two further points must be stressed. First, that the echoes of Montaigne are so numerous in the *Pensées*, not only because the Essays have played a certain part in Pascal's intellectual development, but because he has also intentionally multiplied them, working sometimes, as we know, with his copy of the Essays at hand, and even copying page references on to his slips of paper. Montaigne's ideas and phraseology are intentionally in evidence here, just as they are perhaps intentionally absent from the *Provinciales*, where no turn of phrase, no shade of Montaignesque sentiment or idea is to be found (unless it be in a quotation from poor Le Moine's *Dévotion Aisée*). Secondly the statement that Pascal was to aim at converting his readers by *raisons morales et naturelles*, while only true in a very special sense, helps to remind us that, with its treatment of miracles and interpretation of prophesies, the fideist *apologie* of Pascal is paradoxical in a different way from the *Apologie* of Montaigne, paradoxical just because no *complete* apologia can dispense with a rationalistic method.

If paradox remain in the last analysis, it is not that Pascal has omitted to provide himself with a defence, that defence which is to be found in his ' rhetoric ', his ' Grammer of Assent ', in *L'Art de persuader*, the second section of *De l'Esprit Géométrique*. His point of departure is Méré's distinction of reason and taste, of *esprit géométrique* and *esprit de finesse* : it is also the current definition of *honnêteté* as not merely the ' art of right conduct ' but the ' art of pleasing '. It is Pascal's genius which turns this distinction into that of the ' heart ' and the ' head ', in order to point out that in what concerns a preparation for faith (which can only be given effectively by God's grace) it is more a persuading of the will than a convincing of the understanding that is needed. Since such persuasion (*l'art d'agréer*) is a personal problem, differing with the individual who is to be persuaded, this art has indeed no rules. So that whether these considerations would have found their explicit expression in the *Pensées* or not, it is true that the framework or intention of the first part of the book—the *Préparation à la Recherche* and the *Recherche* of the plan as stated by Filleau de la Chaise et Etienne Périer—is based on Méré no less than on Montaigne : and whatever the general character Pascal might have given to his work, a large proportion of the fragments have, I repeat, a personal destination ; they are designed to appeal to Méré and his friends, students of Montaigne, theoreticians of *honnêteté*. We may add, too, that the *Recherche* is the ' search ', not so much for truths or for the true religion, as the search for *happiness*. For the benefit of his hedonist friends (and Montaigne too is a hedonist, that is the reproach of the *Conversation*) Pascal is to re-enact what he takes to be the quest of Montaigne in order to prove its vanity—the bankruptcy of humanism.

If the framework of the *Recherche* is Méré and Montaigne, its actual steps are Montaigne and Charron—Charron who, despite his ' tiresome divisions ', has a plan whose first chapters prove what Pascal as fideist values in Montaigne.

L'esprit croit naturellement et la volonté aime naturellement ; de sorte que faute de vrais objets, il faut qu'ils s'attachent aux faux.

This *pensée*, itself an example of the way in which Pascal can give a new depth of reasoning to certain remarks of Montaigne, provides the link which unites ' the art of persuasion ' to its psychological complement, Pascal's theory of ' delectation '. It is not only, as Mr. Huxley says, that ' from the fact of change and decay the logic of desire deduces the existence of something changeless ' but that logic of desire is in itself (and without grace) essentially hedonistic, and the realist, Pascal, himself writes elsewhere :

La vie ordinaire des hommes est semblable à celle des saints. Ils recherchent tous leur satisfaction et ne diffèrent qu'en l'objet où ils la placent.

Pascal was to have begun his apology with a preface in which he discussed those who had written of self-knowledge, and it is there that he doubtless intended his criticisms of both Montaigne and Charron to find their place.[1] Following on this, the first part of the work was to be on the ' misery of man without God ', shown by natural light (compare Charron and Marandé). Pascal uses the term ' pyrrhonism ' almost always in the sense of a demonstration of human vanity—' a critique of satisfaction ' in Hulme's phrase, coined with reference to this part of the *Pensées*. It is this emotional fideism which he sets forth chiefly here, its intellectual counterpart, the use of scepticism proper, seems to have its place later. Hence he spends little time on any criticism of sense-perception. He sums the situation up in the long fragment (72) *Disproportion de l'homme*, full of reminiscences of the Essays. Man is double, soul and body ; material things are simple on the other hand ; hence to understand nature seems for ever impossible. To the ideas derived from Montaigne, he adds his famous picture of man placed between the infinitely great and the infinitely small : the appeal of this comparison, too, is obviously mainly emotional.

Turning to self-knowledge, is man any better placed ? No, says Pascal, and proceeds with his catalogues of *puissances trompeuses*. Under the heading : Imagination, he brings forward all Montaigne's reflexions on the fact that pain and pleasure, good and bad, are almost entirely subjective (82). Under the heading Custom, he adapts to his own uses Montaigne's other great weapon for relativity and against intolerance,

Les Pères craignent que l'amour naturel des enfants ne s'efface ?— J'ai grand peur que cette nature ne soit elle-même qu'une première coutume, comme la coutume est une seconde nature (93).

These ideas are used indeed by Montaigne in the way Pascal uses them, above all in the Apology, with which the author of the *Pensées* was especially familiar,[2] but their general inference,

---

[1] I have used the Brunschwicg arrangement of the *Pensées* (Hachette), but those who prefer other arrangements will not find that the general exposé, which is all that is here possible, is invalidated.

[2] It has been suggested that Pascal's knowledge of the Essays was limited almost entirely to the Apology. M. Villey's Appendix to Essays (Alcan 1929) shows that this cannot be maintained.

as has been pointed out, is not by any means always that of inculcating the *vanitas vanitatum* which is Pascal's aim. A more striking example of adaptation comes under the heading : *Divertissement*. Montaigne's ' diversion ', the method of restoring mental or moral balance, becomes yet another striking symbol of human infirmity (e.g. 139, contrast Marandé's use of the term). The familiar themes of inconstancy, diversity and contradiction of opinions and desires are renewed by Pascal's literary genius,[1] and the whole section, it seems, should fittingly end with the supreme puzzle.

Contradiction : mépris de notre être, mourir pour rien, haine de notre être (157).

This part of the *Pensées* is indeed literally built upon the Essays. The fragments concerning the Wager renew the attack upon the *indifférence des athées* from another angle. And here, although echoes of the Essays are still to be found, the initial inspiration as with *L'art de persuader* comes from the gamester, Méré, who, as is well known, proposed *la règle des partis*, the calculation of probabilities, to Pascal, even if Arnobius and, above all, Sebond, in his *Théologia Naturalis*, had sketched a similar apologetic argument. The ' personal destination ' of this argument is so tempting a conclusion, its omission from the plan of Etienne Périer is so striking, that it has been maintained that it was not intended to form part of Pascal's Apology. Without expressing an opinion on this question, it is worth pointing out that the basis of the whole argument (that by natural reason no assurance as to immortality or belief in God can be given) is not what we might term a willing suspension of belief on Pascal's part. With his interlocutor he is agreed that these truths are by reason unprovable. Nay, more, *even by faith* we know *only* God's existence : his nature not at all in this life. Pascal is conscious of the illogical nature of such a position, and he attempts to save it from absurdity by an appeal to mathematical analogy—we know the existence of ' an infinity ' yet not its ' nature '. And since faith itself only informs us of God's existence it is true, for the believer, divinely inspired as he is, and for the unbeliever, that God *n'a nul rapport avec nous*.

The reasons which underlie such a view, no less than its consequences, bring us back to a recurrent theme of this study : anthropomorphism. We have seen the anthropomorphic conception of God denounced again and again, but Pascal has

[1] See especially such reflexions as 114, 115.

taken a final step of the greatest philosophical importance. It is not merely that our justice is not God's justice, but that all our ideas are *quant à nous*, and further that all the most fundamental conceptions of the human mind are self-contradictory. The antinomy, the antinomian character of human nature and human intelligence is by no means the least important side of Montaigne's influence on Pascal. And if God's justice has *no* relation to man's justice, if the rules of conduct which seem right to mere human understanding have no relation to the principles on which the Deity may judge us, if we are to stake our all on preparing for an existence of which we know nothing, the whole *Pari*, which has been condemned as utilitarian, reveals also, treated logically, its own self-contradiction. With the *pari* ends the more purely emotional appeal of the *Pensées*, for we must insist that the mathematical rigour of the Wager is a sham and its intention a disposition of the ' heart '. What shall I do ? asks the unbeliever torn between conflicting emotions. Pretend you believe, replies Pascal, assuming, for the moment, that there are three ways to belief : habit, reason and divine inspiration. Thus after the injunction *ployer la machine*, we are free to turn to the alternative : reason.

Pascal renews his criticisms of rational method. First principles are intuitive, unprovable : *cette impuissance ne conclut autre chose que la faiblesse de notre raison, mais non l'incertitude des connaissances* (282). Yet the truths which remain certain are almost negligible ; that space is three-dimensional and that numbers are infinite—and Pascal goes on to regret that more of our knowledge had not this instinctive or intuitive character—this passive character which divinely inspired belief also has. The position of reason is summed up in his correction of Roannez : No, one does not discover by analysis the reasons which led to such and such a conclusion, and were implicit in one's mind all the time : one finds reasons, or ' rationalizes ' about one's beliefs, without there being a real connexion between the two processes [1] (276).

The main idea of Montaigne used in this part of Pascal's work is, however, that of the two kinds of believers, corresponding to Montaigne's distinction of the vulgar, who believe with-

[1] Compare E. Giselle, article quoted p. 46 : ' Roannez trouve que les discours des mystères sont au dessus de nous, et *quand on parle de la morale nous sommes chez nous*, nous en sommes touchés '. Pascal would doubtless have had his reserves as to the words in italics. Thus Roannez, too, held the fundamental maxim of Montaigne and the whole Montaigne tradition of a ' fideistic humanism '. We know, however, that later in life he appears to have been converted to something like Pascal's own sombre version of Christianity.

out proof, and the really wise who know that no proof can be given in the sense in which the *demi-savants* demand it.

Deux sortes de personnes connaissent : ceux qui ont le cœur humilié, et qui aiment la bassesse, quelque degré d'esprit qu'ils aient, haut ou bas ; ou ceux qui ont assez d'esprit pour voir la vérité, quelque opposition qu'ils y aient (288).

It is in the next section (No. 5 in Brunschwicg's edition) that this notion of the three classes, the two extremes meeting, is specially prominent. This section *De la Raison des Effets* aims at a sort of social philosophy. Injustice and unreason are manifest in society, the simple and ignorant do not see how unreasonable and how unjust : this is *ignorance naturelle* (327). There is an *ignorance savante* which knows the injustice and the unreason, but also that it is better that things should remain as they are—for the sake of peace and quiet. Pascal here combines two ideas dear to Montaigne : conformity and the three classes of men. He adapts the notion of the *arrière boutique* to the necessity of knowing that no social organization has any intrinsic virtue, therefore to *act* one's part with detachment.[1] The laws must be obeyed because this course, instead of changing them, gives the best results. He reproaches Montaigne (unjustly) with having said that the law must be obeyed because it is law. Montaigne and Pascal are really agreed.[2]

The interest of this section is very considerable. This Christian conservatism has a purely utilitarian foundation. The peace and quiet to which Montaigne gives a large place in his ethical ideal is accepted by Pascal so far as social life is concerned, though rejected as mere hedonism in individual ethics. This need not surprise us ; Christianity has a natural tendency to take this line. We can also see how certain portions of this section may be perhaps the development of discussions with Mitton on social justice. What is of first-rate importance, however, is to realize that the rôle of this section and of its heading *la raison des effets* is to show how existing social organization has its adequate ' reason ' in the mere fact that it works—and this in spite of the unreason of most of its features. Hence it affords us a precious analogy with religion : religion too is unreasonable, but it works. It even prepares for the arguments on the figurative interpretation of the Scriptures.

[1] Compare, in *Trois Discours sur la Condition des Grands*, the fable of the King who was not a King (*Opuscules*, p. 233).
[2] cf. *Essais*, III, 13, p. 390. Pascal again hardly seems to have understood Montaigne's irony.

The people, then, in their ignorance are right in their acceptance of unreasonable social organization, unreasonable amusements, unreasonable scales of value in the honours they pay,
but they do not know why they are right nor are they conscious
of their ignorance (328). It is only when a man realizes that
his kind are *visiblement fait pour penser* that he can begin to
have full consciousness of the double character of man. Pascal
presses the dualism of body and mind to the full measure of
the Cartesians, but he at once brings in Montaigne to correct
Descartes. *L'homme est ni ange ni bête* (358). The greatness
of man is not in his thought, except in one sense : that is his
consciousness of his own misery. Thought as such is bankrupt,
le pyrrhonisme est le vrai : not, as we have seen, because all is
uncertain, but because pyrrhonism proves human weakness, and
the dogmatists, by their powerlessness against sceptical criticism,
involuntarily prove it almost as effectually (389, 395).

The critique of virtue which belongs to this part of the *Pensées*
proceeds on lines only too familiar to us from this study. Virtue
is a balance between qualities, or between passions ; it has no
intrinsic value. Moral acts depend on passions, on temperament,
on ethical theories, and all judgements indeed depend on age,
time, place, education. Man remains the enthusiast for absolute
truth and goodness which he seems scarcely able to know (395),
except perhaps by negation (cf. 385). What explanation can
be offered of this double nature, which is capable of good and
capable of hating his own concupiscence ? Knowledge of good
is impossible without faith. Ethics depend on religion (435).
Man still follows universally the goal of happiness : his lack of
success proves that he is lost. Something has happened which
renders useless this impulse.

Then Pascal proceeds to develop the positive part of his
scheme in which Montaigne has naturally little part. Only
Christianity with its incomprehensible dogma of original sin can
' explain ' man's situation. It is an explanation ' which works ',
like the explanation of why conformity and conservatism are
right in spite of the injustices of social life.

True Justice—to each his due—is of God's dispensing. It
has little to do with punishments and rewards in this life : that
is why the persecution of the Jansenist Saints is no sign of God's
displeasure in Pascal's eyes. Nor is the *Deus Absconditus* an
objection, for if God were not hid there would be no merit in
belief. And Pascal's last word on justice is the affirmation that
the purpose of creation itself is the exercise by God of his mercy
and judgement :

Le Monde subsiste pour exercer miséricorde et jugement . . . (584).

Yet even in this part of his work Montaigne's influence may be detected. In certain details, first of all. We have noted the intended quotation of Montaigne on miracles (see also 818). Furthermore, Pascal, unlike so many of his contemporaries, does not seem to have been a reader of the *Relations de Voyage*, and his references to China, Mexico and Mohammedans or to the religion of the savages (594, 599, 817) are taken directly from Montaigne. The general aspect in which Montaigne's influence is to be sought, however, lies in the obsession of the antinomy principle. Of his method he writes :

> Les deux raisons contraires. Il faut commencer par là ; sans cela on n'entend rien et tout est hérétique : et même à la fin de chaque vérité il faut ajouter qu'on se souvient de la vérité opposée (567).
> La foi embrasse plusieurs vérités qui semblent se contredire. Temps de rire, temps de pleurer, &c. (862).

Christ is man and God, the consecrated bread Christ's body and a symbol and commemoration. And there is finally, the great antinomy of faith and reason. Christianity is the true religion because the most *unnatural*, the most contrary to reason ; reason which is itself invalidated by an infinite regress of *pour et contre*.

> Il est bon d'être las et fatigué par l'inutile recherche du vrai bien afin de tendre les bras au Libérateur (422).[1]

Pascal's whole book is intended to badger his reader to that conclusion. And if wisdom itself may lead us towards faith, it is alone Grace—*l'efficacité de la folie de la Croix*—which can save us.
    There is no room to do justice to the *folie* of Pascal or to his *sagesse*, nor to insist on the inhumanity of this ' sick man's religion '. One series of reflections imposes itself, however. There is an important link between fideism and the Calvinistic predestinarianism of the Jansenists. Both involve an essentially passive conception of faith. This, as we see it in Pascal, whose idea of the necessity of a constant renewal of Grace has been compared with Descartes' *création continue*, is indeed equivalent to saying that while I have grace (and without grace no faith) it is not I who act but God who acts in me (cf. Occasionalism). Thus the general character of the doctrine is mystical in tone, and despite their differences with regard to original sin, it is Madame Guyon and the Quietist mystics who are in many respects his true successors.

[1] Note the repetition in 737.

Pascal's own health, his own character, with its demand for an utterly inhuman unity of feeling and purpose, a demand which appears to us like the defence mechanism of a universal curiosity and a passionate nature housed in a body ailing since the days when a ' witch ' was said to have cast a spell on him as a child, these appear perhaps the main factors in his intellectual development. But his contact first with Jansenism, and then with the Essays and their devotees goes far to explain his thought as seen in the *Pensées*. The Essays aid his intellectual growth and bring him, I suspect, first to the position which he outlines as Montaigne's own in the Conversation with M. de Saci ; but Pascal, convinced—or reconvinced—of man's moral bankruptcy as well as of his intellectual bankruptcy—that is where he differs from Montaigne—thus affords us with what we have not yet met in this study, the spectacle of a truly logical fideist.

CHAPTER XXVI

MOLIÈRE AND LA FONTAINE

THE reader will have noted that not only Méré and Mitton but, even in certain respects, Silhon and still more Balzac, from all of whom Pascal derives certain elements of his thought, represent a kind of indirect influence of Montaigne which accompanies a direct influence which has never been in doubt. Still more, in the case of Molière and La Fontaine, the influence of the Essays, real though it is, is merged in a general current of thought in which the part of Gassendi and others of his generation is often indistinguishable from that of the Essays.

The inventory of Molière's library shows that he possessed—along with the Bible, Plutarch, a collection of classical authors, some *relations de voyage*, and a large number of plays, French, Italian and Spanish—a copy of Montaigne's Essays and the two folio volumes of that contemporary sceptic, La Mothe le Vayer. We must also number among his friends Bernier and Chapelle, Gassendi's disciples, the latter the son of Luillier, Gassendi's most faithful patron, and the abbé La Mothe le Vayer, the son of old ' Orasius Tubero '. The claim that Molière shared the private instruction given by Gassendi to Bernier and Chapelle (his school-fellows at the Collège de Clermont) has recently been rejected.[1] It has been shown that the course of philosophical instruction in question was given at Aix in 1651 and not in Paris ten years previously. Even so there is nothing to prevent us still supposing that Molière was privileged to be present at some of Gassendi's private lectures, for what little we know of his life touring in the provinces shows both his presence in Provence during the greater part of that year, and that the roving life was not incompatible with a good deal of enforced leisure. However this may be, there is good reason for taking him as one of those who came directly or indirectly under the influence of the champion of Epicurus, while his translation of part, at least,

---

[1] G. Michaut, *La Jeunesse de Molière*, pp. 67 et seq.

of Lucretius is an undoubted fact. Here indeed we find him in company both amusing and strange, for his fellow-translators of the *De Natura Rerum* include not only the abbé de Marolles and Jean Dehénault, but also Chapelle, his life-long friend, and the abbé Cotin, the luckless original of the immortal Trissotin.[1] It appears that after Molière's death Thierry the publisher refused to add the fragments of the translation to his edition of the dramatist's works ' *les ayant trouvés trop forts contre l'immortalité de l'ame* '.[2]

Despite the insinuation of the publisher, despite the friendship of Dehénault and Chapelle (who have both been considered as free-thinkers),[3] we must insist that what Molière's Gassendism, what his translation of Lucretius, are most likely to imply ' *a priori* ' are some nuance of Christian humanism, hedonistic and latitudinarian, with some tinge of fideism, as we find in St. Evremond. We shall find reasons in his plays for sticking to such a conclusion. But we can never dispose completely of the figure of the free-thinking Molière, because it can always be held that the attacks of his enemies from the first performance of *Tartuffe* (1664) forced him to a discretion which might explain even his presence at the communion-table on the Easter of 1671 and the nuns at his death-bed. Such considerations, however, cannot lead us anywhere. The Molière who concerns us is the Molière of the plays. And though Gassendi may offer us a clue to Molière's conciliation of hedonism and Christianity, there is nothing in the plays which is elucidated by referring to his philosophy.

Yet bearing in mind what has just been said, we can see that those who have discussed Molière's ' philosophy ' have been singularly lacking in prudence on one point. The reflexions of his *raisonneurs*—of a Cléante or a Beralde—are, no doubt, the most explicit representation of Molière's ideas on which we can count, and yet in intention, and often in form, they are an endeavour to express, not Molière's own views, but those of his public—of *les honnêtes gens*. ' Critical comedy ', which Molière created, requires more than any other type of play this appeal of the author to his public, an appeal to a common stock of ideas. We must go beyond these speeches to the conception of the plays themselves and to the secret of Molière's *vis comica*, in order to understand his ideas and estimate what he owes to Montaigne or the Montaigne tradition.

[1] On these translations see Busson, *Pensée Religieuse*, p. 419.
[2] Michaut : op. cit., pp. 78, 79.
[3] Busson (*Pensée Religieuse*, p. 426) is disposed to reject the accusations of D'Assoucy against Chapelle.

The comedies of Molière have their roots in the *commedia dell'arte*, which supplied the dramatist with what has been well called ' a living mythology '. The *commedia dell'arte* is not only characterized by the exaggeration of stock types, but it is also, as M. Fernandez says in a brilliant essay on Molière, *une Jacquerie philosophique* ; not merely in the sense that it is a critique of the erotic Platonism of the Renaissance, the revolt of natural instinct, but it is also the critique of the pedant, of the expert (who is the opposite of *l'honnête homme*), the critique of dogmatism and learning in the name of common sense. Such is the under-lying ' moral ' of this amoral theatre. The whole achievement of Molière has been represented as the result of applying the principle of *castigare ridendo mores* to a form of comedy which knew it not. As it stands, we can hardly accept such a state-ment, yet it does have the merit of referring to a quality which is peculiar to Molière among modern playwrights. For despite the castigation, he somehow avoids the danger which lies in wait for the type comedy dramatist—the moralizing danger. He escapes it because the current ideal of the seventeenth century identifies the good man with the reasonable man, and unreason is naturally ridiculous. The eighteenth century identifies the good man with the man of feeling, and the unfeeling man requires to be placed in very special circumstances before he can raise a laugh, and laughter, together with an ethical ideal, are the twin foundations of satire.

There is much that could be added in developing such a view : how this ' reason ', or rather this reasonableness, is essen-tially the ideal of a century whose admiration of reason, order, moderation and elegance are founded on an existing actuality of unreason, disorder, fanaticism and brutality : how a parallel antimony may be found in the breast of Molière himself. Yet we must first show in more detail and without these brave gener-alizations how the *commedia* evolves in Molière's hands. It is only thus that we can show the meaning of *bon sens* on his lips.

So far as the stock-characters go there is a direct line of development best seen in Harpagon and Argan. The great monomaniacs of Molière, isolated by the inner logic of their own obsession, are the *reductio ad absurdum* of not accepting that pluralism of values which the ordinary man of sense in all ages has implicitly accepted. But they are mainly *comic* by their human failure to be wholly consistent and by the inevitable con-flict with their fellow-men. And this leads us on to the second line of development, the theme of incompatibility, of the diversity of humours. One of the authentic productions of Molière's troop in the provinces was appropriately enough a *Ballet des Incompatibles*. And, as M. Fernandez asks : ' What are Arnolphe and Agnès, Tartuffe and Elmire, Alceste and Célimène, if not Incompatibles ? Less superficially, the characters of Molière are comic because they claim to effect a marriage of things incompatible, for example of authority and love '. The true ' comedy of humours ' which Molière gives us has essentially as its basis the persuasion of the ' diversity of men ' and the *bigarrure* of each individual in himself. If the world's a stage itself, peopled with fools and cranks, the *bon sens* by which we judge the folly of the masks before us would seem to be either the *chacun sa raison* of Régnier or a mere agreement of prejudice, a humble social wisdom, which is nothing more than convention. This is true indeed of these early farces where Molière revived the despised *commedia*, but if we follow the evolution of the themes and subjects which he chooses, from *La Jalousie de Barbouillé* and *Le Médecin Volant* onwards, we shall see take shape before us something to which we can less easily deny the name of philosophy.

The first theme is one of which our forefathers never tired. Horns, their shadow, the fear of their shadow which is jealousy, dominate the landscape of the *commedia*. It is round this theme that some tincture of philosophy, a philosophy of love and then of instinct and custom *versus* reason, first insinuates itself in Molière's work. At least half of these plays contain a condemnation of jealousy. Look at the theme as it emerges in the first scene of *Le Dépit Amoureux* (1656) in the dialogue of Eraste and his valet Gros Réné.

> GROS RÉNÉ. Pourquoi subtiliser et faire le capable
> A chercher des raisons pour être misérable
> Sur des soupçons en l'air je m'irois alarmer !
> Laisser venir la fête avant de la chômer. . . .

and later :

> MARINETTE. Tout le fruit qu'on en cueille est de se mettre mal,
> Et d'avancer par là les desseins d'un rival.

The line of descent leads us next to *Le Cocu Imaginaire* (1660) and to *Don Garcie de Navarre* (1661). The latter, unsuccessful experiment though it is, reveals well enough the ambitions of Molière. In the hierarchy of *genres* which was such a feature of the literary code of the time, the author of Les *Précieuses* was a mere composer of *bagatelles*. Still more, however, the subject Molière chose, the subject of jealousy, seems to indicate a personal preoccupation.

For the amorous Molière, who appears to have enjoyed in the provinces fairly promiscuous relationships with the actresses of his troop, it might well seem that jealousy was but a disagreeable convention. For the man who already in 1659 was secretly in love with a girl more than twenty years his junior,[1] and whom his enemies were to proclaim as his own daughter, jealousy is destined to appear in a new light ; to become the symbol of instinct, of temperament, over which *bon sens*, reason, or a certain ideal of conduct have little or no power.

In *L'Ecole des Maris* (1661) we are still at some distance from such a conclusion. The theme is here presented, perhaps with an eye to Armande's edification. One brother at least is in the situation of the author himself, in love with a girl young enough to be his daughter. But with what ingenuity Molière has shown that brother, the *elder*, as a sage who believes in liberty, in reasonableness, whose maxims of education recall the Essays :

> Soit : mais je tiens sans cesse
> Qu'il faut en riant instruire la jeunesse
> Reprendre ses défauts avec grande douceur
> Et du nom de vertu ne lui point faire peur . . .
> Les divertissements, les bals, les comédies :
> Ce sont choses pour moi, que je tiens de tout temps
> Fort propres à former l'esprit des jeunes gens :
> Et l'école du monde, en l'air dont il faut vivre,
> Instruit mieux, à mon gré, que ne fait aucun livre.

How cleverly Sganarelle is presented as a crusty old young man, jealous, prejudiced, narrow—who even refuses to conform in his dress to the fashion of the day. In *L'Ecole des Femmes* (1662) there is again perhaps an implicit contrast made for Armande's benefit, between Arnolphe, the fiction, and Molière, the man. Arnolphe has conceived his absurd design in order to escape the danger of horns. But in what is the design absurd ? Not in so far as Arnolphe intends to marry a young girl whom he has brought up, for this was precisely the case of both brothers of the *Ecole des Maris*. It is absurd by Arnolphe's original motive, and still more by his methods. He wishes to enjoy all the privileges of parental authority and yet expects to be regarded in the light of a lover and husband. The internal incompati-

---

[1] See the letter of Chapelle to Molière in 1659 (Michaut : *Jeunesse,* p. 181).

bility of this double rôle is emphasized by the fact that, like
Alceste, he is rendered painfully conscious of his own absurdity.
He is the antipodes of Harpagon and Argan or even Philaminte.
It is by their consciousness of their rôle, no less than by the
element of personal dilemma which has gone to their creation,
that Arnolphe and, far more, Alceste seem to us at certain
moments more worthy of pity than laughter.

Le Misanthrope presents the conclusion of the powerlessness
of reason over instinct, passion or temperament, and (though
we are never allowed to forget it as an element in Alceste's
chagrin) on a scale which goes far beyond the theme of jealousy.
We may, therefore, postpone our examination of it. But reason
or *bon sens*, though its power over our own natures may be
limited, still retains its use as the weapon of social criticism.
Here a line of descent leads us from *Le Médecin Volant* to *Les
Précieuses*—and, from *La Critique de l'Ecole des Femmes* onwards,
Molière assumes the task of bringing all professions before the
bar.

Until we reach the *Critique* we do not get beyond the question of women. The *Précieuses Ridicules* is the violent and
perhaps undiscriminating reaction of a man who realizes that the
' chastity ' (*précieuses* and ' chaste ' are synonyms in contemporary phraseology) of these ladies is a sham and, in its obsession
of the *horror of touching*, an imaginative and perverted sensuality.
These *Précieuses* are essentially prudes. Preciosity has another
side, which Molière appears to value in *L'Ecole des Femmes*, and
which brings us back to Mademoiselle de Gournay, if not to
Montaigne. He gives something of a *revanche* to the *Précieuses*
in this play, when he makes Arnolphe's education of Agnès an
attempt to keep her in ignorance, when he makes him laugh at
the idea of marrying *une spirituelle, Qui ne parleroit rien que
cercle et que ruelle.* For Chrysalde replies :

> Mais comment voulez-vous, après tout, qu'une bête
> Puisse jamais savoir ce que c'est qu'être honnête ?
> Outre qu'il est assez ennuyeux que je croy
> D'avoir toute sa vie une bête avec soi. . . .

It is the attack of Molière's enemies on *L'Ecole des Femmes*,
and their scorn for ' mere comedy ' which seem to have revealed
to him the implications of his art and of his ' philosophy '. There
are certain remarks of the *Critique*, which, ostensibly part of a
discussion on aesthetics, seem in the light of later plays to have
a far more general application. One of these is Dorante's *ne
cherchons point de raisonnements pour nous empêcher d'avoir du*

plaisir. A value-judgement of pleasure is essentially individual. *Il faut se laisser prendre aux choses* : the appeal is against the hypostatized ' reason ' of rules (ethical or aesthetic) to the individual ' reason '.   Still   more   important   is   Dorante's   remark apropos of Arnolphe's generosity.   *Il n'est pas incompatible qu'une personne soit ridicule en de certaines choses et honnête homme en d'autres.*   We see its corollary a few moments later where Dorante defending the *transport amoureux* of the last act says : *Je voudrais bien savoir se ce n'est pas faire la satire des amants et si les honnêtes gens même, et des plus sérieux, en de pareilles occasions ne font pas des choses . . . Mais enfin si nous nous regardions nous mêmes, quand nous sommes bien amoureux.* The poor *marquis* finds no reply to this the final argument of the play, but must needs shout (or sing) his opponent down.

Here then we have announced a view of human nature, subtle enough to admit the possible worth of those who may be yet ridiculous, and hence the universal privilege of satire.   The way is open for *Le Misanthrope*, and for *Tartuffe.*

The question of *Tartuffe* is complicated by the fact that the play was actually performed in three different forms.   Whether we accept the ingenious theorizing of M. Gustave Michaut [1] on the original play, he has emphasized what we are apt to forget : that the satire of the play falls almost as heavily on Orgon as on the impostor himself.

Orgon is sincerely devout, although misdirected, and it is in his characterization that we may find Molière's attitude to the ' unco guid '.   The conception of the play centres as much round his obstinate blindness, as round the rashness of the impostor.   We all remember too, the choleric disposition which Dorine delights to provoke and then to taunt (Act II). These are, however, the commonplace jests of all time at the expense of the zealot.   And the same is possibly true of those ' humane sentiments ' developed under Tartuffe's guidance :

> Qui suit bien ses leçons goûte une paix profonde
> Et comme du fumier regarde tout le monde.
> Et je verrais mourir père, enfants, mère et femme
> Que je m'en soucierais autant que de cela . . .

Yet this disregard of natural duties for alleged religious ones is what Orgon puts into practice, when he disowns and curses his own son ; while the tyrannous, dogmatic nature of his temperament, the natural foundation of a zealot, is re-emphasized in the person of his son, Damis, equally violent—and shall

[1] *Les Luttes de Molière*, pp. 59–86.

we add his mother, Madame Pernelle, equally obstinate and exacting ?

More important even than the dogmatism and the violence of the *dévot*, is the other characteristic we have seen emphasized again and again throughout this study—the utilitarian character of ' superstition '. Orgon s sees in the prosperity of his house, since Tartuffe has entered it, a visible sign that he is sent by Heaven. Cléante will bring himself bad luck by criticizing a man of God. The dowry of ' standing well with Heaven ' is the richest he has to offer his daughter. Yet, important as this feature is, it is Orgon's violence which characterizes him best. His renunciation at the end of *tous les gens de bien*, the gesture of physical attack when Tartuffe is being led away by the *Exempt*, best sum up Molière's views of the fanatic. Its humour I have neglected, although the self-abasement mechanism which Tartuffe employs so successfully on him, the aside where Orgon cries *Allons ferme, mon cœur ! point de faiblesse humaine*, the inconsequence of his refusal to allow his daughter to enter a convent (*Mortifier vos sens avec le mariage*), and finally the *faux fuyant*, which will allow him ' truthfully ' to say he has not got his exiled friend's papers, complete the characterization.

From the point of view of the ideas which underlie his characterization, or those which he expresses, Tartuffe is perhaps less interesting. We need only observe his apparent ascetism, his apparent prudery, his apparent isolation from human affections and interests. It is by the false profession of insensibility (for Orgon is infatuated with Tartuffe as Tartuffe with Elmire) and by a sham humility, that the sincere but superstitious zealot and his master, the hypocrite, resemble each other. This professed ideal of isolation is the one new element in a diagnosis of superstition and hypocrisy which is familiar to us in the pages of such *Montaignisants* as Du Lorens, La Picardière and La Luzerne.[1]

The picture, however, is hardly complete without a sketch of *une dévotion humaine et traitable* preached mainly by Cléante (who is accused throughout the play of *libertinage*), and sometimes by Dorine, the first of a succession of characters, peculiarly Molière's own, who represent natural good sense—the ' peasant ' pendants to the true philosophers such as Cléante. Cléante's first maxim—when Madame Pernelle is sufficiently out of breath to let him speak—is a disregard of gossip, and also, as we see when he faced with Orgon, a disregard of outward forms, which

[1] Compare also *l'homme dévot* and the *faux dévot*, as characterized by the Gassendist, Sorbière.

for the *bigot* are the very essence of religion. The *façonniers* of when he speaks are the *formalistes* of Charron, and although he defends genuine zeal as Charron never did, it is after declaring :

> Les hommes, la plupart, sont étrangement faits :
> Dans la juste nature on ne les voit jamais :
> La raison chez eux a des bornes trop petites :
> En chaque caractère ils passent la limite
> Et la plus noble chose ils la gâtent souvent
> Pour la vouloir oûtrer et passer trop avant.

The wisely religious have a humane, a not uncompromising devotion, not fault finding, but content to ' live well '.

Let us take Cléante in a scene (IV, i) where his rôle is to assume Tartuffe's sincerity and to persuade him of his Christian duty of forgiveness to Damis. At the end of the scene it is the question of the morality of accepting the donation which is at issue. Cléante is about to play his trump-card—*La prud'homie*, a moral obligation apart from the ' maxims ' of ' true zeal '. It is at this point that Tartuffe is made to quit the field with superb dramatic irony. The erection of religious obligations into a duty prior to the claims of ethics or of common decency is exquisitely pointed here. The final touch of charity is supplied when Cléante seems willing to assume a sincere remorse on Tartuffe's part. In the last scene he says to Orgon :

> Ah ! mon frère, arrêtez,
> Et ne descendez point à des indignités ;
> A son mauvais destin laissez un misérable,
> *Et ne vous joignez point au remords qui l'accable :*

It is impossible to do justice here to all the implications of this great play, but the traits which characterize the picture of true and false piety offer a brilliant utilization of certain themes we have traced in earlier chapters of this book. The impression of Molière's attitude which I derive from a study of *Tartuffe* is somewhat more complex than some critics have urged. Orgon is ridiculous and sometimes odious, but every indirect means of insisting on the esteem in which he has been held is exploited. There is even enough subtlety in the picture of Tartuffe himself for certain actors to have held that the part is one in which the element of self-deception cannot be ignored. It is indeed on this that depends the full flavour of Tartuffe's employment of religious phraseology in his advances to Elmire. Even if we press this view to an untenable extreme, and maintain that *two types* of the devout are here satirized, it would not follow that Molière is anti-Christian, even in his heart of hearts. The gallery of human types which Molière saw around him contained a sufficient variety of Christians good and bad, for him to pillory certain features and still count on the applause of the genuinely religious.   And if the *Confrérie du Saint Sacrement* were powerful enough to prevent the public performance of the play for five years,[1] we know how they were hated by those who were certainly no *libertins*—nor is it necessary to allege the approval of Tartuffe by men like the Papal Legate, and the King himself.   Finally, of course, Cléante is there, a third type.   He represents the *real* attitude of many contemporaries and friends of the author, but I think that Molière himself, above all when the battle was begun, was, for all his tact, fundamentally a man of too violent a temperament not to feel that Cléante's lack of bitterness, his reasonableness were qualities which, though he may have desired them, he knew well enough he did not possess.   He is Molière's ideal. Such a view lends a new interest to those sermons on moderation which have seemed to some the least attractive feature of Molière's attitude to life.   Whether Cléante is Molière's ideal as well as the one he evidently proposes to his audience, he was created to supply the proof that there is an amiable and human piety which the devout may call *libertinage*, if they choose.

Had *Tartuffe* met with no opposition, *Dom Juan* might never have been written.   Here was a subject which had been presented three times upon the stage since Molière arrived in Paris.[2] Already the seducer of Tirso da Molina had become something of a *libertin* in the free-thinking sense.   The subject made possible an indirect reply to the suspension of Tartuffe.   I will show (says Molière) not only a real *libertin*, but an atheist, so that there shall be no doubt about his wickedness.   Nor is this all, for my hero finally becomes a hypocrite.   The play gives us the true genesis of hypocrites in the atheists and the *débauchés* of yesterday, and Juan himself gives us the 'theory' of a hypocrisy into which no element of self-deception enters.

This play was withdrawn after fifteen performances, and we can judge, from a number of sources, the passages which seem to have caused most offence.   The objections to the play may be reduced to three.   Two of these we may disregard, namely : it was by the author of *Tartuffe*, and that it again dealt with religion upon the stage.   What concerns us is how

[1] Apart from hot heads like the author of *Le Roi Glorieux au Monde*, the opposition, as we see it in La Moignon, was against the *subject* of religion on the stage rather than the treatment in this particular play.

[2] For all details on *Dom Juan* see G. Gendarme de Bévotte : *La Légende de Don Juan* (1906 or abridged edition 1911).

Molière appears to have attempted to forestall all reasonable objections to his *treatment of the subject*, for here we may find certain further indications as to his views on religion.

The most significant difference of *Dom Juan* and the plays of Dorimon and Villiers is not the development of the free-thinking (but not atheistic) young rake into a *grand seigneur méchant homme* whose cynical incredulity is complete. It is the disappearance of the serious arguments on religion which are to be found in the earlier plays. Don Juan himself delights indeed to draw Sganarelle out and make him argue in order to display to his master (and to us) the absurdities of the reasons he finds for his beliefs. Those beliefs, too, in *le Moine bourru* for example, and his faith in medicine are represented as ludicrous enough. But what critic would seriously maintain, as Molière's enemies did (and this is the third objection) that Sganarelle is the one spokesman of sense and piety in the play ? [1] Don Louis, the father, Elvire and even Don Carlos represent this function. But Don Louis and Dona Elvire do not argue : they say ' repent ', ' ask for Grace ', and the veiled figure of the last act seems indeed also the symbol of Grace.[2] Sganarelle, the comic figure of the play, is at once superstitious and *raisonneur*. Molière's prudence and his genius are to be seen in the presentation of an atheist who is *implicitly* judged so, for he thus avoided shocking by anti-religious arguments and could show with more art the cynicism of his hero. But Molière's miscalculation (from a practical point of view as it proved in the event) was, no doubt, the admirable complexity he lends to the character of Sganarelle —good heart but no courage, superstitious *and* also a reasoner on religion. In intention he has given us what may be called a fideist version of the subject.

Dom Juan has the further distinction of being (with the exception of the *Médecin Volant*) the first play in which Molière has a dig at the doctors. The *vin émétique* or antimony which, ill-administered, had killed his friend the Abbé la Mothe le Vayer in the previous year, comes in for a further cut in *L'Amour Médecin* (1665). This play also gives us the first example in Molière's career of personal satire. The four doctors of the play (one of them—Esprit—the cause of La Mothe's death) were the most prominent members of the Faculty, and their names, let alone their ' make-up ', left little doubt as to their identity. Gui Patin,[3] doctor though he be, seems delighted that *on se moque de ceux qui tuent le monde impunément*. Whether or not

---

[1] See G. Michaut, *Les Luttes de Molière*, pp. 184–8.
[2] ib., pp. 169, 170.   [3] ib., p. 197.

a certain personal resentment played a part in the exploitation of this new theme, it is not inappropriate that the long speech of M. Filerin (III. 1), who seeks to calm the dissensions of his colleagues, should derive from a passage of the Essays.[1] Mr. ' Love Dispute ' (his real name was Yvelin) is ready to play false to his name (and nature ?) in order not to discover to the vulgar *la forfanterie de notre art.*

If the attacks of the devout on Molière are surprising in their violence, the spirit in which the doctors received his satire (so often renewed in later plays) appears no less surprising in its moderation. He seems on excellent terms with his own doctor, Mauvillain, the supporter of the same *vin émétique* at which he tilted in *Dom Juan*, in *L'Amour Médecin* and in *Le Médecin Malgré Lui*. We may in some measure attribute this tolerance to the accepted tradition whereby doctors have always been fair game for sarcastic wit. The ill-kept ' mysteries ' of their art, their dogmatism, their cult of authority and tradition, where, behind Hippocrates and Galen, we have the figure of Aristotle himself, made the doctors of the seventeenth century, along with the theologians, the reactionary party of the intellectual world.

With *Le Misanthrope* (1666) we turn to a play which is tinged with some reflexion of the critical years of Molière's life in which it was written.[2] The cares which harassed Molière during this period demanded all the tact, the reasonableness of which the leader of the King's Players and his Upholsterer by Patent were capable. On the interpretation of *Le Misanthrope* this background has its bearing. Alceste and Philinte are in a sense two men Molière himself would like to have been. How he must have longed to run amok like Alceste and tell the *dévots*, the *marquis*, and Armande too, no doubt, just what he thought of them ! Or else to have possessed the calm wisdom of Philinte with its undertone of resignation. The real Molière was neither of these. He was the coaxing, wheedling, irritable, perpetually rushed actor-manager of the *Impromptu de Versailles :—Ah ! les étranges animaux à conduire que les comédiens :* [3] And yet since *autobiographie ne peut guère signifier, en esthétique, que trans-*

---

[1] Molière : *Œuvres* (ed. Mesnard), V, 338 : *Essais*, II, 37, pp. 589, 590. Note that Montaigne's attacks on doctors or rather on contemporary medicine were sometimes taken seriously enough. They were honoured by a solemn refutation in the *Montanus Elenchomenos* (1639) of Jan van Beverwyck, a Dutch physician.

[2] The first act was written in 1664, if we may believe Brossette (Michaut, *Luttes*, p. 203).

[3] I am again indebted for this brilliant analysis to M. Fernandez.

position de l'homme sur un plan d'ordinaire inutilisable, this play reveals Molière to us more profoundly perhaps than any other.

The comedy of friendship, such is the opening note. And the quarrel of friends—were it not that it takes two to make a quarrel. What is friendship if the chance-met fawning stranger can call forth the same response from Philinte as his closest friend ? The comedy of ceremonious politeness, which so irritates the jealous yet singularly trusting Alceste, is soon generalized. The comedy of jealousy, the tragi-comedy of the fact that we love not by reason, choose not by reason, is pursued by Molière in succeeding acts. But the rest of the first act is devoted to the general theme of the play which underlies even the situation between Alceste and Célimène. As Philinte says :

> Je . . .
>   crois voir en nous deux, sous mêmes soins nourris,
> Les deux frères que peint *l'Ecole des Maris.*

This theme is a social one—social and ethical at once, for it is *honnêteté,* and the whole play rests on the double sense of the term. We have seen already what it had come to imply : the good life in its social aspect ; the art of adaptability, of pleasing and conciliating our fellow-men ; the art of personality, one might almost say ; the elaborate equation of temperament, condition, *milieu* with the more universal demands of an ethical code or of common honesty. By the very necessity of his art (to ignore other factors already suggested) Molière goes straight to the crux of the problem. Can honesty always be squared with that other duty of pleasing ? Can we ignore temperament, and the strange incompatibilities it creates ? It is within the framework of such questions that the humour and the occasional pathos of the play develop.

Molière shows a man who is on the point of giving up the attempt to square the ' duties ' of which I have spoken. Why ? Temperament, no doubt, in part, and this explains the comic violence of Alceste's reactions to the initial situation of the play. But these are subsidiary causes. His law-suit shows him how a dishonest man, an upstart too, is treated with the appearance of respect, while only the *honest* man really deserves the *égards* of *honnêteté.* And by the end of the play Alceste has the ' satisfaction ' of knowing that his judges have given a more substantial advantage to his mercenary opponent. The literary professionalism of *Oronte* (*galant homme* who *will* aspire to the quality of poet, despite the code of *honnêteté* itself) puts Alceste's frankness in a purely ridiculous light. And Célimène, *honnête femme* who aims a trifle too much at pleasing, and who may therefore be called *coquette*, is there, not only to put the finishing touches to Alceste's rage and indignation, but to keep him ridiculously cooling his heels in a *milieu* which he is logical enough to see he must quit, if he is to remain true to himself. His incompatibility of nature with Célimène is too obvious to require analysis, but the more general false position in which he stands is stated in an unobtrusive passage, which is *the most objective utterance* he makes during the whole play. To Arsinoé's offer of support, he replied (III. 5) in self-diagnosis :

> Le Ciel ne m'a point fait, en me donnant le jour,
> Une âme compatible avec l'air de la cour ;
> Je ne me trouve point les vertus nécessaires
> Pour y bien réussir, et faire mes affaires.
> Etre franc et sincère est mon plus grand talent ;
> Je ne sais point jouer les hommes en parlant ;
> Et qui n'a pas le don de cacher ce qu'il pense
> Doit faire en ce pays fort peu de résidence.[1]

We cannot do justice to the implications of the play, however, until we consider not only Alceste but also Philinte. Certain passages of arms between them lend a philosophic breadth to the *honnêteté* theme which it would not otherwise possess. If the play itself is founded on the ambiguity of the word *honnêteté*, parts of it appear to offer a similar ambiguity of the word ' philosophy ' or ' philosophic '. Alceste's *chagrin philosophe* gives us the word in what might well be called its Diogenic sense : *cette grande raideur des vertus des vieux âges :* while for Philinte, ' philosophic ' seems at first sight to mean little more than ' making the best of a bad job '. Yet there is a common meaning which Philinte alludes to, when he declares to his friend :

> Mon flegme est philosophe autant que votre bile.

A common meaning which resides in a common view of human nature, and not a flattering one. Their difference is only in the attitude which each adopts in face of the same set of facts. Philinte, with his conformity, his *vertu traitable*, his accustoming himself to take men as they are, has, for all his pessimism, a

---

[1] Quite recently Mr. A. S. Sells, attempting to assess the influence of La Mothe le Vayer on Molière, has maintained that *La Prose Chagrine* (see above, pp. 271–4) has played some part in the conception of *Le Misanthrope*. His evidence is not very impressive, but he might have quoted the above passage as having its exact parallel in the situation which the irritable old Sceptic describes as his own (*Modern Language Review*, 1933).

certain belief in *la parfaite raison* (which he would agree no man ever possessed), and can find the courage to say :

> Tous ces défauts humains nous donnent dans la vie
> Des moyens d'exercer notre philosophie :
> C'est le plus bel emploi que trouve la vertu.

Yet he would admit at bottom that even his philosophy was due to temperament, and Nature had made him the counterpart of his friend, a Democritus to the other's Heraclitus. *La raison* —the word has, again, a strangely un-Cartesian accent on Alceste's lips. He is only too acutely conscious that

> La raison n'est pas ce qui règle l'amour.

He knows that to be jealous with Célimène is to be unreasonable, and yet what an odd figure he cuts with his ' reasonable ' propositions to Eliante.

If this analysis of *Le Misanthrope* has even a modicum of truth, it will be clear that a whole group of themes which we have linked, directly or indirectly, with the Essays, are lurking in the background and demand to be understood, if we are to get the full flavour of the play.

From this play onwards the conflict of reason and temperament is never chosen by Molière as his main theme (unless, as in *Amphytryon and George Dandin*, we are removed to some unrealistic atmosphere). The utter unteachability of the comic ' type ' is certainly a heritage of the *commedia*, but in later plays this powerlessness of reason or omnipotence of temperament seems to be viewed with less and less of an element of indignation. There is no punishment of Harpagon, of M. Jourdain, or even of Argan ; and none is possible. Indeed their whole happiness depends on their illusions. The sting of Molière's satire is almost wholly directed against the social consequences of their illusions.[1]

Le Bourgeois Gentilhomme is the best illustration of this evolution. Behind the rich and farcical humour, there are two more serious elements which have helped to shape the play. The pretensions of the experts—from the *maître à danser* to the *maître de philosophie*—are no less the subject of our laughter than dear Monsieur Jourdain himself. The criticism of the quacks of polite accomplishment finds, on another plane, its continuation in *Les Femmes Savantes*, just as its origin may be seen in the satire of the quackery of the real doctors—or the mimicry of

---

[1] In so far as *L'Avare* is not pure farce, its sting lies in the implicit justification of a son who is forced to rob his father, a situation closely paralleled in Montaigne's *De l'Affection des Pères aux Enfants* (II, 8).

'Doctors despite themselves'. And it is not only in the 'duel' of Nicole, the servant, with her master that we may see Molière's apology of *bon sens naturel* and instinct, but in Jourdain himself, who keeps our sympathy by the inextinguishable *bonhomie* of his nature, his sudden flashes of unperverted pedestrian sanity, his preference for the accomplishments he discovers he has always possessed, and his refusal to abandon entirely his natural character.[1] These are the qualities which, dupe though he is, make him gain our affection at the expense of the fine gentleman who gulls him. Thus we are brought to the second 'lesson' of which I have spoken, one which links this play with the *honnêteté* aspect of *Le Misanthrope ;* a 'lesson' to be formulated in six words : *le bel air ne peut s'apprendre.*

We leave M. Jourdain still isolated in his 'false paradise', confident in his dignity of Mamamouchi, just as our last glimpse of Harpagon is stealing off with satisfaction to see his *chère cassette.*

If we are frank, we must admit that *Les Femmes Savantes*, Molière's attack on all that can be brought under the head of 'preciosity', is to-day almost disconcertingly violent. It is a whole epoch which Molière invites us to laugh at : *Les Femmes Savantes* is the *pendant* of Boileau's 'Satires'. The lampooning of Cotin and Ménage, is indeed the outcome of Boileau's attacks on both authors. In Molière they become the symbols of the generation who were *Maîtres de philosophie*, not of the Jourdains, but of the Philamintes. *Les Femmes Savantes* is, however, much more than this. It is a satire of sham learning, whether in the persons of Trissotin and Vadius or of the egregious women themselves, but it is also the satire of 'angels'. Critics and commentators have always been agreed to see in the play two extremes and a middle party : the women and their mentors, Chrysalde and Martine, and between them, representing the idea of *juste milieu*, Clitandre, Henriette and Ariste. Now this is true enough, if we consider the scene between Clitandre and Trissotin (IV. 3) with its theme of *un sot savant est sot plus qu'un sot ignorant,*[2] its ridicule of obscure latinists, and its defence of a true wit and learning. It is the satire of the 'experts', or pseudo-experts

---

[1] For this last trait, note II, 6. '*Maître à philosophie* ; La Morale . . . Elle traite de la félicité, enseigne aux hommes à moderer leur passions, et . . . *M. Jourdain* . . . Non : laissons cela. Je suis bilieux comme tous les diables et il n'y a morale qui tienne : je me veux mettre en colère tout mon soûl, quand il m'en prend envie.'

[2] Mr. A. L. Sells has tried to show (*Modern Language Review*, 1933, p. 359) that Molière has here paraphrased a passage of *La Prose Chagrine*. This seems quite possible (though nothing more) : but what La Mothe says is merely a repetition of the Essays (II, 17, p. 446 ; III, 8, pp. 191, 197).

over again. It is equally true that when Clitandre declares in a famous passage,

Je consens qu'une femme ait des clartés de tout,

he is speaking for Molière or for *les honnêtes gens*. The attitude is exactly that of a passage of *L'Ecole des Maris*, already quoted and indeed parallel with certain remarks of Mademoiselle de Scudéry herself (see above, p. 341).

If we turn from the question of learning, in men or women, to the question of ' angels ', of soul *versus* body, *ange ou bête*, the distinction between Chrysalde and Clitandre disappears. It is not only Chrysalde who insists *Guénille si l'on veut : ma guénille m'est chère*, but it is Clitandre who, in a passage which definitely recalls Montaigne, exclaims (IV, 2) :

Pour moi, par un malheur, je m'apperçois, Madame,
Que j'ai, ne vous déplaise, un corps tout comme une âme.
Je sens qu'il y tient trop pour le laisser à part :
De ces détachements je ne connois pas l'art :
Le ciel m'a dénié cette philosophie,
Et mon corps et mon âme marchent de compagnie.[1]

The vaunted intellectualism of Armande proves a sham, and the character of Bélise repeats the diagnosis of *Les Précieuses Ridicules*. Even in Philaminte, the Stoical Philaminte, a consistent intellectualism is represented in a purely ridiculous light. The finishing touch is supplied when, having rebuked her husband for regretting the supposed loss of their entire fortune, she continues (pointing to Trissotin) :

Son bien peut nous suffire pour nous et pour lui.

Not sublime, but sublimely comic. Chrysalde and Martine certainly have their laughable side, too, but the sympathy of Molière for both is only too apparent.

This brings us to what may appear disconcerting in the play. If ' feminism ' is a plea for the ' equality ' of the sexes, *Les Femmes Savantes* may be called an anti-feminist play. The situation as Molière sees it is different. It is time for a protest against a ' monstrous regiment of women '. Chrysalde's weakness is symbolic. Philaminte's projects for asserting the claims of women are ridiculous, because those claims have no need to be pressed. It is to the good horse-sense of the servant Martine, dismissed for her ignorance of grammar, that Molière entrusts his final word on the subject.

[1] cf. *Essais*, III, 3, p. 55 ; 5, pp. 144, 145 (top), 148 ; 12, p. 371 ; 13, pp. 443, 448, 449, &c.

It is hardly necessary to enlarge on Molière's `` apology of nature ' in this play. Ignoring (now) the useful analysis of the various aspects of *Les Femmes Savantes*, taking it as (by its subject) the weaving together of these various themes, it is illuminating to compare it with a passage of Montaigne's *De Trois Commerces*, which it repeats with the most extraordinary fidelity. Comment seems almost unnecessary :

Sur tout c'est à mon gré bien faire le sot que de faire l'entendu entre ceux qui ne le sont pas, parler toujours bandé. *Favellar in punta di forchetta.* Il faut se démettre au train de ceux avec qui vous êtes, et parfois affecter l'ignorance . . .
Les savants chopent volontiers à cette pierre. Ils font toujours parade de leur magistère et sèment leurs livres par tout. Ils en ont en ce temps entonné si fort les cabinets et oreilles des dames que si elles n'en ont retenu la substance, au moins elles en ont la mine—à toute sorte de propos et matière, pour basse et populaire qu'il soit, elles se servent d'une façon de parler et d'écrire nouvelle et savante . . . et allèguent Platon et Saint Thomas aux choses auxquelles le premier rencontré serviroit aussi bien de témoin. La doctrine qui ne leur a pu arriver à l'âme, leur est en demeurée en la langue. Si les bien-nées m'en croient, elles se contenteront de faire valoir leur propres et naturelles richesses . . . C'est grande simplesse d'étouffer sa clarté pour luire d'une lumière empruntée ; elles sont enterrées et ensevelies sous l'art . . . Que leur faut-il que vivre aimées et honorées ? Elles n'ont et ne savent que trop pour cela. Il ne faut qu'éveiller un peu et rechauffer les facultés qui sont en elles. Quand je les vois attachées à la rhétorique, à la judiciaire, à la logique et semblables drogueries si vaines et si inutiles à leur besoin, j'entre en crainte que les hommes qui la leur conseillent, le fassent pour avoir loi de les régenter sous ce titre.[1]

Women's true advantage over men lies elsewhere.

The end of the passage differs from even Clitandre in a certain nuance.

Si toute fois il leur fâche de nous céder en quoi que ce soit, et veulent avoir part aux livres, la poésie est un amusement propre à leur besoin.

Poetry is adapted to the female understanding, and Montaigne will further admit (at the most) a tincture of history and practical ethics for the understanding of their own condition. Not so Molière. This difference admitted (and it is a product of the contemporary social situation, an aggravated crisis of the ailment as Molière sees it), it would be hard not to see that *Les Femmes Savantes* derives at least in part from this essay of Montaigne.

It is still more clearly Montaigne who has been drawn upon in the *Malade Imaginaire*. The dialogue of Argan and Béralde

---

[1] *Essais*, III, 3 pp. 50, 51, 52.

(III, 3) on doctors and medicine shows us, for the second time, that it is Montaigne whom Molière has used to formulate his views on the subject.[1] It is not only the repetition of the false promises of doctors, their self-deception, the difficulty of diagnosis, the distinction between men honoured and an art (or science) justly distrusted ; it is also the echo of the same naturalism.

ARGAN. Que faire donc quand on est malade ?
BÉRALDE. Rien, mon frère . . .   Rien. Il ne faut que demeurer en repos. La nature elle-meme, quand nous la laissons faire, se tire doucement du désordre où elle est tombée. C'est notre impatience, c'est notre inquiétude qui gâtent tout, et presque tous les hommes meurent de leurs rémèdes, et non pas de leurs maladies.

The echo continues in the quotation of Molière's own opinion at the end of the scene : *il soutient que cela n'est permis qu'aux gens vigoureux*. But even the ' mock ceremony ', the conclusion of the play, attached to it by the solution that Argan is to become *his own doctor*, provides the parallel with the attitude of Montaigne : if doctoring there must be, employ for yourself, in full knowledge of your own nature, the few harmless remedies that are certain.

Le Malade Imaginaire contains certain indications which are, however, perhaps more important for understanding Molière's ' philosophy '. The author himself knew his end was not far off. A month or two earlier no doctor had been able to save his baby son. Two years before, at the last attempt of the Sorbonne (and the Faculty of Medicine) to suppress by act of Parliament innovations against Aristotle, he had dreamed of a satirical attack on false learning which would have supplemented the *Arrêts Burlesques* of his friends Bernier and Boileau.[2] For him the Purgons and the Diafoirus have acquired a symbolical quality which it is unwise to underrate. The unexecuted ' comedy of learning ' might have given us a whole gallery of doctors of this and that, with a sceptic too, perhaps not after the model of the Mamphurius of *Le Mariage Forcé*, but actually the *raisonneur* of the play. But *Le Malade* does at least give us a whole gallery of medical types, and provides its mitigated sceptic in the person of Béralde.

Can we not go further ? Is *Le Malade* not, in certain respects, the repetition of *Tartuffe* ? The resemblances of Argan and Orgon are not confined to the letters of their names. Here the

---

[1] See above on *L'Amour Médecin*. The Despois et Mesnard edition of Molière (IX, 393 et seq.) gives the necessary references.
[2] See E. Magne, *Une Amie Inconnue de Molière* : Molière et l'Université.

obsession of health, there the obsession of spiritual health, of salvation. Toinette and Dorine, Angelique and Mariane, the whole theme of the daughter's marriage is borrowed, and whole passages of comic dialogue transferred from one play to the other. True, Béline and Elmire are totally different conceptions, but if M. Michaut is right about the first version of *Tartuffe*, with an unfaithful wife . . . ? The repetition of characters and situation cannot be pushed too far, but, such as it is, it raises the question as to whether the play, *bien comprise* (that is to say by a minority) does not hint at the folly, not only of a blind faith in doctors, but a blind faith in priests. Nor would this imply an irreligious Molière, but only a more definite nuance of that anticlerical Molière, whose existence is hardly in doubt.[1]

Whether such a view is accepted or not, we can point to an impressive number of points of contact between Molière and Montaigne : a distrust of learning—of doctors in particular— an acceptance of diversity, of individual idiosyncrasy as the basic fact of human nature and the mark of its oddity, a hatred of dogmatism, a sympathy for the simple-minded and the humble, a profound conviction that soul and body have equal rights and that reason has little power over our own nature, little power to establish more than some humble philosophy of *bon sens*. The *bon sens* of Molière leads us to some conclusion such as that of Montaigne : *Sauf l'ordre, la modération et la constance, j'estime que toutes choses sont faisables par un homme bien manque et défaillant en gros.*[2] A knowledge of Montaigne is necessary to the full understanding of Molière. The influence may be partly indirect, but it is there. Of Gassendi we find nothing specific, and, if we admit all the suggestions of Mr. Sells on the inspiration of La Mothe, we cannot ignore the fact that in almost every case quoted a parallel passage of the Essays could be brought forward.

There is no room to deal so fully with certain friends of Molière. Boileau, who belongs to a younger generation, is often spoken of as a Cartesian. Perhaps ; but the Fourth Satire (to the Abbé La Mothe Le Vayer) and the Eighth repeat all those Montaignesque themes which Régnier had already treated : the vanity of reason, the irreducible nature of individual tempera-ment, anthropocentrism and the folly of mankind. According to Brossette, it was to the Essays that Boileau referred when he wrote of himself :

[1] Compare also in *Les Amants Magnifiques* the satire of astrology, which may be understood *at two levels*—literally or metaphorically.

[2] *Essais*, II, 29, p. 503.

Tantôt un livre en main, errant dans les prairies
J'occupe ma raison d'utiles rêveries.[1]

Nor would it be hard to show of the Boileau of the *Satires* that his ' philosophy ', his attitude to religion and ethics, is full of reminiscences of the Essays. It is beyond the scope of this study to continue our examination of French satire to the end of the century, but two *Bordelais* of whom little is known : Bénech de Cantenac, Canon of Bordeaux, and Du Camp d'Orgas both show how satire—above all on the theme of vanity and the ' critique of satisfaction '—continues in the now familiar vein.[2]

With regard to La Fontaine [1621–95] Montaigne's influence is worth looking into more closely. La Fontaine's character and his *milieu* seem to mark him out as just the man in whom we should expect to find a predestined disciple of Montaigne. The protégé of Fouquet was not only the close friend of Molière, Chapelle, and for a time, of Boileau and Racine, the friend of Madame de Sévigné and Pélisson. With Bernier he shared the hospitality of Madame de la Sablière for nearly twenty years. She, and the Duchesse de Bouillon are two of the links which bind him to a circle which included Ninon, the Vendômes, Chaulieu, La Fare—while Mitton, St. Evremond and La Rochefoucauld are among his friends. It is in this *milieu* that the influence of Montaigne is apparent even at the end of the century. But La Fontaine has named his own masters : Marot, Voiture and Rabelais. Olivet, who had seen his copies of Plutarch and Plato says that it is they who have provided most of the philosophic reflexions of the Fables, and the poet himself has only once referred to Montaigne by name.[3]

Nevertheless, there was another master whose influence La Fontaine did not escape. The *credo* of the *bonhomme* has been sought in the delicious poem which forms the real conclusion of *Psyché :*

O douce Volupté, sans qui, dès l'enfance,
Le vivre et le mourir nous deviendraient égaux ;
Aimant universel de tous les animaux,
Que tu sais attirer avec violence !
Par toi tout se meut ici-bas.

[1] *Epître*, VI.   Reporting Boileau's indication as to the book in question, he continues : ' En effet Montaigne donne lui-même à ses écrits le nom de Rêveries . . .'

[2] See Du Camp d'Orgas, *Réflexions d'un Solitaire sur la Vie et les Erreurs des Hommes*, 1689 (and 1690 under a different title) : Bénech de Cantenac, *Satires Nouvelles* (1690), especially Sat. II.

[3] *Œuvres*, IX, p. 425.   So far as Plato is concerned, note the Preface of La Fontaine (ib., IX, p. 337 et seq.) where he represents Plato as *le père de l'ironie,* the arch enemy of the pedants of his day.

It is another theme, however, equally dear to the poet, round which most of his general ideas may be grouped : the persuasion of the diversity of men, the consciousness of the diversity of opinions and customs, the relativism which goes with it, and the mitigated scepticism which it entails.   What is the lesson of the ' Ass loaded with sponges and the ass loaded with salt ' ?

> C'est assez qu'on ait vu par là qu'il ne faut point
>   Agir chacun de même sorte (II, ii).

again :

>   ce n'est pas sur l'habit
> Que la diversité me plaît : c'est dans l'esprit (IX, 3).

Elsewhere the theme is seen in conjunction with the conclusion of human vanity :

> Les vertus devraient être soeurs
>   Ainsi que les vices sont frères.
> Dès que l'un de ceux-ci s'empare de nos coeurs,
> Tous viennent à la file : il ne s'en manque guères :
>   J'entends de ceux qui, n'étant pas contraires,
>   Peuvent loger sous même toit.
> A l'égard des vertus rarement on les voit
> Tous en un sujet éminemment placées . . .
> L'homme est ainsi bâti : quand un sujet l'enflamme,
> L'impossibilité disparaît de son âme. . . .
>   Tout cela, c'est la mer à boire ;
>   Mais rien à l'homme ne suffit (VIII, 25).

Do we seek another application of the theme ?

> Que j'ai toujours haï les pensers du vulgaire,
> Qu'il me semble profane, injuste, et téméraire,
> Mettant de faux milieux entre la chose et lui
> Et mesurant par soi ce qu'il voit en autrui.

It is thus that La Fontaine introduces the story of *Démocrite et les Abderitains*, the sage Democritus, ' the master of Epicurus ', as he reminds us, who was thought mad by his countrymen. These *faux milieux*, custom and opinion, are treated in a whole series of fables.

> C'est souvent du hasard que nait l'opinion :
> Et c'est l'opinion qui fait toujours la vogue.
>   Je pouvais fonder ce prologue
> Sur gens de tous états : tout est prévention,

Cabale, entêtements ; point ou peu de justice.
C'est un torrent : qu'y faire ? il faut qu'il ait son cours ?
Cela fut et sera toujours (VII, 15).

Note La Fontaine's conclusion, however, on custom, at least.
It is ' vice-nature ', as Donne said, and alas ! inescapable.[1]

Les ames des souris et des belles
   Sont très différentes entre elles.
Il en faut toujours revenir à son destin,
C'est à dire à la loi par le Ciel établie. (IX, 7).

Que sert-il qu'on se contrefasse !
Prétendre ainsi changer est une illusion ;
L'on reprend sa première trace
A la première occasion (XII, 10).

That strange fable *Le Cierge* (IX, 12) offers us yet another
example of

Tout en tout est divers : ôtez-vous de l'esprit
Qu'aucun être ait été composé sur le vôtre,

while a passage of *Psyché* reinforces the lesson. ' You must
imagine me as you would wish me ' insinuates the voice of the
invisible lover.

Oui : mais, repartit la belle, je ne me rencontrerai peut-être pas
avec la Nature : car il y a bien de la fantaisie en cela.   J'ai oui dire
que non seulement chaque nation avait son goût, mais chaque personne
aussi.   Une amazone se proposerait un mari dont les grâces feraient
trembler, un mari ressemblant à Mars : moi je m'en proposerai un
semblable à l'Amour.   Une personne mélancolique ne manqueroit pas
de donner à ce mari un air sérieux : moi, qui suis gaie, je lui en donnerai
un enjoué.   Enfin, je croirai vous faire plaisir en vous attribuant une
beauté délicate, et peut-être vous ferais-je tort.[2]

' To know oneself ' was the old lesson [3] which La Fontaine chose
a few months before his death to sum up and round off his masterpiece ; and we see now a little more clearly what sense the words
of the oracle had for him.

Does La Fontaine compare Alexander with that modern hero,
the great Condé ?   It is the refrain of Montaigne we find upon
his lips :

---

[1] See also II, 18 (*La Chatte métamorphosée en Femme*) ; III, 7 (*L'Ivrogne
et sa Femme*) ; XII, 10 (*L'Ecrevisse et sa Fille*).

[2] *Œuvres* (ed. *Grands Ecrivains*), VIII, p. 70.

[3] See *Le Juge Arbitre, L'Hospitalier et le Solitaire* (*Fables*, XII, 27).

Quand la témérité est heureuse, elle met les hommes au nombre des dieux. On me répondra que celui de qui dépend le salut de toute une armée, ne doit jamais devoir le sien propre à un bienfait du hasard. Toutes ces choses là ont deux faces, aussi bien que la plupart de celles que nous louons ou que nous blâmons tous les jours.
On peut disputer de part et autre tant qu'on voudra.[1]

It is hardly necessary to show La Fontaine's anti-dogmatism, his hatred of pedants, but it is possibly worth quoting in this connexion one of the most original allegories to be found in the Fables.[2] The goddess Discord, banished from Heaven—

> Chez l'animal qu'on appelle homme
> On la reçut à bras ouverts,
> Elle et Que-si-que-non son frère,
> Avecque Tien et Mien son père.
> Elle nous fit l'honneur, en ce bas univers,
> De préférer notre hémisphère
> A celui des mortels qui nous sont opposés,
> Gens grossiers, peu civilisés,
> Et qui se mariant sans prêtre et sans notaire,
> De la Discorde n'ont que faire.

A lodging for the Goddess is finally found at the ' inn of Marriage '. The end of the fable does not here concern us, but the family connexions, the genealogy of Discord, which have astonished the commentators, are familiar enough to us. *Que si que non* is a conception similar to the *Qui et Non* of Charron's *preudhomie artificielle,* the dialogue of reason pitted against reason, of dogmatic affirmation and negation, from which the lesson of relativism (and of fideism) may be learnt. The origin of Discord and Dogmatism is then Property, and La Fontaine's reference to the Savages shows sufficiently the background of thought upon which this allegory is founded.[3]

Having shown how a whole series of themes grow out of the contemplation of the fact or facts of diversity, it will be apparent, on reflexion, that the importance of the animal, the preoccupation with the animal in La Fontaine has far more philosophical interest than has been supposed. It is not only a question of La Fontaine's character and inclinations, nor of the brilliant literary expedient of the fable, rendering possible at one and the same

---

[1] *Œuvres,* VIII, p. 327.
[2] *Fables,* VI, 20. The *Grands ecrivains* Edition suggests one of Gilles Corrozet's Emblems as the La Fontaine's point of departure. This is very doubtful. We have in this allegory one of the rare examples of La Fontaine as inventor of his theme.
[3] On the Savages, see also *Œuvres,* VI (*La Quinquina*), pp. 325, 352, 353.

time an astonishingly outspoken and yet an amiable and friendly satire of human nature.

We have seen in Montaigne and various *Montaignisants* what context 'animal' most often suggests in the seventeenth century. On the one hand, the animal is said to reason. This may be used as a theme for the abasement of human pride, with the usual addition, as in the *Apologie pour Raymond Sebond*, that even if they do reason, reasoning is no great advantage anyhow. The inconsequence of the addition reveals that all along the position 'animals reason' is urged *in view of* a plea for fideism, tolerance or scepticism. Or else, more specifically, as a weapon against anthropocentrism or the presumptuous notion of a *personal* providence. But we have not yet finished with contradictions, for—regarded from another point of view—animals are declared to be wiser and happier *because they do not reason*, because, having no reason, they remain more nearly true to instinct, to the natural law, the *ethos* of their species. The 'primitivism' of Montaigne, the happy savage, the peasant, the admiration for instinct, hedonism and the notion of the importance of individual nature, all lend weight to the theme of the 'happy beast', and all these we find present in some measure in La Fontaine.

We must ask how far this contradiction is present in La Fontaine. Artistically perhaps it hardly arises, for, as has been often said, La Fontaine's animals are at once men and beasts. They symbolize by their different species the diversity of human nature, and its *irreducible character*, and hence show the vanity of serious indignation with the vices and foibles of human beings. Their fallible reasoning is sometimes presented as the satire of human rationalism, human presumption ; sometimes their ingeniosity and resource is presented—often humorously in a syllogistic form—as a theme for our admiration. But what is the real basis of La Fontaine's admiration and genuine affection, as it seems, for the animal world ? Suppose we take the *Discours à Madame de la Sablière* (X, I) where he protests against the Cartesian theory of animal mechanism. Even here the humble reasoning, which is all he argues for, is not represented as an unmixed blessing. What of the Polish foxes and their war-like preparations ? [1] Apart from that mysterious 'soul' which men share in some degree with angels, men and beasts are all alike. It is the same conclusion which we find in *Les Lapins* (XI, 5), dedicated to La Rochefoucauld. Does La Fontaine, then, wholly escape the inconsequence of asking us to 'go to the ant '

[1] . . . Mille inventions D'une pernicieuse et maudite science . . . Exercent de ces animaux le bon sens et l'expérience.

because the ant reasons, while doubting the benefits of ' reason ' ?
Not entirely, owing to his use of the fable as satire, and owing
to the natural implications of his reaction to Descartes.   But
we must not forget that the basis, at least, of his ' theriophily '
is closely connected with his naturalism, with his hedonism,
with a certain nostalgia of innocence, which brings him again
close to Montaigne.

> Humains, cruels humains, tyrans de l'univers
> C'est de vous seuls qu'on doit se plaindre (*Daphné*).

Were we to ask why, as La Fontaine says :

> De tous les animaux, l'homme a le plus de pente
> A se porter dedans l'excès,[1]

the answer is that reason corrupts our natural inclinations.
Animal nature is more *constant* (hence the need for a variety of
species to symbolize the diversity of the single species, man).
We have seen in dealing with Charron some of the implications
of this gambit.   *L'inconstance et l'inquiétude qui me sont naturelles*
explain the fascination of the idea of a *natural* constancy, an
instinctive happiness, for La Fontaine.   It is worth noticing
that he has paraphrased in *Galatée* certain verses of Madame
Deshoulières to which we must return later on in this chapter :

> Que vous êtes heureux, troupeaux, vous ne songez
> Qu'à satisfaire vos envies.

It is the happiness of animals which is the basis of La Fontaine's
' theriophily '.   He makes Momus declare in one of his operas
(with a hyperbole in keeping with his celestial superiority) :

> Le temps de la sottise est celui du bonheur ! [2]

We must not, however, simplify too far La Fontaine's religion
of pleasure.   The sage old man in the second book of *Psyché*
declares to the heroine :

> La véritable grandeur, à l'égard des philosophes, est de régner sur
> soi-même : et le véritable plaisir, de jouir de soi.   Cela se trouve en la
> solitude et ne se trouve guère autrepart.   Je ne vous dis pas que toutes
> personnes s'en accommodent : c'est un bien pour moi, ce seroit un mal
> pour vous.[3]

Again as he makes Gélaste declare in the same delightful story :

> Le plaisir dont nous devons faire le plus de cas est toujours celui

[1] *Fables*, IX, 11.   [2] *Œuvres*, VII, p. 261.
[3] ib., VIII, p. 150 ; cf. the last of the fables (XII, 25).

qui convient le mieux à notre nature : car c'est s'unir à soi-même que de le goûter.

and Gélaste bases on this statement his preference for comedy as against tragedy.[1]

For a man haunted and charmed by diversity, who is keenly aware of his own *inconstance et inquiétude*, the question what pleasure is most suited to his nature admits, of course, no simple answer.

> J'aime le jeu, l'amour, les livres, la musique,
> La ville et la campagne, enfin tout : il n'est rien
> Qui ne me soit souverain bien,
> Jusqu'au sombre plaisir d'un cœur mélancolique.[2]

The central thought of the poem from which these verses are taken is indeed that all pleasures have some cousinage with love, *aimant universel de tous les animaux*. In all there is a sensual element, and love itself, in its widest sense, is that whereby we feel we are alive :

> Les morts sont donc heureux ? Ce n'est pas mon avis ;
> Je veux des passions : et si l'état le pire
> Est le néant, je ne sais point
> De néant plus complet qu'un cœur froid à ce point.[3]

Nothing, however, could be more false than the notion of the author of the *Contes* as a *coureur de femmes*. Certainly no man was less made for marriage, and the traditions of the erotic tale gave him ample opportunity to indulge a somewhat too facile satirical verve. Certainly in love, too, *Diversité c'est ma devise*,[4] but, if we may trust the usual frankness of the *bonhomme*, though he had generally some *Philis* in view, he did not find them, nor wish to find them, so liberal of their favours as his taste for the *gauloiseries* of the *Contes* might suggest. La Fontaine is also the poet of *Adonis* and *Psyché*, where we may find certain exquisite touches which remind us that his conception of love, and his understanding of human nature are too profound for a mere *jouisseur*. I find the best comment on his own marriage in the following sentence of *Psyché* :

[1] '. . . Or y a-t-il rien qui nous convienne mieux que le rire ? Il n'est pas moins naturel à l'homme que la raison : il lui est même particulier ' (cf. the Rabelaisian *Le rire est le propre de l'homme*) ib., VIII, p. 111.

[2] *Œuvres*, VIII, p. 233. Compare these verses with a passage of Théophile quoted above, p. 141.

[3] ib., VI, p. 207 (*Les Filles de Minée*) ; cf. *Fables* XII, 20 (*Le philosophe Scythe*).

[4] *Contes*, IV, 11 (*Œuvres*, V, p. 505).

Qu'on fasse telle mine qu'on voudra, qu'on se querelle, qu'on se sépare, qu'on proteste de se haïr, il reste toujours un levain d'amour entre deux personnes qui ont été unies si étroitement.[1]

There is again a subtle piece of reasoning which falls from the lips of the mysterious Eros and finds its echo again and again in La Fontaine's work :

. . . le meilleur pour vous est l'incertitude, et qu'après la possession vous ayez toujours de quoi désirer : c'est un secret dont on ne s'était pas encore avisé. Demeurez-en là, si vous m'en croyez : je sais ce que c'est d'amour, et le dois savoir.[2]

It is the same apology of uncertainty which we find, for example, in *La Coupe Enchantée*.

Avoir des passions in La Fontaine's case, goes hand in hand with another psychological trait. Morpheus, the god of sleep, holds no small place in his private mythology. That is a commonplace, and yet its significance is lost, if we do not note that for him to sleep is not perchance but almost perforce to dream.[3] To dream—and we can see that day-dreaming is the origin of all those stories of his absent-mindedness—to dream, for such a man as La Fontaine, is to experience a certain effortless Protean life, from which the keenest edge of pleasure, no doubt, but also the keenest edge of pain are absent. It is even the full realization of a certain innocence, which was, in a large measure, his at all times, which even made the charm of his personality—a personality essentially *ondoyant*, capable of *une longue patience* only as a literary craftsman ; an artist, not a philosopher. To attempt to penetrate the mind of such an artist leads one inevitably beyond the question of general ideas to the imponderables of individual temperament. In so far as that mind has been oriented by congenial philosophic themes there seems little doubt, however, that these La Fontaine has found directly in the Essays, and, in part, indirectly in some of the numerous authors who themselves reflect the influence of Montaigne.

As to his religious beliefs we have little to go upon. Towards the end of his life we may note an exchange of letters with St. Evremond in which the latter attempts to characterize La Fontaine's ' ethic ', as he understands it :

S'accommoder aux ordres du destin ;
Aux plus heureux ne porter point d'envie ;

---

[1] *Œuvres*, VIII, p. 101.   [2] ib., VIII, p. 75.
[3] Note, in particular, the letter to his wife (IX, p. 292).

Du faux esprit que prend un libertin,
Avec le temps, connaître la folie ;
Et dans les Vers, Jeu, Musique, bon Vin
Passer en paix une innocente vie ;
C'est le moyen d'en reculer la fin.[1]

The poet, in his reply, writes : ' *Je ne suis pas moins ennemi que vous du faux air d'esprit que prend un libertin. Quiconque l'affectera, je lui donnerai la palme du ridicule.*[2] *Avec le temps* is a restriction which perhaps applies more strictly to St. Evremond than to his correspondent. La Fontaine's repeated ' conversions ' and ' relapses ' in later life are the *crises de conscience* of a man whom religious doubt has perhaps never touched very deeply. The fideist solution of continuity between religion and ethics, no doubt, made it easy for him to ignore certain possible implications of his Epicureanism.

If we wish to see these implications developed, and a certain background against which La Fontaine's treatment of the happy animal theme should perhaps be placed, we have only to turn to two minor writers of his acquaintance, who are characteristic of the *milieu* in which he lived.

Madame Deshoulières [1636–94], some of whose poems were published in 1688, has been given by M. Lachèvre a place alongside La Fare and Chaulieu as *les derniers libertins*.[3] M. Lachèvre makes a great deal of the fact that two of her three children were unbaptized until 1685 (they were born in 1656 and 1666 respectively). The omission seems certainly a fairly clear mark of some independence of mind, and the reparation of the omission (or oversight) in 1685 appears to coincide with other manifestations of ' piety ' such as an ode congratulating the King on the Revocation of the Edict of Nantes. Madame Deshoulières was a student of Gassendi's works, a pupil (it appears) of Jean Dehénault. Among her friends we may number others who have made their appearance in these pages : Des Barreaux, Mitton, La Rochefoucauld, La Fontaine, for example. With the Duchesse of Bouillon she was one of those who staged the *cabale* which attacked Racine's *Phèdre*.

Madame Deshoulières' verses attest on several occasions the influence of the Essays. Their chief interest is perhaps, however, their combination of certain philosophic themes in a manner only hinted at by La Fontaine. Take what is possibly her most celebrated poem, *Les Moutons*, of which the opening verses were

[1] St. Evremond : *Œuvres*, IV, p. 449.
[2] La Fontaine : *Œuvres*, IX, p. 409.
[3] Frédéric Lachèvre : *Les Derniers Libertins*, 1924.

imitated by La Fontaine, as has been said. Strange to say she is almost certainly not the original author of these verses, for they appear in 1661 or 1662 in *Les Promenades de Messire Antoine Coutel, seignieur de Monteaux*.[1] Coutel's version not only antedates Madame Deshoulières' by some sixteen years, but his verses are so much more clumsy that there can be little doubt as to the original author, who appears from another part of his book to have been himself an admirer of the Essays.[2]

The question of the origin of *Les Moutons* is not of immense importance, since the subject was repeated by Madame Deshoulières in other poems, and is thoroughly characteristic of her way of thinking : the combination of two anti-rational themes :

> Hélas ! petits Moutons, que vous êtes heureux,
> Vous paissez dans nos champs, sans soucis, sans alarmes
>   Aussitôt aimés qu'amoureux !
> On ne vous force point à répandre des larmes :
> Vous ne formez jamais d'inutiles désirs.
> Dans vos tranquilles cœurs l'amour suit la Nature,
> Sans ressentir ses maux vous avez ses plaisirs.
> L'ambition, l'honneur, l'intérêt, l'imposture,
>   Qui font tant de maux parmi nous,
>   Ne se rencontrent point chez vous.
> Cependant nous avons la raison pour partage,
>   Et vous en ignorez l'usage.
> Innocents animaux, n'en soyez point jaloux,
>   Ce n'est pas un grand avantage, . . .
> Ces prétendus trésors dont on fait vanité,
>   Valent moins que votre indolence.
> Ils nous livrent sans cesse à des soins criminels :
>   Par eux plus d'un remords nous ronge
>   Nous voulons les rendre éternels,
> Sans songer qu'eux et nous passerons comme un songe.
>   Il n'est dans ce vaste Univers
>   Rien d'assuré, rien de solide :
> Des choses d'ici bas la Fortune décide
>   Selon ses caprices divers.
>   Tout l'effort de notre prudence
> Ne peut nous dérober aux moindre de ses coups
> Paissez, Moutons, paissez sans règle et sans science,
> Vous êtes plus heureux et plus sages que nous.

The disadvantage of reason and the happiness of animals recur in *La Solitude*, in two series of *Réflexions* in verse, and in the *Epître à Monsieur Thévart*, to name only the pieces reprinted

---

[1] Blois, undated. Part of the book was written already in 1649.
[2] ib., p. 173. Three epigrams on the Essays.

by M. Lachèvre.[1] The influence of Montaigne appears more certainly, however, in the *Ballade à St. Aignan* on the omnipotence of opinion, and, in the *Ode à La Rochefoucauld* (1678) where we have a protest against the Stoical idea that pain is no evil, an affirmation of the close interaction of body and mind, praise of a golden age (*où sans guide On laissait les moeurs*) a declaration of the vanity of philosophy. Though the beginning of *Réflexions Diverses* (*Que l'homme connaît peu la mort qu'il apprehende*) derives doubtless in part straight from Lucretius and Seneca and not from a passage at the end of Montaigne's *Que philosopher c'est apprendre a mourir* (I, 20), there are certain other verses in the poem which seem to paraphrase the Essays.[2] We may perhaps conclude that in Madame Deshoulières' case the preoccupation with innocence, with the ' happy animal ', however strikingly or picturesquely presented is subsidiary to the vanity theme of :

> Toujours vains, toujours faux, toujours pleins d'injustice,
> Nous crions dans tous nos discours
> Contre les passions, les faiblesses, les vices,
> Où nous succombons tous les jours.

And while we find certain echoes of Montaigne, there may be also a considerable indirect influence through Dehénault and perhaps Des Barreaux which it is impossible to estimate.

Although the direct attacks on Montaigne grow in number and in violence from 1660 onwards we may still find it recorded how popular the Essays still were round the year 1670. A contemporary scrap-book, already quoted, which voices the opinion of certain people on the outskirts of the Jansenist movement, supplies us with the information that the *beaux esprits* still admire Montaigne—and Charron, too, though good judges put him after Montaigne—but both are beginning to age.[3] Further on we read : *Montaigne est en vogue à présent : il y a peu de bons auteurs français. Montaigne est un des principaux* . . . A hack-writer, who presumably wishes to catch the fashionable ear, still quotes Charron in his *Morale* (1671) and Montaigne in his *Journal de Conversation* (1673).[4]

In another ten years, with the conversion of the King and the

---

[1] *Les Derniers Libertins* : La Solitude, pp. 75, 76, 77 ; Réflexions, p. 88 ; Epître à M. Thévart, p. 90 ; Réflexions Morales, p. 100.

[2] e.g. Strophe VII. (*De qui nous a servi la vue est importune*, &c.) Strophe X (on suicide) ; Strophe XV (*du commerce des sots*).

[3] Bib. Nat. MS. nouv. acquis. françaises. 4333, reproduced in part by E. Griselle : *Revue de Fribourg* 1907–8. Pascal et les *Pascalins*.

[4] *La Morale de Réné Bary*, p. 65, 205, 445, &c. *Journal de Conversation*, pp. 9, 22, 31, Chap. VI (beginning) ; 154–210. cf. also his *L'esprit*

sanctification of the Court, the *beaux esprits* who would still avow their taste for the Essays are mainly to be found in the *milieu* of the Vendôme. We have mentioned the relations of La Fontaine with the ' *société du Temple* ' which is generally considered as the *foyer* of irreligion, where Voltaire learnt his deism. The Epicureanism of Chaulieu establishes (through Chapelle, his master in the art of writing and perhaps also of thinking) a kind of link with Gassendi. Its poetic expression is often similar to that of Madame Deshoulières, who has already given us a pointer as to where we may look for the *Montaignisants* of the late seventeenth century. Chaulieu, however, is fundamentally a rationalist who delights to boast of his freedom from all superstition. I should hesitate to present him as a disciple of Montaigne. The case of La Fare is slightly different—the handsome marquis whom Madame de la Sablière and (indirectly) La Fontaine had reason to know only too well. Although born as late as 1644, we may very briefly consider him here, because he shows how far Montaigne's way of thinking has rightly become identified with some nuance of freethought or of deism, and because he looks forward to Voltaire [1] as well as back to the Essays.

It is only necessary to read the opening pages of his *Mémoires* to see how La Fare's philosophy ultimately derives (with less superficiality than one might suppose) from the Essays. The considerations on the necessary conformity of natural dispositions and principles of conduct, the plea for experience against theory, the causes of the *bigarrure qui se trouve dans le monde*, mistrust of reason—all this is Montaigne seen through the possibly distorting mirror of Théophile and Méré. The themes of La Fare's poems, particularly those only published in 1924 by G. L. von Roosbroeck (and some by Lachèvre) mainly invite comparison with Théophile, La Fontaine and Madame Deshoulières, but here and there *rapprochements* with Montaigne are fairly clearly indicated. The description of the false *Sagesse* of the Stoics recalls a passage of *De l'institution des Enfants*,[2] *La Vieillesse d'un Philosophe Voluptueux* [3] suggests (as well as Horace) certain

---

de Cour (1664), p. 278 : ' Un moderne a dit de bonne grâce . . . parlant de l'immortalité dont nous parlons qu'il n'y avait rien au monde ni de si fortement cru ni de si faiblement prouvé '.

[1] Note in particular his apology of wealth.

[2] Lachèvre, pp. 228, 229 (*La Sagesse Commode*).

[3] ib., p. 234. For a definition of *volupté* see the author of the preface to the works of Chaulieu and La Fare (edition of 1731) : ' La volupté consiste dans une heureuse alliance de qualités qui forment un galant homme, et dans un usage libre, modéré et délicat de tous les biens que la nature et la fortune nous présentent '.

passages of *Des Vers de Vergile*, just as the opening of *Sur la Paresse* would appear to derive from a page of *Du Repentir*.

La Fare, however, like Chaulieu, appears to be at bottom a rationalist in religion, a rationalizing deist of a type which was to become so familiar in the succeeding age. His *Ode à l'honneur de la Religion*,[1] while it shows this, also reminds us of the uses to which these apologists who attacked Montaigne always said the Essays could be put.

> Cet Etre Universel . . .
> Ne veut point qu'à son culte on donne des limites . . .

> Ainsi quand les mortels remplis d'intelligence,
> Qui diffèrent de culte et non de dépendance,
> S'adressent à celui qui gouverne les Cieux,
> Des soupirs enflammés de leurs âmes brulantes,
> Du mélange confus de leurs voix différentes,
> Il se forme un concert *encore plus précieux*.

> Tout hommage est reçu pourvu qui'il soit sincère,
> Les hommes sont nés tous enfants du même pêre ;
> Dès que leur cœur lui parle, ils en sont écoutés . . .

Is this not a paraphrase of that most probable of ' ancient and humane opinions ' which we find in the *Apologie* and which Antoine de Laval discerned as so dangerous from the Christian point of view ?[2]   But, La Fare continues, reason, like the sun, enlightens men, renders them worthy to please the Deity, and is the foundation of their happiness.

> Loin de moi ces esprits faibles on fanatiques
> Sectateurs malheureux de vertus chimériques,
> Sur qui le vrai ne fait aucune impression,
> Qui pensent que ce sont *les choses impossibles*
> *Et les évènements les moins compréhensibles*
> *Qui font le digne objet de la Religion.*

> Chacun a dans son sein une vive lumière
> Qui de l'Esprit divin porte le caractère ;
> Tout ainsi que Dieu même il doit la révérer.

Happy the man who respecting God, and who trusting him, can achieve the harmony of reason and impulse.

> *Jamais dans ces besoins le Ciel ne l'abandonne*
> La Volupté le sert, le calme l'environne
> Et toute la Nature a soin de ses plaisirs.

---

[1] Lachèvre, pp. 243–5. Note that this poem was unpublished until 1924.
[2] See above, p. 35.

The creed which La Fare celebrates—unworthy prophet perhaps—in these somewhat indifferent verses, which end with a symbolical appeal to spread the new gospel, is without much doubt the logical conclusion of the type of humanism popularized by Montaigne, but it is also a conclusion which neither he nor Charron nor the vast majority of those studied here would have found it possible wholly to accept.

With Molière and La Fontaine we have reached a turning-point in the story of Montaigne's influence. To place these writers against the background of the Essays is to replace them in their natural setting, to ' reveal ' them in so far as such classics can still be ' revealed '. We can even point to definite reminiscences of the Essays. But, at eighty or ninety years' distance, it is impossible to deny that the scope and limits of Montaigne's influence on them is merged in that of elder contemporaries and friends, themselves nurtured on the book, despite the protests of theologians and the cavilling of purists. Yet it is not simply a question of the heritage of Montaigne being assimilated or taken for granted. We have reached a turning-point from another point of view. From 1660 a current of reaction against the Essays gathers way until the end of the century—a surface current perhaps—but one whose course and causes we must now examine.

CHAPTER XXVII

ECLIPSE ?

Est-il bon ? Est-il méchant ?

IT has been seen what was the contact of Pascal with the Essays and his reaction. This reaction bears its first-fruits in print, not under Pascal's name but in the *Logique de Port Royal* (1662) by Arnauld and Nicole. The first edition, published in the year after Pascal's death, contains no actual *attack* on Montaigne. In discussing dilemmas, the authors say of the thesis : ' either the soul perishes or goes to a better place ', that ' even Montaigne ' has pointed out that it may go to a worse.[1] Montaigne is quoted on miracles ; even if the first foundation of them is credulity as they pass from mouth to mouth they are more and more firmly believed.[2] This argument is disapproved. Some of Montaigne's considerations in favour of Pyrrhonism, and on the frailty of man are clearly referred to under the heading : ' general propositions imprudently drawn from individual experiences '.

Il est des choses obscures et cachées et l'on se trompe quelquefois grossièrement. Toutes choses sont obscures et incertaines, disent les anciens et les nouveaux Pyrrhoniens . . .
Il y a de l'inégalité dans quelques actions des hommes . . . Il n'est qu'inconstance, disent-ils, que légèreté, qu'instabilité, que la conduite des hommes, même les plus sages. *Nous ne pouvons ce que nous voulons qu'à l'instant que nous le voulons* : nous ne voulons rien librement, rien absolument, rien constamment.[3]

The second edition (1666) of the same book, recast when its authors had been for four years in possession of Pascal's papers,[4] treats our author in a very different manner. Some of the

[1] 1st edition, III, 16   [2] ib., III, 13.
[3] ib., III, 18, pp. 345–8.
[4] Arnauld had already borrowed from *De l'Esprit Géomètrique* in the first edition, according to Brunschwicg (*Pensées et Opuscules*, p. 163).

criticisms seem obviously derived from Pascal : namely on death, repentance, and personal confidences.

Montaigne speaks of himself, showing thus a lack of judgement which corrupts the reason of him who speaks by vanity and self-love, and of him who listens by an aversion for such vanity. Balzac has rightly remarked on his vaingloriousness in boasting that he had a page. He wishes everywhere to prove himself a gentleman and is ashamed of having been a lawyer. This proves that his sincerity is not genuine.[1] Furthermore, he is impious. He says he is incapable of repentance. . . . *Paroles horribles et qui marquent une extinction entière de tout sentiment de religion.* He says he likes to think of death as a plunge into oblivion, speaks of it as *un quart d'heure de passion.*[2] He has attempted to revive Pyrrhonism and wrote a treatise (the Apology) with this express purpose. Montaigne is not only impious, he is credulous, he believes in astrology, and divination :—

son dessein n'étant pas de parler raisonnablement mais de faire un amas confus de tout ce qui se peut dire contre les hommes ; ce qui est néanmoins un vice très contraire à la justesse de l'esprit et à la sincérité d'un homme de bien.

The authors of *L'Art de Penser* seem to forget that a genuine sceptic must be sceptical even about the falsehood of astrology.

This attack ends with a direct invitation to put Montaigne on the Index :

Il est si plein d'un si grand nombre d'infamies honteuses, et de maximes épicuriennes et impies qu'il est étrange qu'on l'ait souffert si longtemps dans les mains de tout le monde, et qu'il y ait même des personnes d'esprit qui n'en reconnaissent le venin.

It is a little ungracious to make such a condemnation when the Essays are quoted with approval on the usual vices of disputes in the very same chapter.

Arnauld and Nicole were not to go without a reply. In the following year (1667) Guillaume Béranger, *bourgeois de Paris*, published at Rouen his *Réponse à plusieurs injures et railleries écrites contre Michel Seigneur de Montaigne.* He says that he had had the intention of publishing a treatise on education, derived from Montaigne, and an anthology of short passages from the Essays when the attack of Port Royal fell into his hands. An arrangement of *De l'Institution des Enfants* and one or two other passages, and 500 paragraphs of from six to twelve

---

[1] 2nd edition, III, ch. 20, §§ 6, 7.   [2] *Essais*, II, 12, p. 360.

lines are printed at the end of this volume without modernization.   The passages are not systematically arranged, and include
obiter dicta, ' examples ', tales, a little of everything in fact.

The answer to the *Logique* is what constitutes the interest of
this volume, however.   Béranger takes, first of all, the accusation of impiety in wishing to revive Pyrrhonism,

afin de se procurer un état de ténèbres qui lui fut agréable et commode
pour appaiser le remords de sa conscience et contenter librement ses
passions.

Béranger denies the existence of any treatise written with such
a purpose.   All that is said of this philosophical opinion in the
Essays is *en forme de devis non d'avis et d'une manière opinante
non instruisante ni magistrale.*   He gives five passages of the
Apology to support this defence, and also quotes Montaigne's
declaration of submission to the Church (I, 56).

Cela, tout au moins, aurait obligé les Lecteurs à épargner Montaigne,
s'ils avaient condamné ses Essais.

As for the other accusations, Béranger remarks that after
blaming Montaigne with angry words—against their own maxims
—they have quoted his opinion on repentance and on death
falsely and interpreted them unfairly.   They certainly appear
to have taken liberties with Montaigne's declaration :

Je puis désirer en général être autre . . .   Mais cela je ne la dois
pas nommer repentir, ce me semble, non plus que le déplaisir d'être ni
Ange ni Caton.

They omit to let Montaigne say that for such matters he has
regret indeed, but no repentance for what cannot be helped.
Béranger makes his point, but he is guilty himself of stupidity
as well as insincerity, in pretending that Montaigne wrote : ' je NE
puis désirer '.   It is untrue and does not even serve his purpose.

Béranger is perfectly justified, however, in his defence of the
other passages of the Essays on death.   Montaigne describes the
horrors of the religious wars : *Je me suis couché mille fois chez
moi, imaginant qu'on me trahirait et assommerait cette nuit là,
composant avec la fortune que ce fut sans effroi.*   He goes on to
say that from the very despair in which he lives there comes a
kind of courage.   *Il m'advient souvent d'imaginer avec quelque
plaisir les dangers mortels et les attendre : je me plonge la tête
baissée stupidement dans la mort.* . . .   Now ! says Béranger,
you detach the last remark from the rest and cry ' out upon
him for a pagan '.

Similarly, when Montaigne writes that death is after all but a quarter of an hour's agony, the authors of the Logic are again deeply shocked, or so they pretend. Is it fair to quote this remark without making it clear that it is a reflexion inspired by the sight of peasants dying like flies in the plague of 1585, and of certain lessons to be drawn from the way they met their death ?

The Logic says of Montaigne's cautionary remarks on miracles beginning : *La vérité et le mensonge ont leurs visages conformes*,[1] that his argument could just as well be turned in favour of miracles. They might, says Béranger, have gone on to point out that Montaigne has used the same argument for that very purpose.[2]

Béranger is sure he can distinguish two hands in the Logic, one unfavourable to Montaigne, the other who secretly admires him but who is too envious to admit his admiration. He concludes : I am the defender of the truth, not of the Essays ; all those who read them will allow that :

Ce Professeur de Logique a eu tort de faire venir en sa classe un Auteur de ce mérite, cent ans après sa mort, pour le traiter publiquement de sot et de ridicule, et d'en faire un sujet de raillerie à ses Ecoliers, comme aussi d'avoir osé écrire qu'il est étrange qu'on ait souffert son livre si longtemps dans les mains de tout le monde et qu'il y ait même des personnes d'esprit qui n'en reconnaissent pas le venin.[3]

Knowing what Béranger perhaps did not know, that the great Arnauld and Nicole were the joint professors of logic, there can be little question, I think, that Arnauld's is the hand which damned, he, the first of the Sorbonne to approve of the Cartesian rationalism, and that Nicole, whom we know from contemporary evidence to have approved of the Essays, if used with care,[4] was the hand which pronounced a qualified blessing.

The *Essais de Morale* of Nicole (1st vol., 1671) contract no conspicuous debt to Montaigne, but the *Education d'un Prince* (1670) has clearly been written with a close knowledge of *De l'Institution des Enfants*. If Montaigne is mentioned, however,

---

[1] *Essais*, III, 11, p. 327.

[2] *Essais*, I, 27 (see use by Raemond and François de Sales).

[3] Béranger : *Réponse* . . . p. 70. His reply ends with a reprint of four appreciations of the Essays. (1) Part of that of Camus, (2) Part of that of Pasquier, (3) Part of the Preface to the Essays by Mademoiselle de Gournay, and (4) a ' Jugement de M.L.D.' (?) reproduced above, p. 299.

[4] v. E. Griselle : *Les Pascalins* (art. cit.) : ' M. Nicole dit qu'il y a mille belles choses dans Montaigne mais qu'il faut le lire avec discernement.'

his spirit is absent—to realize how far absent it is only necessary to read what Nicole has to say of the expression *humainement parlant.* ' It is impossible that most of these humane discourses in which religion is set aside, should not be false.' [1] This ' humanly speaking ' is, of course, the constant attitude of Montaigne. In the *Pensées* which form the sixth volume of the *Essais de Morale*, Nicole has given his final judgement on Montaigne, who is, he says, the advocate of a delicate Epicureanism which ends in brutality as all Epicureanism does. Nicole simply echoes Pascal when he writes :

C'est un homme qui après avoir promené son esprit par toutes les choses du monde pour juger ce qu'il y a de bien et de mal, a eu assez de lumière pour en reconnaître la sottise et la vanité. Il a très bien découvert le néant de la grandeur et l'inutilité des sciences : mais comme il ne connaissait guère d'autre vie que celle-ci, il a conclu qu'il n'y avait donc rien à faire qu'à tâcher de passer agréablement le petit espace qui nous est donné.

God's providence seems to have given us Ecclesiastes and the Essays as awful examples of where this Epicureanism ends.[2]

The attacks of theologians on Montaigne in the second half of the century are numerous, and the importance of the *Logique de Port Royal* is that, with Silhon's *Certitude des Connaissances* (1661),[3] it leads off a regular succession of them. The year after Béranger's defence, Bossuet, just appointed Bishop of Condom, the greatest preacher of the day, denounces Montaigne in a sermon preached on All Saints' Day.

Mais, Messieurs, pour espérer il faut croire . . . Eh quoi ! homme, pouvez vous penser que tout soit corps et matière en vous ? Quoi, tout meurt, tout est enterré ? Le cercueil vous égale aux bêtes, et il n'y a rien en vous qui soit au dessus ? Je le vois bien, votre esprit est si infatué de tant de belles sentences, écrites si éloquemment en prose et en vers, qu'un Montaigne, je le nomme, vous a débitées, qui préfère les animaux à l'homme, leur instinct à notre raison, leur nature simple, innocente, et sans fard, c'est ainsi qu'on parle, à nos reffinements et nos malices. Mais, dites moi, subtil philosophe, qui vous riez si finement de l'homme qui s'imagine être quelque chose, compterez-vous encore pour rien de connaître Dieu ? [4]

[1] *Education d'un Prince* (1671). Montaigne mentioned, pp. 17, 37 ; humainement parlant, pp. 252, 253. Notice *l'honnêteté*, as art of pleasing, rejected for Charity (*De la Civilité Chrétienne*).
[2] *Essais de Morale*, ed. 1755, VI, p. 232. cf. Ste Beuve : *Port Royal* (ed. 1908), II, p. 399.
[3] See above, p. 184 et seq.
[4] *Troisième Sermon pour la Fête de Tous les Saints*, 3me Partie. cf. Silhon, above, p. 181.

A year or two later, in *De la Connaissance de Dieu et de Soi-Même* it is the same reproach against Montaigne. He levels men too effectively to the rank of the animals.

C'est un plaisir de voir Montaigne faire raisonner son oie, qui se promenant dans sa basse cour, se dit que tout est fait pour elle.

What underlies the joke is too serious a matter, however, for mere jesting. It is one of the errors of Celsus, which is being revived.[1]

In 1670 [2] comes the first edition of the *Pensées* with its reflections on Montaigne, and with it the *Entretien avec M. de Saci* (see above). In 1674, *La Recherche de la Vérité* brings a new attack on Montaigne.

After dealing with the general manner in which the imagination interferes with accurate reasoning, Malebranche goes on to mention three authors as examples of the power which an imaginative mind with great literary gifts has over men. These three are Tertullian—whose *De Pallio* is mere rhetoric plus an irrelevant argument by precedent; Seneca, and Montaigne, who both appeal to human instincts—vanity and concupiscence—and thus gain assent to their views without shadow of proof.

Montaigne does not persuade by reasoning, but because he pleases and flatters us. It is true that he did not intend to prove things, but the pleasure which the Essays arouse is ' more criminal than is thought : for it is certain that this pleasure arises principally from concupiscence, and only serves to entertain and fortify the passions '. How necessarily Malebranche's general position involves him in this condemnation is seen by a passage from a previous chapter to which we are here referred by the author. Since pleasure is the mark of any corporal good,

il y a une espèce de nécessité que ces biens remplissent la capacité de notre esprit jusqu'à ce que Dieu répande sur eux une certaine amertume qui nous en donne du dégoût et de l'horreur, ou qu'il nous fasse sentir par sa grâce cette douceur du ciel qui efface toutes les douceurs de la terre.

This particular type of Christian philosophy commits one to a thorough-going asceticism, as a preparation and invitation to the Holy Spirit.

[1] *De la Connaissance de Dieu* (ed. Didot, 1841), V, p. 93.

[2] In 1669 we reach the year of the last seventeenth-century edition of the Essays. This date or 1676 when the book was placed on the Index is rightly the termination of our study. Yet the story of Montaigne's fortunes would be robbed of much interest without a glance at succeeding years, but since from now on we are engaged in some sort of an epilogue, the reader must pardon a certain sketchiness.

Malebranche intends to show, however, that those who admire Montaigne admire him for freedom from a fault from which he is not free, thus correcting perhaps the dangerous ascendancy which the Essays acquire over people. Montaigne, who is praised as free from pedantry, as a man of the world in the best sense, is himself a pedant. For the only reasonable definition of a pedant is one who uses without caution proverbs, sayings and historical examples as if to prove what cannot be proved except by reason. Add to this, vanity, a capacity for making quotations and vigorous but ill-organized imagination—the picture is complete. It fits Montaigne to a T, according to Malebranche.

Montaigne's vanity is at least sufficiently proved by the amount of space he devotes to himself. He must have considered himself a man utterly out of the common to imagine people would want to read a large book mostly about himself. It is criminal to devote so much attention, and the adoration (conscious or unconscious) which necessarily goes with it, to any object but God. If Montaigne did not prove this vanity of his in writing his book, he did so in publishing it. If it was only for his friends, why did he have three different editions of it printed ? Even for his friends and relations, it was a sin to offer them such a lengthy distraction.

Montaigne not only speaks of himself, he praises himself. This is always anti-social for self-praise always causes dislike among one's fellow-men. It is even more vainglorious of him to describe his defects, for these defects are almost always those which the corruption of the age makes into qualities.

Malebranche then sets himself to make a fool of Montaigne out of his own mouth, but with most outrageous unfairness. Montaigne says he had no memory, but elsewhere that he has to learn his speeches by heart, in order not to get tied up in the middle. Therefore he had no cause to complain of his memory. The answer to this (we may note) is contained in the passage which Malebranche quotes incompletely. Montaigne continues : *Mais ce moyen m'est non moins difficile. Pour apprendre trois vers, il me faut trois heures.*[1] Montaigne says he forgets the names of his servants. Has this man, who can learn speeches by heart, got so many then ? He knows nothing of agriculture, and yet he remembers the names and opinions of a host of ancient philosophers. Let us believe Montaigne when he declares his lack of memory, as long as we don't believe him when he claims intelligence and profundity.

[1] *Essais*, II, 17, pp. 432, 433.

Cela pourrait nous jeter dans l'erreur et donner trop de crédit aux opinions fausses et dangereuses qu'il débite.

The other great quality attributed to Montaigne is his perfect knowledge of psychology. But Montaigne was a sceptic: *il était nécessaire de son temps, pour passer pour habile et pour galant homme, de douter de tout ; et la qualité d'esprit fort dont il se piquait, l'engageait dans ces opinions.* How, asks Malebranche (with much logic and little sense), can a man who professes to know nothing have a perfect knowledge of anything? Montaigne did not know the human mind, since he falls into gross errors upon the subject. These errors are a confusion of mind and matter (which can be deduced from the ridiculous opinions he reproduces with a solemn face); a failure to recognize the necessity of the dogma of Immortality, and a belief that, if true, it cannot be proved; and lastly, his notion that animals reason, that we have no essential advantages over them, ' our brothers and companions '.[1]

Malebranche ends with a paragraph in which he professes a desire to be fair to Montaigne. His admirers mistake the beauty of his ideas for their truth:

Ses idées sont fausses mais belles : ses expressions irrégulières ou hardies, mais agréables ; ses discours mal raisonnés, mais bien imaginés. On voit dans tout son livre un caractère d'original qui plaît infiniment : tout copiste qu'il est, il ne sent point son copiste ; et son imagination donne toujours le tour d'original aux choses qu'il copie.

Malebranche appreciates the literary qualities of the Essays, but he is more sincere when he makes it clear, that while he admires much of Tertullian and some of Seneca, he has no great opinion of any part of the Essays.[2]

Malebranche protests against the Essays both as a Christian and as a Cartesian philosopher. Cartesian tendencies, however, do not seem likely to have had anything to do with the placing of the Essays upon the Index two years later (1676). This action was probably the direct or indirect result of the attacks of Bossuet, Malebranche, and perhaps of Pascal and the *Art de Penser*. What, however, was its effect? It is just possible that French publishers may have felt disinclined to reprint an old-

---

[1] Malebranche follows Descartes in regarding animals as machines.

[2] *Recherche*, II, 2, C 3, § 1. Notice Malebranche's criticism of those who believe in sorcery contained in the chapter immediately following. There are real sorcerers, but most of those burnt are the victims of delusion and of superstition. I doubt whether Montaigne influenced Malebranche in this matter.

fashioned book which was disapproved of by the Church; but if there had still been a demand for new editions Amsterdam would have supplied them.

In 1674 Jacques Esprit, once a frequent visitor of Madame de Sablé's *Salon*, obtained an *imprimatur* from the Sorbonne for his *Fausseté des Vertus Humaines*, which first appeared four years later. The book is a Jansenist systematization of the maxims of his friend, La Rochefoucauld. Each human virtue is seen in turn to be a sham, according to the author, because its motives are not completely disinterested, or because they include one or other of ' the passions '. With each is contrasted the corresponding Christian virtue, admirable because its motives are pure—(charity). This remains a mere formula, however, and no attempt is made to reduce all the right motives to gratitude to, obedience to, or love of God. Esprit's book is thus a good example of the position to which a logically minded ' rigorist ' must be driven, but since no interpretation of ' Christian virtue ' is made, it is impossible to say whether Esprit's conception is legalist (the commandments) or what may be called ' Salesian ' (love of God).[1] Esprit adopts the Augustinian idea that ' *le propre de l'homme* ' is not reason but the will.

Montaigne is first taken to task for all he has written in praise of friendship. Human friendship is a commerce, not a virtue.[2] Esprit pretends to give a long quotation from the Essays, which though in inverted commas is no quotation at all, and a pretty serious misrepresentation of what Montaigne has said.[3] Esprit concludes that friendship permits one to be impious, sacrilegious, and to betray a secret. In Montaigne's defence, he says:

Ce qui est cause qu'il s'est égaré dans cette matière, est l'amour qu'il a pour les imaginations belles, grandes et extraordinaires, surtout lorsque dans ces imaginations il y a quelque chose qui le flatte et qui est à son avantage.

(Compare this with Malebranche.)

This is not the only place in which Esprit has misrepresented

---

[1] See above, pp. xxxvii et seq., 131–4.
[2] cf. St. Evremond.
[3] Here is an extract : ' Cette amitié possède l'âme et la régente en toute souveraineté, cette amitié, qui ne peut être qu'unique, découd toutes les obligations. Le secret que j'ai juré de ne pas communiquer à un autre je puis sans parjure le communiquer à celui qui n'est pas un autre, c'est moi. L'amitié que j'ai eue avec Etienne de La Boëtie n'a point d'autre idée qu'elle même, et ne peut se rapporter qu'à soi ' (*sic* !) (p. 63 et seq. cf. *Essais*, I, 28, p. 246).

Montaigne's words. He blames him further on in his book for having suggested that Socrates *ne sentit aucun mouvement de concupiscence.* He again pretends to make a quotation which it is instructive to compare with the original text:

Essais, II, 11, p. 126. [difficulty seems a sign of virtue]

Il me tombe en fantasie que l'âme de Socrates, qui est la plus parfaite qui soit venue à ma connaissance, *serait, à mon compte, une âme de peu de recommandation*: *car* je ne puis concevoir en ce personnage là aucun effort de vitieuse concupiscence. *Au train de sa vertu, je n'y puis imaginer aucune difficulté et aucune contrainte*: je connoy sa raison si puissante et si maîtresse chez lui qu'elle n'eût jamais donné moyen à un appétit vitieux *seulement* de naître. *A une* vertu *si* élevée *que la sienne, je ne puis rien mettre en tête. Il me semble la voir* marcher *d'un victorieux pas et triomphant, en pompe et* à son aise, sans empêchement ne destourbier.

Fausseté des Vertus Humaines (1693, p. 262).

L'âme de Socrate, dit il, est la plus parfaite qui soit venue à ma connaissance, je ne puis concevoir en ce personnage aucun effort de vitieuse concupiscence ; je connais sa raison si puissante et si maîtresse chez lui qu'elle n'eût jamais donné moyen à un appétit vitieux de naitre.

Sa vertu élevée marche à son aise sans empêchement ni destourbier.

Esprit continues after this:

Je rapporte ses propres paroles, de peur qu'on ne croie que je lui impute cette étrange opinion, et afin qu'on voie combien cet auteur était aveugle et peu instruit des vérités de la Religion Chrétienne, puis qu'il réprésente un payen plus pûr et plus parfait que n'en ont été les Apôtres.

Such misquotation is trifling, compared to what follows. Esprit wishes to make out that Montaigne has contradicted himself on this subject. He quotes him, as saying:

C'est quelque chose de ramener l'âme aux imaginations de la vertu ; c'est plus d'y joindre les effets. Toutefois cela n'est pas impossible,— mais de les joindre avec telle persévérance et constance que d'en établir son train ordinaire ; certes en ces entreprises éloignées de l'usage commun, il est quasi incroyable qu'on le puisse. Es vies de ces Héros du temps passé il y a quelquefois des traits miraculeux, mais ils ne pouvaient être naturels ni ordinaires.

This quotation comes from a passage where Montaigne has just described the extraordinary conduct of Pyrrho, who walked on the edge of precipices, and in front of carts, refusing to fear or avoid anything since all things were indifferent.[1] Montaigne, who has shown elsewhere that he cannot understand this stupidity, continues :

C'est quelque chose de ramener l'âme à ces imaginations, . . .[2]

that is, to bring the mind to a belief in this unnatural indifference, and it is to *this* indifference that he refers in the passage quoted by Esprit.   The fact that Esprit has tampered with the text and written *aux imaginations de la vertu*, shows that he was perfectly conscious of his falsification of meaning.   The last sentence of his quotation (*Es vies de ces Héros*) is a pure invention on his part.[3]   Montaigne does believe, indeed, that virtue is natural to man, he is a Pelagian in so far as a Christian at all, that is all the excuse that can be found for Esprit, and it is no excuse for such forgery.

Esprit, however, believes in an ideal of virtue as a harmony, but it is a supernatural state never wholly achieved on earth.

Ce n'est que par la grâce de Jésus Christ que l'homme devient naturel.   C'est elle seule qui lui ôte toutes ses affectations et toutes ses faussetés, et qui donne à toutes ses actions, tous ses mouvements intérieurs, cette justesse qui les rend si harmonieux et agréables : ce qui a obligé Pythagore à dire que la vertu n'est qu'une harmonie.[4]

Hence he subscribes to a good deal of the moral teaching of the Essays.   He notices how Montaigne finds Cato's suicide a beautiful act because it was fitting end to such a life.   He condemns the act, indeed, saying that the notion of fittingness is suitable for the stage, not for life.   Nevertheless, conformity not only of the inner and outer life but of speech, action, character and office or dignity into a harmonious whole does seem to him an important part of Christian perfection.[5]   His final judgement on Montaigne is the exact opposite of Pascal's.   His moral teaching is fine in conception but beyond the powers of man, except when aided by grace.

If adverse criticism of the Essays appears to grow in bulk in the years between 1670 and the end of the century, there is

[1] *Essais*, II, 29, p. 504.
[2] See for all this *Fausseté*, p. 262 et seq.
[3] ib., p. 467.   Notice p. 475 his ridicule for the idea of natural goodness under the guise of the *vieux gaulois* or that other fiction, the golden age.
[4] ib., p. 369.   (See also on Montaigne and suicide, end of chapter on friendship.)
[5] ib., *De la Gravité*.

still Madame de Sévigné to write with delight of unexpectedly finding a volume of the Essays :

ah ! l'aimable homme ! qu'il est de bonne compagnie, c'est mon ancien ami, mais à force d'être ancien il m'est nouveau. Je ne puis pas lire ce que dit le Maréchal de Montluc du regret qu'il a de ne s'être pas communiqué à son fils, et de lui avoir laissé ignoré la tendresse qu'il avait pour lui, sans avoir les larmes aux yeux . . . Mon Dieu, que ce livre est plein de bon sens.

Or in the same year, 1679, *Je suis ici, ma fille, toute fine seule. J'ai de bons livres et surtout Montaigne. Que faut-il autre chose quand on ne vous a point.*[1] It is a piece of news when Charles de Sévigné is *raccommodé* with Montaigne, and the one fault to find with the abbé de Chavigny, just made bishop of Rennes, is his aversion for the Essays.[2] Her granddaughter Pauline is too young at fifteen for such books, though.

A l'égard de la morale, comme elle n'en ferait pas un si bon usage que vous, je ne voudrais point du tout qu'elle mit son petit nez ni dans Montaigne ni dans Charron, ni dans les autres de cette sorte : c'est bien matin pour elle. La vraie morale de son âge, c'est celle qu'on apprend dans les bonnes conversations, dans les fables, dans les histoires, par les exemples : je crois que c'est assez.[3]

It is worth quoting the above since it is sometimes made out from this passage that Madame de Sévigné considered the Essays a dangerous book. There is no sign of that I think ; Montaigne and Charron are simply not suitable for Pauline's age and tastes.[4]

Besides Madame de Sévigné there is still La Bruyère, a pessimist who owes much to the Montaigne, Pascal, La Rochefoucauld tradition, to protest against the critics of the Essays :

Deux ecrivains (he says) dans leurs ouvrages ont blâmé Montaigne que je ne crois pas aussi bien qu'eux exempt de toute sorte de blâme : il paraît que tous deux ne l'ont estimé en nulle manière. L'un ne pensait pas assez pour goûter un auteur qui pense beaucoup : l'autre pense trop subtilement pour s'accommoder de pensées qui sont naturelles.[5]

It is generally agreed—and I think correctly—to see in La Bruyère's remark a reference to Balzac and to Malebranche.

[1] *Lettres* (ed. Grands Écrivains), VI, 40, 41, 111.
[2] ib., IV, pp. 353, 358.
[3] ib., X, p. 2113. See also for references to the Essays VI, 432 ; X, 215.
[4] But a few months later she does not consider Nicole's Essays, which she so admired (Charles said the style was *comme qui mangerait trop de blancmanger*) are at all unsuitable for Pauline (IX, p. 315).
[5] *Caractères* (ed. Chassang, 1876), I, p. 31 (Des Ouvrages de l'Esprit).

Elsewhere in his chapter, *De la Société*, La Bruyère has given an imitation of Montaigne's style.[1] His interest in individual psychology, in which—with a different type of genius, St. Simon —he seems alone at the end of the century, may have been sharpened and perhaps even aroused by his acquaintance with the Essays, but there appear to be few direct traces of this influence in the *Caractères*.

There is still room for an *Esprit des Essais* in 1677, for a collection of *Pensées de Montaigne* in 1700, republished in 1701 and 1703, but these are the only texts of Montaigne published from 1669 to 1724. The preface to the *Esprit* begins respectfully :

Le mérite de Monsieur de Montaigne est si connu qu'il n'a pas besoin d'être recommandé par de nouveaux éloges . . .

The preface to the *Pensées*, twenty-three years later opens thus :

Il est peu de si mauvais livres qu'il ne s'y trouve quelque chose de bon : et peu de si bons qu'il n'y ait quelque chose de mauvais. Montaigne n'a pas manqué de censeurs et l'on ne peut guère ignorer que c'est un Auteur fort équivoque et fort mêlé.

The intention of the *Esprit des Essais* is to cut out quotations and digressions while offering a minimum of change in the disposition and even the orthography of what is left. This gives us some strange results. *De l'Exercitation* (II, 6) ends with an account of Montaigne's accident, the long addition of 1595 on the self-portrait does not appear. So too in *De la Cruauté* (II, 11) all that does not deal with cruelty is left out. A similar treatment is meted out to *Des Boiteux* (II, 11). The Apology is reduced to a dozen pages but with a certain amount of skill. Where the editor has decided on the impossibility of cutting out all digressions, he has added to the original title of certain essays : thus we find : *Sur les Vers de Virgile ou plutôt de l'Amour et du Mariage : Des Coches ou plutôt de la dépense des Princes et de l'industrie du nouveau monde*. The only important alteration of a text which I have noted is at the end of II, 3 (*Coutume de l'Ile de Céa*), where a definite condemnation of suicide as cowardly is added.

Artaud, author of the *Pensées de Montaigne propres à former l'esprit et les moeurs*, undertakes a similar task, but although many passages from the same essay generally appear together the physiognomy of the original is even more hopelessly lost. The *Journal des Savants* extended a welcome to both these adapta-

[1] *Caractères*, I, p. 145.

tions of the Essays—the book, it thought, evidently, was better purged—and the spirit of the times is seen in its echo of Pascal's condemnation.

La principale fin de Montaigne en écrivant ses Essais fut de tracer son portrait et de se faire connaître. Quel besoin le public avait-il de cette connaissance ? Quelle nécessité qu'il fut informé des travers de son esprit, et ses pensées vaines, de ses idées fausses, de ses opinions dangereuses, de ses passions folles et insensées ? [1]

Vigneul Marville, however—the one passable writer, according to Voltaire, produced by the Benedictines—though a severe critic of the Essays, disapproves of such enterprises as *L'Esprit de Montaigne* : Balzac, he says, found a happy excuse for Montaigne's digressions, and a happy formula for his genius, like that of those classics of whom it is said they were *maximi ingenio et arte rudes*, but Marville notes that since the time when Sorel (whom he quotes) defended Montaigne from his critics, Pascal, the *Art de Penser* and Malebranche have all condemned him.

Il est difficile qu'un livre examiné et censuré par de si redoutables plumes ne tombe pas dans le mépris, cependant Montaigne a encore ses partisans, mais ils ne sont plus en si grand nombre, et ses trois derniers censeurs lui ont enlevé la meilleure partie.[2]

So much for Marville's estimate of the position of the Essays on the threshold of the new century. Eight years earlier his own judgement of Montaigne seems more unjust :

Le Génie de Montaigne est de tout risquer, bon sens, Religion, conscience, doctrine, pour faire valoir une pensée forte et une expression hardie.[3]

In 1701 the Protestant Charles d'Ancillon is no less severe.

L'ouvrage qu'il appelle ses Essais est un livre dangereux rempli de venin et d'irrégularités. Je n'ai guère vu d'Auteur qui ait eu occasion d'en parler qui n'ait été à peu près de ce sentiment.[4]

D'Ancillon enumerates some of them, Pascal, the author of the Logic, Malebranche, Balzac, putting the worst construction on

[1] *Journal des Savants*, 1677, p. 185 ; 1701, p. 436.
[2] *Mélanges d'Histoire et de Littérature* (1699), ed. 1725, II, pp. 31, 32 (cf. I, pp. 163–6, 340).
[3] *L'Education, Maximes et Réflexions de M. de Moncade*, 1691. The *education* of this imaginary character certainly owes some details to the Essays (see especially opening pages) also p. 250.
[4] *Mélanges de Littérature*. Amsterdam, 1701, pp. 415–17.

what each of them has said : even Sorel has admitted the Essays
are not fit reading for every one. Finally

Montaigne débitait deux mauvaises maximes ; savoir premièrement qu'il n'y a point de paroles sales ; secondement que toutes les
actions des Payens n'étaient pas corrompues. M. Esprit les a très
bien détruites dans son livre de la Fausseté des Vertus Humaines,
Tome 2. Le Cardinal du Perron appelait les Essais de Montaigne le
bréviaire des honnêtes gens. Il ne faut pas s'en étonner, car on sait
qu'il n'était pas un Chrétien des plus scrupuleux.

In 1704 a new book appears with Montaigne's name in the
title : *La distinction et la Nature du Bien et du Mal : Traité où
l'on combat l'erreur des Manichéens, les sentiments de Montaigne,
et ceux de M. Bayle.* The author, Father Gaudin, a Carthusian
like Marville, believes that Montaigne and Charron held there
was no distinction between good and evil, ' founding the duties
of justice and social life only upon custom, on the laws of each
country, and upon temporal circumstances, thus establishing the
indifference of all human actions '. They set all religions on the
same footing and approved of them all, largely as political institutions, hence morality appears to them essentially founded
on the laws and customs governing any society. Gaudin directed
his attack in this respect on Charron even more than on Montaigne,
unlike any other author dealt with since Chanet. He ends his
remarks with the following paragraph :

En voilà bien assez sur le Chapître de Montaigne et de Charron, deux
auteurs surannés, et à mon sens du nombre des plus déraisonnables : on
en voit divers exemples, à l'égard de Montaigne, dans l'Art de Penser et
dans plusieurs autres ouvrages anciens et modernes. Cependant ils
sont estimés et goûtés dans le monde, moins par ce qu'ils ont de bon que
par ce qu'ils ont de mauvais.

Hence he fully approves the enterprise of Artaud in his *Pensées
de Montaigne.*[1]

In 1706 an Oratorian, Bernard Lamy, in his *Démonstrations
ou Preuves de la Vérité et de la Sainteté de la Morale Chrétienne,*
attacks similarly the hedonism of Epicurus, Montaigne and St.
Evremond.

Whatever the exact value of these various statements as to
the neglect of the Essays, they at least imply a change from the
respect shown by earlier critics whatever their dislike. The
hostility of all these critics from Pascal onwards must be set
down mainly to a realization that Montaigne's philosophy was

---

[1] op. cit., p. 25 (see the *Journal des Savants'* compte rendu. 1704.
p. 303).

fundamentally incompatible with Christianity, at any rate in the forms then held. With some of these authors Montaigne's chief crime is his belief in the natural goodness of man, or, better, in the capacity of man for a good life attainable by his own efforts. This is true of Pascal, of Esprit. Along with this there is also the aggravation of his hedonism.

In the first half of the century the main ground of theological attack on Montaigne was connected, however, with his fideism and his comparison of man with the animals, which, intrinsically important as a protest against anthropocentrism, was originally part of the expression of that fideism in the Apology. Despite exceptions, theology was becoming more and more Cartesian and rationalistic in the second half of the century, whereas we have seen what fideist elements were present in the thought of some of Montaigne's earlier critics. Was the succession of attacks on the Essays, from the publication of Silhon's *De la Certitude des Connaissances Humaines* in 1661 and the second edition of the *Art de Penser* in 1666, the result of this change over to a theological rationalism ? [1] I think it was largely so, and that just for this reason the Essays are often referred to as ridiculous : for Arnauld Montaigne's pyrrhonism is ridiculous, for Bossuet his opinion on animals, for Malebranche his doubts upon the immortality of the soul. It is for them unnecessary to refute this side of the Essays since they feel sure of their ground. This was the time when a certain Cartesianism held the field, as Voltaire says in connexion with Bayle, a Cartesianism which had already begun to fall into discredit before the end of the Regency, though it left enough confidence in a theological rationalism to facilitate the task of the *philosophes*.[2] It was against this enemy that Bayle fought in his Dictionary (1697) and in his many pamphlets. It was the measure of his success that he prepared the way for the reception of Locke's empiricism in France, the empiricism which completed the ruin of the Cartesian ' innate ideas ', the one part of Descartes' philosophy which had been really acceptable to Christian apologists. Bayle is the great representative of Montaigne's way of thinking at the end of the century. The question of the influence of Montaigne on him lies outside the scope of this study, but his

---

[1] For Cartesian influence, see especially works published round 1700 by Pierre Poiret (*Fides et Ratio Collatae*), Régis (*L'Usage de la Raison et de la Foi*) and especially the protestants, De la Touche Bernier and Jacquelot (the enemy of Bayle).

[2] Voltaire (*Le Siècle de Louis XIV*) quoted by A. Tilley : *The Decline of the Age of Louis XIV* (1929), pp. 395, 396.

love of quoting the Essays, and quoting just the texts which seemed most dangerous to Christian apologists may be quickly seen on reference to the *Œuvres Diverses*.[1]

We have followed the attitude of Christian apologists towards Montaigne from Florimond de Raymond down to Gaudin, Lamy and Bayle. So far as the question of fideism or rationalism in religion is concerned, the general movement during a hundred years has been away from fideism, but the movement is no uniform one until the Cartesian *innéisme* becomes generally accepted, which cannot be much before 1680 or 1685 and even then there is the exception of Huet,[2] Simon Foucher, and of Bayle himself—whose sincerity may, of course, be questioned. Before this time both the fideist and rationalist tendencies are reflected. The difference is that before the period of Cartesianism every mind of any acuteness we have met is more or less conscious of the inadequacy of the arguments put forward in defence of the principal dogmas of religion. Only that single man of genius, Pascal, accepts wholeheartedly Montaigne's fideism, which he transforms into something not only logically reconcilable, but at one with his particular type of Christianity. He does it by carrying over Montaigne's *dénéantise de l'homme* from the intellectual into the moral sphere. That is a solution only possible to those who share to some extent Pascal's temperament.

The change of tone toward Montaigne which may be marked

---

[1] *Œuvres Diverses* (1727), cf. II, p. 331 (on the rights of conscience) ; p. 400 (against torture) ; III, p. 36 (ascertain facts before offering explanations : *Essais* III, 11, p. 326) ; p. 118 (on belief, and the illusion of belief) ; p. 578 (on witchcraft) ; IV, pp. 837–9 (defence of Sceptics) ; and finally the ingenious appeal in his *Reply to Renaudot* (IV, p. 743) :

' Après tout oserait-on dire que mon Dictionnaire approche de la licence des Essais de Montaigne, soit à l'égard du pyrrhonisme, soit à l'égard des saletés. Or Montaigne n'a-t-il point donné tranquillement plusieurs éditions de son livre ? Ne l'a-t-on pas réimprimé cent et cent fois ? Ne l'a t-on pas dédié au grand Cardinal de Richelieu ? N'est-il pas dans toutes les Bibliothèques ? Quel désordre ne serait-ce pas que je n'eusse point en Hollande la liberté que Montaigne a eue en France.' See also ib., II, p. 318, an imaginary (?) Crisante to whom Bayle replies, both letters full of the Essays. See in *Dictionnaire* : arts. Charron, Simonide and Manichéisme.

[2] Huet expresses a temperamental dislike to the Essays, as old as the book itself when he says : ' Quand il avance quelque sentiment hardi et sujet à contradiction, *Je ne la donne pas pour bon*, dit il, mais pour mien : et c'est de quoi le Lecteur n'a que faire, car il lui importe peu de ce qu'a pensé Michel de Montaigne, mais de ce qu'il fallait penser pour bien penser ' (*Huetiana*). Huet, who nevertheless admired the Essays, and whose copy with some annotations of no great interest is in the Collection Payen, thinks, however, that Montaigne's *désinvolture*, his lack of method, has helped his popularity in France.

from the publication of the Logic of Port Royal, cannot, however, be put down entirely to this swing away from fideism.
It cannot even be put down to the success with which Pascal,
Nicole and Esprit had shown the contradictions of Montaigne's
humanism and Christian ethics (as generally understood). It is
as literature that the Essays are less highly esteemed, it is the
decline of Montaigne's literary reputation which brings about
the change of attitude from a respectful hostility to an open one.

And yet the very violence of these attacks and the statements of various authors even up to the beginning of the eighteenth century show that, in spite of no new editions of the Essays
appearing in the press, Montaigne is still widely read. The
Huetiana, presumably composed in the nineties, still speak of
*cette grande vogue dans laquelle il a été pendant plus d'un siècle
et où il est encore aujourd'hui.* Jean Jacques Bernard a few years
later affirms equally that, in spite of his enemies, *Montaigne sera
toujours aimable et toujours lu.* One is almost tempted to wonder
whether in 1669, the saturation point of copies of the Essays
having been reached there were not a sufficient number of
second-hand copies on the market to meet the new demand.
This, however, would hardly explain the fact that both Coste's
London edition of 1724 and the Paris edition of the following
year were privately printed for subscribers.

The reputation of Montaigne as a literary artist was long in
reviving in spite of the indebtedness to him of such figures as
Voltaire, Diderot, Rousseau and even Holbach in the following
century. In his *Discours de Réception* at the Academy, it is
Montaigne's *style* which Voltaire feels called upon to defend, and
even in 1763 the *Journal des Savants* puts Charron's *Sagesse*
above the Essays both for its language and its method of composition.

In following the history of such a book as the Essays, in
tracing its fortunes and its influence there is no *end*, unless it be
the year and day of writing ; there are only halting-places. My
chosen limits 1580–1669 have been involuntarily expanded to
cover, even if sketchily so far as its last years are concerned, the
whole of the seventeenth century. This period, together with
the earlier Renaissance, forms the transition from the medieval
to the modern world—characterize, if you will, by such names
as the age of religion and the age of science, the age of faith as
contrasted with the age of reason. Such terms serve to convey,
at all events, the contrast to which we refer. The Renaissance
popularized what had been the argument of the Averrhoist com-

mentators of Aristotle from the thirteenth century onwards ; that faith and reason were two separate spheres, perhaps they contradicted each other, but they could not influence each other. To maintain such an attitude involves the use of reasoning against the claims of reason : this is what is done in the Apology of Raymond Sebond. Reason, however, demands some positive task, some sphere of its own. This is given it by Montaigne and even more by Charron : the sphere of conduct even more than that of empirical science.

The consequences of this view, which is the essence of Montaigne's philosophy, have been seen in those who came under his influence and in those who rejected it. For those who *wished* to believe what the authority of the Church taught and yet saw that this teaching had no rational foundation, this division of spheres provided a way out. For those few who did not believe nor wish to believe, this attitude was equally valuable ; it was thus that fideism worked in the interests of the liberty of thought. It has been seen how many of the most important writers of the seventeenth century availed themselves of this solution of the difficulty, without fully realizing for the most part, how provisional it was.

It was necessarily provisional except for those who, like Pascal, could go the whole hog. So soon as ethics were recognized as not the same as religion, right conduct not the same as piety, humanism had a foothold which it was bound to increase. The characteristics of Montaigne's humanism were its hedonism, its humanitarianism, and its aestheticism expressed by the ideal of the organization of the whole personality of the individual.

The influence of the first of these was very great, but it has nothing peculiar to Montaigne in it. It united with the revival of Epicurus by Gassendi to form a powerful current of opinion, to which, except for the earlier part of the century, it has not been possible to do justice.

The influence of the second was seen to be the earliest of all the aspects of the Essays to make its effect felt. In the form of a protest against torture, against the persecution of witches and sorcerers, against cruelty to animals, it came into conflict with views backed in those days by the authority of the Church. Montaigne's critique of anthropocentrism in the Apology and elsewhere, his reminder that animals were our brothers, added special importance to this last side of his humanitarianism.

The humanitarian spirit is also visible in the ideal of *l'honnête homme*, the civilized man, as I should translate it. Montaigne's influence here too has been seen, especially in the aestheticism of Méré and La Rochefoucauld, and the hedonism of St. Evremond. Here again the last years of the century if studied in detail would doubtless afford evidence that the influence of Montaigne was not then confined to the last-named author and to Bayle. *L'honnêteté* is the one form in which Montaigne's emphasis on the organization of personality has much effect. As a psychologist he seems to have suffered during this period from the popularity of the type-psychology of the theory of the four humours.

The temporary eclipse of Montaigne's popularity—as to which I have made some reservations—seems to have been produced by the influence of two men, Descartes and Pascal, to which literary taste may be added as a contributory cause. Descartes' influence on theological rationalism effected a strong reaction against the fideism of Montaigne as dangerous to the Church. It was not so dangerous as the humanism of Montaigne against which Pascal reacted. Pascal's attack inspired, as has been seen, those of most of the other authors of the second half of the century, but just as the theological rationalism of 1700 went down before Bayle and Locke, so the rather narrow religious spirit, which was the legacy of the defeated but not annihilated Jansenists, became ridiculous and odious in the eyes of the age of reason, and behind the *philosophes* the shadow of Montaigne may be not seldom discerned.

BIBLIOGRAPHY

I. Manuscripts, &c., Consulted

British Museum C 2897. Edition of the Essais with Notes by Van Veen (Langelier, 1601).

Bibliothèque Nationale : MS. nouvelles acquisitions françaises, 330, f. 243 (Garaby La Luzerne. Poems).

Bibliothèque Nationale : MS. nouvelles acquisitions françaises, 4333 (' Pascal et les Pascalins ').

Bibliothèque Nationale : Collection Payen. No. 637–40, 647, 648, 650, 682, 683.

II. Books of the Sixteenth or Seventeenth Centuries Quoted in the Text or Notes

A.C. Discours sur les Sentiments Communs d'Aujourd'hui. 1653.

Ailly, Abbé d' : *Maximes.* 1678.

Amirault, Moise : *De l'Elévation de la Foi et de l'Abaissement de la Raison.* 1650.

Ancillon, Charles d' : *Mélanges de Littérature.* Amsterdam, 1701.

Angot de l'Eperonnière : *Exercises de Ce Temps.* Ed. 1924.

Anon. : *Quatrains de la Vanité du Monde.*

Anon. : *Les Quatrains du Déiste* (v. Belurgey).

Anon. : *Maximes, Sentences et Réflexions Morales.* 1687. (Attributed to Méré.)

Arnaud, Antoine (et Pierre Nichole) : *L'Art de Penser.* 1662 and 1666.

Artaud : *Pensées de Montaigne.* 1700.

Aubigné, Agrippa d' : *Histoire Universelle* (ed. Ruble. 10 vols.).

Audiguier, Vital de : *La Philosophie Soldade.* 1604.
　　Le vrai et ancien Usage des Duels. 1607.
　　Diverses Affections de Minerve. 1625.

Authomne, Bernard : *Commentaires sur les Coutumes Générales de Bordeaux.* 1621.

Balzac, Jean Louis Guez de : *Œuvres.* 2 vols. 1665.
　　Premières Lettres (ed. Bibas and Butler). 1933.

Bardin, Pierre : *Essai sur l'Ecclésiaste.* 1626.
　　Pensées Morales sur l'Ecclésiaste. 1632.
　　Le Lycée, Ed. 1634.

Barclay : *Icon Animarum.* 1619.
　　Argenis. 1621.

Bary R. : *La Morale de*, 1671.
Journal de Conversation. 1673.
L'Esprit de Cour. 1664.
Baudier, Michel : *Histoire de la Religion des Turcs.* 1625.
Histoire du Serail. Ed. 1631.
Histoire de la Cour de Chine. 1631.
Baudius, Dominicus : *Epistolae.* Ed. 1636.
Poemata. 1607.
Bayle, Pierre : *Dictionnaire.* 4 vols. 1697.
Œuvres Diverses. Ed. 1727.
Pensées sur la Comète. 1682–1704
[Belurgey, Claude] : *Les Quatrains du Déiste* (in Lachèvre : *Le Procès de Théophile,* Vol. II).
Béranger, Guillaume : *Réponse à plusieurs Injures et Railleries écrites contre Michel Seigneur de Montaigne.* 1667.
Bernier : *Abrégé de la Philosophie de Gassendi.* Lyon. 1684.
Requete des Maîtres és Arts . . . 1671.
The History of the Late Revolution of the Empire of the Great Mogul, &c. Ed. 1676.
Besoldus, Christoph : *Opus Politicum.* 1641.
Binet, le Père : *Essay des Merveilles de Nature.* 1622.
Œuvres Spirituelles. 1620.
Bodin, Jean : *Colloquium Heptaplomeres* (ed. Chauviré). 1914.
Paradoxe sur la Vertu (trad. fr.)
Les Dix Livres de La République. 1576.
Boileau Despréaux : *Satires.* Ed. 1932.
Boisrobert : *Epîtres.* Ed. 1921. 2 vols.
Bossuet : *Correspondance* 15 vols. (ed. Urbain 1909–1925).
Œuvres (ed. Didot, 1841).
Boucher, Jean : *Le Bouquet Sacré ou Voyage en Egypte . . .* (1613 ?)
Mariage de la Vertu avec la Religion. 1622.
Les Triomphes de la Religion Chrétienne. 1628.
Bouchet, Guillaume ; *Les Sérées* (ed. Roybet, 1879).
Browne, Sir Thomas : *Religio Medici.* 1642.
Bruno, Giordano : *De Umbris Idearum.* 1582.
Bussy Rabutin : *Mémoires.* 1693.
Caillière, F. de : *Traité de la Fortune des Gens de Qualité.* 1661.
Campanella : *De Sensu Rerum.* Ed. Frankfurt, 1670.
Campion, Henri de : *Mémoires* (Bibliothèque Elzévirienne).
Campion, Nicolas de : *Entretiens sur divers Sujets . . .* 1704.
Camus, Jean Pierre : *Les Diversités,* 11 vols. 1609–18.
Vol. V. Ed. 1620. Douai.
Homélies Festives. 1619.
Homélies Dominicales. 1616.
Alexis. 2 vols. 1625.
Pétronille. 1626.
Voyageur Inconnu. 1630.
Hermante ou Deux Hermites Contraires. 1639.

L'Esprit de Saint François de Sales. Ed. 1840.
Acheminement à la Devotion Civile. 1625.
La Syndérèse. 1629.
De l'Unité Vertueuse. 1630.
Cantenac, Benech de : *Satires Nouvelles.* 1690.
Cardanus : *De Subtilitate.* 1561.
Champaignac, Jean de : *Physique Française avec un bref Traité de l'Immortalité de l'Ame.* 1595.
Sommaire des Quatre Parties de la Philosophie. 1606.
Chanet, Pierre : *Considérations sur la Sagesse de Charron.* 1643 ; 1644 ; 1666.
Traité de l'Esprit de l'Homme. 1649.
Chapelain, Jean : *Lettres* (ed. Tamizey de Larroque). 2 vols. 1880.
Charron, Pierre : *Toutes les Œuvres.* 1635.
De la Sagesse selon la vraie copie de Bordeaux. Ed. 1665.
On Wisdome, tr. Samson Lennard, 1615 ?
Caussin, Nicolas : *La Cour Sainte,* 1624.
Colletet, Guillaume : *Vie des Poètes Gascons* (ed. Larroque).
Conrart, Valentin : *Correspondance* (ed. Kerviler 1881).
Corneille, Pierre : *Œuvres* (ed. Grands Ecrivains). 12 vols. 1862–1868.
Costar, P. : *Lettres.* 1658.
Entretiens de Costar et de Voiture. 1655.
Cotin, Charles : *Discours à Théopompe sur les Forts Esprits de ce Temps.* 1629.
Théoclée. 1646.
Cureau de la Chambre, Marin : *Caractères des Passions.* 1848.
Cyrano de Bergerac, Savinien : *Histoire Comique de La Lune*: *Les Etats du Soleil* (ed. Jacob 1857).
Œuvres Diverses, 1654.
Dehénault, Jean : *Œuvres* (ed. Lachèvre, 1922).
Delrio, Antony : *Disquisitionum Magicarum Libri Sex* (French Translation, 1611).
Descartes : *Œuvres* (Adam et Tannery). 12 vols. 1897–1910.
Discours de la Méthode (ed. Gilson). 1930.
Des Barreaux, Jacques : *Poèmes Libertins* (ed. Lachèvre). 1907.
Des Caurres, Jean : *Œuvres Morales et Diversifiées.* 1575 and 1584.
Desmarets, Roland, (Maresius) : *Epistolarum Libri, II.* 1655.
Du Bosc : *L'Honnête Femme.* 1632.
Du Camp d'Orgas : *Réflexions d'un Solitaire.* 1689.
Du Lorens : *Satires.* 1624 (and 1646).
Dumoulin, P. : *L'Anatomie de la Messe.*
Héraclite ou de la Vanité et Misère de la Vie Humaine. 1608.
Dupleix, Scipion : *La Liberté de la Langue Française.* 1651.
Éthique. 1617.
Durand, Etienne : *Méditations* (Le Livre d'Amour d'Etienne Durand 1907. Ed. Lachèvre).
Du Vair : *Traités Philosophiques.* 1606.
Du Verdier : *Bibliothèque Française.* 1585.

Esprit des Essais. 1677.

Esprit, Jacques : *La Fausseté des Vertus Humaines.* Ed. 1693.

Expilly, Claude : *Les Poemes de.* Ed. 1596 : and 1624.
Plaidoyers. 1608.

Faret Nicolas : *Nouveau Recueil de Lettres.* 1627.
Vertus Necessaires à un Prince. 1623.
L'honnête Homme. Ed. Magendie. 1925.

Favre, Antoine : *Quatrains Moraux.* 1582.

Firmianus, Petrus (Zacharie de Lisieux) : *Genius Saeculi.* 1656.

Fitelieu : *La Contremode.* 1642.

Fontenelle : *Dialogues des Morts.* 1683.

Forget, Pierre : *Sentiments Universels.* 1630; 1646.

Fornier, R. : *Discours Académique de l'Immortalité.* 1619.

Fortin de la Hoguette, Philippe : *Testament ou Conseils Fidèles.* 1648 and 1655.
Catéchisme Royal. 1650.
Les Eléments de la Politique. 1663.
Correspondance (ed. Larroque).

François de Sales : *Œuvres* (ed. Annécy). Vols. I–III. 1892.

Galerie des Peintures, La. 1663.

Gamaches, Charles de : *Le Sensé Raisonnant sur les Passages de l'Ecriture Sainte contre les Prétendus Réformés.* (Without place or date.)

Garaby de La Luzerne, A. : *Les Essais Poétiques.* 1638.
Sentiments chrétiens, politiques et moraux. 1642 ; 1654.
Satires Inédites. Rouen, 1888.

Garasse, François : *Doctrine Curieuse des Beaux Esprits.* 1624.
La Recherche des Recherches. 1622.
La Somme Théologique. 1625.
Nouveau Jugement de tout ce qui a été dit et écrit contre le Livre de la Doctrine Curieuse. 1625.

Gassendi : *Opera.* 6 vols. 1661.

Gaudin, I. : *La Distinction et la Nature du Bien et du Mal* . . . 1704.

Gilbert : *De Magnete.* 1600.

Godet, Louis : *Apologie des Jeunes Avocats.* 1613. Chalon.

Goulart, Simon : *Trésor d'Histoires Admirables.* 1600 : 1604.

[Goulart, Simon : ed. *Les Essais.* Lyon, 1595.]

Gournay, Marie de : *Le Promenoir de Monsieur de Montaigne.* 1594.
L'Ombre de Mademoiselle de Gournay. 1626.
Les Avis ou Présents. 1641.
Préfaces aux Essais. 1595 ; 1598 ; 1617 ; 1635.

Gravelle, Fr. de, Sieur d'Arpeutigny : *Abrégé de Philosophie.* 1601.

Grenailles, F. de : *L'honnête Garçon.* 1642.
Le Bon Esprit. 1641.
La Mode. 1642.

Guyon, Louis, Seigneur de la Nauche : *Diverses Leçons.* Ed. 1610.

Lord Herbert of Cherbury : *De la Vérité.* 1639.
De Religione Gentilium. 1645.

Huarte, Juan : *Examen des Esprits* (ed. Chappuys).
Huet, Pierre Daniel : *Traité Philosophique de la Faiblesse de l'Esprit Humain.* 1723.
Huetiana. 1722.
Jacquelot : *Conformité de la Foi avec la Raison.* 1705.
Joly : *Remarques sur le Dictionnaire de Bayle.*
Journal des Savants from 1667–1730.
La Bruyère : *Caractères* (ed. Chassang). 1876.
La Croix du Maine : *Bibliothèque Française.* 1684.
La Faille, —de : *Portefeuille.*
La Fare : *Mémoires* (ed. Petitot).
    Unpublished Poems (Van Roosbroeck). 1924.
La Fons, J. de : *Le Dauphin.* 1608.
La Fontaine : *Œuvres* (ed. Régnier). 1883–1893.
La Mothe le Vayer : *Cinq Dialogues : Quatre Dialogues.* Ed. Trévoux.
    Œuvres. 2 vols. 1663.
    Deux Dialogues (ed. Chefs d'Œuvres Méconnus). 1922.
    Soliloques Sceptiques. 1670.
    Hexaméron Rustique. 1670.
    Mémorial de Quelques Conférences. 1669.
La Motte Messemé, Fr Le Poulchre : *Le Passetemps.* 1595 and 1597.
    Les Honnêtes Loisirs. 1587.
Lamy, Bernard : *Démonstrations ou Preuves de la Vérité et de la Sainteté de la Morale Chrétienne.* 1706.
Lanclos, Ninon de : *Correspondance Authentique.* Ed. Colombey. 1885.
Lancre, Pierre Rostégui de : *Tableau de l'Inconstance et Instabilité de toutes choses . . .* 1610.
    Tableau de l'Inconstance des Mauvais Anges et Démons. 1612.
    Le Livre des Princes. 1616.
    L'Incrédulité et Mécreance du Sortilège pleinement convaincue. 1622.
    Du Sortilège. 1627.
La Noue, François de : *Discours Politiques et Militaires.* 1587.
La Primaudaye : *L'Académie de.* 1581.
La Rochefoucauld : *Œuvres* (ed. Grands Ecrivains). 4 vols. 1873.
Launay, J. de : *De Varia Aristotelis Fortuna.* 1656.
Laval, Antoine de : *Desseins de Professions Nobles et Publiques.* 1605.
La Vergne, de : *Essais de Poésie.* 1643.
Le Moine, Pierre : *La Dévotion Aisée.* 1656.
Le Page : *L'Homme Content.* 1679.
La Touche-Bernier : *Préservatifs contre l'Irreligion.* 1704.
Lescarbot, Marc : *Histoire de la Nouvelle France.* 1609.
Lestoile, Pierre de : *Journal* (ed. Brunet). 12 vols. 1875–1896.
Lipsius, Justus : *Opera Omnia aucta et recensita Vesaliae.* 4 vols. 1675.
Locke, John : *Works.* 1727.
    Essays concerning Human Understanding. Ed. Fraser. 1894.
Loisel, Antoine : *De l'Œil des Rois.* 1596.

Loryot, F. : *Fleurs des Secrets Moraux.* 1614.
Malebranche : *La Recherche de La Vérité.* 1674.
Marandé, Leonard : *Le Jugement des Actions Humaines.* 1624 and 1635.
Ariades. 1629.
Abrégé de l'Histoire d'Ariades. 1630.
Abrégé de Toute la Philosophie. 1642 ?
Les Inconvénients du Jansénisme. 1654.
Réponse à la seconde lettre de M. Arnauld. 1655, &c.
Marguérite de Navarre : *Mémoires* (Coll. Chefs d'Œuvres Méconnus).
    1920.
Marolles, Michel de : *Mémoires.* 1656.
Suite des Mémoires. 1656.
Les Six Livres de Lucrèce. 1659.
Matthieu, Pierre : *Tablettes.* 1610 and 1620.
Mazarinade : *Ovide Parlant à Tieste.* 1652.
Maynard, François : *Poésies* (ed. Cohen). 1927.
Menagiana. Ed. 1715.
Méré, chevalier de : *Conversations du.* 1669.
Discours de la Justesse. 1671.
Discours. 1677.
Lettres. 1682.
Le Cahier du (Revue d'Hist. Litt. 1923-4).
Œuvres Posthumes. 1701.
Œuvres Complètes (Boudhors). 1930.
Mersenne, Marin : *Quaestiones Celeberrimae in Genesim.* 1623.
L'Impiété des Deistes. 2 vols. 1624.
La Vérité des Sciences. 1625.
Questions Théologiques, Physiques, Morales et Mathématiques. 1634.
Miraeus, Audebertus : *Vita Lipsii* (ed. Antwerp, 1609).
Molière, J. B. Poquelin de : *Œuvres* (ed. Despois et Mesnard). 1873.
Michel de Montaigne : *Les Essais* (ed. Villey, 1922 except where
    otherwise stated).
Les Essais (Paris folio 1595).
Les Essais, Lyon, 1595.
Les Essais, Lyon, 1598.
Les Essais, Lyon, 1617.
Les Essais folio 1635.
Les Essais (edition Municipale, 1905-30).
Les Essais (ed. Courbet et Royer). 1872-1899.
Les Essais (ed. Didot. Panthéon). 1872.
Ephémerides (ed. Payen : Documents sur Montaigne No. 3). 1855.
Journal de Voyage (ed. Ancona). 1889.
La Théologie Naturelle de Raymond de Sebond. 1569.
The Essays. English Translation by E. J. Trechmann. 1927.
L'Esprit de Montaigne. 1677. *Pensées de Montaigne* (by Artaud). 1700.
Naudé, Gabriel : *Apologie pour les grands personnages faussement
    accusés de magie.* 1625.
Considérations sur les Coups d'Etat. Ed. 1668.

Avis pour dresser une Bibliothèque. 1627.
Syntagma de Studio Liberali. 1633.
Épistolae. Geneva 1667.
Bibliothèque Politique. trad. française. 1642.
Naudiana. Ed. 1700.
Le Mascurat. 1650.
Nervèze : *Epîtres Morales.* 1598.
Nicole, Pierre : *Education d'un Prince.* 1670.
Essais de Morale. 25 vols. Ed. 1755.
(and Antoine Arnaud) : *L'Art de Penser.* 1662 and 1666.
Ochino, Bernardino : *Il Catechismo.* 1561. Basle.
Pascal : *Œuvres* (ed. Grands Ecrivains). 14 vols. 1903.
Pensées et Opuscules (ed. Brunschwicg). 1922.
Pasquier, Etienne : *Lettres.* 1618.
Œuvres. 1623.
Pasquier, Nicolas : *Le Gentilhomme.* 1611.
Patin, Gui : *Lettres* (ed. Réveillé Parize 1846, and ed. Triaire 1907).
Pelletier : *La Nourriture de la Noblesse.* 1604.
Pellisson, Paul : *Histoire de l'Academie* (ed. Livet). 1858.
Pellisson, Georges : *Mélanges de Divers Problemes.* 1647.
Perrot D'Ablancourt : *Recueil de Diverses Harangues* 4me Partie.
    Bruxelles. 1682.
Preface to *L'Honnête Femme.* Ed. 1633.
Perrot de la Salle : *Gigantomachie ou combat de tous les arts et sciences.*
    1593 (and 1599).
Plantin, Christopher : *Correspondance.* 1916. Antwerp.
Plassac, Josias Gombaud de : *Lettres.* 1648.
Poiret, Pierre : *Fides et Ratio Collatae.* 1707.
Racan, Honoré de Bueil, marquis de : *Œuvres* (Bibliothèque Elzé-
    virienne). 2 vols. 1857.
Rampalle, Sieur de : *Discours Académique : Que le Monde ne va point
    de mal en pis.* 1639.
Raemond, Florimond de : *Erreur Populaire de la Papesse Jeanne.*
    1587, 1594.
De l'Antichrist. 1595.
Histoire de l'Héresie. 1605.
Recueil de Pièces en Prose. Paris, Charles de Geret. 1661.
Réfuge, Eustache de : *Traité de la Cour.* 1616 and 1619.
Régnier, Mathurin : *Satires.* (Ed. Poiterin). 1875.
Régis, P. S. : *L'Usage de la Raison et de la Foi.* 1704.
Renaudot : *Recueil Général des Questions Traitées és Conférences du
    Bureau d'Adresse.* 1638–60.
Rohault : *Entretiens sur la Philosophie.* 1671.
Rousseau, A. : *Nouvelles Maximes.* 1679.
Sablé, Madeleine de Souvré, Marquise de : *Maximes.* 1678.
Saint Amant : *Œuvres* (Bibliothèque Elzévirienne). 2 vols. 1855.
Saint Evremond : *Œuvres* (ed. Desmaizeaux. 1739. Amsterdam).
Œuvres Mêlées. 1680.

Saint Sernin, Jonatan de : *Essais.* Allde, London.
Sainte Marthe, Scévole (II) de : *Elogiae.* 1602.
Sarazin : *Œuvres.* 1656 : and ed. Festuguière. 1926.
  Nouvelles Œuvres. 1674.
Sarpi, *Vita del Padre Paolo*, Leiden. 1646.
Scaliger, Joseph : *Correspondance Inédite.* 1881.
Scaligerana : *Editio Altera.* Cologne, 1667.
Scudéry, Madeleine de : *Conversations sur Divers Sujets.* 1680.
  Clélie. 10 vols. 1654–60.
Segraisiana : ed. 1731.
Sévigné, Madame de : *Lettres* (ed. Grands Ecrivains). 1862–6.
Silhon, Jean : *Les Deux Vérités* . . . 1626.
  De l'Immortalité de l'Ame. 1634.
  Le Ministre d'Etat. 1631.
  De la Certitude des Connaissances Humaines. 1661.
Sirmond, Antoine : *De Immortalitate Animae* . . . 1635.
Sorbière, Samuel : *Lettres et Discours.* 1660.
  Relations, Lettres et Discours. 1660.
  Sorberiana. 1695.
Sorel, Charles : *La Bibliothèque Française.* 1664.
  Le Berger Extravagant. 1622.
  Histoire Comique de Francion. (ed. Garnier).
  La Science Universelle. 1668.
Tabourot des Accords : *Les Bigarrures.* Ed. 1640.
  Quatrième et Cinquième Livres des Touches. 1588.
Tallemant des Réaux : *Historiettes* (ed. Monmerqué et Paris). 1857.
Théophile de Viau : *Œuvres* (Bib. Elzévirienne). 2 vols. 1856.
Thou, J. Ad. de : *De Vita Sua* (ed. in French 1717).
  Historia temporis suae (ed. 1630).
Tristan L'Hermite : *Le Page Disgracié* (Bibliothéque Elzévirienne).
Vauquelin des Yveteaux : *Œuvres.* 1921.
Vermandy, Pierre de : *Scepticismus Debellatus.* 1697.
Vigneul Marville : *Mélanges d'Histoire et de Littérature.* Ed. 1725.
  L'Education, Maximes et Réflexions de M. de Moncade. 1691.
Vion Dalibray : *Poésies.* 1656.
Voiture, Vincent : *Œuvres* (ed. Roux, 1856).
Yves de Paris : *La Théologie Naturelle.* 1635.
  De Jure Naturali. 1658.
  Le Gentilhomme Chrétien. 1666.

III. Some Modern Works Consulted

Allier, Raoul : *La Cabale des Dévots.* 1902.
Archives de la Gironde, XXIV.
Aragonnès : *Mademoiselle de Scudéry.* 1933.
Armaingaud, Dr. : *Introduction to the Essays.* 1924.
Atkinson, Geoffrey : *Relations de Voyage au XVIIᵐᵉ Siècle.* 1924.
Barach, K. S. : *P. D. Huet als Philosoph.* 1862.
Bartholomess, Ch : *Huet ou le Scepticisme Théologique.* 1849.

Berthelot, R. : ' La Sagesse de Shakespeare ' (*Revue de Metaphysique et de Morale.* 1924).

Borinski, K. : *Gracian und die Hof-Literatur in Deutschland.*

Bonnefons, P. : *Montaigne et Les Amis.* 2 vols. 1892.

Brett, G. S. : *Gassendi*, 1908.

Bremond, H.: *Histoire Littéraire du Sentiment Religieux en France.* Vol. I. *La Querelle du Pur Amour.* 1933.

Brunschwicg, L. : *Le Progrès de la Conscience.* 1927.

Burnet, John : *Early Greek Philosophy.* 1908.

Busson, H. : *Les Sources et le Développement du Rationalisme dans la Littérature Française de la Renaissance.* 1922.
La Pensée Religieuse Française de Charron à Pascal. 1932.

Campagnac, E. T. : *The Cambridge Platonists.* 1901.

Chamaillard, E. : *Le Chevalier de Méré.* 1921.

Chinard, G. ; *L'Exotisme Américain dans la Littérature Française au XVIme Siècle.* 1911.
L'Amérique et le Rêve Exotique. 1913.

Cohen, Gustave : *Ecrivains Français en Hollande.* 1920.

Collas, George : *Jean Chapelain.* 1912.

Coppin, J.: *Montaigne traducteur de Raymond Sebond.* Lille. 1925.
Etude sur le Grammaire et le Vocabulaire de Montaigne. 1925.

Dezeimeris, R. : *Pierre de Brach.* 1858.

Espinas : ' Pour L'Histoire du Cartésianisme ' (*Rev. de Métaphysique et de Morale.* 1906).

Faure, H. : *Antoine de Laval et les Ecrivains Bourbonnais.* 1870.

Fernandez, Ramon : *De la Personnalité.* 1928.
Molière. 1930.

Feugère : *Mademoiselle de Gournay.* 1843.

Foucault, M. : *Les Procès de Sorcellerie devant les Tribunaux Séculiers.* 1907.

Gilson, E. : *Études de Philosophie Médiévale.*
La Liberté chez Descartes et la Théologie. 1913.
Revue Philosophique. Mai-Juin. 1924.
La Pensée Médiévale dans la Formation Cartésienne. 1930.

Griselle, E. : ' Les Pascalins ' (*Revue de Fribourg.* 1907–8).

Grubbs, H. A. : *Damien Mitton.* 1932.

Haag : *La France Protestante.* 1848–1859.

Habasque, F. : *Episodes d'un Procès de Sorcellerie dans le Labourd.* 1911. Biarritz.

Hauser, H. : *François de la Noue.* 1892.

Hubert, R. : *Rousseau et l'Encyclopédie.* 1928.

Hulme, T. E. : *Speculations.* 1924.

Ivanoff, W. : *La Marquise de Sablé et Son Salon.* 1927.

Jones, L. P. : *Simon Goulart.* 1917.

Jovy, E. : *Pascal et Saint Ange.* 1927.
Pascal et Silhon. 1927.
Deux Inspirateurs peu connus de La Rochefoucauld. 1910.

Kerviler, R. : *Étude sur la Vie de François La Mothe le Vayer.* 1879.

Lachèvre, Frédéric : *Le Libertinage au XVIIme Siècle* (Le Procès de Théophile : Des Barreaux ; Cyrano de Bergerac ; Dehénault, &c.). 11 vols. 1910–1924.
Lecky : *History of the Rise and Influence of Rationalism in Europe.* 1865.
Leroy, Maxime : *Descartes, le Philosophe au Masque.* 1929.
Magendie, M. : *La Politesse Mondaine.* 2 Vols. (undated).
Magne, E. : *La Rochefoucauld.* 1923.
   Ninon de Lanclos. 1925.
   Une Amie Inconnue de Molière. 1924.
Maine, Sir H. : *Ancient Law* (Pollock's Edition).
Maritain, Jacques : *Le Songe de Descartes.* 1930.
Merlant, Joachim : *De Montaigne à Vauvenargues.* 1914.
Michaut, Gustave : *La Jeunesse de Molière.* 1923.
   Les Débuts de Molière. 1923.
   Les Luttes de Molière. 1925.
Millan, A. L. : *Voyage dans le Midi.* 1807.
Nisard : *Le Triomvirat Littéraire au XVIe siècle.* 1852.
Nitze, W. H. : *Revue de l'Histoire Littéraire de la France.* 1927. (Art. on Molière).
Ogden, C. K. (and I. A. Richards) : *The Meaning of Meaning.* 1923.
Payen, le Docteur : *Documents sur Montaigne,* No. 1, 2, 3. 1847–56.
Prat : *Maldonat et l'Université de Paris.* 1856.
Philipot, M. E. : *Noel du Fail.* 1914.
Richards, I. A. : *Practical Criticism.* 1929.
   (with C. K. Ogden) : *Meaning of Meaning.* 1923.
Richou, G. : *Inventaire de la Collection Payen.* 1878.
Roth, Leon : *Correspondance of Descartes and Ch. Huygens.* 1926.
Rougier, Louis : *Les Paralogismes du Rationalisme.* 1920.
Roux, Marquis de : *Pascal en Poitou.* 1920.
Sabrié, J. B. : *Pierre Charron.* 1913.
   Les Idées Religieuses de Jean Louis Guez de Balzac. 1913.
Sainte Beuve : *Histoire du Port Royal.* Ed. 1908.
Schiff, Mario : *Mademoiselle de Gournay.* 1910.
Sells, A. L. : ' Molière and La Mothe Le Vayer ' (*Mod. Lang. Rev.* 1933).
Smuts, J. C. : *Holism and Evolution.* 1926.
Strowski, F. : *Pascal et son Temps.* 1907.
Tamizey de Larroque : *Florimond de Raemond.* 1867.
Tilley, A. : *Literature of the French Renaissance.* 2 vols. 1904.
   The Decline of the Age of Louis XIV. 1929.
Vianey, Joseph : *Mathurin Régnier.* 1896.
Villey Pierre : *Les Sources et l'Evolution des Essais.* 1908.
   XVIme Siècle : Sources d'Idées (Plon). 1912.

INDEX OF PROPER NAMES

SUBJECT INDEX

451

Society, disadvantages of, 255, 265, 340 ; possible without religion, 284 ; duties to, 93, 160, 185, 345

Sorcery, 23, 39–43, 125, 179, 244–6, 249, 258, 259, 277, 291, 375, 417 note, 425, 428 ; impotence produced by, 5, 7, 42, 108 ; and feminism, 58

Soul, nature of, 42, 177, 278, 283
— immortality of, xix, xxii, 38, 42, 167, 175, 180–4, 187, 201, 227, 231–4, 236, 237, 253, 263, 267, 281 note, 283, 365, 377, 414 ; doubted, 144, 145, 152, 153 ; denied, 154 ; unprovable, 85 note, 159, 185, 256 note, 277–9, 301, 353, 370, 406 ; this doctrine condemned, 129 note, 165, 168, 177, 180, 417, 425 ; how proved, 177

Spectatorship, 217, 218, 220, 221, 226, 227

Stoicism, xx, xxxviii, 20, 21, 71 note, 93, 108 note, 134, 137, 188, 200, 201, 203, 208, 213, 224, 226, 253, 263, 289, 293, 316, 392, 406, 407 ; Montaigne's, q.v.

Style, prose, 38, 73, 183, 274, 280, 290, 296–9, 303 note, 336, 337

Suicide, 35, 331, 406 note, 420 note, 422

Superstition : founded on unworthy conception of God, 85, 86, 152, 153, 177, 270 ; as confusion of observance and virtue, 71, 153, 247, 270, 384 ; condemned, 143, 144, 147, 149, 158, 159, 161, 168, 175, 176, 242, 248, 249, 256, 272, 277, 280, 281 note, 291, 294, 301, 356, 382–4, 386, 407, 408 ; all religion, without divine grace, 84 ; and intention, 86, 94 note ; saint worship, 143, 144, 148 note, 156, 161, 277 ; indulgences, 156, 270

Symbolism, 216, 218 note, 230, 231, 254

TABULA RASA (theory of knowledge), xix, 30, 113, 127, 173, 198, 240, 254

Talcum powder, 52 note

Taste, literary, 337, 381, 382 ; moral, xxxiv, xxxix, 135–7, 140–2, 332–4, 347, 356, 357, 368

Taxation, 125, 138, 161 note, 251 note, 272

Temperament : theories of, xxxvi, xxxvii, 86, 99–103, 163, 207, 429 ; attacked, 166, 183, 189, 190, 248 note ; influence of, on life and morals, 67–70, 113, 136, 137, 139, 140, 150, 160, 191, 227, 274, 277, 280, 324, 335, 340, 344–7, 352, 357, 380, 390, 391, 395, 398, 401, 402 ; influence not paramount, 206 ; and dreams, 268 ; in education, 271, 311, 312 ; in literature, 116, 121, 336 ; knowledge of, necessary to honnête homme, 314, 317, 318, 328, 332–4, 346, 347, 388

Theft, how punished, 251 note, 269

Theology, xiii–xxiv, 37, 38, 126, 127, 216, 234–6, 239, 289, 313 note ; attacked, 45, 292, 293, 315 note, 354, 355 ; no science, 213, 262 ; and feminism, 57

Tolerance, toleration, xxv, xxvi, xxxiii, xl, 33, 34, 36, 37, 45, 91, 124, 136, 137, 145, 147–50, 155, 160–3, 189, 199, 235, 244, 246, 248, 253, 261, 263, 281, 289, 308, 311, 313, 321–4, 329, 335, 355–7, 384, 400, 426 note

Torture, examination under, 5, 6, 246, 263, 426 note, 428 ; punishment by, 13, 14, 269

Travel, and books of, influence of, 11, 91, 174, 213, 214, 223, 244, 246 note, 255–9, 261, 276, 289, 290, 299, 309, 317, 374, 376

Trinity, doctrine of, xix, 172, 239, 366

Truth, all, revealed, 83, 84, 127, 128, 197, 219, 240, 273, 274 ; this doctrine condemned, 182 ; no ' necessary ', 235, 240 ; none self-evident, 262 ; self-evident, negligible, 371 ; criteria of, 173, 201 ; search for 211, 240, 241, 272 ; of human knowledge self-contradictory,

Truth :
216, 219, 220 ; wisdom not the attainment of ultimate, 272 ; notion of, discussed, 254 ; inapplicable to drama and epic, 255
Type-psychology, *v.* Temperament

UNIVERSALITY, *v.* Consent, Universal
Utilitarianism, xxx, 69–71 note, 203, 239, 241, 242, 247, 251, 255, 259, 317, 324, 332, 343, 345, 352, 356–8, 360 ; attacked, 363 ; of Montaigne, xxxvii, xxxviii ; in religion, 143, 144, 181, 182, 336, 371, 383 ; in politics, xxxvii, xxxviii, 13, 69, 247, 248, 373

VANITY (and Folly) of man, xxvi–viii, 16, 30, 31, 33, 36, 37, 47, 112, 113, 119, 120, 125–7, 128, 136, 137, 144, 145, 153, 154, 158, 161, 196–8, 202, 203, 206 note, 250, 251, 269, 279, 280, 316, 318, 342, 343, 366, 367, 369, 370, 373, 389, 395–7, 405, 406 ; why affirmed, 81, 82, 198 ; Montaigne's use of theme, 183, 184 ; special use of theme, 203–5, 247 ; condemned, 82, 120, 168, 172, 193, 241, 301 ; defended, 170, 363
Vengeance, 67, 70, 71, 248, 285
Verities eternal, 234, 235, 240
Vice, 66, 92, 121, 140, 284, 333 ; useful, 191, 265, 343, 344 note
Virtue : heroic, based on conflict, xxviii, xxx, xxxi, 14, 21, 56 note, 60, 94, 199, 200–3, 334, 352, 389, 390, 401 (*v.* Harmony) ; pagan, xxi, xxxix, 156, 167, 175, 176, 182, 248, 250, 265–7, 419, 420, 424, 425 ; and innocence, xxxi, 140, 141, 154 note, 282, 283 ; conscious or unconscious, xxxi, xxxii, 56 ; its own reward, 21, 133, 153, 159, 175, 247, 308 ; not so, 181 ; if natural, 264, 316, 420 ; and natural law, 95, 96 ;

Virtue :
pleasurable, 121, 282, 283, 308, 317, 343, 356, 380 ; independent of circumstances, 136 ; dependent on weather, 141, 142, 202 ; on faith, 203 note, 348 note, 418 ; critique of, 264, 265, 343–5, 373, 418–20 ; virtues incompatible, 160, 397 ; *Vertus Vicieuses*, 69, 70, 343, 344, 418
Vocation, Descartes', 215–22
Voyage, the imaginary, 257–9 (*v.* Travel)
Vows, 224 note, 283 note
Vulgar, xxxiv, 68, 69, 189, 199, 248, 274, 275, 286, 323, 372, 373, 397

WAR, 181, 255, 284, 340 (*v.* Pacificism)
Wisdom : identified with philosophy, 66, 211, 212, 215, 223 ; according to Charron, 92–9 ; its starting-point, 82, 147 ; lessons specified, 66, 67 ; simplicity of wise, xxxi, xxxiv, xxxv, 161, 271 ; wisdom in ignorance, 106, 174 ; resists tyranny, 93 ; based on *maîtresse forme*, 99, 271 ; based on diversity of actions, 322 ; and folly, 16, 137, 147, 161, 196, 345, 358 ; gay if sceptical, 253 ; consists in *douceur de moeurs*, 272 ; in peace of mind, 324
' Wisdom, Pastoral ', conception of, xxxi, xxxii, 87–9, 128, 129, 281, 323, 331, 371, 372 ; variants on, 166, 223, 271 ; and temperament, 89, 99, 161
Witchcraft, *v.* Sorcery
Women : prejudices against, and sorcery, 40, 41 ; excellence of, 109, 110 note ; Indian, 290 ; and temperament, 345 ; religion and, 354 ; and *honnêteté*, 333, 334, 360 ; feminism, 55–9, 341, 381, 392 ; *précieuses*, 381, 391–3

ZEAL, condemned, 93, 94, 155, 266, 267, 382–4